# DENALI

## Deception, Defeat, & Triumph

# DENALI

## Deception, Defeat, & Triumph

To the Top of the Continent

The Conquest of Mount McKinley

The Ascent of Denali

Dr. Frederick Cook, Belmore Browne, & Hudson Stuck
with commentary by Art Davidson

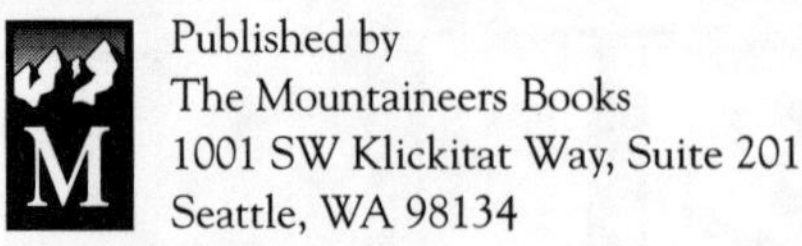
Published by
The Mountaineers Books
1001 SW Klickitat Way, Suite 201
Seattle, WA 98134



First edition, 2001

*To the Top of the Continent* was first published in 1908 by Doubleday, Page & Company.
*The Conquest of Mount McKinley* was first published in 1913 by G. P. Putnam's Sons/The Knickerbocker Press.
*The Ascent of Denali* was first published in 1914 by Charles Scribner's Sons, and again in 1977 by The Mountaineers Books.



Published simultaneously in Great Britain by Cordee, 3a DeMontfort Street, Leicester, England, LE1 7HD

Printed in Canada

Editor: Kathleen Cubley
Cover and Book Designer: Kristy L. Welch
Layout Artist: Gray Mouse Graphics
Mapmaker: Red Shoe Design (page 6)

Cover photograph: *Mount McKinley, Denali NP, AK* © John Warden/Index Stock Imagery
Frontispiece: *Mount McKinley near sunset—from the west at 41,000 feet (neg. 7975)*
© Bradford Washburn

*Library of Congress Cataloging-in-Publication Data*

Denali : deception, defeat, and triumph / Frederick A. Cook, Belmore Browne, Hudson Stuck.-- 1st ed.
p. cm.
ISBN 0-89886-835-1 (hard cover)
1. Mountaineering--Alaska--McKinley, Mount. 2. Cook, Frederick Albert, 1865-1940--Journeys--Alaska--McKinley, Mount. 3. Browne, Belmore, 1880-1954--Journeys--Alaska--McKinley, Mount. 4. Stuck, Hudson, 1863-1920--Journeys--Alaska--McKinley, Mount. 5. McKinley, Mount (Alaska)--Description and travel. I. Davidson, Art, 1943- II. Cook, Frederick Albert, 1865-1940. To the top of the continent. III. Browne, Belmore, 1880-1954. Conquest of Mount McKinley. IV. Stuck, Hudson, 1863-1920. Ascent of Denali.
GV199.42.A42 M32252 2001
796.52'2'097983--dc21

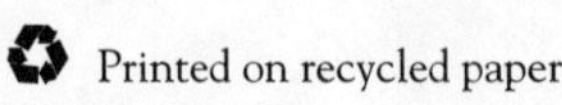
Printed on recycled paper

# CONTENTS

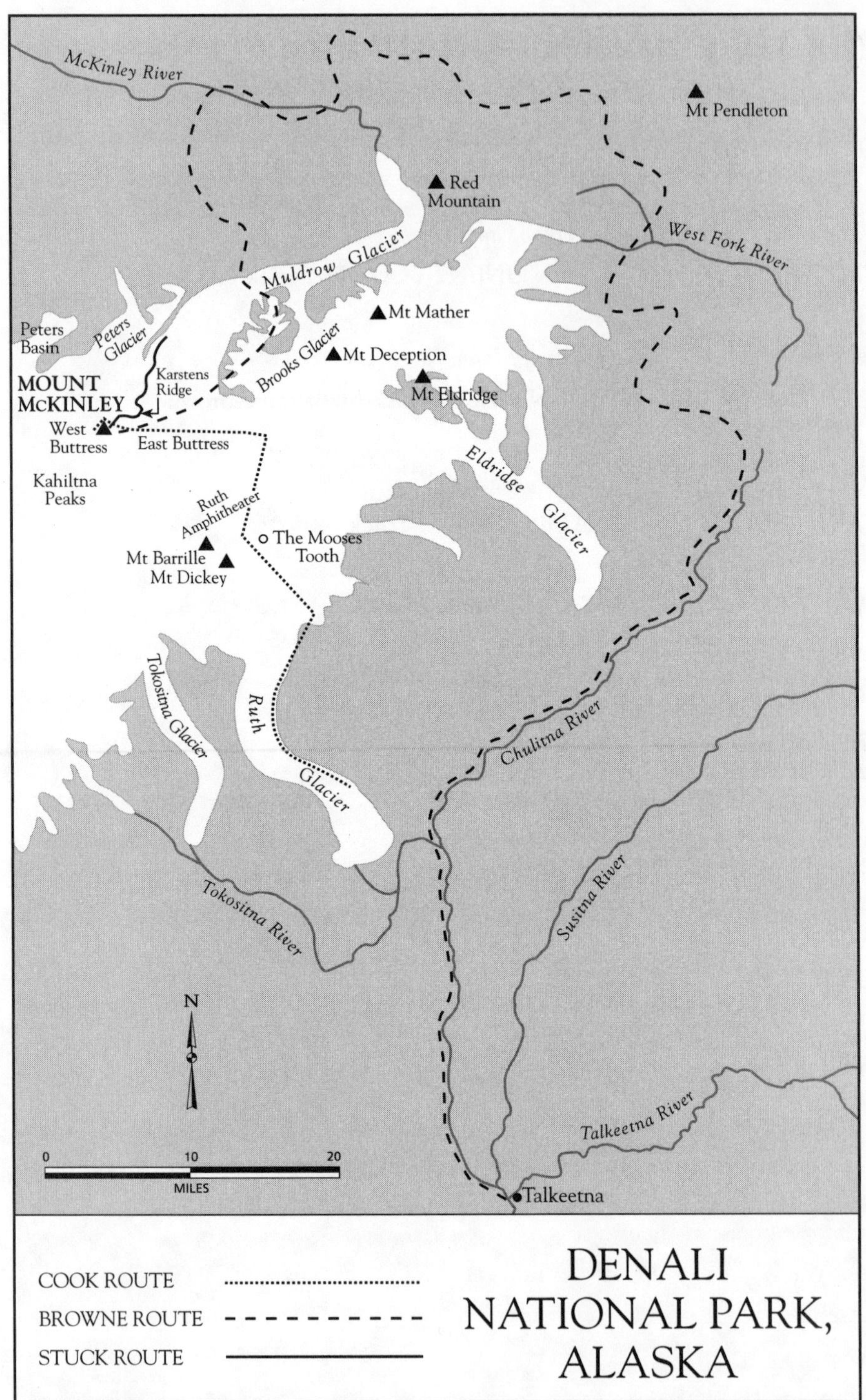

McKinley River
Mt Pendleton
Red Mountain
West Fork River
Muldrow Glacier
Mt Mather
Peters Basin
Peters Glacier
Brooks Glacier
Mt Deception
Karstens Ridge
Mt Eldridge
MOUNT McKINLEY
West Buttress
East Buttress
Kahiltna Peaks
Eldridge Glacier
Ruth Amphitheater
The Mooses Tooth
Mt Barrille
Mt Dickey
Tokositna Glacier
Ruth Glacier
Chulitna River
Tokositna River
Susitna River
N
Talkeetna River
0
10
20
MILES
Talkeetna
COOK ROUTE
BROWNE ROUTE
STUCK ROUTE
DENALI NATIONAL PARK, ALASKA

# FOREWORD

*To the Top of the Continent. The Conquest of Mount McKinley. The Ascent of Denali.* Each of these books is a classic in its own right—evoking the rigors of that fascinating, if fleeting era when the age of exploration merged with modern climbing. Just reaching Mount McKinley required the skills of a Meriwether Lewis. One faced flooding rivers, quicksand, muskeg bogs, and grizzlies before ever setting foot on uncharted glaciers and ridges.

Together, these three books form the cornerstones of one the greatest controversies in the history of mountaineering. No less than three groups claimed to have made the first ascent of Mount McKinley, or Denali, as many prefer calling North America's highest peak.

The first was Dr. Frederick A. Cook: *To the Top of the Continent* describes his 1903 reconnaisance and 1906 ascent. Next, in 1910, Tom Lloyd set out with some winter-hardened miners from Fairbanks: he called their group the Sourdoughs and claimed they reached the top. Belmore Browne, who didn't claim to reach the summit, nevertheless jumped into the controversy, writing *The Conquest of Mount McKinley* about his 1910 and 1912 expeditions to disprove Dr. Cook and climb the mountain himself. Finally, Hudson Stuck mounted an expedition in 1913; he recounted his climb in *The Ascent of Denali*.

Who was the world to believe? The distinguished Dr. Cook, a veteran of polar expeditions and a founder of the American Alpine Club? Belmore Browne, a young artist with a sense of adventure? Hudson Stuck, an archdeacon and cannon of the Episcopal Church? Or a bunch of Sourdoughs who had never held an ice axe and who claimed to have planted, of all things, a fourteen-foot spruce pole on the summit?

The beauty of The Mountaineers Books publishing these three books in one volume is that it brings these incredible men and their times back to life in ways that the books by themselves never could. Today, we look at a map of Denali and see the names of the early climbers: the Wickersham Wall, Harper Glacier, Archdeacon's Tower. Here, striding through the pages of this trilogy, we find these very people, James Wickersham, Walter Harper, and Archdeacon Stuck, so alive and filled with a passion for high places. Today, we can fly to Alaska and tackle Denali on a three-week vacation—sorting our brightly colored gear in Talkeetna and waiting for a break in the clouds so we can catch a thirty-minute ski-plane flight to one of the mountain's glaciers. The sheer, raw beauty of Denali is still there. Crevasses still lurk beneath the snow. The ice is still steep, the air thin. But much of that marvelous mystery of the unknown has slipped away.

Here, I think, is the real magic of this trilogy: it rekindles our sense of the unknown. Here are stories within stories that bring to life just how hard it would have been for us to climb the mountain back then. In the 1880s, Denali and the Alaska Range remained such a mystery that a government survey said, "What the country north of Cook's Inlet is like, no civilized man can tell. Indians tell us stories of mountains visible for hundreds of miles."

At the turn of the century, the highest of these fabled peaks was known by no fewer than five names: Denali, Doleyka, Traleyka, Bulshaia Gora, and Densmore's Peak. By the spring of 1903, it was being called Mount McKinley, for William McKinley who would become the twenty-fifth American president, and the rush to reach its summit was on.

In mid-May of 1903, Dr. Frederick A. Cook left New York City with a heady sense of the acclaim he hoped to find on the high, wind-swept slopes of a mountain five thousand miles away. With Cook was Robert Dunn, a writer he hoped would chronicle his ascendence to the top rank of explorers.

About the same time Cook's train was pulling out of New York, Alaska's frontier judge, James Wickersham, set out on the very first attempt to climb McKinley. He had recently moved his court from Eagle, Alaska to a ragtag mining camp on the Tanana River called Fairbanks. From here he could look south to a great peak shimmering in the distance. He would recall that, "From the moment we reached the Tanana Valley the longing to approach the mountain had been in my mind."

On May 16, with flags flying and a dance band playing, Wickersham left Fairbanks, provisioned with flour, bacon, beans, dried apples, and prunes along with a hundred pounds of rolled oats for the mules he hoped would help his men bushwhack their way to the base of the mountain.

They woke one morning to find fifty Indians and a hundred malamute dogs staring at them. When the Indian leader asked if they were climbing the mountain to find gold, Wickersham said, "No, we merely go to seek the top, to be the first men to reach the summit." Great laughter ensued as the Indian told him, "You are a fool."

Foolish or not, the notion of climbing a mountain for its own sake was something new and not easily understood. Wickersham himself was a thoughtful man with a keen sense of adventure. His attempt to climb Denali fell far short of the summit. Yet even in retreat, Wickersham seemed to savor every moment he spent on the mountain: "The midnight sun which lighted our way home, although far down in the north, was yet high enough above the horizon to tint the upper half of Denali a soft rose color."

Meanwhile, Dr. Cook was making his way to Alaska, stopping off at the Yakima Reservation in Washington State to buy some pack horses. He landed on the shores of Cook Inlet in mid-June to find he had fifteen unruly, half-broken cayuses and another 250 miles of uncharted hills, tundra, and black-spruce bogs between him and the mountain. Before the summer was over, Cook had made an incredible 750-mile circumnavigation of the McKinley massif, a feat that wouldn't be duplicated for another seventy-five years. He also managed to climb about a thousand feet higher on Denali than Wickersham. Cook returned to New York triumphant. Though he made no claim to have reached the summit on this trip, he was making his mark as a man among the great men of his time. The great Norwegian explorer, Roald Amundsen, who had been trapped in the Antarctic with Cook, said, "[he] was the one man of unfaltering courage, unfailing hope, endless cheerfulness and unwearied kindness."

Praised by one of the greatest explorers of all time and now returned from the untracked wilds of Alaska, what was there not to admire about Dr. Cook? Yet, even as he moved about New York society and easily found sponsors for his return to McKinley in 1906, the first hint of a darker side appeared. Curiously, the first aspersions on his character came from the very man he thought would loft him to the heights of an Amundsen.

"This is the story of a failure," wrote Robert Dunn in his 1907 book *The Shameless Diary of an Explorer*, a withering expose of Cook's 1903 sojourn to Alaska. In a presentient moment, he wrote that Cook, "has the feat accomplished before starting. He will not hear of difficulties, and when his unreasonable dream of success balks, or turns out a nightmare, he is all weakness and dependence."

Cook returned to McKinley in 1906 and through the pages of *To the Top of the Continent* we can follow him step by step. This time he brought along a strong young man named Belmore Browne, who would become his nemesis. When their attempt to reach the summit faltered, the expedition appeared to be over. They broke camp and returned to the shores of Cook Inlet. Then, inexplicably, Cook wired his New York sponsors: "AM PREPARING FOR A LAST DESPERATE ATTEMPT ON MCKINLEY."

Returning with only Ed Barrill, Cook climbed, "From cliff to cliff, from grotto to spire, from cloud to cloud, up and up farther and farther into the whirling vapors." We are there with Cook in his moments of undistilled, if self-imagined glory, knowing all the while he was taking the first fateful steps down that dreary road to infamy.

When told that Cook had reached the summit, Browne was incredulous. He knew the terrain. He knew the difficulties. He knew Cook had been gone only eight days and couldn't have possibly reached the top. Barrill had as much as confided to Browne that they had faked the summit. But how could he prove it?

Browne's *The Conquest of Mount McKinley* reads like a detective story. He pursued Cook's claim with the methodic persistence of a forensic detective and it paid off. He spotted a fatal flaw in Cook's ruse: one of his "summit" photos showed a mysterious bit of ridge in the background. Browne reasoned that if he retraced Cook's route, he might find the telltale ridge and locate the spot where Cook took his dubious photo of Barrill. Though he thought he found the spot, the controversy would rage on.

Browne also gives us a riveting account of his own heartbreaking attempt to make the first ascent with his friend Hershel Parker. At 19,000 feet, they saw the summit: "It rose as innocently as a tilted snow-covered tennis court and as we looked it over we grinned with relief—we *knew* the peak was ours!"

But in their excitement, they hadn't noticed the southern sky growing dark. With every step the wind increased. Browne reached the top of a small rise and suddenly, "I was hit by the full fury of the storm. The breath was driven from my body . . . I couldn't go ahead. As I brushed the frost from my glasses and squinted upward through the stinging snow I saw a sight that will haunt me to my dying day. The slope above me was no longer steep . . . all I can say is that we were close to the top."

Browne and Parker were not the only ones trying to climb Denali in 1910. Tom Lloyd and his buddies from the gold fields were convinced that Cook hadn't reached the summit and that they could. Opting for the much faster winter trails, the Sourdoughs left Fairbanks on December 22 with dog teams and horses. "Our Boys will succeed," said the *Fairbanks Times*, "they've got the route figured out and they'll show up Dr. Cook and the other 'Outside' expeditions."

By February 27, they'd established a camp on the mountain and went back down to the flats to hunt moose and caribou for more food. They weren't seen or heard from until Lloyd walked into Fairbanks on April 11, announcing that all four of them had reached both the north and south summits and had left a spruce pole on the north summit as proof. But without photos and with the Cook controversy in full swing, few believed him.

The third remarkable book in this trilogy is *The Ascent of Denali*, Hudson Stuck's account of his 1913 climb. While Cook seemed driven by a quest for fame and Browne to set the record straight, Stuck's venture on Denali seemed to be an extension of his life's work. At the beginning of *Ascent*, he tells us that he is "concerned much more with men than mountains," and that his "special and growing concern is with the native people of Alaska, a gentle and kindly race, now threatened with a wanton and senseless extermination, and sadly in need of generous champions if that threat is to be averted."

Traveling by riverboat in summer and dogsled in winter, Stuck took his Episcopal ministry to hundreds of tiny, out-of-the-way native villages. It's no coincidence that his helper would be a bright, trail-savvy young native; nor that he would invite this twenty-year-old, Walter Harper, to join him on Denali.

"He was adept in all wilderness arts," Stuck said of his protege. "An axe, a rifle, a flaying knife, a skin needle with its sinew thread with all these he was at home; he could construct a sled or a pair of snow-shoes . . . and could pitch camp with all the native comforts and amenities as quickly as anybody I ever saw."

As Stuck's party climbed higher on Denali (he insisted on calling the mountain by its native name), Harper was usually in the lead. And it was Harper who spotted evidence that the Sourdoughs had come this way three years before: "I suddenly looked up to the ridge that was running down from the north peak and to our great surprise I saw it standing out against the blue sky. The pole was about twelve or fourteen feet long."

The Sourdoughs had planted a spruce pole on the summit after all; unfortunately for their place in history, it was on the slightly lower north summit. Had these brash young men known the south summit is a bit higher, they almost certainly could have climbed it.

Stuck, with Harper leading the way, would make those final, first steps to the summit. That night, in wonderful understatement to Cook's soaring prose, Harper wrote in his journal: "Soon after we started, the grade got so steep that we were compelled to zigzag, and although we had our creepers we had to chop steps . . . It was one o'clock when we got to the top. I was ahead all day and was the first ever to set foot on Mt. Denali."

Part of the beauty of this trilogy is that we can be there with the protagonists, listen to their words, and try to ferret out the truth for ourselves. Did the Sourdoughs actually make the first ascent? Were Parker and Browne so close they could have almost reached out and touched the top?

Where did Cook's climb, and his life, go awry? The careful reader may be able to find the very point at which his narrative veers from a detailed, straightforward account to the more obtuse and florid telling of his final steps to the "summit."

The enduring enigma is not whether Cook reached the summit, but what possessed him to perpetrate a hoax. I'm reminded of a friend who retrieved a locked safe from a prospector's abandoned cache. At first, he thought he'd crack it open to see what was rattling around inside. He decided instead to keep it locked, the mystery stayed intact. So it is with Cook, who professed his innocence to the end and carried to his grave the mystery of what compelled him to invent his own demise. We are left wondering what was rattling around in the dark corners of his psyche.

Reading between the lines of this trilogy—listening, really listening, to the voices of these great and greatly different men—we may discern some of the deeper truths about what draws us to mountains, though we sometimes suffer mightily and struggle to our last breath to return.

*Art Davidson*
*Alaska*
*April, 2001*

*Art Davidson made the first winter ascent of Denali, which he recounts in* Minus 148°: The Winter Ascent of Mt. McKinley. *He is also the author of* Endangered Peoples, Light on the Land, In the Wake of the Exxon Valdez, *and a book of poetry,* Moonrise Over Denali. *He lives with his family in the Chugach Mountains near Anchorage, Alaska.*

# Dr. Frederick A. Cook: Deception

When Frederick Cook sat down to write *To the Top of the Continent* in 1906, he had already made four polar expeditions and been to the wilds of Alaska twice. In 1903, he had completed an incredible 750-mile circumnavigation of Denali, after which he helped found the American Alpine Club and was elected president of the Explorers Club. Then, in the summer of 1906, he had returned to Denali, purportedly climbing to its summit. Cook was at the peak of his career—well-known, respected, and able to finance expeditions at the drop of his black bowler hat.

Cook's status in society was all the more remarkable given the deprivations of his youth. Here, in a childhood straight out of Dickens, he began his life-long struggle with the vagaries of triumph and defeat. His father died of pneumonia when he was five, condemning him, his mother, and his brothers to unremitting poverty. With tremendous force of will, he scraped his way through college and then medical school. In 1890, at the age of twenty-four, he married and a child was soon on the way. He opened a practice in Manhattan, but during the first six months only four patients came to see him. Then his wife died while giving birth; the baby also died.

Alone and stripped of everything he held dear, Cook knew the pain of Job: his life's fateful lesson was that all his hard and honest work had come to naught. As a diversion Cook took to reading stories of explorers and faraway places. One day in 1891, he noticed in a newspaper that Arctic explorer Robert Peary needed a surgeon for his next expedition. Cook wrote a letter of application. Peary accepted. And there it was—with a few strokes of his pen, Cook had vaulted himself from the bleak realities of his daily life to the larger-than-life realm of explorers.

And so it was, years later, in the summer of 1906, that Cook found himself trudging back from Denali with fellow explorer Belmore Browne—worn-out, swatting mosquitoes, and no doubt feeling defeated after failing to reach the summit. On his 1903 expedition he'd made a successful reconnaissance; and he rhapsodized that whoever conquered Denali would, "be amply rewarded, but he must be prepared to withstand the tortures of the torrids, the discomforts of the north pole seeker, combined with the hardships of the Matterhorn ascents multiplied many times."

On this second trip, in 1906, Cook may have felt more pressure to reach the summit and become this larger-than-life explorer-climber-conqueror. Others might easily shrug off such a defeat; it was only a climb after all. But in Cook this failure may have conjured up the desperations of his youth. It must have come to him in some despondent moment—why not wrest triumph from defeat with a few more strokes of the pen and claim he had made the top? At that moment, he may not have thought of it as deceit, but merely a convenient way to fulfill his rightful destiny.

The dark recesses of Cook's mind remain a mystery. But we do know that he penned a telegram announcing that he was making one last desperate attempt to reach the summit. Then, leaving Browne behind and returning to Denali with Ed Barrill, he dictated entries for the diary of his sole companion. All that remained was writing a book securing his claim—and his place in the pantheon of explorers.

Cook no doubt intended *To the Top of the Continent* to be his masterpiece, and in its own convoluted way it is. The book opens with an accurate, if somewhat melodramatic, account of his 1903 expedition "through primeval forests, across and against rushing glacial streams, over marshes and tundras, on to tumbling glacial ice, up into the frosty mist of the upper world." The second half of the book chronicles the 1906 ascent to the "summit," the crowning, if tragically flawed keystone around which he tried to build his career. When this false story began to crumble, so would his life.

As a book, *To the Top of the Continent*, published in 1908, is a new genre of sorts—part fact, part fiction, with no footnotes to indicate where one begins and the other ends. The mystery of its deceit is as poignant and intriguing today as when that first copy landed in Fairbanks and miners from the Kantishna diggings tried to find the place where true description was replaced with vague, imaginative writing. And within this mystery emerges the larger mystery of Cook himself—and why he felt compelled to perpetuate this deceit.

*Art Davidson*

# TO THE TOP OF THE CONTINENT

## Discovery, Exploration and Adventure in Sub-arctic Alaska, The First Ascent of Mt. McKinley, 1903–1906

---

By Frederick A. Cook, M.D.

*Author of "Through the First Antarctic Night"*

*Chevalier of the Order of Leopold I*

*Member of the American, National,*

*Philadelphia, and Belgian Geographic Societies*

*President of the Explorers Club*

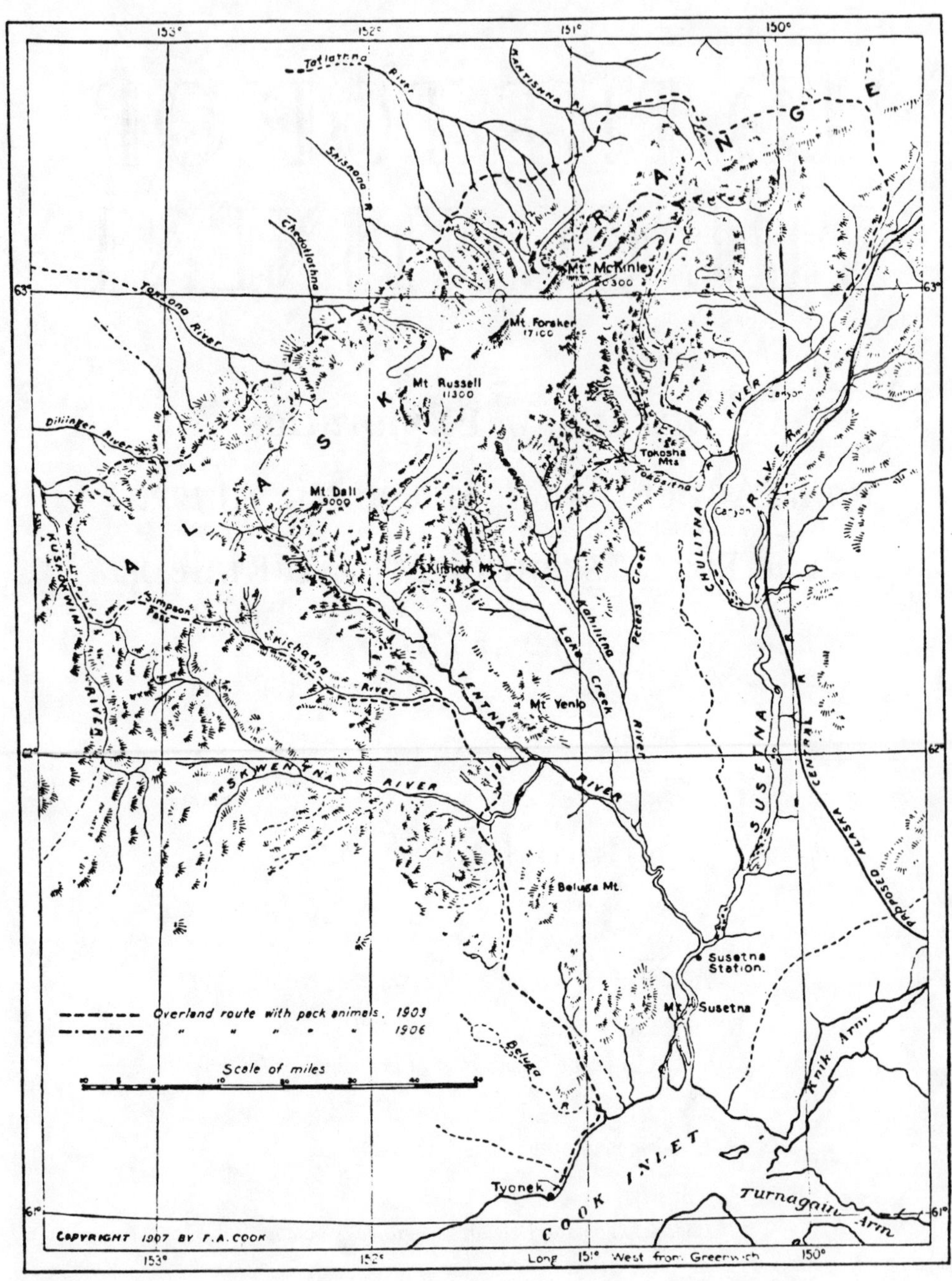


DR. COOK'S DETAILED ROUTE MAP TO MCKINLEY'S SUMMIT

*First published in* Harper's Monthly Magazine, *May 1907*

# CONTENTS

# INTRODUCTORY

In the development of the project for the conquest of the mountain which this volume narrates, a series of barriers arose which seemed almost unsurmountable. A great mountain was rediscovered in an unexplored district and christened in honour of our late President, William McKinley. Preliminary investigation proved this mountain to be the highest peak in North America. Hidden in the heart of Alaska, far from the sea, far from all lines of travel, this newly crowned alpine rival pierced the frosty blue of the Arctic within reach of the midnight sun. The recognition of the pre-eminence of this peak, together with its fitting designation, framed a national mountaineering challenge which we took up fully realising the strenuous task which it entailed. The mere effort of getting to the base of the mountain with sufficient supplies to prolong the siege required the exploration of thousands of miles of trackless wilderness. Unlike most other big mountains this giant uplift rises suddenly out of a low country and the climb begins over ice torn by crevasses and weighted down by sharp stones. Above were 19,000 feet of unknowable troubles, wherein the rush of the crumbling, tumbling earth with its storms and snows must be guarded against. Such an expedition involved most of the difficulties of arctic travel and all of the hardships of high alpine ascents multiplied many times, but with the working incentive of pioneer adventure, and with the spiritual exhiliration of discovery, all these obstacles, it was hoped, would eventually be bridged.

Mountaineering as we assume it in this venture is a department of exploration, and as such it is worthy of a higher appreciation than that usually accorded it. Among our British cousins there has long been an admirable spirit of mountain adventure which has developed into a well-defined sport. In America there has recently grown a similar appreciation of alpine ascents. This is made clear by the vigorous growth of the Alpine, the Appalachian, the Mazama, the Sierra, and other mountain clubs. Mountaineering is too often put down as a kind of dare-devil sport, of risky feats on cloud-piercing pinnacles; but in climbing there is an inspiration expanding with the increase of vision which is capable of much development. In the records of high ascents there is not only the glory of the pioneer spirit of conquest, but also data for scientific research as well as fascinating studies in art. When primitive man climbed the nearest hills to get a better view of the animals he sought, the sport of climbing began. When he extended this climb to higher hills to note the lands beyond, then the science of geography was born, but when he returned and conveyed to others not only the glory of his enlarged horizon but the spirit of the outlook then the climbers' art was established. The succeeding generations, wandering into new areas and expecting always the end of the world just beyond the horizon, have climbed mountains that they might see into the mysterious lands beyond. Seeing no abrupt termination, men have moved on, have climbed other mountains, have looked farther over the globe, until to-day there is the prospect of wireless telegraph stations reaching from peak to peak, from pole to pole.

The mountain climber and the arctic explorer in their exploits run to kindred attainments. The polar traveller walks over uniform snows, over moving seas of wind-driven ice; his siege is long and his main torment is the long winter darkness. The mountaineer reaches heavenward over the snows of cloudland. His task is shorter but more strenuous and his worst discomfort is the task of breathing rarefied air. In the general routine, however, both suffer a similar train of hardships, which hardships are followed by a similar movement of mental awakening, of spiritual aspirations, and of profound and peculiar philosophy. Thus the stream of a new hope, of dreams and raptures is started, and this stream seeks a groove down the path of life forever after. It follows that he who ventures into the polar arena or the cloud battlefield of high mountains will long to return again and again to the scene of his suffering and inspiration. This return habit or migratory spirit is a curious study in one of the first primitive instincts and its most potent factor is the joy of discovery and exploration. Mountaineers and polar explorers are thus members of a widely separated family, and they should be brought closer together as brothers in a new school of pioneer adventure. We have much to learn of each other.

The exploration of the Alaska Range was not seriously attempted until the Klondyke stampede of 1897 indicated the mineral prospects of the adjoining territory. Gold had earlier been found in the Cook Inlet district but the interior from the Inlet to the Yukon was a terra incognita. With the surprising speed of the new gold rush various government reconnoissance expeditions were directed into this area of mystery. At about the same time the gold diggers pressed up the Susitna and among them was W. A. Dickey, who in 1898 sighted a big peak, christened it Mount McKinley, and guessed at its altitude with surprising correctness as 20,000 feet. A sketch of the mountain with notes was sent to the New York *Sun* and the data thus falling into the hands of the noted geographer Cyrus C. Adams were placed on record.

A good deal has been said bearing on the wisdom of placing a modern name over a landmark that would seem to have been recognised and named for ages. We have taken much trouble to clear this point, but up to the present have been unable to trace a name which was previously used to specifically designate this particular peak. The Russians applied the name *Bolshoy*, meaning big, to many high mountains, and this name was given to the peak in question with its companion peaks in the central group. Thus Bolshoy was the general name for the highest section of the Alaska Range. The Susitna Indians gave the name *To-lah-gah* to the same group. Therefore the new name Mt. McKinley finds a proper setting to a fitting monument as a token of appreciation to the memory of one of our greatest statesmen.

The titanic slopes of ice and granite of this most majestic of American summits rise out of the low wet wilderness of mid-Alaska, dividing the game and gold countries which will soon be trailed by the prospector and the nimrod, dividing also the tributary waters of the Yukon, the Kuskokwim, and the Susitna, Alaska's greatest rivers. From the west the giant cliffs rise suddenly out of an ancient glacial shelf extending hundreds of square miles. Here good grass is found in abundance, and herds of caribou graze along the edge of the timber line. At the heads of countless glacial streams the moose nibbles sprigs. In the endless fields of blueberries the huge grizzly bear grunts in peace, and along the foothills in great white zigzags the snowy mountain sheep climbs to untroubled joys. To the north-east and south-west the higher slopes are continuous with a narrow saw-toothed ridge ten thousand feet high. The approaches from the north and east are guarded by a wide belt of mountains rising to altitudes of twelve thousand feet, but from the south-east there is an unobstructed view. From the banks of the Susitna River the mountain stands out a huge succession of cliffs weighted down with all the snow it can possibly carry. Many glaciers receive the ceaseless downpour of avalanches from the misty heights, and these glaciers extend to amphitheatres where the clouds deposit their frozen vapours carried from the warm Japan current.

The task of getting to the base of this mountain is a prodigious venture which offers very many difficult obstacles to the transportation of men and supplies. The prospective conqueror of this immense uplift must pick his path through forest and marsh, to one of its many glaciers, and then begin the climb at 2000 feet or lower. He ascends for miles over sharp broken stones and then up a slope of séracs and arâtes, around gloomy cloud-rubbed rocks, up into the most desperate cold that man has encountered.

We tried not to underestimate the arduous task or the unavoidable hardships of our assumed mission. Months were spent in preparation to use human energy to the best advantage and with the greatest economy. Our ultimate success was due mainly to this preliminary preparation. For the purpose of our enterprise the usual mountaineering equipment was quite impossible, for our limited means of transportation, and likewise the assistance of alpine guides seemed of doubtful value because of the prolonged task of difficult exploration in low countries before the alpine work was to begin.

The food and fuel supply for a prolonged ascent over icy slopes will always prove a difficult problem. In this phase of our work we were greatly helped by the experience in polar effort. After many years of experiment I have about concluded that all the gastronomic needs are best supplied by pemmican, biscuits, and sugar. A few minor accessories might be added but this is all that is absolutely required. For fuel we burned wood below 3000 feet, kerosene for the preliminary exploration among the foothills, and alcohol for the high camps.

The entire equipment for the climbing expedition differed radically from that usually carried, but the special things which led to success were a light Shantung silk tent and a combined robe and sleeping bag, together weighing but eight pounds.

With this refinement of climbing equipment we were able to be independent of guides and of porters, for the necessary weights which we transported were so reduced that with fifty pounds on each of our backs we were completely outfitted for a campaign of two weeks. It is not often that a more prolonged siege is necessary from a base camp.

For the pioneer work of the low country we were guided by the experience of the exploring parties of the U. S. Geological Survey and the needs of the prospectors. Our food supply here was flour, bacon, beans, and the various accessories which the gold diggers have found best. For transportation we secured pack horses east of the Cascade Range; semi-wild, hardy animals that endured the hardships of Alaska very well. For river transportation we built a special river boat able to cope with shallow swift streams. This double system of transportation was of vital importance to us.

In the run of failures and successes which marked our conquest, I was nobly supported by two loyal parties of able assistants. No great task of exploration can succeed without a strong bond of helpfulness extending to the leader and to the family of workers. The unselfish energy expended by every man in my parties was very commendable. We did have our minor differences, but in the main the interest in the success of each expedition was ever foremost. To these men and to a number of warm friends who at home have assisted in the enterprise is due a large measure of praise.

*Frederick Albert Cook.*

*670 Bushwick Ave., Brooklyn, N. Y.*

# PART I

# The Expedition of 1903

ROBERT DUNN, RALPH SHAINWALD, MRS. F. A. COOK, DR. F. A. COOK, FRED PRINTZ

*The party of 1903*

Frederick A. Cook, M.D.

## CHAPTER I

# With the Breath of the Tropics into the Arctic

We had planned to go to the top of the continent, to the summit of Mt. McKinley. This is, perhaps, the most inaccessible of all the great mountains of the world; but it is also the centre of one of the most fascinating areas of rugged wilderness. The huge ice-corniced granite cliffs rise in successive tiers out of a gold-strewn low country, over which wander bear, moose, caribou, and other big game animals. The middle slopes are swept by a sea of storm-driven clouds, and above, far above the usual cloud line, there is a new world of silent glory and snowy wonder. Peak upon peak, range upon range, the great uplift continues to rise into the blackness and mystery of the arctic heavens. Our route is through primeval forests, across and against rushing glacial streams, over marshes and tundras, on to tumbling glacial ice, up into the frosty mist of the upper world. The obstacles are many, but the splendid prospective achievement of the conquest is in fair proportion to the magnitude of the task.

Alighting from the luxurious Northwestern Limited we began our conquest by a jaunt into the primitive at North Yakima. Here we secured from the Indians fifteen pack-horses of the kind which we believed to be best adapted to the rough life of Alaskan mountaineering. The Yakima cayuse has a hard struggle for subsistence in high sterile country, and if properly trained and of good size he works well and endures the northern hardships with less chances of breaking down than animals raised in an easier environment. At Seattle we spent many anxious days in selecting food and equipment. We found the prices there reasonable, and the tradesmen admirably prepared to fit out such ventures as ours.

In due time the expedition with its many needs was on board the quaint Alaskan coaster, the steamer *Santa Ana*. The ropes were cast off at dawn on the morning of June 9, 1903, as the whistles started a run of noises that must have awakened the whole town. Men were on the docks cheering for their parting comrades en route to the new Eldorado of gold and hope; men on board were giving a parting shout to their less ambitious fellows ashore. All of this human howl was followed by a chorus from horses, cattle, pigs, dogs, and chickens on board, giving a taste of wild, animal excitement in keeping with our mission. We were soon gliding over the silvery surface of Puget Sound and, as the dark spirals of smoke rose from the city through the still balmy air into cloudless skies, we got a superb glimpse of the huge forests along the shore-line, and, far beyond, the magnificent snow-crested peaks of the Coast Range. Mt. Tacoma with its poetic mountain solitude, and its sublime vapour drapery of purple and gold, was slowly sinking into the broad green expanse. All on board were on deck dreaming of Alaska and the return a few months hence with pouches of gold and a wealth of other hopes. Good weather followed while the landscape improved with our progress "down north and up along." The

Along the Alaska coast near Sitka

rugged, snowy heights of Vancouver Island, ever wrapped in storm-clouds, made a striking contrast to the sunny, quiet waters of the inland sea which laps the soft green shores of British Columbia. Thus we followed the warm, vapour-charged breezes, the breath of the tropics, along the evergreen shore-line of Alaska with the north-ward sweep of the Pacific into the icy air of the Arctic.

A short stop was made at Juneau early in the morning of the fourth day, and from there delightful weather followed us to Sitka. During the night we steamed easily among the magnificent mountains under a sky ever changing from tones of blue and purple, the prow sending up ripples in glittering waters which reflected the snowy peaks of the arctic world in close contrast to the dense green verdure along tempting shore-lines. The night effect was nearly that of the higher polar zones. There was its silvery brightness, its inspiring stillness, its elusive grandeur, plus the joys of dense forests but without frigid discomforts. Near Sitka we saw two little deer sporting on a sandy beach apparently unconcerned at the sight of a big ship with its noise and smoke.

Sitka is the most picturesque and the most original of the coast towns of Alaska. Its numerous historic reminiscences, its church, its old Russian architecture, and its totem poles, will long make it a mecca for tourists, but as a business town the outlook is not cheerful. The fur trade is no longer profitable, its fisheries are controlled by large canneries. The rival mining excitement in other cities has left Sitka a lonely town interesting for its life of a past decade.

On leaving Sitka most of us went to bed to await Neptune's call, for here we plunged from the quiet inland waters into the always unruly waters of the Gulf of Alaska. The weather proved unexpectedly good, and the *Santa Ana,* though her decks were crowded with lumber, coal, cattle and horses and other live stock, rode the big seas with ease and grace while Captain Schage, ever on the alert for the comfort of his charges, made life easy and interesting. Early in the morning of the 15th the curtain of mist was raised from the Fairweather Range. During the night the needle peaks of Baranoff Island vied with the easy slopes of Edgecomb volcano for notice, but now the giant snowy crests of this unknown cluster of great peaks compelled our attention. At the sound of the ship's triangle at eight, we paced the decks and discussed the principal peaks of the Fairweather and St. Elias groups. Mt. Fairweather was in all its glory of glitter and colour. A bunch of pearly clouds partly screened the sun, allowing silvery beams of light to dart upon glacial slopes, while the waters near the ship were strewn with spouting whales. Mt. Fairweather resembles Mt. McKinley in is general environment and also in main outline. We noted three possible routes to its summit and plotted the mountain for a possible future exploration.

Mt. St. Elias with its companion peak Mt. Logan and the great maze of glaciers and lesser mountains next took our attention. Mt. St. Elias is a huge pyramid rising out of an immense area of glacial ice about forty miles from the sea, while Mt. Logan, a great whaleback of snow in Canadian territory, twenty-five miles beyond St. Elias, among a sheen of giant peaks, is plainly noted as the greatest of the coast peaks. Mt. Logan is over 19,000 feet high and is therefore the second highest peak in North America. Its ascent and exploration offer many difficulties because of the arduous task of approaching its base. Nevertheless, if supplies were moved to the base in the end of February and early March, the lower areas might then be explored while food caches were appropriately placed, and later the final climb might be made by a quick assault.

The coast from Mt. St. Elias to Port Valdez is less picturesque, but more useful. Placer gold, copper, coal, and petroleum are among the minerals which have just at present created a boom. No less than four railroads are here in the course of construction, all aiming at the resources of the interior of Alaska, but mostly the copper of the Copper River Valley. Two of these roads are to start from points near the delta of the Copper River, one from Valdez, and one from Seward. Each terminus has had, or is expected to have, its boom. Valdez was made to survive while its railroad was being projected on paper; later, the town discovered itself, made a trail to Fairbanks, located copper in Prince William Sound, and now the people have a substantial town which originally was little more than a hope for the future. The same can be said of Seward.

With a lighter cargo and less animal life we steamed over the mirrored waters of Prince William Sound with its fascinating reflections of glaciers and snow-streaked mountains, around Kenai Peninsula into the great gulf named in honour of its discoverer, Captain James Cook, Cook Inlet. A delightful run of a few hours among grassy islands where blue foxes are farmed took us to Seldovia. This harbour is a quaint little basin surrounded by a few Indian log huts with grass thatched roofs, a Russian church, and several trading sheds.

We left Seldovia with the first glimmer of dawn, aiming to catch the ingoing tide at Anchor Point. The night was cloudy, but now the sky cleared and a warm glow spread over the cold waters of Cook Inlet. Mt. McKinley, two hundred and forty miles northward, was just visible, a mere tooth of ice biting the arctic skies. The volcanoes, Chinabora, Illiamna, and Redoubt, were all sending columns of steam, but they did not portray signs of warmth. Illiamna and Redoubt were particularly frigid. Great mantles of ice encased their giant slopes to within two thousand feet of the sea level. The Cook Inlet shores showed signs of an earlier season than did the coast from Sitka to Seward. Indeed, from Seward northward and to the utmost reaches of Cook Inlet the advanced stage of vegetation betrays the greater effect of the Japan current. The snow here had been melted several weeks, grass was thriving, the alders, willows, and birches were in new dress, and the overtime work of the sun in high latitude was everywhere in evidence.

Tyonok, a little row of log huts, dignified by more pretentious storehouses of the Alaska Commercial Company, was not sighted until we were within ten miles of the sand spit upon which it is located. Behind it we noted a bank perhaps four hundred feet high with curious lines upon it. Here we saw as we got nearer cultivated gardens, planted on steep slopes because at that angle the greatest heat would be absorbed. These gardens are said to be "planted with a shotgun, and dug out by landslides." Beyond this embankment there is a wide spread of timbered tableland

TYONOK

which ends in the foothills of Mt. Spur, a snow peak nearly 11,000 feet high. The foothills and associated peaks of this mountain are so extensive that it would be safe to say that Mt. Spur has the largest base of any mountain in North America.

At 2 A.M. we dropped anchor in the rushing tidal current a half-mile off shore. Among the huts in Tyonok wolfish Eskimo dogs chased each other, sounding their harrowing howls. This, with the whistle of the *Santa Ana,* brought out a few half-clad, half-awake Indians. On board ship everything was life and bustle, men and horses after a long sea voyage had reached their destination; henceforth a keen battle was to be fought with the sterner elements of nature. All were bent on exploring, some for gold, some to find the haunts of new game, and others to climb America's giant peak. To the east, sharply silhouetted against the orange glow of dawn, we saw Kenai Peninsula, the curious line of ice-crested mountains of

GUIDING A HORSE ASHORE, COOK INLET

uniform height. To the west and south-west, under a dark purple sky, rose the rugged outline of the Alaska Peninsula. The most noticeable features of this sheen of cold, hard mountain expanse were the smoking volcanoes of Illiamna and Redoubt. The icy mantle of Illiamna was glowing with the fire from the rising sun. Redoubt spouted flames and vapours and gave a suggestion of life and heat to what appeared to be a land of death and frost.

The shore-line of the head of Cook Inlet was screened by a blue haze, but several times during the night of twilight we got a peep of a snowy crest which pierced the blue dome far northward. This peak like a star on a cloudy night would blink and disappear with marvellous quickness. It did not seem to us as being very far away, nor did it give the impression of great altitude, but there was a mystery about the thing which kept one's attention pointed. This in reality was Mt. McKinley, one hundred and fifty miles away, the ultimate destination of the impatient adventurers on board the *Santa Ana*, the new Eldorado of the big game hunter, the gold seeker, and the mountaineer.

I found it interesting to try to note the reasons why men go to this far-off northland to fulfil the ambitions of the prospector, the hunter, or the mountaineer. The three classes have no interest in common, and no sympathy for each other; each argued that the other's longing should be satisfied nearer home; but the somewhat similar train of troubles in prospect for them made a kind of brotherly bond to help each other. We were all the wildest kind of dreamers.

Soon we began to throw the horses over to swim ashore, but the tide was so strong and the water so cold that the poor creatures were nearly exhausted before they scented the shore. The long ocean voyage had prepared the animals doubly to appreciate the sense of security of land and its growth of luscious green grass. Their ears quivered, their heads raised, and their feet were light when green fields and new forests were once more before them.

We had now come five thousand miles only to find that the enormous task of getting to the base of the great mountain had but just begun. Thus far our voyage had been one of pleasing surprises greatly enjoyed by all, but now we had arrived at the parting of the ways, and also came the parting of friends. Mrs. Cook had accompanied us thus far and was eager to go farther, but in the anticipated hardships of the overland trip it did not seem to be prudent to risk the discomforts, so she wisely decided to limit her exploring ventures to the more congenial coast in the vicinity of Valdez. Captain Schage and several other friends bade us a hearty farewell, then the old steamer turned seaward and we were left to work out the task of transporting ourselves and supplies over regions of forests, marshes, and mountains to the heart of Alaska.

By this time I had gotten acquainted with the men of the party, and it was now clear to me that I had made no mistake in the selection of the personnel. At any rate the manly faithfulness of each was clear and while we must have personal differences of opinion, as do the members of every pioneer expedition, the determined union of forces displayed on this first day of hard work was never broken.

CHAPTER II

# From Volcanic Fires to Frigid Jungle

We had quite an exciting adventure in training our semi-savage horses to submit to carrying packs. The long period en route by train and boat, being fed on oats and cooped up in small boxes, did not tend to a taming tendency. First the Indian dogs tormented them, and later the flies and mosquitoes sapped their blood, and now we were trying to harness the excited animals. They had about decided that this new land promised trouble and they resented with tooth and hoof. For two days we packed the cayuses and they unpacked themselves, kicking us and the packs around the old army barracks in lively Western style. Ronzo, the most wicked of the horse desperadoes, escaped so many times and made such dangerous plunges that we thought it prudent to give him his freedom. Finch, the energetic storekeeper of the Alaska Commercial Company, said that he would school him to a better life, but Ronzo's heels were too light and when we returned four months later he was still the hero of liberty, roaming at will in the forests toward the fires of Redoubt volcano.

Packed with one hundred and fifty pounds each the horses were started northward on the morning of June 25th along the beach of Cook Inlet. The animals were frisky and set a rapid pace. Soon after noon we reached the end of an extensive flat meadow which marked the beginning of the low country of the delta of the Beluga. Here we found in abundance the three necessities of camp life, grass, wood, and water, and soon decided to camp. On the following day we set a course through a jungle out of which the snow had just melted, to the first bank above the delta about five miles from the mouth. Here we saw a large brown bear on the opposite shore pitching salmon on the beach. The bear paid no attention to us, and since we were not in need of either his skin or his meat we did not interrupt his sport. Successive schools of white whales (belugas) ascended the river, cutting the oily, chocolate coloured surface of the waters in a vigorous but graceful manner and spouting jets of vapour with a sound that reverberated from shore to shore, breaking the silence of an otherwise desolate wilderness.

The Beluga River takes its name from these white whales ascending its waters. From the miners who have prospected its shores to the source we learned that the river is about thirty miles long and starts from two deep lakes. These lakes are supplied by glacial streams coming from the mountains to the north and east of Mt. Spur. Great overhanging glaciers are above the last of these lakes and the frequent earthquakes shake down extensive masses of ice, which, falling into the lake, cause the river to rise with a dangerous suddenness. One of these strange floods occurred in winter when the temperature was 40° below zero, and all the river was covered with ice. Suddenly the ice and the flats were flooded and the miners who were sledding up the river barely escaped by climbing trees, for a flood at such a temperature makes a sweep of death to all living things.

The Beluga is very shallow at its mouth but at high tide moderate-sized boats with a draft of not more than four feet can cross the delta. Above the stream deepens and narrows to about four hundred feet. It is navigable for about ten miles and

INTO THE CHULITNA CANYONS

with dories much farther. This would make a splendid area for a small exploring party. Bears are very numerous and the chances for other game are good. The opportunities for original discovery are not surpassed by many other regions. Placer gold, copper, and coal exist here, in tempting quantities. The river winds through a densely forested low country where botanical enthusiasts and collectors of small life are likely to make many discoveries. In the lakes should be found rare specimens and in the mountains above there are new unmapped snow peaks and glaciers enough to satisfy the most ardent alpine climber.

From Tyonok a boat was sent to the Beluga to ferry the men and the packs. This task about completed we took the lead horse, fastened to him a long rope, urged him into the river, and paddled slowly across stream, while the other horses were forced to plunge in from a cut bank. They gathered in a bunch, snorting, and tried to get back to the shore from which they started. Failing in this they took to the stream for the green meadows opposite where the lead horse was towed as a decoy. They climbed out on the soft marshes and here they saw many fresh bear tracks which interested them very much. With their noses to the footprints they started in a hasty pursuit like dogs on the chase.

The route which we had outlined to the western slopes of Mt. McKinley was one explored and advocated by Alfred H. Brooks of the U. S. Geological Survey. From the Beluga there was an old Indian winter trail close to the head waters of the Theodora River over bald hills to the head waters of the Talushulitna River, and from thence keeping a general north-western course to the head waters of Canyon Creek, following this creek to the Skwentna River. Descending the Skwentna to a point about a mile below the lower canyon and crossing here the trail wound around the shell hills over an old trail cut by Lieutenant Heron. We aimed to cross the range through Simpson Pass into the Kuskokwim and from there, above the tree line and close to the Alaska Range we expected to find a trail to Mt. McKinley.

Under the direction of Dunn the pack train was started over the Indian trail for the Skwentna. I estimated that it would take about seven days to cover this sixty miles of very difficult travelling through dense forests over marshes and tundras. We anticipated considerable difficulty in getting a boat to the Skwentna ford in time to ferry the packs across without delay. Though I should have preferred to join the pack train the uncertainties of the boat mission were so great that I assumed the responsibilities of that campaign with Miller as my associate. In our small dory loaded to the gunwale we drifted quickly along the cut banks of the Beluga in oily brown waters, out through the delta with its great stir of bird life into the rushing tide ripples of Cook Inlet. We thought we had gauged the tide time rightly, for in the Inlet tide not time rules every movement by land or sea. Ashore progress is only possible along the sandy beach at low tide; by water, since the tidal current is eight miles per hour, everything goes with it. We aimed to strike the tide high and so go over the great flats into the delta of the Susitna River. The river is about five miles wide at its mouth with but two or three navigable channels very difficult to find. While searching for these channels the tide suddenly went out and left us high on a vast mud flat. In a few minutes we found our boat glued to a pasty clay a mile from shore and three miles from the receding tide waters. This was exactly what we had tried to avoid, for we knew that the rising tide was likely to come with the wild sweep of a destructive boa, filling our boat before she could rise from the sticky clay.

The ensuing night caused us a great deal of anxiety. Our first concern was to devise some plan to raise the boat on planks so the coming tide would not find us pasted to the clay. This was soon accomplished and then we sought some wood for a camp-fire. A good portion of the night was spent in brewing tea, cooking beans, and baking bread while we watched carefully the weather signs. For an incoming wind with the tide would mean destruction to us. We took turns in keeping up the watch for the coming danger.

This night with its run of uncomfortable premonitions was nevertheless strikingly impressive. The sun sank under the rugged snowy peaks of the Tordrillo Range, leaving a warm rosy after-glow over everything. Even the mud which, ordinarily black and repulsive, covered our surroundings glittered with reflected colours. Redoubt volcano, eighty-five miles south, in a cloak of violet snow, belched huge tongues of fire and clouds of vapour. One hundred and twenty miles south, still plainly visible, was Mt. Illiamna, clear cut, its cone of bright purple snow standing against a sky of dark purple-blue. Then as the eye glanced across the great expanse of rushing waters of Cook Inlet it rested upon a sea of fascinating blues and purples and violets, flooded by the rose and gold of the parting sun. Far off to the west, under a haze of blue, were the curious mountains of equal height, characteristic of the Kenai Peninsula. To the north Mt. Susitna, dull, black, and gloomy, wrapped in storm clouds, apparently but a stone's throw though fifteen miles away, and to

Redoubt Volcano, Cook Inlet

the eastward of it the great broad delta of the Susitna River, covered by a dense verdure, almost tropical in luxuriance. It was a scene which rapidly changed in colour and interest as the long twilight of the arctic midsummer night advanced.

In the morning the tide came and lifted us as easily as it had left us, and then we pulled for the left fork of the Susitna River. We soon found that the current of the river was too strong for rowing, so we tried towing. At noon we came to a small Indian settlement, where we got an Indian boy by the name of Stephen to assist us. Stephen proved to be an expert boatman, but our troubles increased with every mile of advance. The water got swifter and deeper, too swift to paddle and too deep to pole, while the cut banks and overhanging brush made lining almost impossible.

On the morning of July 2d, after nearly four days of the hardest kind of river boating, we reached Susitna Station, a small trading post twenty miles up the river. The weather had been uniformly bad, cold and wet, but it did not prevent the gnats and mosquitoes from doing their worst. These persistent pests followed us over the waters in clouds, with a buzz that drove us to the verge of madness. Our hands and faces were so badly bitten that we developed serious forms of inflammation, followed by pain, fever, and torture indescribable. All this in spite of great care in protecting ourselves by "dope," veils, gloves, and a mosquito-proof tent. I have seen mosquitoes and allied pests in all parts of the world, but the Susitna denizens are certainly in my experience by far the most desperate in their attack upon man and beast.

THE SUSITNA CHIEF

At the Station we secured Evan, an Indian friend of Stephen, to assist us; we also obtained a better river boat. We had arranged to meet the pack train at a point fifteen miles up the Skwentna River in a week after leaving the Beluga. We had spent five days in ascending the Susitna twenty miles, and now there were sixty miles of worse water ahead of us before we could join our party. Our Indians told us that it would take twenty days to meet the horses.

Soon after leaving the Station we pulled up the Yentna River, a great glacial stream a half-mile wide draining most of the eastern side of the Alaska Range.

Poling and towing, rowing, pushing, and by all kinds of devices, we averaged twelve miles daily. The fifteen miles up the Skwentna River to the canyon, which we were told could not be made in less than a week, was covered in one long day. On the morning of the 8th of July, we pitched camp on a small island in the Skwentna River, two miles below the canyon, the appointed place to meet the pack train. Nothing was observed of our companions, though we expected them to have been in waiting several days, till noon of the same day, when we heard a voice and soon we saw the horses moving along the southern side of the river. The Skwentna is here about three hundred yards wide, and plunges over a gravel bed at the rate of eight miles per hour. The men and outfit were quickly ferried over, but we had considerable trouble in swimming the horses. One unfortunate animal was carried down-stream five miles, and was only finally secured by the great skill and diligence of Printz; but the animal was so nearly exhausted that it never recovered its normal strength, although it followed us to Mt. McKinley.

The course taken by the pack-train from the Skwentna River was almost due north twenty miles over swampy spruce-timbered country to the Kichatna River about four miles above its mouth, and to this point it was also necessary to take the boat.

# CHAPTER III

# Westward Through the Alaska Range into the Kuskokwim

The descent of the Skwentna River was immensely exciting. In less than two hours we rushed over fifteen miles of foaming rapids, jumping boulders and snags and gravel bars with a rush that made us hold our breaths. In ascending the Yentna we discovered that the river in the vicinity of Mt. Yenlo split into several slews making large picturesque islands. To study this curious distribution of river waters and the edge of the Alaska Range through which we were about to seek a pass we ascended Mt. Yenlo or *Tahliktoh* as the Susitna Indians call the mountain. It was also expected that from here we would be able to get a good view of Mt. McKinley and its environments from the south and east.

We landed on the east side of the Yentna at a point where the main river is nearest the southwest base of the mountain. After making camp under birch trees we left Evan to guard the boat from floating driftwood and our food from bears, while Miller and Stephen joined me in the first alpine adventure. A broad marshy meadow was first crossed. Here we sank to our knees in pools while the brush and high grass made progress difficult and slow. In the centre of this marsh we found a chain of small lakes in which we saw salmon trout darting about. On the surface of these lakes we were surprised to find pond lilies and along the edge were beautiful yellow and purple flowers. The soft green verdure and the warm colours of the mountain were superbly reflected in the mercurial surface of the water, but in our comforts we were not in harmony with the deceptive congeniality. The water was just above the freezing point, we were saturated to the skin by the wet grass, and in sinking waist deep into pools we had become coated with mud. Mosquitoes in clouds were settling upon us, and the normal chill of the frigid jungle was approaching with the setting sun.

In trying to pick the most promising ground we noticed that a grizzly had been through there on a similar mission. We followed his foot-prints and soon discovered that his course was good enough for us. We argued that this bear was probably aiming for the blueberries above tree line, or the ground rats at the top of Mt. Yenlo, and after eating bacon and beans, as we had for two weeks, we were ready to accept bear diet or even bear steaks as a delightful change.

Miller and Stephen, with their guns always ready, turned their eyes expectantly from side to side, but they saw only the fool-hens. Bruin had good sense; he knew where the ground was best, and, better still, he led us to the only place where the lakes could be crossed. As we reached the base of the mountain the trail was lost and then we picked a course through a dense forest to an elevation of two thousand eight hundred feet; five hundred feet more were made through grass five feet high, and there on an old glacial shelf we pitched camp at midnight.

Early on the morning of July 12th, we tumbled out of our silk tent, and with a few roots we made a fire over which we melted some snow for a cup of tea, and then, over steep grassy slopes, we made the final ascent to the top. From here we had a most magnificent view of the easterly slope of the Alaska Range, and of the vast expanse of fertile lowlands. It was a view of the least known but probably the most picturesque area of Alaska.

Mt. Yenlo rises out of a wide expanse of low marshy country. The mountain is a narrow ridge running north and south with several peaks, the highest point being the most northern one, about five thousand feet. Our position was near the centre at an elevation of four thousand two hundred feet.

The top of the mountain was covered with short grass and some moss. The blueberries just under the crest of the mountain were not yet ripe. Here and there were banks of winter snow still resting in sunless places. Hundreds of ground rats were darting about, and when there was no wind we were tortured greatly with mosquitoes.

The grizzly had preceded us and dug out many ground rats and our Indian boy followed his haunts with visions of bear steaks. The mosquitoes were so troublesome that we found it difficult to manipulate our instruments, but soon there came a breeze out of the long blue waters of Cook Inlet which swept the little pests from our immediate neighbourhood. Taking advantage of this little puff of air we set our cameras, levelled our theodolite, and arranged the other instruments for a round of observations. These observations when worked out did not alter the essential features of the remarkable map made by Brooks and Reaburn, but we were able to fill in several blank spots.

We now saw that the Yentna River which we had ascended divided its waters between the Skwentna and the Kichatna around three large islands. These islands and indeed all of the lowlands looked like carefully cultured parks. There were belts of high spruce, birch, and cottonwood trees along the water and inside of this dark green belt, usually but a few hundred feet wide, was a level area beautifully covered with a profuse growth of light-green grass. Circles of alders and willows and small lakes covered with pond lilies made the park-like picture complete. No city park could give a more beautiful and carefully planned artistic effect than this impenetrable wilderness to the east and west of Mount Yenlo. Our position was high and far enough away to prevent a critical view, for in reality no tropical jungles could be more dense than the chaos of underbrush in the narrow belt of forest. The beautiful light-green meadows were marshes over which man or beast could only travel with the greatest difficulty. Later we learned to our hearts' content that this enticing landscape so beautiful to look upon offered us the tortures of countless devils—mosquitoes, horse-flies, gnats, and marshes, thick underbrush, icy streams, and never-ceasing rains all combined to make life thoroughly miserable for us. In this misery we lost our earlier enthusiasm for the bird's-eye view from Mount Yenlo.

Our admiration of the great Bolshoy group, which as seen from that point is surely the most remarkable range in North America, was heightened from every other point of observation, though we did not again get so comprehensive a view. Sixty miles northward Mt. Foraker, a double ridge, acted as a barrier to the westerly drift of clouds. A little to the eastward, seventy-five miles away, was Mt. McKinley, a huge beehive loaded down with prodigious quantities of snow. East of Mt. McKinley we saw a group of mountains from five thousand to ten thousand feet high, separated by deep narrow gorges. Mt. Russell is a sharp ice-sheeted pyramid piercing the sky about seventeen miles south-west of Mt. Foraker. About twenty miles below appeared Mt. Dall, also a pyramid, mostly free of snow, with the rock strata clearly marked though forty miles away.

Midway between Mt. Dall and Mt. Russell we noticed a cluster of sharp peaks east of the main range with an average height of about eight thousand feet. These I have named Bryant Peaks in honour of my friend and co-worker, Mr. Henry G. Bryant, Secretary of the Alpine Club.

The Yentna takes its head waters from the glaciers in the vicinity of Mt. Dall, Mt. Russell, and Bryant Peaks. In the rolling foothills south-east of Mt. McKinley we noticed a depression which we afterwards learned was the bed of a large glacial stream, which flowing easterly and joining the streams from Ruth glacier empties into the Chulitna River above the lower canyon. This uncharted river is called by the Indians *Tokositna*.

The origin of the Skwentna River was easily seen from Mt. Yenlo. Out of the high icy mountains west of Alger Peak and north of Mt. Estelle the waters descended; uniting with those of the opposite side they pour into a canyon; but a few miles below, the waters rush out and spread over a wide flat, narrowing again to a second canyon below. The Skwentna is about eighty miles long and three hundred feet wide near its mouth, and is navigable with dories for about forty miles. The last fifteen miles of the stream flows through a low country to the Yentna. There is placer gold and lignite coal found along this river.

The Kichatna, taking its first milky waters from Fleishmann and Caldwell glaciers, takes a course nearly parallel to that of the Skwentna, through a deep gorge, and pours over a succession of rapids almost its entire course, emptying into the Yentna opposite Mt. Yenlo. The river is about fifty miles long and about one hundred and fifty feet wide near its mouth; navigable with dories for only about ten miles. Gold is found at a point just beyond navigation. Up the valley of the Kichatna we saw continuous streams of great, fluffy, cumulus and nimbus clouds drifting through the range to the arctic slopes beyond. To follow these clouds with our dreams of mountaineering conquests is the next adventure.

At breakfast we ate our last food. We expected to get to the river for lunch, but it took us nearly all day to get to the section of the mountain necessary for our observations. At lunch Stephen got for us some ground rats, saying they were good for white men but not for Indians. We tried roasting them on a stick, and while we were not enthusiastic as to their palatableness, we agreed that rats were not bad. We descended in about two hours and found Evan haunted by all kinds of spirits—saying it was no good for an Indian to be left alone.

We ascended the Kichatna River late that night, July 13th, so late that it proved too dark to find a camping place. It was a welcome sound when at eleven o'clock we heard voices and saw the camp-fire of our companions on the south bank of the river, in a swamp among spruce trees. On the following morning we crossed the stream, and found a better camping ground. Dunn reported much difficulty in crossing the low, wet country. The horses were frequently mired, and both men and horses showed signs of a hard time. After a day's rest the horses were started with light packs up-stream along the soft ground of the banks and over many slews to the first high ground. The boat, with an increased load, followed. Our camp on the evening of the 5th was on a foothill about ten miles from the mouth of the river. From here our Indians were sent back. They were good faithful helpers, and we would gladly have taken them farther, but they were eager to return to their fishing grounds, and we could not have carried food enough for them had they continued with us.

Our route now lay westerly along the Kichatna and this in many respects proved to be our most difficult trail. Continued rains, thick underbrush, rapid streams, and difficult slopes, as well as horse-flies and mosquitoes, all combined to retard progress. Our horses soon failed in strength and were so sick that we could march them only three hours every second day. Their legs were very much bruised and lacerated by the brush, their skins so badly bitten by horse-flies and mosquitoes that they developed a kind of blood poisoning. Our packer called the disease distemper, but I am inclined to ascribe the entire trouble to direct poisoning through open wounds. A somewhat similar affection is commonly known among the Indians and prospectors who are much bitten.

The scenery up the Kichatna was usually hidden from us by the dense forests and thick clouds which drifted into the pass. Occasionally we got a glimpse of rounded mountains, three thousand to four thousand feet high. To the south we observed frequently high picturesque peaks in unexplored areas. We longed to investigate this region, but our main object compelled us to press onward. As we rose out of the Kichatna we got a glimpse of the first remarkable scenery at close range—to the north, a great brown tongue of ice, Caldwell Glacier, nearly two miles wide, with arms reaching to unknown heights between steep, snowy slopes. The water which comes over, under, and through this glacier with a mad rush gives origin to the Kichatna River. Before us was the broad, green depression, with black, cloud-crested, slaty peaks to both sides, six thousand feet high. This valley leads to several passes through the Alaska Range—one to the south, which Brooks discovered; another westerly named by Lieutenant Heron, Simpson Pass; and there is probably still another between the two. Before entering Simpson Pass, we crossed a milky stream, which came from a cavern leading to Fleishmann Glacier. This glacier in size and surroundings is similar to Caldwell and its drainage joins the same river.

It had rained almost incessantly from the time we left Tyonok. The men were always soaked to their skins, their boots were continually filled with ice-water, and the horses were wet and bleeding from wounds, but in spite of all this we slowly pushed our pack train up the Kichatna into the divide which had been crossed by Heron and Brooks, camping among the cottonwood trees near the head waters of the Kichatna.

In the pouring rain, on July 27th, we started the pack train up the steep treeless slopes over which the clouds pressed through the range. It was an old gathering basin, part of a huge ice system which once filled the valley of the Kichatna. Blueberries were very abundant and so were signs of bears. We saw one as we got well into the mountains, and we quickly had visions of bear steaks; but the bear also saw us, and betook himself out of range. Moose, caribou, and sheep tracks were abundant. The tracks of Heron's pack train where it crossed here five years previously were still visible and also those of Brooks's horses. We camped at an altitude of about four thousand feet along the northern side of the valley one mile east of Fleishmann Glacier. It was a miserable camp with rain and snow being driven by violent gusts of wind, and with only small green willows to burn, but the pass which we aimed to follow had as yet not been located and we did not care to travel through the frosty mists to the dangerous cliffs and overhanging glaciers as we broke through the range.

During the brief periods of clearing we saw gaps through the range and the deep blue of the Kuskokwim skies beyond. To the southward was Brooks's Rainy Pass, but we wanted a more northerly route. To the northward there was a promising gorge but this proved to be a blind pass leading to a kind of ice-cap. In our scouting about we saw a gap north of Brooks Pass which offered a workable route but in seeking Heron's trail, we went close to the face of Fleishmann Glacier, and from there was noted a deep cut choked with clouds. We explored this and found it to be Simpson Pass for which we had been looking. With this happy news we returned to our shivering colleagues at camp and ate an extra ration of bacon and beans to celebrate our luck.

Very early on the following morning we gathered the horses, who seemed to enjoy the frosty air because of the freedom from mosquitoes, and packed for the plunge into the Kuskokwim. We crossed a huge ice bridge and turned sharply to the west over a grassy meadow marking the divide, into a little stream. This stream was hardly more than a leaping jet of spring water, but its volume increased quickly. Soon we descended to alders and willows of moderate size, and there the stream had grown to a vigorous brook and plunged into a desperate looking canyon. We sought a trail over the walls above the canyon and crossed from side to side as required by the slopes. The splendid spruce forests of the Kuskokwim were seen soon after crossing the divide, and to get to these was our day's mission, but the distance was deceptive; men and horses tumbled down slopes all that day—until almost too tired to move their feet. The march was continued for fifteen hours without stopping to eat lunch. Late at night as the sun was gliding northward we stumbled into the broad expanse of the Rohn River. It was a deep and swift glacial stream, but just beyond were big green trees and on the steep grassy slopes above hundreds of white mountain sheep were seen grazing in groups. The possibility of juicy sheep meat made us forget all the discomforts of the day.

Our camp here was better in its anticipation than in its realisation. After various kinds of gun luck we had but one old Winchester in working order, and it did not shoot straight at long range. The sheep were wise enough to be watchful and no meat was secured, but it was satisfactory in a way just to see them wander at long range, over snow-streaked mountains. Moose and bear tracks were abundant but we were too hard pressed for time to do much hunting. In the low country fool-hens, ptarmigan, rabbits, and squirrels were abundant. Food for the horses was very scarce in this region near the Kuskokwim and the horses in consequence greatly failed in strength. There was, however, one great redeeming feature in the life west of the range—this was the entire absence of horseflies and mosquitoes.

Two days' march brought us to the Kuskokwim River, among mountains six thousand feet high, appropriately named, because of their colour, Terra Cotta Mountains. Here our lot was unfortunate. The horses again failed because of the scarcity of grass, and worse still, John Carroll, who had been ailing for some time, found that he could no longer keep up with the pack train, and returned, taking with him one horse to carry his provisions. Our party now consisted of five men and thirteen horses; the horses each carrying about one hundred pounds.

Just ahead of us at this time was Egypt Mountain, a pyramid of red sandstone; a little farther north, Farewell Mountain; and beyond the great green expanse the spruce covered valley of the Kuskokwim. Soon after passing Egypt we bid farewell to the Kuskokwim, and set a course above the tree line north-easterly along the northern slope of the Alaska Range. Here the grass improved; blue-berries and game were abundant. Horses and men were well fed, and accordingly rapid progress was made.

CHAPTER IV

# Through the World's Best Big Game Country

We now entered Nimrod's dreamland. To the west were ten thousand square miles of unexplored territory. We made no attempt to press into this, but from our various high points of outlook we could see that it was a low, rolling, spruce-covered country. We noted that the south fork of the Kuskokwim drains the western side of the Alaska Range, as does the Yentna from the east. Its waters, however, descend into the great sluggish volume of the lower river and reach the Bering Sea, by a broad, dangerous delta.

Our route was along the edge of this timber, north-easterly parallel to the Alaska Range for several hundred miles. To the east there was a surprise at every turn. Range after range of rounded foothills rose to beautiful snowy crests. Great gorges and canyons with rushing milky streams led to the tongues of unnamed glaciers. Below a sub-arctic forest of mystery with its unknown small life and fur-clad animals; above the paradise of the bear, moose, caribou, and sheep.

We had now, in spite of various trials and difficulties, gone about one half of the distance to Mt. McKinley. In an air line this distance would probably be one hundred and fifty miles, but in reality we had covered more than three hundred and fifty miles over the worst kind of trail imaginable. Our outfit had been wet constantly and our food was beginning to show the effects of the bad weather and bad treatment. To the present we had secured very little game. Birds and fish, it is true, were abundant, but as a rule we had not the time to hunt or fish. Our hopes, however, were good, for now we were about to enter a region where the signs of large game were such that we must stumble over fresh meat.

We turned our backs to the Kuskokwim, with its famine of grass, to the great evergreen expanse beyond Egypt and Farewell mountains on the morning of August 2d. An icy wind followed us, but we soon entered a dense forest. At noon we broke through thick brush and came out upon the wide flats of Jones River. Here we found some grass, and though we had made but a short march our horses were too hungry to travel farther. This camp was particularly agreeable to both men and horses. The animals had their first good feed for several days, and with an abundance of blueberries and partridges we too had a good dinner. In exploring above camp we saw game signs everywhere, but as yet nothing big had gotten in range of our inefficient gun.

Rising higher and closer to the range we crossed several dry, barren ridges, and descended to the southern fork of the Dillinger River. Here we secured a young brown bear, and gloried in bear steaks, bacon and beans, and delicious brown biscuits baked in the reflector. As the sun sank into the burning gold of the Bering Sea that night we were tired but enthusiastic as to the outcome of our undertaking.

A quantity of bear meat was packed as we started on the crisp morning of August 5th. The weather since crossing the range was much better than along the eastern side of the mountains, though a few clouds were still pressing from the east through narrow gaps between snow peaks, and these poured brief but severe rain showers over us. The temperature was usually about 50° and the humidity increased rapidly as we went northward. We were now above brush; the ground was hard but the land became more and more irregular as we pressed towards the Tonzona River. Steep climbs and disheartening descents were necessary to keep to a good general north-easterly course.

From the Jones River to the Dillinger River we crossed a very irregular country over the depressions of low rolling foothills into marshy gullies. As we neared the Dillinger we passed through a beautiful green expanse, spotted by many small clear lakes, and here our scent for game became keener than ever. Many reported sights of moose proved to be illusions, but game trails crossed everywhere, and finally as the pack train rose over a mountain Printz hurriedly came back to the lead horse for the rifle and, while men and horses remained motionless, then advanced behind a row of rocks. There were four or five shots in rapid succession and then rising to spot the luck we saw that a big brown bear had fallen and we thought him dead, yet when Printz advanced knife in hand to get his skin the bear quickly picked himself up and vanished in the brush where we dared not follow.

Our camp that night was on an elevated bench above the lakes. Having made a long march we were too tired to do much hunting, but we watched the shores of the blue lakes with a hungry interest. The howl of the wolf, the bark of the foxes, and the giggle of the fool-hens and ptarmigans made the night air ring with weird noises which the horses did not relish. Our route during the next day took us over fresh moose trails which had been trampled to the depth of two feet below the level. We had lunch in a big patch of blueberries at the side of a river somewhat larger than Jones River. The stream rises out of a great gap through the range which seemed to be a pass for the moose and caribou to the east. Taking the drainage of the many small lakes it flows westerly, emptying into the Kuskokwim about one mile north of the mouth of Jones River.

Rising out of the Dillinger we saw several caribou and tried them with our rifles, but they only shook their heads and ran gracefully into the upper valleys. Later on, however, while crossing a nameless stream beyond the Dillinger, we saw a pair of horns winding among the big boulders up-stream and making an air line for our pack train. No one would take the gun for they had all tried and failed. Printz insisted that I try a shot; I did so, dropped the animal and thereby established confidence in the old Winchester, and incidentally my own reputation as a marksman was made. During the rest of the trip, with new confidence in the gun, our larder was kept supplied, but I did not again risk my reputation as a shot.

Over mountains ever higher, and slopes continuously more difficult, we pressed on for the Tonzona River. The weather was clear and warm and game was in evidence on every side, but now we secured it with such ease that the pack train was seldom interrupted in its march. Above us were long lines of white sheep moving in sunny patches of new green grass, below herds of caribou moving up the banks of small streams for the new grass in the uplands.

Late in the afternoon of August 8th, we rose to a saddle at an altitude of about five thousand feet and from this place we saw for the first time, from the west, the distinctive peaks of the main range. Mounts Russell and Dall were easily recognised from the score of lesser peaks. To the south of Mt. Dall we noted several wide gaps out of which pour the head waters of the Dillinger and the Tonzona rivers. Clouds drifted through these gaps as they did through Simpson Pass and Brooks Pass. There seemed to be signs of good passes from the Tonzona to the Yentna.

As the sun poured its parting rays on the shining spires of Mt. Russell we rose to a dome-shaped mountain and beyond saw for the first time the broad expanse of the gravel bars of the Tonzona. The great low cuts through the mountains, making a canal for the clouds from the east, were now seen to better advantage. Beyond the Tonzona was an easy rise to a table-land and along the edge of this were huge boulders giving the impression of the houses of a big city. This table-land was the shelf of an old glacier which extends to and beyond Mt. McKinley. We descended very quickly along a steep slope winding around cliffs into a small stream which led us into the big cottonwood and spruce forests, to the side of the Tonzona. From this camp we saw our first moose. It crossed the stream near camp and rising to a green hummock within a few hundred yards above us from there looked down upon the stir of horses and men with evident curiosity. We did not need meat and could not carry his great spread of horns as a specimen, and therefore the animal was not molested.

East of the range the camp life was a torture. Continual rains, hungry mosquitoes, dense wet brush, and frequent icy fords made our daily adventures so difficult that we had neither the time nor the disposition to dwell on the few pleasant phases of the boundless wilderness through which we forced a trail. But along the northern foothills all this changed. The weather was good, the mosquitoes were absent, the whole aspect of life was better, and with all this was the happy environment of a new world of big, wild animals roaming about undisturbed by man.

In this northland, where dusk and dawn run together, men get into the real swing of nature and close to each other's hearts at the camp-fire. There is something about the crackle of the fire, the inspiration of the blaze, and the long frosty nights of twilight, which bares the breast of each camper to the scrutiny of his companions. At the club a man may be a good fellow superficially, with the veneer of a make-believe spirit of human brotherhood over a selfish centre of commonplace discord, but in the sub-arctic wilderness this is impossible. Naked manliness under togs that are stripped and dried at the evening round-up with the aroma of the spruce and the music of the forest wilds, is the ultimate necessity of every adept.

If a man has been an artist, with system and order in the daily routine of his home life, he is sure to get a large measure of admiration from his comrades, for he gathers and disseminates bits of light that dispel the fatigue of the hard day's trail; but the haphazard chap who has run the life of a literary hack bewails his misfortunes, makes copy, secretes his observations of interesting things, and makes life tiresome by his egotism. As a discloser of manly character the camp-fire surpasses the confession booth.

On the morning of August 9th, we packed the decreasing loads on the horses and cut trail through a wide belt of large trees. The Tonzona was here divided into a number of rushing streams. For each crossing it was necessary to mount the horses, and we had become quite expert at this kind of fording. All our things were packed in water-proof bags, and when about to ford we would make a running jump, alighting behind the packs. If the prospective ford proved a swim, as was often the case, we held to the pack ropes as best we could. In crossing the coffee-coloured waters of the Tonzona two streams were found to be very deep, and at one of these, after losing considerable time seeking a place to ford, we at last plunged in for a swim. Men and horses were carried down-stream a long way. Two animals turned over in midstream and their riders struck out for the shore, leaving the horses to follow. It was a warm, sunny day, but this swim in glacial waters made us feel like travellers en route to the Pole.

With garments soaked to our skins and with shoes full of water we continued the march. There was not time to change, nor had we the extra clothing, for these fords were so frequent that being wet was by this time regarded as a part of the game of getting to Mt. McKinley. Indeed we had adapted ourselves to this semi-aquatic system of travelling. We wore no hats, only very light clothing, and short shoe packs. After a swim we shook ourselves and hurried along to warm up and dry out by the increased action of the march. Men will get used to this kind of life after awhile and enjoy it, but in the schooling one hears a great deal of sulphurous language.

Climbing out of the Tonzona we rose about two thousand feet over the edge of an old moraine among giant boulders. Here were extensive patches of large, delicious blueberries and also bright green spots of new grass. Men and horses with equal zest bent to the fruits of the soil. After half an hour the horses were rounded up and with grunts of mingled satisfaction and protest the ascent was continued to the great treeless plain above. On this grassy expanse, looking over the numerous lakes of the lower plains, we saw many caribou, feeding with the contentment of cattle on our Western prairies.

To get to moose, caribou, or mountain sheep was now only a matter of shifting the line of march. The best and most direct travelling was over this glacial shelf at heights between three and four thousand feet. Travelling thus, caribou were sufficiently abundant to supply our larder without interrupting the long marches. In descending to the timber line along the head-waters of the streams we saw moose.

THE MT. MCKINLEY CARIBOU

When making a cut behind the first foothills we saw great bands of mountain sheep, while everywhere there were fresh signs of bear. Here, wandering with primeval freedom, were the largest of the big game animals. Surely, it is the finest game preserve in all the world.

It behooves us to protect these splendid animals against the cruel slaughter which blots the history of wild life in the past decade. Game preservation is too long a subject to take up here, but my admiration for the noble creatures that run to untroubled joys along the west of this range impels a word of caution. Some game law must be framed for this undisturbed wilderness will soon be spotted with the blood of innocent creatures to satisfy the murderous lust of man's instinct to kill. The present game laws of Alaska are a farce in their effect. They favour the Indian and the prospector but permit the wholesale extermination of the game.

The only result of this law is to keep big game hunters out of that territory and to make a closed field for the Indian and the prospector to slaughter at will.

There is room for a good deal of discussion on the relative merits of allowing special privileges to the Indian, the prospector, or the nimrod. The spirit of the law and the generally accepted theory is to curb the outside hunter and allow the native a free hand with minor restrictions. This theory in Alaska is a misfit. The Indian about Cook Inlet and the Alaska Range is to-day, and always has been, a fish eater. He secures his yearly supply of salmon with such ease and despatch that for his own use he does not seriously trouble the game. It is only since the advent of the white man with rapid-fire guns and a market for skins that he has taken to the hunt of big game. The ultimate object of this chase is easily gotten revenue, not meat. The prospector with a privilege paramount to that of the Indian is not more worthy of free meat. I admire the brave type of manhood displayed by the prospector in his quest for gold in the difficult northlands, but he follows his calling with a purely selfish lust for gold. Wealth secured, he goes to other climes to spend it. Is it not enough that Alaska should allow him to carry away its mineral riches? Why should he have a free entrance to nature's larder?

Now as to the nimrod, let us examine his claim to consideration. He starts on an expedition which, physically, is much like that of the gold digger, but he does it on a larger scale. He hires a corps of men, takes a large outfit, spends thousands of dollars, not to kill, as is the common impression, but to enjoy wild life at its best. His return is a trophy for two, a collection of pictures, and a note-book full of memoranda, all of which is a permanent record of use to future generations. The nimrod's claim to consideration is at least as good as that of the Indian and prospector, and the law in my judgment should be so reconstructed.

There is another phase to this subject from the standpoint of real and not fancied protection. The hunter is a lover of animal life, his destruction is limited to a few males with large heads, which does not seriously affect reproduction; while the Indian and the prospector slaughter indiscriminately, females and young, and all living things. Furthermore the hunter is usually an explorer, making contributions to the annals of natural history and geography. His eye is trained to useful observations and the results of his adventures are published. Publicity is the best remedy for any abuses and where the hunter enters the gross infraction of game laws cannot remain a guarded secret as it is in Alaska to-day.

The present law prohibits the exportation of heads and skins. The hunting season is limited and the number of animals allowed each individual is stated. Professional hunters are absolutely barred by the first provision, and so far the law is a success. But the exclusion of the friend of the game animals makes the lot easy for the local destroyers. Near the head waters of the Skwentna River there are thousands of square feet covered with moose hair to the depth of three feet. Here Indians have massacred hundreds of moose in the deep snows, taking only the skins for souvenir moccasins, leaving heaps of heads and tons of meat to rot. Kenai Peninsula, right under the eye of men paid to enforce the law, is a brilliant example of the working of the present law. Moose and sheep meat is everywhere exposed for sale at all times of the year, and all over the Peninsula one finds many magnificent heads strewn about in the wilderness. At Seattle, Wash., Alaska game heads are on sale at reduced prices. These heads I suppose were transported by aërial navigation, for the steamship companies rigidly exclude heads from returning freight.

It would seem reasonable that the best way to prevent the present wanton destruction of game in territory bordering on Mt. McKinley should be a law which would be fair to all—a law providing for a short open season, prohibiting the destruction of females and their young, and allowing the hunter to take out his heads. A very high license should be charged and efficient game wardens should be kept in the field. The Indians and the prospectors, the greatest enemies to the game, should be carefully watched, for if these are allowed to shoot every moving thing as they do now, any law, however well its framing is in theory, in practice must prove a farce.

CHAPTER V

# Up the Slopes of Mt. McKinley from the Southwest—The First Defeat

With an abundance of fresh meat for the men and good grass for the horses and a great undulating treeless country before us, long marches were possible. On the evening of August 11th, we rose to a bluff as the setting sun softened the great waving sea of evergreen forests, extending into the unknown world of the Kuskokwim. Along our line of march the land now became much more irregular. The glacial rivers as we neared the big mountains increased in numbers and size, and the tree line ascended somewhat higher along the streams into the foothills. Heron Glacier was noted just below, pouring huge quantities of ice and rock and water out of the great gold-fringed clouds which hung on the lower slopes of Mt. Foraker, while its three peaks of ice were softened by a warm afterglow. From points near here we got the first glimpse of the top of Mt. McKinley. Its contour was a surprise to us for it indicated a double system of peaks not shown from the east or the west. We could see only the upper four thousand feet over the ice-crested shoulder of Mt. Foraker, a double system of gable roofs placed side by side with the eastern apex slightly higher. The slopes were shingled by plates of ice which were continuous with the surface of a glacier carrying the drainage down from the median depression. Here was the roof of the continent; the prize of our conquest, seemingly within grasp, and our ambition, cooled by fifty-one days of wet feet, warmed to a new enthusiasm.

We pitched camp on the side of the vigorous stream which rushes out of the grottos of Heron Glacier. Through the waving leaves of the big cottonwood trees we watched the veiling and unveiling of the polished cliffs of Mt. Foraker, with its awe-inspiring cornices chiselled in graceful curves of alabaster. As the beans boiled and the aroma of the bacon and fresh bread drifted with the chill of twilight the echoes of the explosive noises of Heron Glacier sent a thrill of the arctic battlefield to our hearts.

A march of three days over whaleback ridges ploughed by vanished glaciers, took us to a point on a tributary of the Tatlathna River, about fourteen miles north-west of the crest of Mt. McKinley. Our camp was placed beside a foaming stream at an altitude of twenty-six hundred feet, along the edge of the last willows. A mile below we noted the zigzag of the upper line of the spruce forest which we had skirted for two hundred miles. To the east a succession of glacial benches rose gradually for about five miles to an altitude of four thousand feet and there began the sharp pyramidal foothills which are characteristic of this area. In wandering about the camp we saw a great deal of interesting life; mosquitoes and flies were absent, but bumble bees attacked us several times. There were squirrels and marmots, and the bears were so numerous that we never felt safe without firearms at hand. An occasional wolf-track was seen and one wolf was bold enough to come right into our camp. Caribou grazed about like domestic cattle, and moose were always expected in the willows. Mountain sheep were more common in the regions north-east and south-west of Mt. McKinley. Perhaps the most remarkable bit of life we saw here was a family of black foxes following us at long range like dogs, and retreating to their earth mounds when we took up the chase.

While here a violent storm swept our camp and we were kept rather busy in holding up the tents and nursing a willow fire. The stream rose with alarming swiftness. Our tents were on a flat not more than three feet above the foaming stream. When we turned into our sleeping bags that night we felt anxious about that rising stream. Shainwald had such premonitions of a coming flood that he devised a safety signal. Placing a small log at a point near our level he attached to it a rope and this rope was taken in his tent and fastened to his toe. The wind blew violently that night and the rain poured down in torrents. Just before dawn Shainwald felt a jerk at his toe. He quickly called all, but we were already lying in pools and when we arose we stumbled into cold water. There was no great danger at this time but in the haste and bustle of moving camp to higher ground we were thoroughly awakened.

Our position was particularly favourable for a promising attack upon the south-west ridge of the big mountain. Before beginning the climb we decided to spend two days in rest and final preparation.

In fifty-four days we had marched a tortuous course of five hundred miles through swamps and forests, over glacial streams, up and down mountain sides, through a trackless country. We had travelled afoot while the horses carried our supplies. In this march we had hoped to get to the mountain by the first of August, but had been delayed a great deal through the illness of the horses during the early part of the trip. The season was now advancing rapidly; storms were beginning to pour down from Mt. McKinley with a great deal of rain; the temperature ranged from 45° to 60° F. and the glacial streams were much swollen. Still, our position seemed so favourable, and the ascent of the mountain appeared so easy from our point of observation, that we felt certain of reaching the summit within a few days.

Our days of rest were spent in making final preparations for the alpine work. We had carried with us a sufficient quantity of hard biscuits for the mountain ascent, but these biscuits had been so much in water and were so often crushed by accidents to the pack horses that they were worthless. We were now compelled to devise some kind of bread for the high altitude, because there bread could not be baked. It occurred to me that we might bake our bread in the usual way with the tin reflector, and then toast and dry it, after the manner of zweiback. For this purpose I detailed Dunn and Miller to go down the river a few miles where they could procure spruce wood, and within twenty-four hours they had successfully baked sufficient bread, and toasted and dried it thoroughly for mountain work. This I think is a new thing in mountaineering and it certainly proved excellent for our purposes.

Our mountaineering equipment was very simple and extremely light. As food for each man we allowed pemmican, 1 1/4 pounds per day; zweiback, 4 oz. per day; sweetened condensed milk, 4 oz. per day; and some tea. We had also a small quantity of cheese and erbswurst; both of these, however, proved unsatisfactory. Pemmican, bread, tea, and sweetened condensed milk seemed to satisfy all our wants. For fuel we had wood alcohol to be burned in aluminum stoves, and also petroleum to be burned in a Primus stove. The latter proved by far the more successful. We carried no dishes except a few cups, spoons, pocket knives, and one kettle, in which we melted snow to get water for our tea.

There was nothing unusual about our clothes, except a large eider-down robe (the down adhering to the skin of the birds). The robe was so arranged that it could be made into either a sleeping bag or an overcoat. Our tent was made of silk, after a special pattern which I devised for polar work. It was large enough for three men and weighed three pounds. Each man carried a regular alpine axe, and in his rucksack he was to carry his sleeping-bag, glacier rope made of horsehair, provisions, and a general outfit for a ten days' stay in the mountains. This weighed forty pounds.

Mt. McKinley presented a formidable face from our camp. The upper ten thousand feet were, during the day, usually wrapped in dark clouds. The best view was obtained when the sun was lowest, and by far the most impressive view was during the long hours of the blue twilight. In the bright light the mountain seemed dwarfed. The foothills, the glacial depressions, and the striking irregularities were then run together into a great heap of mingled snow and rock, but the feebler play of light at dawn and sunset brought out all of the sharp edges, the great cliffs, the depressions, the lesser peaks, and the difficult slopes. To the north-east there was a long ridge with a gradual ascent, but this ridge seemed impossible as a route to the summit because of several lesser peaks, which appeared to bar the way. To the south-west there was a more promising ridge, also interrupted by a spur, which however we hoped to get around. The western face of the great peak between these ridges, above twelve thousand feet, was an almost uninterrupted cliff of pink granite, so steep that snow could not rest upon it. Hence the only way to the summit from the west as we understood it at that time was along the south-westerly ridge.

Aiming for this ridge, we moved our entire camp with the horses along the southern bank of the river to a point on the main stream where it came from a huge moraine. Crossing here, we ascended into a narrow valley four thousand feet, and there pitched our camp. Here the grass was abundant, and the outlook for an easy ascent was good, but the rain came down incessantly. On the following day, with five horses, the entire party pushed over a series of moraines to a glacier which started from an amphitheatre. The ice travelling was quite difficult for the horses; deep snow and numerous crevasses made the task tedious and very dangerous. We pitched our camp at an altitude of seven thousand three hundred feet on the glacier near a part of the wall of the amphitheatre to the south-west, the only place where the slope permitted an ascent. During the night a great deal of snow fell, and on the following morning we left our horses, and in the snowstorm ascended this slope to eight thousand three hundred feet, only to find that farther progress was absolutely cut off by a chasm the cliffs of which we afterward learned led down with a sheer drop of two thousand feet into the bed of Peters Glacier. The horses were sent to the last camp while we remained on the glacier another night, and explored the area for a route out of the gathering basin; but the only outlet was toward Mt. Foraker.

Defeat for our first attempt was now evident. There was no way over the gap in the shoulder upon which we had risen. We were, however, able from here to get an occasional peep between the clouds into a new world of great action and sublime beauty. The remarkable glacier on which we camped marked the beginning of the first of a series of interesting discoveries. Its gathering basin was a crescent in shape, about five miles wide, and walled by frowning cliffs from two thousand to three thousand feet high. Small overhanging glaciers and never ceasing streams of avalanches carried the condensation down from above while a constant train of clouds descended into the gap, dropping cargoes of snow. Thus the output of the glacier was continuously augmented. The stream was about seven miles long. By right of exploration to us fell the privilege of assigning a name, and accordingly we inscribed in honour of our colleague "Shainwald Glacier."

Rising over a low divide out of Shainwald Glacier toward Mt. Foraker we saw two other glaciers with streams about one mile wide running parallel to each other. The first came from a system of snowfields from the Mt. McKinley slopes. The second came from an amphitheatre of Mt. Foraker. Both these glaciers had large quantities of black moraine uniformly strewn over them. This moraine we believed to be slate, therefore differing from the northern glaciers where the moraine was granite. These glaciers from above appeared to offer good routes for an attack upon either mountain, but we had not with us sufficient supplies to prolong the siege over a circuitous route. We therefore descended out of a region of perennial snows into one of perpetual rains at four thousand feet. The base camp was quickly taken down and packed and then we started for the golden lowlands where the sun was seen to shine as we looked between the clouds. Rising to a commanding foothill southward we were able to see that there would be great difficulties in rising out of the lower country to the glaciers that looked promising from above, so we now decided that the few remaining days of the closing season would be better spent by an ascent over the ice of Hanna Glacier.

In this sudden descent from eight thousand feet to three thousand feet we noted a languid, feverish feeling, a weakening as if convalescent from a serious illness. We soon learned to accept this descent of spirits with the descent of slopes as an aftermath of every climb.

CHAPTER VI

# Against the Western Face of Mt. McKinley—The Second Defeat

In shifting camp twenty-five miles from a line at right angles to the south-west of the base to a similar line to the north-west base we spent two pleasant days in travel and exploration. This march over a rolling treeless country gave us time and opportunity to study the face of the great mountain. Looking at the peak in the light of our first experience the magnitude of our task was more and more impressed upon us. Making a camp in the edge of the last spruce, within a mile of the moraine of Hanna Glacier, at an altitude of three thousand feet, we made preparations for our next assault upon the ice-armoured slopes.

Mt. McKinley as seen from this camp presents a stupendous sheen of granite cliffs and ice-walls. The foothills rise out of an old glacial shelf at four thousand feet elevation, and about ten miles from the crest of the saddle which makes the double peak of the west. The first hills are rounded by glaciation, but these are quickly succeeded by a few pyramidal peaks scraping the lower clouds at six thousand feet. These foothills lead to Roosevelt Ridge, which extends along nearly the whole western face of the main mountain and is separated from it by Hanna Glacier. Ordinarily the clouds sweep the slopes from six thousand to twelve thousand feet, and thus blot out the upper line of Roosevelt Ridge and the huge gap made by Hanna Glacier between it and Mt. McKinley, giving the great uplift the appearance of gradual easy slopes. But the cloudless skies of night and morning alter the prospect to one of sharp contours, interrupted arêtes, and successive cliffs of rock and ice. Roosevelt Ridge, which has an altitude of seven thousand feet in the north-west, gradually rises to twelve thousand feet in the south-west. Its crests are blanketed by sheets of ice with huge cornices and overhanging glaciers to the west, and to the east many tributary glaciers carry ice-tongues into Hanna Glacier.

With our mountain equipment and some firewood packed on four horses we crossed the glacial stream not far from where it rushed out of the great green caverns of the face of Hanna Glacier. The waters boiled among large granite boulders freighted from the heights by the movement of the glacier, and after tumbling over widening bars of glacial silt, the stream narrowed, plunged into a canyon, and disappeared in the great green expanse. This river makes the McKinley fork of the Kantishna, which carries the northern Mt. McKinley drainage to the Tanana, en route to the Yukon and the Bering Sea.

On the north shore we found signs of a fresh camp. It was the first signs of human life which we had seen for more than two months. Leaving the horses to graze among stunted willows we examined the camp carefully. We had about decided that it was an Indian camp when a wrapper of a kodak film was found. We were not prepared to believe that Indians carried cameras, and sought diligently for some other signs. A pair of blue overalls and some woollen socks were found, which even yet was not conclusive. In the ground we saw the footprints of a mule, and then we concluded it was a railroad survey party. This was agreeable news, for it relieved the tension of our shortage of supplies. The main privation from which we suffered at this time was the lack of salt. Early in the campaign the horses located the salt and ate it during a single night. This did not interfere with the alpine work; in the climbing diet salt was rigorously excluded because of its faculty to produce thirst where water could not be easily obtained, but in the lower country, without bacon, and without salt, fresh meat and beans did not promise a relish for our enjoyment. Under a bush Printz picked up an old rusty covered tin can. Raising it for a better examination it was found to be full of gray granules, which we took to be arsenic, a part of a bird-collector's outfit. It might be salt, but who would taste it? If salt it was worth its weight in gold, but we had no chemical way of testing it. The relative chemical qualities of arsenic and salt were heatedly discussed, and finally some one took the risk of arsenical poisoning by putting some on his tongue, ready to spit it out quickly. With a broad grin he exclaimed, "It is salt!" and everybody at once shouted for joy. This camp we later learned was made by Judge Wickersham.

Taking a course parallel to Hanna Glacier we soon found splendid caribou trails leading in a straight line to the base of Mt. McKinley through the gap forced by the glacier. Blueberries were abundant, but they were frozen and those of us who ate them in quantities developed a serious form of indigestion. The grass had a similar effect upon the horses, as it was also frozen. Following the same trail along the glacier for eight miles we pitched camp on the evening of August 24th within a mile of the base of the frowning cliffs of the main mountain. Here the glacier made a sharp turn and we now saw for the first time that the huge stream of ice swept the whole north-west face of Mt. McKinley and this stream as a highway offered the best route to the top.

To the east of Hanna Glacier Mt. McKinley rises in an alternate series of precipitous granite cliffs and overhanging glaciers for fifteen thousand feet; and to the west in similar cliffs and glaciers Roosevelt Ridge, a wide imposing line of mountains from seven thousand to twelve thousand feet high, extends for twenty-five miles parallel to Mt. McKinley. Below Roosevelt Ridge to the west are three rows of foothills over which there is a successive descent to the lower glacial plain at three thousand feet.

As we were pitching the tents we noticed a big grizzly bear on our trail. He leisurely wandered over the bars of the glacial stream to the little green island where we aimed to make our base camp. We had with us plenty of fresh meat, so we did not need his carcass, nor did we want his skin, but we did not like his boldness nor his familiarity.

The great quivering mass expanded to alarming proportions as he neared the camp, and his funny dance on his clumsy hind legs, while his forepaws waved an evident desire for a handshake, was not at all funny to us who were trying to bluff the bear by putting up a brave front and a firm stand without firearms. We had only ice-axes as weapons of defence, and as the bear rose to his haunches the second time we backed up to a boulder, from the top of which we expected to defend our skins; but the bear was considerate: after eying each one separately, and then taking a side glance at the horses, he rose, sniffed the air, and turned into a great basin for the highlands, from which he watched the curl of the smoke of our camp-fires, while the aroma of caribou steaks kept his nose pointed. Our sleep that night was troubled by bear thoughts and the thunders of avalanches.

From this camp we started for the upper slopes with the climbing equipment packed in the rucksacks. Under heavy packs we crossed the miniature mountains of broken stone to a narrow tongue of ice which ran wedge-shape down the centre of the glacier. The lower ten miles of this glacier are completely buried under an irregular cover of moraine. The travelling was extremely difficult over the glacier, though not particularly dangerous. The temperature was near the freezing point. There was bright sunshine on the higher slopes, but into the glacial gap drifted frequent clouds, and under these it was dull and gloomy. Toward night the clouds drifted over us so frequently that we found ourselves in an almost continuous snow-storm. Icy winds made a whirl of snow through which it was difficult to spot the crevasses. At the lower drop of a great sérac we separated. Dunn and Miller returned to the base camp, while Printz joined me in a desperate attempt to find a way through the maze of gaps and pinnacles. There was no way over the top, so we descended into a great blue cut, and from this we ascended into other crevasses, following one after another to the better ice above the sérac. At an altitude of eight thousand feet we rose above the settling clouds and burst into the arctic world, with all its glory of glitter and frost, and continuing our march through deep snow to an altitude of nine thousand feet we pitched the silk tent on the glacier within two miles of the south-west arête upon the ascent of which our future fortune depended.

The temperature was ten degrees below the freezing point and the bitterness of midwinter was in the air. We heard water far down in the crevasses, and determined to find some if possible, for we were too thirsty to wait for snow to melt. Furthermore, we desired to save the precious fuel which we had carried thousands of miles for use in this cloud-world. Opening out our sleeping-bags, we drew them as robes around our shoulders, and with a tight line we sought for water along the crevasses. Under a circle of new ice near the tent we found a miniature lake, and from it we first filled up, and then our aluminum can was filled. In the tent we made our robes into bags, crept in, and started the alcohol lamp and fried caribou steaks. Later tea was served. Outside an arctic blast rushed down the glacier, and avalanches from every side made the night air ring. There was discomfort and real danger at hand, but we were warm and at ease within the silk walls of our tent.

Dunn and Shainwald were expected to meet us here on the day following, but owing to some delay they did not come. We explored the upper reaches of the glacier and outlined the line of attack which we aimed to pursue in the next climb.

All glaciers in the Alaskan Range have a high gathering basin, out of which descends the first ice which starts the frozen stream with its freight from cloud and peak. There are two general systems in which all of these basins may be classed. In the breaks through the range, or in the passes between high peaks along the range where clouds are driven through gaps, moisture is condensed in large quantities, and snow-fields form as a result. These snow-fields sometimes make one general basin for several glaciers, but usually there is a separate field or a plurality of fields for each stream. The other type starts from an amphitheatre, or a chain of amphitheatres, over the cliffs of which the clouds are interrupted by still higher slopes. Hanna Glacier belongs to this latter type. Its main amphitheatre is in the south-west corner of Mt. McKinley, and from it, at nine thousand five hundred feet, the train moves around the polished granite, following irregularly between Mt. McKinley and Roosevelt Ridge, taking avalanches, tributary glaciers, and direct cloud deposits in its course for twenty-five miles.

From a point near our camp we heard avalanche after avalanche thunder down the great slopes, and we felt the glacier under us shake as if moved by an earthquake. This noise of rock- and snow-slides and the quiver of the earth are characteristic of Mt. McKinley. We heard or felt them everywhere near the mountain, and the danger from this source was very great.

On August 29th we made our first assault on the slope of the main peak, selecting again the south-western ridge, which from every observation of the mountain offered the only chance to gain the summit. In Hanna Glacier our altitude was eight thousand feet. We began the ascent in the track of a harmless avalanche of soft snow. This gave us a good slope for a few hundred feet, and then we were forced to cut steps up a slope ranging from forty to sixty degrees. Our greatest difficulty was not the work of chopping steps in the ice, but the effort of removing fourteen inches of soft snow before we found trustworthy ice upon which a safe footing could be made. Slowly but steadily we advanced against a freezing wind charged with drift snow, until the setting sun forced us to seek a camping place. We found nowhere a level place large enough for our tent, so we were compelled to dig away snow and cut down the ice for a tent flooring. This camp was at nine thousand eight hundred feet. The day following the slopes were steeper and the difficulty of cutting steps greater, but we rose to eleven thousand feet, where we were again compelled to cut a camping floor to keep from rolling down three thousand feet.

Camp was pitched in a hole cut out of the steep icy slopes; we nestled closely to get warm under eider-duck skins, and over hard blue ice. A frosty blast of wind was blowing hard crystals of snow against the silk walls of the tent, making a metallic noise. There were four of us as tightly pressed together as sardines in a box. From each there came a cone of breath which rose in curious circles to the top of the tent, and there the moisture was frosted, falling in beautiful crystals only to add misery to our condition. All at once some one who had peeped out exclaimed, "My God! look at that!" and as quickly as we could get something around us we all went out to see the thing which stopped the jerky breath of our emotional companion. It was certainly a view to enrapture a mountaineer, but we were not comfortable enough to absorb its tremendous scenic importance. A cutting wind drove little ice needles down our necks, and under our wraps in a manner to dispel poetry. But we took the thing in quickly, as a hungry man does food, and then crept back under our furs to digest it.

Behind us were the awe-inspiring successive cliffs of Mt. McKinley, its glittering spurs piercing a dark purple sky nine thousand feet above us. The great mountain presented all the phases of the most terrible conflict of elements. Hundreds of avalanches were thundering down the sides of the giant peak, with trains of rock and ice followed by clouds of vapour and snow. Against this chaos of awful noise and lightning movement there drifted a steadily moving fleet of snow-charged clouds. Vapours were dragged down and set into violent agitation by the swift currents of the avalanches. At high altitudes we got only an occasional peep through a rift in the clouds, but this peep was full of gloomy mysteries. It was a sheen of melancholy, the noise of a great war scene, a death-dealing breath storming down every ravine. It was a scene which in our position, with the low temperature, made one's marrow shrink. But the outlook in the other direction was quite the reverse. Here the colour was cheerful, the movement, though exciting, was rhythmical, and configuration of cloud and land, though on a gigantic scale, was enticing, while the depth of perspective led the mind on to dreams of happy fairy-lands.

Before a lilac curtain, feebly dashed with gilt, the sun was rapidly drifting, edging northward, soon to plunge below the cloud level at our feet. Seemingly but a step down, though two thousand feet below, was the upper line of a curious sea of waving clouds glistening like liquid gold, the waves crested with long lines of pearl.

Over this strange sea-like cloud-world, there were many fascinating optical illusions. Now we saw a mountain rise, move, explode, and vanish, then we would see a lake vague in outline, rich in colour, surrounded by an amphitheatre of ice-corniced mountains so near that we could almost touch some spurs. As we had about made out the strange picture, it dissolved into another, like the views of a stereopticon. Thus the scenes ran with all kinds of pictures to suit the fancy and imagination of the observer. Perhaps the most deceptive thing that I saw was the upbuilding of a giant peak, which for a time seemed to rival Mt. Foraker. It slowly rose out of a particularly brilliant area of the cloud line in the south. It seemed as if the lime-light was turned on this particular spot, and for a long time I could not keep my eyes away from it. The surface quivered, a huge spray was thrown up, and then a spot slowly rose dragging up with it irregularly most of the level around it, and the surface raised, burst, leaving a ragged edge somewhat like the opening through the paper-covered hoop pierced by a circus rider. Through this opening rose a vague velvety outline of a mountain, the ragged edges settled, leaving foothills, ridges, valleys, and gullies with sharp cliffs next to the mountain. It was a bird's-eye view of an exact replica of Mt. Foraker. But as the air cooled all the outlines were sharpened, all the optical illusions vanished, and this particular mountain settled rapidly, leaving a rift through which we saw, seven thousand feet below, a blue expanse of glacial ice.

The temperature steadily fell from twenty to twelve; the entire cloud level settled and had more the appearance of a quiet sea, but the glitter of gold remained, though cooled by a gauze of blue. While our great mountain and all its fantastic illusions vanished with the falling mercury there remained to the south-west two large mountains, and we almost expected them to disappear but they did not. We soon recognised these as the great peaks, Foraker and Russell. Mt. Foraker, twenty miles away, a cross-ridged, ice-crested mountain, seventeen thousand feet high and Mt. Russell, a pyramid of ice-plated rock forty miles south west. At nine thousand feet the slopes of both mountains were hugged by a sea of clouds.

On the day following we shook ourselves out of the snow and examined the disheartening slopes above. The entire scene had changed. There was a succession of shadowed granite cliffs and glacial walls which ran up into the glowing sky. A few

CUTTING STEPS IN THE ICE AT 11,000 FEET

luminous cloud shreds were dragging their edges along the icy spurs at about sixteen thousand feet. The western side of the giant peak was bathed in a frigid blue, but from the east there came a warm rose glow, which soon enveloped the mountain and made the thing enticing.

Dunn and Printz had already made up their minds that farther progress up the difficult slopes and into the coming winter was impossible. There was much to support this view; snow was falling almost constantly, the icy storms were sweeping the spurs, and the stilly blackness of the polar night with its awful cold was daily thickening and lengthening. We had, however, plenty of mountain food, and if we could only find some safe and sure line of attack there was yet a chance for success.

The ridge upon which we were camped at eleven thousand feet led with an ever-increasing slope to a granite cliff which did not appear unclimbable from below. But at close range and in a good light we could see that farther progress on the south-west arête was impossible. There were successive cliffs for four thousand feet. Beyond we saw a gradual slope leading to the western peak. Over the glacier which came from the gap between the eastern and western peaks there was also a promising route. After a careful search we were compelled to acknowledge

BREAKING CAMP ON THE SOUTHWEST RIDGE AT 10,000 FEET
*Steps were cut for 3,000 feet up this steep wall*

defeat, for there was no way around the succession of sheer granite cliffs.

Leaving some pemmican and fuel here to ease our packs we descended quickly over the steps previously cut, reaching our camp on the glacier at eight thousand feet on September 1st, as the parting sun threw piercing blue shadows over us. From here on the following day we made a desperate dash of twenty-nine miles over the ice and moraine to the face of Hanna Glacier.

## CHAPTER VII

# Northward Through the Range and into the Chulitna

We had aspired to get to the top of the great mountain and the many hardships served to increase the tension of a nervous excitement which was fired by momentary surprises and inspirations in wonderful scenes. The spirit of discovery ran with our aspirations and the ascent. Here we breathed the free air of the Arctic, while the eye wandered over the snowy grandeur to the broad green splendour of the lower game lands, the visual senses drinking to intoxication while the spirit communed with nature in moods of severe playfulness. We had gone into an upper world, into the battle-ground of terrestrial and celestial forces. We had coped with a superior foe and our battle was half won when the auxiliary forces of our adversary, the advancing run of winter and its awful night of frost, called a halt.

As we descended from our second attempt we were made to realise by frozen grass and increasing snowstorms that the season for mountaineering had closed; furthermore, the north wind convinced us that if we wished to get out of the country before the long winter and the night stilled the sub-arctic world about us, we must quickly reach the head waters of some big stream. We did not care to go to the Yukon, because in doing so we would cover explored territory. We could not return as we had come, because horse feed along the western slope of the range was already frozen. We were not yet ready to leave Mt. McKinley, provided we could only linger at some point where our retreat would not, as was likely in our present position, be suddenly cut off. Altogether, our purposes would seem best served if we could cross the range and get into the Chulitna Valley; but the possibility of such attainment seemed doubtful, in the time at our disposal, unless we were fortunate enough to find a pass within a few days' travel. Accordingly, we resolved to make a desperate attempt to cross the range to the eastern slope, and in the event of failure in this, our alternative was to make the deep waters of the Toklat, and travel thence by raft to the Tanana River.

Though thwarted by an insurmountable wall, we had ascended Mt. McKinley far enough to get a good view of its entire western face. The walls of the main mountain rise out of Hanna Glacier, which sweeps the western slope. Avalanche after avalanche rush down the steep cliffs and deposit their downpour of ice, rock, and snow on the glacier. Beyond Hanna Glacier is a remarkable ridge of lesser mountains, extending about sixteen miles parallel to the great mountain. Its altitude is seven thousand five hundred feet at the north, and it gradually rises to eleven thousand nine hundred feet at the south. The ridge is weighted down, with all the ice it can possibly carry. Many glaciers grind down the gorges on both sides, and along the western slope every cliff is heavily corniced with ice. The altitudes of the lower clouds here range from six thousand to ten thousand feet, and when looking at Mt. McKinley from the west, during the greater part of our sojourn, we could see only this great ridge, the main mountain being usually obscured under heavy clouds. For this unique geographical feature I have placed in honour of our President the name "Roosevelt Ridge." West of Roosevelt Ridge is a series of snow-free foothills, mostly pyramidal in shape. We descended a dome-shaped mountain six miles south of this ridge, from which place we made our final attack. The mountain referred to is entirely covered with ice, and its summit reached an altitude of fourteen thousand feet. This will appear on our map as Mt. Hunter in honour of Miss A. P. Hunter of Newport. In the eastern end of Roosevelt Ridge there is a huge amphitheatre, in which rises a glacier about two miles wide and six miles long; this glacier, in honour of one of our companions, received the name of Shainwald Glacier. Over Shainwald Glacier we had made our first ascent to an elevation of eight thousand three hundred feet.

As we were about ready to start on our uncertain effort to cross the range we found ourselves deserted by six of our horses. In their eagerness to get grass the animals had wandered down-stream toward the main valley of the Kuskokwim. The seven remaining horses were easily able to carry our reduced packs, so we allowed the wayward ones to seek their fortunes in lowlands among the caribou and moose.

On the morning of September 4th we started on our weary march along the western foothills above the tree line. The slopes were long and difficult, and the travelling after our mountain experience proved very tiresome. Every sudden descent from the high altitudes produced a feeling of languor, with difficult heart action. This aftereffect of mountain work was to us much worse than any effect of ascending altitudes. So much was the fatigue felt that as we ate lunch on a prominent hill we picked out our evening camp only a few miles away. The lunch was eaten with some relish, because we were hungry and had worked hard. It was the usual meal of boiled caribou ribs, cold and without salt; also without bread, or anything else except glacial water. While we were picking the bones our horses were searching little depressions for a few sprigs of grass which had not been frozen, and as they were being rounded up we saw several caribou. Printz with a rifle and Shainwald with a revolver crept stealthily around a hill into a ravine and soon we heard a volley of shots. We followed with the horses and took the choice bits off a fat bull. Within an hour we were headed for the willows of a small creek, and here the nimrods spied and secured a moose, which was a very good excuse for shortening our day's march. So we camped in moose haunts in a swamp where we built a huge camp-fire and ate an incredible amount of moose steaks while our horses climbed the neighbouring hills for the vanishing grass.

Packing our horses on the following morning with an abundance of fresh meat, we then took a course for Muldrow Glacier, beyond which we hoped to find a pass. In two days' marching seven hours daily over tundra, we reached the terminal moraine of this great glacier, and we then marched south-easterly to examine the mountains. Our course hitherto had been close to that of Brooks and Reaburn, and their map, though quickly made, was found to be remarkably correct. But now we were to traverse absolutely unknown territory, and the task thus became doubly interesting, though much more difficult. In our course we first discovered a glacial stream pouring through a canyon only a few hundred feet north of Muldrow Glacier. We followed the stream into a broad valley, and there learned that the river was the output of a system of glaciers among a cluster of sharp peaks seven miles east of the Muldrow Glacier.

As we left the lateral moraine of the big glacier, travelling on the gravel bars of the newly discovered river, we moved through a great broad basin, which we later discovered extended nearly fifty miles north-easterly. To the east were snow-capped mountains from seven thousand to ten thousand feet high, while to the west were brown weatherworn mountains from five thousand to seven thousand feet in altitude. The valley had a general width of seven miles and an average elevation of four thousand feet: and I named it, in honour of one of our companions, Dunn Valley. On September 8th we camped in the canyon of a small stream at the base of a rounded black mountain, to the west of which we hoped to be able to find a pass.

After a hasty meal of unsalted moose-steaks I asked Printz and Dunn to join me in an ascent of the mountain before us, which we called Black Head. The climb was steep, but not difficult, and on the way we found many tracks of grizzly bears, caribou, and mountain sheep. In the course of an hour we reached the summit at an altitude of five thousand four hundred feet. From here we had a magnificent view of a great expanse of country, upon which it is probable no human eye had rested before. Thirty-five miles to the south-west, looking across unnamed mountains twelve thousand feet high, we saw the summit of the unconquered culminating peak of North America. The upper walls of this great uplift from this side had for us a new aspect. An almost constant stream of clouds swept over and around the mountain from the east, and a blue electric glow softened the rough outline. Now and again we could see the summit, and from here it resembled very much the crown of a molar tooth. Four tubercles were distinctly visible; the saddles seen from the west formed two, and to the east were two rather higher and more distinct. These tubercles of this giant tooth are separated by large glaciers, whose frozen currents pour down very steep slopes. If it were not so difficult to get at this side of the mountain, we reasoned that here the upper slopes might offer a promising route.

Apparently continuous with Mt. McKinley, and extending north-easterly far beyond our position, there was a sharp icy ridge in which we saw several mountains over ten thousand feet high. We thought we could break through this ridge about ten miles northward from our position, but the prospective pass which we had seen from below was only a small valley walled off by the main ridge. About eight miles up the valley we saw the benches of a large stream and on the banks spruce trees. The sight of spruce raised hopes of a big camp-fire and a good camping-ground with better prospects of grass for our poor, half-starved horses. Along the upper slopes, in the most inaccessible places, we saw long lines of snowy dots zigzag on the sunny rocks; these were mountain sheep in great numbers, but our larder was too well stocked and our time too precious to seek them. Around us and toward the unnamed brown mountains northward we saw innumerable ptarmigan.

After plotting our course for the following day, we descended and camped among some scrub-willows. Here we found coal in the stream's bed, and near by signs of petroleum. On the day following we moved our pack train to the river we had seen from Black Head, but, much to our disappointment, the southerly outlook here did not promise a pass. Beyond, the main valley widened, the glacial streams became more numerous, willows were larger, and signs of game more abundant. Our camp on the 9th was near a salt-lick, where many animals had congregated to eat the salty soil. The drainage all along Dunn Basin was northward into the Toklat River. The connecting A-shaped valley forming the basin had been carved out by some ancient glacier. To the eastward the basin ended in a series of hills, and there we felt that we were certain to find a pass. On the10th we camped on a large stream at the end of our newly discovered basin, and from here, looking southward, we discovered a wide cut through the ridge. Through this opening, over a glacier, came the moist easterly winds. The horses were desperately hungry and were bent on deserting us. To guard against this we set up a watch through the night, but in the dense blackness of midnight they escaped and back-trailed. On the morning of the 11th, while Dunn and Printz searched for the horses, Shainwald and I explored the prospective pass. In an hour we had ascended the face of the new glacier and walked over ice very much crevassed. Ahead were two possible routes to cross the range—to the north and to the south of a nunatak which projected above the glacier. We gradually rose to an elevation of six thousand one hundred feet, crossing hundreds of crevasses in a thick snowstorm, and as we came to the end of the easterly arm of the glacier the snow-cloud vanished, the weather cleared, and with a good deal of pleasure we looked down into the green valley of the Chulitna, the main tributary of the Susitna River. The descent however, promised to be very difficult for our horses, though possible in an emergency like ours.

We next sought a course through deep, soft snow around the nunatak to the westerly arm. A cloud of snow swept the glacier, and so thoroughly blotted out the huge mountains to each side that we were compelled to travel by compass. For nearly two hours we marched up this arm, keeping our glacier rope tight, almost expecting to drop into a crevasse any moment. Suddenly we broke through the clouds and just beyond Shainwald's toes appeared the brink of a precipice with a perpendicular drop of three thousand feet. We quickly stepped back, and then beheld the most desolate mountain wilderness which it has ever been my privilege to behold. Here were the easterly foothills of the McKinley group, black ragged peaks, dotted by spots of fresh snow. We were at an altitude of seven thousand feet, and these mountains were a little higher. The most remarkable feature was their apparently uniform height of about seven thousand five hundred feet. Over this expanse of jagged peaks there drifted heavy silver-edged clouds. Sometimes we could see over them, at other times under them, but at nearly all times through them. This remarkable effect also induced a mirage, which drew up some mountains to such heights that we could see huge needles of rock so far above us that we believed ourselves discoverers of several peaks that rivalled Mt. McKinley.

As we turned, the clouds were now for a time swept out of the divide by a strong northerly wind, giving us a good view of the glacier over which we had advanced in a snowstorm. It is about eight miles long and somewhat less than two miles wide. The highest mountains on each side are eight thousand feet, and from these several small tributaries pour down their frozen output. This new glacier I have named Harvey Glacier, in honour of Mr. George Harvey.

The drainage from Harvey Glacier spreads out into numerous channels over a great bed of glacial silt about a mile wide. This takes a course almost due north across Dunn Basin, and then it enters a canyon, after which it probably takes an easterly course to the Toklat River.

Nearing the centre of Harvey Glacier, we met the recovered pack-train, carefully guided by Dunn, Printz, and Miller, between two great pillars of granite, which mark the gates of the divide. From here the task of getting the horses over and around wide crevasse became extremely difficult, and as we ascended higher the horses frequently slipped into wide gaps, deceptively bridged by snow. Our horses, however, were now pretty well used to all kinds of hardships, and, though they were thoroughly frightened by frequent falls into dangerous cavities, they carried their packs nobly and safely over the divide.

The most difficult task for the horses, among their long series of hard adventures, was the descent from this glacial pass. In less than two hours they came down three thousand feet at an angle sometimes too steep for the men. It was a route over

Harvey Glacier
*Over which a new pass was discovered*

sharp stones, ice, and frozen ground; but the animals, with their feet and legs cut and bruised—leaving bloody stains everywhere in their trail—followed us without being urged toward the green fields of the lower valley. We were lucky enough to cross a green slope of long young grass just as we were aiming to strike camp, and from here the famished animals refused to be urged on, so we quickly removed their packs that they might eat to their utmost capacity. It was their first feed of grass which had not been frozen, for more than two weeks.

CHAPTER VIII

# Fording, Swimming, and Rafting the Chulitna

~

As we tumbled out of the clouds which were compressed and driven through the newly discovered pass, we left behind us for a time the icy winds of the early winter, but the gloom of the coming arctic night, was daily thickening. From seven thousand feet we suddenly dropped to three thousand feet, into an unknown land; so far as we knew there were neither Indians nor prospectors within one hundred and fifty miles. What the future had in store for us could only be guessed at; we had seven horses thin and hungry, but the country over which we were about to move promised at least sprigs of willows and cottonwood trees upon which the hardy creatures could subsist. The land, however, was not a horse country, at least not to the south in the direction in which we must push to the coast. Every little stream from the great range cut a huge canyon across our track. The only chance was to keep close to the Chulitna, ford and swim and cut a trail through the thick underbrush, pushing south quickly and desperately to rafting water before the advancing winter imprisoned us in the heart of Alaska.

The food supply, though not dangerously low, was such that we were anxious to get to Cook Inlet quickly. Along the western side of the range we could count on game to supply our larder, but along the east there was no such security of a supply. Before crossing the range we counted on the uncertainty of game in the Chulitna and packed our horses with all the moose and caribou meat that could be carried. This meat, now two weeks old, was not particularly appetizing, and furthermore we must eat it without salt, for our last find of salt was now exhausted. There was no longer any flour, sugar, or bacon. Indeed our meals were made of highly coloured and highly scented moose steaks and beans, both without salt, and tea, mixed with

HORSES FORDING
*Into tumbling glacial streams and through a frigid jungle. In the effort to get to Mt. McKinley we were drenched with ice-water continuously for three months.*

dried onions, without sugar or milk. The food was satisfying, but it did not go down easily.

We had carried a fair supply of wholesome food, but there is a limit to transportation facilities in this kind of pioneer work. Hunger is the great call for action to all life in the northland, and it was ours more keenly than ever at this moment. The dogs and horses and wolves and foxes, all seeking to satisfy the same pang, helped themselves from our scant supply, and now we must either seek their sources or sacrifice our horses. There was ever before us the possibility that we might be detained for the winter as was Lieutenant Heron, and this outlook with our food supply nearly exhausted and our clothing in tatters with neither coats, shoes, nor hats caused much anxiety, while as a precaution against starvation or freezing we carefully guarded a few necessities. The matches and ammunition were securely packed in several waterproof coverings, for with a liberal supply of these in a land where food and game could be secured we felt safe. We also reserved a supply of our alpine food sufficient to support us for about one month; thus with the horror of the winter before us there was still the hope of ultimate sustaining powers. Our food prospects without salt were not pleasing to the palate, still we could keep the inner fires burning.

At breakfast on September 9th, these thoughts took definite shape while I watched the anxious solicitude on the chilled faces of my companions. Our camp was in the first willows below the descending snow line. A piercing frost had caused us to shiver all night, and as we came over to the feeble glow of the willow campfire there was an exchange of confidences which clearly ran to premonitions of an arctic winter imprisonment. The flat taste of the meat, the insipid and repulsive saltless beans, and the onion tea did not allay this spectre of hard luck. In the midst of all this perplexing care there was one redeeming note of joy. Our horses for the first time in weeks were lying in tall green grass, with stomachs full, grunting with delight which sent gladness through our despondent hearts. Good, faithful creatures, how we were attached to them at this time! They had followed us through forest and tundra, over icy rivers into the snow clouds of the big mountain. They had learned to climb steep slopes and to cross glaciers which I never would have believed possible for a horse. They were almost human in their loyalty to the aim of our expedition and as each man had a special reason for his friendship for a special horse, to see the horses full and happy was to manifest the best wishes for our animal friends.

The horses having been packed with the precious remnants of the season's supplies, we started along the small glacial stream which drained the pass, and as we neared the timber line we took a southerly course over tundras and rolling hills into a clear stream. We followed this creek several miles into a canyon but could not keep this course because of the narrowing of the canyon and the large boulders. Ascending to the brim we still kept a southerly course along the edge of the cliffs to a high bluff overlooking the valley of the Chulitna near its main western tributary. We had covered about fifteen miles, had gotten blueberries and currants, and were offered ravens and ptarmigan. The march though difficult and tiresome cheered us up very much for though we saw no large game we found good grass for our horses and saw that we were nearing large rivers which we knew would take us to tide-water swiftly.

Around a bright fire of stunted spruce we watched the sun settle behind the saw-tooth ridge through which we had just come. A brilliant afterglow softened the jagged peaks and warmed the shivering blue of the high snow sheets. There was much colour in the lowlands, the cottonwood trees were golden, the willows had changed to red, the mosses were fired by orange and cardinal, the spruce and alders were darkening. It was all remarkably beautiful but it led to the thought of an early winter which we were not prepared to face. That night a beautiful moonlight sent a thrill of exaltation through us as we watched the cloaks of snow in changing hues of blue and purple. The foxes barked, the ravens screeched, the ptarmigan laughed, and at long range we heard the cry of wolves and the rumble of avalanches. It was an interesting shrieking wilderness to which we felt like adding the cry of human voices.

As the moon sank into a glacial cut with a great dark cloud the east paled, the fresh snow of the peaks glittered in gold, the tree tops brightened, but the frost increased. With the rising sun there came a rush of wind out of the glacial basins

Bridgman River

*The junction of Bridgman River and the Chulitna*

that made our teeth chatter. At the morning camp-fire with a cloudless sky we were able to study the new surroundings to good advantage. Looking westerly we saw a large gap through the range which seemed to offer a better pass than the one we had taken. Below this gap were three sharp snow peaks about nine thousand feet high, and a few miles eastward a sharp black peak. Large glaciers were noted here collecting the combined precipitation. We discovered from another point that out of the main gap came another glacier. The streams from these glaciers united with other streams to make a large river. This river has been named in honour of my friend and arctic colleague Mr. Herbert L. Bridgman, of Brooklyn. Bridgman River takes a south-westerly course about twenty miles from the range, then plunges into a canyon and joins the clear stream from the broad pass, making the Chulitna.

In our next march the underbrush was so thick and the canyons so numerous that we were forced to take the sand-bars of Bridgman River for a highway.

Getting into this glacial stream we found excellent travelling, but the slews soon narrowed, and led us into a canyon with walls three hundred feet high. The rushing milky waters among richly tinted cliffs crowned by trees in beautiful foliage made a picture sublimely fascinating; but just at this time we were not so much interested in landscapes as we were in making rapid progress. We were still anxious to examine Mt. McKinley from the east, and all our energies were bent on getting to the mountain as quickly as possible. The low mountains about were blanketed by newly fallen snow, and the temperature was falling to the freezing point every night. We desired to get out of this canyon, and cut a trail, but we dared not lose the time. Fully knowing the danger of following an unknown stream through a canyon, we still had no alternative.

We marched down-stream, crossing from bank to bank as the river turned, to find footing for our horses. At first these crossings were not difficult, but the stream gathered force very rapidly. On the second day's march down-stream the horses were compelled to swim at almost every crossing, and it was necessary to cross the river thirty to forty times daily. The men tried to ride the horses, behind the packs, but in swift streams they were frequently thrown off. For three days we swam and forded this icy stream, and then we were aroused to the dangers of the task through an accident in which a man and a horse were carried down-stream and thrown against a cliff. A similar accident was likely to occur at any time. The horses could

OUT OF GREAT BLUE CAVERNS AND OVER PRECIPICES, THE GLACIAL WATERS POUR WITH A MADDENING RUSH.

not be taken much farther. For the safety of ourselves and our outfit we now sought to build a raft.

The Chulitna proper is formed by the union of the glacial stream, Bridgman River, down which we came, and a clear-water stream of somewhat less volume, the latter draining the extensive low country towards the head waters of the Cantwell River. About two miles below this fork the canyon was considerably broken down, and here we found small flats covered with tall cottonwood trees. In the absence of better wood we camped here and built a raft. The cottonwood trees were fifteen inches thick, about eighty feet high, remarkably straight, and free from limbs. We cut logs thirteen feet long and carried them to a convenient launching place, where we fastened them with cross-bars, lashed by ropes, making two tiers about eight

Rafting

feet wide. After the raft was finished we learned to our sorrow that it would barely carry two men. The wood was evidently too heavy for raft-building.

Printz and Miller floated the raft, while the others followed with the horses. The stream got larger, more rapid, and ever more dangerous to swim. After having gone only two miles we saw dry spruce trees a short distance westward up a large creek of clear water. Here we camped and built two good rafts, and then came the sad task of leaving our horses. Good, faithful animals they had been; it seemed heartless to leave them to meet an almost certain death, either as a result of deep snow or from the onslaught of wolves. Each man had among the animals one or two pets, and no one had the boldness to deliberately kill any of the noble creatures. The grass was good here, and we argued that when the deep winter snow came they might possibly dig under it and find a bare subsistence. On this clear stream, about eighteen miles north of the big glacier, we left seven of the finest and most faithful horses that ever traversed the wilds of Alaska. We afterwards learned that all the animals were still living after two winters.

Taking to the rafts, we quickly descended the Chulitna through a series of small canyons divided by cross-canyons. Early in the afternoon of September 19th, we camped on a bar about eight miles southeast of the moraine of a great glacier. The lower end of this glacier had been partly charted by government parties, but nothing was known of its upper reaches. We now set for ourselves the task of exploring this glacier, and over it the eastern slopes of Mt. McKinley, which had not yet been seen by us.

Somewhat later we discovered a smaller glacier about twenty-five miles south which drains the eastern slopes of Mt. McKinley. These two glaciers I have named in honour of my wife and daughter, the larger Fidèle Glacier and the smaller Ruth Glacier.

With our outfit and supplies for three days packed in our rucksacks, we ascended the terminal moraine on the following morning, and then climbed for eight miles over the most wonderful accumulation of glacial débris that I had ever seen. At the first bend we left the glacier, and ascended the steep slopes of a series of mountains, from which we hoped to see the course of the glacier and the eastern face of the great peak.

## CHAPTER IX

# Down the Susitna—Around the Alaska Range

Though our mountaineering ambitions were hopelessly frustrated we had succeeded in pushing around and through the Alaska Range over unexplored country. We therefore added a good deal of material to the annals of pioneer research. Before leaving the cloud piercing spires of Mt. McKinley we had planned to make a rapid reconnoissance of its eastern approaches and thus obtain data for a future expedition. For this purpose we now followed Fidèle Glacier into the foothills, seeking to reach a favourable point of observation.

We climbed to an elevation of six thousand feet, but then our progress was barred by cliffs. From here, however, we were able to map Fidèle Glacier and a large mountain area. The glacier starts from the north-east ridge of Mt. McKinley and flows almost due east for fifteen miles, where it receives a large arm from the north. Five miles south-east of this another arm swells the bulk of the great icy stream, and then it takes a circular course, swinging toward the Chulitna. Its face is about seven miles wide, its length is about forty miles, and the lower ten miles are so thoroughly weighted down by broken stone—the product of landslides—that no ice is visible. It is thus the largest interior glacier of Alaska, and it probably carries more moraine material than any other known glacier.

Mt. McKinley from the east gives a much clearer impression of great altitude. We could not see the lower ten thousand feet, but the upper slopes though difficult are more nearly accessible than those of the west. The upper ten thousand feet are rounded like a beehive, and three spurs offer resting places for glacier ice, over which it was thought a route to the summit might perhaps be found.

The season had now so far advanced that if we cared to avoid being detained for the winter, we saw that we must take to our rafts quickly and descend the Chulitna

River. We had still to raft sixty miles of an unknown stream. Our supply of provisions was nearly exhausted, we were hatless and almost shoeless, and our clothing was torn into rags.

Returning to the rafts at noon we quickly packed our belongings to start down-stream. The river as we descended split into numerous channels and spread over a wide flat. Rafting was very difficult,— the water was so shallow that the rafts went aground every few miles. To float them we were compelled to jump into the water and push. The raft would suddenly slip into deep water and we would be forced to hold on and crawl out on the logs like water rats. This rafting life was very exciting—plunging from wide foaming rapids into the boiling deep of narrow channels, at a railroad pace, under overhanging trees, over great boulders, and into dangerous log jams. We were kept dodging dangers from every side, the raft with its precious load of records and instruments was under water often, but we were making good progress to the coast, and all of our hardships were belittled by this pleasant prospect.

About twenty miles below Fidèle Glacier we noted the moraine of Ruth Glacier which pours its ice through a deep gap leading to the northern face of Mt. McKinley. From the glacier came a vigorous stream—the Tokositna; and at this junction the Chulitna made a sharp bend easterly and soon after an equally sharp turn southerly, plunging into a second canyon. As the rafts went rushing through the canyon on the following morning, judging from the rapid drop of the river bed and the abrupt walls of the canyon, we began to look for dangerous falls. The river so far as we knew had not been rafted or boated before and there was good ground for expecting a Niagara below. To guard against such a drop we kept a rope coiled and a man ready to jump off and swim ashore. The prospect for the swimmer was not a pleasant one but we were not forced to test the method of precaution.

As we were emerging from the gloomy canyons we spied two tents on a bar of silt. The sight of these tents created quite a commotion among the rafters. It was the first speck of human life outside of our own party either white or red which we had seen in nearly four months. Aside from the joy of meeting a fellow-creature in a far-off wilderness, we were keenly interested in the chances of getting needful supplies. Not that we were nearing starvation, for we had plenty of moose meat, pemmican, and beans, but we had nothing else. With a good deal of excitement we pulled ashore and found there two groups of prospectors sluicing gold. They believed themselves the only people in this part of the world and we were pretty sure that we were the only adventurers about Mt. McKinley. A good deal of explanation followed while we were marched to a tent where some one detected the odour of fresh bread and bacon, things foreign to our camp for some time. The miners had had no fresh meat for three months but they had everything else which we wanted and we had an abundance of moose meat, somewhat black and gamey because of its long journey from the west, but still it was meat. In exchange for this meat we got sugar, tea, salt, and tobacco. We were told that the river was clear below, that we could reach the trading post at the station with our rafts in two days.

We lost very little time for the water in the river was lowering and the temperature was falling fast. There were still thirty miles of the troublesome Chulitna, with its tumbling shallow streams, before we could get into the deeper water of the Susitna. In coming out of the Chulitna we ran aground often, and were frequently entangled in snags. A few miles below the forks we camped at a point from which we got a splendid view of the four great peaks of the Bolshoy group.

Looking over a low tree-covered country we saw rolling foothills leading to sharp black peaks and beyond the perpetual snow of the Alaska Range.

Floating down the Susitna was a delight compared to our troubles on the Chulitna. The beautiful autumn foliage, the clear winter air, the migrating birds, and the absence of mosquitoes made rafting down this great river of mud a fitting termination to a series of very hard exploits. At the station we secured an old dory and in it we paddled down the lower Susitna through the delta into the treacherous waters of Cook Inlet. We arrived at Tyonok on September 26th, just four months after our start. In that time we had walked over seven hundred miles, and by boat and raft we had travelled three hundred miles; we had explored a good deal of new territory; we had ascended Mt. McKinley to eleven thousand four hundred feet, encircled the McKinley group, and had made a fair geological and botanical collection. Altogether we had done all that determined human effort could in the short interval of an Alaskan summer.

Mt. McKinley offers a unique challenge to mountaineers, but its ascent will prove a prodigious task. It is the loftiest mountain in North America, the steepest mountain in the world, and the most arctic of all great mountains. Its slopes are weighted down with all the snow and ice that can possibly find a resting place, but unlike Mt. St. Elias, the glaciation is not such as to offer a route over continuous ice. The area of this mountain is far inland, in the heart of a most difficult and trackless country, making the transportation of men and supplies a very arduous task. The thick underbrush, the endless marshes, and the myriads of vicious mosquitoes bring to the traveller the troubles of the tropics. The necessity for fording and swimming icy streams, the almost perpetual cold rains, the camps in high altitudes on glaciers in snows and violent storms bring to the traveller all of the discomforts of the arctic explorer. The very difficult slopes combined with high altitude effects add the troubles of the worst alpine climbs. The prospective conqueror of America's culminating peak will be amply rewarded, but he must be prepared to withstand the tortures of the torrids, the discomforts of the north pole seeker, combined with the hardships of the Matterhorn ascents multiplied many times.

# PART II

# The Expedition of 1906

THE MIDDLE NORTHEAST SLOPES

*Where avalanches tumble from slopes unseen to depths unknown*

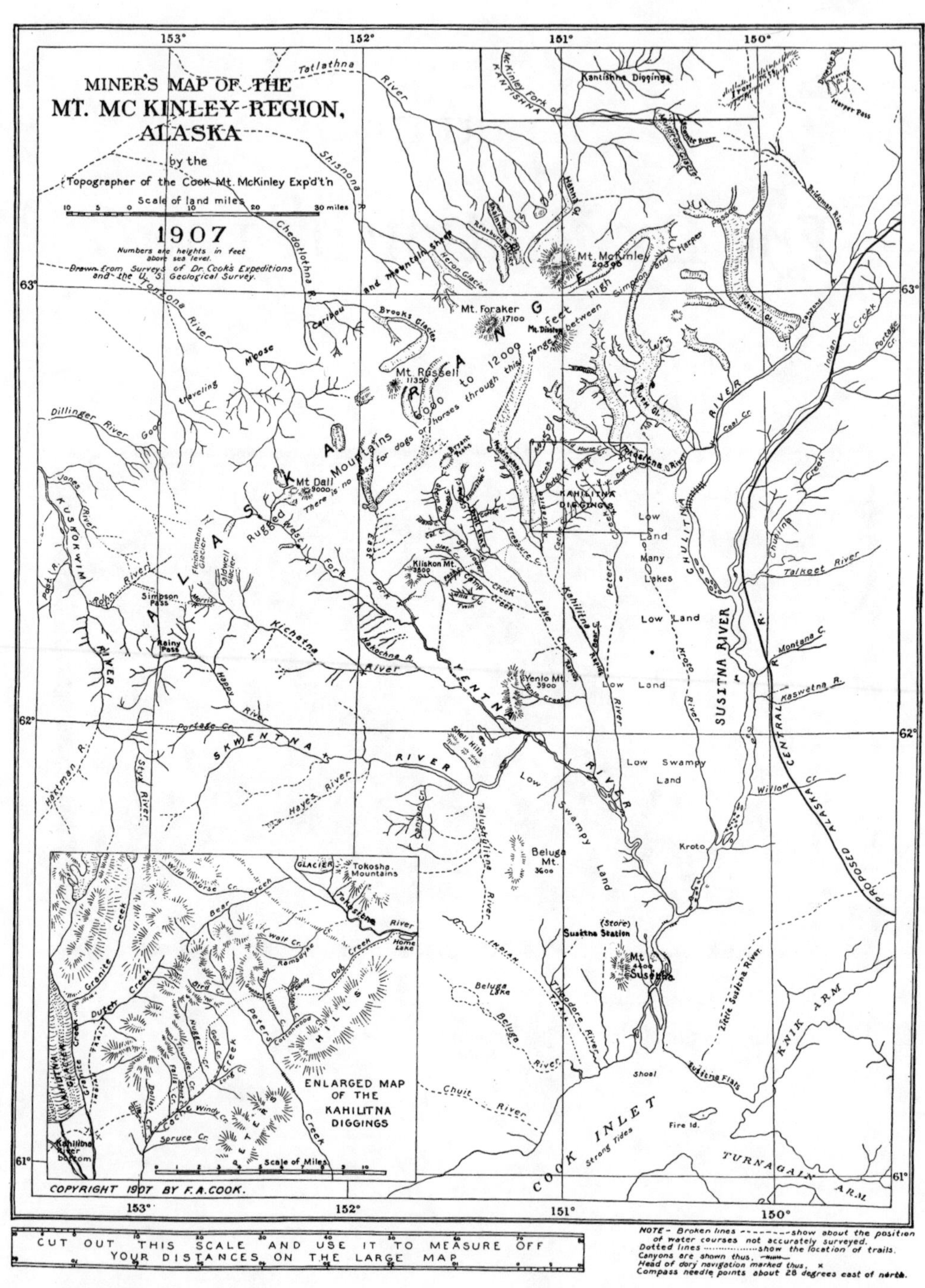


MINER'S MAP OF THE MT. MCKINLEY REGION, ALASKA

CHAPTER I

# With the Prospector into a New Gold Country

The opportunity to renew the attack on Mt. McKinley did not again present itself until the spring of 1906. I had taken up mountaineering to offset the home-destroying call of the Arctic but this first taste of mid-Alaskan life with its sheen of mountain magnificence, its haunts of big wild animals, and its gamble in gold and copper mines instilled an intoxication worse than the return habit of polar travellers. Alaska to-day is a land of boundless opportunities. It is the richest gold-bearing region in the world. Copper and other minerals promise great return. The fisheries and the big game will interest many for long years; but to mountaineers it is sure to be a stamping ground in the immediate future, for those who like ourselves are bent on first ascents.

While at Seattle, outfitting for our second alpine campaign, we soon became infected with the restless spirit of the prospectors. All Seattle and the Pacific coast was on the verge of a renewed Klondyke stampede, but no focus had been fixed for the rush. The greatest enthusiasm was directed towards the district surrounding Mt. McKinley, and the head waters of the Kuskokwim, the Kantishatna, and the Yentna were specifically outlined as promising ground. All of this was happily in line with our work of climbing and exploration.

After a month of great anxiety and hard work there was a sudden lull, the engines puffed, and the steamer *Santa Ana*, with a cargo of Alaskan dreamers, including ourselves, their weird outfits and horses, was en route for the great land of promise, the golden north.

Gliding softly through Puget Sound on the morning of May 16th, we admired at long range the snowy crests of the coast mountains, comparing the various peaks with Mt. McKinley against which our efforts were directed. Along the rugged shores of Vancouver Island, into the remarkable chain of evergreen islands, through an inland sea of quiet grandeur to Juneau, four days and three nights we breathed a balmy atmosphere, feasted upon wonderous scenery, and learned much of the mission of Alaskan travel. Every one was after gold or copper or tin, or some mineral which was to bring sudden and easy riches. Poor fellows!—all intoxicated with the gold fever, or yellow peril as we styled the prospector's spirit. Four months afterward many of these men returned depressed, melancholy, and cursing their fate, but in another year they will again be on the same chase after the elusive glitter of the yellow metal.

Juneau is the new capital of Alaska. It has long been the business centre of south-eastern Alaska but Sitka had previously retained the government and its honours mostly because it was in earlier days the most active town. Juneau owes its present importance to the great quantities of low-grade gold-bearing quartz discovered in its vicinity. The town is seemingly set in steps cut out of steep mountain slopes, picturesque beyond description, but with the present outlook of earthquake results, the town site is in great danger. It would need but a slight shake to bury the city under mountains of rock. Juneau people however ridicule this idea quite as the people of Valparaiso did, and are perfectly willing to trust to fate. The *Santa Ana* tied to the dock early, but the town was open full blast. The big Treadwell stamping mills on Douglass Island were sending up huge cones of smoke. From the chimneys of almost every house of both towns there came jets of smoke rising into the clear crisp air between the great cliffs which surrounded the vicinity.

The run to Sitka was serenely delightful, but the town had profited little during the three years which intervened between our visits. A new series of totem poles had been erected. The Greek church had been painted, but the place presented a study for the tourists interested in the Alaska of yesterday. To the passengers of the *Santa Ana,* the prospector, the nimrod, and the mountaineer, who were interested in the modern awakening of Alaska, Sitka had little to offer. In leaving Sitka we plunged from the quiet inland seas out on the ever stormy swell of the Gulf of Alaska, and then the drift of conversation rose from seasickness to the bigness of Alaska.

Like all new countries Alaska is overrated and underrated by the pioneers. It is put down as an arctic desert or as a semi-tropical Eldorado. As a matter of fact this great northland has within its boundless limits both the worst arctic temperature and the most agreeable temperate climate. In the interior north-east it is colder in winter than at the North Pole, while the south-west, moderated by the Japan current, has a climate comparable to that of Baltimore.

Alaska is a large country. Its coast line with its enormous indentations is said to be equal to the circumference of the globe. It is twelve times as large as the State of New York. It contains some of the greatest rivers of the world, and there is surely no place on earth where there are such picturesque mountain areas.

We stopped, among other places, at Orcha, and since everybody was eager to get to Cordova, a new boom town from which a railroad is projected into the Copper River country, we followed the excitement. After wading through mud and swamp we finally found ourselves in a narrow gorge near a small lake, a central street lined on both sides for three hundred feet by shanties and tents filled by men in various stages of intoxication, all trying to sell town lots and whiskey. Browne and Parker entered one place more attractive than others where a phonograph was noising popular airs. Browne asked for the cylinder "Absence Makes the Heart Grow Fonder." The bartender sang out in a loud voice: "We ain't got it, but we have what makes the jag grow longer."

There is a great difficulty in getting men to work on the Alaskan railroads. Agents of the road secure men at Seattle, furnish them with transportation and other expenses, and send them to Alaska. These men as a rule are of the hard luck type, ready to jump at anything in haste and regret at leisure. On the *Santa Ana* there were about one hundred men for the Alaska Central Railroad at Seward, and most of these yielded to the boom spirit at Cordova, remaining to work on the Copper River Railroad. When we arrived at Valdez and Seward, about one half of the people were eager to rush to Cordova to take advantage of the boom while the others were eager to get to the Yentna diggings. We might easily have secured two hundred recruits for the effort to climb Mt. McKinley, but previous experience had taught me that prospectors eager to get to a new diggings are of little use as helpers in an exploring enterprise.

At Seldovia we were forced to transship to a smaller steamer to take us up Cook Inlet. We anchored off Tyonok on the 9th day of May, and began at once to establish ourselves on shore.

Our outfit was a very large one. We were prepared to push a party of ten men to Mt. McKinley and continue a siege for five months. A double system of transportation was planned for this purpose. A pack train of twenty horses purchased from the Yakima Indians as before was to move supplies across country, and a specially constructed motor boat was planned to ascend the large easterly rivers. Our food for the low country was similar to that of the prospector—flour, bacon, beans, and the various accessories packed in waterproof bags of fifty pounds each. There is no dock and no lighter at Tyonok. So our things were thrown into dories and pushed through the surf by Indian boatmen to a wide sand spit. While some of the party watched this task and kept a check on our baggage, others were preparing the horses for their exciting plunge. The animals were raised in slings and lowered into the rushing cold waters to swim ashore. With the motor boat and dories we tried to guide the snorting animals to the nearest beach but often they chose their own way and gave us an exhilarating chase.

Several horses were nearly lost in this effort, only the speed of the launch and the ingenuity of our packers Printz and Barrille made their rescue possible. Later the vessel steamed closer to the shore and went aground to make the task of the horses easier and then they were quickly thrown over and as quickly the shivering

PORTER SKETCHING CONTOURS FROM ABOVE THE CLOUDS

creatures swam for the shore, but as they did a group of Indian dogs that had assembled made an assault. Many of the first horses turned their hoofs at the howling creatures, but later another assault was made and the wildest horses stampeded, four towards Mt. Redoubt and two northward along the shore.

One half of our baggage and outfit was put into the launch and then the boat was anchored in the stream; the other things were taken ashore by the Indians under the guidance of Mr. Finch, the local storekeeper. In due time we packed our things from the mud of the beach, made a pile above high-water line, covered it to keep the rain and the dogs off, and then pitched a big tent and placed in it a Yukon stove burning coal which we gathered from the beach.

Without any special orders on my part every man quickly devoted himself to his special vocation. Porter with his numerous instruments hustled about to get the local time, the latitude and longitude, and also a base line for triangulation. Parker with the hypsometer and barometers made sea-level observations for future altitude determination. Miller with all kinds of cameras posed the Indians and snapped picturesque effects. Altogether it was a busy day.

CHAPTER II

# Preparations for the Cross-Country March—Motor-Boating in Cook Inlet

At about three o'clock May 30th, as the sun was dashing the Kenai sky with crimson, and the countless dogs began their morning howl, we crawled from the blankets and tumbled out into the frosty air. The scene was superb; the big volcanoes Redoubt and Illiamna, dressed in snowy cloaks of purple blue, belched columns of dark vapour, while the purple waters of the Inlet gently lapping the gravel bars and the sky perfectly clear promised a good day; so leaving Printz, Barrille, and Beecher to corral the horses, while Parker and Ball were to do some unpacking, all others embarked on the launch and turned the screw to kicking us toward Mt. McKinley to transport the first load of supplies up the Susitna River.

The launch had been built in Seattle along lines necessary to cope with the shallow, swift streams rushing down the eastern drainage of Mt. McKinley. She was forty feet long, seven feet wide, with an extreme draft of twenty inches. The model was somewhat after the lines of a Peterborough canoe. The power was supplied by a twenty-five horse-power Automarine engine (Lozier) with the propeller in a tunnel. The boat was also fitted for oars and sails. The engine weighed 775 pounds, and the entire boat but three thousand pounds. A river boat on the Susitna needs also to be a good sea boat, for the waters of Cook Inlet are very treacherous. As a powerful river boat and a safe sea craft our launch was a great success.

With the tide running eight miles per hour and the speed of the launch about twelve miles per hour, we rushed up Cook Inlet at a pace that seemed like railroad travel. In less than two hours we reached the head of Cook Inlet and then with a diminished speed we moved over the endless tide flats of the delta, and though the

BEECHER, PARKER, PRINTZ, BARRILLE

river has a mouth five miles wide we missed the main channels and found ourselves en route for Knick when the tide turned. At last we noticed an opening into the low meadows from the east and following this we ascended the muddy waters still on bars of silt, in water less than three feet deep. We were aground every few minutes and thus drew up water thickened with mud which fouled our check valves and filled the cylinder jackets with clay which soon baked. This was a new trouble for a power launch to contend with and it proved to be our greatest trouble throughout the summer.

With two men sounding we managed to find channels where we were just about able to get through, but the task was a most difficult one. In about two hours we got into deeper channels, and then it took us four hours more to ascend ten miles against a very swift stream to Susitna Station.

The Station had changed much since our last visit. The Indians had decreased in numbers and pitched their camps near the trading post. Several new log huts were seen scattered among the trees and brush. The town now had a saloon, a trading post, and a roadhouse. Altogether there were about twenty prospectors' shacks and an equal number of Indian camps. The rush for gold toward Mt. McKinley made the Station an important place.

Mr. Frank Churchill, the manager of the trading post, very kindly placed a log cabin at our disposal, into which we placed our boatload of things, and in it also we camped for the night. The next morning at about ten o'clock we were ready to start down-stream, aiming to catch the tide at the mouth of the river at about noon.

Having had so much trouble in going aground we decided to add a river pilot to our party. Stephen, the son of the Chief, was secured. He was a trustworthy and intelligent young man who had been in our employ on our previous expedition. Stephen took the helm and guided us very well, jumping tree trunks and gravel bars as occasion demanded. The shore line was rushing past at the rate of fifteen miles an hour and after a half-hour of Indian pilotage we decided that a better knowledge of power boating was more important than an expert knowledge of the river bottom. So Miller took the wheel. We had much trouble at this time; mostly because the pump was often being fouled by the great quantity of glacial silt suspended in the water. The carbureter, too, was giving trouble because of water in the gasoline, and our downward trip was far from a happy one. Fortunately it was easy for us to ship oars and thus control the boat as she floated down-stream while the engines were being adjusted.

Porter desired to climb Mt. Susitna and Browne volunteered to join the venture. They desired to go light as the launch was expected back in two days, and therefore little food was taken with them when they left us at Alexander, a deserted Indian village. Since we had been much delayed we hastened down-stream to catch the tide by the westerly channel. The boat now ran splendidly, but as we neared the tidewater through the delta we noticed that the tide was already going out fast, but we kept on, our pilot saying it was all right. Passing out of the river and heading past an island upon which a barrel was placed we found the water rather deep, six to eight feet. With the brown water boiling behind us we went along in great glee, but soon after real dangers were at hand. The water shallowed, a heavy sea rolled under the bow, the engine stopped, the boat pounded lightly, we were aground, and the tide was fast going out. In less than half an hour there were fifty square miles of muddy flats about in place of the chocolate-coloured water. There was no shore-line within five miles of us, nor was there wood or water. We tried the surface water before it left us, and found it drinkable, though salty and thick with mud. We took the precaution to dip up a pail of this before it left us. We drank this water and ate some crackers, then threw out an anchor and without blankets we spread life preservers on the floor and tried to sleep until such time when the tide might return and lift us off.

The night proved dark and the clouds came out of Turnagain Arm with a speed which indicated a blow. We slept little but listened to the roar of the great

BROWNE

waves as they neared us. At about twelve o'clock midnight, the boat was afloat and soon after we put on power and headed the swell and the wind. The seas rose and the wind increased and white caps formed on every side. I suggested to our pilot that we make for Fire Island, but Stephen said, "I think all right, river good," from which we understood that he thought a course back into the river and later for Tyonok was all right but that he preferred to return to the river. We didn't like the idea of heading for ten miles of mud flats in the darkness with a howling gale behind us. So I said, "River no good—Tyonok good." He replied with a grunt and some Indian mutterings which I took to be swear words for the tone in which the utterances came was not indicative of good humour. But for Tyonok we headed. The seas now began to break over the bow and the wind carried the spray into Stephen's face with an ugly force. With each rush of water the boy would grunt and let drop an ugly Indian word. After about a half-hour at the wheel Stephen said, "Me plenty sick," and Miller and I might have said, "Me too," but we did not confess. We had been nursing the engine, for either the pump or the carbureter was balking frequently. The boat had no ballast and under the violent pitching of the sea we were only able to crawl around in the dark, not daring to light a lantern because we detected gasoline vapours. Miller took the wheel to relieve Stephen and he too got soaked from head to foot in the first few minutes. By two o'clock there was a little burst of light in the east and now we figured we were far enough away from the dangerous shallows to set a course for Tyonok. The altered course brought the seas to our fore quarter but we could not use full power because the boat would hit the seas dangerously hard. Thus we took the seas as easily as possible while the tide carried us southward. By daybreak, about 3:30, we pushed behind the spit at Tyonok, dropped anchor, and blew our fog horn for a boat to take us off. We were hungry, exhausted, and cold, but Prof. Parker had the cook prepare a meal for us before we got ashore, and food never tasted better.

The six horses which had stampeded were still at large; no trace having been found of them. To make the search more thorough we decided to run the launch fifty or sixty miles south on the next tide and land wherever we could to trail the horses. Ball was sent in saddle along the sandy shore-line, while Printz and Barrille joined me on the launch. As the people of the town were starting their fires we were again on the rough waters. The weather was improving, but Turnagain Arm still had a steel-coloured lustre in its clouds, and vapour plunged into the Inlet, which did not promise good weather; but we were so eager to start the pack train on its long trail overland that we could not afford to wait. We passed in among the big boulders of Trading Bay and noted the dangers at low water. Here the beach is wide and the steep sandy bank three hundred feet high leads to a plain covered by spruce, birch, and cottonwood trees. In this bank in various places we saw thin strata of lignite, a coal in which the fibre and bark of trees are easily made out, but it seems to burn well and is said to be good steaming coal.

The first twenty-five miles of this beach had been searched as we hastened on to Redoubt Bay. Then far out in the mud flats we saw some tracks but after a long search we decided that if the horses were to be found we must seek grassy lowlands near the point which separates the two bays. Here we met Ball, whose luck was like ours. He had secured no definite trace of the horses. We built a camp-fire and ate lunch, allowed the tide to go out, leaving the launch on the tide flats. Our campfire was spread by a sudden gale into a forest fire close to which we tried to keep warm, but the combination of smoke and wind drove us into the boat for shelter. After the wind subsided we began another search for the horses, but could find no further trace except the tracks which had been followed up to the outer tide flats. Late that night as the tide was about half in we abandoned the horse chase and started for Tyonok. The wind came in gusts and the sea came up in dangerous hills. The night was not dark but the light was of such a quality that we could never be sure of our bearings. The launch laboured heavily in the tumbling seas and we were quickly exhausted, for we had been three days and three nights without proper rest or sleep, and food had been only taken as the conditions permitted. Upper Cook Inlet has no harbours and seeing that the sea was too rough to make Tyonok and get ashore, we ran under a point of land below Tyonok, dropped anchor, and rode out the storm. The sea had broken over the boat so much that the floor and about everything on board was wet, but we spread the life preservers out and on these we slumbered for about two hours. With the change of the tide the sea eased, the wind ceased, and a warm sun made the icy volcanoes glitter at six o'clock. On the morning of June 2d we tipped the anchor, headed the tide, and by eight o'clock we were again at Tyonok.

## CHAPTER III

# Through the Valley of the Yentna—Climbing Tumbling Waters in a Motor Boat

The programme for our campaign, as it had been formulated to the present, was to explore the head waters of the Yentna River first, and from there we expected to get either by the westerly or an easterly route to the southwest arête of Mt. McKinley. From what we had seen of this area from Mt. Yenlo we had many reasons to suppose that there was an easy pass from the Yentna to the Tonzona. Our efforts were accordingly directed toward the big break in the Alaska Range forming the Yentna Valley. The horses were to go with light packs cross-country to a point at the head of navigation, while the boat with most of our equipment was to go up the Yentna as far as possible.

We decided to spend the day in loading the launch for her second trip up the river and also to help the packers prepare the pack outfit for its great tramp through brush and forest, over marsh and glacial streams.

At about noon June 3d, Printz, Barrille, and Beecher mounted their horses and we turned the others loose. The train of fourteen horses bounded northward at a rapid pace, only a few of them carrying packs consisting of supplies for thirty days and a folding canvas boat for crossing streams. All the other things were to be carried by the launch to the head waters of the Yentna. It was expected the two horses that had been chased northward would be found along this trail.

As the horses galloped up the beach toward the Beluga River the launch was started in the same direction. The sky was somewhat hazy, but the sea was as smooth as a glacial lake with a glimmering silvery surface. The quiet town of Tyonok with its busy prospectors was soon left behind. The pack train moving at a good pace was seen for some time edging along the great high banks. The boat cut the waters at an astonishing speed and in less than two hours we entered the mouth of the Susitna, a distance of thirty miles, and in another hour we were at Alexander anxiously looking for Porter and Browne who had been awaiting us with empty stomachs and eager eyes. They had known nothing of our horse troubles or the Cook Inlet storms.

Four days had passed since we left them, and after the first two days they began to realise their isolation. With but two days' food they had left the launch to climb Mt. Susitna, and when their task was accomplished the last was eaten and then it was a skirmish for food in a deserted town where but one thin, hungry dog broke the spell of loneliness. Hulligans, a kind of small fish, were coming up stream in great numbers, and in an old house some oats belonging to the Alaskan Central Railroad were discovered. The oats and the fish prepared with a hungry man's ingenuity made luxurious food for two days. But then it seemed as if they might be obliged to stay weeks; and the oats and fish diet did not seem a cheerful prospect. However, they occupied themselves sketching the local bits of nature, and when the launch puffed up the river a heavy weight of distress vanished.

We ate lunch at Alexander and then headed up the swift current for the Station. The weather was such that only now and again did we see the bald top of Mt. Susitna with its long tongues of winter snow still resisting the summer heat.

Mt. Susitna is an important landmark. In clear weather we seldom lost sight of it within a range of fifty miles from either side. With easy slopes the mountain rises out of a low, marshy country to an altitude of four thousand four hundred feet about fifteen miles above the mouth of the river. In its summit there are said to be copper deposits. At its base is the little town of Alexander with a shifting Indian population, getting its subsistence from the run of salmon and trout.

The run of the hulligans proved very exciting. We noted a ripple close to the shore and soon discovered that the dash of water was produced by a small fish about seven or eight inches long. We followed them mile after mile expecting to pass the excited train, but it was a continuous performance, they first rushed over and under roots, through submerged brush, up into the air, and down with a splash, always seeming to race with the launch. Mr. Porter's thoughts ran to mathematics, he figured that the train of hulligans was twelve inches wide and six inches deep and that it probably extended a hundred miles. Estimating the number of fish in a cubic foot at ninety-one and one half, he went on to so many millions that he gave it up, suggesting that we try and catch some. The launch was run close to shore, and its speed reduced to about that of the fish, then Porter, Parker, and Miller grabbed pell-mell, bringing up handfuls of wriggling, silvery creatures, until the floor of the boat was alive with the catch. Browne was asleep in the stern while all this excitement was making the air hilarious. He was the accredited naturalist, and it was thought that he should join the sport. It occurred to some one that the fish should wake him; and at once his blankets were alive with them; he awoke with a start and struck out as if to swim, believing himself in water, which shows that a man's notion of fish and the sense of swimming are closely associated.

The launch under full power threw up the muddy spume in angry whirls and pushed forward with a force inconceivable against rushing waters. In six hours' actual running time we reached the Station, beating all records for boats of all kinds on the same run. The prospectors coming over the route regard it as good luck if they can pull or pole or push their boats up this stream in six days. Here with the kind permission of Mr. Churchill we again camped for the night in his log cabin.

In our excitement after hulligans we jumped a log, bent a blade of the propeller, and twisted the rudder. Browne volunteered to fix the rudder, but the task proved disheartening. To take it out he found it necessary to get into the icy waters to his waist, and to replace it he was compelled to get under the boat. With a spirit not discouraged by glacial waters, the thing was fixed, at no expense, with two baths thrown in.

We blew our horn early on the morning of June 4th, to assemble for a start at nine o'clock. The Indians, the prospectors, and hangers-on at the Station came out to see the boat take the stream. About three hundred yards above the Station the river narrows and turns, shooting the waters past a huge bluff with a dangerous swiftness. No boat heretofore had been able to stem this current. In one way or another they have been compelled to seek a roundabout way, but our reputation had gone before us and would we try it? We had so far been able to negotiate all rapids and this did not seem much worse than others which we had made, so we said, "Yes, we will try."

Over-confident of our success we put on the switch and were off, but somehow we did not rush into the current in the usual way, but we went on. As we neared the bluff Browne boldly headed for the swiftest water, it shot over the bow and down stream we went. Pushing into the eddy at the Station ashamed of our performance we threw over a line and the people ashore were good enough not to make amusing capital out of our failure. We examined the engine carefully to discover the reason for the lack of power and soon found that the clutch was slipping, and that the propeller was fouled by small sticks in the tunnel. The propeller was reversed a few times, the sticks drifted away, then everything was carefully adjusted for our second effort, the explosions came full and free, the boat quivered with its usual life, and this time all of the town moved up to the higher banks to see our battle with the rushing waters. Browne kept the split between the eddy and the current until about two hundred feet from the bluff and then heading out slowly, the rushing waters flushed the decks and threw the boat far out into the gurgling stream, but the launch kept going up stream—our reputation was now redeemed and we were permitted the favourable prognostication of the sourdoughs.

The Yentna pours its silt-laden waters into the Susitna about two miles above the Station. It drains the great area from Mt. Spur to Mt. Foraker and it is the last of the great river beds to attract attention as a placer gold-field. The launch pushed up this stream with greater ease than up the Susitna. The rapids were less treacherous, and the waters are mostly crowded into one main channel. During most of the day we pressed along low banks thickly covered with alders, willows, and cottonwoods, but in the afternoon the banks rose, spruce trees were more in evidence, and here we saw the sticks of old Indian camps, also many signs of miners' camps.

At about four o'clock the low clouds which hung over us for several days lifted, and, looking backward, Porter located Mt. Susitna. We had gone about twenty-five miles against a six-mile current. The trip had been delightful and not at all fatiguing, but a bluff coming in sight, and the topographer desiring some observations from it of Mt. Susitna, we decided to land and enjoy our first real wilderness camp.

It was one of the most impressive spots on the Yentna. The river was about seven hundred feet wide and plunged into a deep gorge below, while above to the west were steep banks crested by spruce and birch. To the east were islands covered with cottonwoods, alders, and willows separated by sluggish slews which formed a part of the delta of the Kahilitna. The launch was tied to a tree, and the camp equipment was quickly passed out. Parker discovered that some one had preceded us and had cut wood. Browne and Miller soon had a cheerful camp-fire under a big birch tree, flour was mixed in the prospectors' pan, and out of the reflector in a few minutes we took twenty brown biscuits; this with bacon, potatoes, and tea completed our bill of fare.

In our rambles about camp we discovered a log cabin on the bluff and a good trail to it. There were differences of opinion as to a choice of sleeping places, some preferred the boat, others the log cabin, and still others a small tent under a spruce tree. The mosquitoes were just beginning to be active, and we anticipated a mild first assault, but they quickly surrounded us in countless millions, driving us to despair with a song and a sting that made the camp ring with sulphurous words. Here were all the varieties of insect life suddenly released from their dormant state, most of them seeking the first blood, and under our thin skins they found what was to their liking. We tried mosquito dope, gasoline, coal oil, creosote, and other things but all to no avail. From this time until we were well up in the snow line these little pests were to us deadly enemies and they were never idle.

The sun sank under the cones of the spruce and left a glitter of gold on the glossy brown waters. Mt. Susitna was clear cut against a purple sky. The rushing waters, the crackling fire, and the forest noises were keyed to a harmonious pitch, but the skeets coming in black swarms out of the grass kept us in a perpetual torment. There was a bright twilight through the night, so bright that we could read ordinary print in our silk tents at midnight. Early in the morning a very heavy shower of rain stilled the mosquitoes but made all the camp thoroughly uncomfortable.

On the morning of June 6th the dark rain-clouds separated, and for a brief period there were spots of sunlight floating down the river. Shivering around the camp-fire we took up the momentous question of christening the boat. The discussion was rather heated in its first stages and the names advocated were Bolshoy, the Russian and Indian name of the McKinley group of mountains; Tyone, Indian for Chieftain; Tyonet, Indian for the king Salmon; also Yenlo, Yentna, Mountaineer, Yellow Peril, and Come-and-Get-It. After due discussion the vote was unanimous for *Bolshoy*.

At 7 o'clock we slipped the rope and pushed up stream. Browne and Miller took turns at the wheel while Parker did the soundings. Porter arranged the kitchen box on the stern and from there, undisturbed by the excitement of navigation, he took his angles with the prismatic compass thus plotting the river and its banks as we went along. But above all, what interested us forward was the calm pleasure which was pictured on Porter's face as the launch with sharp bounds rushed over swift waters and brought to his gaze a changing and highly coloured landscape. To myself fell the peculiar task of posing as captain and acting as engineer. To be captain was easy, for my crew were good river men, but my duties as engineer necessitated a careful watch upon the many phases of gas-engine operation. By making slight adjustments, however, the engines puffed away hour after hour with the ease and regularity of clock movements. Each hour we were climbing up stream a distance which it would take a river dory several days to accomplish.

The scenic effect improved as we rose. During the second day from the Station Mts. Yenlo and Kliskon rose into view. Over the lower skyline of the spruce and birch trees, we now noted the foothills of the Alaska Range, but the great central uplift was still veiled by dark clouds. On this day also we passed nearly all of the large tributaries of the Yentna. One, the Kahilitna, a glacial river taking the drainage of a huge glacier from Mt. Foraker, runs through the centre of the new gold country south of Mt. McKinley. Eight miles above the Kahilitna we

MOTOR BOATING IN THE NORTH COUNTRY WHERE DUSK AND DAWN RUN TOGETHER

passed Lake Creek, arising from a large lake south of Mt. Russell. Twelve miles above this we passed the mouth of the Skwentna coming from the glaciers amid the unknown mountains north of Mt. Spur, and early on the morning of June 7th we passed the mouth of the Kichatna which drains the Simpson Pass district. After ascending beyond these four tributaries the Yentna was still as large as the Hudson above tide water, and its waters poured over gravel bars at the rate of nearly seven miles per hour.

We followed the Yentna it its great sweeps and curves over a wide expanse of silt. This silt was washed out of the high mountains of the north in former ages, and to-day the same silt, though covered by forests, is being cut away and deposited into other places lower down. The quantity of this glacial wash held in suspension is inconceivable. In places where the current is rapid the consistency of the water approaches that of syrup. This peculiar faculty of the Yentna in tearing down and building up explains the very frequent changes in the channel of the stream. It explains also the origin of the many islands and slews so characteristic of the Alaskan glacial rivers.

Youngstown, a kind of mythical miners' camp, the supposed head of navigation, was our ultimate destination. But we were a long time locating the town. Indeed the town was unable to locate itself, for it drifted with a shifting population of miners. At about ten o'clock we saw a big dory drifting down the stream. A corpulent miner with all kinds of things was in the boat. To our question, "How far to Youngstown?" he answered: "It used to be twenty miles above, but it just moved. I have the town in the dory and am taking it down the stream." He also said the river was not navigable above, but our soundings gave from three to four feet of water, and so long as we could find thirty inches, our boat could kick along.

By going aground often, jumping snags and dodging sweepers, we managed to get to a point on the west fork about forty miles from the headwaters. Here we secured the *Bolshoy* to a cut bank, built a cache, placing in it most of our provisions, and on the bars we erected a big tent.

The tent and its surroundings we named "Parker House" in honour of our coworker Prof. Parker. The river above Parker House spread over a wide expanse of quicksand. This shallow rift extended about three miles, and beyond the river narrowed and would have been navigable for several miles had we been able to get our boat above the shallow.

A huge camp-fire was built for comfort, and another fire for cooking. We gathered around the fires and talked about our luck in climbing the rushing waters, our picturesque surroundings, the signs of game, and the next effort to find a pass through the range. The work of the day had been exciting. We were tired, cold, and hungry. Nearly everybody helped the cook to prepare a great feast. The menu in preparation was as follows: Biscuits baked in the reflector, with a Yentna gold and brown finish, pork and beans, fried bacon, fried eggs, mashed potatoes, tea. As this was about ready Browne introduced the call "Come and get it." This was continued as a meal call during all of our adventures.

CHAPTER IV

# Discoveries About Mt. Dall and the Yentna Headwaters

We had hardly finished the meal when we noted a rather strong icy wind blowing from the north, and with it the clouds drifting up the valley vanished. These vapours in our trip up the Yentna obscured the big mountains of the Alaska Range. Soon after the high clouds also withdrew, leaving a central zone of stratus films. Above this line of clouds we were suddenly surprised by the mirage of peak after peak of giant proportions, all seemingly near and looming up so very high that any one of them could have been mistaken for Mt. McKinley. Below, were the steep green slopes of the foothills, separated by large rounded valleys, in several of which could be seen the blue surfaces of great ice streams, from which came the brown waters of the Yentna. There were four notable peaks after the mirage had disappeared. These were Mts. McKinley Foraker, Russell, and Dall. All were freshly covered with snow, but Mt. Russell seemed most remarkable because of its nearness and regular pyramidal shape. To the westward of Mt. Dall we were now able to pick out several distinct breaks in the range, and to explore these to discover a pass to the westward was our next effort. On the afternoon of the same day, June 9th, we determined to start for the Pass. We estimated that we were forty miles from the divide, and we planned to cover as much of this as possible by poling or lining a twenty-foot canvas boat. Stocking our boat with a supply for five men for ten days we left Parker House in charge of Prof. Parker and began the arduous and dangerous task of pushing up the tumbling waters of the Yentna. Prof. Parker was to make a round of observations and direct the building and stocking of a large main cache. Mr. Porter had already measured the base line, and had also secured meridian and latitude observations. The topographer was thus in a favourable position to begin a plane-table survey of the unexplored territory through which we were about to travel. My companions in this scouting party were Porter, Browne, Miller, and Armstrong, the latter having joined us on the river to prospect the new territory through which we aimed to go. The boat was not heavily loaded but it gave us much trouble in towing, and we soon discovered that for glacial rapids a canvas canoe was a failure. With four men on the line and one in the stern with a steering paddle we just managed to get along about a mile an hour. Our troubles were numerous, being frequently mired in quick-sand, stumbling over treacherous drift wood into deep icy waters, fording rapids, and fighting the mosquitoes, were but a few of our hardships. The thing was however exciting, and was taken with good cheer.

As the sun settled under the snow peaks of the west we witnessed the first of the remarkable series of sunsets which gladdened our hearts for weeks to come. We were approaching the time of the longest day and also nearing the arctic circle, the combined effect of which was to give us a long day of intense heat with frequent showers, a short night, frosty and clear with the sun just under the northern mountains throwing flames of orange and gold against a sky of purple. We camped that night on a bar where driftwood was plentiful, and in a near-by pool clear water was found which was a discovery indeed, for though water was to be found everywhere, clear water, free of glacial mud, was indeed rare.

As the chill and twilight of the night settled over us the bright camp-fire was doubly appreciated. A bit of canvas was spread on the sand in the lee of a log and upon it in an appetising array were steaming beans and bacon, bread, and tea made of clear water for all to "come and get it." Our clothing was soaked with ice water from head to foot, and until the cheer of the fire and the thought of hot food were impressed upon us we were thoroughly miserable. That night in the silk tents we were well housed from the mosquitoes, and in the morning as we awoke among the roaring ice waters, the camp-fire and the warm breakfast proved a fetching inducement for early rising.

By noon of the 10th we reached the limit of profitable canoe navigation. The boat had been dragged over gravel bars so much that the outer canvas was worn through in several places, requiring immediate repair. We were now about eight miles above Parker House, and here the river makes a sharp turn. Leaving Miller and Armstrong here to repair the boat and prospect for gold, Porter and Browne joined me on a venture to seek a pass. The outlook from here was favourable. Winds and clouds were rushing into gaps through the mountains at a point about thirty miles westward. To reach and examine these gaps we packed into our rucksacks our equipment of sleeping bags, tent, food for seven days, and instruments, in all weighing thirty pounds. Starting late in the afternoon of the 10th we set a course into the narrowing valley of the west fork of the Yentna travelling over gravel bars and benches, fording slews occasionally, but no big streams. The frequent stops which Porter required to set up his plane table gave us a welcome breathing spell. The tracks of bears, moose, and wolves aroused us to a spirit of the chase, while the bewildering mountain slope with roaring falls and cataracts echoing from side to side revealed nature in its wildest aspects.

After having covered about seven miles we spent the night in our little tents pitched on a sand bar, and before the sun had dispelled the chilly shadows of the big mountain of the north-east we were again on the march with our packs. At noon we found the sun so hot that it was thought best to camp for a few hours to rest, to dry out our clothing, and to eat a hearty meal. We had crossed and recrossed the main stream with great difficulty. The icy waters were here wide and deep, but the shores were so precipitous, and the underbrush so dense that we were compelled to take the river bottom, fording and swimming as the occasion required.

At four o'clock in the afternoon we again took up our burden and marched into the opening of a canyon, but the waters here proved too deep and too swift to ford. After vainly searching for an easy crossing we were finally forced to camp, having made only ten miles for the day's effort.

We took to the brush on the next day to avoid fording and swimming. The stream was very dangerous, the alders the worst we had seen, and though we found an old bear trail it took us all day to make an advance of three miles.

Early on the morning of the 14th it rained heavily in the mountains. The river was high, but we could not afford the time to wait for better weather. Our first task was to cross a stream, the worst that we had seen. We tried in vain for a good ford and at last Browne in a desperate spirit plunged into the raging torrent, lost his footing, turned several summersaults, was carried downstream some distance, and only saved himself by landing on a submerged boulder. Porter and I followed with better luck, but it was agreed that we would cross no more such streams. We tried hard to be true to our resolution, but other streams barred our way and must be negotiated. In four hours we had gone about eight miles and were blocked from farther progress by rapids increasing in force and depth. We calculated that with horses all these waters would be easy, so it simply remained for us to explore the pass far enough to be reasonably sure that we could get through the range. To determine this point finally we now decided to climb the mountains to the south to an altitude where we might see through the range. We crossed a deep channel and began the climb wet to our hips, with boots full of ice water. The slopes were steep, while the underbrush was as dense as tropical verdure, and on hands and knees we climbed and crawled between branches. The mosquitoes were maddening, and the devil-clubs filled our clothing with needles. Before we had ascended two thousand feet our trousers were torn in strips and we were thoroughly exhausted. A rest of an hour while observations were being made and another hour for lunch changed our fatigue into renewed enthusiasm; for at this time we saw that if we could reach an old glacial bench about a thousand feet higher, and about four miles west, we could get a view which would satisfy us as to the possibility of getting our pack-horses through the range. We reached this position in about two hours, and there pitched the tent. Wood was scarce here, but we found roots, bits of brush, and moss sufficient to prepare our food. We had now reached the limit of time and food-consumption which we had allowed ourselves, so this must be our last day of advance. It rained, snowed, and hailed a great part of the night, but the early morning as usual was bright and clear.

Our position here was unique. The foaming waters of the Yentna were more than two thousand feet below us, rushing from bluff to bluff in a system of unexplored canyons which for perpendicular cliffs and superb mountains of great altitude surpassed the glories of the Grand Canyon of the Colorado. To the south were huge snow-capped mountains unnamed and unexplored, among them large snow basins feeding glaciers of the Yentna and Kuskokwim. To the north was a curious mountain about six thousand feet high with five pinnacles. The main Yentna waters came out of canyons on both sides of this mountain. To the south above the canyon we could see the rolling hills of the western slopes of the range. To the north of this mountain was a wide low gap through which the clouds of the Kuskokwim drifted, and beyond this gap were high mountains leading up to

Mt. Dall. The passes existing on both sides of the mountain with five pinnacles seemed promising from every view we had, but no pass is a pass until some one has passed through it. We could have gone through afoot, but we had neither the time nor the food supply, and, after all, our object was only to ascertain with reasonable possibility if the pass was practicable for pack-horses. Of this we now felt sure, and laboriously returned to Parker House over-confident of our ability to cross the range by the new pass with our horses.

## CHAPTER V

# Into the Yentna Canyons

We were now waiting for the arrival of the pack-train. Miller and Ball had been sent to the Kichatna to meet the packers and guide them above the timber line, along the bald slopes, and down to our camp in the Yentna. The days of waiting were spent by cutting trail from the river to the grassy upper slopes. Porter and Browne camped high up in the mountains to study topography and game, and had several exciting experiences. Porter took his instruments to the top of a commanding peak and set up his plane table to sketch a round of contours. While his attention was fixed on distant peaks, he was disturbed by the approach of a big brown bear with a cub. There was not room for Porter and the bear on the peak, and Porter had no weapon with which to enforce his prior claim, so he quickly grabbed his instruments and with long strides he descended over the sudden drop of snowbank. The coming of a violent storm made farther retreat necessary for both Browne and Porter, and the map was never completed.

In the course of a week after our return to the Parker House we heard one day the sound of the bell-mare's bell and the axes cutting trail through a dense spruce and birch forest, and soon after saw Printz, the chief packer, tumble into a stream from a low bank. The water was deeper than he had calculated, so he had quite a tussle to dodge the horses that plunged in after him. Men and horses scrambled out on a sandy bar, and with them came clouds of mosquitoes. Here these pests greeted us and we greeted our companions from whom we had been separated for three weeks, and the reunion was an occasion for a special feed and rest.

Printz with Barrille and Beecher had had a hard time in the cross-country tramp to reach us at the Parker House, a distance of one hundred and thirty miles, over marshes, through thick underbrush, and across several big glacial rivers. The horses were reduced in numbers, and those that survived were weak, thin, and sickly, due mostly to the incessant torment of mosquitoes and horseflies. The six horses stampeded by the Indians' dogs were not recovered, and to make matters worse, while feeding near the Beluga River the herd wandered over a grassy plain under which a stratum of lignite coal was burning. Some of the horses broke through the surface and were mired in the fiery coal. Six were badly burned, of which three were shot, but the others after careful nursing recovered. Now there remained but eleven horses of a splendid pack-train of twenty animals, and some of these were not strong enough to carry packs.

On the 25th of June we packed the horses with supplies which we hoped to place in caches along the western side of the range for later use by our hunting party. We also packed an outfit and supplies for an assault upon Mt. McKinley from the slopes north of Mt. Foraker. The weather had been very warm for several days, melting the winter snows in the high mountains rapidly, and there was also a great deal of rain during the night. The river in consequence was rather high and we could not afford the time to wait for low water, nor could we guess when the water would become tow. We started to follow the Yentna into the pass as we had previously gone afoot. We had not gone far before we noticed that the Yentna offered perils even with horses. The pack-train of eleven horses, carrying about one hundred and fifty pounds each, with eight men scattered among them, was in good control. The men and horses rushing over seething rapids into a land unknown made a picture of pioneer life as primitive as that of the early Western frontiersmen.

While the horses were thoroughly trained to carrying pack they had not yet adapted themselves to the new trick of fording rivers with the double load of pack and man. In following the Yentna it was necessary to ford so often that we could not stop and unpack, nor did we aim to trouble the animals except in crossing dangerous places. As we neared a deep slew each man took his favourite horse and led him into the ford, mounting on the run. This kind of adventure proved very exciting. Most of the horses bucked with the first attempt and plunged into deep swift water with a wild splash. If the swim was short and the rider had good presence of mind the task proved merely exhilarating, but if the swim was long, and either man or horse became panic-stricken, then there was trouble for all.

This panic in the depth of swift water, which is the same as that in the breath of avalanches at high altitudes, is a dangerous state of mind, for it defeats the ability for quick action upon which the security of life often depends. Some men soon school themselves to its elimination, but with others the thing becomes more overwhelming with every experience. Rushing glacial streams have a peculiar effect upon every one is who much around them. There is a run of human passion which goes with tumbling waters. Most of our party felt the spirit of this peril of the rapids, for as we breathed the icy spray of the swift streams some became stimulated and talkative and others quiet and melancholy. Thus each swim of the Yentna left its imprint of intoxication.

In the first three miles the fords were only waist-deep and few men took the trouble to mount, but as the river turned westerly the many slews united, making one large river about three hundred yards wide. Picking what we supposed would be the best ford, Printz, Browne, and Porter started. They got along splendidly until the horses began to swim and were carried down stream, landing on the opposite shore along a cut bank among roots and fallen trees. The men climbed out, and after a good deal of trouble succeeded in dragging their horses out also. Most of the other horses were bucking and could only be urged into the water with great difficulty. To allow for the drift down stream the rest of us started into the water farther up, with results even more disastrous than the first.

At the next ford we were more careful. A trail was cut for a mile through dense alders and willows, which served the double purpose of obviating a swim and warming the men after their shivering water adventures. Coming out of the jungle we found a camping spot on a bar where driftwood and clear water were abundant, but the grass was insufficient. From the driftwood a big fire was made. Soon we forgot the discomfort of the cold water and warmed to home topics.

During the next day we were able to avoid dangerous fords, and, with an agreeable camp under magnificent cascades, the peril of the rapids was for a time dispelled by the more distant music. The next day, however, troubles returned with double force, for as we pushed into the mountains the river took a zigzag course from bluff to bluff and ruffled up in mid-stream tumbles.

The worst experience of this day and the most dangerous of the entire trip unfortunately fell to the lot of the man who feared the run of glacial waters most. As the river made a sharp turn from cliff to cliff we were forced to cross two narrow slews where the water moved with a rush that made us hold our breaths. In the first crossing nearly every one had got into trouble and scrambled out of the bubbling rapids with the feeling that he had just escaped an icy grave. The next slew was more encouraging. Here it was wider and gave us more room to clear the cliffs if by chance we were taken down stream. Four men crossed with some difficulty, but by just missing a swim. Prof. Parker mounted Billy Buck, the horse that had gained the reputation of being the best river animal. Billy Buck started in somewhat lower than the other horses, became confused in mid-stream, lost his footing, went down stream and under. For a few seconds both the Professor and the horse were out of sight. Suddenly the Professor bobbed up, struck for the shore, and was pulled out by Barrille at a time when he had about given up the game. The head of the horse was seen as the seething waters swept the cliffs, but we followed the stream with anxious eyes for some distance without seeing the unfortunate animal again. We were certain the horse was lost but thought his pack must drift ashore somewhere. In the pack were a number of things indispensable to our work, but the thing desired most was Browne's rifle, which was lashed insecurely over it. Two scouting parties were sent down stream to seek the pack, and a few miles below they found Billy Buck feeding along in tall grass, with his pack still properly balanced and the rifle somewhat scratched and dented but still in working order.

The unexpected rescue of Billy Buck made our camp ring with enthusiasm, but the day's experience, with the narrow escape of Parker, proved that greater caution was necessary in the future fords. Our camp here was near a clear stream, where Porter secured some trout. The foothills rose in successive slants almost perpendicularly. Near the stream bed were a few spruce, birch, and cottonwood trees, and some scattered patches of grass. The middle slopes were covered with alders and the upper benches were remarkable for new green carpets of grass, while just above, at six thousand feet, was the line of perpetual snow.

When the sun broke through the haze and vapour it was suffocatingly hot, but the almost continuous train of clouds which ran through the range in the direction of our prospective pass kept up a gloom of local showers. The nights were bright but chilly, and the winds were unusually strong. The extremes of heat and cold were keenly felt and the difficulties of advance were such that an air of uncertainty and mystery was necessarily cast over every plan of action.

The mouth of the canyon of the Yentna was but eight miles away and the next day's camp was to be pitched in a bunch of big cottonwoods within easy striking distance of the opening. With good weather and good luck we reached this camp soon after noon.

It was evident that much scouting must be done before a pass could be forced here with heavy packs. A cache was built, a permanent camp was made, and good feeding grounds were sought for the horses.

The morning of June 29th opened with spats of sunlight, which drifted hurriedly along the valley. The temperature was 43° and a strong wind came out of the canyon in hard puffs. The problem of the day was to determine finally the possibility of getting through the range. We entertained strong hopes of doing so, but the canyons were still unexplored, and with our unfortunate water experience we prepared cautiously for the desperate task. Browne, Barrille, and Printz were invited to join me in the endeavour. The four best river horses were selected, and without packs and without saddles we started for the plunges.

Our camp fellows gathered at the gates of the canyon and watched the horses take the first series of rapids. The water was deep and swift, but the swim was very short. As we pushed into the narrowing gap of the cut the streams came together with augmented force. To gain footing on the bars it was necessary to cross at every turn. We had expected to swim much and therefore wore as little as possible. A bathing suit would have been to our liking, but the icy water and the frost of the shadows in the canyons, with a biting wind, made our wet clothing almost harden to armour plates. After each swim we dismounted, shivered, danced about, and hurried along to the luck of the next crossing.

About two miles up stream the main canyon turned to the north of a remarkable peak with five points. Here the river forked, the northerly stream heading towards the Tonzona River while the southerly stream, with a lesser canyon, led towards the Dillinger River. Both courses must be explored for a pass. Browne and Barrille were sent to examine the Yentna–Dillinger gap, while Printz and the writer sought to push into the Yentna–Tonzona canyon.

Toward the Tonzona the walls of the canyon rose in successive tiers to seven thousand feet. For sheer cliffs and dazzling contrast of colour the scene surpassed that of the Grand Canyon. The gap narrowed as we advanced, the stream deepened until at last three miles above the forks we were halted by the plunging torrent with no place for a footing for man or beast. We found some tracks of moose, bear, and mountain sheep, but the footing was too insecure for our horses. With no safe practical way to get through this canyon we returned to the forks and followed Browne and Barrille into the other canyon, westward to the limit of horse travel. This canyon was less picturesque, but it offered better facilities for travel. To each side of the canyon there was a bench, the shelf of an old glacier, beyond which we saw a rolling grassy country at an altitude of about three thousand feet. It was, however impossible to rise out of the canyon with our horses to this bench, and therefore this pass would also be impracticable for the pack-train, though men with light packs could get through. Unless we could push along supplies sufficient for several months it was useless to continue the search for a break through the range, and therefore we abandoned the pass-seeking undertaking.

The return proved to be a very dangerous adventure. The sun had thrown its fire on the glacier all day, and the river swelled with leaps and bounds. We had no great difficulty until after we passed the forks; then the horses refused to take to the water. Printz made seven or eight attempts with his Billy Buck, and each time the horse turned to the near bank. In one of these attempts my Roan followed, struck out with a desperate lunge, and crossed. This left a wide torrent between us, and the noise of the rushing water was such that we could not hear each other. After several more attempts Printz took his horse to a break in the canyon and, signalled that he would try to return along the brim.

There were still five dangerous crossings to be made before leaving the canyon, and to do this alone was taking a desperate chance, but there was no alternative. The next crossing was accomplished without much trouble, though Roan refused for a long time to make the attempt, but the next swim induced me to quit water ventures for that day. In urging the horse into the water he suddenly lost footing and struck out, but the current was such that he turned over so quickly that he hardly knew what happened, and I had no time to argue either with Roan or myself when I found myself groping at the horse's stomach with his legs dashing out with wild darts. I let go; whether I prudently decided to quit the horse or unconsciously let go I do not know, but the next moment we were side by side, snorting and puffing and reaching out for the shore.

Roan was carried down only about one hundred feet, and then reached out over big boulders to a sand bar, where he stood and watched me drift with the rushing waters toward a cliff. It seemed as if I could never reach that shore, and as

I was about to seek the bottom the stream brushed the rocks with such force that it was impossible to hold the feet down. Feeling that the grip of death was at hand a last effort was made, which landed me on the boulders as the current turned to press into a tunnel. For some minutes I remained face down on those boulders, so nearly paralyzed from cold and exhaustion that I was unable to stir. With increased consciousness there was also an added sense of cold, and as I walked over to the horse I noticed that he too was shivering. It was but a mile to the end of the canyon, but I had not the courage to test the more dangerous crossings below.

Finding some good grass in a gully I left Roan, intending to reach camp over the brim and expecting to come after him in the morning, when the river would be lower. The ascent out of the canyon was a very difficult one, but I had not gone far before the horse pushed his nose under my arm and proved that he could climb as well as a man. Together we made a zigzag course to the top, but there our trouble was even worse. The brush was so thick that it was difficult to push through, and I had nothing but a pocket knife with which to cut a trail. Crowding between alders the horse followed, seeming to share with me the eagerness to get away from the rapids. Finally we reached camp, where we found Printz against a blazing camp-fire thawing out. Browne came along about an hour later having shot a brown bear, and having had the same experience which fell to our lot, but Barrille with his horse was left in the canyon

An expedition was organised for the relief of Barrille with other horses and ropes, but he refused to be rescued that night while the water continued to rise, and the temperature lowered, and asked to be left until low water in the morning. As the sun rose Printz took Roan and went to the relief of Barrille. The water was so low that both were able to ride on one horse without swimming. Barille had been twenty-four hours without food or sleep but he had a well-rounded experience.

Our adventures in the canyons proved that a farther effort to cross the range here with supplies was hopeless. There still remained a glacier leading to Mt. Dall along which there appeared to be a break through the range, but this was not practicable with horses, and therefore of no use to us.

We returned to Parker House to devise some other line of attack. The pass-seeking adventure was a hopeless failure, but the many discoveries of glaciers, mountains, and rivers were sufficient reward for the hard experiences.

## CHAPTER VI

# Northward to Mt. McKinley over New Gold Diggings

Failing to force the Yentna Pass our next route to the west was along the Kichatna and through Simpson Pass. But before such an attempt could be made the horses must feed up and be allowed time to recuperate. The long drive overland from Tyonok and the hard life in the Yentna with very little grass all along so reduced the pack-train that the animals were unable to assume the hardships of the mosquito-pestered Kichatna. There were three arguments which induced us to try a reconnoissance northward to Mt. McKinley. In prospect it did not seem a difficult horse trail, and food was abundant. Therefore the horses would rest and regain strength for the more serious effort later to the west. The country over which we were to travel was the new dreamland of the prospector, and our exploration of it would give a map of what was a blank on the charts, and above all it was the most direct route to the base of Mt. McKinley, a distance of seventy miles.

With these points in view we refitted from Parker House for a month's campaign. From the highlands to the west of the Yentna we had previously picked a trail for the first stage of this journey. Between the two forks we must cross five miles of jungle, then cross the east fork of the Yentna, and ascend Mt. Kliskon. To cut trail Browne, Printz, and Miller were sent out early in the morning of July 3d. The pack train followed in the afternoon. The water was high and we had still to cross several deep streams of the west fork, in each of which we got thoroughly drenched. In the jungle over the newly made trail travelling was at first good. There were large spruce, birch, and cottonwood trees and a dense underbrush of willows and alders. Now again we rose and to a hill where the light fell through the narrow gap between the trees and illuminated luxurious grass fields to which the horses ran with delight. Around some erratic boulders we found wild currants and cranberries. Squirrels and fool-hens made the air ring with a note of life, while bear trails and moose tracks kept the nimrods keyed up to a pitch of excitement, but we were too busy to hunt.

We had counted on crossing this neck of land in a few hours but we were misled. Our bird's-eye view from above indicated a soft green wilderness with a decorative park-like grouping of the spruce, the alders, and the cottonwoods. There were many deep slews and marshes which we did not see until we plunged in muddy waters. Finally as the chill of night increased and the song of the mosquitoes saddened, we were confronted by a deep stream with cut banks on both sides, which we could not cross. We camped on the bank of the slew, and before morning the stream rose and the whole jungle seemed to be afloat.

In the pouring rain we started to find some ford but we waded for miles through brush and mud without being able to cross. Another slew drove us back until we wearied of doubling upon our back trail. It was an innocent, quiet-appearing band of water not more than one hundred feet wide. In a desperate mood we resolved to cross it. When men slip and stumble over roots and entangling willows in ice water waist deep for hours the thought of a swim comes as a sort of relief. But some of our men could not swim and others who could were so cold that they did not dare to venture.

Two horses voluntarily plunged in, and with loud snorts they struck out for the other shore. The poor creatures with our instruments and matches and sugar and other precious things swam about for a long time before they were able to gain a footing on the opposite shore. Completely exhausted and nearly frozen to death they finally reached bottom in the brush but were unable to drag themselves out of the deep water. In my eagerness to get to these sinking animals I tried to mount my horse without taking off his heavy pack and urged him into the water. He was a good swimmer but objected to being mounted while carrying a pack saddle. We edged along to find a favourable jumping-off place. Without my consent the horse jumped a fallen tree and bucked me several feet into the air after which I went down to what seemed like several leagues of wetness. When I had a chance to catch my breath I found myself drifting down stream within reach of my struggling horse. Separately we struck out for the other horses in trouble. Browne and Printz felled a tree and managed to cross on it, as did also Prof. Parker, but they sank to their necks before crossing and might have swam over with less discomfort. All the others managed to cross holding to a pack strap or the tail of a horse and made easy work of it. To the other side of the slew we waded through a flooded flat grabbing the limbs of trees, monkey fashion, to keep from having our feet glued to the mud bottom. We all breathed a sigh of relief when we rose on to a ridge where we found a good bear trail going our way. Bears usually went our way but they only came our way when we were unarmed.

Soon after we saw the beautiful green slopes of Mt. Kliskon and the wide flats of the east fork, and now it remained only for us to find a ford to be able to get up into the mountains and out of this detestable floating lowland with its pests of mosquitoes and its run of icy waters. But the hope of a better country was very slowly realised. Indeed when we did get into the high country we still had water troubles of another kind.

We jumped out of the jungle on to the bars of silt and began to cross the river. We forded for several miles across stream, up and down, taking one slew after another, all over dangerous quicksands, where the horses would mire and tumble and roll amid stream with the packs. The last stream was about five hundred feet wide, very swift and deep. This we could not attempt, reduced as we were by the day's troubles. There was an alluring camping spot about two miles south and to it we betook ourselves over the many slews which we had to cross. From this camp we saw several miners' tents on the other shore. After a rest and a meal we managed to signal to the strangers to bring a boat and ferry us over. The horses without packs were run into the main river and swam splendidly, but they were carried a long way down stream. These tents marked the location of what had been intended as a miners' town, but the east fork was not found to be navigable to that point, and therefore the town moved down stream eight miles.

Rain or storm did not as a rule delay our advance but our next day's march was over the miners' trail, climbing steep slopes through dense underbrush. It rained every day at some time. During a stay of two days with the miners there was no interruption in the downpour. With swollen mountain torrents and wet brush before us we were forced to await better weather. From the prospectors we gathered that there was a trail for eighteen miles over the mountains to Sunflower, a miners' camp and beyond the country was said to be possible everywhere for horses.

We packed our horses on the morning of the 7th for the climb of Mt. Kliskon. It was still raining, but in the course of an hour the rain stopped, the air thickened, and a wet dew blackened the day. As we edged along a roaring mountain torrent, cold whiffs of wind brushed the jungle and flooded us with a freezing drip. The ground was soft and little angry streams rushed at us from every ledge. The horses after their long rest set up a lively gait but soon the feeble animals fell back and before rising out of the timber line they were exhausted. Two sorrels rolled down hill for several hundred feet with their packs. We gathered up the bags and again put on the diamond hitch but both animals collapsed. The horses' packs were then removed, and the train moved along up a steep incline through grass six feet high to a camping place under the birch trees along the edge of the tree line.

It was about noon when we camped. The freezing wind eased, the sky cleared, and a bright warm sun soon changed the shivering atmosphere into one of surprising warmth and scenic grandeur. The gap through the Yentna canyons was choked by clouds bunched tightly and hurrying rapidly to the west. The great winding bed of the Yentna visible for fifty miles was marked by a wide zone of trees and above were extensive meadows of tall grass running to mosses and lichens and snowy peaks. The horses sank in the grass grunting with a joy of fulness. The men stretched lines around twin camp-fires and dried out their clothing which had been wet for weeks. With a fill of bacon and beans, rice and curry, and beautifully browned biscuits, all around the soft blazes of a birch camp-fire, with a superb outlook, the tormenting rapids with their frigid perils were left far behind. Life had indeed for us a new aspect.

It rained most of the night and in the morning we were pelted with hail. Good weather does come occasionally but like the gold it is found in small bits. Our prospective route from here was along easy grassy slopes, around bunches of alders into a saddle. With bright hopes we packed for Sunflower. Local showers flushed us as we rose but these did not bother us as much as did the increasing pools in the muskeg. We naturally supposed that as we got to the top of the mountain the water and mosquitoes which followed us everywhere through the low country would leave us, but not so, it was water everywhere with an increasing sacrifice of blood for the omnipresent insects.

For mountaineering in Alaska one requires a good deal of dexterity in dodging water. Along the sea level the waters have an inconvenient way of tumbling over you unexpectedly, and one looks forward with delight to the time when in ascending rivers the wind-pitched swell of the ocean can do no harm. On the rivers one gets entangled in snags and goes aground so often that it becomes a constant swim to keep the boat afloat. Leaving the river bed one plunges into a dripping underbrush and gets a shower bath with shivers compared to which swimming glacial streams is easy. Beyond the forest and the brush we break through beautiful carpets of moss into water and mud, waist deep. Rising out of the floating lowlands into the magnificently painted uplands we prepare for the luxury of dry feet. The camp-fire is built, we dry out, scrape off the accumulation of mud, and continue our ascent into the hills, but the water follows us. It spouts out of the side hill, it shoots over the rocks, it oozes from everywhere. On the top of the mountain we fall into it. Along the rivers far below we were forced to climb trees to get out of the water. In coming up it rushed out at us. On the top it bubbled up at us. Even above the clouds we did not get away from the water, for then snow fell on us from a clear sky. Water from below, water from above, water everywhere. To climb Alaskan mountains we should be web footed and duck-feathered and wing-finned like the penguin.

During this amphibious climbing several horses failed and we were again forced to carry their packs after a half day's travel. Camp was pitched in the saddle on a little dome which sloped to quivering marshes. Around a carefully nursed miniature fire of green willows we tried to absorb hard-earned comfort. To the north was the snow-streaked summit of Mt. Kliskon, and from one of its glacial worn shoulders we hoped to get a look at Mt. McKinley, with a peep into the run of troubles before us for the next few days. The tents were pinned down on the hummocky muskeg, and on it we folded ourselves like pocket-knives to fit the particular ditch which fell to our lot. It rained most of the night, and the hills, only a few hundred feet above, were blanketed with fresh snow. As we crawled out of the tent to straighten out the kinks in our twisted bodies we saw the horses leisurely browsing in new spots of green, where the winter snow had but recently melted. The air was flavoured with a wintry bitterness, but the following clouds and the crimson sunbursts indicated better weather. A day of rest was declared for the horses while we scattered to explore the country about. Parker and Browne climbed to the summit of Mt. Kliskon. Porter and Barrille moved from peak to peak to make a topographic outline. With Miller and Beecher I prepared to climb the nearest peak to plan our future movement. We ascended the most northerly peak over easy grassy slopes to its summit. The altitude was 3500 feet. It had rained and hailed during the night, but the day was clear with a cold wind driving out of a northern snow field. To the west the view was obscured by other peaks. To the north and east there was an unobstructed spread of scenic surprises.

The three greatest peaks of the Alaska Range, Mts. Russell, Foraker, and McKinley rose out of a wild maze of peaks and gaps. The middle slopes were being swept by a few clouds which gave the peaks an unnatural height. About Mt. Russell we noted high snow fields and to the east of Mt. Foraker a wide open space which we took to be the gathering basin of the glaciers since given the names of Yentna and Huntington. There was what appeared to be a southeasterly ridge extending from the easy upper slopes of Mt. McKinley which interested us very much, but

Mt. Disston and the gathering basins east

this later proved to be an optical illusion, for instead of a continuous ridge it was a line of peaks including Mt. Disston, all separated by narrow canyons. To the eastward there was a great rolling country extending from the sharp snow-streaked foothills downward by easy stages to the lakes and marshes and forests that parallel the Susitna. This is the new gold country known to the miners under the name of the Yentna diggings. As we searched with our glasses along the creeks we saw several miners' tents, and about ten miles away on a bluff to the side of a large creek we noted five tents and this we took to be Sunflower.

About three miles beyond Sunflower, we saw a beautiful lake out of which poured the water and the gold of Lake Creek. This lake was surrounded by a great green expanse that appeared like finely cultured farm lands with fruit trees and waving fields of grain. And about four miles beyond there was a deep depression through which poured the Kahilitna River.

Plans were now made for the future line of march. The pack train must descend about one thousand feet and move over a muskeg to the lower edge of the lake, ford Lake Creek, and continue over similar country to the Kahilitna and from thence westerly through the lower foot-hills to the south of Mt. McKinley. With this itinerary in view Beecher was sent back with instructions to the packers to proceed to Sunflower, while Miller and I pushed on to examine the land over which our next march was to be made. We had left camp without carrying lunch, intending to return in a few hours, but the hours passed rapidly, and we descended and stumbled over the muskeg to the first miner's camp. We saw no one around, and as our appetites were sharpened and we were tired we invited ourselves to the hospitality of the camp.

There was a cache built of logs and raised on the stumps of four trees. It was a picturesque little hut, out of the reach of bears and wolves, and almost out of the reach of miners. We improvised a ladder and found under a canvas roof a large supply of flour, bacon, and beans. A curious log cabin with a canvas roof was next examined. It had luxurious furnishings for a prospector's shack. A sled was raised for a table, there was a block of wood for a chair, and two raised beds of roughly hewn wood and brush. A Yukon stove completed the fittings. All kinds of delicacies were hidden under the beds and about the corners. Tins of condensed milk, cans of meat, jars of marmalade, butter, and biscuits. We had been without food for ten hours and to stumble upon such an array of tempting things was beyond our power to resist. We helped ourselves to a modest lunch out of the open tins when we discovered the following legend:

> *Notice.*
>
> *This camp is the property of Sam. Wagner, and anybody coming along is welcome to use camp. Leave it as you find it and pack away what you bring. Use your own provisions as these don't grow here. If any one steals anything from here, he will be treated with a gun as a common thief in accordance with the law of the land.*
>
> *Sam. S. Wagner*

With the food choking us we started for Sunflower to face the law of the land. It was a leg-breaking run of five miles over hummocks, into soft marshes, through brush that tore our clothing in strings, and across deep, swift streams. At Sunflower we were heartily received by the miners, and Mr. McDonald, the principal promoter of the new stampede, invited us to his overcrowded camp to await our pack train. As we were adding to the previously unfinished meal Sam Wagner joined us. We explained our misdeed at his camp and he eased our consciences by inviting us to a smoke.

Just why this camp was christened "Sunflower" it is hard to conceive. Before entering its spruce studded and brushy confines we were forced to ford several icy streams and as we ascended the bluff the cold water dripped from our torn shirts and trousers. With chattering teeth and boots full of cold water we were attacked by clouds of mosquitoes who took advantage of our reduced courage. The spirit with which one enters Sunflower is not in accord with the conception of a land of sunflowers.

## CHAPTER VII

# Over Gold-Strewn Lowlands to Mt. McKinley from the South

In the course of two days during which it rained constantly the pack train came along and Prof. Parker reported having had a terrible time crossing marshes. The grass however was good and in spite of hard work the horses steadily improved. At noon on the 12th we started for the Kahilitna, under the guidance of the Indian Susitna Pete, "he of many devils," whom McDonald loaned to us for three days. Pete infused new humour in our camp life but his appalling laziness was a bad example for the discipline of our party. Pete had never seen pack-horses at close range before, and he took a keen interest in the animals. Furthermore he was openly inquisitive as to our motives in bringing so many men and so large an outfit into a wilderness where even his own people could not subsist. His contact with the miners led him to the conclusion that the new invasion was for gold. There could be no other incentive to push so desperately into a land of hardships. Pete had himself found a hatful of nuggets which he sold for four hundred dollars, and he agreed to guide us to where gold was "heap plenty." We told Pete we were not after gold, and asked him to guide us to the top of the big mountain, to which Pete did not reply but cast at us a searching eye, thinking perhaps that either we did not tell the truth or there was something wrong with the arrangement of our heads. After a little better acquaintance he seemed to prefer to believe that we shammed a dislike for gold.

With Pete in the lead the horses struck up a lively gait out of Sunflower, over grassy swamps, around beautiful lakes in which floated pond lilies, through widely separated groups of spruce trees around which roamed ptarmigan with their chicks just leaving their nests, to Lake Creek. Here Pete sat down and waited to see what we

SUSITNA PETE

*He of many devils, who places the spirit world around Mt. McKinley*

would do. There was a raft of two logs tied together by suspenders in the lower lake, and this was captured by Parker and Browne for crossing. As they pushed out into the current, the suspenders broke, the logs separated, and the rafters were forced to straddle both logs, and pole in an exciting fashion. Parker had lost faith in the fording of the cayuses, and took to rafting as a relief from the peril of the rapids, but this rafting experience brought him back to his horse with renewed friendship. The other members of the party each secured his favourite cayuse and prepared to ford or swim as was our habit in the Yentna. The horses were urged to jump with men and packs from the bank into what seemed a shallow stream, but it proved to be just short of swimming water. Pete instead of guiding us watched each horse to see where he could pick an easy crossing and then pulling up his hip boots he followed in water that was not more than knee deep. Just before stepping ashore he stumbled into a pool and sank to his neck. We pulled him out sputtering Indian swear-words and prepared to continue the march, but Pete insisted on building a camp-fire to warm up and dry out. We were about as cold and wet as Pete, but the pack train could not be halted on such a pretext. We must warm up with increased exercise.

Late at night we came to an edge of a bluff and beyond we saw the face of a large glacier from which rushed the first waters of the Kahilitna. We descended about seven hundred feet and pitched camp in the basin. On the following day we crossed the river, edging along to get the water as shallow as possible in small slews. We were two hours crossing this river as the water was spread over an area of over three miles. Keeping close to the northern side of the glacier we cut trail through small spruce and dense underbrush over an old moraine. We camped at a point where eighteen years before the Susitna chief had hunted moose. But so far as we were able to find out the place had not been visited since. The next day we rose out of the brush and timber, left the glacier, and followed a stream which the miners have named Dutch Creek.

Camping in a bunch of cottonwood where Pete declared there was lots of gold we panned the creeks and found colour but no pay dirt. The pools were alive with trout and bear tracks were so numerous that no one would venture away from camp without a gun. Pete declared there were seven moose beyond the next ridge, and that ahead there were plenty of caribou. He started out to do big shooting but he returned in a few hours without meat, still asserting that there were moose and caribou beyond the next range.

The march of the following day took us over the watersheds, through the head waters of Dutch Creek into Bear Creek. Descending Bear Creek we came to a sudden opening of a "U" shaped valley on a bluff from which we were able to gather the first knowledge of the land to the south and east near Mt. McKinley. Two huge glaciers poured through parallel gaps and their waters, passing around a group of jagged peaks, which Pete called *Tokosha*, united to make the Tokositna River. Upon one of these glaciers we hoped to find a highway to Mt. McKinley. We descended about a thousand feet, cut trail through a dense jungle of willows and alders, and camped in the basin of the Tokositna.

Pete had been with us his allotted time and was told that he might return to the miners' camp, but he enjoyed our camps and our food and above all he was still thoroughly inquisitive as to our motives. The mountain-climbing project he was

CAMP SCENE ON NEW GOLD DIGGINGS

*In the low country south of Mt. McKinley, an area of 3,000 square miles was explored.*

not inclined to take seriously, but he also began to doubt our mission for gold, for he showed us gold and we did not stake the ground as did the prospectors. Instead of using the picks, the shovel and pan, we went about with pencil and paper and all kinds of instruments, which he did not understand. The cameras, the barometers, the thermometers, the prismatic compass, and all of the other apparatus came in for a careful scrutiny. When the topographer got out his plane table, theodolite, and steel tape and began to measure a base line, then Pete looked up with a sigh of relief, for according to his understanding we were measuring off claims.

While peeping through the telescope of the theodolite, Pete thought he discovered a bear digging out a ground rat far up in the mountains. His face lit up with a knowing expression. At last he had discovered our real vocation. All of this strange apparatus was to locate wild animals and in some mysterious way to place the gold deposits on a map, and for several days he made himself comfortable about camp at our expense to verify his guesses at our mission. As a guide Pete was a failure, for our horsemen preferred to pick their own way. But as a character study he made a splendid model.

We had about reached the limit of advance by pack train, therefore in our future efforts we must make pack animals of ourselves. The horses were left in charge of Printz to graze in the lowlands while a scouting trip was planned to the top of a system of foothills from which we hoped to outline our future campaign. We expected to follow the glacier far into the foothills, and then climb some peak offering a favourable outlook, but the lower glacier was impossible because of its troublesome hills of moraine material.

The stream was too deep and swift to ford and it rushed out of a canyon in which we could not gain a footing. As a last resort we cut trail through the lower brush and climbed to an old glacier shelf at twenty-seven hundred feet. Following this bench northward for several miles we climbed to the top of a peak eighteen miles south of Mt. McKinley. Pete had not been asked to join the party but he followed our tracks, and as we got to the difficult climb over steep slate slopes we waited for him to catch up. Since he was with us in the role of a guide and helper, I turned over my rucksack to him but he protested against carrying it saying his feet were sore and his shoulders pained. The pack remained on his back, however.

The first outlook from the summit was disappointing. Dark clouds screened the higher foothills and also the middle slopes of the great mountain. Parker and Browne climbed another peak and as they neared the top, for a few brief moments the southerly face with its death-dealing plunges of sheer granite cliffs was unveiled. After a quick but careful examination Prof. Parker pronounced the mountain unclimbable from the south and east, and advised against any further advance from that side with a view of climbing. I was inclined to coincide with the Professor but desired to camp at our point of observation to watch the walls of the great mountain with its easterly environment under changing conditions of light and shadow. For this purpose Browne volunteered to stay with me. While the mountaineering aspect of our project was discouraged by the first views, the chances for important exploration had increased, and to this end orders were sent with the returning men to move the main camp with the horses to the side of the lateral moraine at the base of the mountain upon which we were encamped.

The silk tent was soon erected, the teapot filled with snow, and the alcohol lamp cheered the frosty air. The sun sank under the clouds behind a system of new mountains. The glory of colour and contour was beyond the reach of the camera, and beyond our powers of interpretation. We were permitted only to see bits of fascinating landscape through openings in the screen of vapour, wherein we noted huge cornices showered by gold and great gaps levelled by a liquid-blue and purple. We drew the robes about us and peeped out every few moments. The clouds seemed to settle and freeze to the icy armour of the mountains.

The purple haze faded with the afterglow and a milky whiteness spread over the great naked peaks with a sky-line of the purest alabaster which remained all night as the sun edged along the north pole. During the night the temperature was low and the wind strong, but we were so eager to see the changing run of light and colour of the weird, fantastic figures over which the eye ran to the glimmer of dawn that our shivers seemed only as pauses in the reading of the poetry of an arctic dreamland.

The overwhelming bigness of the whole scheme of new mountain wilderness did not impress us until the first beams of light burned on the sky-scraped peaks, and shot through gaps into the yawning cuts which separated the buttresses from each other. The light and colour which during the night were so soft and delicate now became as savage as the cliffs that were illuminated. Blinding darts shot out from a thousand snow slants and shivering shadows of indigo sent a wave of gloom to our hearts. Mt. McKinley with its fifteen thousand feet of successive cliffs rose out of a crumbling, tumbling sheen of lesser peaks to the level of the gods.

A larger surprise than all this was the discovery of a huge peak midway between Mt. Foraker and Mt. McKinley, but much nearer our point of observation. We had seen this peak from several points, but were inclined to put it down as a part of the general uplift around the base of Mt. McKinley, but now we clearly made out that it was a giant peak in the midst of a separate group of mountains, divided from the others by an intrusion of slate. This mountain was christened Mt. Disston, in honour of my friend Henry Disston. Beyond a part of the south-east ridge of Mt. McKinley we noted Mt. Hunter, which loomed up as a great mountain from our line of ascent from the west in 1903, but from the south this was seen to be a spur of the main mountain. Between it and Mt. Disston there was noted a narrow but deep gap through which Ruth Glacier sends an arm to the south shoulder of Mt. McKinley. To the south and west of Mt. Disston there is another wide break where we believe Huntington Glacier sends arms to a system of gathering basins.

Mt. Disston has three peaks, the highest of which is 14,970 feet high. Its very remarkable position in the path of an endless train of heavily laden clouds coming out of the warm Japan current and drifting along the Alaska Range makes it a barrier. The great bunches of vapour sweep against Mt. Disston, condense, freeze, and the resulting snow scatters in the hundreds of amphitheatres that feed the great glaciers. The easterly drainage of Mt. Disston is sent by numerous tributaries into Wyckoff Glacier, which is about two and one half miles wide and twenty miles long.

From our better acquaintance of the approaches of Mt. McKinley and its precipitous walls we were not able to come to a more hopeful climbing prospect than that so forcibly expressed by Prof. Parker though we gathered much other data for future use. Descending to Wyekoff Glacier we met the pack train and pitched camp beside a huge boulder in the upper edge of the willows. Here was good grass for the

Mt. Disston and Mt. McKinley from a foot-hill 90 miles south

horses and we planned to give them a long rest while the easterly approaches to Mt. McKinley were being explored.

The climb of Mt. McKinley was now put down as a hopeless task but we determined to devote about a week to the study of Ruth Glacier and to the general exploration of the easterly foothills. Mr. Porter selected for a series of observations the ridge separating the two glaciers.

Parker, Browne, and Barrille joined me in an effort to cross this ridge to explore Ruth Glacier into its tributaries. With the camp equipment in our rucksacks we started on the morning of July 21st. The weather was remarkable for its short chilly rains and spells of burning sunshine with a smothering heat. Our route over the glacier was through hills of sharp fragments of granite and quartz, around great caverns, over ice tunnels where the glacier waters roared with a mad rush en route to the lower country. We were three hours in crossing, and the task should have completed the day's work, but we were eager to rise to some eminence where we could see the curtain rise and fall with the dusk and dawn.

Out of the glacier we climbed through brush and high grass, over the blueberries and flowers of the old glacial moraine, crossing bear trails every few moments. We had passed so many bear tracks that this did not now excite our curiosity.

We had taken no rifles, but Porter and Browne had had such exciting experiences with the inquisitiveness of this race of bears that they insisted on being armed with Luger pistols. With the ambition of a nimrod Browne kept far in advance. We were leisurely trailing into a deep gulch along a picturesque cascade to a point where the stream forked. Browne descended to the waters, crossed, and ascended on a ridge between the streams. We picked an easier way along the right bank close to steep slopes to the other side of the gulch where was a high ridge with more gradual sides marked by bunches of alders. We were bending our heads and shoulders under the heavy weights of the rucksacks when Barrille shouted "Bear!" Every fellow at once braced up and looked about for a rock or a tree to climb, but there was nothing in sight to climb except big mountains so we bunched up and watched the coming of Ursus with a tight grip on our ice axes. The great mass of brown plunged down with an alarming speed, turning somersaults in the high grass, edging around precipices, and vanishing in bunches of alders, coming like a dart through gaps to hummocks, down and down, ever nearing the noisy stream which separated him from Browne. He was making a bee line for us, but we had gotten new courage and had planned a line of defence with our ice axes. Along the crest of the bluff which must be climbed to get to our flesh Browne had the only gun, the Luger pistol. We called to him to save the day and our necks, but he did not understand. He had not seen the thing and the rush of the twin streams was such that he could not hear what we said. The bear was fording the waters as we called, and began to ascend Browne's ridge as he came toward us to ascertain the cause of our excitement. The bear came over the edge of the bluff and Browne met him. They were face to face, not more than twenty feet apart. Though excited Browne quickly drew his Luger and took a slow careful aim. We impatiently listened for the shot and watched for its effect on the bear—but nothing happened. The bear stood still, so did Browne, for what seemed to us several minutes, and then Browne slowly backed about fifty feet, sat down in the grass, and watched the bear. For a time we believed Browne had gotten out paper and pencil and was calmly sketching Bruin, but we soon discovered that he was awfully busy with his Luger—and then unexpectedly the thing went off. The bear jumped into the stream and Browne emptied his Luger to no effect. With the bear on the run we gathered new courage and rushed forward to head him off with the hope that he would take a course parallel to Browne's ridge where another shot might be more successful, but the bear avoided his chance acquaintance and took to the high hills, where Porter awaited him over a plane table with equally elusive results.

Rising out of the bear haunts we camped in a saddle from which we could see both glaciers. Two days and two nights were spent along the ridge with splendid results for Porter from a topographer's standpoint, but no new mountains or glaciers or routes to Mt. McKinley were discovered. The weather was daily assuming a wintry aspect. The snow line was descending and new ice forming every night. The combined result of this reconnoissance proved to us finally the hopelessness of further mountaineering from any point of attack which could be reached before the coming winter closed the gates to the upper world. In this spirit we returned to camp to devise a plan for further exploration.

CHAPTER VIII

# With the Descending Cloud Waters Back to the Sea. The Party Scatters

Our study of Mt. McKinley seems to indicate that the only possible line of ascent is along the north-east ridge, which we believe most accessible from the west. To reach this ridge, but more especially to reorganise, and collect big game specimens on the Arctic Slope, is our next problem. In returning over the gold country we have decided to leave Porter with two assistants, two horses, and several caches of food to complete the map of the new country, after which he is to return by raft to Susitna Station.

The horses were now in splendid trim. The long rest and the young tender grass near the glaciers infused them with a new spirit. With light packs the return march over our old trail was rapid. Pete left us at Dutch Creek to go to his camp on Cache Creek. While building a cache on the Kahilitna bluff on the evening of July 28th, two days later, Pete stumbled into camp under a big pack and exclaimed, "Glacier busted!"

In crossing the Kahilitna we had noticed that the river was very much higher and concluded that something had gone wrong with Pete's water devil far up in the big mountain. But now Pete explained it all. He called our attention to the basin of a large lake to the north side of Huntington Glacier. In our northward trip the water in this lake was almost level with the glacier. This water had now burrowed a tunnel under the ice and had joined the other rushing torrents to swell the Kahilitna.

In crossing Lake Creek the next day Pete decided to try a horse and ford as we did. He selected a bay mare, young and active, in fact too much so for the other

The Face of Huntington Glacier
*Waiting for the unveiling of Mt. McKinley*

members of our party. The mare was easy to approach and Pete had no trouble in being friendly. Barrille helped him mount, the mare shot off like an arrow into mid-stream, Pete was game and held on. Suddenly the horse stepped into shallow water and bucked. Pete went several feet into the air and landed in deep water. A wave of suppressed merriment ran along the line.

The pack-train moved on to Sunflower. Here we camped at noon to study the miners' luck. Gold had been found everywhere, but there was food nowhere. Most of the miners had come in with about a week's supply on their backs and this was hardly sufficient to reach a creek and scratch for colour. Most of these prospectors were leaving in a disgruntled humour. Barrille and Printz in fishing with rifles secured four salmon weighing about forty pounds each, and we fell to salmon so enthusiastically that we did not care to eat fish again for weeks.

While packing for our return to the Yentna, Pete requested to be allowed to follow us with his squaw, who had been left at Sunflower, and without further talk brought all of his belongings to be packed on our horses. There were several deep streams to cross on this trail, and Pete, either from a sense of humour or from a sense of devotion, secured the bay mare to ferry his wife over the cold waters. The mare only followed him a few hundred feet and then dragged him through the bushes and left him besmeared with mud. The boys persuaded him that the mare objected to his red sweater, and he promptly took this off and packed it away, but he was not able to approach the mare again. Barrille gallantly loaned his horse to Pete to ferry his wife over the river, but afterward it was difficult to persuade the squaw to dismount.

As we neared the Yentna, Browne and Miller volunteered to join me in the venture of getting to Parker House while the pack train moved along to Youngstown. Our mission was to take the *Bolshoy* and all the supplies down stream. Horses could not be used, for we were anxious to conserve horse strength for the westward trip. We found a miner who ferried us across the main river, but after that we were left to our swimming capacities to cross the swollen slews. We reached the Parker House late in the afternoon of July 31st, after the most detestable water adventures of the entire trip. The slews were high, the whole jungle was afloat, and we were in water for about three hours. We determined never to repeat this experience.

About Parker House the whole river had changed. The easterly streams were very much larger and the main westerly slew had been reduced to a mere rush of small rapids. Around the launch a new bar had formed which nearly left the boat stranded in a blind slew. We built a camp fire to thaw out, then prepared to fit the boat for her descent to Youngstown. It was nine o'clock and the sun had settled into the Kuskokwim before we were ready to start, but the afterglow was bright and the July twilight was promising. Furthermore the ten miles of swift waters to Youngstown would take us only an hour. We dragged over bars, under overhanging trees, over roots, and plunged into the wider river near the forks, with the speed of an automobile. But here, when we felt at ease, our troubles began. The *Bolshoy* went aground on one bar after another; finally we threw out both anchors in disgust, and at three o'clock we dropped on the sands in the light of a big camp-fire for a few moments' rest. When we awoke the chocolate waters were fired by the rising sun and we were buried in the feathery ashes blown from the cottonwood fire. We were several hours digging the boat out of the new deposit of silt in mid-stream and at last, freed by the main force of the current, we pressed on to join our companions at Youngstown.

Barrille was left in charge, and John Dokkin, a miner, was added to our expedition. Barrille and Dokkin were to cut trail into the Kichatna and prepare for the westerly trip while the others of the expedition went down the Yentna in the *Bolshoy*.

Under less than half power we averaged fifteen miles per hour in our plunge with the descending cloud water to the sea. If our motor-boat adventures up stream were a joy, the downward rush was a sport with the wildest kind of excitement.

The *Bolshoy* pushed cautiously over the bars of the delta of the Susitna River into quiet Cook Inlet waters. In jumping snags and shooting rapids down the swift icy waters we broke the rudder and bent all the blades of the propeller. We might have beached the launch and replaced the propeller, but the rudder was beyond repair. We had rigged the stern so two men could steer with oars, and in the river this makeshift worked very well. Since the screw was pushing us along at the rate of eight miles per hour, and the boat was in perfect control, we decided that it was safe to risk a passage over the thirty miles of treacherous sea with a tide of eight miles per hour to Tyonok. We had no ballast. The first ten miles were covered quickly, but we noticed that a sea was rapidly rolling out of the east. Two miners' dories were seen edging the increasing whitecaps (one of these has not been heard of since). Turnagain Arm, which is the storm centre of Cook Inlet, did not look bad, but the increasing force of the wind and sea coming out of it made us anxious. A few steel-coloured clouds, separated by bright glistening bands, came hurrying out of the narrow gap. The cloud effect was odd, though not particularly suggestive of a storm—but the storm came quickly. The little bunches of steel-coloured vapour were hurled at us as though from a cannon. The seas with our course gave us a broadside which made the little craft turn and twist and crack until we felt that she must go to pieces. We were now compelled to take the seas on the quarter, making a zigzag course. This brought the breaking, tumbling water aboard. Browne and Printz on the poop steering with care were twice nearly swept over into the boiling waters, and to secure them they were fastened by lines to the deck. The engines balked somewhat because of the violent commotion of the boat, the low temperature, and the mud of the cooling waters. Two were kept busy at the engine, and all under cover were miserably seasick. In our desperation we tried to run into the Beluga River out of the storm, but the endless low flats with mountains of sea breaking over them did not look inviting. The Chulitna, another river, was our next hope, but as we allowed the wind and sea to carry us into the bay we noticed that the dangers were even greater than at the Beluga River—seas which we estimated were fifteen feet high rolled under us and broke on the beaches but a few hundred feet away. One went over us and for a second the entire boat seemed to be under water. Some one exclaimed at this moment, "Beach her!" but since flats extended five miles from shore, with a blast pitching us on shore and a sea breaking everywhere, we were not in a beaching mood. But we must do something quickly. Tyonok but five miles south was to us as impossible, with the onshore wind and the raging sea, as Chulitna. To cross Cook Inlet to the windward shore was our only hope, but this was not an agreeable prospect. The night with its awful storm and blackness was before us. With men lashed to the deck who might be swept off, and with no harbour within two hundred miles, we thought it best to push from the land out into the night and into the gloom of the continued storm.

The wind now came in gusts, but with a force that held us on the crests of swells as the engines were pushed to do their best. The rise and fall of the launch at this time was sickening. Tumbling from the seas she would crack as if she had struck, a rock, and frequently Prof. Parker said, "What have we struck?"

In spite of our efforts to cross the inlet the strong tides carried us southward, and as we neared Tyonok the seas became choppy, the wind eased, and the prospect of making a landing seemed worth trying. We pushed under a spit, dropped anchor, lowered our little fourteen-foot canvas boat, and in it Browne and Printz pushed through the breakers into the river. Mr. Finch, with a crew of expert Indian boatmen in a big dory, came and took us off. We had weathered the worst storm of the season in the north country without a rudder and with a crippled wheel! It was an experience which none of us cared to repeat, but it was a fitting addition to our other hardships. For more than two months we had been in icy streams and drenched by cold rains in the uplands. Cold water was ever about us whether on sea or land. Indeed, Prof. Parker pronounced the effort of ascending Mt. McKinley a marine task.

In the middle of August there were various changes made in the personnel of the expedition and in the working programme. Prof. Parker, unable to remain longer with us because of the necessity of his returning to his college duties and other business matters, left us. The projected trip through the range into the game country along the western slopes was abandoned and various parties were scattered for collecting specimens of animal life and to survey new districts. Owing to our repeated failures and the advancing winter we decided that our energies for the short period of the remaining season would be better spent in exploration than climbing, and to this end our plans were now made.

At this critical moment, when we were anxious to get to work quickly to carry out the new plans, the *Bolshoy* was Hobsonized. To weather a storm she was taken into the creek behind Tyonok. All the other small craft of the Cook Inlet fleet followed, and finally the big stern-wheeler *Caswell* ran into the mouth of the river and went aground. The tides were "nipping off" and we were thus hopelessly locked in the river for an indefinite time. After waiting nearly a week we took our boat overland and prepared to push up the Susitna to continue our work.

## CHAPTER IX

# Up the Susitna and Chulitna by Motor Boat

In dragging our boat overland the circulating pump was broken in such a way that we could not fix it. Anticipating such an accident we had provided ourselves with an extra pump, but to adjust this we were compelled to take the *Bolshoy* to the machine shop of the Kaselif Salmon Cannery. Through the kindness of Mr. Witherbee the pump was fixed, and then preparations were made for the final trip against the easterly torrents of Mt. McKinley.

Though it is agreeable to come out of the wilderness of the interior to the semi-civilisation of the coast occasionally, we usually found the coast environment induced ill-health for a time.

In the pursuit of our routine we were almost constantly wet with ice-water. For two months we travelled with wet feet. In rain or sunshine, in wind or calm, we went without coats for the simple reason that with increased clothing we carried more water and therefore were less comfortable than with light simple garments which would dry out easily. We slept in dripping jungles, on floating marshes, in wind-swept clouds, on wet snow, and in perennial frost, always with the worst element about us. Surely here were conditions to cause colds, rheumatism, pneumonia, and all kinds of winter diseases, but we never enjoyed better health. No colds, no rheumatism, and no sickness of any consequence was reported. But when we returned to the outposts of civilisation and warm dry beds, breathed the comfort of good shelter in luxury, were glutted with food and prevented from taking our accustomed exercise, we promptly suffered from headaches, toothaches, colds, tonsillitis, neuralgia, and all kinds of physical troubles.

Our immunity from disease is a lesson in physiology worthy of more minute examination. The real cause of taking cold lies in the balance between the production and radiation of heat. Likewise the real cause of many of our most troublesome diseases, like headaches, insomnia, rheumatism, gout, neuralgia, and many minor complaints lies in the difference between the process of assimilation of nutritive fluids and that of the elimination of waste products. With an active life like ours in the wilderness every function of the body is called into service and there is soon established a normal equilibrium in the movement of cellular construction and destruction. Under these conditions the processes of repair and waste are active and new cells are fitted into the fabric strained under tension; worn-out tissues are removed, and the process of normal health proceeds without interruption because of a compelled rhythm in all of the usual functions of life.

How different are the life-sapping conditions of modern city life. Physical exercise is prohibited by the limits of space and the ease of mechanical locomotion; mental energy is strained to cope with the maddening pace of this material age. The stomach is abused by unnatural foods, the liver and kidneys are hardened by poisonous drink, the lungs breathe a hothouse, germ-cultivated air, the muscles wither from disease, the whole splendid cellular organisation is disarranged in an endeavour to fit man into an artificial environment for which animal life was never intended. The misfits result noticeably in the breaking down of some important department of biologic association, and disease follows. If mountaineering has no other recompense than to act as a means to arouse dormant functions and to establish a normal balance in the laboratory of human economy, it is a boon to mankind.

Owing to the lateness of the season and the non-arrival of other members of our party, we now decided to abandon the projected trip into the Kuskokwim and scatter the party to collect game specimens in more accessible places, and to continue the work of exploration. Browne and Beecher were sent into the mouth of the Matanuska River to get moose, mountain sheep, and goats. The *Bolshoy* pushing up the Yentna quickly reached the camp at Youngstown on August 28th.

From there Printz and Miller were sent into the valley of the Kichatna with five horses, also to gather game specimens. Four horses were sent to Porter to ease his task of transportation and then, taking Barrille and Dokkin, I descended the Yentna to the Station to refit for the next stage of the work.

As a final task for our season's work I now determined to explore the river systems and glaciers to the east of Mt. McKinley, and to examine the northern arête for a route to the top of the mountain for a possible future ascent.

With a full load of food and gasoline the *Bolshoy* was pushed up the Susitna. The upper waters had not before been tried by a motor boat and the miners doubted the ability of our launch to climb the rapids. The river was moderately high, but there was before us the chance that the early frosts would suddenly stop the melting glaciers from sending down their output and so reduce the rivers that we would be unable to get down stream.

The scenery was rapidly changing from its run of dark green to the warm colours of autumnal foliage. Beyond the delightful line of birch and spruce along the shore the eye rested upon a wide expanse of muskegs cushioned knee-deep by fluffy verdure in delicate colours of green and brown pegged down with buttons of cardinal. The currants and the cranberries had withered; the bears had left the river and the berries to dig out the fat ground rats near the tops of the foothills; the beavers and rabbits were active; ptarmigan were descending from the snowy highlands and moose and caribou tracks were seen in the silt along the river. Altogether this race for time against the tumbling waters and the advancing winter night was very interesting.

The Susitna, like the Yentna, is divided into many slews, and pours its brown waters over a broad expanse in great graceful curves, but it has a very much more difficult current to stem. The average mid-stream current is about seven and one half miles per hour, and to dodge the swift water proved a great task. Perhaps the worst feature of the Susitna is its manner of spreading over wide flats and then rushing in rifts over bars that extend across the river without a deep channel anywhere, thus offering swift and very shallow water, which is extremely difficult for a power boat.

We ascended the first sixty miles in two days without any great trouble, but in entering the Chulitna we lost a day because of the shallow water. Trying one slew after another, we were stopped in each as we were about to push into the main stream. Finally we took the most westerly channel and lined the boat for a few miles, dragging her over bars when necessary by placing an anchor out and pulling in the rope by the capstan. About ten miles above the forks the Chulitna narrows to one deep, swift channel where low rolling hills lead to a plateau through which the river has cut a narrow channel with canyons three hundred feet high.

The scenery in the lower river is rather tame. The valley is wide and the trees along the river prevent a view of the great spread of the Susitna lowlands, but now we have risen in altitude considerably and are able to look over the lower valley to

Ruth Glacier
*The Tokosha Mountains*

the snow-streaked Chugach Mountains. Ahead the foothills close in on the stream and in the occasional clearing the big peaks of the Bolshoy group are visible. The rock of the canyon appears to be grey wacke. Above the canyon, which is about five miles long, the river spreads out, and as it nears the Tokositna it turns abruptly to receive its waters.

Pushing the launch up the Tokositna to the first stream from Ruth Glacier a camp was made within easy reach of the terminal moraine. We had gone about half way through the boiling rapids. The big boulders here indicate that Ruth Glacier at one time extended at least four miles beyond its present moraine. The river above would have been navigable by lining for a few hundred feet, and beyond the waters seemed to be deep and easy for about twenty miles farther. Preparations were made to stay here for several weeks. Barrille built a crude pier for the boat, of drift logs weighted down with boulders. This was necessary because of the sudden rise and fall of the glacial waters, also because of the swell produced by the rapids. Dokkin was so fascinated by the place that he prepared to winter, intending to start mining operations there in the spring.

CHAPTER X

# Discover a Way to Reach the Summit of Mt. McKinley—Preparations for the Climb

After a preliminary examination we were convinced that our position was a very fortunate one. The limits of navigation had not been reached on either river, but for our purposes it was not desirable to push the launch farther. Within three miles of our landing was seen the end of Ruth Glacier, and through its gap we were able to make out a line of attack to the north shoulder of Mt. McKinley, from which we now discovered a way to reach the summit of that mountain.

With the *Bolshoy* safely harboured we began to establish a base camp. The surroundings here were agreeable: To the east, but a few miles distant, were the bold uplands and the wooded lowlands of the Chulitna and Susitna valleys; to the west the new gold country, the foothills of the Alaska Range in which we had left our topographer; to the northwest, forty miles away, far above the clouds, the summit of Mt. McKinley, the Top of the Continent, the Ultima Thule of our ambition.

In going up the Chulitna we noted carefully every snow-slope of the big mountain. We had already changed our minds as to the impossibility of climbing the mountain. Three promising routes were carefully plotted in our note-books, with all possible landmarks. We aimed to tabulate these routes at long range so thoroughly that if we were caught in a storm while climbing we could still travel by this previously noted line of landmarks.

The weather during the entire summer had been the worst ever noted along the eastern side of the range. Continuous cold drizzling rains made the work of exploration and climbing nearly impossible, but now there was a radical change: the thermometer fell to near the freezing point in the lowlands, and above two

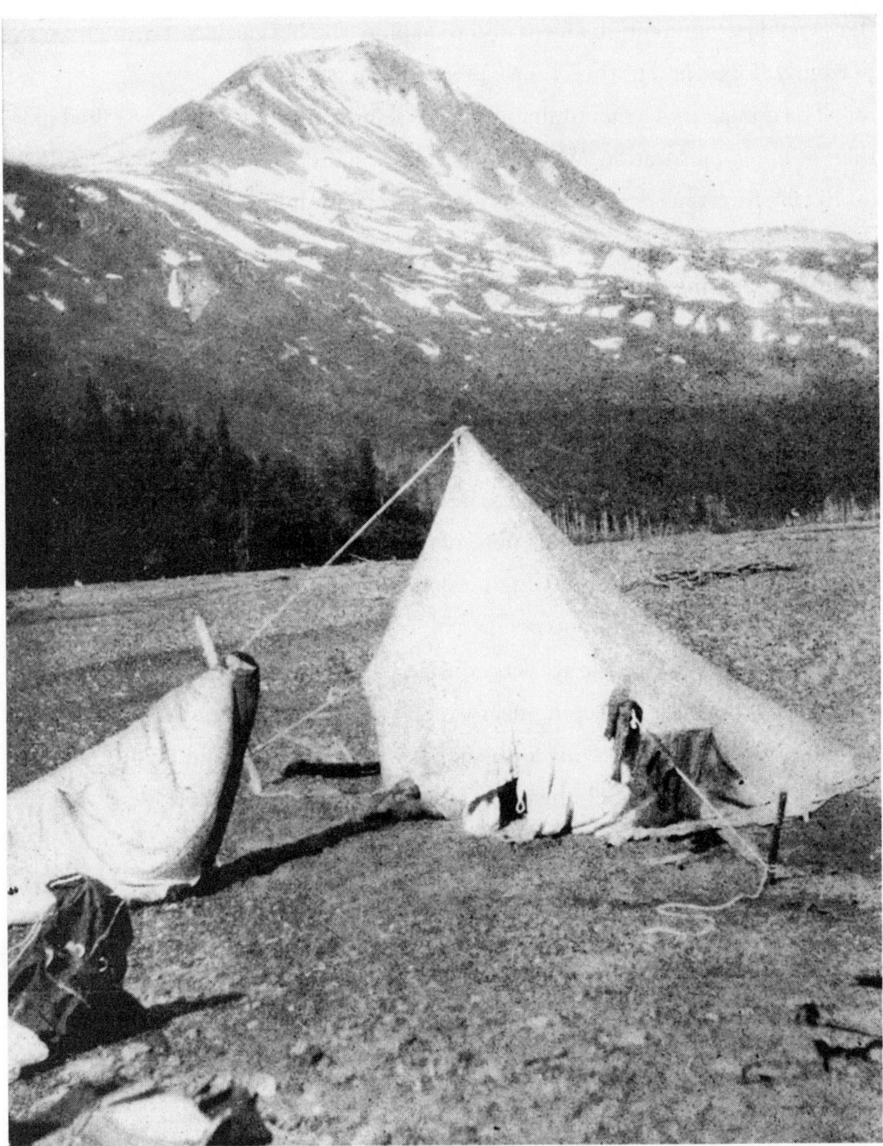

THE SILK TENT

thousand feet the winter snows were beginning to accumulate. There was a dryness and briskness to the air which aroused anew our ambitions to climb Mt. McKinley.

Our intentions, however, were not to climb to the top. The winter, with its heavy snowfall, its death-dealing avalanches its storms and awful cold, was too far advanced in the upper world. We hoped only for an opportunity to discover a route that would permit a future ascent and to explore the big glaciers starting from the northerly slopes, and to this end we prepared our equipment.

The conquest of a mountain of this size so near the arctic circle required more than ordinary preparation. We had no guides and no porters, and no camp followers to take from our shoulders the usual hardships of alpine ascents. The very great difficulty in moving supplies to the base of the mountain prohibited such assistance. In preparing our equipment I had determined to break away from the established method of mountain climbing by reducing the number of my party and by changing the working equipment. The work in prospect as we had originally planned it required not days, but weeks and perhaps months, during which we must sleep on storm-swept snow-fields, and for the prolonged siege we must carry food, fuel, and shelter on our backs. With blankets, heavy tents, and tinned food such a project would be impossible. To meet the need of reduced weights and increased efficiency I had invented a new silk tent which weighed but three pounds, was large enough for three men, and required no pole.

That we might be able to sleep on ice in low temperatures Mrs. Cook had made for us three novel sleeping-bags which were a great success. With a woman's ingenuity three robes were made in such a way that they could be buttoned together and hooked up along the edge, making a sleeping-bag. However, it was not only a sleeping-bag but an overcoat besides. The outer section was made of cravenette, the inner section of camel's hair blanketing, and the middle section of the skins of eider duck covered both sides with Shantung silk. These robes could be

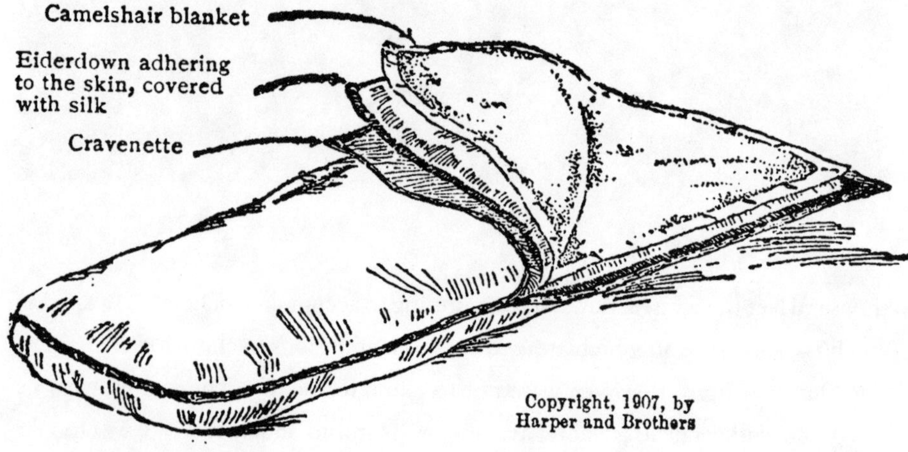


SLEEPING-BAG/OVERCOAT

EDWARD BARRILLE WITH THE CAMEL'S-HAIR SECTION OF THE SLEEPING BAG AS A PONCHO

used separately or together as ponchos, and with belts they made a perfect garment. We carried no coats or waistcoats. The sleeping-robes furnished us all the protection that we needed.

We did no relay work or double-tripping. We moved no heavy tents nor other cumbersome equipment. Rapid marches, light packs, and but the prime necessities of camp life were to be our method of action. We aimed to carry on our backs about forty-five pounds each, and this pack was to contain all our needs for ten days. We were thus independent of each other and independent of a base camp or a supporting party.

We spent a day in the preparation of this pack. Our clothing needed some mending, and to bake the right kind of bread required a good deal of study. Crackers and all kinds of factory-made biscuits are in my judgment not only troublesome to transport, but their nutritive value is decidedly inferior to properly made bread. In the first attempt we were forced to invent some kind of mountain bread, and we then tried to imitate zweibach, which proved very good. In the preparation of any food for a high altitude one has always to keep in mind that such food should not require cooking nor should it contain a particle of moisture. Ordinary bread would freeze so hard that it would require hours to thaw it out, consuming precious fuel which must be carried on the back. Our experiment here resulted in the invention of a biscuit which I would recommend for any work where the temperature is low and fuel scarce. We mixed the dough in the usual way with baking-powder but omitted shortening. This dough was divided into little bits not larger than a good-sized marble and baked in the reflector by a hot fire until quite brown, then the reflector was moved farther from the fire and by slow heat the biscuits were dried and hardened. No grease was put in the pan nor in the dough.

Distributed as expedition baggage we carried a silk tent, rubber floor-cloth, tent pegs, three aneroids barometers, two thermometers, one prismatic compass, a watch, and a 5 x 7 camera with six film packs, the total weight of which was twelve pounds. This was distributed among the different packs.

The luggage which fell to each as common baggage was:

Food: twenty-one pounds
Fuel: two pounds
Sleeping bag: five and one half pounds
Sleeping stockings: eight ounces
Alcohol stove: two ounces
Aluminum pail, cup, spoon, and pocket knife: four ounces
Horsehair rope: one pound

Ice axe: three and one half pounds
Rucksack: three pounds
Expedition baggage: four pounds

Thus the total weight for each climber to carry was somewhat over forty pounds. We carried no extra clothing except one pair of sleeping socks. As we left the boat we wore medium-weight suits of woollen underwear, heavy flannel shirts, short trousers, puttees, four pairs woollen socks, shoe packs, and a felt hat.

We had underestimated the arctic effects of even the low altitudes and had not our bags been made in sections which, as ponchos, furnished a splendid protection against the awful cold above, we could never have been able to begin the climb.

With all these things snugly packed in our rucksacks we started from the *Bolshoy* where the altitude was 1000 feet, on the morning of the 8th of September. It was a bright clear day with the temperature near the freezing point. But a few hundred feet from camp we saw fresh moose and bear tracks. We followed these tracks a short distance, and then discovered a blazed trail cut by the gold seekers. This trail led to Ruth Glacier, and after crossing several icy streams in which we got wet above our waists we found to the north side of the glacier an old caribou trail where travelling was excellent.

As we followed these game trails a sharp wind was blowing and the air had a touch of winter bitterness in it. The great chasm out of which the glacier poured its frozen product was roofed by masses of dark gray clouds ranked closely and hurrying swiftly. The curious tunnel between cloud and glacier, through which we saw snowy peaks, was weird and gloomy but our attention was fixed upon it for it was the track of our future efforts.

On the evening of the second day we took to the ice, crossed the first northerly tributary, and camped on a beautiful moss-carpeted point about fifteen miles from Mt. McKinley.

As we crossed the glacier and jumped the crevasses. Dokkin developed quite a fear of the bottomless pits and said that he would prefer not to trust his life to the security of his footing. Barrille and I had been on glaciers before and did not entertain the same fear. Indeed we regarded this glacier as one particularly free of danger and hardship. Its surface was unusually smooth. We had about determined that the limit of our effort would be the top of the north arête at 12,000 feet; from there we

*Mt. Church* *Mt. Grosvenor* *Mt. Johnson* *Mt. Wake* *Mt. Bradley*
FIRST FIVE OF THE TWELVE NEW PEAKS OF RUTH GLACIER
*Camp at 5,000 feet*

believed that we could thoroughly outline the glacier drainage and also a route up the mountain. For this purpose Dokkin was not needed, and since he wished to prospect for gold in the lowlands I sent him back with instructions to read the base barometer and to place emergency caches along the glacier.

The snow on the glacier was hard and offered a splendid surface for a rapid march but the advantage of its hardness was offset by the treacherous manner in which it bridged dangerous crevasses. As we advanced these snow bridges increased and we held to our horsehair rope with more interest.

As the sun settled behind Mt. McKinley and threw a shivering blue over the mammoth glacial canyons about us the tent was pegged down on the mossy shelf. Here our eyes first danced to the dazzling glows and the wild notes of enchantment and despair of a snowy cloud world. We were making discoveries in every direction. The gates of a new world of arctic splendour had opened. In line with the magnetic needle the glacier continued with graceful curves and like a thing of life, its arms reaching up to the easterly outline of the great monarch of mountains. To the west of this snowy bosom of ice our anxious eyes ran from peak to peak of wondrous mountains entombed by gauzy films of gold. With utter amazement we counted twelve cone-shape peaks in an air line all 12,000 feet high, the last a pinnacle in the huge northern arête making a barrier to the conquest of Mt. McKinley. To the east of this wonderful line of frosted and polished cones there was another row of less regular but sharper peaks with sheer walls of yellow granite down which avalanches plunged for 5000 feet without a shelf.

The scene changed every minute, clouds came and went swiftly. The blue changed to purple, the purple to lilac, and at last a black veil of sadness dropped over this new world of arctic evanescence.

With this peep into the frosty splendour of our future camping environment we knew that at this camp we would leave behind the last traces of life, for in the icy altitudes above neither plant nor animal life could subsist. We were eager to celebrate this departure from life by a feast with the greatest possible comfort, for feasts and comforts as we understood them would be impossible in the upper world!

Under the silk tent was a soft carpet of moss in delicate shades of brown and green and red. From this moss we were able to make a cheerful fire and thus save the precious alcohol which we had carried thirty miles for a fire higher up. Among the lichens of the upper rocks we heard the shrieks of numerous ptarmigan. After some delicate manoeuvres that would do credit to a mountain goat, Barrille secured five of these with his rifle. To make the birds palatable proved to be a task more difficult than the hunt. With wet moss we could not get fire enough to broil the birds. To cut them and make a kind of soup was our only resource but we had no salt and no flavouring material, and the thought of a parboiled bird without salt was not pleasant. We filled the aluminum pail with snow, cut the meat in small strips, and as the snow melted we tossed in the meat. After boiling for about an hour and a half, Barrille tasted the meat and said it tasted like oysters without lemon. I tasted the soup and it was impossible. We had carefully eliminated salt from our food because of its tendency to produce thirst. Barrille put in some pemmican which gave it a sickening sweet flavour. I added some crumbs of bread which helped a little. Finally Barrille said, "Let's put in the mixture some sugar and tea and our feast will be complete and it will save us the wait for the tea after." I yielded to the sugar and tried it, and to our great surprise this seemingly impossible mixture passed our palates without protest. A sweet soup with sugared meat, what joys it brought us! But we never repeated the experiment.

The night was dark and gloomy. There was an occasional fall of snow from the low clouds sweeping along the surface of the glacier. From a long distance there came low-pitched rumbling noises like that of a farm waggon over a rocky road. These were the premonitory warnings of the avalanches. Sharp winds were piping frosty notes through granite crevasses but in our silk tent and buttoned in our eiderdown bags with stomachs full of sweet soup and sugared ptarmigan, we were serenely happy.

Dawn came with a weird blue glow from the west. The high frosted foothills to the east brightened and warmed to an orange tint but there was a long arctic twilight with an oppressive stillness interrupted by sharp explosive noises due to the

Over the moraine of Ruth Glacier

*The lower ten miles of this, and most of the McKinley glaciers, was completely covered with moraine.*

movement of the glacial stream. In this twilight we saw the stars through the silk mesh of the tent as clearly as at night in lower lands. The outlines of the mountains were also clearly seen through the tent while we were resting comfortably.

As we turned out of the tent the glacier and the mountains toward the Chulitna were for a short time free from the usual drift of clouds. The great tongue of ice descended four thousand feet in about thirty miles. The lower ten miles of the ice was completely covered by a thick spread of finely broken granite and slate thrown up in huge hummocks. There were curious lines of moraine running in parallel courses above. The striking differences in colour of these rock streams distinguishes this glacier from all others. The black of the slate, the buff of the granite, and the blue of the ice made a run of attractive, contrasting streams.

The Tokositna mountains with their sharp spires stood out in bold relief against a bunch of vapours moving hurriedly into the glacial cut. The wind on the glacier was westerly but these clouds moved in the opposite direction, indicating a contrary upper drift of air currents which explained the usual cloudiness.

We made an early start over the moss to the mountains of lateral moraine. Climbing the big boulders we studied the séracs through which our course forced us. The ice in the dim morning light looked enticing from a picturesque standpoint; great blue crevasses crossed the glacier and huge points of ice rose like the pinnacles of the polar pack. We enjoyed the scene but as a highway the outlook was discouraging. The hair rope was securely fastened about our waists and then we descended into the widest of the crevasses, picking our way in the blue depths below across the glacier. Rising out of this frigid gap to the main surface of the ice we found the snow hard and a fairly clear spread of ice for miles ahead. The crevasses were still numerous; those visible were easily evaded, but those invisible were at times unintentionally located by breaking through snow bridges. Big cumulus clouds pressed against the southern slopes of the twelve peaks, but the narrow sky of the big blue canyon into which we were pushing was perfectly clear. A strong wind rolled from off the ice of the great mountain and it pierced us like the blast of an arctic winter. It was not until noon that the sun broke through the narrow gaps of sky-piercing foothills and then we changed our course to the north side of the glacier. The awful frost of the dense blue shadows combined with the icy head wind made advance rather difficult. The bright burning sunbeams falling on the glittering snow of the other side of the glacier were equally uncomfortable, for

Scene of glaciers, peaks and cliffs

*Shoulder of Mt. McKinley, a cliff of 8,000 feet. Ruth Glacier, a freight carrier of the cloud world. The Great White Way, where the polar frosts meet the Pacific drift of the tropical dews.*

now there fell from our faces big beads of perspiration, which froze in icy pinnacles on our garments.

Because of the splendid progress made we allowed ourselves the luxury of a mid-day lunch. We tried to set up our alcohol lamp in a big grotto, but deflected currents of air so blew the blue flame that the heat was lost. The tent was set up and in it we brewed a pot of tea, ate pemmican and biscuits, and rested for two hours, and then as the sun sank behind the big cliffs of the main mountain we took up the march again into the frosty shadows. Before dark we pitched the tent on the glacier at an altitude of 8000 feet within a few miles of the northern ridge, the summit of which, 4000 feet above, was at this time our ultimate destination.

CHAPTER XI

# To the Northeast Ridge—In a Snow House at 12,000 Feet

From here the stupendous wonder aroused by the titanic uplift sent a thrill of amazement over us which carried its note of fear and admiration for many days.

Just as Mt. Tacoma surpasses all other American mountains in quiet softened grandeur, so Mt. McKinley transcends in savage magnificence and in colossal proportions all mountains of the world. While there are other mountains greater in altitude, still these are a part of a general elevation, and as individual peaks the great mountains of the world are less attractive.

There are mountains where the blend of colour, the scale of dripping waters, the waves of balmy breezes run to music and poetry and quiet aesthetic inspirations, but there is no such play on the senses here. Mt. McKinley is one of the severest battle-grounds of nature, and warfare is impressed with every look at its thundering immensity. The avalanches fire a thousand cannons every minute and the perpetual roar echoes and re-echoes from a hundred cliffs. The pounding of the massive blocks from ledge to ledge in their mad descent makes the whole mountain world quiver with battle spirit.

We had every reason to be pleased with our rapid progress to this camp. In three days we pushed thirty-five miles into the foothills of an unexplored country and were now in a better position to attack the mountain than at any previous time during a siege of three months.

The main glacier here narrowed and turned sharply to the south-east, sweeping the whole eastern slope of Mt. McKinley. Feeders pulled the snows out of

MT. BARRILLE: THE NORTHEAST RIDGE

numerous amphitheatres and the main tributary sent prongs on to the great northeast arête. Indeed the gathering basins of the glacier were arranged like the leaves of a tree and huge limbs connected them with the parent mass of ice, completing the circulatory system from cloud to sea.

We realised the serious aspect of our next ascent into a region of cloud and storm, but we were now prepared for all contingencies. We had seen the great mountain from every possible side during our various campaigns. Along the west we had followed the face of the mountain for twenty-five miles. Along the east we had circled the base close enough to study carefully the giant slopes. Every glacier, every pinnacle, everything that could possibly be seen as a landmark or a route had been carefully charted. We knew that we could not possibly carry into the clouds a sufficient supply to permit of halts during storms. We must make progress and climb every day. Cloud obscurity or storms must not delay us and to be able to be thus independent of weather we must always know exactly where we were and know also the workable route and the dangers above and below. These points were splendidly

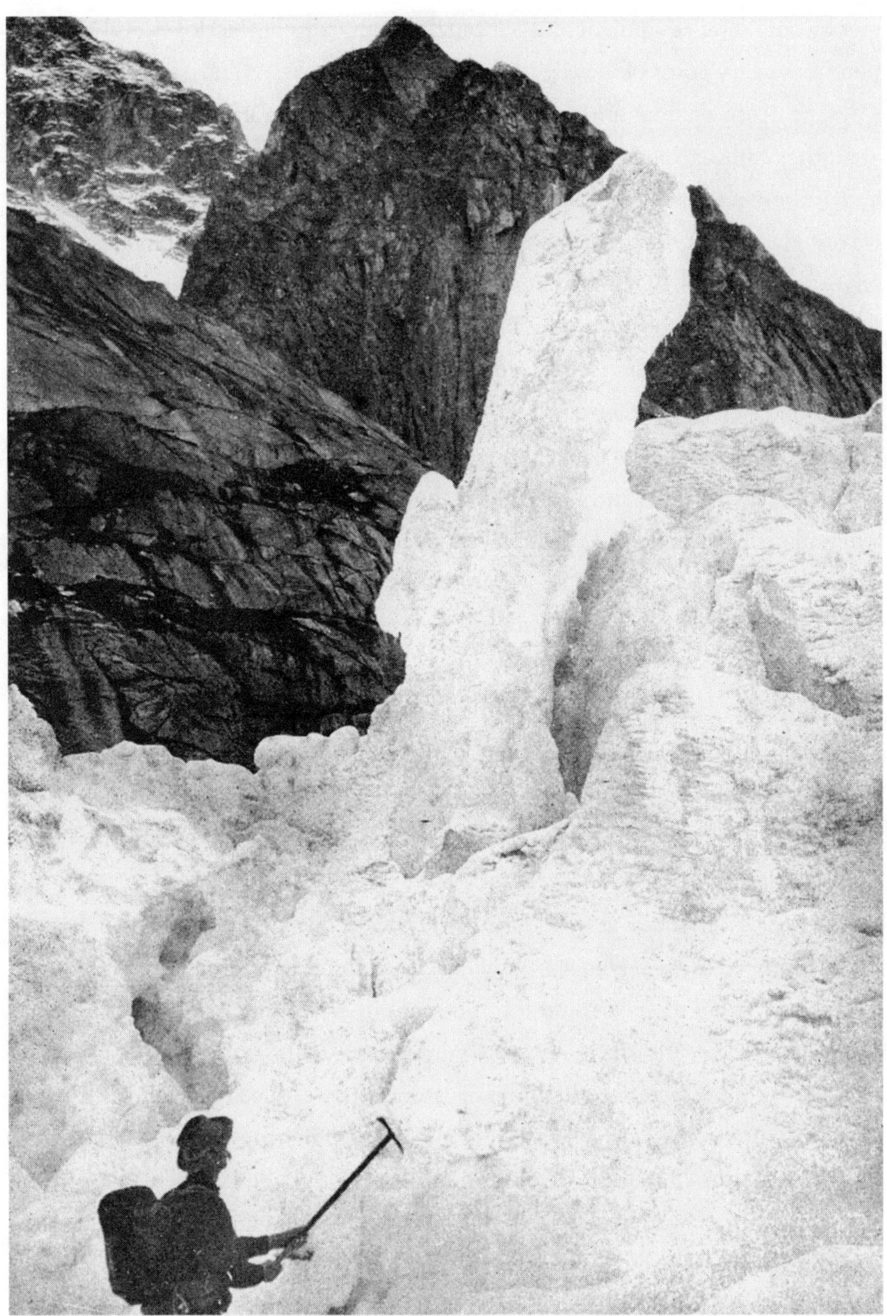

INTO THE BREATH OF DEATH-DEALING AVALANCHES

*Picking steps over treacherous ice and snow, around polished spires, up and up to the heaven-scraped granite of the top*

met by our arctic equipment and our rapid sketch maps of the slopes of the mountain from every point of view.

The death-dealing spirit of the avalanches created more anxiety here than at any other camp, though we never failed to note this danger. The night was dark and we were restless like soldiers on the eve of a battle. Snugly wrapped in our bags we rested well, but slept little because of the violent thunder of avalanches and the angry rush of winds. Out of black clouds from the invisible upper world there rushed with the noise of a thousand cannons and the hiss of a burning volcano indescribable quantities of rock and ice mixed with snow and wind. The tumble from cliff to cliff, from glacier to glacier down the seemingly endless fall was soul-stirring to the verge of desperation. The glacier under us cracked, the whole earth about quivered as from an earthquake, and as we tossed about in our bags the snow squeaked with a metallic ring. That third night we felt as if we were at the gates of Hades. We were about ready to quit and seek a more congenial calling. But dawn brought its usual inspiration. The temperature fell to zero, a heavy fall of snow cleared the gloom out of the sky, and a bright orange glow softened the depressing chaos of cliffs and spires into a sheen of sparkling splendour. While in our bags breakfast was prepared and eaten, and as the sun broke through the granite gap we tumbled out, rolled up our bags and tents, packed all in our rucksacks, secured the life line to our waists, and with axes in hand we started over the fresh snow for the cliffs of the northern arête.

The gaps of the crevasses widened, and the ice became more irregular, but the snow improved as we advanced. We chose the lateral moraine of the sérac of the first glacial tributary as a route into an amphitheatre. Here we found ourselves rising into the breath of avalanches too numerous and too close for our sense of security, but there were no other lines of ascent, so we pushed on into the gathering basin and into the clouds. The sunlight and snowy brightness were soon obscured by a curious gray-blue mist. The frosty chill of blue shadows and also the warm glow of sunbeams were absent and in their place a humid chill which is the usual effect of the cloud-world. With an eye on some rock we picked our way through mists, over dangerous séracs, to the frowning cliffs that made the circular rim of the amphitheatre. Here at noon we dropped in the snow, ate some pemmican, and rested long enough to permit the clouds to part and give us a peep at the cliffs above. We were thirsty, but it would take more than an hour to melt snow, and

AN AMPHITHEATRE
*A typical gathering basin of the Mt. McKinley glaciers*

this delay we could not afford at this time. There was no place to camp in the regions above unless we reached the top of the ridge and we still had about two thousand feet of step cutting and unknown trouble above us to a possible resting place. We rose farther and farther into the ragged edge of quickly drifting clouds. Rising from ridge to ridge and from cornice to cornice we finally burst through the gloomy mist on to a bright snow-field upon which fell the parting glow of the sun settling into the great green expanse beyond the Yukon. We were on the divide, the wall between the Yukon and Susitna.

It did not take us long to discover that we were on the battle-ground and in the firing line of clouds from the tropic and the arctic. The winds came in gusts now from the east and then from the west; with each change there was a fall of snow and a rush of drift. This locality did not appeal to us as a camping ground. In seeking for a sheltered nook we found a place where the snow was hard enough to cut blocks with which to build a snow house. In less than two hours

In a snow house on the Northeast Ridge, 12,000 feet

our dome-shaped Eskimo igloo was completed and thereby shelter and comfort were assured us for the time of our stay on the ridge.

The ice axes were driven into the snow, a rope was stretched, and on this line we hung our wet stockings and puttees. We had previously learned that the best way to dry things out was to allow them to freeze and on the following morning to shake off the frozen moisture. Everything else was taken inside the snow walls and a block of snow was pulled in as a door.

In the snow dome we were splendidly housed from the wind and drifting snows. Even the deafening rush of the avalanches was muffled. The temperature outside was below zero but we were perfectly comfortable within. Thin sheets of rubber were spread on the floor first, the silk tent and all our outer clothing were next put down. The sleeping bags were placed on this and into them we crept with the confidence of enjoying a warm restful night. Our shoes and cameras and other bulky things were rolled up in our rucksacks and used as pillows. This done the snow camp was complete.

For the culinary process Barrille packed the aluminum pail with fine snow while I filled the lamp with wood alcohol. Soon the happy buzz of the numerous blue jets lowered the snow line and more snow was added. During this time we rested comfortably in our bags and braced our teeth to the hard fragments of tallow and dried beef. We had a sickening empty feeling and ravenous appetites and felt like spending the night in filling up. We were not at all particular as to the menu. I have heard mountain climbers speak of the difficulties of digestion; this was not one of our complaints, anything to fill the gap would have been appreciated. Fortunately pemmican changes a hungry man's mind very quickly, and this with tea and biscuits raised an atmosphere of contentment which could not have been equalled by a course dinner. We lived a simple life indeed.

Little streams of snow drifted through the cuts between the blocks that night, but we rolled over now and then, shook the snow from the flap about our faces, and renewed our slumber with even increasing joys. At the end of twelve hours we woke up with a gastric emptiness which called for immediate attention.

As we crawled out of the snow house we noted to our surprise that the clouds below had separated and were drifting northerly, leaving unveiled the unexplored mountains and glaciers, the study of which completed our main mission.

Cloud and Cliffs, 13,000 feet

*Climbing and camping during gloomy days and frosty nights in storm-driven clouds*

Here to the east we noted the burial place of a great system of clouds which, arising out of the warm waters of the Japan current far away to the south, drift poleward, and are interrupted by the sky-scraping peaks of the Alaska Range. A local current of air carries the clouds north-east and drags them from one glacial depression to another, over ridge after ridge, and peak after peak, until the beautiful forms of the clouds are torn into shatters and drift in sections to the surface of a glacier, dropping tropical humidity to augment the arctic output of the stream of glacial ice.

The west of the mountain presents a face twenty-five miles wide with one great glacier (Hanna) sweeping the entire reach. Here, too, we noted the destination and the final resting place of an endless train of active clouds. These clouds came out of Bering Sea and the Arctic Ocean, drifted against the range a hundred miles southward, and then like the clouds from the east they too were carried along the western side of the range by a north-east current. Thus the vapours of the tropics were precipitated to the east while the vapours of the Arctic were precipitated to the west. Here then is the meeting place of the frigids and the torrids. In every gulch, glacial gap, or valley the local winds rolled down from the upper slopes carrying down torn bits of clouds, with the result that there was a never-ceasing rush up and down, to and fro, in the cloud world. But by far the most interesting battle was along the saw-tooth cuts of the great north-east ridge. Here we noted a ceaseless warfare between the pale arctic clouds and the dark Pacific clouds. There was a great deal of change on the ridge in barometric pressure as we had noted, winds rushed over the ridge from the Susitna valley to the Kuskokwim and vice versa with a dangerous suddenness, carrying along clouds and drifting snow in huge quantities. All of this could be easily seen from our fourteen-thousand-feet ditch, while we shivered and hoped for better times. With the upper clouds on both sides of the range moving along the general trend of the mountains, the lower clouds drifting away from the range, and the battle of angry vapours over the arête, there was a wilderness of commotion in the cloud world which quite dazzled us.

## CHAPTER XII

# To the Brink of an Arctic Inferno—A Night in a Ditch at 14,000 Feet

In about an hour we had completed our observation and then we turned for a look at the upper slopes for a route to the top. A few stratus films were brushing the snowy crests above, and the sun poured a wealth of golden light over the giant cliffs, illuminating the rushing snow of the plunging avalanches with a wild fire. Along the east among the cliffs that had seemed impossible from below there were several promising lines of attack along narrow overhanging glaciers and over steep ice-sheeted ridges. Every possible route however from this side was seen as the eye followed it to the summit to be crossed somewhere by avalanche tracks. Along the west there was a similar danger from the sweep of the ceaseless downpouring rock and snow. Our only chance, and that seemed a hopeless one, was along he cornice of the north-eastern arête upon which we were camped. For some distance there was a smooth line of crusted snow with a sheer drop of about 4000 feet to either side. At about 13,000 feet this line was barred by a huge rock with vertical sides of about 1000 feet. Beyond this rock there were other cliffs of ice and granite, and beyond this was a steep arête over which we could go from the west to the northern face on to a glacier and into a valley between the two majestic peaks which we now saw graced the summit.

After so many failures along lines of attack which looked good from a distance we concluded that to determine the feasibility of this route it would be necessary to pick a way around the big rock and into the median depression of the mountain. If we succeeded, however, in doing this we might as well prolong our siege and try for

THE EASTERN CLIFFS OF MT. MCKINLEY

the top. We had food and fuel enough for this, but the winter was so far advanced that the venture seemed imprudent.

With a half notion to climb to the summit, but with a more determined resolution to pick a route for a future ascent, we adjusted our rucksacks and life line and started on the morning of September 12th along this cornice. Soon the big southern clouds swept the mountain and we were left to grope among the spires in the misty blue of the cloud world. We found a way over a narrow cornice around the big rock and then we dug and scratched for a footing among the ice blocks in the narrow gorges between sharp pinnacles. With the dimness of the light and the limited range of vision we could not determine here the prospective course of avalanches, and this uncertainty gave us a great deal of anxiety. Our course was very irregular, winding around granite walls into gloomy séracs, over dangerous snow bridges, the climb becoming more impossible with every step.

Out of an amphitheatre with its crescentic walls of granite polished by the ice of ages, over tumbling blue-ribbed streams of ice into the aërial mystery of sweeping

In the solitude of the cloud world

clouds, groping for hours in the frosty night, picking a sure footing among treacherous cliffs, we at last broke through the clouds and climbed on to a wind-rasped cornice for a rest.

Every moment some colossal block thundered out of the clouds followed by a rumbling train of snow and ice. With bumps and roars and hisses, the seething run of débris came from cliffs unseen and plunged into echoing depths inconceivable. For days and months and years and centuries these reducing trains have been at work thus by chemical action, by the winds, by the sweep of the clouds depositing snow, by the action of the ice melting, by the spreading of ice in the rock crevasses, by the general expansion and contraction of heat and cold, by the force of gravity. The time must come, if this cooling earth lasts long enough, when this great majestic tier of chiselled granite above the clouds will all have settled into an ugly mound, a mere forgotten grave of an alpine monarch.

We continued our steep ascent farther and farther into the icy clouds curling above our heads up the knife edge of the north arête, around a great spur, from cornice to cornice, cresting sheer cliffs over which there was a sickening drop of ten thousand feet, into the mystery of a lower arctic world, and then began the awful task of making a ladder for two thousand feet. With eternity but an easy step below every moment of this climb we went from hanging glacier to snow slopes, from blue grottoes to pink pinnacles, from security to insecurity, with the thundering rush of avalanches on both sides. If there ever was a more disheartening task it has not been my misfortune to be confronted with it.

We would have been glad enough to return and give up the task at this time but night was near and the little light that remained was blotted out by the gloom of a coming snowstorm. To return over the dangerous cornices in the dark was impossible. To camp anywhere within reach was equally impossible. For self-preservation we must move up out of the dangerous area. Keeping the rope tight we chipped steps as near the ridge as was possible and remained sheltered from the wind. One hundred steps and Barrille took the axe, then another one hundred steps and it was my turn. We could not see the slopes above for more than a hundred yards, and below everything was obscured by twisting clouds and drifting snows. It was black at seven o'clock. We dropped into the steps from sheer exhaustion. There is a limit to human endurance, and we had reached that limit, but where could we rest and live for the night? There were snow slopes not far away, but they were swept by avalanches. The safest place was along the steep arête.

Our axes had been kept chopping steps all day, and our rise in altitude was very little, but we got beyond the barriers and out of the area of windy cliffs and frigid crags out on a steep snow-sheeted arête.

We uttered a sigh of relief as we rose on the icy steps of our Jacob's ladder, out of the gloomy dangers from below to the upper edge of the cloud zone. We uttered a good many other sighs of despair before the night was spent. The little colour which we were able to note between the cloud rifts indicated sunset. It was 7:20 by the watch, the mercury stood at 11° below zero, and the compass pointed to the tip of a new peak above the clouds 28° east of north, the only mountain visible. The thin blue haze about us was thickening to a colder blue, ragged outlines of torn cloud filaments were noted, crystals of snow fell as we rested and talked of the chances of camp or shelter on a cloud-swept slope too steep for a seat. The blackness of night was thickening fast and its chill increased in penetration with the decrease of the light. We knew that we could not descend to a sheltered spot, for there was none within the day's climb. The darkness was too far advanced and we were too nearly exhausted to risk a farther ascent into the unknown dangers above. The slope upon which we had cut steps and seats in the ice was nearly 60° but the ice was secure, the snow firm, and the danger from avalanches small. As a duty to ourselves and our families we had no alternative but to dig into the icy side of the mountain and hold on for the night.

In this side-hill ditch we fitted ourselves securely with a view to the effects of slumber movements. For if we slipped from the ditch we would plunge thousands of feet through the clouds to the smoky depths of an arctic inferno. We wrapped ourselves in a bundle with all of our belongings including the silk tent, then lashed the bundle to the axes, which were securely driven into the ice and in this way we held on for the night. The fine snow drifted down our necks and into the cracks of the dug-out, but we did not dare to move for fear the snow would fill the gap, crowd us out, and we would be left to hold on to the axes to stay us from a death plunge.

Avalanches thundered down from both sides at close range. The night was very long and stormy. There were frequent rifts in the clouds through which we saw clusters of stars framed by silvery films of vapour—beautiful pictures in the retrospect, but we were then not in a humour to appreciate the glories of our outlook. We were interested more in the break of day and in the chances of getting to a place of greater security. The thought of going to the top of the mountain was dispelled by the misery of that awful night. We were too tightly bundled to disagree actively, though we spent wakeful hours in mild arguments. We agreed, however, on two points: we must hold on, freeze to the ice if possible, and with the first light make for the low country, abandon mountain climbing, and take to a better life. But with the break of day with its fetching polar glory all of this disheartening note of abandonment and danger changed. Now our determination to retreat resolved itself into a resolution to go to the top.

With the chill of dawn the upper clouds froze to the slopes, while the lower clouds settled lower and lower into the maze of glacial canyons. Through these lower clouds there was a burst of fire and with it the great glittering spires above blazed with a glow of rose. This glow lasted but a short time, then the normal frost of purple and blue submerged every hope of feeling heat or seeing warmth in colour. As we dragged ourselves out of this icy ditch of terrors we were able to see that we had passed the barriers to the ascent. The slopes above were easy, safe, and connected, but the bigness of the mountain was more and more apparent as we rose above the clouds. Instead of our having to climb one mountain we were forced to deal with peak upon peak and mountains within a mountain. The task enlarged with the ascent. Rising over crest after crest we finally reached what seemed to be the top of the mountain. But it was only a spur, and beyond it were many other spurs. The air became clearer and sharper with every step, and our exhaustion, mostly the result of sleeplessness and anxiety of the previous night, was increasingly felt.

Soon after noon we swung from the arête easterly to the glacier. Here owing to fatigue progress was slow.

The snow was hard and the slope such that little step-cutting was now necessary. Along the glacier to the gathering basin near the summit the prospective route rose in easy slants to our goal. Above it was perfectly clear, but below there was an ever-changing drift of cloud obscurity in which we had spent two days of despair. If torment is the test of Hades then the habitat of Mephisto was in that cloud-world at our feet.

There is a sinister and savage ferocity along the middle slopes of shelves and cliffs and clouds and storms that is accentuated by a precarious footing as well as by the rush and thunder of avalanches. Everything was snow covered as we looked over the sheen of death and destruction. There was absolutely no semblance of life in sight and it seemed months since we left the comfortable camp-fires. If it were a mountain of skulls it would not convey a more forcible sense of gloom.

In picking a way among the séracs we soon found that our muscles refused to work. Though the climb was easy we could not gather enough energy to continue the ascent. The night in the ditch and the prolonged expenditure of energy along the middle slopes had pressed us to the verge of collapse. Under these circumstances it seemed best to seek a good camping spot on the glacier with a view to resting for a day to recuperate and store up force for the final spurt of the upper ascent.

CHAPTER XIII

# Glory and Desolation above the Clouds from 16,300 to 18,400 Feet

~

We found a level space in a small amphitheatre where the snow was hard enough to cut blocks for a snow house, and though the view was magnificent beyond anything previously seen we turned our backs to visual glories and crept into the snow hut and into our bags to prepare for food and a long rest. While the alcohol lamp spent its feeble heat against the pail of snow we dozed, to dream of far-off comfort, awaking every few moments to the chills of an icy reality. Through the door we peeped at the changing sheen of gloom of the lower world.

For desolation it would strain the English dictionary to describe it, but there are shades of desolation as there are grades of intoxication. Last night the note of abandon was soul destroying. From our dug-out in the treacherous drop the outlook and the world about was desperately gloomy. To-night with the sparkle and glitter of the snowy world above the clouds, illuminated by glowing stars that hang like huge arc lights from a black sky, we see another phase of desolation, one full of hope, inspiration, and promise.

In the lower climb there was a thrill which fired ambitions. The beauty of the naked cliffs raised us to a pitch of ecstasy which made us forget fatigue, but in the upper world all of this was changed. It was a region of harmony in colour and contour. A suffusion of light with subdued colour blends to frosty shades. A softening of contours by a flooding of snow crystals fills the ugly gaps and rounds off the sharp corners. But nevertheless it is a region of pulseless eternity where the spirits with the clouds fall to earth in weeping sadness. The lack of movement, the oppressive stillness, the absence of every speck of life impressed upon us the fact that

IN THE SILENT GLORY AND SNOWY WONDER OF THE UPPER WORLD, 15,400 FEET

we were utterly alone; the only breathing creatures in a great expanse of mystery far above the habitable world.

As the stifling blackness of night was bleached by the blue of dawn the whole weird run of unreality changed. The upper world of silent glory and snowy wonder was beyond human interpretation. We have a similar white world of deathly glory in the low polar wilds but there the clouds are above and there is sometimes a glow of warm colour, but here the clouds are below, the sky is black, and a frosty steel-coloured light is poured over the sparkle of the snow-fields. There is however a weird fascination in this curious supra-cloudland. It is difficult to grasp the thread with which it rolls up its spool of mysteries, but to me the most striking is the paradox of light and colour: at your feet a dazzling whiteness, overhead a dense blackness, in space a gloomy neutral play of dull blues.

When I was a boy I had a distinct notion of the geography of heaven and of the regions above the clouds. The splendid colours of sunbursts, sunsets, and indeed all brilliant displays were manifestations of the glory of heaven, which I placed among the clouds. I did not know that there was a cloud-world rather close to the crust of the earth, and beyond, far beyond the blue sky which we believed to be the limit of space there was a great unknown without colour or light! In later years I was inclined to push the actual location of heaven into this mysterious void far away, but to-day I am bound to confess that I believe the spiritual future which we in a figurative way style heaven is very near the terrestrial surface.

As we ascended into this cloud world we thought of angels in light attire with wings, and of an easy world of rare glory. But how different was our realisation. As the great bunches of vapour which we call clouds brushed against us along the middle slopes we were submerged by a gloomy darkness preceded and followed by icy gusts of wind while the incessant showers of fine snow made a weeping spectacle. This environment of the cloud world was indeed opposed to a heavenly or even a congenial spirit. We were in desperate mood, without poetry or aesthetic appreciation; with heavy packs on our backs, treading a path through deep snow up dangerous slopes, where wind drove snow into our faces, down our necks, withal a depressing monotony of colour, and with no safe place where we could rest our weary bones. From cliff to cliff, from grotto to spire, from cloud to cloud, up and up farther and farther into whirling vapours we pushed until at last when we thought night had dropped over us, we suddenly burst through the clouds into a glistening pearly twilight with stars hanging low like electric lights. The brilliancy of this glittering half light was new to us, the darkness of the sky was even more surprising. This however as we learned later is one of the natural conditions of the land above the clouds. The snow here was such that we were able to build a snow house and in it we packed ourselves for a long rest.

As the stars were beginning to fade on the following morning, the sixth day of our climb, we kicked out the snow block which made our door, and crawled on to the crackling surface. The temperature was 15° below zero. The light increased rapidly, and the oppressive stillness contrasted strongly with the noisy rush of avalanches below. The marvels in this new world of ice were slow in penetrating our frosty senses. Even after we began to appreciate the anomaly of things we questioned our perceptions. We were surely in a land of paradoxes. Here looking down ever so far below, we could see a sea of clouds whose upper filament waved in the gold of the rising sun, while above us was a dark gray-blue sky with the stars still visible. The snow and the rocks glittered with a weird brightness seeming to come out of the earth—darkness above, light from below; things were certainly topsy-turvy. This supra-cloud world is a land of fantasy, of strange other-world illusions. Here summers are winters and winters are what a polar traveller believes Hades ought to be.

Starting from camp, at 16,300 feet, picking a trail around successive séracs, our progress was good. We still felt the bad effects of our overworked muscles on the lower climbs; but we hoped to be able to push on to the summit that day. However the increasing altitude, the very low temperatures, and the lack of nerve energy all combined to make our ascent extremely difficult.

During the frequent breathing spells we examined the upper reaches of the mountain. We had seen the summit from various sides, but we were not prepared for the surprise of the great spread of surface. From below the apex appears like a single peak, with gradual slopes. From the northern foothills we had previously discovered two distinct peaks. But now, from the upper slopes, we saw that there were several miniature ranges running up to two main peaks about two miles apart. To the west a ridge with a saddle, to the east a similar ridge, with one main peak to the south-east. This peak was the highest point, and to it we aimed to take our weary spirits.

Compared to our lower climbs the slope here was ridiculously easy, but the work was hard, out of all proportion to the seeming difficulties. After slowly making a hundred steps we puffed like race horses on the home stretch, and were forced to stop and gasp for breath; another hundred steps and another gasp, and so on. We tried to pull ourselves together in a renewed compact to rise, but do what we could, cheer each other as we could, the thing seemed impossible, purely because of our inability to raise one foot above another. Our legs were of wood and our feet of stone. After prodigious efforts we were forced to camp at 18,400 feet with not enough energy left to talk or to eat.

The silk tent was pitched in a gathering basin under the shadow of the topmost peak and as we crept into the bags we were so reduced by frost and the awful breath-reducing struggles that we were but half conscious of the surroundings.

The circulation was so depressed that it was impossible to dispel the sense of chilliness. Increased clothing or bed-covers did not seem to make much difference. The best thing to dispel the shivers was hot tea. The alcohol-lamp was not a success at this altitude. But with a good deal of nursing we succeeded in melting snow enough for our drinks. The water boiled at a point so low that the tea was weak and never too hot. Indeed, if we desired the real flavour of the tea, it was necessary to eat the tea-leaves.

It was a restless and exciting night. Restless, because the task of breathing less than one half an atmosphere and pumping blood through collapsing arteries abnormally taxed our powers. Exciting, because with heaving, pulsating bodies we felt as if the end of life had come and the door of heaven was about to open.

This last night of the climb was one which we will long remember. We were not able to see anything with a normal perspective until long after midnight. Unable to sleep we were only permitted to rest in a semi-reclining position with shoulders raised, in which attitude the heart was eased and breath came and went with less effort.

We had to contend with a very difficult combination opposed to our comfort. With our strength reduced by the lower climb, with no reserve energy, with a low temperature to which were added the natural depressive effects of great altitudes, we were indeed much handicapped. Though the temperature was only 16° below zero, in its effects it was colder than 60 below at sea level. The shivers of this night with the pumping, thumping hearts and the spasmodic breath will always stand out as the worst torment of our endeavour.

Words did not freeze and tumble about us as did the words of Mark Twain's hero at the north pole, who found himself knee-deep in his own eloquence, but as we raised the flap from our faces we did find ourselves nose-deep in the frost of our own breath.

We believed this to be our last camp but the outcome of our final assault was not at all a hopeful one. In a critical examination of ourselves we found that all of the pleasurable sensations had merged with the strain of the terrible task of climbing, but there was still the mechanism of duty which pushed us upward. The courage born of inspiration, the enthusiasm arising from anticipation, and all of the spirit of the joys of the pioneer ascent had been put into the slavish bent to press one foot above another to the summit.

CHAPTER XIV

# To the Top—The World in White and the Heavens in Black

Long before dawn we rolled out of the sleeping bags, crept out of the tent, and then placing the robes about our shivering shoulders we studied the brightening blue of the topmost pinnacle of the Alpine North Pole. I never saw a more impressive spectacle. The peak loomed up like a giant mountain in the curiously deceptive light before dawn. In reality it was but two thousand feet above our camp, a mere fraction of the altitude of the great mountain, but in our enfeebled condition the peak appeared as high and as difficult as the entire uplift from the first camps. As the darkness merged into twilight the sky brightened, but as the sun rose the sky darkened and the cold increased.

With numb fingers and teeth chattering we packed our sleeping bags and a light emergency ration in the rucksacks and then with a grim determination we started for the culminating peak. The sun soon rose far above the green lowland beyond Mount Hayes and moved toward the ice-blink caused by the extensive glacial sheets north of the St. Elias group. Our route was over a feathery snow-field which cushioned the gap between rows of granite pinnacles. During most of this part of the ascent we were in frosty shadows where the cold pierced to the bone, but when we did rise into the direct sunbeams there was a distinct warm sensation. Ten yards away, however, in another shadow, the air was as cold as during the polar night. The sunbeams seemed to pass through the air without leaving behind a trace of heat, similar to the effect of an electric spark through space.

A magnificent spread of an other-world glory ran in every direction. A weird world in white, with stars fading in gloomy blackness. Far below were milky waves of clouds and still farther down ugly gaps of indigo into which the vapours settled to their last resting-place. At the present writing I am tempted to enlarge on the awe-inspiring grandeur of this scene, but at the time we were too miserable to spend even visual energy on mere scenic effects.

An advance of twenty steps so fagged us that we were forced to lean over on our ice-axes to puff and ease the heart; another twenty steps and another rest, and so on in a life-racking series of final effort.

The last few hundred feet of the ascent so reduced our physical powers that we dropped on to the snow, completely exhausted, gasping for breath. We had gone so near the limit of human endurance that we did not appreciate the proud moments of the hard-earned success. Glad enough were we to pull the eider-down robes about us, and allow our thumping, overworked hearts, as well as our lungs, labouring in less than half an atmosphere, to catch up. We puffed and puffed, and after a while the sickening thump under the left fifth rib became less noticeable. Breath came and went easier, and then the call of the top was again uppermost. It was an awful task, however, to pick ourselves up out of the deep snow and set the unwilling muscles to work pulling up our legs of stone. The mind was fixed on the glitter of the summit, but the motive force was not in harmony with this ambition.

Just below the summit we dropped over an icy shelf on the verge of collapse. After a few moments we gathered breath and courage and then for the last stage the life line tightened with a nervous pull. We edged up along a steep snowy ridge and over the heaven-scraped granite to the top. AT LAST! The soul-stirring task was crowned with victory; the top of the continent was under our feet. Our hands clasped, but not a word was uttered. We felt like shouting, but we had not the breath to spare. The thing that impressed me first was the noble character of Edward Barrille, the bigness in heart and soul of the man who had followed me, without a word of complaint, through hopelessness to success; and then after several long breaths the ghastly unreality of our position began to excite my frosted senses.

Curious experience this. It was September 16th, the temperature 16 degrees below zero, the altitude 20,390 feet. The Arctic Circle was in sight; so was the Pacific Ocean. We were interested mostly, not in the distant scenes, but in the very strange anomaly of our immediate surroundings. It was ten o'clock in the morning, the sky was as black as that of midnight. At our feet the snow glittered with a

THE TOP OF OUR CONTINENT
*The summit of Mt. McKinley, the highest mountain of North America. Altitude, 20,390 feet.*

ghastly light. As the eye ran down we saw the upper clouds drawn out in long strings, and still farther down the big cumulus forms, and through the gap far below, seemingly in the interior of the earth, bits of rugged landscape. The frightful uncanny aspect of the outlook made us dizzy. Fifty thousand square miles of our arctic wonderland was spread out under our enlarged horizon, but we could see it only in sections. Various trains of morning clouds screened the lowlands and entwined the lesser peaks. We could see narrow silvery bands marking the course of the Yukon and the Tanana, while to the south, looking over nearby clouds, we had an unobstructed view. Mt. Susitna, one hundred miles away in a great green expanse, was but a step in the run of distance. The icy cones of the burning volcanoes Redoubt, Illiamna, and Chinabora, the last two hundred miles away, were clearly visible with their rising vapours. Still farther the point of Kenai Peninsula, and beyond, the broad sweep of the Pacific two hundred and fifty miles away!

A record of our conquest was, with a small flag, pressed into a metallic tube and left in a protected nook a short distance below the summit. A round of angles was taken with the prismatic compass. The barometers and thermometers were read, and hasty notes jotted down in our note-book. Most impressive was the curious low dark sky, the dazzling brightness of the frosted granite blocks, the neutral gray-blue of space, the frosty dark blue of the shadows, and, above all, the final picture which I took of Barrille, with the flag lashed to his axe, as the arctic air froze the impression into a relief which no words can tell.

The descent was less difficult, but it took us four days to tumble down to our base camp.

Dokkin, during our absence having grown enthusiastic about the chances of gold and copper mining, asked to be grub-staked. We had food enough for one man for a year, and left this with our companion to seek his fortune in the newly explored regions. The *Bolshoy* descended the river quickly and, taking the scattered parties from the Susitna Station on the next day, we pushed on to Tyonok, and to Kenai, and from there southward by the regular steamers.

# Belmore Browne: Defeat

Belmore Browne's *The Conquest of Mount McKinley* (1913) draws together three of the most exciting and pivotal pioneer expeditions to Denali. Browne's first trip was with Dr. Cook in 1906; it was here, left behind after their first failed attempt, that he came to suspect Cook was fabricating his ascent to the summit. Next came his 1910 and 1912 expeditions with Herschel Parker; they had two objectives—to prove that Cook was lying and to make the first ascent themselves.

To appreciate the tension under which *The Conquest of Mount McKinley* was written, it's helpful to have a sense of the intrigue happening behind the scenes. In the winter of 1906–1907, following their Denali expedition, Belmore Browne was convinced that Cook's ascent was a hoax, but he felt he should wait to confront Cook until his official story appeared in print. However, by the time *Harper's Monthly Magazine* ran the story in May of 1907, Cook had quietly slipped out of New York, embarking on an ambitious expedition to reach the North Pole. Browne was forced to bide his time: "By our own ideas of fair play," he said, "we refrained from publishing anything derogatory to the Doctor's character while he was absent, and unable to defend himself."

When Cook's book, *To the Top of the Continent*, was released in 1908, Browne immediately spotted a discrepancy. The summit photo in the book showed a distant ridge that was missing in the *Harper's* magazine photo. Evidently, with Cook on his way to the Arctic, this crucial photo hadn't been cropped to eliminate the telltale ridge. With this tantalizing bit of evidence, Browne felt sure he could find the peak where Cook had taken his "summit" photo and prove it was a fake. We can imagine his mounting frustration as he waited for Cook to return from the Arctic.

Browne must have been mystified by Cook's triumphant arrival. On September 1, 1909, a cablegram announced: "DR. COOK REACHED THE NORTH POLE." As Cook's ship approached New York on September 21, it was surrounded by a flotilla of boats crowded with cheering celebrants. *The New York Herald* described it as "a demonstration of popular confidence and enthusiasm without parallel in the history of the city."

Cook's euphoria would be short-lived. Within a few days, Robert Peary, once Cook's mentor, announced that he had reached the North Pole—and that Cook had come nowhere near the pole. For the moment, public sentiment remained with Cook. A poll showed that 73,238 people believed Cook; only 2,814 believed Peary's denunciation of Cook.

Peary's accusation would throw Belmore Browne into the middle of the polar controversy. Since one patch of snow and ice looks much like another, proving or disproving that someone reached the North Pole is no easy task. People reasoned that if Cook was lying about Denali, he was probably lying about reaching the North Pole. So Browne's case against Cook's Denali ascent became the crux of the erupting polar controversy.

The Explorers Club arranged a meeting between Browne and Dr. Cook, but the doctor begged off, claiming that the long strenuous months in the Arctic had affected his memory. He promised to return in two weeks with his notes, but he didn't show. Ed Barrill, his only companion on their "summit" climb, recanted their story.

The pendulum of public opinion was rapidly swinging away from Cook. Still, hard evidence was needed to refute him once and for all. Browne made plans to return to Alaska with Herschel Parker to gather this very evidence—and to climb Denali if they could. The two friends returned from expeditions to Denali in 1910 with convincing photographic evidence of Cook's duplicity. In this objective they succeeded brilliantly, but climbing to the summit proved to be a more elusive goal.

Reading *The Conquest of Mount McKinley*, we realize that Browne and Parker were pushing the boundaries of mountaineering. Approaching Denali from the south, it took them months of exhausting bushwhacking and river-fording just to reach the base of the mountain, where the challenges of route finding began. All the while, they were experimenting with new equipment and techniques.

It also fell to Browne and Parker to figure out what kind of food would work best at altitude. Had they not relied so heavily on pemmican, which they discovered is all but indigestible above 12,000 feet, they could have waited out the storm that stopped them just short of the summit in 1912. Then again, if they had waited, they almost certainly would have been crushed by the colossal avalanches that were triggered by a major earthquake that struck the day after they left the mountain.

"There is little doubt," says Bradford Washburn, pioneer mountain photographer and dean of American mountaineering, "that the Parker-Browne expeditions of 1910 and 1912, undertaken in the heat of this controversy, were the longest and most arduous mountain expeditions in which American mountaineers have ever taken part."

*The Conquest of Mount McKinley* is their story—and, although a storm defeated their summit bid, this is ultimately a story of triumph—a triumph of their honor, ingenuity, and perseverance.

*Art Davidson*

# THE CONQUEST OF MOUNT MCKINLEY

By Belmore Browne

# CONTENTS

Behring Strait
Arcti
Norton Sound
2°
A
L
A
Kuskoquim
Ri
BEHRING SEA
Bristol Bay
ALASKA PENIN
0 25 50 100 150 200 250
APPROXIMATE SCALE OF MILES

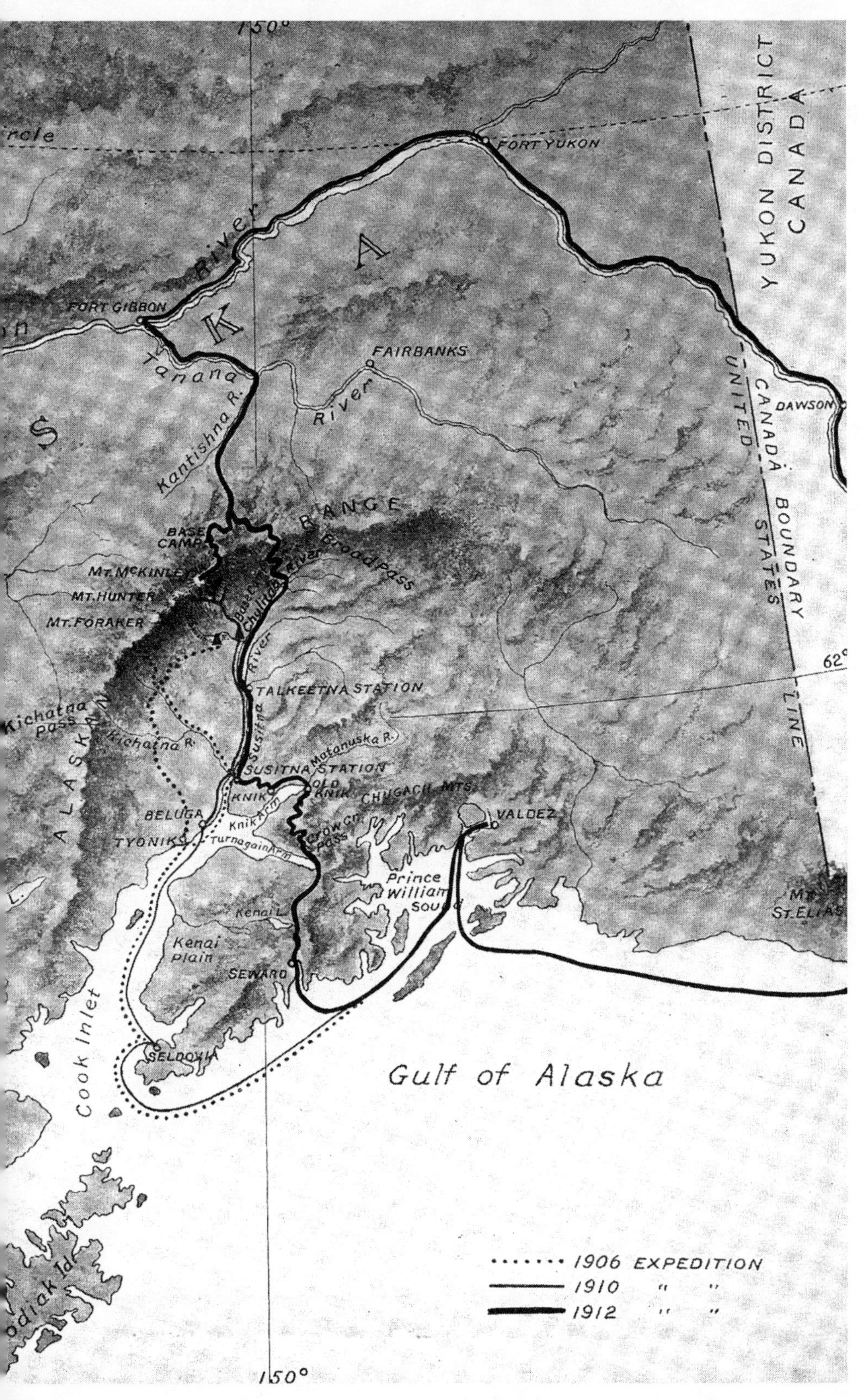
150°
FORT YUKON
YUKON DISTRICT
CANADA
River
A
FORT GIBBON
K
Tanana
FAIRBANKS
River
Kantishna R.
DAWSON
UNITED STATES
CANADA
BOUNDARY LINE
RANGE
BASE CAMP
Broad Pass
MT. McKINLEY
MT. HUNTER
MT. FORAKER
Chulitna River
Susitna River
62°
TALKEETNA STATION
Kichatna Pass
Kichatna R.
Matanuska R.
SUSITNA STATION
KNIK
OLD KNIK
CHUGACH MTS.
ALASKAN
BELUGA
Knik Arm
VALDEZ
TYONIK
Turnagain Arm
Crow Cr. Pass
Prince William Sound
Kenai L.
Mt. St. Elias
Kenai plain
SEWARD
Cook Inlet
SELDOVIA
Gulf of Alaska
Kodiak Id.
1906 EXPEDITION
1910 " "
1912 " "
150°

# FOREWORD

More than seven years have passed since I sat down in a smoking-car on the Canadian Pacific to enjoy a morning pipe. After several weary days we left the monotonous prairies behind and were climbing upward through the beautiful foothills of the Canadian Rockies.

Sitting opposite to me was a man whose eyes never left the rugged mountainsides as they flew by the window. As I studied my companion I knew that his interest in the mountains came from a deeper feeling than the casual curiosity of a tourist, and while the train sped on we talked of mountains and mountain craft. From the Canadian Rockies our talk drifted back to other ranges we had known, and then I told of how, from high mountain camps in distant Alaska, I had looked longingly northward to where the great cloud-like dome of Mount McKinley—America's highest mountain—hung above the Alaskan Wilderness.

And then I found that my companion was planning an attempt on Mount McKinley's summit the following year, and when I left the smoking-car, I had cast my lot with his.

It is interesting, in looking backward, to see how small events can change the entire course of our lives. This book is the result of that chance meeting, and my companion in the smoking-car—Professor Herschel Parker—has since been my "pardner" on many a rough wilderness trail.

To those of my readers who have never felt the lure of the mountains, I will give a few reasons for our undertaking so strange a task. The primal force at the base of all exploration is the call of the wild. Without this deep-seated love of adventure men would never be willing to meet the hardship that is waiting for them in the wilderness. But in addition to this there are many different sides of exploration, any one of which taken by itself is of sufficient interest to draw a man from civilization. I know of no task more absorbing than the mapping of an unknown territory; there is nothing more stimulating to the imagination than watching the growth of rivers and mountain chains on a topographer's plane-table. Equally absorbing is the geological interest of "new country," which runs through the whole gamut of human emotions from the frenzy of the gold-mad prospector to the unselfish enthusiasm of the geologist.

Then come the daily study and companionship of the wild life, from the smallest bird that dares a flight of thousands of miles to rear its young during the short arctic summer, to the big game herds that roam the storm-swept mountainsides.

But always dominating man's endeavours is the struggle against the forces of nature—this is *Life*—and when all is said, this is the world-old magnet that draws alike scientist, explorer, prospector, mountaineer, and hunter. This was the force that brought the men who joined our ventures, and they came from every walk of life.

Without the love for the unknown they would never have undergone the hardships they bore so cheerfully, and the material reward they received was not sufficient to repay them for even one day of the weeks of toil and danger they endured. Without men of this kind, nothing would be possible, and in looking back on those wild, free days in the open I realise that my happiest memories are of the sun-tanned faces of my old companions.

It is my hope to convey to the reader in the following pages a faithful impression of the wild lands we saw and the joys and sorrows that we experienced in our three struggles with North America's grandest mountain.

In compiling this book I am indebted to Alfred H. Brooks, of the U.S. Geological Survey, for valuable passages and notes taken from his report to the Department of the Interior; to the Outing Publishing Company, and the *World Today Magazine* for the use of photographs previously published by them.

B.B.

*New York City*

*January 18, 1913*

## CHAPTER I

# Description of Mount McKinley

*The difficulties of reaching the mountain—Polar condition of glacier travel—Comparison with other mountain ranges—Geographical position—Early history of mountain—Russian accounts—Indian fables—Early explorations by American prospectors—W. A. Dickey's description of the mountain—Public interest—United States Government explorations—Brooks and Reaburn make their long journey—Judge Wickersham attempts the climb—Dr. Cook makes his first attempt to scale peak—Result of explorations.*

Mount McKinley is the highest mountain in North America. There was a time not long past when this fact was disputed, but the increase in knowledge concerning Alaska and the fact that all of its large rivers have been explored proves conclusively that no unknown mountain approximating Mount McKinley in size can exist; for high mountains form extensive ice-fields, and these in turn necessitate large rivers to drain them.

This great peak, rising 20,300 feet above the sea, is formed by a gigantic mass of granite that was forced upward through the stratum of slate that overlaid it. On many of the lower peaks close to the mountain this stratum of slate is still in position, giving them a strange, black-capped appearance.

The granite of which the mountain is composed is of a light tan colour, and at a distance its grim cliffs take on a pinkish hue which gives the mountain a delicate atmospheric appearance that differentiates it from all other mountains, and stamps it with a beauty and grandeur of its own. One of the principal difficulties to be overcome by the mountaineer in climbing Mount McKinley is the low altitude from which it rises. It is safe to say that all of the known mountains in the world of the same height rise from plateaus of considerable elevation. This is particularly true of South America and Tibet where high mountains are plentiful. In both of these countries the mountaineer has reached an altitude of at least 10,000 feet before his climbing difficulties commence. On Mount McKinley the difficulties are exceptional. The only routes to the southern face lie over glaciers thirty miles in length—there are no other possible routes.

If a party were to follow these glaciers in the winter time, dogs could be used to draw the provisions, but in the summer time it is necessary for the climbers to transport everything on their backs. After crossing the thirty miles of ice and snow, the only explored glacier broadens into a piedmont glacier 5000 feet in altitude, so that the climber is still confronted by 15,000 feet of ice and snow! On the northern face there are places where the mountain's icy flanks sweep down to 3000 feet leaving 17,000 feet of mountain to rise above the plain. While it is a difficult matter to judge the exact line of perpetual snow, on account of the yearly changes in the climate, and the local climatic changes on different sides of the range, one can measure accurately the point where the glacier ice ends, and an average of the glacier snouts would place this line at about 2500 feet. As the mountain ranges that separate the glaciers are too rugged to follow, the climber is forced to take to the ice at a low altitude, which necessitates polar equipment, and the transportation of large quantities of provisions. In the Andes, particularly, the conditions are incomparably easier, as any one will realise after reading Stuart Vine's account of his ascent of Aconcagua, 22,860 feet. During the climb his feet never touched snow, and his Swiss guide, having no use for his ice axe, left it on the summit as a memento for the next comer.

Herman L. Tucker, a member of our 1910 expedition to Mount McKinley, went to South America the following year with the Yale Peruvian Expedition. While in the Andes he joined in the ascent of a 20,000-foot mountain and in a letter to me he stated that they reached the summit of the peak with less exertion than we expended in reaching an altitude of only 4500 feet on Mount McKinley.

Geographically Mount McKinley seems to have been placed "in the most inaccessible position obtainable." It lies just north of "sixty-three" where "there is no law of God, nor man," and it is bisected by the 152d meridian, forming the apex and geographical centre of the great wilderness south of the Yukon and west of the

Tanana rivers. Its glacier waters cool the Yukon on the north via the Kantishna and Tanana rivers and the Susitna on the south via the Tokositna and Chulitna rivers.

The nearest salt water, Cook Inlet, is 140 miles from the southern face as the crow is supposed to fly.

The Alaskan Range, of which Mount McKinley forms the crowning peak, is the most inaccessible and least known mountain range in Alaska. But for the insignificant break at Lake Illiamna which separates it from the mountains of the Alaska Peninsula, it would sweep in a grand arc from the Aleutian Islands to the headwaters of the Tanana River.

My first view of Mount McKinley was from the deck of a small steamer on Cook Inlet. The mountain rose like a dim cloud on the northern horizon, two hundred miles away. This view took me back in imagination to the days of the Russian explorers when the mountain and the great wilderness that guards it were

MOUNT MCKINLEY FROM THE CHULITNA RIVER. ABOUT 43 MILES AWAY.

wrapped in mystery. What thoughts the dim cloud-like shape suggested to Shillikoff and his wild companions we can only conjecture, but to this day in the Indian lodges many a weird tale is told of the mountain giant. If you can earn the confidence of the aged Indians they will tell you of days when the earth was covered with water, and how a god who was chasing his eloping sweetheart threw a rock with intent to kill, and how that rock rose above the falling water and stands to this day—the incomparable Doleika. And they tell of later days when Doleika belched flames and smoke, but unfortunately there is nothing to bear out this fable, for McKinley is not a volcano. "Doleika," or "the big mountain," the Susitnas call it, while the Aleutes speak of it as "Traleika." The Russians named it "Bulshaia," meaning "big."

Talkeetna Nicolae, chief of the Susitnas, told me a story that was handed down from the olden days, of a Russian adventurer who tried to reach Doleika and died miserably in the Kichatna swamps. The mountain has always been holy ground to the natives, and to this day the surrounding country is supposed to be haunted and the abode of devils.

In speaking of the Indian names for Mount McKinley, Brooks writes as follows:

> *No one can know how many generations of natives have wandered over this region, but it seems certain that the indigenous population was greater at the first coming of the white man than it is now. As the natives depended largely on the chase for subsistence, they must have frequented the slopes of the Alaskan Range, and the adjacent lowlands, for this is one of the best game regions in the North-west. Much of the range formed an almost impassable barrier between the hunting-ground of the Cook Inlet natives and that of the Kuskoquim Indians. It does not seem to have been named, for the Alaskan Indian has no fixed geographic nomenclature for the larger geographic features. A river will have half a dozen names, depending on the direction from which it is approached. The cartographers who cover Alaskan maps with unpronounceable names, imagining that these are based on local usage, are often misled. Thus the Yukon Indians called White River the Yukokon, the Tanana natives called it the Nasina, the Kluane Indians called it the Nazenka, and the coastal tribe of Chilkats had still another name for it. No one of these can be said to have precedence over any other.*

*The immense height of Mount McKinley must have impressed the Indian. It was used as a landmark in his journeys. With its twin peak, Mount Foraker, it is interwoven in the folklore of the tribes living within sight of the two giant mountains. The tribes on the east side of the range, who seldom, if ever, approached it, termed it Traleyka, probably signifying big mountain. Those on the north-west side, who hunted the caribou up to the very base of the mountain, called it Tennally.*

Captain James Cook, who discovered the great inlet that now bears his name, did not catch a glimpse of the Alaskan Range as the mountains that rise so majestically above the water on a clear day were obscured by fog. The honour of the first mention of the range belongs to George Vancouver, one of Captain Cook's officers. He caught sight of the range from Knick arm at the head of Cook Inlet and in speaking of it says:

*The shores we had passed were compact; two or three small streams of fresh water flowed into the branch between low, steep banks, above these the surface was nearly flat and formed a sort of plain on which there was no snow and but very few trees. This plain stretched to the foot of a connected body of mountains, which, excepting between the west and north-west, were not very remote; and even in that quarter the country might be considered moderately elevated, bounded by distant stupendous mountains covered with snow and apparently detached from each other; though possibly they might be connected by land of insufficient height to intercept our horizon.*

In speaking of this description, Brooks says that:

*Even Vancouver failed to mention specifically the two high peaks which tower above the range, though the description "distant stupendous mountains covered with snow, and apparently detached from each other" undoubtedly refers to Mount McKinley and Mount Foraker.*

In 1834, a Russian mate by the name of Malakoff ascended the Susitna River, but it is improbable that he reached the forks as he made no mention of the Alaskan Range.

Possibly the story handed down by the Susitna Indians concerning the Russian who died on the Yentna may have reference to one of Malakoff's men, for he was the only Russian who made an attempt to explore the Mount McKinley region.

That the Russians knew of the Alaskan Range there is no doubt, as Brooks says, "Grewingk, who summarised the geography of Alaska in 1852, indicates on his map the axis of such a range, to which he gave the name of Tchigmit Mountains."

Dall named the Alaskan Range. He was one of the engineers appointed to find a route for a telegraph line; he did not come close to the range, but saw it from a distance.

In speaking of the first mention of the big mountain by Americans, Brooks tells us that:

> *In the fall of 1878, Harper and Mayo ascended the Tanana a distance estimated at 250 to 300 miles, which would bring them to the present town of Fairbanks. This was the first exploration of the Tanana by white men. They reported the finding of alluvial gold in the bars of the river and also that there was a high snow-covered mountain plainly visible to the south; this, of course, was Mount McKinley.*

Later on Brooks says:

> *In 1889, an Alaska pioneer, Frank Densmore, with several others, crossed by one of the portages from the lower Tanana to the Kuskoquim.*
>
> *About the same time another prospector, Al. King, made the same trip. Densmore must have had a glorious view of Mount McKinley. Apparently it was his description of it which led the Yukon pioneers to name it Densmore's Mountain, and as such it was known on the Yukon long before any one realised its altitude.*

In 1885, Lieutenant (now Major) Henry T. Allen crossed from Copper River to the Yukon, and in his story he says: "The range south of the middle part of the Tanana contains some very high snow-clad peaks."

Although the mountain was known among the pioneers along the Yukon, no news of it had as yet reached the outside world. W.A. Dickey, a young Princeton graduate, was destined to wake the mountain from its long sleep, and give it the prominence it deserved.

In 1896, with one companion, he "tracked" a boat up the Susitna River. He and Monks, his partner, were prospecting for gold, and in the course of time they reached a point where from some bare hills they got an open view of the Alaskan Range with Mount McKinley towering above it. With remarkable accuracy he estimated its height at 20,000 feet, and on his return to civilisation he wrote a newspaper article describing the location and grandeur of the great peak, which he called Mount McKinley.

A few years ago I asked Mr. Dickey why he named the mountain McKinley, and he answered that while they were in the wilderness he and his partner fell in with two prospectors who were rabid champions of free silver, and that after listening to their arguments for many weary days, he retaliated by naming the mountain after the champion of the gold standard.

MOUNT MCKINLEY (VIEW FROM THE SOUTH-EAST)

*The south-western ridge where we attained our highest altitude is shown on the left.*

After its rediscovery Mount McKinley again faded back into oblivion, for while it was known to a few prospectors who had pushed their way into the wilderness, no man had as yet reached its base.

In 1898, many additions were made to the knowledge concerning the Alaskan Range and Mount McKinley. Geo. H. Eldridge and Robert Muldrow led an expedition up the Susitna. Muldrow, the topographer, made a rough triangulation of the mountain that verified Dickey's estimate.

J. E. Spurr and W. S. Post of the Geological Survey ascended the Skwentna, a western fork of the Susitna, crossed the Alaskan Range, and eventually, after many adventures, reached Bering Sea.

The War Department despatched Captain (now Lieutenant-Colonel) F. W. Glenn to Cook Inlet to explore a route to the interior. His party reached the Tanana and retraced their steps via the Matanuska and Delta rivers.

In the same year a party led by W. J. Peters, to which Brooks was attached as geologist, was traversing the Tanana River on the north. In summing up the year's work Brooks says:

> *These surveys of 1898 had circumscribed an area of about 50,000 square miles which was still unexplored. Within it lay Mount McKinley, the highest peak on the continent, as the general public, hitherto sceptical as to its reported altitude, was beginning to realise.*

In looking backward over the history of the big mountain, it seems strange and unfortunate that the name of McKinley should have been attached to it. Any of the Indian names, or the Russian name of Bulshaia, would have been far more appropriate historically as well as sentimentally, while if any proper name was used it should have been named after Densmore, the old pioneer whose vivid word pictures of the mountain's grandeur made it known to the old-time prospectors along the Yukon.

And so five years went past before Brooks and Reaburn made their famous pack-train trip from salt water to the Yukon. Starting from Cook Inlet they broke through the Alaskan Range by a pass on the headwaters of the Kichatna River, and following the northern slope of the Alaskan Range they mapped the country as they advanced. Their route allowed them to take horses directly under the towering ice slopes on Mount McKinley's northern side and their triangulations placed the mountain's height at 20,300 feet.

The data collected by Brooks and Reaburn formed the first accurate report ever made of the Mount McKinley region, and as the mountain became better known men began to stir to the challenge of its virgin summit.

The first of these was Judge James Wickersham. Nothing to my knowledge has been written concerning his expedition. He started from the mining camp of Fairbanks on the Tanana River and used pack-horses to transport his supplies. The party was not prepared in any way for alpine work of so severe a nature, but an attempt was made to scale the mountain in the vicinity of the most westerly of the glaciers flowing north from Mount McKinley, which they named Hannah Glacier.

The second expedition to attempt the conquest of Mount McKinley was led by Dr. F. A. Cook, in 1903. Following the route blazed by Brooks and Reaburn, his party made an attempt on the peak in the vicinity of Hannah Glacier. The attempt ended in failure and the party retreated towards the Tanana and finally forced their way through a low pass, well to the eastward of the mountain. On reaching the southern side of the range they abandoned their horses, and by the aid of rafts eventually reached their starting-point on Cook Inlet.

While the men of this party accomplished a fine feat of wilderness travel, the results of their labours did not add materially to the knowledge of Mount McKinley, for the party was in no way prepared for the alpine side of their venture.

This was the history of the mountain and the attempts made upon it at the time that Professor Parker and I began to plan our first effort to climb it. As I will make clear later, the mountain was so difficult to reach at that time, that, in the light of later knowledge, the earlier attempts to climb it were relegated to the plane of reconnaissance trips, as no promising route to the summit had been discovered. At the time of our first expedition, therefore, the problem of *reaching* the mountain offered as many difficulties as *climbing* the mountain, and it was this perplexing problem that we determined to solve.

CHAPTER II

# The 1906 Expedition

*The first motor-boat—Assembling the pack-train of Indian cayuses—The trip to Cook Inlet—Brief history of Cook Inlet—The trip to the head of Cook Inlet—Unloading the horses—Horses attacked and scattered by Indian dogs who took them for moose—Hunting the lost horses—The pack-train starts inland on its long journey to the head of the Yentna—The motor-boat starts up the Susitna River—Porter and I climb Mount Susitna—Starvation on returning to river—The party joins us—Adventures in the rapids of the Susitna—Catching fish with our hands—Arrival at Susitna Station.*

It was on the 17th of May, 1906, that Professor Parker and I started on our first attempt to climb Mount McKinley.

Professor Parker had joined forces with Dr. F. A. Cook in New York City. Dr. Cook at that time was already well known from his trips to the Arctic and Antarctic regions. As he had also made a trip to Mount McKinley we followed his advice in everything pertaining to our coming adventures and allowed him to choose the line of attack.

At this time the pack-horse was the only method of transportation that had been used in reaching the mountain, and we therefore secured a pack-train of twenty carefully chosen horses from the celebrated stock-ranges east of the Cascade Mountains in the State of Washington. The horses were all of the Western type, and they were all chosen for their strength and endurance. In addition, however, we were equipped with a shoal-draft motor-boat for use on the glacier rivers. On our way to Alaska, the horses were housed in specially constructed stalls on the forward deck

THE 1906 EXPEDITION SWIMMING THE PACK-TRAIN ACROSS THE YENTNA RIVER (FROM A DRAWING BY BELMORE BROWNE)

of the steamer, and the motor-boat was also placed on deck where we could finish some of the necessary carpentering details.

We were a party of seven men. Dr. Cook and Professor Parker were the organisers of the expedition. Cook had raised a good sum of money from a well-known Eastern sportsman, who was to join us in the autumn for a hunt for big game. Professor Parker advanced a substantial sum to defray the original expenses and at a later date he again advanced a substantial sum. The expedition therefore was really financed by Professor Parker and the Eastern sportsman, who, as it turned out later, was unable to join us.

As a "packer," or "Cargodor," we had Fred Printz, the veteran of Brooks's 1902, and Dr. Cook's 1903 expeditions. He was a small active man, as hard as nails, and probably as good a wilderness pack-train man as ever threw a diamond hitch. As a helper he had brought Edward Barrill, who was as tall as Printz was short, and who was also an excellent packer. Walter Miller was our photographer. He had been with Dr. Cook in 1903, and had had much experience in taking photographs in the open. All the topographical work was done by Russell W. Porter, who had been the topographer for the Baldwin-Zeigler Expedition. I joined the expedition as a freelance through Professor Parker's invitation. As our steamer ploughed northward we spent the days in doing the countless little things that are necessary in getting a large outfit into shape for entering the wilderness. As most of our work was on deck we could enjoy the magnificent mountain and glacier views through which we steamed and we looked forward eagerly to the day when our struggle with the wilderness would commence.

Finally after many days of steaming we reached Seldovia, a little village at the mouth of Katchimac Bay on Cook Inlet. Here we left the big steamer and boarded a smaller vessel. Our horses were reloaded and our launch was lowered into the water and towed up the Inlet.

A trip of about seventy miles brought us to Tyonik, a settlement of five or six houses, and the point where our labours were to commence.

The first difficulty was in getting our horses ashore. Their Indian blood made them difficult to handle, and as we had to lash them into slings and drop them overboard, we had an exciting time.

Once in the water the horses were left to look out for themselves, but at this point a totally unexpected interference occurred. A large pack of Indian dogs came down to the beach and attacked the horses as they landed. The dogs had never seen horses and thought evidently that they were a queer new species of moose or caribou. In the meantime we were all busy and when we eventually got all our duffel ashore and the tents pitched it was too late to round up our horses. The result was that some of them got so far away that we were unable to catch them all, as the large marshes covered here and there with dense brush made finding them a hopeless task.

Dr. Cook's plan was to divide the party into two units, a horse- and a launch-party. The horses were to go overland to the headwaters of the Yentna River, where they were to meet the launch-party, when an advance in force would be made on that unexplored portion of the Alaskan Range in the hope of finding a pass that would lead us to the northern side of the range.

In view of Dr. Cook's having already failed on the northern approach of the mountain I am to this day unable to understand why he was willing to risk the finding of an unknown pass when there was a good pass on the head of the Kichatna River on the line of march that the pack-train were to follow. The result of this plan placed the finding of a pass in a place of the first importance, whereas the climbing of Mount McKinley was our one reason for undertaking the journey. Had the exploration side of finding a new pass been worth the risk we would have improved our chances greatly by sending the horses through the Kichatna pass and attempting the new pass on foot, for, as any one knows, a man can go where a pack-train cannot, and in view of later knowledge I know that a small party of strong packers could have crossed the range at the head of the Yentna.

We, however, accepted the Doctor's plans without question, and while the horses were being rounded-up Russell Porter and I began the topographical work by making a trip to Mount Susitna.

To reach the mountain we proceeded up the Susitna River a distance of about ten miles to an old Indian village called Alexander. The Susitna Valley is broad and flat and the delta of the river runs through a wilderness of marsh and mud flats in countless channels and "slews." Mount Susitna is a granitic boss rising about 4000 feet above the level valley and its isolated position makes it one of the most important landmarks of the region.

After putting us ashore at Alexander the launch returned to Tyonik to secure our outfit and start the pack-train on its long journey. The launch-party were to return to Alexander and pick us up in two days. As the launch turned downstream we waved good-bye and shouldering our packs began the ten-mile tramp to Mount Susitna. We found an old Indian trail that led us through beautiful deep woods broken now and then by beaver meadows. On one of the old beaver dams I found an otter trap that had been left set by some Indian—this is a common habit with them—and a little bird had stepped on the pan and had been caught between the steel jaws.

After a long tramp we came to the base of the mountain and pitched our camp in a beautiful little cañon below a waterfall. After a frugal meal I left Porter in camp and climbed up to the last scree slope below the crest of the mountain. After lighting my pipe I found a soft seat and gave myself over to the enjoyment of the beautiful view. It was my first climb of the year and with it came the wonderful feeling of exhilaration that sweeps over you when you stand alone on a mountainside after months spent in civilisation. The delta of the Susitna was spread out below me like a huge map and as I looked through the fast dimming light I thought that I could see a boat beyond the marshes on the waters of the Inlet.

It turned out later that it was our launch that had been caught on the tide flats, and when the tide came in again it was accompanied by a heavy sea and our companions had an unpleasant time of it before they won back to Tyonik. As we were to climb the mountain next day I did not go on, but returned to camp in the dusk and joined Porter in front of a cheery camp-fire.

The following day dawned dark and grey; Mount Susitna was hidden in a dense mass of mist and as we expected the launch we returned to Alexander. The launch had not returned and we spent our time wandering about the deserted village.

Susitna Indian boy in Susitna birch-bark canoe

Our provisions were about gone and when we awoke to another day we began to bestir ourselves in the hunt for food. Three foodless Susitna natives glided past in their tiny birch-bark canoes on their way to a moose range on the headwaters of the Alexander River. We spent the day in drawing and Porter made some triangulations of Mount Susitna. Robins were singing everywhere and the air had a cool clean smell of mountains and evergreens. In almost all the northern rivers there is a small fish that runs at certain seasons on their way to the spawning beds. They are called hooligans by the Alaskans, and they average about six inches in length. The hooligan run was beginning at this time, but as we were separated from the main river by a back water we could not reach the main school of fish and had to satisfy ourselves with the fish that had died. We found that by splitting the stranded fish and eating only the upper side which had been cured by the sun and air, they tasted very good. We also found some oats in an Indian cabin and after roasting them we were able to extract a kind of brown water which Porter optimistically called coffee. In our hunt for fish we were joined by a starving Indian dog. He had been abandoned by his Indian owner and was pitifully weak from lack of food. In his suffering he reverted to the wild state; treating us with the greatest suspicion, and giving vent three times a day, morning, noon, and night, to the long wolf howl. Finally, after we too had reverted to wolves—in appetites at least—we heard the welcome exhaust of a motor and our launch shot into the river. There was quite a party aboard as in addition to Professor Parker, Dr. Cook, and Miller our expedition had been augmented by two new volunteers, Captain Armstrong, and Russell Ball, who were anxious to prospect on the headwaters of the Yentna.

Our plunge into the wild life had already resulted in some interesting adventures. The boat party had completed the work to be done at Tyonik, and I will set down the account of what happened, in Dr. Cook's own words:

> *Porter desired to climb Mt. Susitna and Browne volunteered to join the venture. They desired to go light as the launch was expected back in two days, and therefore little food was taken with them when they left us at Alexander, a deserted Indian village. Since we had been much delayed we hastened downstream to catch the tide by the westerly channel. The boat now ran splendidly, but as we neared the tidewater through the delta we noticed that the tide was*

*already going out fast, but kept on, our pilot saying it was all right. Passing out of the river and heading past an island upon which a barrel was placed we found the water rather deep, six to eight feet. With the brown water boiling behind us we went along in great glee, but soon after real dangers were at hand. The water shallowed, a heavy sea rolled under the bow, the engine stopped, the boat pounded lightly, we were aground, and the tide was fast going out. In less than half an hour there were fifty square miles of muddy flats about in place of the chocolate-coloured water. There was no shore-line within five miles of us, nor was there wood or water. We tried the surface water before it left us, and found it drinkable, though salty and thick with mud. We took the precaution to dip up a pail of this before it left us. We drank this water and ate some crackers, then threw out an anchor and without blankets we spread life-preservers on the floor and tried to sleep until such time when the tide might return and lift us off.*

*The night proved dark and the clouds came out of Turnagain Arm with a speed which indicated a blow. We slept little but listened to the roar of the great waves as they neared us. At about twelve o'clock midnight, the boat was afloat, and soon after we put on power and headed the swell and the wind. The seas rose and the winds increased and whitecaps formed on every side. I suggested to our pilot that we make for Fire Island, but Stephan said, "I think all right, river good," from which we understood that he thought a course back into the river and later for Tyonik was all right but that he preferred to return to the river. We didn't like the idea of heading for ten miles of mud-flats in the darkness, with a howling gale behind us. So I said, "River no good—Tyonik good." He replied with a grunt and some Indian mutterings which I took to be swear words for the tone in which the utterances came was not indicative of good humour. But for Tyonik we headed. The seas now began to break over the bow, and the wind carried the spray into Stephen's face with an ugly force. With each rush of water the boy would grunt and let drop an ugly Indian word. After about a half-hour at the wheel Stephen said, "Me plenty sick," and Miller and I might have said "Me too" but we did not confess. We had been nursing the engine, for either the pump or the carbureter was balking frequently. The boat had no ballast and under the violent pitching of the sea we were only able to crawl around in the dark, not daring to light a lantern because we detected gasoline vapours. Miller took the wheel to relieve Stephen and he too got soaked from head to foot in the first few minutes.*

*By two o'clock there was a little burst of light in the east and now we figured we were far enough away from the dangerous shallows to set a course for Tyonik. The altered course brought the seas to our fore quarter but we could not use full power because the boat would hit the seas dangerously hard. Thus we took the seas as easily as possible while the tide carried us southward. By daybreak, about 3:30, we pushed behind the spit at Tyonik, dropped anchor, and blew our fog-horn for a boat to take us off. We were hungry, exhausted, and cold, but Prof. Parker had the cook prepare a meal for us before we got ashore, and food never tasted better.*

*The six horses which had stampeded were still at large, no trace having been found of them.*

*To make the search more thorough we decided to run the launch fifty or sixty miles south on the next tide and land wherever we could to trail the horses. Ball was sent in saddle along the sandy shore-line, while Printz and Barrill joined me on the launch. As the people of the town were starting their fires we were again on the rough waters. The weather was improving, but Turnagain Arm still had a steel-coloured lustre in its clouds, and vapour plunged into the Inlet, which did not promise good weather; but we were so eager to start the pack train on its long trail overland that we could not afford to wait. We passed in among the big boulders of Trading Bay and noted the dangers at low water. Here the beach is wide and the steep sandy bank, three hundred feet high, leads to a plain covered by spruce, birch, and cottonwood trees. In this bank in various places we saw thin strata of lignite, a coal in which the fibre and bark of trees are easily made out, but it seems to burn well and is said to be good steaming coal.*

*The first twenty-five miles of this beach had been searched as we hastened on to Redoubt Bay. Then far out in the mud-flats we saw some tracks but after a long search we decided that if the horses were to be found we must seek grassy lowlands near the point which separates the two bays. Here we met Ball, whose luck was like ours. He had secured no definite trace of the horses. We built a camp-fire and ate lunch, allowed the tide to go out, leaving the launch on the tide-flats. Our camp-fire was spread by a sudden gale into a forest fire close to which we tried to keep warm, but the combination of smoke and wind drove us into the boat for shelter. After the wind subsided we began another search for the horses, but could find no further trace except the tracks which had been followed up to the outer tide-flats. Late that night as the tide was about half in we abandoned the horse chase and started for Tyonik. The wind came in gusts and the sea came up in dangerous hills. The night was not dark but the light was of such a quality that we could never he sure of our bearings. The launch laboured heavily in the tumbling seas and we were quickly exhausted, for we had been three days and three nights without proper rest or sleep, and food had been only taken as the conditions had permitted. Upper Cook Inlet has no harbours and seeing that the sea was too rough to make Tyonik and get ashore, we ran under a point of land below Tyonik, dropped anchor, and rode out the storm. The sea had broken over the boat so much that the floor and about everything on board was wet, but we spread the life-preservers out and on these we slumbered for about two hours. With the change of the tide the sea eased, the wind ceased, and a warm sun made the icy volcanoes glitter at 6 o'clock. On the morning of June 2d we tipped the anchor, headed the tide, and by eight o'clock we were again at Tyonik.*

*The programme for our campaign, as it had been formulated to the present, was to explore the headwaters of the Yentna River first, and from there we expected to get either by the westerly or an easterly route to the southwest arête of Mt. McKinley. From what we had seen of this area from Mt. Yenlo we had many reasons to suppose that there was an easy pass from the Yentna to the Tonzona. Our efforts were accordingly directed toward the big break in the Alaska Range forming the Yentna valley. The horses were to go with light packs cross-country to a point at the head of navigation, while the boat with most of our equipment was to go up the Yentna as far as possible.*

*We decided to spend the day in loading the launch for her second trip up the river and also to help the packers prepare the pack outfit for its great tramp through brush and forest, over marsh and glacial stream.*

*At about noon June 3d, Printz, Barrill, and Beecher mounted their horses and we turned the others loose. The train of fourteen horses bounded northward at a rapid pace, only a few of them carrying packs consisting of supplies for thirty days and a folding canvas boat for crossing streams. All the other things were to be carried by the launch to the headwaters of the Yentna. It was expected the two horses that had been chased northward would be found along this trail.*

*As the horses galloped up the beach toward the Beluga River the launch was started in the same direction. The sky was somewhat hazy, but the sea was as smooth as a glacial lake, with a glimmering silvery surface. The quiet town of Tyonik with its busy prospectors was soon left behind. The pack train moving at a good pace was seen for some time edging along the great high banks. The boat cut the water at an astonishing speed and in less than two hours we entered the mouth of the Susitna, a distance of thirty miles, and in another hour we were at Alexander anxiously looking for Porter and Browne who had been awaiting us with empty stomachs and eager eyes.*

Our preparations were now complete. The pack-train with light packs had begun their overland journey, and our launch heavily loaded with supplies began to "buck" the swift waters of the Susitna. As soon as we reached the boat Porter and I went for the food lockers and after a good meal I hunted out a soft spot on the dunnage bags astern and fell asleep. I was awakened from my nap by a cold, wiggling, squirming sensation, and as I sprang to my feet I heard roars of laughter and found that I was covered with hooligans. While ploughing up the river the launch had run into a dense mass of these fish and all on board had begun to throw them into the boat with their hands. The fish were in such enormous numbers that we soon had several hundred. About thirty miles from the mouth of the Susitna we came to Susitna Station, and the bank was lined with prospectors and Indians as we came in front of the town. Our boat caused much interest as we had made the fastest trip on record between Tyonik and Susitna Station, and there was much talk as to whether we could buck the swift current of the upper river. We had sprung our propeller on a snag coming up the river and after two trips overboard I returned cold but successful and our new propeller gave us no more trouble.

There were many Indians about, and scaffolds lined the banks weighted down with long fringes of dried hooligans. The Susitna birch-bark canoes were everywhere, flitting light as leaves through the swift water. We saw quantities of prospectors heading for the great unknown interior, and dreaming of creeks with golden sands. Stories of gold filled their conversation—of men made rich in a day, but the gold was always "behind the ranges" on "some other river"; if they were there they would be satisfied.

INDIAN CACHE AT SUSITNA STATION

## CHAPTER III

# The Journey Up the Yentna River

~

***Difficulties of navigation—Youngstown—The head of navigation—Our reconnaissance party advances up the Yentna Valley—Dangers of fording glacier streams—We reach the mountains—Discovery of what appears to be a possible pass—Our food gives out—Hardships of our return to base camp—Building trail for the pack-train—Porter's escape from a bear—The arrival of the horses—Loss of four horses in a burning coal-vein.***

One hundred yards above the Station you meet a savage eddy where the combined waters of the Susitna and Yentna foam around a high bluff.

As we started our engine the following morning the Station's population gathered below the bluff to see how our boat would behave in the white water. I kept well inshore to get the benefit of the eddy but our engine did not seem to drive us with its usual vigour, and when we struck the white wall of water that roared around the point the current threw us back and we rounded up ignominiously at our old anchorage. Something was wrong, and after a search we found that the propeller tunnel was choked with snags. After the engine was reversed everything was clear and we ploughed strongly upstream past our dubious audience. This time I eased her head very slowly and when we hit the white water it came boiling over our bows, but after the shock we moved steadily along and followed by hearty cheers from the bank headed for the mouth of the Yentna.

As we pushed our way up the Yentna our difficulties and enjoyment increased. The great snow-fields of the Alaskan Range began to show to the westward. When one is travelling in the lowlands life in time becomes monotonous. The swamps and sluggish "slews" shut you in, fringes of ragged spruce form the horizon, and the low songs of rushing rivers serve only to accentuate the silence. These first glimpses of snow and ice called to us as a well-watered land would call to one who has travelled in a desert.

The Yentna is a typical Alaskan river—turbid, swift, snow-fed, and full of treacherous sand-bars that are formed by the accumulation of silt from the glaciers. The meaning of the word Susitna is "the river of sand" and in this respect the Yentna resembles it. The navigation was getting to be a problem due to the swiftness of the water and the numerous sand-bars. It was necessary to keep a man sounding with a pole, and even then we often struck submerged bars or snags. At night we camped on exposed islands as the mosquitoes were beginning to be troublesome. There was little sign of big game; we would see now and then where a moose or bear had wallowed through the soft mud, and at night we sometimes heard the soft bugle-calls of wild swans—but that was all.

On the lower Yentna we met a few prospectors "tracking" their river boats against the pitiless current and once a boatload of bronzed "sour-doughs" drifted past us headed for the "outside" and the delights of civilisation. These men will undergo any hardship to reach a country where gold is reported. Once let the whisper of yellow sands drift through the forest to their eager ears and everything is forgotten but the wild joy of "hitting the trail" and the frenzy of the stampede. "If there was any gold on McKinley," one of these prospectors said to me, "you'd find a camp there damn quick!"

At Susitna Station we had heard reports of a mining camp called Youngstown away up on the South Fork of the Yentna and as we passed these occasional boatloads of prospectors we always hailed them with the cry of "Where's Youngstown?" and they would always answer, "Away up on the South Fork." At last when we were well up towards the forks we saw a lone prospector drifting downstream and as we hailed him with the familiar question he called back, "Youngstown is here in the boat with me—I'm takin' the burg downstream!" He was the last man to leave the camp and having by himself formed its entire population he naturally thought that he represented the whole camp.

During all our twistings and turnings Porter had mapped the river from his lookout station on the stern deck. By this time we had passed the South Fork and we were now forging slowly up the North Fork. At last the day came when our little boat could go no farther. On a point near by was wood in plenty for "cache" and fire, so we made camp and called it "the head of navigation." During the last mile of travel we had great difficulty in making progress and we were driven to all sorts of strange expedients for ascending the swift water. In one particularly swift rapid, Miller and I carried an anchor upstream and stood on it in the ice-cold water while our companions helped the engine by hauling in on the capstan.

After making camp we busied ourselves in getting ready for our future work. Our launch, which we had christened the *Bulshaia* after the Russian name for Mount McKinley, was drawn in to the bank behind a protecting sand-bar; caches were erected; Porter measured a base line and took angles on Mount Kliskon and Yenlo; and everything was done to make the camp comfortable.

The pack-train was, in the meantime, working slowly across the benches of the Alaskan Range and would not arrive for many days. We could follow the valley of the Yentna with our eyes as it wound away between grim snow-covered mountains, and it was now our duty to explore this valley for a possible pass to the Kuskoquim, before the arrival of our cayuses.

After a council we decided to push on immediately. The Doctor, Porter, Captain Armstrong, and I started on this trip, leaving Professor Parker and Ball at our base camp. On the first stage of the journey we tracked our supplies in a canvas boat, but one day's work in the swift water convinced us that our boat could not stand the hard usage, so we camped and again divided our party. We left Captain Armstrong and Miller in this camp, and Dr. Cook, Porter, and I shouldered our packs and pushed on into the unknown. We took food for three days in pemmican, erbswurst, tea, beans, and bacon. Besides the food and sleeping-bags we carried a tent, and Porter's topographical instruments. I carried a 30:40 carbine.

Shortly after leaving our base camp we caught our first glimpse of Mount McKinley—a great majestic dome, rolling up cloud-like from the Alaskan Range; then the mountains shut us in and we settled down to work.

Before us stretched a great glacier valley; four miles broad; flat as a floor; and swept bare to rock and sand by the fury of the spring overflows. At intervals great snake-like glaciers swept back among the rugged mountains. The rushing river was broken into dozens of snarling streams, that were always deep and swift enough to be troublesome. At times the rivers ran from one side of the valley to the other and we had either to climb the mountainsides or ford the swift water. The hillsides were covered with dense alder thickets, and with packs on our backs, we made slow headway. Once we chopped our way for three hours through the thickets, and at the end we had scarcely a mile to show for our toil. Usually we held to the middle of the valley and forded as best we could. When we found streams that were unfordable we had to follow them until a ford was found. The water was mostly glacial; at noon the streams rose swiftly from the melting of the snow and ice under the warm spring sun, and we were often forced to wait until midnight and ford when the water was less dangerous.

At that time of the year it was never dark and we travelled at all hours. After a day's travel we met two prospectors. On seeing the moving spots through the heat waves that danced above the level gravel bars I thought they were wild animals of some kind, and moved to intercept them. When I approached, I saw that the men were in a small shoal-draft river boat, headed downstream. The roar and rattle of a glacier river separated us, but I could hear them yell: "The glacier streams are runnin' on edge up above—yuh can't cross 'em." I yelled back that we had already forded the west branch, and that we were going on. They watched us dubiously as we started off, and did not answer the "So long" that we shouted across the water. These wilderness meetings stimulate the imagination, and the memory of them stays with you for years; for an instant two human beings meet; wondering at the unseen forces that have brought them together they converse intimately of their hopes and fears, and then without any reason they part, never to meet again. I have often thought of these two men, and of why they warned us to turn back.

When we travelled at night the mountains took on an added grandeur and solemnity. Through the heat waves of midday they hung like mirages in the sky and the glare of the sun on the snow- and water-washed rocks was blinding. Our camps scarcely deserved the dignity of the name: a small tent; a wisp of smoke from a brush fire surrounded by steaming, ragged clothes; some black pots, and three sun- and smoke-browned men hugging the fire—that was all. At a short distance we were nothing but an indistinct blur in the shadow of the mountains. A few chips and blunt axe marks on fallen trees is the only impression that we made on the valley of the Yentna.

Our real excitement came when the valley narrowed up. We found the rivers growing swifter day by day; the gravel was giving way to large boulders, and we were forced more often to the rugged mountainsides.

By this time we had all had narrow escapes while crossing the streams. A man with a heavy pack is helpless when he loses his footing in bad water and is "rolled." He is lucky if he reaches the bank with no worse hurt than torn and bleeding hands, and a bruised body. The Doctor and Porter used Alpine Rhuksacks—a poor contrivance for wilderness packing. They do not hold enough, hang badly when full, are unsteady, and are dangerous in swift water as they can not be loosened quickly. I used a home-made adaptation of the "Russian Aleute" strap, to my mind the easiest and safest strap in the world. We were wet to the skin constantly, and dried our clothes at night, sitting more or less naked about the fire during the process. The wilderness too had set its brand on us; we were as dark as Indians except where the mosquito bites had blotched our faces with red, and our hands were hard and swollen from contact with rocks and devil's-club. We were a rough-looking crew. One day I reached an island in the centre of a river that had held us all night. The further channel looked unfordable, and as the Doctor and Porter were far away I tried to get back. But I had waded downstream to the island and found that I could not return against the current. To make matters worse the hot sun was striking the snow-fields and the roar of the water was growing steadily louder. I then made a determined effort to reach the bank but the water swept me from my feet and I was rolled. My hands were cut open by the rocks and my pack nearly choked me, but I could not afford to let it go and held on until I reached my island again. I then attracted the attention of the Doctor and Porter with a rifle shot as we had enough rope to get my pack ashore and I could then swim the channel.

As they were coming toward me I decided to try the further channel, and after a most exciting ford I gained the further bank. After my companions had joined me we headed across the valley—we had had about all the fording we could stand.

Luckily we had reached the point where we could take to the hills for we were opposite a large glacier that headed near Mount Dall and beyond we could see our Mecca—the cañon of the Yentna. On it depended all our hopes; if we could get horses through or around it, our route to McKinley was assured. The indications of a pass were favorable. The mountains seemed to fall away to the westward and—best sign of all to a mountaineer—a long, low line of clouds drifted steadily southward through a gap in the range.

We were beginning to worry about our food. We were now three days out from our base, and the first half of our journey was still far ahead of us. We had only taken three or four days' rations, as we thought that we could get a glimpse of the pass from some high mountain. The windings of the valley made this impossible, so we took our belts in a hole or two and went on short rations.

We climbed the mountains west of the cañon. As the range was fairly smooth we travelled above brush line, and followed on parallel to the course of the valley. The scenery was of great grandeur and beauty. Far below us spread the Yentna Valley with its savage streams wandering like silver ribbons across its brown floor.

Ahead the cañon ran like a jagged gash across a cup-shaped basin, and we noticed with misgiving that most of the water came from the cañon.

Beyond the valley a large glacier wound around a grand delta-formed peak, and to the westward lay the tangled mass of mountains that we wanted to cross. They had a more cheerful atmosphere than the silent valley. Hoary marmots whistled at us from their sheltered homes in the rock slides. Bear sign was fairly plentiful, and ptarmigan feathers lay among the willows. We had hopes of finding sheep, but we did not expect to find any until we reached the western side of the Alaskan Range.

We progressed very slowly; the sun was hot, our packs heavy, and the climbing was difficult. A shoulder of the mountain hid the view to the westward, and we panted on with the optimistic idea that once beyond the ridge we would see the Kuskoquim. Before long we encountered a deep gorge that barred our path, and we were forced to climb higher. Other obstructions came in their turn until we were no longer of the earth, but moving in that sphere where the valleys are a haze below you, and your only companions are the wind-swept rocks and snow-slides.

At last, at the foot of a cliff I found white mountain sheep hairs. It meant many things to me—the excitement of the chase, fresh meat, and the knowledge that we were within reach of the Kuskoquim. The snow-slides increased as we advanced, and on one of them, a wicked slope of snow that lay at a dizzy angle, the Doctor had an unpleasant experience.

Porter and I were above and crossed where the slope was not dangerous, but the Doctor was careless and crossed at a place where the soft snow sloped downward until it was lost in the valley haze. After starting he was afraid to turn back and we were unable to help him. By chance he was carrying a small axe and after a breathless period of step chopping he got across, a wiser and more experienced man. At the next shoulder we camped by a mossy pool below a snowbank, and after climbing the hill above us we could see the rounded sheep mountains of the

Kuskoquim! It was a wonderful feeling to stand there and look out over the unknown mass of mountains.

But even at that height the mosquitoes were troublesome, so with my rifle lashed to the plane-table tripod we pitched our little tent and rolled into our sleeping-bags.

Camps above timber-line are cold and cheerless. We had no fuel, and our food consisted of dry fruit and hardtack washed down with ice-cold water.

Early the next morning we were seated on a grassy shoulder where we could see the pass to better advantage. Porter did some topographical work and the Doctor and I made a moss fire, and studied the country below. As far as we could see the route looked possible for pack-train travel. Beyond us the cañon split. One fork flowed in a westerly direction toward the Tonzona River; the other fork headed between two large mountains, and offered a possible route for our horses. Between the forks stood a mountain of great beauty. It rose from dim mile-long sweeps of scree and sheep meadows, far below us, to a rugged pinnacled top that stood clear cut against the evening sky and scattered the clouds broadcast.

Since finding the sheep hairs I had been continuously on the lookout for moving white spots. When one realises that even to a well-fed man sheep meat is a delicacy, one can understand with what longing we searched the mountainsides.

By this time we had been on short rations for three days and all the food remaining consisted of a half-pound sausage of erbswurst, a handful of tea, and a quarter of a pound of bacon. Our fruit, bread, and sugar were gone, our work was still uncompleted, and we were four long days' travel from our base camp.

After talking things over we decided that we would climb down the mountainside and explore the cañon. There was no use in going farther but it was useless to go back without seeing whether or not the horses could follow the cañon bed. The descent to the cañon was the most difficult task that we encountered on the reconnaissance. We were weak from hunger, and the mountain fell off in numerous precipices, and was covered with dense jungles of twisted alders and devil's-club. We travelled mostly on our hands and knees, our packs catching in the brush and our hands and bodies swollen from bruises and devil's-club thorns.

We hoped to find good "going" in the bed of the cañon, but looking down from a great height is always deceiving. When we reached the bottom we found to our despair that the stream was dangerous and unfordable. So swift was the water that in a ford I attempted I could scarcely keep my feet in water that was only knee deep. We were famished and exhausted, so we built a fire of driftwood and cooked our precious erbswurst. The cañon was a dreary spot; the roaring of the water was deafening, and cold damp winds swept down from the snow-fields above. After our meal and rest we shouldered our packs, and the thought of our base camp, with food and companions, eased our climb from the gorge.

The retreat was a repetition of the first trip, but rendered more difficult by our lack of food. The lack of food did not seem to detract from our ability to travel but we were all more or less unsteady on our pins, and while we talked ceaselessly of food, I can say that I was less hungry on the last day than I was when our food first began to grow scarce. My greatest desire was to lie down in the sun and sleep. Our only disappointment was the lack of game, and over our fires at night we talked of the sheep steaks and "caribou butter" we would eat when we reached the Kuskoquim. One evening at dusk I jumped a bear, but the thick brush prevented a shot.

We reached our camp after eight days of travel and ran the swift current to the head of navigation. Great changes had taken place since our departure. A strong cache was completed, a trail marked "Wall Street" ran along the river, and over the main tent was the sign "Parker House."

Now the question before us was meeting the pack-train and getting the horses through the swamps and timber to the open sand-bars. We first dropped the *Bulshaia* downstream, to a sheltered "slew," and then started our trail to timber-line. It took us four days to complete the trail, and then we settled down to await the horses.

Trail chopping is always interesting, but it is hard work. Ours wound ever towards the mountains; now following an old moose trail, or the rut left in the wet grass by a passing grizzly; now we would make a detour to avoid destroying a song bird's nest, then slash our way through twisted alder thickets toward some big spruce, where the brush would be thinner.

As you rise you begin to catch glimpses of snow-fields above, and the rivers far below you. When the trail wound around a bald hill we would take a smoke, looking out over the silent lowlands, and say, as we wiped the sweat from our faces, "Three hours more and we'll be above the mosquitoes." But this was rank optimism for we never were. We finally camped on top of a snow-capped mountain, and the mosquitoes swarmed about us.

After the trail was finished Porter and I camped above timber line while he continued his topographical work, and in this lonely camp he had his first adventure with an Alaskan brown bear.

We had had a wet day's trail chopping through the willows when we pitched our tent on a mountainside above a deep valley. As I came out of the tent the next morning I saw a brown bear and a cub in the amphitheatre below me. Hastily pulling on my wet socks and drawers, I warned Porter and started down the mountainside. On reaching the bottom of the valley I could no longer see the bear, and after a careful stalk I heard a hail from Porter.

On reaching camp he told me that the bear had either winded or heard me and that she had run uphill through a little draw and had blundered into our camp. This second meeting with mankind had frightened her badly and Porter added that the cub seemed pretty tired by the time it reached the mountain top. After breakfast Porter climbed the mountain to take some angles, and I stayed in camp and dried out our wet duffel. After a while I heard a noise below me, and to my surprise Porter appeared climbing slowly uphill. He was tired out, scratched and torn from contact with brush and rocks, and as soon as he regained his wind he told me his story. On reaching the mountain top he had followed a narrow arête that joined the mountain to the main range. On this narrow ridge he had been charged by the bear, and it was probably due to the fact that he rushed instantly down the steep mountain that he did not lose his life. I picked up my gun and climbed at my best speed to the mountain top. On reaching the narrow arête I found the tracks in the snow where the bear had pursued Porter, and after leaving him she had returned to her cub and continued along the arête towards the upper snowfields. Before I had gone far a terrific storm swept across the Susitna Valley. The lowlands turned as black as night, and the wind shrieked and moaned among the cliffs. Great flashes of lightning followed by earth-shaking crashes of thunder shook the mountains and the air was full of the noise of falling rocks and avalanches. At times I had to cower among the rocks so strong was the wind and lashing rain. After a miserable night we returned to base camp, and the next day the pack-train arrived. Only eleven out of the fourteen animals had survived the hardships of the journey, and ill-luck had dogged their footsteps from the start. At the first camp out of Tyonik the horses had been turned out to graze; now the coast line at that point is seamed with veins of coal, one of which had in some mysterious way caught on fire, and into this hidden oven some of the horses blundered.

Printz told me later that strangely enough the horses made no effort to extricate themselves when they felt the burning embers, but crouched down, trembling. They were all rescued eventually, but only two out of the six animals that were burned were able to travel. The rest were relieved of their suffering along the trail.

CHAPTER IV

# The Attempt to Cross the Alaskan Range

*The advance up the Yentna Valley—Dangers of swimming loaded horses across the glacial rivers—Professor Parker's narrow escape—We reach the cañon of the Yentna. Exploration of the cañon—Dangers in the cañon—I kill a bear—Barrill and I see the Kuskoquim Sheep Mountains—Our retreat through the cañon—Our horses give out—Barrill spends a night in the cañon—Retreat to base camp.*

We lost no time in pushing forward. Captain Armstrong and Ball returned down the Yentna in the canvas boat, and we moved up the valley with our entire outfit.

The work of swimming loaded pack-horses across glacier rivers is the most dangerous form of exercise that I have ever indulged in. The horses served as pack-animals and ferry-boats. We were forced to swim the animals with their packs on, and we either sat behind the packs, or held on to the ropes while we were in the water.

Several times members of our party were in imminent danger of drowning. In some of the fords the horses swam eighty to one hundred yards, and this distance, in swift ice-water, is trying to man and beast, but the short fords in savage swimming water are more nerve trying, and the legs of the horses suffer from stumbling about among the sharp rocks. At times the river banks were steep and after a hard swim the horses would be unable to climb out, then, unless we "kept cool"—not an easy thing to do in glacier water—trouble would result. Professor Parker probably had the narrowest escape. He was crossing a swift chute of water above a rapid that lashed the base of a high bluff. The Doctor, Printz, and I had crossed safely, and the Professor was half-way across when his horse turned around and lost his footing.

Ed Barrill fording the east branch of the Kahiltna River

Luckily the current swept Professor Parker past a point and Barrill helped him ashore, but the horse disappeared from view in the rapids. We thought the animal was dead and as soon as we had pitched camp, Printz, Barrill, and I returned down stream to find the horse and recover the pack. We rode on horseback and to our great surprise we found the horse alive about a mile below our camp. His pack was intact, and my rifle which I had pushed under the cinch ropes was in working order. I was riding a powerful roan that Dr. Cook used in fording and as our lost horse was on an island I forced the roan into a rapid well above. This was a different thing from riding a heavily loaded horse, and the great roan took me down through the white water as if I weighed nothing—it was a thrilling ride. After landing on the island I put the pack on the roan and brought both horses to the mainland, and we returned joyfully to camp.

Our camps were picturesque in the extreme. They were usually situated on a bar of the glacial rivers. The camp-fires were built in the great piles of driftwood that the river brought down during the spring freshets. The men moved half naked, like savages, in the crimson glow, while above the haze of the valley the Alaskan Range stood clear cut against the evening sky.

After several days of hard, wet travel we reached the cañon that was the deciding factor in our crossing the range. We had overcome all the difficulties of summer exploration: swift water, trail chopping in heavy rains, camps without horse-feed, quicksands, swamps, and mosquitoes. We made camp near the mouth of the cañon and prepared for a mounted reconnaissance.

The following morning the Doctor, Printz, Barrill, and I mounted four of the strongest horses, and entered the cañon. We and the horses were stripped down for the struggle with the water. We rode mountain pack-saddles, as they are good to hold on to in rapids.

At the first ford in the cañon we realised the danger and difficulty of the undertaking. The water was swift and white and our horses shrank in fear from it. Our misgivings proved to be well founded, for not one of us was able to return to camp by way of the gorge.

Barrill led and after we had made six desperate swimming fords, the cañon split. The Doctor and Printz took the smaller or right-hand fork and Barrill and I followed the left. The right-hand stream swung to the east and carried "fresh water," showing that there was no glacier at the headwaters. Our stream carried the original dirty glacier torrent, which grew swifter as we advanced until it required all our courage to make us drive the horses into it. At the last of six cruel crossings we came to a glacier that completely dammed the cañon. It was of a deep bluish green colour and the river spouted upward from a great cavern in the face of the ice. Scattered about us were tons of granite that had fallen from the cliffs above, and now and then a crash heard above the thunder of the water would tell us of a new arrival.

We had realised long before that it would be impossible to take a pack-train through the gorge, but the interest of our explorations, added to a man's natural dislike for turning back, led us on. Barrill unlashed an axe from his saddle, and I carried my rifle. We left the horses securely tied, and chopped steps across the glacier. We found that the stream tunnelled under the ice, and above the cañon grew narrower and we were forced to climb the walls.

About two hundred yards above the bed of the gorge we found sheep sign, while ahead of us, as we climbed, we could see miles of sheep pasture, everlasting scree slopes, and a great ridge that shut off the view of the pass.

As we advanced we found more sheep sign than I have ever seen before or since, and the promise of game put strength into our tired, water-soaked legs.

Finally we reached a high knoll that overlooked the valley and we sat down to take in our wild surroundings. Suddenly as my eyes were roving over the valley I saw a large brown bear cross an opening in a thicket below us. Barrill was unarmed, but in the excitement of the moment he followed me downward. The bear was travelling steadily along the mountainside, and I waited for him on a steep slope. When he came into view his great, dark hulk stood out in strong relief against the blue haze of the valley. At the first shot he rose on his hind legs and a second shoulder shot sent him crashing down the mountainside. Below us was a little knoll which commanded the whole hillside. From this point of vantage I could see that bruin had rolled into a dense jungle of alders that grew in the wildest confusion among the great boulders of an old moraine.

I saw that when I reached the thickets I would not be able to see about me, so I asked Barrill to direct me from the hillside. The bear's trail showed plainly until I reached the masses of brush and rock, where it disappeared. Glacial erratics weighing many tons lay scattered all about, making it impossible either to move rapidly or see any distance; the grim wildness of the spot made it a fit background for a bear killing. At last I found arterial blood and following it through the dense brush came again to fault in the shadow of an upright shaft of granite. Not a sound broke the stillness, and knowing that the bear was hard hit, and close at hand, I decided that he was dead. I therefore called to Barrill and asked him if I was on the right track, and he answered that the bear ought to be close to the spot where I was lying. The brush made moving in an upright position an impossibility. I had just raised my rifle to crawl farther when I heard a slight noise, and turning quickly I saw a great brown head rising slowly through the brush about ten feet away. The bear did not utter a sound, and his small eyes gazed steadily into mine as I pushed my gun through the branches and fired. He rolled down the mountainside and when I reached him he was dead. Since then I have understood why so many accidents happen while tracking wounded bears, for while I was close enough to touch him with a fishing-rod, I was unable to see him among the tangle of rocks and branches.

Barrill soon joined me and while we were preparing to skin our prize we made an interesting discovery; the bear's chest and belly were a patchwork of ugly wounds. Some of the cuts had festered and despite our hunger we could not bring ourselves to eat the meat. As the beast was thin and weighed close to 700 pounds, the bear that inflicted the wounds must have been a powerful adversary.

After leaving the bear we climbed about one thousand feet and on reaching a high shoulder we could look down onto two passes that led to the Kuskoquim. Our cañon split again and between the forks rose a high rounded mountain. We lay for a few minutes looking sadly and yearningly towards that promised land, our "happy hunting ground," and then we slowly turned towards the back trail, for while we were through the worst part of the range, we knew that horses could not follow us. This is the only time as far as I know that men have crossed through the Alaskan Range between Mount McKinley and the passes at the head of the Kichatna.

We were filled with anxiety on nearing the cañon, for the sun had been melting the snow, and the deep, sullen roar from below told us that the stream was more dangerous than it had been in the morning. Our fears were realised when we reached the gorge. The stream below the glacier was now a seething ice-laden torrent, and it looked impassable.

We would have waited for the water to subside, but night was approaching, our poor horses had weakened perceptibly since morning, and we ourselves were tired and our food was gone—we had to go on. Barrill, who had undergone the strain of leading in the morning, asked me to lead now, and I did so gladly. Our poor horses were terrified, but it was pathetic to see the eagerness and bravery with which they undertook the cruel task. There was no wild scramble or panic with them—they knew the danger of the water, and they made the most savage fords slowly and cautiously.

My horse, "Ferry-boat," had carried Fred Printz and me across every ford that we made on the Yentna and I have never seen a horse who knew water better than he. He lacked strength, however, and it was a lesson to me when I saw the intelligence of the faithful old animal in these moments of danger.

In each ford a misstep would have cost us our lives, but the noble animals braced themselves against the ice and current with splendid courage and intelligence. On the gravel bars between the fords our horses left a trail of blood, but on they went never hesitating. I did not touch Ferry-boat's head during the entire trip, but his pointed ears were always turning towards me as I cheered him on.

We expected an easier time when we reached the main cañon, but to our horror it was a raging flood. Horses and men alike were weak and numb from cold, but in we went. As I was searching the further bank there was a splash behind me; Barrill's horse had fallen and he and his mount swept past me in a smother of foam. At times I could see nothing but the swirling water. Once I saw Barrill's hat on the

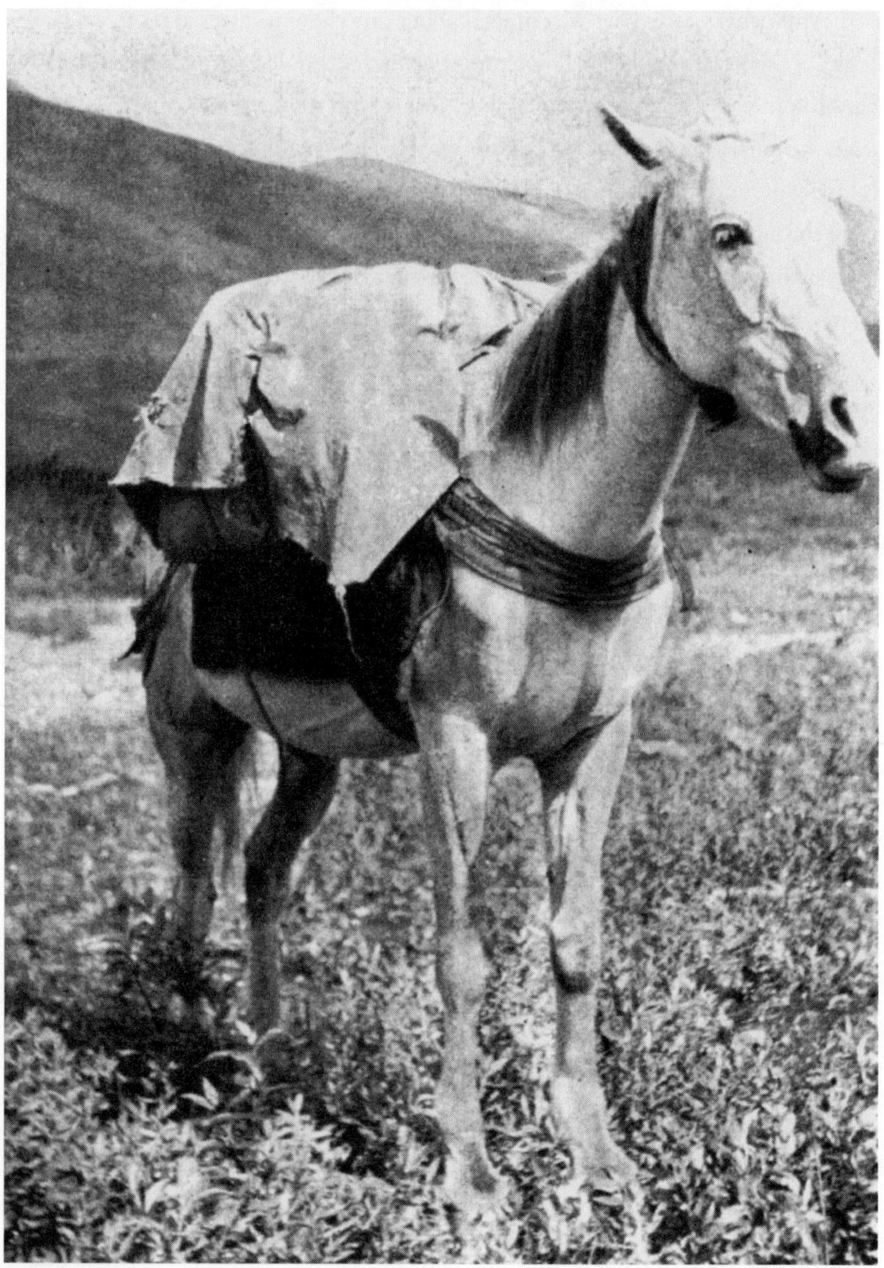

FERRY-BOAT

*This horse carried Fred Printz and the author in addition to his pack over most of the bad fords of the Yentna River. This photo was taken at a time when many of our horses were exhausted and unable to carry anything.*

crest of a roller, and then instantly his horse's hoofs appeared lashing the white water, and then down I went into the choking, freezing flood. At last after feeling blows and hearing the sound of rushing water in my ears I felt the convulsive heaving of Ferry-boat's body and I found myself on the rocks. I lay there some time and then raising my head I saw Barrill below me. There is something terrifying about savage glacier water, and it was getting dark, as well, and a freezing wind was sucking through the cañon. I remember that my pockets were full of ice dust from the river. The cold seemed to sap the life from us; our energy and courage were gone, and we urged our horses into the next ford in a kind of stupor.

We made three more fords, and then Barrill's horse pulled him from the water on the very edge of the black cliffs, and mine staggered ashore just above.

Our next attempt was the last; Barrill's horse collapsed after going into the river and wallowed ashore on the same bank, and I by leaving Ferry-boat's back and swimming landed safely on the opposite bank. Ferry-boat was done for and I started to lash him as he lay, but I couldn't do it, and eased him by taking off his saddle.

Barrill, wisely, refused to make another attempt. We could not talk as the thunder of the water drowned our voices, but as I knew that he had matches and firewood I waved good-bye to him and began to climb the cañon walls. As I climbed, Ferry-boat tried to follow me, and as I gained the crest I could see him standing by the river watching me wistfully. Barrill stayed in the cañon all night. The next morning the river was unusually low and Printz brought Barrill to camp without having to swim the current, and our horses followed.

On reaching camp I found that the Doctor and Printz had also had a dangerous experience in the cañon, and after having their horses rolled in the rapids, had returned to camp over the cañon walls. The stream they had followed ended in a box-cañon and they reported that there was no possibility of breaking through the range in that direction. This strenuous day ended our attempt to cross the Alaskan Range. The only chance left to us was to return to our base camp and from there strike out along the southern foothills of the range towards Mount McKinley. Our retreat was enlivened by quicksands, high water, and trail chopping.

On the last day we forded all of the united streams of the West Fork.

The quicksands were our principal difficulty, and some of the horses sank so deep that only their heads were visible above the water. Even the land some distance from the river was soft, and in pack-train parlance would "bog a snipe."

## CHAPTER V

# The Start Towards the Southern Side of Mount McKinley

***We cross the Yentna Valley and climb Mount Kliskon—We find prospector's and gold-bearing streams—Our horses begin to weaken—We are joined by an Indian—We reach the Tokositna glacier—A night on a mountain peak—An adventure with a bear—Exploration of the McKinley glaciers—We give up hopes of climbing Mount McKinley—The retreat—Arrival at Youngstown—The boat and pack train are reunited.***

We lost no time at base camp, and after chopping at rail across the valley to the East Fork, we started for Mount McKinley. We crossed the East Fork, swimming our horses, at the site of Youngstown, and after two days of heavy rain we drove our horses across Mount Kliskon, a rounded hill about 3000 feet in height. The country was soft, the mosquitoes lay in black clouds, and our horses were exhausted.

While the horses rested for a day we climbed the highest part of Mount Kliskon, and were repaid by a magnificent view of the Alaskan Range. From Mount McKinley on the north-east to the volcanoes Redoubt and Iliamna in the south-west stretched an unbroken chain of jagged peaks and glistening snow-fields. Then we dipped into a low country splashed with black lines of spruce, and cut by rushing streams. We found grayling, trout, and salmon, no end, and added them to our simple bill of fare. Deep in the moss we found that antlers of two giant moose that had locked their horns while fighting and died miserably. Our horses struggled bravely through the swamps but they were growing pitifully weak.

I remember one day in particular when we traveled all day and made only two or

THE LOCKED SKULLS OF TWO GIANT MOOSE THAT FOUGHT AND DIED

three miles. Sometimes we would have several horses "bogged down" at one time, and while we were unpacking, pulling out, and repacking these animals, others were becoming bogged in the swamps. Work of this kind, when the northern sun is hot and the mosquitoes hang in dense clouds, is hard on all hands, but it is the sight of the horses that you are fond of growing weaker day by day that makes you hate the lowlands and the cruelty of lowland travel. At "Sunflower Creek," a gold-bearing stream, we found a new settlement of a few miners. We also picked up an Indian, "Susitna Pete" by name, who said that he could guide us to the big mountain. As a piece of local colour he was a great success, but as a guide his services were of no value. While fording a beautiful stream called Lake Creek by the miners Susitna Pete told us an interesting story. He said that in the lake at the head of the stream there lived an enormous fish. The fish was so large that it could eat caribou. A friend of his once followed four caribou so relentlessly that they were forced to swim the lake to escape, and while the hunter stood on the mountainside sadly watching his escaping quarry the huge fish rose to the surface with a hissing sound and—swallowed the caribou. I asked him why some Indian didn't kill it, and he answered, "Indian no ketchum—too big—some day white man he sit down long time—maybe ketchum." At the great glacier that heads the Kahiltna River we had some cold, dangerous fords, as we forded just below the ice tongue.

We then climbed to timber line and swung towards Mount McKinley. The country changed to high, rolling caribou hills, minus the caribou, and one sunny morning a brown bear ambled amiably into camp while we were eating breakfast.

At the head of the Tokositna (the river that comes from the land where there are no trees) we found two glaciers. Susitna Pete said that the smaller glacier was called Kahnicula by the Susitnas. It headed in a nest of rugged mountains. The other glacier was large and extended far into the range towards Mount McKinley.

We were now close to Mount McKinley and as the country was too rough for pack-train transportation, we turned our horses loose by the side of the Tokositna glacier, and prepared for the real struggle. First the Doctor, Professor Parker, and I climbed a high mountain west of the Tokositna glacier that gave us an unobstructed view of the southern and western faces of Mount McKinley.

At the first glance we all saw that the scaling of the peak was a hopeless undertaking. We knew only too well the weak condition of our commissary, and between us and the mountain was a tangled, chaotic mass of rugged mountains and glaciers. The night air was already beginning to have the tang that presaged the coming of frost, and we knew that with the coming of the frost our horses would die.

From the point where our camp was, the climbing of Mount McKinley would be a summer's task—if it were climbable. We could see the southeastern, southern, southwestern and a part of the western faces of the great peak, above an altitude of about 9000 feet. Below that the walls were hidden by the rugged peaks of the main range.

There was a steady drift of clouds moving across the great ice slopes, and with hopes of a better view the Doctor and I decided to remain on the peak all night. After Professor Parker had left us we pitched our mountain tent with the entrance facing the mountain, and after a cup of tea we rolled ourselves in our sleeping-bags and prepared for our long vigil. It was a wonderfully impressive experience. Lying on top of the sharp peak we looked straight out through space to the icy walls of this wilderness giant. The night air had a chill clean tang, and as the cold crept downward the sound of falling water ceased until the whole world seemed steeped

MOUNT MCKINLEY AS IT LOOKED FROM OUR NEAREST CAMP IN 1906

in frigid silence. The mountain stood out clear cut against the northern sky and as the hours passed the clouds settled slowly in the cold air until we saw the whole sweep of the mighty mountain. As we watched we talked in whispers, and we agreed that even a summer's campaign might be too short a time to allow of a complete traverse of the southern base.

As the cold increased an occasional, deep, thunderous roar would sweep, echoing back and forth, across the range and we would know that an avalanche had fallen from the grim ice walls. From our aerie we could see a grand unnamed peak that rose to a height of about 15,000 feet on Mount McKinley's south-eastern side, and for want of a better name we spoke of it as "Little McKinley." From our point of view, south-east, the mountain looked absolutely unclimbable. Our only possible chance was to work farther north and east across the Tokositna glacier and attempt to reach the Eastern Arête, but the country we had to cross was gashed by great parallel glaciers; it was a discouraging outlook.

In my original magazine article I place our position too far to the east. Porter had not yet completed his map of this region and I made my observations largely by guesswork. I spoke of the Eastern Arête as the Northeastern Arête, as we did not know at that time that there were three great ridges falling from the North-eastern face of the mountain. In this book I will speak of this ridge as the Southern Northeast ridge.

We started across the Tokositna glacier after two days' delay on account of rain. We carried heavy packs and the travel was difficult as the glacier was about two miles wide and covered with crushed granite, which ranged in size from coarse sand to blocks the size of a house. The glacier rises in the vicinity of "Little McKinley" and it is the main feeder of the Tokositna River. Bounding the glacier on the north and east was a high mountain ridge, which we climbed. From the top of the ridge we secured a good view of McKinley.

North of our ridge was another huge glacier that seemed to come from Mount

THE VIEW OF THE BIG GLACIER AS IT LOOKED FROM OUR CLOSEST CAMP TO MOUNT MCKINLEY IN 1906.

*The glacier can be seen coming through the great gorge on the left. The amphitheatre glacier, or glacier no. 2 as we called it in 1910, can be seen on the right. It was on this glacier that Dr. Cook took the fake photographs of Mount McKinley.*

McKinley, and after talking it over we decided to use this glacier as a reconnaissance route.

On our first trip to the high dividing ridge we advanced in force. Professor Parker, Dr. Cook, and I were to make a reconnaissance, while Porter with a helper was to carry on the topographical work. Printz and Barrill packed loads to the summit of the ridge and then returned to camp to guard the horses.

As we were climbing the ridge I had an amusing adventure. A brown bear and I divided the leading part between us, and we were ably supported by a large company that made up for their lack of training by their remarkable enthusiasm and lung power. The scene was set on the grassy mountainside aforementioned, and the jagged peaks of the Tokosha Mountains formed the background. The comedy opened with the discovery of a brown bear by the main party. They had no arms but their ice-axes, which on the whole are not suited to bear-hunting. They at once began shouting to attract my attention, as I was about four hundred yards ahead of them and had in my possession a high-power pistol. This weapon of ill omen was a patent arm covered with complicated safety stops, and filled with ingenious machinery. It was guaranteed to shoot a whole broadside in three seconds, and was sighted up to a mile—if it had been sighted on a ten-foot range it would have served my purpose better. I was carrying it for Professor Parker and had not practised with it.

When I heard the shouts of the main party I accepted the leading role, and starting towards them, soon discovered the bear. I was on a grassy hillside, and the bear, unconscious of the excitement he was causing, was digging at a squirrel burrow in a little ravine between me and my comrades. Just above him was a granite boulder, and selecting this rock for a stalking mark, I began the approach. I could see my companions—six in number—sitting in an interested line, and a thrill of pride swept over me as I thought of the large audience that would witness my triumph.

Everything went splendidly at first; I reached the rock without alarming bruin, and on looking over it I saw him busily at work, not more than fifteen feet away. Without losing a minute I aimed my infernal machine at his shoulder, and pulled the trigger. Nothing happened! From this point on to the curtain of the farce, the bear held the centre —and all four corners—of the stage. I was so close to him that I was afraid to move away for fear that he would charge me, so I sat down back of the rock and tried a rapid-repair-act on my pistol. The bear in the meanwhile had

Our mountain base camp by the side of the big boulder on the Tokositna Glacier

discovered my companions, who, realising that something had gone wrong, began to execute a "song and dance" with the idea of distracting the bear's attention. Their plan succeeded for he left his digging and stalked past me and sitting down about ten feet away began to study my companions, turning his head from side to side. He was now directly between me and my companions. Luckily for them I had removed the magazine during my repairing operations, or I might have added homicide to my other sins. At last the bear turned around and saw me, and as long as I live I never expect to receive such a disgusted look as that bear gave me. I sat in as apologetic an attitude as I could, with the pistol in one hand and the magazine in the other. After giving me a thorough looking-over, he turned slowly, the hair on his back standing in a stiff ridge, and stalked away.

As soon as I was sure that he was leaving, I returned to my repairing, and succeeded in driving the loosened magazine home. The gun went off like a bunch of fire-crackers, and the bear, wild with terror at the noise, dashed downward towards my companions. They began to take immediate notice, and for a few minutes there was a sound of shouting and a dizzy blend of figures on the mountainside, and then silence once more settled among the hills. Whether they were afraid of my pistol or the bear I will never know, for I wisely decided to let the matter rest—I had had enough excitement already.

That night we camped on the summit of the ridge, and weathered a savage wind and rain storm. We had anchored our tent with boulders and ice-axes. The view from the mountain was beautiful; two thousand feet below us on either side were giant glaciers, and over them the black storm clouds tore themselves to shreds against the cliffs. We had a wild night and our tent rattled like a sail in a storm.

On studying the big glacier we saw that to reach it we would have to cross either an ice wall or a swift glacier river. We tried the river first but the water was too strong for us. We followed the stream until it plunged into a great cavern in the ice wall.

Below the cavern the wall continued around the base of the Tokosha Mountains. The ice wall was formed of solid green ice covered with great granite slabs, and as we could see from the ridge as far as our food supply would allow us to travel, it would have been a foolish risk to attempt the wall. We skirted the wall as far as the Tokosha Mountains without finding a break, and then returned to our camp. The Tokosha Mountains are a magnificent mass of sharp knife-blade peaks that form the dividing wedge between the lower ends of the two great glaciers. We named them Tokosha after the Tokositna River which encircled the base of the range.

The weather was cold and rainy, our enthusiasm was gone, and as Dr. Cook was expected at Tyonik to meet the Eastern sportsman who had partly financed the expedition, we turned our faces towards the base camp. Porter in the meanwhile was hard at work on his map-making, and he joined us a day later at the base camp.

During all our wanderings Susitna Pete had been consumed with curiosity about our reasons for entering this country. To our answers that we wanted to climb Doleika he shrugged his shoulders with an air of amused tolerance. White men always wanted gold, and Pete decided that the search for gold must be our mission. He therefore told us of creeks where we might find the precious metal, and retired in outraged dignity when we showed no enthusiasm. Porter's topographical instruments mystified him greatly and he finally decided that in some way those mysterious instruments were connected with the thing we sought. One day Porter set up his theodolite by the side of the glacier and took some angles. On leaving the theodolite for a minute we were amused to see Susitna Pete eagerly place his eye to the telescope. In an instant his body stiffened with excitement—he had seen a

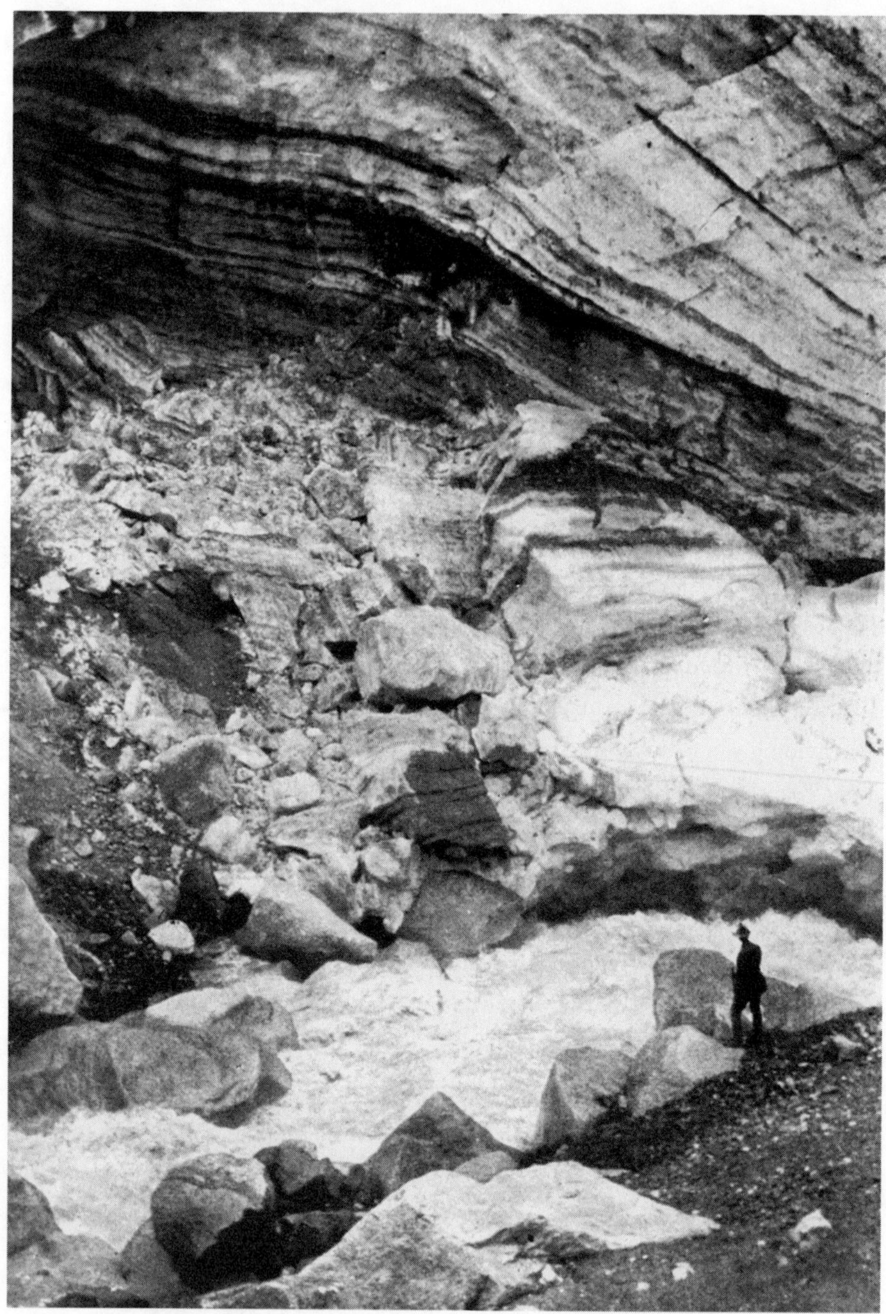

The ice wall on the western side of the big glacier that we followed to Mount McKinley in 1910. The torrent in the foreground plunges under the ice and disappears.

bear; the theodolite must therefore be a new and marvellous instrument for the finding of big game! Porter at once rose in Susitna Pete's estimation, and we were no longer bothered with questions.

Our retreat was carried out in the "devil may care" spirit that comes over men whose chief purpose in life has been removed.

We no longer had to exert all our energy of mind and body towards the overwhelming mania of speed, regardless of cost. We drifted, rather, as a band of gypsies would, as free and irresponsible as children. Laughter and rough jokes tippled back and forth along the pack-train, and we learned to play wild, shrill marching tunes on the turned edge of a red willow leaf.

The horses, as a whole, had improved slightly in condition, but it was due more to the light loads they were carrying than to a return to strength. Horses furnish the chief topic of conversation among pack-train men, and the argument as to which type and colour of horse shows the most stamina is a world-old bone of contention. For example Brooks in his most interesting account of his long pack-train drive from Cook Inlet to the Yukon says:

"Experience proved that the buckskins, bays, and sorrels had more endurance than the black, or, especially, the white animals.

"The white horses suffered most from mosquitoes and were the first to give out."

After many hard trips with pack-horses in different parts of the West my

WHAT STARVATION AND THE ALASKAN MOSQUITO CAN DO

experience has brought me to an almost totally different conclusion. For instance I never remember having packed a sorrel that was worth his salt. On our trip to Mount McKinley the two weakest horses we had were sorrels. As far as buckskins and bays are concerned I heartily concur with Brooks but I would also place roan horses at the head of the list. But strangest of all in view of Brooks's statement is my experience with white horses, for on every trip where I have driven a horse that proved to be a particularly strong and faithful animal, it has been a white horse. As an example I will take our beloved "Ferry-boat." This faithful old animal did double duty throughout our long trip. Fred Printz and I worked together in choosing the many fords along our trail and when we forded we both used "Ferry-boat"—hence his name. We usually took turns in the fords, one of us holding to the pack-rope while the other rode behind the pack. Even with this handicap he was one of the best swimmers and weight carriers that we had.

Ferry-boat went through the strain of the cañon swimming without any apparent ill effect, while the sorrels were spared this arduous experience.

These contradictory experiences lead me to believe that the *kind* of a horse is more important than the *colour* of a horse. In our pack-train there were times when individual horses were practically incapacitated by the mosquito hordes, and yet Ferry-boat at no time seemed unduly distressed, and stood the ordeal as well as the best.

These reminiscences take me back to an amusing feature of pack-train driving. At the beginning of every pack-train journey each man chooses a particular animal as his personal charge. In very rough country he leads the horse, if necessary, and when a river is encountered he fords on his own favourite. To "jump" another man's horse at a ford would be a deadly insult. As time goes on each man's fondness for his favourite horse grows stronger. He saves every little delicacy, such as a small piece of bacon-rind, or a mouldy biscuit, for his own animal, and sees to his comfort in every way. It is not strange then, under the circumstances, that a man's opinions become slightly biassed, and in my loyalty to white horses I know that I am strongly influenced by my affection for Ferry-boat.

Susitna Pete had left for parts unknown while we were exploring the glaciers near Mount McKinley. We did not see him again until we had returned across the glacier streams of the Kahiltna glacier and were camped on the plateau that lies west of the river. He joined us in the evening and he was wet and tired from his struggle with swift streams. He told us that after we had crossed, the glacier had broken, and that the streams were almost unfordable. By "broken" he meant that the glacier had flooded. There are many of these "flood glaciers" in the north, and they are a source of great danger. The glaciers are so formed that they block or dam certain valleys or cañons. In these natural reservoirs the water begins to gather, until in some cases large lakes are formed. All goes well until the movement of the glacier changes the location of the ice dam, by the formation of a crevasse, or a crevasse moving in front of the reservoir. A mighty flood ensues. It comes without the slightest warning and the effects are often felt in the lowlands far below. After the flood has occurred the valley or reservoir remains dry until it is once more dammed by the moving ice, and the water rises once more until another break in the ice wall allows the flood to escape.

After Pete had joined us we pushed forward over our back trail. We reached Sunflower Creek the following day.

We were joined at this time by Mrs. Susitna Pete—a typical Susitna Indian woman, and she was the innocent cause of one of the most amusing incidents that occurred during our travels. As we reached a stream on the first day that she joined us, one of the men gallantly lifted her onto one of the horses. It was a new and unexpected pleasure to her and thereafter she always expected a lift whenever we reached a stream. Instead of being gratified at his wife's comfort, Susitna Pete was envious. He told us that he too wanted to ride. Now all our fording horses were in use. We had with us, however, a small bay mare. She was as wild as a hawk, and although almost every man in our party had tried to ride her, every attempt had ended in failure. We at once became certain that providence had been saving the bay mare for Pete, so we ran to help him. One man held the mare's head, while two men grasped Pete. At a given word Pete was hoisted onto her back and the head man turned her loose.

Before she really began to buck Pete was in the water, and he came out of the ford with his Indian stoicism rudely shaken. To his questions as to what had caused the trouble the men told him that the mare's impoliteness was undoubtedly due to the fact that his red sweater had frightened her. On reaching the next ford Pete without a word removed his red sweater. With ill-disguised attempts to hide our amusement Pete was again hoisted onto the mare's back. On this occasion there was a high bank above the water and as the mare cleared the bank she arched her back and gave a mighty buck. Pete went so high that we thought he would never come down and when he finally hit the water he did so in a cloud of foam; As the laughter ran back and forth along the pack-train we heard a shrill cackle from the head of the line—it was Mrs. Susitna Pete in a paroxysm of mirth over her husband's downfall. To our amusement she little realised that there was a difference between horses, and she was firm in her conviction that Pete's ill-luck was due alone to his lack of horsemanship.

After an uneventful trip we once more gathered at the site of Youngstown.

At this point we were confronted by several difficulties. In the first place Dr. Cook wanted the horses driven down the river to the Kichatna, as he wanted to use them on a hunt when he was joined by his sportsman friend. As a second attempt on Mount McKinley that season was out of the question, Professor Parker decided to return at once to New York.

Dr. Cook urged me to stay with him and help to make the hunting trip a success, and I agreed to do so. Porter and a prospector hired for the occasion remained in the Lake Creek country to finish the map of that portion of the Alaskan Range.

There was an old camp site some miles below us on the main river, and thither the main party drove the pack-train. Dr. Cook, Miller, and I started across the valley of the Yentna to get the launch and take it downstream where we were to rejoin our party.

We had a hard trip as we had to cross on foot the many streams that cut the valley, and in one or two instances we had to swim. The water was bitterly cold. Miller could not swim, and we got him across the largest, channel by felling trees from each bank and helping him across. We finally got so chilled that we had to build a fire in a swamp. We placed the fire on a platform of sticks and stood in the water while our bodies became warmed by the cheerful flames.

On reaching the boat we had a huge meal and turned energetically to putting the *Bulshaia* in commission. After a day's work we had everything in order and started downstream.

The channel was so narrow and the water so swift that I would have done better by taking the boat down backwards, but I attempted to gain time, and paid for it by hitting a "sweeper" below a sharp turn in a rapid. "Sweepers" are the curse of Alaskan river navigation, and they are feared by every one who has engaged in this form of travel. A "sweeper" is any tree that has had its roots undermined by the current until it has leaned far out over the stream. They are usually spruce trees, and they are found, as a rule, over-hanging the swiftest and most dangerous reaches of the northern rivers. Many a prospector or trapper, rafting to the sea, has had his raft overturned by one of these treacherous obstructions and has lost his life or his outfit. When we struck the sweeper it bent the iron stanchions that formed the cabin, and Miller, who was standing on the stem deck, was nearly swept into the river.

In our desire to reach our companions we travelled too late, for in the dusk it was hard to choose the right channel, and I ran the boat aground. We waded ashore and spent a miserable night, lying on the rocks, without blankets, by the coals of a driftwood fire.

On the morning after our accident we began the discouraging task of hauling the *Bulshaia* off the sandbar. We worked as follows. One man would carry an anchor well astern and sit or stand on it while the others would haul on the capstan. We would make about one foot in a half-hour, but in the end patience won and we were soon at the old camp-ground where we rejoined our companions. We left Barrill behind at this camp. He was to await our return and take care of the horses until we ascended the Kichatna on our hunt for big game.

On the way down the river we carried away our rudder on a snag, and I fitted two large steering chocks on the stern and from then on we steered the *Bulshaia* with large sweeps.

## CHAPTER VI

# The Return to the Coast

*We descend the Susitna River—Porter is left behind—Barrill is left to guard the horses—Arrival at Susitna Station—The boat accident in the Kahiltna cañon—Adventures during the storm on Cook Inlet—Professor Parker returns to New York—We go after big game—Printz and Miller ascend the Kichatna River—Dr. Cook and Barrill ascend the Susitna—Dr. Cook claims the ascent of Mount McKinley—Professor Parker and I prepare for another attempt.*

We reached Susitna Station on August 1st. Coming down the river we had heard rumours of a boat accident that happened in the Kahiltna cañon, and, on reaching Susitna Station, we met some of the men who had gone through the terrible experience.

Five miners were coming down the Kahiltna River in a boat. One of them was an experienced river-man, the others knew little or nothing about small boat navigation. Before reaching the Kahiltna cañon the experienced riverman tried to coach his companions in the safest method of running the cañon, but they laughed at his suggestion of running the boat through stern first, and he finally gave way to their optimistic viewpoint. All went well until the boat was nearly through the cañon walls, when a large partly submerged boulder appeared ahead. As they were rowing with the current the boat was moving with terrific speed and the steersman being in the upstream end of the boat had little or no control over the craft.

They struck the rock with great force, and the boat was broken to pieces. The men managed to cling to the rock and eventually they succeeded in drawing themselves out of the rapids.

There was, however, only a very small portion of the rock exposed above water, and on this tiny surface one man at a time could partly dry his chilled legs; the rest were forced to stand in the icy water.

One of the men decided that death by drowning was preferable to a living hell. Almost naked he took to the water and by the aid of a portion of the boat which had stuck on the rock, he succeeded in reaching the shore. Before him was a long journey through the most rugged part of the Alaskan wilderness, and yet he finally reached a miner's cache or cabin and found food. The other men faced their fate amid the roaring waters of the cañon. I believe that four days went by before the impossible happened. What those dark chilling nights must have meant to the men, no one but they will ever know. One day when hope was gone and death had marked them for his own, a boat shot downward through the white water. For an instant the bronzed miners that manned her looked in horror and surprise at the huddled group on the submerged boulder, and then the current swept them on.

But they returned and with the aid of a tracking line eventually rescued the men from the rock. They were brought down, in easy stages to Susitna Station, where we found them on their return. They were in a pitiable condition, and their legs were black and swollen from the long immersion in glacier water, but I believe that they all recovered. The North holds hidden thousands of these tales that will never be written. But the more you see of the Alaskan prospector, the more you admire his breed, for these men pay a thousand-fold more in toil and suffering than the treasures that they win are worth.

From Susitna Station we ran quickly to the delta on our way to Tyonik. As we entered Cook Inlet we encountered a good-sized sea. I was familiar with the dangers of navigation on this part of the Inlet, for, besides hearing many tales of the terrific winds that sweep down from the great fiord known as Turnagain Arm, I had on more than one occasion sailed on different parts of the north coast in small boats.

Turnagain Arm is known locally as "the Cook Inlet compressed-air plant," and the greatest danger results from the savage winds beating directly on the Susitna flats, which extend across the head of the Inlet for many miles. Any heavy wind blowing on these shallows builds up mountainous seas. After leaving the delta the wind began to blow with great force. The sky above Turnagain Arm had a sinister look and knowing that we were in for trouble I called the Doctor out and advised him to turn back while there was yet time.

Printz and I were steering the *Bulshaia* from the stern deck with sweeps. The body of the boat was covered with canvas which was stretched lightly over iron stanchions. After a look around the Doctor said that we might as well keep on, for in case we got into trouble we could run into the Beluga River. Now the Beluga River was a small river that ran into the Inlet in the centre of a great expanse of level marshes. At low tide the mud flats extended for miles into the Inlet, and I felt certain that it would be an impossibility for any man to follow the tortuous channel through the heavy sea. Printz however said that he knew the channel, but later on I found that his knowledge of the river was gained by having swum pack-horses across it on two occasions! I however agreed and once more eased the *Bulshaia's* head towards Tyonik. The seas rose rapidly and Printz and I had to be lashed to ring-bolts in the deck or we would have been swept overboard. We had a small canvas canoe inverted over the canvas house and lashed in place with small ropes. Suddenly a savage puff of wind caught the canoe, broke the lash ropes, and carried it off to leeward where it filled partly with water.

After this exhibition of what the wind could do I realised that we could not make the delta or Fire Island, our only two possible shelters, as our canvas house would not stand the strain of driving into a head sea.

The storm increased steadily. Do what we would we could not keep all the seas from breaking over our frail canvas house, and on two occasions solid green combers rolled over us.

If the canvas had broken or a stanchion given way we would have filled. Printz had had no experience with boats, and told me between the waves that were striking us that he preferred the "hurricane deck of a cayuse."

Opposite the Beluga River we ran in to take a look and the sight we saw was what I expected—a great white line of foam-crested breakers were thundering onto the shoals a mile out from shore—there was not a break to be seen.

As we swung the *Bulshaia* back on the Tyonik course, the engine gave a dry cough and stopped. We were on a dangerous lee shore, our engine was red hot, and our ground-tackle consisted of one thirty-pound anchor. It was an unpleasant predicament. The only thing Printz and I could do was to keep the boat's head up wind, and as we were standing in the open we could see that the sea and wind were driving us rapidly towards the line of breakers.

The engine trouble was due to the glacial silt in the river filling our pumps and stopping the water circulation.

Our engine was an expensive and powerful automarine engine but it was built for clear water and fair-weather boating; it was in no way fitted for the rough conditions found on the Alaskan seacoast.

Through the canvas door we could see the men working at the engine. The pumps had to be removed and cleaned out and the engine cooled off before we could start again. Some of the men were seasick, and the boat was pitching heavily.

By this time we were only about one hundred yards from the outer breakers and I was figuring on what would make the best buoy in case our engine balked, for in that case it would have been "every man for himself and the devil take the hindmost." At last they began to crank the engine, and after several trials the exhaust grew regular and we began to wallow through the seas and leave the white breakers behind. With thankful hearts we squared away, but I soon realised that we would be helpless at Tyonik. It was an unprotected anchorage and we would be unable to land. I therefore called to the Doctor and advised him to take the launch across the Inlet, where we could anchor in the lee of the bluffs. He answered that there was a small creek near Tyonik and that we might run into it. I advised against it as I knew the entrance and it was difficult to enter in good weather, but the Doctor insisted, so Printz and I pulled on our sweeps and we headed for the river. To get a view of the river entrance we had to run into the surf, and in an instant a huge comber caught us and swept us with terrific force towards the bar. As we were shooting along the *Bulshaia's* head began to pay off. I pulled on my sweep with all my strength, and yelled at Printz to do likewise, but we could not hold her. Our sweeps were dragging bottom as the big wave passed us. The next roller caught us in a smother of foam but the *Bulshaia* shook herself free and we began to creep offshore, meeting wave after wave until we passed the line of surf. The water at times had swept us from our feet and if we had not been lashed to the deck we would have been washed overboard. The Doctor was a little chastened after this experience, and we took the bit in our teeth and headed for the south side of the Inlet. Night was already upon us and I had no liking for a lee shore in the darkness. As we plunged along through the dusk I began to be aware that the waves were losing their force. In a short time I was sure of it—the great Cook Inlet tide was cutting down the swell, so we once more turned the *Bulshaia's* head towards Tyonik.

We arrived opposite Tyonik in inky darkness. A heavy swell was breaking on the beach, and there was no sign of life to be seen. As I knew the lay of the land by the loom of the bluffs against the sky, I got into the little 12-foot canvas canoe and Printz lay between my feet for ballast.

I backed in slowly until I caught a big wave that shot us in to the beach. I had warned Printz to jump the minute we struck, but as the roller that had carried us broke into foam a number of dark form's loomed out of the darkness and we were carried boat and all above the reach of the surf. A keen-eyed Aleute hunter had seen the *Bulshaia* against the black sea, and had told Durrell Finch, who ran the A. C. Co. trading post. He in turn had called out all the population, which was composed mostly of Aleutes, and they had stood by to aid us as we ran the surf. Finch then gathered a crew of expert Aleute boatmen and they succeeded in getting through the surf in a dory and taking off our companions. In the meantime Printz and I had been taken in hand by Red Jack, a well-known Cook Inlet character. We had been wet to the skin for hours and were numb from the cold. Following Jack to his cabin we got out of our wet things while our host prepared generous glasses of hot whisky, and the next thing I remember was that it was morning, and that we were all glad to be on land. The storm was one of the worst in years, and we were lucky to get through as easily as we did. A dory, containing three men, that we met and spoke on entering the Inlet was never heard of again.

The western coast line of Alaska is always treacherous on account of the big tides and tremendous glacier-bred winds, and after one or two experiences of this kind a man learns that discretion is the better part of valour.

Professor Parker now returned to New York and Dr. Cook accompanied him to Seldovia to meet his friend. He returned alone from his journey stating that the Eastern sportsman could not join us, and we therefore began to make new plans. Dr. Cook was anxious to secure some specimens of big game for an Eastern museum and as he had a large party he decided to split it up into small units and send it in search of game. Printz and Miller were to take some horses and go up the Kichatna. I had remained in Tyonik from a desire to see more of the Alaskan Range. Had the hunting trip been carried out as we expected we would have all crossed the Kichatna Pass and I would have then seen the Kuskoquim country.

Dr. Cook however decided to take Barrill and a new hired man and prospect the upper Susitna River to see if reaching Mount McKinley by that route was feasible. He asked me if I would go up the Matanuska River on the northern slopes of the Chugach Mountains and collect some zoölogical specimens for him. I told him that if he contemplated exploring the southern foothills of Mount McKinley I would prefer going with him. He answered that he would do no exploring outside of seeing whether or not the water route was practicable and he again urged me to aid him with his game collection. I agreed to help him, and went aboard a small steamer that was lying at Tyonik on her way to the mouth of the Matanuska.

The details that follow are hard to understand and harder yet to write about. But for the sake of truth and in order that posterity may be able to judge correctly the events that followed, I feel it my duty to put down every detail of what followed my departure.

Before leaving Tyonik I invited Dr. Cook aboard to take luncheon with me, and while he was on board or while the boat was at Seldovia he sent the following telegram to a well-known business man of New York City:

"Am preparing for a last, desperate attack on Mount McKinley."

I proceeded up the Matanuska and the Knik rivers and returned after a short and successful hunt to Seldovia.

Printz and Miller were the first to join me. On the head of the Kichatna River they had found miles of tangled brush and morasses. The poor horses grew too weak to travel and the report of a rifle echoing through the silent spruce forests was their only requiem.

The death of the horses left Printz and Miller without means of transportation, until they reached the Kichatna River and built a raft. They finally reached Susitna Station after a narrow escape from death by drowning, and proceeded by boat to Seldovia.

At this time we heard the rumour that Dr. Cook and Barrill had reached the top of Mount McKinley. We knew the character of country that guarded the southern face of the big mountain, we had travelled in that country, and we knew the time that Dr. Cook had been absent was too short to allow of his even reaching the mountain. We therefore denied the rumour. At last the Doctor and Barrill joined us and to my surprise Dr. Cook confirmed the rumour. After a word with Dr. Cook I called Barrill aside, and we walked up the Seldovia beach. Barrill and I had been through some hard times together. I liked Barrill and I knew that he was fond of me for we were tied by the strong bond of having suffered together. As soon as we were alone I turned to him and asked him what he knew about Mount McKinley, and after a moment's hesitation he answered: "I can tell you all about the big peaks just south of the mountain, but if you want to know about Mount McKinley go and ask Cook." I had felt all along that Barrill would tell me the truth, and after his statement I kept the knowledge to myself.

Dr. Cook was detained at Seward by a lawsuit over a pack-train, and he kept Barrill with him. The rest of the party returned to civilisation

I now found myself in an embarrassing position. I knew that Dr. Cook had not climbed Mount McKinley. Barrill had told me so and in addition I knew it in the same way that any New Yorker would know that no man could walk from the Brooklyn Bridge to Grant's tomb in ten minutes.

This knowledge, however, did not constitute proof, and I knew that before I could make the public believe the truth I should have to collect some facts. I wrote immediately on my return to Professor Parker telling him my opinions and knowledge concerning the climb, and I received a reply from him saying that he believed me implicitly and that the climb, under the existing conditions, was impossible.

I returned to New York as soon as possible and both Professor Parker and I stated our convictions to members of the American Geographical Society and the Explorers' Club.

Many of these men were warm friends of Doctor Cook. We, however, knew the question was above partisanship, and were willing to give Doctor Cook every chance to clear himself. Nothing official had as yet been written by Dr. Cook, and before we could make any formal accusation against him it was necessary for us to wait until his account of the climb was published. Before his book was published, however, Dr. Cook sailed secretly to the North. Both Professor Parker and myself were present at the gathering of the Explorers' Club when his farewell telegram was read. It was rather significant in view of the fact that he had many good friends in the club that no applause or signs of enthusiasm followed the reading of his message.

After the appearance of Dr. Cook's book Professor Parker and I found ourselves in possession of irrefutable proof that Dr. Cook had made countless misstatements in his description of the route he followed to the mountain, and the equipment he used. Many of the misstatements we knew to be downright falsehoods. We were influenced, however, by our own ideas of fair play as well as the suggestions of our friends, and we refrained from publishing anything derogatory to the Doctor's character while he was absent, and unable to defend himself. During his absence in the North Professor Parker and I were planning another attempt to climb Mount McKinley.

The reader will remember the excitement of Dr. Cook's return and the Polar controversy that followed, and I will skip all the public details of this period of Dr. Cook's notoriety.

In looking back on that remarkable controversy I am still filled with astonishment at the incredible amount of vindictive and personal spite that was shown by the partisans of Doctor Cook. Men who had never seen an ice-axe or a sled-dog wrote us reams of warped exploring details and accused us of untold crimes because we had dared to question Cook's honesty.

I was visiting Professor Parker at that time and scarcely a day went by when we did not receive abusive anonymous letters. In the face of this blind public partisanship, we realised that we would need more than documentary and circumstantial evidence to convict Doctor Cook irrevocably. The Polar controversy had put an entirely new light on our claims against Cook. Originally our claims against him were really more or less private and personal. While Mount McKinley was a splendid mountaineering prize, our attempt to climb it had been in the nature of a sporting proposition. We did it for the love of adventure and our attack on Cook was simply a question of mountaineering ethics. But the North Pole was an international prize, that had claimed the heroic efforts, and lives, of the explorers of many nationalities for many years. There was no sport here—it was a question of international importance.

We did have a chance to convict Dr. Cook of fraud before a committee chosen by the Explorers' Club. Both Professor Parker and I were called as witnesses and Doctor Cook appeared. A well-known man opened the meeting by telling Dr. Cook that he was not to consider himself in the light of a guilty man being tried to prove his innocence, but rather as an honest man who was being given a chance by his friends to clear himself from suspicion.

I can truthfully say that the majority of the men who formed the committee were men whose sympathies were, at that time, with Dr. Cook. But Dr. Cook refused to testify before the committee. He said that his hardships in the long Polar night had affected his memory and that he could not answer any questions without consulting his diary.

He asked for two weeks' time, and before the expiration of that time he had disappeared. At this time we were busy on our plans for our second attempt to scale Mount McKinley, and the last chapter of the Polar controversy will be found in the following account of our 1910 expedition.

# CHAPTER VII

# The 1910 Expedition

***Plans—The motor-boat* Explorer*—Arrival at Seldovia—We reach Beluga—The rival expedition—The break-up of the ice—We reach Susitna Station.***

When Professor Parker and I decided to make a second attempt on the southern face of Mount McKinley we were influenced by three distinct desires. In the first place we had actually underestimated the difficulties of travel on the southern glaciers, and, knowing that the water route was the easiest way of reaching the big mountain, we thought that if we failed on the southern face (which from our knowledge of the mountain seemed probable) we would still be able to swing the Southern North-East Ridge and attack the mountain from that new and untried quarter. This north-eastern approach we knew to be the most promising line of attack, but it was at this point that our other plans entered and forced us to choose the southern.

Our principal reasons for attacking the southern side consisted first, in duplicating Dr. Cook's photographs and settling once and for all time his Polar claim, and secondly the mapping of the impressive mass of peaks and glaciers that guard the great mountain's southern flanks. The northern side had already been mapped by Brooks and we, therefore, looked forward eagerly to adding this chaos of mountains and glaciers to the map of Alaska. The northern also was more inaccessible than the southern side. We knew that we could reach the southern approach in the summer time in time to benefit by the good weather. In the late summer the snow-fields throw off such an immense amount of moisture that the big mountain is continually wrapped in clouds which would double the difficulties of an attack, or, possibly, render a successful ascent impossible. Our starting point for the northern approach would have to be Fairbanks, which is the largest town on the Tanana River, and 160 miles north-east of the big mountain. Now it is extremely easy to reach Mount McKinley from Fairbanks, if you go in the winter time and use dog teams. But neither Professor Parker nor I were able to make a winter trip at that time. In the summer, the Fairbanks approach is practically out of the question, for in using horses one would be forced to wait until the snow had gone, the ice broken in the streams, and the grass abundant enough to insure feed for the stock. These complications would delay the final climb and the early summer months would be wasted.

The suffering of our pack-train in 1906 had made us resolve to do without horses on our next venture, and I, therefore, turned all my energy toward the designing of a boat that could carry heavy loads through the rushing rapids of the northern glacier rivers. Knowing that the head of navigation would be at least thirty miles from the mountain, we also enlisted a party of exceptionally strong packers, as all our provisions would have to be carried on our backs across the glaciers. It was a boat and back-packing proposition.

Professor Parker, Professor Cuntz, and the writer were fellows of the American Geographical Society and we had the official sanction of that society, and reported to them on our return. We also represented the Explorers' Club, as members. On this trip as on our other two, Professor Parker and I jointly led the expedition. For while Professor Parker advanced most of the expedition expenses, I outfitted the party and led the expedition in the field.

The outfitting of a large party in the North is a laborious affair that necessitates an intimate knowledge of wilderness conditions. Our river outfit differed in no way from the usual Alaskan outfits. But our mountain equipment, with the exception of somewhat lighter clothing and sleeping-bags, was the same as that used in Polar work.

Our party consisted of eight men: Professor Parker; Professor J. H. Cuntz, of Stevens Institute, who was our topographer; Valdemar Grassi, of Columbia University; Herman L. Tucker, of the United States Forestry Service; Merl LaVoy, of Seattle; J. W. Thompson, who handled the boat engine; Arthur Aten, of Valdez, Alaska; and the writer. Our party was the best equipped expedition from a mountaineering point of view that had ever been organised in America. We left Seattle on the 5th of May. Our boat, which we had named the *Explorer*, after the Explorers'

Club of New York, was run down under her own power from Tregoning's shipyard, near Seattle, to the steamer, and hoisted on to the upper deck.

After a busy but uneventful trip we once more found ourselves in the familiar harbour of Seldovia.

At this point we left the steamer and transferred all our belongings to a smaller boat called the *Tyonik*, for our voyage up Cook Inlet, and the *Explorer* made her maiden plunge into the cold northern waters. We tried out the engine in Seldovia harbour and although it had not yet "found itself" we got some splendid bursts of speed out of her, that gave us confidence in our ability to conquer the rapids of the glacier rivers. The engine had a powerful exhaust and during her trial spin the *Explorer* made so much noise that we were much amused on returning to the ship to find that she had been nicknamed the *Exploder!*

Seldovia is the principal port on Cook Inlet. A few warehouses flanked by the grass-thatched Russian Aleute cabins face the beach. The harbour is wonderfully protected and the coast line being of rock formation many little rock islands rise above the beach, like miniature fortifications. To the east the rocks rise in lines of cliffs that tower above the sea, and here in the summer time the northern sea-birds nest in thousands. Close to the town, groves of Alaskan spruce insure firewood to the inhabitants, but as the hills roll upward, these give place to the almost impenetrable jungles of Alaskan alder, which in turn disappear below the perpetual snowfields of the surrounding mountains.

Below the town you come to the burial-ground where three-armed Greek crosses speak mutely of the early Russian days. Bidarkas—three-hatched kyaks—and dories line the beaches as the Seldovian travels by water and seldom penetrates the alder thickets of the back country.

At the head of the bay a salmon river furnishes the native population with food, for the Aleute takes life easily and gives hardly a thought to the morrow.

As hunters they are of little use, although with careful handling they make fair packers and camp followers. But in their long sealskin bidarkas they are at home, and they brave the most savage seas in these light boats that a man can raise above his head with his two hands.

On landing from the steamer, I asked for two young Aleutes with whom I had hunted the Kenai Mountains in days gone by. "They went to sea in a bidarka"—my aged informant answered—"and they fastened to a white whale, but the harpoon line caught on the bidarka's prow and when the whale sounded they went to Heaven."

To save time, the *Tyonik* towed the *Explorer*, and our trip down the Inlet proved to be an eventful one. Off Anchor Point at the edge of Katchimac Bay the wind began to blow, and before long there was a heavy sea running. As the *Explorer* was shoal draft and as light as a feather the least tug on the towing line would make her shoot forward and overrun the cable.

It finally grew so rough that communication was cut off between the two vessels, and Herman Tucker and I found ourselves marooned. Luckily there was a gasoline blow-lamp and a crate of eggs aboard or we would have had a hungry time. Tucker manufactured a sort of basin out of an oil tin and after filling it with eggs he would hold it over the blow-lamp and we would have a meal in short order. The navigation was most difficult, and on several occasions I thought that the *Explorer* was doomed. She would overrun her cable so far at times that the bight would be far astern, and as she lost headway and the *Tyonik* took up the slack, the cable would come taut with tremendous force. I managed to save the bitts from being torn out by running her off at an angle as we shot forward, and then when the rope tautened with a jerk some of the force was expended on pulling the *Explorer*'s head around. It was touch and go for a long time and the night seemed to last for ever, but we reached Beluga safely. Durrell Finch and the A. C. Co.'s store had left Tyonik, the scene of our landing after the storm in 1906, and had taken up a new stand on the Beluga River, which was the same river that we tried unsuccessfully to enter during the 1906 storm. On this day, however, the sea was as smooth as glass and we moved slowly up to the new wharf and after a hearty greeting from Finch and Red Jack we began to unload our equipment.

Finch told us that the ice had not yet come out of the Susitna, or any of the rivers, and he showed us from where we stood the white cakes massed in the Beluga River above the wharf.

As we had to wait for the ice to break we gladly took possession of an empty log cabin and began to keep house.

Cook Inlet is such an imposing sheet of water that I find it difficult to dismiss it with a few words. It is the largest estuary in Alaska and its lonely beaches and the towering snow-covered mountain chains that encircle it give it an atmosphere of wildness and grim desolation that is even more impressive than the more picturesque fiords farther south. The Kenai Peninsula forms the Inlet's southern boundary, and as the mountains break down towards the sea they flatten out into the rolling timber-covered country that enjoys the distinction of being the world's best moose ground. In fact the Kenai Peninsula is a wonderful big game range, for in addition to the moose that range the lowlands, the mountain meadows are dotted with bands of the white mountain sheep.

The northern side of the Inlet follows the base of the Alaskan Range for a distance of seventy miles. While these mountains that tower above the sea are extremely impressive they seem dwarfed by the two great volcanoes, Iliamna and Redoubt, that raise their snowy steam-crowned summits far above the main range.

There is scarcely one good harbour on the northern side of the Inlet and the erosion of the mountains has built up great flats of mud and sand that complicate navigation.

As you approach the head of the Inlet, the mountains break away and the water blends almost imperceptibly into the marshes and flats of the great Susitna delta. On account of the extreme tides this part of the Inlet is particularly dangerous, and many men have lost their lives by being caught in small boats among the savage seas that break miles from shore on the shallow mud-flats.

Near the north-eastern end of the marshes a narrow opening allows the sea to rush into two arms that are called Turnagain and Knik Arm. Turnagain Arm received its name from the old navigator Captain Cook, who after repeated efforts to ascend it in his search for the mythical north-west passage, gave up in despair and turned back to the Pacific.

This fiord and its sister Knik Arm are still true to their old reputation and the savage glacier-bred winds still lash the seas to froth, and the tide bores can still be heard miles away as they come roaring in between the narrowing mountainsides. It was one of these savage glacier gales that threatened us with destruction in 1906, and on account of its propensity for breeding dirty weather Turnagain Arm has earned the descriptive title of "The Cook Inlet Compressed Air Plant."

The Beluga River is named after the Beluga or white whale and as the tide comes in, their glistening bodies can be seen shining in the sunlight as they come to the surface to breathe. Their oil is highly esteemed by the natives of Alaska, who use it for cooking purposes and the preservation of fruits or berries. I have eaten it at times while living with the natives but the oil has a strong rancid taste that does not appeal to a white man's palate.

The Beluga River has its source in a rugged portion of the Alaskan Range and it enters the Inlet through the north-western portion of the Susitna marshes. Small amounts of gold have been found along the river but never as yet in paying quantities. It is a "salmon-river," however, and during the run of fish its banks are the home of the great Alaskan brown bear. Where it enters the sea it passes through the great marsh that is famous for its mosquitoes and wild fowl. I have seen marshes many miles in extent literally covered with geese, brant, ducks, and snipe, and during our stay at Beluga the wild fowl made a welcomed addition to our simple bill of fare.

Reorganising was an easy matter, for each man saw to his personal duffel, and I had packed all the expedition food in marked packages, in the order in which they would be wanted. After the *Tyonik* left, the *Explorer* was made fast at Finch's dock and I slept on her at night in case the ice came down without warning.

Shortly after we were settled the river-steamer *Alice* arrived. It was her first year on the Inlet, and she had been sent up by the A. C. Co. to carry freight and passengers to a new trading post at the upper forks of the Susitna. This trading post was called Talkeetna Station after the Talkeetna River which joins the Susitna at that point. On this steamer was a rival Mount McKinley expedition which had been sent out by the Mazama Mountaineering Club of Oregon. The expedition consisted of four men: C. E. Rusk, the leader; Cool, a guide; Rogec, a photographer; and Ridley, an ex-forest ranger. They were to proceed to Talkeetna Station on the *Alice* and then ascend the Chulitna River in a poling boat, until they reached the nearest approach to Mount McKinley's southern side. They were a pleasant party of men, and the friendly competition that existed between the two expeditions added greatly to the amusement and interest of our adventures.

A few nights after the departure of the *Alice*, I was awakened by Finch, who told me that the Beluga had broken and that the ice was coming. We turned out all hands instantly and armed with long pike poles began an exciting battle with the ice. The stream of small bergs was ceaseless and at times they came with such force and in such numbers that the wharf was threatened and we feared for the *Explorer*.

The beautiful long northern twilights had begun, and across the marshes a great silver moon hung in the sky while behind us the east was rosy from the scarcely hidden sun. The "break-up" on a northern river is a sight worth travelling far to see. And yet I doubt if there have been any more beautiful from an artistic standpoint than the breaking of this small river. The clear floes came sweeping down in a stately procession and as the moonlight or the warmer reflection of the rising sun struck them they gleamed and flashed like precious gems. The ice, weakened by the spring heat and torn from its hold on the river-beds by the fury of the water, moved as majestically as an army, that, beaten and retreating, still keeps its dignity and courage. Phalanx after phalanx, winter's beaten cohorts swept to the sea, and as we fought the floes the harsh clanging calls of wild geese told us that they too knew that winter was gone and that the water-lanes were open.

For two nights we fought the ice, snatching a few hours' rest when the flood tide backed the water up, and then saying good-by to our friends at Beluga we headed for the Susitna.

The Inlet was comparatively free of ice but the instant we entered the Susitna we began to meet floating masses of broken bergs and all the way to the Station we had to dodge swift-moving floes. In 1906 we had followed the northern channel but we were told at Beluga that almost all the water was coming down the southern channel, so we did not pass Alexander, where Porter and I had dined on dead hooligans in bygone days. I brought the *Explorer* from the delta to Susitna Station, a distance of about thirty miles, without touching bottom once, a feat which I never accomplished in the *Bulshaia*. The difficulties of navigation were increased by the ice-floes and made the ascent of the swifter portions rather serious work.

At the Station we met a lot of old friends. The camp had changed to quite a little village. The A. C. Co. had erected a large store and warehouses, but the Indian cabins were still in evidence. We found the stern-wheel steamer *Alice* moored at the river-front, and I imagine that the scene resembled some of the river-scenes on the Mississippi in the old days of the fur traders. We left a recording barograph with Mr. Wood of the A. C. Co., and he was to wind it at regular intervals and replace the marked sheets. Professor Parker and I enjoyed a civilised dinner, which boasted a chicken as the *pièce de résistance*, at the home of Doctor Kevig. The

Doctor and I were old friends as we had run 150 miles of the Stikine River in an Indian canoe several years before.

The *Alice* had had a narrow escape coming up the river; an ice jam had broken and they were just able to escape destruction by running downstream and darting into a small tributary called Willow Creek. The ice was still running in large quantities and we decided that we would lose no time by waiting over a day as we could then make better speed.

It was interesting to watch the river. Dirty masses of bar ice were sweeping and grinding towards the sea; here and there brilliant glittering phalanxes of clean ice showed where some distant mountain tributary had broken free and sent its clear covering to the main river, while great tree trunks and fields of drift spoke mutely of the overwhelming power of the spring thaw. As you looked you knew that every stream in every distant wilderness valley of the interior had risen at the call of summer and burst its winter bonds. But as you looked you thought too of the miles of river that stretched before you, and of the hard knocks your boat and engine would receive before the flood was beaten.

## CHAPTER VIII

# The Ascent of the Susitna and Chulitna Rivers

*Difficulties of northern motor-boating—The* Alice *passes us—We arrive at Talkeetna Station—We pass the Mazama expedition—Difficulties of navigation—Accidents—We reach the Tokositna River.*

Of all the problems in northern motor-boating, the choosing of an engine proved to be the most serious. If you take a cupful of glacier water and let it stand until it has settled you will find that about one fifth of the fluid is composed of the finest kind of pulverised silt. This silt is the natural tailings of nature's stamp-mill and is composed of glacier- and water-crushed rock. In the water-cooling systems used in gasoline engines, this silt clogs the cylinder water-jackets, and as your engine heats you have a very perfect but undesirable imitation of a brick-kiln on your hands. This was what occurred during the storm of 1906, and since then I have taken a frenzied interest in the different water-cooling systems. The continuous rain and humidity of the Alaskan Range likewise affected our electric batteries. Another difficulty that we encountered was the lack of gasoline in the Cook Inlet ports, and as the steamers that carry gasoline only run at long intervals, the fuel question was a constant annoyance.

With all these harrowing details in view we turned our eyes in 1910 toward kerosene engines, and finally selected an 18 h. p., two-cylinder engine that developed 26 h. p. when tested.

It was the uncertainty concerning the power and reliability of this engine that made me dread the struggle with the swift water.

As the *Alice* was going directly to Talkeetna, eighty miles up the river, Professor Parker took passage on her and we agreed to meet him later.

We left Susitna Station on May 26th and once again I found myself steering a boat along the crowded river bank towards the eddy that roars around the bluff. But this time the deep steady exhaust promised us power to spare and when we struck the white eddy wall the *Explorer* took the lashing foam over her bow and kept steadily on. Many of the "old timers" were sceptical about our ability to "buck" the Chulitna, but I had had more experience with engines in swift water than they and I knew that if we could get water enough and the engine did its work, we would win our fight with the river.

Now the navigation of swift water is fairly safe as long as you are careful and do not hurry. In bad water all men will, of course, use caution and do their utmost to keep away from danger, but in ordinary water this is not the case; time is of value, and a good river-man, by using his knowledge of currents and eddies, and by the skilful handling of his boat, will cover many more miles in a day than an overcautious man who holds to the main current.

On the first morning out the *Alice* passed us; we were having some slight engine trouble at the time and Captain Malmquist, who had taken a lot of interest in the *Explorer*, gave us a derisive whistle as he forged ahead.

Our greatest joy was in the return to wilderness camps and the exhilaration of our struggle with the river. The long spring days were a great help and during the three days that we spent in reaching Talkeetna, I stood at the wheel for fourteen, fourteen and a half, and fifteen hours respectively. As we advanced the beautiful peaks of the Talkeetna Mountains seemed to follow us on the south-eastern horizon, while Mounts McKinley, Foraker, and Roosevelt (as Mount Hunter is known among the prospectors) stood up grandly against the northern sky. As you watched the great cloud-like shapes hanging above the blue foothills, it was hard to realise that they were in reality stupendous masses of rock and ice.

We arrived at Talkeetna Station only five hours behind the *Alice*. Professor Parker was overjoyed as the river-men prognosticated that we would not show up for two days, but the *Explorer* was running like clockwork and we beat the small boat record by twelve hours. On the way up the river the *Alice* had rescued a prospector whose boat had been crushed by the ice while he was descending the river. He was sighted early in the morning, sitting on a log-jam in the river, a few hundred yards from the main channel. He appeared to be so weak that he could scarcely sit up, and he took no apparent interest in the approach of the steamer. In speaking of the rescue, Mr. Rusk, of the Mazama party, says:

> *The* Alice *was quickly landed a short distance above, on a little sandy island. Pilot Gordon and mate Blair jumped into a dory and went to the man's aid. He was brought aboard, put to bed, and given some light food. He proved to be one John Schmidt, and had been on the jam for six days and nights in such a cramped position that he could not keep entirely out of the water. Having started from Talkeetna in a small boat just after the ice went out, he overtook the jam at this point. Just as he reached it, it broke and swamped his boat. He managed to get onto the logs, where he remained until saved by the timely arrival of the* Alice*. This same man and a companion were wrecked at this identical spot in the spring of 1909 and remained on a jam for several days, until they were rescued. In fact the boat which they had on the first mishap was still lying on the island and it was now taken aboard the steamer. Twenty-four hours longer on the logs, and Schmidt would undoubtedly have been beyond help; but, as it was, he soon recovered from his trying experience.*

On our arrival at Talkeetna, we saw Schmidt sitting on a stump by the river, and we could see by his distended appearance he had been making up for lost time in the food question.

The Rusk party had left a few hours before, so not to be behindhand we waved good-by to our new friends and headed for the mouth of the Chulitna.

Many rivermen who had heard of the Chulitna cañon questioned our ability to run it in the *Explorer*.

The Rusk party were using a poling boat, a slow but sure way of reaching the Tokositna, and we were overjoyed, therefore, on entering the Chulitna to see the smoke of their camp-fire a short way above us on another branch of the river. After supper Professor Parker and I walked across the valley to where we could see their camp but several rushing streams kept us from paying them a visit.

The following morning things began to happen at the very start. Usually an accident on a northern river comes like a thunderclap out of a clear sky, and almost invariably the cause of the trouble is some minor accident that, taken by itself, *under ordinary conditions*, would be of no consequence. In the delta of the Chulitna the river is cut up into so many small channels that the water is extremely swift and shallow. After breaking camp we were trying to force our way up one of these narrow chutes where there was no room for manoeuvring. At last I sent four men ashore with a tracking line, and with the extra pull that they exerted we began to make headway. Everything was going finely, when suddenly the tiller line broke. In an instant the trackers were pulled off their feet, and the current swept us over a submerged bar, and crushed the *Explorer* against the bank.

Making the boat fast we gave her a thorough examination and found that the propeller was broken, the tunnel badly scarred, and the shaft worn. Nothing but a complete overhauling would fit us for our fight with the Chulitna cañon. Our first duty was to haul the stem out of water, and as the *Explorer* was lying with her bow upstream, we had to turn her around. As the current was exceedingly swift, we were afraid to let the current take her bow around, so we made a line fast to the bites with the idea of easing her. After anchoring the stern firmly we cast off the bow, but a battleship's hawser would not have held against that current, and when we finally succeeded in pointing her stern upstream, we had broken our hawser, torn the bitts out by the roots, and nearly hurt a man who got tangled in the line.

THE EXPLORER AFTER THE ACCIDENT ON THE CHULITNA RIVER

Before turning her, we had unloaded all our duffle—a good-sized job in itself. Then, after hauling the *Explorer's* stern out of water with the help of a dead man sunken in the frozen gravel, and a block and tackle, we recorked the tunnel, and sheathed it with tin from kerosene cans. We then put in a new steel shaft and propeller, melting our babbit in a frying-pan over a fire made from native coal that we picked up on the river bar.

At this point I realised the difficulties that confronted us and decided to sacrifice everything aboard that we could possibly do without. This extra duffle we placed in a cache against our return. Twelve hours later, with a new tiller-line insuring our steering-gear, we were flying up the Chulitna with everything in better working order than before the accident.

During the afternoon we were prospecting a bad rapid for a route, when Thompson shut off the engine and yelled: "Throw out an anchor!" We were about fifty yards above bad water so we dropped two anchors which we always carried on the forward deck ready for instant use. The current ran with such force, however, that we dragged our anchors, and came up with a thud on a bar at the head of the rapid. In a case of this kind it is "Every man overboard!" and into the water we went. The water under her bow where we had to work to push her off was about three and a half feet deep, and so swift that we could scarcely stand against it without holding on to the *Explorer*. When we began to push, we had to stoop and the rushing glacier water ran over our shoulders. Working over a boat under these conditions is about as unpleasant a task as I know of, and when the day is cold and raw, with downpours of rain drenching your back, the roar of the rapids is not loud enough to drown the explosions of "language" from the workers. When we finally got the *Explorer* into deep water, we found that in some mysterious way the tail shaft had become loose and would have slipped out into the river had not Arthur Aten grasped it with his bare hands—he was a truthful man who said, "It is the unexpected that always happens."

Our third camp was made where the distant spruce-crowned walls of the Chulitna Valley began to come together.

Besides forcing most of the water into one channel, the narrowing walls told us that we were approaching the cañon of which we had heard so many wild tales. On the following morning therefore we made an early start. Little by little the bluffs increased in height and drew together until the whole river was rushing and boiling along in one channel. At last we came to a rock point and beyond we could see the river sweeping around other straight rock walls, and we knew that we were at the foot of the cañon. I ran the *Explorer* into a large eddy below the bluff and we gave her a thorough overhauling.

When everything was shipshape the exhaust began to thunder and we were off. I cut straight through the big eddy and a great spout of spray flew up when we hit the swift water, but the *Explorer* ploughed along, and I drove her diagonally across the current to an eddy on the farther bank. Here we picked up headway again and once more we drove in clouds of spray across the river and caught an eddy above the big bluff.

In this way, using every eddy and backwater, we shot back and forth, slowly climbing the current as a salmon climbs a fish-ladder. It was thrilling work and a large part of the pleasure came from the magnificent way in which the *Explorer* behaved.

With my hands on the wheel I could feel every vibration of the staunch little craft, and there was a splendid exhilaration in feeling the steady force of the propeller as the white water drove against us. As commands would have been drowned in the roar of the rapids, I had installed bells, and Jack Thompson stood with every nerve on edge for the first clang of a signal.

In this work in swift water I have often noticed a strange fact for which I am unable to give an explanation. In very swift water it sometimes happens that the boat will come to a standstill. For a minute maybe you will not gain an inch, and then, just as you are beginning to give up hope and are searching the river for a new point of attack the boat will begin to climb. Very slowly at first, inch by inch, she will force her way along until, with the help of her momentum, she ploughs steadily upward past the dark bluffs. I know that there is some simple explanation for the boat's seeming increase in power, but we used to say that the *Explorer* had playful moods and would not exert all her strength until she had to.

At the head of the Chulitna you get your first smell of the snows, and as we came out of the cañon's walls the grey clouds lifted and we could see the great blue foothills of the Alaskan Range, running up to the everlasting snow-fields.

Above the cañon the river was difficult to navigate. Cañon water is swift but it is usually deep, and as a rule you have more difficulty in the swift shallow rapids. The valley of any Alaskan river the size of the Chulitna is usually several miles broad and as flat as a table. Through this level waste of water and gravel the river forces itself in countless channels that change from day to day, and the helmsman must be skilful indeed who unerringly chooses the right course. You may be speeding up a fine stretch, in a broad channel, when suddenly the river will split. One branch will follow a dense fringe of timber that marks the edge of the valley, while the other may lead across the broad valley, where you know there are scores of channels crisscrossing back and forth. If the streams are of equal size you must put all your experience to work in choosing the right course. The masses of driftwood and snags that rise above the water can be seen a long way off, and they usually indicate the location of the largest channels.

"Cut" or straight banks usually indicate deep water, and the points of forest land that run far out on the gravel bars will give you an idea of the location of the main channel.

The best-looking channels, however, are often "blind" at either the upper or lower end; for instance many small streams may overflow from a main channel and join each other one by one until a mile below they form a stream that appears to be as large and navigable as the true channel. A man coming upstream may easily choose the "blind" channel, and, being unable to see far ahead on account of the flatness of the valley, he will continue until the water gives out and he is forced to go back. As he has not room to turn his boat around he has to drift slowly backward, and when he finally reaches the main river again an hour has been wasted.

Sometimes we found places where the river was divided into three or four main branches of the same size, and we would patiently try them in turn. Occasionally they would all seem equally hopeless. The first step in a case of this kind is to find the branch with the shortest shoal. Two of the crew should then stand beside you—one to port and one to starboard, and take constant soundings with slender poles. The rest of the party should move forward at the command of the captain to counteract the sag of the boat's stern when she runs into exceptionally shallow water.

We passed a miserable spot of this kind above the Chulitna cañon. I could not get deep soundings anywhere and was forced finally to choose the most promising channel and ring "full speed ahead." As the water began to shoal I called the men forward, until finally I had Professor Cuntz sitting on the bow like a figurehead with his legs dangling alongside the cutwater. LaVoy and Grassi were taking soundings, and for what seemed an hour to me they kept calling, "Two feet!" "Two feet!" To relieve the monotony they would occasionally call, "Two feet—who'll make it three?" And then, sadly, as the shoal continued, "Two feet—no takers."

In this rapid our propeller was touching bottom for long periods, and there is no sound more harrowing than the grating of a grounding propeller; it comes up through your feet from the quivering hull and rings a danger signal in your brain far louder than the roar of the exhaust, the cries of the sounders, or the snarling of the rapids.

Glacier water is an opaque, milky-looking fluid, that hides every inequality of the bottom, and you must depend on your eyes to find the signs that denote a deep channel. These signs consist of minute differences in the formation of the surface waves, and they can only be learned by experience. When you see the surface "boiling," you know that you have at least three feet, and as the boils increase in size you know that the water is deepening.

When you see rough water sliding into large, oily eddies you know that the water is running over a shoal into a deep channel. The signs are many and the differences are often so minute as to make a description misleading. The best training for river-work is "tracking," as then you are forced to look for shallow water to wade in, and when a bath in ice-water is the result of a mistake, a man is inclined to study the current with fervid interest. Eventually you will be able to approximate closely the condition of the bottom by "the look o' the water."

Shoal water is always dangerous, while cañon navigation, provided you have a fast boat, is fun in comparison. The terrific force of the water, however, makes careful steering imperative. There were times in the Chulitna cañon, while we were taking the big swells, that the water swept across our forward deck, but these struggles with white water between grim cañon walls are the pleasantest part of northern motor-boating, and the memories of the breathless moments when you hung poised in the suck of the rollers will remain with you for years.

There is another side of river navigation that embodies all the excitement and danger without the dramatic setting of the cañon work. On all the northern rivers you will encounter long straight chutes of the current that rush past "cut banks" covered with dense timber. The current in these places is often almost irresistible and the only method of making appreciable progress is by hugging the banks. As all the soil in the bottom lands is composed of fine silt, these banks are continually caving in, and as the banks melt away the forest trees come thundering down, throwing up great spouts of spray as they strike the rushing water. On the day that we left Talkeetna, a large cottonwood tree fell as the banks caved in and just missed the *Explorer*'s stern.

Equally dangerous are the submerged snags, which, luckily, can be traced by the waves and whirlpools that mark their hiding-places.

Navigating swift water among the snags and "sweepers" requires the greatest mental concentration, and your course is a constant series of problems in distances, pressures, and speeds. You may be barely holding your own in the racing stream with a half-submerged snag bellowing six feet astern of your propeller, a sweeper hanging over you, whose lower branches had to be chopped off to make a passage-way for the boat, and a log jam ahead around whose jagged edges the current is torn to foam. At these times the helmsman cannot take his eyes, even for a fraction of a second, from the current ahead, as a failure to "meet" an over-boil of the current would mean disaster. He must depend on his crew for intelligence concerning the progress of the boat. Standing with your eyes glued on the water while your companions cry, "She's holding her own! She's holding her own! She's going back a little! Now, she's going ahead!" is exciting enough to make your hair turn grey.

We passed a point on the Chulitna where the water shot between two points with terrific speed. I tried twice, by dropping astern and then hitting the current full speed, to climb the swift water. On my second failure I saw that the water above some big snags had overflowed among a grove of small cottonwood trees, and on the third attempt I drove the *Explorer* through the cottonwoods on the edge of the swift water. Our propeller was beating an insane tattoo on the saplings, and left a trail of match-wood behind, but we got through.

In another rapid our progress was arrested by a large spruce sweeper. Just above the sweeper was an eddy that was the key to the successful navigation of the rapid. By forcing our boat to full speed we could just beat the current, and LaVoy threw the bight of a line around the tree trunk. With our engine still going to take some of the pressure from the straining line we hung to our precarious anchorage while LaVoy chopped through our evergreen obstruction. When the tree fell it was sucked under instantly by the rushing water and we had a clear road to our coveted eddy.

As the reader will understand, this kind of work is a great strain on the best of boats or engines, and where chances such as these are taken accidents are sure to result. It was for this reason that I took so many extra engine parts and propellers, and we made good use of them before we said good-by to the rushing waters of the Chulitna.

After we had crossed the large flats above the Chulitna cañon, we kept to the left of the valley and watched for the mouth of the Tokositna. As we advanced the great spires of the Tokosha Mountains broke through the clouds, and my thoughts flew back to the day in 1906 when we crouched in our mountain tent above the Tokositna glacier and gave the range its name. The river that we were now looking for—the Tokositna—was the river after which we had named the range.

The Chulitna River now swung to the north-east, following the foothills of the Alaskan Range, and at the bend we caught our first glimpse of the great glacier that drains Mount McKinley's southern ramparts, and then a streak of white water showed where the Tokositna came rushing into the Chulitna. With a feeling of exultation we headed the *Explorer* up "the river that comes from the land where there are no trees," and an hour later we had come to the end of our long water journey.

There were old choppings on the bank where we landed and on going ashore to prospect for a camping place we found a well-constructed but tiny cabin. In all probability it was built by Dokkin, the prospector, who accompanied Dr. Cook and Ed. Barrill to this point and remained after their departure to trap and prospect for gold. It was a good camp-site, for a dry bar just above a cut bank gave us both deep and shoal water for docking or hauling out the *Explorer*, and a grove of spruce trees furnished us with firewood and boughs.

The excitement of our journey up the Chulitna had driven all thought of the Mazama expedition from our minds. But as the navigation became easier, I studied the banks carefully for "tracking" signs, and as I was experienced in this form of travel the results told me that no one had ascended the river before us. With the knowledge that we had passed our rivals we were filled with delight, but there was no personal feeling in our happiness; it was merely the gratification of having won a race, although our success following the prognostications to the contrary from the river-men gave me a certain satisfaction. The race, however, was only begun for the Mazamas were also headed towards the ice-crowned summit of McKinley, and our friendly rivalry was not yet over, although we had won the first heat. Had it not been for this fact, I would have gladly run the *Explorer* downstream and given Mr. Rusk and his men a helping hand.

## CHAPTER IX

# The Advance Up the Big Glacier

~

***Parkersburgh—Reconnaissance trips—Trail chopping—Packing—Ascending the glacier—We travel at night—We send back for more food—Gas poisoning.***

As the little cabin that Dokkin had built on the banks of the Tokositna River was to be our home during the summer, a description of its position in relation to Mount McKinley will not be amiss. Our camp was situated thirty-seven and a half miles from Mount McKinley. The country between it and the mountains was a piedmont gravel bed that extended along the base of the Alaskan Range. This strip of low-land was covered with typical Alaskan forest growth except where the treacherous muskegs lay, and at frequent intervals glacier- and snow-water streams rushed down to the Tokositna. A few miles away in an air line rose the terminal moraine of the great glacier that was to be our roadway to the big mountain. The moraine was covered with rock and soil for a long distance back from the glacier's tongue and on this precarious foothold groves of spruce and tangled jungles of alders grew. The ice in reality continued much farther than one would suppose as the carpet of forest growth hid the dividing line. On one of my reconnaissance trips I was forcing my way through the masses of undergrowth and moraine débris well down toward the valley floor, when, to my surprise, I came upon a wall of solid ice one hundred feet high that had forced its way upward through the earth.

From the tongue of the glacier rushed a quantity of glacier-streams, and as the weather grew warmer the overflow of water from the huge masses of ice filled the streams until they were well-nigh impassable. The great glacier itself was shrouded in mystery. Dr. Cook had named it the Ruth glacier but the name had not "taken" and to this day the great ice-river stands nameless on the Government maps. There is a lot of sentimental foolishness connected with the naming of geographical features, and it is strange to note how little taste or forethought is shown by the average man when it comes to naming national monuments. These great mountains, rivers, and glaciers are firstly the property of all the people, and secondly, as they form important geographical monuments or dividing lines, they should when possible be given historical or descriptive names. The Board of Geographical Names in Washington was organised with this point in view. In the use of proper names lies the principal source of trouble, for a large number of the names found on the map are the names of people who are of little interest to the general public. In the use of proper names those of famous or illustrious men or women only should be used, and wherever possible a name that carries an historical significance. An excellent illustration of a geographical monument, bearing an illustrious and at the same time an historical name, is the Malaspena glacier. On hearing the name for the first time the traveller will inquire into its origin. And in the ensuing description he not only hears for the first time of the exploring feats of this early navigator, but obtains, as well, a glimpse into the early history of this portion of the Alaskan coast. This name, therefore, serves two purposes: it is a monument to a brave man, and it reminds us of the early history of that bleak coast. The name of the Susitna River will serve as an example of a descriptive name that is historical as well; Susitna means in the language of the Susitna Indians, "the river of sand" or "the sandy river." No name could be chosen that better describes the natural peculiarities of this great stream, and at the same time it will perpetuate through centuries to come, not only the name of one of the Alaskan tribes, but a sentence from their language as well. No one can belittle the importance of geographical names after giving the matter due thought, for America is filled with "horrible examples" of this thoughtless manner of conferring names; the highest and most beautiful snow-clad mountain in the United States is known by the misspelled name of an Englishman who never saw the peak and whose only important historical connection with our country was as an enemy.

With this human weakness in view Professor Parker and I strove to refrain from complicating an already complicated state of affairs by abstaining as far as possible from conferring personal names that might or might not remain, and in our explorations in the Mount McKinley region we spoke of the natural landmarks by such titles as their forms suggested, or by numbers in the order in which they occurred. The large glacier which we followed to Mount McKinley we spoke of as the "big glacier," and in view of the fact that the United States Government has conferred no name upon it, I will still speak of it as the "big glacier" for purposes of identification.

Our first duty on the completion of our water journey was to dry-dock the *Explorer,* so that Thompson, who was to remain at the base camp, could make such slight repairs as were necessary. This feat was easily accomplished with the aid of rollers and a block and tackle.

With the *Explorer* in a safe place we could turn our thoughts towards the important work, which was the location and construction of a good trail to the top of the big glacier. This duty necessitated a thorough knowledge of the country and I therefore divided our party into three units of two men to explore separate routes to the ice.

This reconnaissance constituted our first real wilderness day, and as an example of the importance of physical training it is worthy of a few remarks.

The day's work consisted in travelling through brush, soft snow, swamps, and glacier streams for about ten hours. With the exception of one or two men who put a biscuit in their pockets we took no food with us. The day's work was in no way difficult, for we carried no loads; our condition from *the civilised standpoint* was splendid; we were well-fed, sun-browned, and fairly hard—and yet we all came into camp *thoroughly tired out*. Two months later, after our adventures on Mount McKinley's icy flanks, we came down through the same stretch of country. The snow however had melted, leaving dense thickets through which we had to chop our way; the mosquitoes hung in clouds; and four of us, Grassi, LaVoy, Tucker, and I, were carrying packs running from 95 to 120 pounds. From the civilised standpoint *we were not well-fed* and we did not look well—our eyes and cheeks were sunken and our bodies were worn down to bone and sinew; and yet we came into camp as fresh and happy as children, and after a bite to eat and a smoke we could have gone on cheerfully.

On the following day we followed out our best reconnaissance line and chopped out a good trail to timber-line. This brought us out on the bare morainal hills that lie on the northern side of the big glacier, and as we turned campward we could see an easy approach to the back of the great ice-river. We had reached our base camp,

THE TERMINAL MORAINE OF THE BIG GLACIER. TOKOSHA MOUNTAINS IN DISTANCE.

which we had named Parkersburgh, in Professor Parker's honour, on the 31st of May, and on June 5th everything was in working order and we had advanced 625 pounds of mountain duffle to camp 2. The distance separating our camps as we moved forward always depended on the character of the country. We usually counted on advancing two loads per man per day; one in the morning and one in the afternoon.

We increased the weight of our packs as our bodies grew accustomed to the toil, and on June 6th we carried seventy-pound loads comfortably. In packing we worked systematically and each man of the packing squad knew just about what his share amounted to. Grassi, LaVoy, Tucker, and I carried the bulk of our equipment, although both Professor Parker and Professor Cuntz gave us much appreciated aid.

Packing, when a man carries all he can stagger under, is one of the most exhausting occupations in the world. Only men of sound build and physical courage ever succeed in becoming expert weight-carriers. You can never tell from a man's looks how much he can shoulder, although short, compactly built men are usually the strongest. Men of over six feet in height are seldom able to carry heavy loads, and the best packers usually stand between five feet five inches and five feet ten inches.

Our packing squad was particularly well fitted for this arduous toil. Valdemar Grassi had held the strength test of Columbia University to within a short time prior to his joining our expedition. He was the tallest man in our party, standing close to six feet, and he weighed, in condition, about 176 pounds. He was used to the active forms of outdoor sport, but he had not as yet had any experience in the gruelling labours of a wilderness life. He learned quickly and carried heavy loads.

Herman L. Tucker was inured to the hardships of a life in the open. He was stockily built, standing about five feet ten inches in his shoe-packs. The muscular development of his lower limbs was unusual, and he carried heavy weights with ease and rapidity.

Merl LaVoy had spent his whole life in the open, and with one or two exceptions he was the best packer that I have ever travelled with. He stood about five feet ten inches and strangely enough his body showed only normal physical development, although he was capable of far more physical hardship than the average frontiersman.

OUR PACK TRAIN LEAVING CAMP 2

*From left to right: Aten, Tucker, Parker, Cuntz, La Voy, and Grassi*

I was the smallest member of the packing squad, standing five feet six inches and weighing about 145 pounds when in training.

The task that confronted us was a journey of thirty-seven and a half miles in an air line over glacial ice and snow. But as we travelled the distance was much farther. Our outfit at the beginning of our journey weighed about 1200 pounds.

In carrying our loads we used an adaptation of the Russian-Aleute pack-strap of my own make. It was composed of padded canvas, and when it was adjusted over the shoulders, the principal weight came on the chest strap. There was no possibility of chafing, and the harness was light and easily adjusted. Whenever heavy loads are carried the "tump-line" or forehead strap is a necessity, as a heavy weight can be borne on the head and neck.

There are many pack-bags or sacks on the market but they are only useful for ordinary camping trips. In really serious packing the loads carried are so heavy and of such bulk that a pack-bag of a restricted shape is useless. Our personal belongings were stowed in waterproof bags and in addition each man carried a waterproof pack cover.

The bulk of our weight was in pemmican and alcohol, and the cans were packed in wooden boxes. Until our backs got hardened to the toil, they were raw from the

TUCKER AND THE AUTHOR PACKING AT GLACIER POINT, SHOWING OUR METHOD OF CARRYING LOADS

constant contact with the hard wood. But bearing pain with stoicism must be one of a packer's attributes, and for this reason good packers are made—not born. Our alcohol was denatured and undrinkable, and on one occasion one of our party was heard to say that he wished it was "good-natured." Our pemmican was the usual kind, consisting of pulverised raw meat mixed with sugar, raisins, currants, and tallow.

We drank nothing but tea while we were on the ice. Coffee is rarely used in the wilderness.

Our work progressed steadily until on the 6th of June we had our first accident. On the way home from camp 2 I slipped on a rotten log and sprained my ankle so badly that LaVoy, Grassi, and Tucker carried me to camp. I kept my ankle in glacier water and although the swelling did not disappear for six months I was soon able to travel and carry loads of eighty pounds. By the 9th of June we had advanced all our equipment to camp 3, and a part of it to camp 4, which was situated on the edge of the big glacier.

Since leaving Beluga we had been keeping pace with the vanishing snow; but in the shadow of the Alaskan Range it was still winter and we were forced to use our long Susitna snowshoes between camps 3 and 4. Back-packing in soft snow is hard work, but the snow below timber-line was really an advantage, for it covered the dense thickets of alder and willow.

On June 11th we had our last wood-fire. We had packed 1200 pounds of mountain duffel to the back of the glacier and from there on we were to travel through Arctic surroundings. The conditions were the same as those that prevail in the lowlands in the early spring when travelling is attempted only in extreme cases. During the day the snow turned to wet slush that clung to our snowshoes until they dragged like leaden weights. Our packs averaged seventy pounds at this time but we carried more as our muscles hardened.

The glacier was rough and cut up into innumerable hollows, lakes, and sharp ridges, and under either the blazing sun or the weird blue light of the northern night the contours blended into flat masses. We all began to suffer from snow-blindness, and finding a good trail under such conditions was largely a matter of chance. We were comforted somewhat, however, by the knowledge that the going would be better when we reached the hard-packed mountain snow, and a glimpse now and then of Mount McKinley, as it shook off its mantle of clouds, and towered clean cut against the northern sky, would encourage us to greater efforts. After one experience with packs under the hot sun we rested during the heat of the day and travelled at night. The change benefited us in two ways; it saved our eyes, and the snow grew firm from the frost.

Camp 5 was situated on the northern edge of the glacier. A high range of mountains formed the glacier's northern wall, while directly opposite rose the beautiful Tokosha Mountains that ended in the great ridge on which Professor Parker and I had camped in 1906. I climbed the mountain behind our camp and in addition to a good view of the glacier found a large brown bear who objected to my society and left me to the enjoyment of the magnificent scene. As the travelling conditions seemed to be growing worse our thoughts turned to an old sled that we had found beside the cabin at Parkersburgh and in the hope that it would aid us in advancing our supplies, Professor Cuntz and Aten returned for it.

Even under the weight of a heavy pack the night travel had a great fascination for me. We would move slowly along across the great sombre snow-fields. The silence was absolute and the slow, rhythmic crunching of our snowshoes seemed but to accentuate the quiet. I do not remember ever having seen skies of greater beauty; they were green, or claret, or golden, and under this light the grey snows seem to spring into life, and change to every shade of blue and purple. After we had dropped our precious loads we would trot back to camp with the long rolling snowshoe gait, and trudge slowly away under a second heavy load. The work was monotonous but we never knew monotony for always the great saw-tooth ranges that guarded McKinley beckoned us on.

Professor Cuntz and Aten rejoined us at camp 6 with the sled. But to our disgust the temperature refused to drop as night came on and we were unable to use it as the snow was too soft. They also brought us the news that the Mazama expedition had reached the Tokositna.

On the night of June 15th it rained, and after breaking a long trail to the top of a *serac* or ice fall, we were forced to give up and lie shivering in our damp bags, for the trail did not freeze and we could not pull the sled over it. When daylight came we arose and by a combination of back-packing and sled-work we advanced our camp to the face of the serac. The snow was wet and our exertions terrific. At 2 A.M., we crawled exhausted into our bags and slept until morning. The scenes through which we were moving were of Arctic desolation; great green blocks of ice rose high above our camp and stupendous ice-covered mountains surrounded us. In addition to Mount McKinley we could see Mount Foraker—17,000 feet, which is called Mrs. McKinley by the Indians; and Mount Hunter, 14,960 feet.

Mount Hunter, as it is called on the United States Geological map, is the same mountain that Dr. Cook and I saw and spoke of as little McKinley when we spent the night on the peak west of the Tokositna glacier in 1906. The name Mount Hunter is unknown to the Alaskans and in 1910 it was called Mount Roosevelt by the prospectors of the Susitna watershed. We were now about opposite our last ridge camp of 1906, and strangely enough the views of the glacier that I had obtained at that time were a benefit now, although four years had passed, for the seracs ahead of us cut off all view of our route. The weather too combined with the glacier to hold us back, and before we reached our eighth camp, we had been held by several severe snow and wind storms.

I had been studying the food question from day to day, and despite our original 1200-pound outfit, I began to realise that if we intended to climb Mount McKinley we would have to conserve our food. We were averaging about a mile a day in advancing our camps, as we had to make so many relays. Something radical had to be done, so we sent back Grassi, Aten, and LaVoy, with instructions to get more food. We would in this way be using less mountain food, and would eliminate the useless drain on our commissary due to the constant delays in our reconnaissance work.

Camp 8 was at the top of the first system of seracs and from this point we could get a good view of the glacier ahead. On account of a heavy snow-storm we only advanced a half march from this camp and Professors Parker and Cuntz, after carrying forward their own belongings, decided to spend the night, so we pitched a tent for them before returning and called the new camp "camp 8B." The following morning dawned beautifully clear, and we started early with heavy packs for camp 8B. There had been a snow-storm during the night and even our fresh trail was smoothly covered by the white mantle. It was with the greatest surprise, therefore, that as I approached the tent, I saw a fresh deep-ploughed trail leading from the tent to the distant mountains. But my surprise was even greater as I drew near and noticed that the fresh trail did not lead from the tent. Turning off to examine it, I found the explanation. The trail had been made by a great brown bear!

Professors Parker and Cuntz were still sleeping and as I wished them good-morning, I laughingly asked them if they knew that they had had a visitor during the night, and Professor Parker answered: "Why, yes; I heard one of the boys moving about, and asked him to come in and get warm, but he went away without answering me." When he and Professor Cuntz saw the kind of visitor they had invited into the tent they were glad indeed that their invitation had not been accepted!

It was at this camp that we divided the party and sent the men to base camp for more food. In many letters that I have received from sympathisers with Dr. Cook, I have been told by these gentlemen (that have never back-packed on a glacier) that there was no reason why Dr. Cook could not have climbed Mount McKinley and returned to the Tokositna River with a forty-pound pack. If the reader will compare with the map the numbers of days that we and the Mazama party spent in following the big glacier, they will understand, I am sure, that no rules of travel can be applied to ice work. One little serac, not indicated on any map, may block the advance of the most determined party; one small crevasse may detain a party for hours; or one mountain storm hold the travellers storm-bound for days. On the first night after the division of our party we encountered a large crevasse that was filled with running water. At last Herman Tucker found a point where a huge glacial erratic had bridged the chasm and we were able to cross in ease and safety. Fearing that more streams would intervene and cause us trouble, we headed once more for the edge of the glacier, and pitched our ninth camp on the snow-covered moraine. At camp 9 we underwent one of the most unusual and unpleasant experiences that it has been my ill fortune to be subjected to. On the night of June 18th it began to sleet and blow. Cold followed, the temperature dropped below freezing, and the storm increased to a blizzard. We lay helpless in our sleeping-bags, listening to the lashing of the wind and snow on our tent. On the next day the storm continued. On several occasions we had difficulty in lighting our alcohol stoves, but we reasoned that the frozen tent was air tight and after enlarging the aperture in the door the stove burnt well. We all felt badly during the afternoon, but we attributed our troubles to lack of exercise. The glaciers and mountains presented a desolate sight through the wind-driven clouds of snow and mist. About 8 P.M. I began to feel so weak that I determined to go outside, storm or no storm. I had been conscious for a long time of an unpleasant feeling of depression.

Later my mind was filled with queer illusions. Finally I staggered to my feet and went outdoors. As the cold air filled my lungs a feeling of relief came over me and then my mind was stunned as if some one had struck me on the head with a club. I remember sinking to my knees although I fought to stand uptight. I saw, as in a dream, Professor Parker come out of the tent, stand for an instant, and then fall headlong in the snow, and lie there motionless. Without surprise I heard my own voice, a long way off, calling to Tucker and then—nothing. How long the unconscious spell lasted I do not know but I was brought to by hearing Professor Cuntz calling my name. I tried to answer but at first no sound came, although eventually I succeeded in making myself heard.

He could not find me at first as I had slid down the moraine and under a great granite boulder, but when he came to me he brought a steaming cup of hot tea. After the welcome drink I crawled to the top of the moraine, and saw both Professor Parker and Tucker lying in the snow. But with the help of Professor Cuntz's tea they too soon revived and we gathered in a miserable group beside the granite boulder. We were attacked by nausea and vomiting, and later by violent spasms of shivering. Later we returned to the tent and drank more tea, and after a good sleep we seemed none the worse for our adventure. The cause of our unpleasant experience was the use of alcohol stoves in a small tent where the oxygen had already been exhausted by our breathing; carbon monoxide gas resulted and we were lucky to recover as easily as we did. We attribute Professor Cuntz's immunity to the fact that he was sitting upright, working on his topographical notes, during the greater part of the day and as his head was above the small aperture in the door he received some fresh air. We profited by the experience and thereafter when we were stormbound we thoroughly ventilated the tent at frequent intervals.

CHAPTER X

# The End of the Polar Controversy

***We arrive at Glacier Point—We duplicate Dr. Cook's pictures—We find the peak shown in his "summit picture"—We explore Glacier No. 2—We find the fake peak.***

From the summit of the moraine where camp 9 was situated, we were able for the first time to see the head of the lower portion of the big glacier. The first tributary glacier entered from the south-west side. This was the glacier that I had chosen as the *probable* site of Dr. Cook's Mount McKinley photographs, and had indicated as such in a sketch which was copied and published by the *Metropolitan Magazine*. But on closer scrutiny the mountains did not resemble Dr. Cook's photographs as they were covered with what appeared to be perpetual fields of deep snow. The second tributary glacier joined the big glacier from the north, and here we saw at once a striking resemblance to the type of mountains shown in Dr. Cook's photographs, reproductions of which I carried with me. We were also influenced to some degree by the map of this glacier shown in Edward Barrill's affidavit, in which he shows that Dr. Cook's photographs were taken on this glacier which we called "glacier 2."

But we realised that Barrill's testimony could not be believed by many people as he had confessed to having made misrepresentations concerning his Mount McKinley climb. We, therefore, determined to depend on our own investigation and on Dr. Cook's photographs alone in our search for evidence.

Between these two tributary glaciers stood what we called at our first glance "the great gorge." The great gorge was formed by two lines of magnificent peaks that rose in jagged lines above grim walls. Through this aperture poured the main stream of the big glacier, and under the heavy cloud banks we could see the crushed

Glacier No. 2

*The glacier on which Dr. Cook took the fake pictures of Mount McKinley. The short arrow indicates the Fake Peak. The long arrow indicated the cliff shown opposite page 239 in Dr. Cook's book [shown on page 164 of this book]. Called McKinley Cliff by the 1910 expedition. This is a duplicate of the picture opposite page 197 of Dr. Cook's book [shown on page 169 of this book].*

chaotic seracs formed by the terrific pressure of the ice against the cliffs.

The point of land between the great gorge and glacier 2 we recognised from Dr. Cook's and Ed. Barrill's description as the point on which they camped, and we spoke of it as "Glacier Point." Between camp 9 and Glacier Point the glacier ice had formed a great eddy. Large snow-covered hills of crushed rock had been forced up by the pressure of the ice and between lay deep hollows, some of which were filled with water later in the season. Over this mass of glacial débris lay a treacherous covering of soft snow. Herman Tucker and I were carrying eighty-pound packs and in sliding down and climbing up these steep hills we had many a bad fall. More than once one of our party would break through into the holes between the boulders, and become so hopelessly tangled with pack and snowshoes that he needed assistance to get out. On one of the snow slopes that swept down from the high peaks we saw a big brown bear, possibly our visitor of camp 8B.

After an exhausting day's work we reached Glacier Point. Our camp was pitched in a deep morainal hollow, and we looked across the void to dim blue ice walls capped by the serac of glacier 2.

We intended to explore glacier 2 on the following day but it was stormy, so we returned to camp 9. In returning we held to the centre of the big glacier and found excellent travelling, and escaped the rough surface of the moraine; we therefore packed all our belongings from camp 9 to the centre of the glacier in order that we might profit by our new route. After forming the depot we returned to camp 8B for a third relay. We also needed "babiche" with which to mend our snowshoes, and we took this opportunity of leaving a letter for our companions, telling them which route to follow, as they had been gone a week, and we were beginning to get worried. I was attacked by snow-blindness while we were "filling" our snowshoes and we were forced to remain at camp 8B that night. We had left a mountain tent standing at this relay station and we found that it was necessary to move it as the

THE GREAT GORGE VIEW FROM GLACIER POINT

exposed surface of the snow melted away so quickly that it left the tent standing on a high snow pedestal that would have collapsed eventually.

We carried heavy packs to camp 9 and Tucker and I exchanged them for our regular seventy-five pound relay loads and pushed through to Glacier Point. Our idea was to bring up at least a month's outfit in food and alcohol, and then we would be free to advance up the great gorge to Mount McKinley. The long stretch of glacier over which we did our relaying was as lonely and silent an expanse of country as I have ever tramped through. At night the fog would cling to the mountains so that from our dim trail you could see nothing but the blue snow melting away into the mist. After several hours of packing through this cold, blue solitude, the monotony would become almost unbearable. I remember trying all sorts of things to keep my mind occupied. Probably the most successful expedient was reciting poetry, in time to the clicking of your snowshoes, for the faster you recited the faster you travelled. The monotony of this kind of work seems to have a hypnotic effect on the traveller. I remember one night when Professor Cuntz fell into a deep sleep during the short rests we made at half-hour intervals. Talking, or yelling, did not have any effect and I was forced to shake him into consciousness.

Several brown bears had wintered among these great expanses of ice and snow, and we found their tracks leading downward towards the lowlands.

On June 27th we intended to explore Glacier 2, but the weather was cloudy and we devoted our energy instead to moving our camp out of the hollow. We established our twelfth camp on the edge of the great gorge, making a rise of four hundred feet in altitude. We were now worrying constantly about our companions, as they were several days overdue and we feared that an accident had occurred.

We had packed to the edge of the great gorge:

19 6-lb. cans of pemmican
1 3/4 cases of hardtack
2 lbs. of Lipton tea
35 lbs. of Erbswurst
35 lbs. sugar
70 cups beef tea
22 lbs. raisins
12 gals. of alcohol

In addition we had two mountain tents complete; alcohol stoves, pots, ice axes, mountain rope, ice-creepers, cameras, and a large supply of films, snowshoes, etc. This amounted to more than twice as much food, per man, as Dr. Cook and Ed. Barrill had when they started from the Tokositna River, and we were already half-way to Mount McKinley. Dr. Cook said that he and Barrill carried forty pounds, and Barrill told me that they carried less, as Dr. Cook's pack was appreciably lighter than his. But accepting Dr. Cook's figures we can allow them an outfit of eighty pounds. An allowance of fifty pounds for food out of the original eighty would be liberal, but we must remember that out of this fifty pounds we must subtract at least ten pounds for fuel. This would allow them twenty pounds of food per man, at the most, and the weight of cans, sacks, cooking utensils, and a stove would reduce it still more.

On June 28th we made an early start to explore glacier 2. But before going into the details of our method of tracing Dr. Cook, a few words are necessary to explain to the reader the photographic and topographical mistakes, or blunders rather, that Dr. Cook had made. When his book, *The Top of Our Continent*, was published, we found that it contained conclusive proof that he had not ascended Mount McKinley.

Opposite page 227 is a photograph purporting to be "The Summit of Mount McKinley, the highest mountain of North America, altitude 20,390 feet."

The camera that took this photograph was, as any experienced mountain photographer can tell at a glance, *pointing upward*, and yet in the right-hand lower sky-line of this picture appears the dim outline of a second *rock-capped peak*, which any mountaineer would recognise as a mountain as high, or higher than the rock called the summit of Mount McKinley.

Now as every sign of rock ceases a thousand feet below Mount McKinley's summit, this photograph in itself constituted absolute disproof of Dr. Cook's story, and yet he was careless enough to print a second photograph which shows this telltale "lower right-hand sky-line peak" in its relation to the surrounding mountains, *and Glacier Point!* Comparison showed that both of the pictures were taken from nearly the same point. Our knowledge of the country, therefore, enabled us to locate Dr. Cook's fake peak before leaving New York, and later events showed that we were only about one hundred yards out of the way in our reckoning.

It was four years after Dr. Cook's visit that Professor Parker, Cuntz, Tucker, and I arrived at Glacier Point.

Our food statistics were all that was necessary to tell us that we were close to the scene of Dr. Cook's mountaineering operations. Glacier No. 1 was, as I have before stated, eliminated from our explorations as there were no peaks there that resembled Dr. Cook's photographs. The perpendicular walls of the great gorge were ample evidence that he could not have made the pictures there. This left only the northern, or northeastern, amphitheatre glacier, or glacier No. 2, as the locality in which he could have taken his photographs.

With our eyes on this glacier, the great gorge, and the great peaks that rose above the gorge, we began to study Dr Cook's pictures. We did not have long to wait, for in Dr. Cook's illustration which is published opposite page 239 in his book, was the answer to all our questions. This photograph showed the great peaks above the gorge including the second or telltale peak, the main serac below the great gorge, Glacier Point, and glacier No. 2 in the foreground. It was on June 22d that we reached Glacier Point and as we pitched our tent in the "morainal hollow" the view that we saw was the same as that shown in Dr. Cook's photograph opposite page 197, and we could tell by referring to this picture that he had taken the photograph from a knoll about three hundred feet above us.

Our mountain detective work was based on the fact that no man can lie topographically. In all the mountain ranges of the world there are not two hillocks exactly alike. We knew that if we could find one of the peaks shown in his photographs we could trace him peak by peak and snow-field by snow-field, to within a foot of the spot where he exposed his negatives. And now, without going out of our way, we had found the peaks he had photographed, but we had found as well from the photograph opposite page 239 that at the time that he took that picture he was not going towards Mount McKinley but that he was high up among the peaks at the head of glacier No. 2—*at least a day's travel out of his course!*

There was only one explanation for this fact and that was that close to where this photo was taken we would find the fake peak! From Glacier Point we could see several high mountains that looked as if they might prove to be the one we were looking for, and a cliff which stood above a saddle had a familiar look to us. The distance however was too great for a definite decision and we decided therefore to make a reconnaissance.

As we climbed the serac on glacier No. 2 we began to leave Glacier Point well below us, and by the time that we reached the upper snow-fields we had made two important discoveries. The first was that as we increased our altitude, peak No. 2 was not hidden by the intervening summits of Glacier Point.

This proved to us that if peak No. 2 was, as we believed, the same peak shown in the right-hand lower sky-line of Dr. Cook's fake photograph of Mount McKinley, we were travelling in the right direction to reach the spot from which he made his exposure. The second discovery was the confirmation of our suspicions that the cliff we had seen from Glacier Point was the same cliff shown on the left side of the photograph opposite page 239. The scent was growing warm.

There was one fact that puzzled us. We had been under the impression that the peak Dr. Cook climbed and photographed was a moderately high peak, and yet as we advanced we could see no peaks worthy of the name in the vicinity of the cliff. For we had decided that this cliff must be close to the fake peak.

It required but a short advance, however, to relieve our minds on this point, for turning to Dr. Cook's picture of the cliff with peaks 1 and 2 showing in the distance, we read: "Scene of Glaciers, Peaks, and Cliffs—shoulder of Mount McKinley, a cliff of 8000 feet. Ruth Glacier, the freight carrier of the cloud world. The Great White Way where the polar frosts meet the Pacific drift of the tropical dews."

Just what Dr. Cook intended by a "a cliff of 8000 feet" we can only surmise, but the top of the cliff actually rose about 300 feet above the glacier, and its altitude was only 5300 feet above sea-level! After this discovery we no longer expected to find that the Doctor had actually climbed a high peak—climbing with printer's ink was far easier. We had now reached the base of the saddle that led on its southern end to the cliff. We called a halt for luncheon, and as we ate our hardtack and pemmican we studied the country about us. Looking back at the cliff I was struck by a remarkable profile of William McKinley. The likeness was so perfect that on asking one of my companions what the outline of the cliff suggested to him, he replied without the slightest hesitation, "William McKinley." For purposes of identification, therefore, we named it McKinley cliff.

A few minutes later we began the ascent of the snow saddle on the way to the snow cornice on top of McKinley cliff. Professor Parker had started a few minutes before, and, as we neared the top, we saw him breaking down a small snow cornice that led to a small rock outcrop near the top of the saddle.

This cornice led in the direction of the summit of McKinley cliff, and as we turned to follow the saddle we heard Professor Parker shout, "We've got it!" An

McKinley Cliff on left. Glacier Number 2 in foreground. Glacier Point on right. The Big Glacier in distance. McKinley Cliff rises about 300 feet above the glacier, and is situated 20 miles south of Mount McKinley.
*This same view is printed opposite page 239 of Dr. Cook's book and is labeled "Scene of glaciers, peaks and cliffs. Shoulder of Mt. McKinley, a cliff of 8,000 feet. Ruth Glacier, a freight carrier of the cloud world. The Great White Way, where the polar frosts meet the Pacific drift of the tropical dews."*

instant later as the cornice came into line with the rock we saw that it was true—the little outcrop of rock below the saddle was the rock peak of Dr. Cook's book, under which he wrote, "The Top of our Continent—the Summit of Mount McKinley; the highest mountain of North America—Altitude 20,390 feet."

While we stood there lost in thought of the dramatic side of our discovery, Professor Parker walked to the top of the rock at the point where Barrill had posed when Dr. Cook exposed the negative. His figure completed the picture. Then we gathered around the photograph that Dr. Cook had taken and traced the contours of the rock by its cracks and shoulders. As our eyes reached the right-hand sky-line there stood peak No. 2—the rock-ribbed peak on which we had based our denial of

Dr. Cook's claim, and by which we had traced his footsteps through the wilderness of rock and ice. After taking a few photographs we sat down on the rocks in the warm sun. Avalanches were booming and thundering among the mountains, and the view of Mount McKinley, twenty miles away, across the blazing whiteness of the glacier far below, and up above the lines of grim knife-hacked ridges, was a picture of such sublime beauty that our powers of appreciation seemed benumbed.

Away and away to the south-eastward through the dim blue summer haze shone the snows of the inland plateaus that stretched from the Talkeetna Mountains to the end of the eastern horizon. On the north-east the horizon was broken by the tangled ice-armoured peaks of the Alaskan Range. Not a peak there was named and little did I think as I turned away that in two years to come we would be fighting the winter storms and unravelling the mysteries of that ice-bound wilderness. And yet, with all their grimness, the views held a hint of tender beauty, and

THE AUTHOR PHOTOGRAPHING THE FAKE PEAK.
*Tucker standing where Barrill stood. This view including the author is used for a special reason. As short a time ago as March, 1913, a geographer accused the author of painting (by hand) the views of this peak with which we convicted Dr. Cook!*

the lowlands called to us with their promise of green meadows and hunting grounds as yet untouched by man.

The peaks about us were remarkable for their broken character; I have never seen peaks so seamed and disintegrated by the forces of nature. Rock pinnacles rose about us that looked as if a breath of wind would send them crashing and rumbling to the glaciers far below.

We rolled some big boulders over the cliffs and watched them leaping and spinning down, down, among the cliffs until they crashed with a great thudding splash into the snow-fields far below, and from the snow-fields in turn snaky snow-slides would slither down to the lower glaciers. Sliding snow has a nasty look and sound—there is something sinister about it—like the noise of a snake in dry grass.

The "fake peak" was covered with far more snow than it was at the time of Dr. Cook's visit. His photographs were made in September, while we visited the peak in June. On our return trip in July, we revisited the peak and obtained more photographs, The July exposures show the contours of the rock far better than the June exposures, but Dr. Cook's September pictures show that the snow cap had completely melted away and that some new snow had settled in the crevices.

CHAPTER XI

# The Great Gorge

*LaVoy joins us—News of the rear-guard—We advance up the great gorge—Hanging glaciers—Avalanches—The rear-guard joins us—LaVoy's narrow escape—Aten leaves us—We enter the "big basin"—First near view of the southern walls of Mount McKinley—Reconnaissance trips—We advance toward the Southern North-East Ridge.*

On the way to camp I ran ahead to boil tea and as I struck into our old trail below camp 12, I saw fresh man tracks in the snow, which I found had been made by LaVoy. He was waiting for us at camp. His eyes were tight closed by an attack of snow-blindness, and after treating them with boracic acid and cocain, he told us of his adventures since he had left us. Aten, Grassi, and he had had an uneventful and pleasant trip to Parkersburgh. They had at once begun the preparation of food, which consisted in boiling quantities of beans and drying them. The drying operations, however, had been postponed for several days by heavy rains and cloudy weather. The delay resulting from the bad weather had been augmented by the flooding of the glacier rivers, and they were unable to reach the big glacier until the waters had subsided.

While waiting at the last ford they had been overtaken by the Mazama expedition, who were just beginning their arduous relaying towards the big mountain. As our men had comparatively light loads to carry they had come through quickly to camp 8B. They had then begun the relaying of the provisions that we had left behind, while LaVoy had pushed forward alone to learn our plans and to tell us the news.

After his eyes had recovered and he had rested he returned over the back trail.

We began at once to push relays of provisions up the great gorge, and to escape the unlucky numeral we called our next camp "Hanging Glacier Camp."

Our route led us along the foot of magnificent cliffs that towered straight above us, grim and majestic. Against the rocks pressed the stupendous ice-wall of the big glacier—its surface broken and crushed into countless crevasses and dazzling pinnacles. Sweeping down from cloud-land we saw the first of the many hanging glaciers that, like frozen Niagaras, bring down the surplus ice harvests of the upper snow-fields. The almost unearthly grandeur of these walls would have made Doré throw down his brushes in despair, as they were more weird and awe-inspiring even than the pictures of his mind. As the setting sun lowered, great, pointed shadows, such as cathedrals or enchanted castles might cast, would zigzag across the cliffs, and creep in deep blue ribbons across the lower snow-fields. The lights changed constantly as one great peak after another shut off the sunlight, and, very slowly as the shadows joined, the great gorge took on the deep blue mantle of night; it was then that the twisted towers and broken masses of the seracs loomed like fantastic frozen forms through the dusk, and added a weirdness and wildness to the scene that I have never seen equalled. As we moved cautiously across the cliffs above the ice grottoes and dropped our loads below the hanging glacier we were overcome with the wildness and the silence of our surroundings; at times we had heard deep cracking noises, as some ice-pinnacle was crushed to bits by the pressure of the upper snow-fields, but these sounds were swallowed up among the deep grottoes and crevasses.

But suddenly, along the cliffs, a soft murmur ran that swelled, and swelled, until the cañon was echoing to a roar as of thunder, and a great cascade of snow came sweeping over the distant walls, leaping from one cliff to another, breaking into a thousand streams, until it slid with a sighing sound far out onto the blue floor of the glacier. This was the voice of the great gorge, and we grew to know it well; for as we pushed our way towards Mount McKinley, the sound of avalanches became a part of our lives, and we never ceased to thrill to the magic of this mountain music.

After bringing up all our belongings we made a reconnaissance, on the rope, and without packs, to find, if possible, a route across the rough side of the glacier to the centre where the surface was smooth.

After worming our way among a maze of deep crevasses we were successful, and by the following day we were camped in the centre of the ice river with an open road before us to Mount McKinley.

We could now advance our entire outfit in three relays, and after the second day in the gorge we had reached the top of the long slope that begins to lead down to the serac at the mouth of the gorge. Beyond the glacier was fairly level and as the fog lifted we saw a beautiful sight. The glacier stretched ahead of us as level apparently as a floor for about five miles. The snows of ages lay untouched, sheltered by the huge cliffs that towered in long straight walls on either hand.

Through this great funnel we could see what we thought must be the base of Mount McKinley. We could see also that well ahead of us the cañon walls broke away and that there was a large basin of some kind, and then the mountain fog came creeping down and we pushed on by the loom of the side walls. I found two little birds that had died while trying to cross the Range. One was a warbler of some kind; it was mottled with black and grey, and it had a yellow topknot, and splashes of yellow on each side of its breast. The second was a smaller bird of the warbler family; it was yellow all over with the exception of a black-cap. The poor little things looked so out of place among those grim surroundings that it made one wonder at the power of that instinct which animated the tiny things and brought them to this lone spot over thousands of miles of mountain ranges. In a distance of about two miles we passed ten distinct cascading glaciers that swept down from heights of several thousand feet. These views we caught through rifts in the fog as we tramped back and forth over our relay trail; but the distant views were hidden from us and we could see nothing of the country ahead. There was an atmosphere of mystery in tramping forward through the dense fog; the uncertainty of where we were going, the uncouth loom of the men's figures as they rolled forward in single file, the death-like silence between the thunderous crashings and echoes of the avalanches, all combined to give a feeling of unreality and mysterious adventure to our toil.

In appearance we bore no resemblance to the party who had left civilisation only two months before. Our faces were burned almost black by the glare of the sun on the ice-fields, and were seamed and hard from the severity of our toil. Our clothes too reflected the needs of our unusual calling. Our legs were wrapped in puttees or bound with rawhide and our rubber shoe-packs were bound to the long,

La Voy Cuntz Grassi Tucker Parker

*The 1910 party in the "Great Gorge."*

upturned Susitna snowshoes. Wool or fur caps or hoods covered our heads, while every man wore snow goggles, or possibly, if the day was warm, a red or blue handkerchief with rough eye-holes cut in it. The fault in almost all of the glasses or goggles that one buys is that there is no ventilation, which results in the glass sweating and renders them useless. The only satisfactory manufactured glass is also the cheapest on the market; it has a wire-net frame that fits closely around the eye socket, and for ordinary work it answers rather well. The glare of the sun on the northern snow-field is terrific; it has to be seen—or felt—to be appreciated.

Although we were at comparatively low altitudes in 1910, I have seen the glare so strong that a man was afraid to step out of a tent, even for an instant, without first covering his eyes.

Trail-breaking under these circumstances is an ordeal, and as I did the leading for the advance party, my eyes were almost constantly affected by snow-blindness. The slightest shadow or dark spot on which a man may rest his eyes proves a relief, as much of the trouble comes from being unable to find anything on the wide snow-fields on which to focus the eyes. I have often tossed a burnt match or cigarette butt on to the snow in order to enjoy the relief of having something definite to look at. For this reason the days when the sun is shining through a dense fog are the most dangerous, as the leader is forced to strain his eyes in trying to pierce the fog in the search for dangerous crevasses, or landmarks of importance. On foggy days there were times when, maybe for an hour, the only line I could get on our course was the light of the sun through the fog, and trail-breaking under these conditions invariably resulted in snow-blindness. Speaking from my own experiences I am of the opinion that no permanent injury results from snow-blindness. I have had more than twenty attacks without, so far as I have been able to discover, suffering any permanent harm. From personal observations on northern snowfields I have learned to recognise two distinct forms of this unpleasant malady. The most common variety comes on slowly. The eyes water excessively and at the same time feel dry, as if they were filled with emory dust. The pain is sometimes excruciating and may in serious cases last several days. In bad cases I have noticed that the stomach is affected and the sufferer is unable to eat. Boracic acid and cocain, or boracic acid and zinc sulphate, are the best remedies known to me. The sufferer by bearing the pain that results can see by forcing his eyelids open; it is the pain that closes his eyes and renders him blind. The second variety comes on quickly and rarely lasts a long time if the patient takes the necessary precautions. No pain to speak of is felt, but total although temporary blindness results. One summer on the snowfields of the Behring Sea coast my companions and I were attacked by snow-blindness. Having no medicines with us, we were driven to experimenting and secured some slight degree of comfort from placing tea-leaf poultices over our eyes. The care of the eyes in northern exploration is a question of the greatest importance, for, under certain conditions, a man's safety or possibly his life may hang on his ability to see clearly.

I have never met a man who was immune from this painful malady and so far as I have been able to discover the colour of a man's eyes does not affect his susceptibility to the glare of the snow.

On the 4th of July we were awakened by the crash and thunder of avalanches. It seemed as if Dame Nature was striving to make up for our lack of firecrackers. The cañon walls had suddenly disappeared and although we could see nothing but grey walls of mist we had the feeling that something new had happened and that

FOURTH OF JULY ON THE EDGE OF THE BIG BASIN

we had arrived *somewheres*. This strange sensation continued as we pushed our camp forward over the fog-draped waste of snow. After a hard day's work we succeeded in bringing up all our belongings and established our sixteenth camp.

Early the following morning we were awakened by "the creak of snowshoes on the crust," and then we heard a voice calling, "This is the Mazama party." We were all taken aback, for although the rivalry between us was a friendly one, we were nevertheless anxious to hold our lead. While we were unfastening our tent door, however, a suspicious whispering was going on outside and then to our delight we heard Grassi and LaVoy laughing.

Aten joined us later and we had a great "pow-wow and potlatch." They had overtaken us with light loads from camp 14, and they had lots of news to relate. The last news of the Mazama party was that they had heard them shouting close to camp 8B, but they had not seen them.

LaVoy had had an unpleasant experience between camp 9 and Glacier Point. He and Grassi were following our old snowshoe trail across the great plain of snow, and were unroped, and widely separated, for our trail lying plain before them seemed a guarantee of safety. LaVoy, who had been plodding along for an hour under his heavy pack, stopped to rest as he was some distance ahead. When Grassi had approached within hailing distance, LaVoy again started ahead. He had taken only a few steps when the snow broke under him, and he fell. The first thing he remembered was being under water, fighting for air, and almost helpless in the tangle of his pack and snowshoes. During the fall he had broken one of his snowshoes, and his pack, consisting of sixty pounds of beans in two waterproof sacks, and some odds and ends, swung over his head. His nerve did not forsake him, and after what to him seemed centuries, he reached the surface and grasped a shelf that the water had worn in the icy wall. To the fact that his pack consisted of dry beans he probably owes his life, for the beans being buoyant brought him to the surface; had his pack consisted of sixty pounds of pemmican he would have drowned. In the meanwhile Grassi was plodding along with his head bent low under the strain of the rump-line. Raising his eyes finally, he halted with amazement—LaVoy had vanished! Pressing forward he saw the hole in the snow. Visions of the horror of the crevasses they had passed crossed his mind, and in an agony of fear he rushed along the trail. As he neared the crevasse he heard LaVoy's voice, and for an instant was overcome by the reaction of the fear that had gripped him. By this time LaVoy had freed himself from his load, and with the aid of the ropes that Grassi now lowered to him, he sent up his pack and scaled the fifteen feet of ice wall and stood shivering on the snow.

Now, on the big glacier there are three distinct types of crevasses. First, crevasses that sink to the very bowels of the glacier—great blue chasms that are so deep that you can see nothing but a blue void; secondly, crevasses filled with icy stalagmites upon which a falling man would be impaled; and lastly, crevasses that fall sheer to subglacial torrents, the bellowing of which between the deep ice walls sends the cold shivers down a man's back. Some of the ice caverns were open, others were partly covered by snow cornices, while a few, and these we dreaded most, were completely hidden with snow. Usually there was a slight depression or discolouration of the snow that warned us of the hidden danger; but sometimes—as in LaVoy's case—the snow lay smooth and white across the death-trap. Luckily the crevasse that came so near to being LaVoy's sepulchre was the only one in the many hundreds that we saw that was filled with stagnant water. Had it been like the others he would have been ground to pieces by the subglacial torrents, or his body would now be lying frozen in the depths of the big glacier.

After a good rest at our camp the rear-guard returned to camp 14 for their last relay, while Aten continued his journey to base camp. As we had not expected to add him to our party we had made no allowance in special clothing or sleeping-bags for an extra man, and we were now beginning to reach an altitude where warm clothes and sleeping-bags were a necessity. Among other things that the rear-guard had left with us were fifty pounds of cooked beans. They were mouldy and sour so we spread them out on canvas sacks to dry. They had a peculiar taste, but by mixing them with erbswurst we were able to use a fair amount, although Grassi and Tucker were made ill by the sour bean diet and suffered from abdominal cramps.

It was not until our arrival at camp 17 that we were able to study any of the surrounding mountains, and then the fog only raised a few hundred feet. We could see a great plain of snow surrounded by mountain slopes that blended with the mist, but we were as yet unable to tell where the best point of attack lay. After a day's absence, Grassi and LaVoy returned with their last relay loads. Aten had left them at camp 14 and departed for Parkersburgh. This reunion and the final relay loads placed us in a position to devote all our energies to the attack on Mount McKinley. In food and fuel we had:

55 qts. of alcohol
25 1/2 6-lb. cans of pemmican
32 lbs. of sugar
10 lbs. of good beans
30 lbs. of sour beans
30 lbs. of erbswurst
3 lbs. of tea
4 lbs. of bacon
80 lbs. of hardtack
21 lbs. of raisins
Beef tea ad lib.
Food total 228 lbs. or 38 lbs. per man
Fuel total 96 1/4 lbs. or 16 lbs. per man

The above were the rations that we had carried to within two miles of the base of the southern cliffs of Mount McKinley, after thirty-six travelling days.

In comparing our food supply with Dr. Cook's own figures, we find that on leaving the Tokositna River at the very beginning of his journey he and Barrill only had twenty-one pounds of food and two pounds of fuel per man. Dr. Cook is not a humourist or we could picture him smiling, while writing the following description of his equipment: "In preparing our equipment I had determined to break away from the established method of mountain climbing by reducing the number of my party and by changing the working equipment."

On the 7th of July we awoke under a clear blue sky and at 3 A.M. we were preparing for the day's work.

We had split the party into two working units. Each unit handled an equal portion of our equipment and occupied a separate tent. This system simplified the division of rations and added to our travelling efficiency. Professor Parker, Herman Tucker, and I formed the first party; and Professor Cuntz, Valdemar, Grassi, and Merl LaVoy completed the second. The second party was instructed to explore the base of the mountain on the western side of the glacier while we started over the blue snow-fields towards the eastern cliffs.

Dense cloud-banks still clung to the main cliffs, but the indications pointed to a clear day and we expected to discover the right line of advance before nightfall. As we plodded forward over the snow, Tucker began to complain of serious abdominal pains, and before long the cramps grew so severe that he was forced to lie in the snow until the attacks had passed. We returned to camp at once and left him well wrapped up in his sleeping-bag. As we left camp for the second time, the clouds lifted and we secured our first near view of Mount McKinley. We were awestruck at its immensity and grandeur and as we swept the giant cliffs with our eyes we began to search for promising climbing routes. We could also see the whole system of cliffs and glaciers that guarded the southern approach. The great gorge opened into a great piedmont glacier which lay in the form of a basin below the great peaks and cliffs that hemmed it in. The "big basin" was about 5000 feet in altitude and it stretched like a level floor to where the Mount McKinley glaciers brought down their loads of ice and snow.

Directly upon this level plain rose Mount McKinley—15,000 feet of rock and ice and as the sun began to creep across its face the distant thunder of avalanches came to our ears. At the first glance we were overjoyed by seeing what appeared to be several climbable routes to the summit. But on using our binoculars we found that the intense glare of the sun combined with the similarity of colouring of the mountain rock, hid much of the bad climbing by making the nearby mountain masses melt into and flatten the approaches to the summit.

It was only by using powerful binoculars and the greatest care that we could see some of the great breaks between the huge snow-fields. After carefully studying the southern face we could see that it was unscalable. The great South-Western Arête looked climbable up to an altitude of about 15,000 feet, but at that point it joined the main peak below as savage and hopeless a mass of cliffs as I have ever seen. The north-eastern approach seemed to be the most promising. We could see a great ridge leading to the summit, and on this ridge we hung our hopes. As we did not know, at that time, that there were three north-eastern arêtes, we spoke of it as the North-East Ridge but it is really the Southern North-East Ridge. In order to study the country better, Professor Parker and I crossed the big basin and climbed a ridge that came down from a tangled mass of peaks that lay directly under Mount McKinley's southern walls. These peaks were attached by sharp ridges to a great dome-shaped buttress that forms one of the most important landmarks of that region. On reaching the top of the ridge I removed the rope which we had been wearing for our mutual safety. The ridge led up to a big snow-field and as I was crossing it the snow broke under me and I just caught myself on my outstretched arms. By feeling carefully with my feet I located one wall of the crevasse and Professor Parker gave me the end of his ice-axe to pull on. On looking into the hole that my body had made I could see a deep blue void with some dark rock masses far below. I reversed the proceeding a few moments later by helping Professor Parker out of another crevasse, and after that we always wore the rope. The country we were in was literally seamed with crevasses and it would have been criminal carelessness to have taken even a few steps without the protection of the rope.

From our lookout point on the ridge we could see that we would have to cross two jagged mountain ranges to reach the Southern North-East Ridge. As this was impossible from the food point of view alone, we turned our eyes farther east and there we saw two great snow *cols*, or saddles, that swept up gently from steep seracs to a height of about 11,000 feet. It was the only promising way out of the great amphitheatre in the direction of the Southern North-East Arête and we decided to attempt it at once.

While making these observations we had been sitting among some rocks at an altitude of 7000 feet. Directly opposite stood the great dome-shaped buttress that supports Mount McKinley's base and under the heat of the warm sun it presented an inspiring sight; from every cliff, snow-slope, and rock-runnell, avalanches were roaring down on to the glacier floor below, and the very air seemed to pulsate to the crash and thunder of the falling snow. In all of the well-known mountain ranges of the world the snow melts away during the summer. In cases where it does not disappear it becomes hard and packed under its own weight and gives a firm, safe footing to the climber. Mount McKinley, however, is so far north and the snow-fall is so great that the snow never gets in this desirable condition.

The cliffs are overhung and powdered with unnumbered tons of soft snow, and at the slightest touch of the sun the great cliffs literally *smoke* with avalanches. The sight is beautiful beyond words from a spectacular point of view, but when your object is the scaling of these selfsame cliffs the sight is not conducive to peace of mind. On our return to camp we were relieved to find that Tucker was feeling better, and we at once began our preparations for the advance on the great seracs below the 12,000-foot cols. While we were at work we saw our companions returning home across the snow-fields.

They were a long way off when we first saw them and it was a fascinating sight to watch the tiny specks growing larger and larger until they materialised into men. It was light almost all night while we were at the base of Mount McKinley; the advance and retreat of the night shadows went on with scarcely a pause, and sometimes we would be uncertain whether the alpine glow on the big mountain's icy crest was the light of the rising, or the setting sun. The dazzling whiteness of the snow-buried peaks made the contrast of sunlight and shadow the more beautiful.

## CHAPTER XII

# The Great Serac—First Reconnaissance

***Explorations in the big basin—Night travel—Arrival at the base of the great serac—Avalanche—Fog—We fail to find a route—Return to main camp—News of the Mazama expedition—Puddings—Books—Short rations.***

The following afternoon found Professor Parker, Tucker, and the writer well up towards the base of the great serac. As we rose to the upper snow-fields the sun set. Deep shadows crept up from the distant lowlands, and the big basin turned into a deep blue sea of mystery. Mount McKinley rose between two giant peaks that framed it and as the shadows deepened its crest took fire from the distant sun. We pushed forward while our snowshoes began to sing on the frozen crust, and as the cold increased the silence was broken by the falling of ice on the cliffs.

There is a mysterious attraction about night travel on these northern snow-fields that is hard to explain; the clean, cold smell of the night air, the loom of great peaks against the night sky, the bigness and freedom of the everlasting snow-fields, and the excitement of the life, all combine to make a lasting impression on the minds of those who have travelled there.

As we approached the walls of ice their great size began for the first time to dawn on us, and we realised at once that even if we succeeded in finding an easy route to the snow-fields above, our food supply was scarcely equal to the magnitude of the task, for after crossing the 11,000-foot cols we would still have the whole sweep of the great ridge to negotiate.

We arrived at the base of the seracs after midnight and proceeded to make camp.

The serac rose sheer above us for 1000 feet, and we knew that beyond the first wall lay others that would bar our path. Against the sky stood pinnacles and spires of blue ice, broken into weird and fantastic shapes. As the biting cold of early morning crept downward we could hear the ice groaning and settling and now and then a deep cracking noise would run along the blue walls. Taking off our frozen packs and rope we broke and scraped away the thick crust, and began our mysterious "tent dance." In pitching our tents we always had to first stamp down the soft snow in order to insure a firm floor when the sun came out. Beginning with our snowshoes we would stamp out a circle in single file. When the surface was hard and smooth we would remove our snowshoes and stamp the snow down with our shoe-packs, and level it off finally with another snowshoe pounding. This operation resembled some heathen war-dance; seen through the frost-mist we must have looked like mountain elves engaged in a propitiatory dance to some glacier demon. When the floor was pounded flat we would stretch our tent and fasten the corners and sides with ice-axes and snowshoes.

Our beds and war-bags were passed inside, and the alcohol stove filled and lighted. After everything outside had been stowed neatly we would fill our pots with snow, and retire into our new home. Then the sleeping-bags were spread on top of waterproof covers, our bundles of damp socks were hung on the centre-pole above the purring stove, and pipes and diaries were brought out; in a few minutes, a warm human shelter would stand on the ice, and for the first time the silent glaciers would echo to the sound of human voices and laughter. By this time we had become experts at camp-making. I remember once noting the time when we began to make camp; no one was aware that I was timing the operation, and there was no unusual hurry; yet only fifteen minutes elapsed before we were all inside our tents with our beds spread out and snow melting over the alcohol lamps.

After our arrival at the base of the "great serac" we ate a hurried breakfast and went outside in the hope of seeing a promising route over the ice-wall. To our surprise we found that a dense fog had settled, and the crust was so hard and dry that we could run about on it in our sleeping-socks.

This was a novel experience to us after our weeks of snowshoe work and we enjoyed it to the full. After three hours' sleep we commenced preparations for our attack on the serac, but on opening the tent-door we again looked into a dense wall of fog. We waited an hour and just as the mist began to rise, a heavy snowstorm swept over us. After the snow had passed we began our climb, but on approaching the foot of the serac the sun broke through the clouds and in a few minutes avalanches began to thunder downward, and we retreated once more to our tent. We saw that nothing could be done until nightfall, and gave ourselves up to the rare delight of a day's rest. It was Professor Parker's birthday, and in honour of the event we made our first attempt at cooking pemmican. The result so far surpassed our wildest hopes that life took on an added interest, and the concoction which we named "Professor Parker's Pemmican Pudding" became one of our standard rations. I have copied the recipe from my diary in case the reader should ever find himself in a similar position.

> *PUDDING FOR THREE MEN*
>
> *First soak 3 broken hardtack in snow-water until they are soft. Add 60 raisins and pemmican the size of 4 1/2 eggs. Stir slowly but energetically until the mess is thoroughly amalgamated. Boil slowly over an alcohol stove, add 3 tablespoons of granulated sugar, and serve in a granite-ware cup.*

During the afternoon we slept and played chess. We did not need to look outside for the avalanches kept up a steady war that told us that the seracs were unclimbable. After hearing the noise one could not but wonder at the terrific forces of nature. No foundry or machine shop could be noisier than this great wall of ice; avalanches breaking from the walls struck the cliffs with a noise like artillery, and then crashed and rumbled downward until you would have thought that an army was firing small arms and rapid-fire guns. The serac avalanches are distinctly different from the great mountain avalanches, which start with a dim murmur, that grows and swells until the cliffs echo to the mighty roar, which slowly dies away among the peaks until silence reigns again.

During the afternoon the sun beat down upon the ice with such force that the heat was almost overpowering, and yet two hours later a snow-storm struck us and I was suffering from the cold inside my sleeping-bag, although I was clothed in two undershirts, two woollen shirts, sleeveless sweater, sleeping socks, trousers, woollen hood, and gloves. The remarkable side of the temperature on Mount McKinley is the extreme changes of heat and cold that one feels without a corresponding change being noticeable in the thermometer. The maximum heat recorded by our party on the southern Mount McKinley glaciers was 52° in the sun, and the minimum temperature was 28°. Under a temperature of 50° the glaciers became blinding sheets of white light and the sun burnt like fire; it was unsafe to take a step without snow-glasses, and our skin peeled off like parchment. But the instant that you stepped into the shadow of a moraine, or mountain, you felt the chill of the ice creeping over you. I have seen fresh snowshoe tracks frozen hard on the bottom and sides, where they were shaded, while the exposed snow was soft as slush from the heat of the sun.

We lay snow-bound under the great serac for one and a half days and finally at 3:45 on the morning of July 11th we began to chop our way up the face of the ice-wall. It was the most unpleasant and treacherous climbing that I have ever experienced, for instead of the serac being solid the ice was so rotten that you could bury an ice-axe to the head in ice blocks that looked perfectly safe.

Shortly after we left camp it began to snow, and after more than two hours of Herculean labour we came to a mass of ice gorges and grottoes below a high perpendicular wall. I was forced several times to hew doorways between the ice blocks with my axe. Skirting the wall to the right we came out on a platform that overlooked a deep gorge. Here we were halted by perpendicular ice-walls sixty feet high. While we were studying the problem, Professor Parker read his barometer and found that we were 1200 feet above our camp, although we had not yet reached

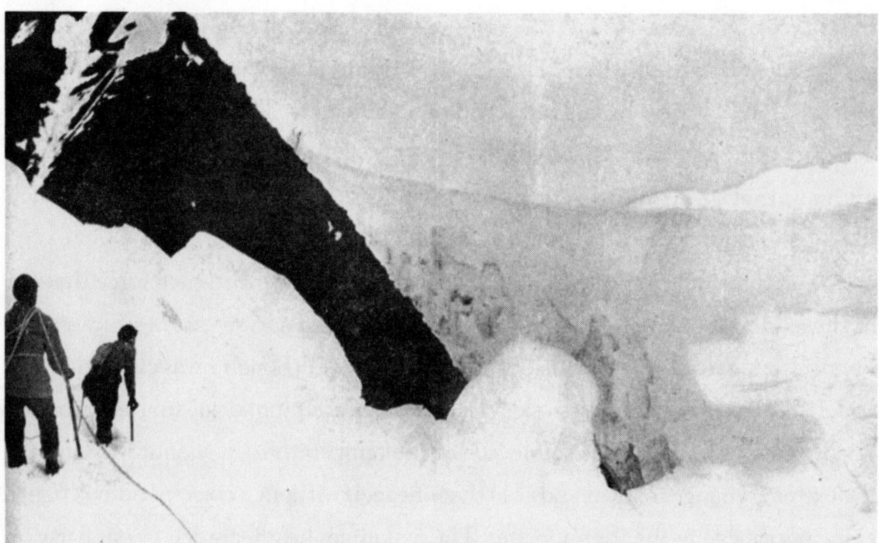

Night climbing on the Great Serac. The rising sun can be seen striking the mountain top on the right.

the top of the first break in the serac. Turning to the left we began to follow the ice-wall but a dense fog shut us in and as the rising sun began to shine through it, we retreated as quickly as possible from our unpleasant surroundings. On the lower slopes the heat of the sun through the white mist began to send down avalanches. The heat was terrific, our clothes were wet with sweat, and yet to our surprise the temperature in the sun was only 48°!

We had only enough food for one more day so after a pemmican pudding luncheon we slept, in order to be fresh for a night attempt on the great serac, as our experience had convinced us that there was too much danger during the day. The night that followed will live long in my memory, for it was my first experience in night climbing in the north. We left camp at 9 P.M., with our complete mountain equipment, for a last attempt on the eastern end of the great serac. I led by as straight a course as I could hold until we had risen 600 feet above camp. At that altitude I was afraid that my steps would not hold, as the ice was rotten—in fact in the worst climbing condition I have ever seen. After a traverse to the right, we followed a good ice *couloir* that led between giant ice blocks, but above we had to pass under a sixty-foot ice cliff where we could see that avalanches had been falling during the day.

This climbing was too difficult to be undertaken with packs, but although we had given up hopes of finding a relay route at this point in the ice-wall our interest in our explorations urged us forward. At an altitude of 1000 feet above our camp we entered a glacial amphitheatre surrounded by perpendicular ice-walls—a frozen cul-de-sac, and as gruesome a spot as I have ever entered. One great block of green ice rose like a snake's head from a narrow base to a height of sixty feet and leaned drunkenly towards us. Fifty feet above us a rotten ice-bridge sagged from a shattered berg to the main wall, and as we looked a cold mist crept over us and everything was blotted from sight. It was midnight when we reached our turning point and as we sat fog-bound, an avalanche broke loose on an ice slope far above us. We could see nothing, and the roar grew louder and louder, like the sound of a fast approaching train. We were decidedly uncomfortable until it swept into a frozen gully beyond us, and we listened thankfully to the ice blocks crashing and thudding on the snow-fields far below.

On our return to camp we saw one of the most magnificent mountain pictures that I have had the good luck to witness. The fog had begun to fade away as we approached our tent. The main mountain masses were indistinct blue shapes looming against the dark sky. Along their great flanks films of clouds lay like frozen veils. High above the main ranges rose the dim majestic shapes of Mounts Hunter and McKinley, and as we watched McKinley's crest began to glow; at first with the merest tinge of warm colour, as if it was turning to gold from internal heat; then, little by little, the alpine glow crept downward until Mount Hunter was crowned with fire. Other peaks began to catch the sun in turn until above the great foreground of nocturnal gloom the great crests glowed like gems. We stood spellbound under the frozen cliffs and it seemed to me as if nature had for a moment drawn aside a veil and allowed us to look on one of the mysteries of the universe.

On our return to our companions we left our tent opposite a promising break in the western end of the great serac, as we had planned to return at once with more food and make another attempt to cross the 12,000-foot col.

During our absence the second party had advanced all our belongings well up towards the base of the serac, but as our outlook was so discouraging we decided to leave the bulk of our equipment there until we had completed our explorations. During our absence, Rusk, the leader of the Mazama expedition, had visited one of our rear camps. He had pushed forward without a pack and returned to his own party after a short visit. He reported that their food was nearly exhausted and that they would soon retreat to the Chulitna. He also stated that his party had been unable to locate "Dr. Cook's fake summit of Mt. McKinley" on account of cloudy weather, but he assured Grassi that since he had travelled over the big glacier, his sympathies were no longer with the Brooklyn explorer, and that finding the fake peak was superfluous evidence.

The following account of Rusk's meeting with our rear-guard was published by him, after his return to civilisation.

> *We had now made six camps in reaching this spot and the mountain (McKinley) was still unclimbed and, what was worse, unclimbable with our present equipment. We had only sufficient food left to last two or three days. There was nothing we could do but secure a lot of photographs and make a few reconnaissance trips, with a future ascent in view. We raised our tent at Camp Morden shortly before noon of July 12th. Rojec, while skirmishing for pictures, thought he saw figures moving about on the snow a mile or so to our*

*north. With the glasses, I soon made out a camp to which I started. After travelling perhaps a mile and a half, I found Professor Cuntz, Grassi, and LaVoy of the other expedition, who welcomed me warmly and opened a can of pemmican for my especial benefit. They intended to remain two weeks longer although their supplies, especially their alcohol, were running low. Parker, Browne, and Tucker had been gone for three days endeavouring to find a route by which to attain the north-east ridge of the mountain. Whether or not the expedition would attempt the ascent now depended largely upon the result of this reconnaissance. After a brief but pleasant visit I returned to camp, and we did not see the members of the other expedition again to talk with them while we remained on the glacier. Our relations with the Parker-Browne party had been of the most friendly character, and the best of feeling prevailed between us.*

While Mr. Rusk's remark concerning our food supply was accurate in the light of the discoveries that we made later while trying to reach the Southern North-East Ridge, we still had as large a supply of fuel and food as I had thought nccessary when undertaking the climb, for at our nineteenth relay camp, within one mile of Mount McKinley's southern cliffs, we had:

20 6-lb. cans of pemmican
$2^1/2$ cases of hardtack
20 lbs. of erbswurst
20 lbs. of sugar
Ample tea
Ample beef tea
12 gals. of alcohol

This would have lasted us twenty-five days, which would have been an ample allowance had we found a climbable route to the summit, but as it turned out, a food allowance of fifty days would have made little or no difference in our attack by the south approach, as we were surrounded by mountain ranges that, from a freight transportation point of view, were practically unclimbable.

This brings to my mind a fact that is seldom realised, and that is that the most dangerous and difficult trips are usually those that end in failure. While things are going smoothly and the chances of success seem good, the mental satisfaction of the explorer eases the difficulty of the toil or the suffering of hardship. But when things go wrong a man is driven to taking risks in a frantic endeavour to win success, and the mental depression which follows failure is as hard to bear as bodily suffering.

In swimming the cañon at the head of the Yentna in 1906, and again in the serac climbing in 1910, we ran risks that were out of all proportion to the direct benefits to be gained, but we took these risks in a spirit of desperation while trying to surmount insurmountable obstacles, and wrest success from failure.

On trips such as ours the work is so arduous that at the end of the day or night's work you are usually too tired to talk much or play games. Occasionally during the delays caused by fogs or blizzards, we would summon enough energy to play chess or tell stories. But our principal diversion was reading for the one-hundredth time one of our travel-worn books. "Pigskin libraries" or other luxuries permissible on exploring expeditions by ship in the Arctic, or caravan in the tropics, are out of the question in the rugged mountain ranges that we traversed. Early in the journey when we were cutting the covers from the few books we possessed to save weight, some wag referred to the collection as our "Near-skin library" and the name stuck. What few books we carried were public property and were handed on from man to man in a sort of endless chain. Our only hope was that we might forget what we had read in order that we might enjoy it over again when it returned to us. Nothing was too commonplace to read; advertisements even were acceptable and we read the list of instructions on the Kodak film wrappers until we could recite every paragraph by heart. Our books had been collected in a haphazard way, according to the personal choice or caprice of each member of our party, and I must admit that our list in no way resembled President Eliot's of Harvard. Our two favourite authors were Shakespeare and Omar Khayyam (Fitzgerald edition) and among other books we had Epictetus, some of Browning's poems, some of Emerson's essays, and *The Reveries of a Bachelor*. I know of nothing in this world that will produce a stronger attack of melancholia than reading *The Reveries of a Bachelor* on a fog-draped glacier!

We lacked ordinary comforts even more than we lacked amusements. Our tent floors were 7 x 8 feet, and as the tents were only seven feet high and came to a point there was practically no standing room. The tent floors were always wet from the snow soon after they were laid, and we were driven to all sorts of expedients in keeping our sleeping-bags dry. Extra covers or articles to sleep on were extremely scarce, and mountain rope, rubber-shoes, or anything that could be secured was utilised in the construction of waterproof mattresses.

Keeping our belongings dry was perhaps the most difficult of our many housekeeping problems. During snow-storms, or the long days on the trail, our clothes became covered with snow, which melted when we entered our tents. As each man wore at least three pairs of the heaviest wool socks, and as there were three or four men in each tent, there were always eighteen heavy, damp socks to be suspended from the centre pole. After the socks were fairly dry, we usually put them in our sleeping-bags and dried them out by the warmth of our bodies. The principal benefit of this plan was that in case the socks did not become dry they were at least warm when we put them on in the morning. Alcohol was so precious that we could not use it for drying purposes, except in cases where it was possible to combine drying with cooking.

Our life in these tiny tents on the cold wastes of snow and ice was disagreeable and cheerless in the extreme. Quarrels and disagreements frequently occur in the wilderness under conditions far more pleasant than those we laboured under and it redounds greatly to the character of the men who composed our party that not a single unpleasant incident occurred to mar our pleasant relations. The two expeditions to Mount McKinley organised by Professor Parker and myself are the only serious expeditions that I have ever taken part in where no unpleasant incidents occurred. While this result is due largely to the type of men who joined our ventures, the management of an expedition is of the greatest importance in eliminating friction and producing *esprit de corps*.

Experience actually gained through hard knocks on many a long trip is requisite in a leader who handles bodies of men in the wilderness. This includes a knowledge of human nature, and the causes that produce friction. The fundamental cause at the bottom of all the dissensions that have occurred in the history of exploration is *selfishness*. There is only one way to positively eliminate unpleasantness, and that is by guarding absolutely against selfishness. The leader who refuses to recognise this fact is foredoomed to failure. Under the heart-breaking toil and brutal hardships of a life in the open the longing for comfort becomes an obsession; the craving for certain kinds of food—sweets in particular—becomes too strong for some men to resist; it is a well-known side of human nature that in Alaska is described by the term "Sugar Hog." While it was possible for us to guard against the "Sugar Hog" by using extreme caution in the selection of our men, I nevertheless devoted much of my time to seeing that the men shared equally in everything. It is an impossibility for any one who has lived the life of civilisation to realise the self-denial and self-sacrifice that men are called upon to show under primitive conditions. When a man has reached the stage of hunger where he would gladly fight for a lump of sugar, it requires the highest kind of self-sacrifice and honesty on his part to deal justly with his companions. The most liberal man in civilisation may be the most selfish under primitive conditions, for to be unselfish in the wilderness often means that you must actually undergo bodily suffering and discomfort, while in civilisation one often gains much by giving.

One of the best methods of insuring justice to every man is by putting the entire party on rations the instant they leave civilisation. Many men make the mistake of thinking that rations are ordered to save the food supply, but this is not necessarily true. The greatest benefit to be derived from rations is *that every man shares equally*. Any real man will starve when he knows that his companions are starving too. But the instant that the slightest whisper of suspicion runs through a party, it becomes demoralised and the gaunt spectre of the "Survival of the Fittest" becomes their master. The instant a party goes "on rations" the necessity for "fast eating" disappears, and an atmosphere of peace and security prevails.

In 1910 we worked on a very small food allowance. Each man received one pound of pemmican and three hardtack biscuit each day. In addition we had a practically unlimited quantity of tea, but our sugar was rationed at the rate of two flat teaspoonfuls per man per meal. We existed and performed the hardest labour on this allowance for fifty consecutive days, but I can truthfully say that I consider it the minimum food allowance permissible.

We reserved our raisins for the actual climb, but as soon as we reached the big basin and saw the difficulties that confronted us, I rationed the raisins in small quantities. Our erbswurst was used as a luxury from time to time and we usually drank it as a "night-cap" before going to sleep.

While we would have been more comfortable had we eaten more, it is interesting to know that we accomplished the severest toil on such a small amount, for the average young man in civilization eats twice as much without doing any physical work to speak of.

There was one amusing side to the food question and that was the constant conversations on eating that we carried on. To have heard us one would have thought that we were an exiled party of epicures and gourmands. The universal topic of conversation was *food!*

We would be lying in our bags, resting up after a hard day's pack, when one of the men would say—apropos of nothing—"I went on a week-end visit in the country once and I wolfed so much roast beef that later when some squabs on toast and salad came in, I was full-up and only made a bluff at eating them!"

After a long silence pregnant with sympathy and understanding some one else would regale us with a like harrowing tale, until our voices would grow weaker and weaker, and we would fall asleep—to dream possibly of ice-cream sodas and chocolate éclairs.

With these painful details in view the reader may form a faint conception of the tremendous excitement that swept over us on the discovery of the delights of cooked pemmican. Had we discovered a method of making diamonds we could not have felt more elated, and with feverish impatience we awaited the time when we should initiate our companions into the delights of "Professor Parker's Pemmican Pudding." The chance came at our reunion at camp 22. We had kept the discovery a profound secret, and as meal-time approached we could hardly control our excitement. At the proper time I entered their tent and told them that they were invited to a party, but that in view of our being in starvation country, they were called upon to make a contribution of their allotted rations. They demurred slightly at the last clause in my invitation, but eventually the rations were turned over, and I re-retired to our tent. Professor Parker, Tucker, and I at once began the preparation of our gastronomic secret. In the meantime, we had made a second valuable discovery. Professor Cuntz had brought (for medicine purposes) a small flask of brandy as far as the big basin. The temptation was too great to resist, and after due deliberation, I commandeered it for the good of the whole. At the appointed time the pudding began to steam and we called to our mystified companions. It was with the greatest difficulty that the six of us crowded into the small tent. As the pudding was ladled into our granite-ware cups it was covered with sugar and a teaspoonful of brandy poured on top. Professor Cuntz, LaVoy, and Grassi ate the first few spoonfuls in dubious silence, but soon an expression of beatific contentment crossed their sun-browned faces and it was not until their cups had been emptied and *licked dry* that they gave their enthusiasm free rein. Finally, after a long, contented silence, LaVoy said: "No wonder you fellows stayed so long on the big serac."

## CHAPTER XIII

# The Great Serac—Second Reconnaissance

***We attempt the west end of the ice wall—Avalanches and crevasses—Night climbing—We reach the top of the serac—Impracticability of the route for relaying—We return to our companions—Report of the rear party—We make the first ascent of Explorers' Peak—We climb 10,300 feet on the South-West ridge—We retreat to the Big Basin.***

On the thirteenth of July we started out for the western side of the Great Serac, and at 11 P.M. of the same day we were inside our tent below the cold walls. During our absence the rear-guard were to explore the central glacier on Mount McKinley's southern side. We had no hope of finding a route from this glacier, as it headed directly under the stupendous ice walls of the big mountain. But a few great ridges that hid the glacier's source gave enough uncertainty to the venture to make it worth while.

Shortly after two o'clock of the morning after our arrival at the ice-fall we were chopping our way up the steep slopes of the serac. Eventually we found a good cold-weather route to the top of the first ice-fall; but avalanche tracks warned us to beware of the route when the sun shone. Swinging towards the western col we rose to an altitude of eight thousand feet only to find ourselves thwarted by a second serac gashed by immense crevasses. The great rents in the ice stretched between almost perpendicular walls of rock. Across the face of the western cliffs we could trace a large vein, but as the formation was not promising for valuable minerals we were glad to pass it by, for it would have taken nothing less than a mine of pure gold to tempt us under those avalanche-swept slopes. As we retraced our steps and studied the serac for a new route, the day broke, and the rumble of avalanches followed the march of the sun across the range. We turned at once, for we dreaded the steep slope that separated us from camp, and during the descent the snow began to get *greasy* and the noise of slides came from every side. We were glad when we reached our tent.

This failure to reach the left-hand col convinced us that there was little use in remaining longer at the base of the serac. But during the morning we had seen a very steep snow-slope leading up on the right-hand side of a wedge of rock that split the serac. It was out of the question to climb it in the daytime, but we thought that at night it might be possible. The route, even if we succeeded in reaching the top, would be too difficult for use as a relay route, but the desire to scale the serac had become a personal matter with us, and Herman Tucker and I therefore decided to have one more try.

As soon as the great white walls began to freeze, we left camp. We climbed quickly, except where snow-slides had swept away the footholds we had made in the morning, which had to be re-chopped. High upon the last big traverse, one thousand feet above our camp, we turned to take a last look at the tent, a tiny dark pyramid far below. Prof. Parker was standing outside watching our progress. Lowering my voice purposely, I said "Good-night," and such was the deathlike stillness of the frozen cliffs and plains below that he heard me as if I had been standing by his side, and his answering call of "Good-night and good luck" reached us like the strokes of a clear bell. We turned then to a snow couloir before us, a hidden crevasse broke under me, but Tucker was used to the job and swung back on the taut rope until I reached firm snow again.

Roughly our plans were as follows. This Great Serac leads to the only snow pass on the south-eastern side of Mount McKinley. The great terraced granite ridges that form the big mountain's southern walls are unclimbable. Our only hope then was to find a way over the high passes by way of the Great Serac. Twice we had tried earnestly and failed, at Reconnaissance Camp 1, to reach the right-hand col of the glacier.

Our third attempt had failed when we had encountered the crevasses, and the venture that we were now engaged in was in the nature of a forlorn hope. At first everything went well. We made a long traverse and found a deep couloir between ice walls that led us to a good elevation. Without knowing it, however, I had swung too far to the right, and suddenly we came out on a level snow ledge and found ourselves looking directly down the grim walls. One look into that frigid basin, with the dim blue snow-fields far below, sent us on a long traverse to the left. Here we found the route we had chosen from below. The climbing began to be very steep, and we were again forced to make a traverse that took us below a huge ice wall, over snow that was literally ploughed by the ice blocks that had fallen during the day. The night was very cold, and before we had climbed half way up the slope, our axes were encased in ice and our mittens were as hard as boards. At the head of the steep slope we entered a chaos of crevasse ends and intervening ice masses that puzzled us until we turned a sensational corner above a deep cavern, crawled below a ten-ton icicled overhang, and crossed a rotten snow bridge that led us into the bottom of a snow-filled crevasse. Here we were cheered by seeing what appeared to be the smooth floor of the upper glacier. After some more strenuous climbing we came to an ice cavern that crossed our crevasse, and we had to chop steps again until we reached the top of the left-hand ice wall and then—we stopped. Below us on both sides lay crevasses, one of which sank deep into the heart of the glacier. There was only one thing that we could do. Herman lowered me down the wall of the largest crevasse, after we had crawled on our stomachs across a narrow snow bridge from which we could look down into the blue depths of the ice river. As I went down I chopped deep foot-and-hand holds, which Herman descended in. Then began the weirdest pilgrimage of my life. Following the snow-smoothed floor, we advanced between walls of ice that in places rose seventy feet above our heads. We passed crevasses end on, and looked far into their frigid depths. Blue grottoes led into the ice glittering with stalagmites and stalactites of blue-black ice, and one glance into these caverns of deathlike cold and silence was enough to turn one's skin to goose-flesh.

It was midnight, and the first cold blue sheen of dawn was creeping along a distant snow dome that was framed by the walls of our frozen roadway. We kept on until we came to a second crevasse that wound away into the snow-fields. We could see that there was an hour's work ahead of us before we would be out of the crevasses, and the thought of the sun catching us on the steep slopes far below sent us hurrying over our back trail. At our highest point we were two thousand feet above our camp, and we reached our camp at 2 A.M. after as strange a night's adventure as I have ever experienced.

After two hours' sleep we broke camp, and with our belongings on our backs started downward towards our companions.

The Great Serac had beaten us, but there was no regret in our minds as we snowshoed away over the hard crust, only a feeling of gladness that our hard toil on the treacherous ice walls was finished.

On the way to camp we stopped to admire the great central glacier that enters the big basin from Mount McKinley's cliffs. We were talking of exploring it on the following day when Tucker said, "There are some men on the glacier now!" Looking where he pointed we could see three tiny specks winding among the crevasses far away on the edge of the broken ice-fields. They proved to be our rear-guard, and as they joined us soon after we reached the tent, we had much to tell and learn. The central glacier, they told us, was broken by tremendous crevasses, and Grassi remarked that "to cross the glacier we would need a portable steel bridge with a span of 150 feet."

The reconnaissance work of our rear-guard and our own explorations on the Great Serac ended our hopes of reaching the Southern North-East ridge; the main southern cliffs, too, needed but a glance to convince us that they were impossible; the only hope left lay in the direction of the South-Western Arête. This great arête extends a long way from the big mountain. It rises steeply to a high altitude, possibly twelve thousand feet, and then extends for several miles, like a great wall, until it joins the main peak of Mount McKinley.

So far our chances looked fairly promising, but at the point where the ridge joins the mountain, great cliffs sweep down from the main summit, and these cliffs are too dangerous and too difficult to climb.

On the western side of the great basin a narrow glacier-filled gorge leads up to the lowest portion of the South-Western ridge. On one side the stupendous cliffs of Mount McKinley rise thousands of feet above the glacier's frozen floor, while the opposite wall is formed by a separate group of very steep and rugged mountains, whose steep cliffs are continually sending down avalanches into the blue depths. We determined to explore this glacier, and while we knew that our chances of scaling the mountain were poor, we hoped to at least attain a "respectable" altitude.

Before "turning in" for a much-needed sleep we stood outside of our little tents and talked, and enjoyed the wonderful mountain views that surrounded us. On the eastern side of the big basin stood an isolated peak. It was beautifully formed and rose to an altitude of about three thousand feet above our camp. As we stood talking, our eyes were drawn to this mountain. Its steep snow and ice slopes called to us with the world-old challenge, and Grassi—who had as a boy learned to swing an ice-axe among the Swiss Alps—sighed as he studied the mountain and expressed a wish to stand on its corniced summit.

The idea was received with enthusiasms. For weeks we had been doing the hardest labour yet devised by man; furthermore, we had done the labour in hopes of climbing Mount McKinley; our only reward had been serac and glacier climbing, which is dangerous without being sport; it was time that we had some fun. We held a council of war on the spot and decided to attack the peak after we had had some sleep.

We awoke late in the afternoon. The long blue shadows were beginning to creep eastward across the snows of the big basin. As night came on, the air began to bite, and we ate our pemmican in confidence of a good crust to travel on. We were not disappointed, and at 11:22 P.M. we moved out in a long line towards the peak we were going to attack.

EXPLORERS PEAK, CLIMBED BY THE 1910 EXPEDITION

We were divided into two parties of three men, only this time the rear-guard under the leadership of Grassi went ahead. We moved quickly through the cold air, our snowshoes making a fine noise on the hard crust. At the base of the first steep pitch of the western arête of our peak, we cached our snowshoes and began the climb.

Grassi worked hard from the start and from the start it was stiff climbing as the lower slopes were so steep that we had to traverse continually between a small serac and some rocks that lay to our left. After reaching a fair altitude the arête became corniced, and we gave the edge a wide berth until we reached a broad snow-saddle, where we ate a second breakfast.

The mere fact of climbing for pleasure exhilarated us, and so incessant were the jibes and jokes that were tossed back and forth between the two parties that if there had been any one in the silent basin far below they would have thought that an afternoon tea had been transplanted to the icy mountain side! We enjoyed the frolic to the full, and when Grassi, poised on a corner of solid ice, called down that there were two routes to choose from—"A safe, and a sporty route," we all clamoured for the "sporty" one. We advanced slowly over a very steep slope of nearly solid ice that swept downward two thousand feet. The tops of the great peaks about us were beginning to turn pale from the coming of dawn and the big basin lay as still as death, like a deep blue lake, far below. Grassi's step-cutting gave us time to fill our eyes and minds with the beauties about us. From the start the night had been crystal clear. Mount McKinley had towered over us since we left camp, and just above its crest a planet—the only one we had seen for more than a month—hung in the blue-black sky. Far below us now, across the big basin ran the black walls of the great gorge, whose gloom deepened the purple of the snows. We had "raised" the Tokosha Mountains by our climb, and their distant forms brought back memories of our boat and camp far down in the spruce forests beyond.

We reached the snow-saddle at 2 A.M. and, turning in our steps, we saw a sight that none of us will ever forget: buried in gloom, as the ranges were, McKinley's summit was catching the first pink flush of the morning sun. Nothing could be more beautiful than the glories that followed the march of the sun across those icy mountains. As the pink deepened, the higher snows seemed actually to burn, and deep stately shadows began to creep across the giant walls. We would turn in the still cold to our work of step-cutting only to be stopped by an ejaculation of wonder from one of the party, and turning we would see a new peak burning in its sun-bath. Mt. Hunter began to catch the sun next, and in an instant its stupendous ice slopes were turned to yellow and gold.

Later a film of clouds sweeping in from Cook Inlet added beauty to the scene, but fearing that Mount McKinley would be hidden I made several exposures of the big mountains between 2 and 2:30 A.M. The fact that these photographs, as well as some that I had taken previously on the Great Serac, at night, were successful, will give the reader an idea of the strength of the northern light. Finally, after what seemed like hours of step-cutting, we reached the summit, and our triumphant cheers were swallowed up in the great silence about us. The summit was corniced, and the wind made it necessary to shelter our hypsometer in a rhuksack while we boiled it. Our barometers registered an altitude of eight thousand feet. The fact that we were twenty miles from timber, and that every foot of our climb had been on ice or frozen crust will give the reader an idea of the difficulties of mountaineering in the Alaskan Range. On casting about for a name for the mountain we thought

On the top of Explorers Peak with Mount McKinley in background. From left to right: Grassi, Cuntz, La Voy, Tucker, Parker.

of the Explorers' Club of which several of our party were members. Our fellow-members of this club had made its influence felt from the North Pole to the Antarctic continent, and in memory of their great work we called the mountain "Explorers' Peak."

On the return Professor Parker, Tucker, and I went ahead. When we reached the ice corner above the lower ridge I left the rope and waited with my camera to take a photograph of the second party as they came down over the steep ice slope. They had been detained on the upper ice-field and it was bitterly cold where I stood in the shadow of the peak. Finally ice and snow fragments began to hurtle past me. One piece came buzzing toward me, so I put my camera in an ice step and caught it as it passed me. I will never be so foolhardy again! It seems inconceivable that so small a piece of crust could gather such force. My hands ached for hours afterwards, and to my added disgust the picture that I waited so patiently to take turned out to be a double exposure!

We arrived at camp after an absence of nine hours, and our return to the arduous work of relaying was lightened by the memory of the day of sport.

On July 17th, we returned to the centre of the Big Basin and began to prepare for our advance on the South-West ridge. We had in provisions: $8^{1}/_{2}$ gals. of alcohol (21 days for 6 men); $15^{1}/_{2}$ 6-1b. cans of pemmican ($15^{1}/_{3}$ days); $14^{1}/_{2}$ lbs. of raisins; $12^{1}/_{4}$ lbs. of sugar; $17^{1}/_{2}$ lbs. Erbswurst (3 days); 340 hard-tack biscuits (19 days for 6 men).

The reader will see that we could have remained on the ice twenty-one days longer—at a pinch—or as long as our fuel lasted. As it was we arrived at our base camp eighteen days later, and on the lower glacier we "ditched" some of our fuel when we got within striking distance of Parkersburgh.

After completing our preparations for the morrow we crawled into our sleeping-bags for a short sleep. But when we awoke we were dismayed by hearing the wind howling about us and the snow beating on our tents. Another long night and day dragged by to the accompaniment of howling wind and drifting snow, then a third, and a fourth. We lay in our bags, most of the time, resting and conserving our strength for the hard days to come. We played chess occasionally or checkers, or between fancied lulls in the storm we dashed hastily from one tent to the other. Our tents were so small that when one man went calling we usually exchanged him for a visitor so that every one would be comfortable.

While a short rest is always welcome to men who are working hard, these long periods of inaction were distasteful to us, for we knew that we would pay for it with tired backs and weary muscles when we began to carry packs again. One of nature's inexplicable laws is that while it takes weeks to get a man into good condition only a few days of sloth or inaction are required to spoil his wind and soften his muscles.

But every storm must cease and on the afternoon of our fifth day the sun shone on a glistening world. The Big Basin and the surrounding mountains were white with their new covering but the bright sunshine revived our spirits and we were a happy crew as we filed away through the soft snow. We laid a straight course for the deep gash in the western mountain wall, that was to be our roadway to the great ridge.

At nightfall we entered the glacier-choked gorge and as we began to climb the lower seracs Tucker and Grassi complained of stomach and eye trouble, the result probably of our enforced inaction during the storm. As they did not improve we camped until morning. With the break of day we continued and our advance up the ice-river was spectacular in the extreme. Stupendous rock walls rose on either

MOUNT HUNTINGTON AND THE GLACIER THAT WE FOLLOWED TO THE SOUTH-WEST RIDGE

THE SNOW WALL THAT PREVENTED OUR REACHING THE TOP OF THE SOUTH-WEST RIDGE

side. I have never seen cliffs of more grim and savage beauty. Where they were broken they were incrusted with ice and snow, and with the deep thunder of avalanches in our ears we chose our route cautiously and swung wide of the overhanging snow-fields.

The steepness of our ascent told us that we were approaching the base of the South-West Arête and on reaching a smooth step in the glacier we halted and made camp, for a heavy fog hid the upper snows.

In the evening the fog lifted and through a rift we caught a glimpse of a great wall of ice—the end of the South-West Arête—blocking the end of the cañon. The ridge was about three miles away and looked unclimbable.

The following day we awoke to the familiar sound of snow and wind. On looking out we could see nothing but wind-driven clouds of ice dust; but the deep roar of an occasional avalanche would tell us that the mountains were still there.

On the following morning we found that the bad spell of weather had at last broken.

Professor Parker, Tucker, and I left camp at 4:40 A.M. and the others followed us in half an hour. The travelling conditions were splendid, as there was a hard crust, but we carried our snowshoes to come back on in case of a thaw. There are four glaciers emptying into the northern side of the main gorge. They cascade down from the cliffs of Mount McKinley and head in huge *box-cañons* the walls of which rise in places to a height of five thousand feet above the glacier. About a mile above camp there was a serac which we "swung" to the left. At this point the main gorge was about one half a mile broad, and the largest of the tributary glaciers faced us on the farther side of the ice fall. We had just gained the top of this serac when an exclamation from Professor Parker halted us. We turned instinctively towards Mount McKinley's grim cliffs and then we were as men turned to stone. The whole of the great cliffs of the box-cañon appeared, at first glance, to be on fire. Unnumbered thousands of tons of soft snow were avalanching from the southern flanks of Mount McKinley onto the glacier floor five thousand feet below. The snow fell so far that it was broken into heavy clouds that rolled downward like huge waves. The force of the falling mass was terrific and as it struck the blue-green glacier mail it threw a great snow cloud that rose like a live thing for five hundred feet; whirling in the wind the avalanche had caused, the white wall swept across the valley, and almost before we were aware of it we were struggling and choking in a blinding, stinging cloud of ice dust. For a long time we crouched with our feet braced far apart and our bodies bent over our firmly planted ice-axes, and when the air finally cleared the walls were still smoking and rumbling under the masses of falling snow. It was a most impressive example of the terrific force of gravitation, and when we finally started onward we were thankful indeed that we had not ascended the right-hand side of the glacier.

We could now see that the glacier ended in a box-cañon. The side walls were formed by the great cliffs of Mount McKinley on one side, and the equally grim cliffs of a second mountain range on the other; the end of the box was formed by the South-West Arête. The arête dipped down, forming a col, but the walls were too steep to negotiate. If the climbing of Mount McKinley had depended on our scaling this slope, and if we could have counted on cold weather, we might have accomplished the feat. But the yawning *bergschrunds* and particularly the overhanging fields of soft snow that scarred the lower slopes with avalanche tracks made the risk too great.

Below the final basin we travelled through a maze of huge crevasses, and while

THE COL OF THE SOUTH-WEST RIDGE OF MOUNT MCKINLEY

crossing one of them on a long snow bridge, Tucker broke through. I had already crossed, on my hands and knees, to distribute my weight, so that Tucker was between Professor Parker and me and we held him easily until he extricated himself. Many of these crevasses were so deep that although the walls seemed perpendicular we could see nothing but an inky blue void below.

Once below the col the travelling was safe, but a high wind had arisen that blew clouds of snow from the upper ridges, which settled in soft drifts into which we sank to our knees. It was regular winter weather and long "mare's-tails" of snow streaming to the leeward of the higher ridges added to the arctic aspect of the scene. We stopped below the col for a second breakfast, and after chopping a hole in the ice and sheltering it with our bodies we succeeded in boiling a hypsometer. Our barometers placed us at ten thousand feet.

Before long the wind had begun to moderate and by the time we attacked the col, the weather was quite pleasant.

We rose five hundred feet over avalanche tracks and finally came to a halt directly below the lowest point of the great ridge. What wouldn't we have given to rise five hundred feet more and look out over the other side! Beyond, just out of our sight, was an absolutely unknown mountain wilderness. Mounts Foraker and Hunter we knew would be in sight, and could we have only climbed a little higher we would have secured a view that no man has ever looked on, or probably will ever look on. We were at an altitude of about 10,300 feet when we stopped. A *bergschrund* stretched across the ridge above us, and the constant sound of falling ice warned us from the cliffs on either hand. This was the end of all our labour—10,300 feet; it seems like a small thing on paper, but we knew what every foot of the 10,300 had cost—and were content.

As we stood looking off across the tangle of jagged peaks and gleaming snow-fields I was conscious of a feeling of reluctance to leave it all. The glacier we had climbed wound downward in a deep gash to the Big Basin far below and as a final payment for our toil every peak in that alpine wilderness stood clear cut against the sky. We stood there a long time drinking it all in, and then Tucker said, "Every step that we take from now on, means green grass, trees, and running water!" With his words the longing for the lowlands swept over us; Mount McKinley and its ever-lasting snow-fields were a thing of the past, and we started downward from our last climb with light hearts. As we tramped along we swung towards a small shelf of rock that broke through the ice on the glacier's edge. It was "pink McKinley granite," an actual part of the great mountain, and we broke off samples with our ice-axes to take back over the long trail. As we rested our companions passed us on their way to the col—tiny black specks, they looked, against the immensity of the mountain masses that rose about them. Climbing out of the snow gully below the rocks we could place our hands on the cold granite slabs and as we passed we each patted the old mountain on the back, as it were, in farewell.

We reached camp at 1 P.M. having made 3500 feet of altitude during our climb. We snowshoed the last mile through the slush the northern sun had made and I ended the morning with a snow bath, which is the only luxury that the snow-fields have to offer. After the return of our companions we lay down for a short rest, and then a long steady "hike" brought us to our old camp in the centre of the Big Basin.

Everything was bustle and confusion as we prepared for our final tramp to the lowlands. Each man's belongings were thoroughly overhauled and each useless article thrown aside after the closest inspection.

The instant anything is thrown aside it becomes public property; each frayed sock and worn shoe-pack is carefully balanced against its mate, and every ounce of unnecessary weight is eliminated. I remember an amusing incident that occurred in 1910 which I have often seen repeated. While breaking camp one morning

Professor Parker regretfully discarded an old pair of trousers. On reaching the spot I was overjoyed to find that they could boast a solid seat and untorn knees. I made an exchange on the spot, and as I looked back some minutes later I saw Printz marching proudly along in my trousers while what remained of his former pair decorated a willow bush. The condition of Printz's original pair is too awful to contemplate!

Before leaving our last camp we made a careful survey of the surrounding mountains. Professor Cuntz had been busy taking the angles and elevations of the surrounding peaks and as the great number of mountains made it difficult to describe with accuracy the individual mountain masses we decided to name three of the most important peaks that rose above the Big Basin.

On the east stood a magnificent mountain that rose in the shape of a rock-ribbed, ice-incrusted throne, above a broad base whose lower snow-fields had been carved into buttresses by the glacier winds. This peak we named Mount Hubbard after General Thomas H. Hubbard, president of the Peary Arctic Club, whose life-long interest in exploration has been of such great benefit to mankind.

The highest peak on the eastern edge of the Big Basin we named after Professor Huntington, president of the American Geographical Society, under whose auspices we had undertaken the exploration of Mount McKinley's southern glaciers.

Directly under the southern cliffs of Mount McKinley stood a third peak that we wished to name. It was a magnificent cliff-girdled pile that formed in itself the main southern buttress of the McKinley massif. The naming of this peak rested with our entire party and the name chosen was that of Daniel Carter Beard, the father of the world-celebrated Boy Scout movement, and a man who has endeared himself to every American man and boy through the pages of *The American Boy's Handy Book*.

We conferred proper names on these peaks as it was impossible to choose descriptive names that would not be confusing among such a chaos of unnamed mountains, and the names chosen were in each instance those of men who had either directly or indirectly contributed towards the exploration of this region.

Our last hour in the big basin was celebrated by the first bonfire that has ever reddened those lonely snowfields. By gathering together each infinitesimal piece of wood from our pemmican and chocolate boxes we succeeded in making a respectable fire and we joyfully gathered around to enjoy the grateful warmth.

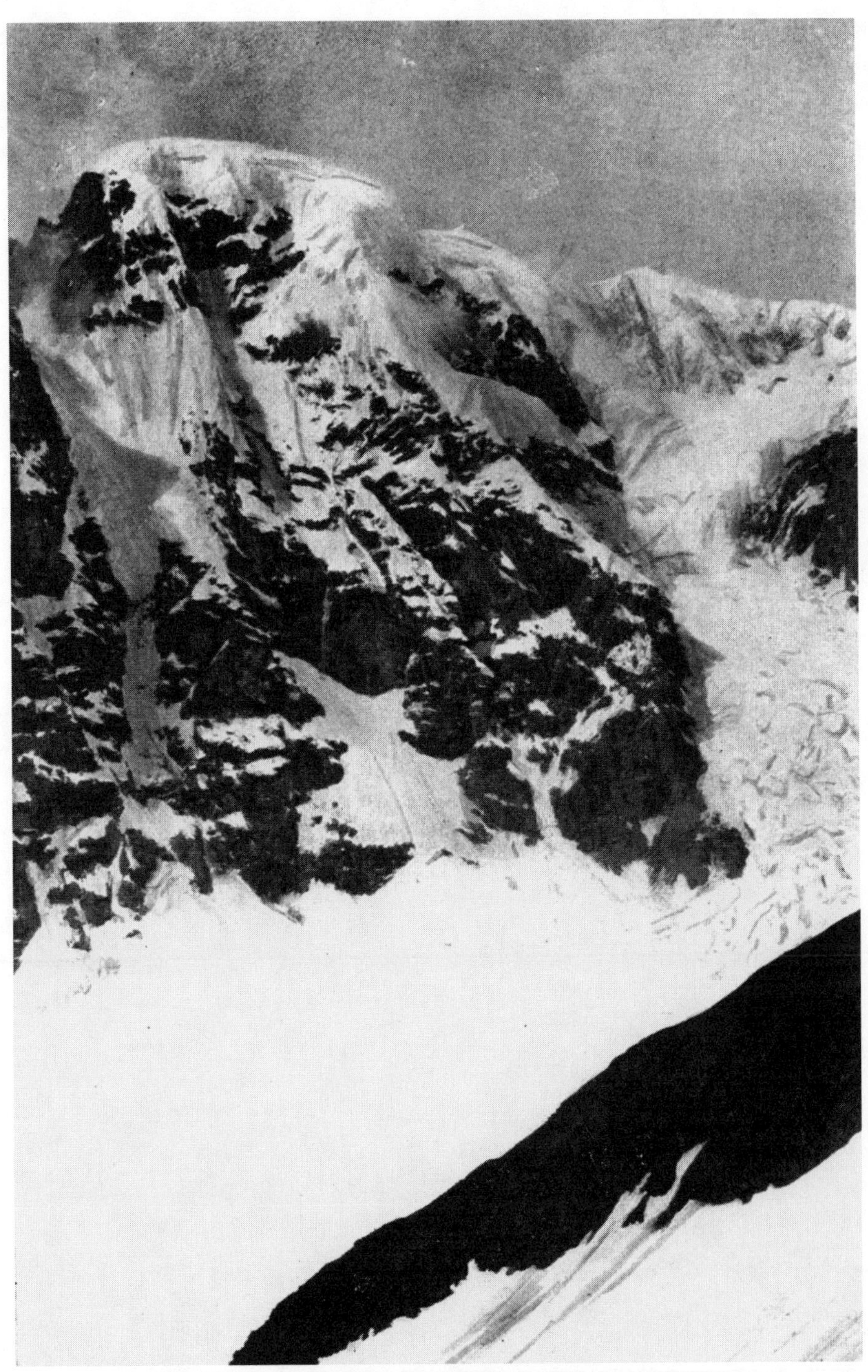

Mount Dan Beard, Mount McKinley's main southern buttress

On the following day we said farewell to the trampled area of snow that had, for so long, been our mountain base camp. It had been a hard pull. In reaching it we had endured many hardships. We had given our best efforts and every foot of progress had been won by the sweat of our brows, and by this toil we were unashamed—yes, even proud in a small way of our work, for we had mapped and explored a part of what is probably the grandest mass of rugged peaks on the North American continent.

Every man had done more than his share, and after forty-two days on the ice we were living in greater comfort and amity than we were on that day so far away when we had said good-by to the lowlands.

## CHAPTER XIV

# The Retreat to Civilisation

*We leave the Big Basin—We re-photograph the "fake peak"—Changes along our route—The joy of running water and wild flowers—We reach timber—Remarks on packing and physical condition—Arrival at Parkersburgh—The feast at "Wreck Island"—Talkeetna Station—The man hunt at Susitna Station—We arrive at Seldovia.*

We left our old camp with seventy-five pound packs and in two hours we reached a point well down between the walls of the great gorge. The travel was all downhill, and as we picked up and passed our old relay camps, we realised to the full the difference between relay travel and straight packing. We sometimes travelled in one march a distance that it had taken two days to cover when we ascended the glacier.

On the second day we reached Glacier Point and camped by a snow-water lake that had formed during our absence. We crawled into our sleeping-bags at 1:30 P.M. and at 4:40 we were up again as we wanted to revisit Dr. Cook's fake peak while the weather was good.

The day was perfect, with no wind and a bright sun for photographing. While crossing Glacier Point we encountered some sun-bared turf where moss, grass, and purple lupine were growing luxuriantly, and the very look of the beautiful spring carpet to our snow-worn eyes acted as an intoxicant. Dropping onto the ice again we pushed on steadily to the fake peak. We found that the snow formations had changed considerably during our absence. But there was still a good deal more snow than Dr. Cook's September photograph showed. We secured the photographs without delay and the following morning found us on the march again.

On the lower glacier everything had changed and instead of blinding sweeps of snow we now found bare ice seamed with countless crevasses. During our midday's rests we brought out a worn pack of cards and played bridge whist for candy, to be paid when we reached civilisation, but the craving for sweets from which we all suffered was aggravated instead of appeased, and even the winners drew small consolation from their good fortune. On August first we found grass growing in considerable quantities among the rocks of the glacial moraines and we derived a considerable amount of satisfaction from eating the soft stems. We were "vegetation-mad" and to us even the poorest little wild flower was a thing of exquisite beauty. As we neared the glacier's snout we were greeted by the dim greens of the nearby mountain slopes and by an alpine lake we found the fresh tracks of a small band of caribou that had come up out of their summer retreats in the foothills.

At last the great day came when we dipped down over the last ice-field and found ourselves on the bank of the glacier stream that swept the base of the ice. We did not hesitate before taking to the water, for on the farther bank we could see the gleam of dead willow branches and as the warm flames leapt about our steaming clothes we laughed with joy and chattered like children, for we were once more in "God's country" and our fifty days of glacier travel had come to an end. In the deepening dusk the glacier's form loomed black against the night sky. There was something sinister and repellent in the grim loneliness of the scene, and we turned with thankful hearts to our willow fire. As LaVoy said, "Looking back at the dead ice walls was like looking back on a misspent life."

At this time, with base camp only a day's march away, I wish to say a few words about our physical condition after our long ordeal. In the first place we were in magnificent condition and yet according to civilised standards we looked weaker than when we first reached the ice. In civilisation when a man's cheeks are full and smooth and his body also runs to curves people say, "Doesn't he look *well?*" On the trail we could say with greater truthfulness, "Doesn't he look ill?" Our faces were hatchet-thin, our eyes sunken and wrinkled from days of squinting over blinding snow-fields, and our bodies worn down to bone and sinew. But every unnecessary ounce of flesh *and muscle* had been burned away in the fire of constant toil, until each tendon worked as smoothly and evenly as the well-greased parts of an engine. One would naturally suppose that our lower limbs in particular would have shown a noticeable increase in size, but, if anything, they were smaller than when we left civilisation.

A fact of even greater interest is that we were living comfortably on a smaller food allowance than we consumed on our march up the glacier.

With these facts in view the work accomplished on the following day will prove of interest. When we broke camp on our last "drive" to Parkersburgh, LaVoy, Tucker, Grassi, and the writer shouldered packs weighing between ninety and one hundred pounds. After going about a half-mile, we came to a food cache left by Aten and Thompson in case of need, and knowing that there was no food to spare at Parkersburgh we picked up this cache, which included a tent, axe, tin buckets, beans, etc. This raised the weight of our packs to between ninety-six and one hundred and twenty pounds, weighed with scales on our arrival at Parkersburgh. With these loads we travelled through alder thickets so dense that we were forced to chop out a trail, and over bogs where we sank to our knees in the sticky mud. High water had washed away our bridges and we forded swift water waist deep and climbed gravel banks on our hands and knees, and yet we reached camp as fresh and happy as a band of children. We could have repeated the journey with ease, and yet it was in covering this same stretch of country, under far better conditions, that we became so tired on the first day of our arrival. In stating these facts I am not holding up our labours as an example of weight carrying—under different conditions we could have carried much more; the point of interest is that we accomplished the labour more easily on a small food allowance, and after weeks of toil, than we did when well fed and fresh from civilisation.

Our arrival at Parkersburgh was a joyful event. To us the green cottonwood groves and flower-spangled river banks were a paradise, and the cosy tent with its log walls a veritable palace. Our food supply was low, but the evening meal of baconless beans, sugarless tea, and sour-dough biscuits was a Lucullan banquet. That night as I lay in my warm blankets listening to the familiar roar of the Tokositna the two previous months seemed a strange jumbled dream—bitter cold camps in the snow—the roar of avalanches—dreary hours under a rump-line—and dim stretches of blue snow under the night sky came back to me in queer disjointed pictures; but the whole was already an intangible blend of memories that had faded away to form what men call *experience*. Now our minds clung eagerly to the future:

the song of "glacier glutted rivers," the smother and roar of the cañon we would "shoot"—but above all to our treasure trove—our cache on the gravel island hard by the Talkeetna. The last thing I remember hearing before falling asleep was LaVoy's voice beseeching an all-wise Creator to keep our potatoes from spoiling until we reached the cache.

Our last day on the Tokositna began with "the crack o' dawn," and by night we were encamped well down towards the mouth of the Chulitna. We tried frantically to reach our cache but the river gainsaid us. In the swift water we had to come down backwards, letting the current do the work while Thompson gave a "kick" with the propeller now and then to keep steerage way. The gravel bars, too, gave us trouble. When you are ascending a river and run aground it usually occurs at the foot of the shallow, and the current will help you to get off. But in descending a stream when you strike a gravel bank you usually lodge on the upper end and at every movement of the boat the current forces you into shallower water. In cases of this kind we reached deep water by "sluicing." Several men would carefully sound the shallows about us for the deepest channel. Having once decided on a route we would move the *Explorer* in the following manner. Taking the bow we would either move or lift it to one side of the current. This would deflect the rushing water and in a short time it would make a channel on the exposed side of the boat. When the water was deep enough to suit our purpose we would push the *Explorer's* bow in the

THE *EXPLORER* STRANDED ON THE GREAT FLATS FORMED BY THE SILT CARRIED DOWN BY THE SUSITNA RIVER

opposite direction and as the current cleared away the gravel under her she would slip into the new channel and move downstream a foot or two. In this slow manner we would sluice a channel through the shoals until we reached deep water. We moored the *Explorer* to the bank well after dark.

It was a peaceful spot and yet before the night wore through we were destined to have one more adventure.

In the inky blackness LaVoy zealously attacked an "adult" dead spruce for firewood, which breaking sideways, as dead trees can, came crashing down on the *Explorer*'s bow. The majority of the party were aboard wrestling our supper from a brace of oil stoves. Luckily a coil of cable on the bow saved the boat from damage, but in the resulting kick of the *Explorer*'s stern our hot cakes and beans went skyward.

Now our party included men of many diverse temperaments. In moments of excitement Grassi depended on volcanic outbursts of Italian to sooth his feelings. Professor Cuntz boasted a deaconship but in moments of stress he has been known to say "My gracious!" as we can all bare witness. Professor Parker being a scientist was coldly accurate in his remarks, while Tucker's speech flowed along with an *abandon* that was positively refreshing! Thompson's diction in moments of mental exhilaration resembled the purr of a contented motor. LaVoy and I, being safe in the gloom of the forest, could give our entire minds to the ensuing babel and when silence at last reigned he turned to me and said, "It's an education to travel with a bunch like ours; when anything *good* happens you can listen to a whole dictionary!"

We needed no alarm clock to wake us next morning for the luxuries in our cache called to us with a voice that drowned all other thoughts. We slipped quickly downstream and soon a gleam of white among some cottonwood trees told us that our hour of joy was at hand. We moored the *Explorer* by a gravel island but the Chulitna had eaten out some new channels and our canvas canoe was launched and sped away through the rushing water. We stood on tiptoe watching the retreating figures, and as they reached the cache our anxiety was boundless; but soon the welcome hail of "Everything's O. K. !" came across the river to our eager ears, and in an instant we were all at work gathering firewood and preparing for the coming feast. By the time that our stove was going, the boat arrived and we unloaded the treasures it contained in the same ecstasy with which children empty their Christmas stockings! We were actually ravenous, and as jars of chow-chow, cans of maple-syrup, and tins of meat appeared we hugged them in our arms and danced delirious dances on the sand! One of the great truths of life that one learns to understand in the north is that it is well worth while to go without the things one wants, for the greater the sacrifice the greater the reward when the wish is consummated. I have eaten with all manner of hungry men from the sun-browned riders of the sage to the bidarka-men of the Aleutians, and I have feasted joyously on "seal liver," "seagull-omelets," and "caribou spinach"; but never have I seen men eat more, or better food!

We started standing up, and wiped the stove clean; then we refilled our pots, pans, and oven, and made a clean sweep of that—sitting down; we ended conservatively—*on our backs!* Then we lay "as we had fallen," and with the sound of glacier water in our ears and the warmth of the northern sun in our faces we slept the whole day through.

Now we knew that Talkeetna Station would be populated, for in addition to Dyer who ran the A. C. Co. store, there would be Indians coming in from their summer camps. One detachment had passed us while we were repairing the *Explorer* on our way up the Chulitna. They had drifted past us in boats made of the green skins of moose and caribou. The primitive canoes were loaded to the gunwales with men, women, children, and dogs, and in the bow of each sat an Indian man tapping the river bottom with a slender pole and searching the channel for dangers that might wreck his frail craft. Your northern red man is a master of the craft of travel. After the salmon-rim on the lower rivers have filled their caches with food for man and dog they await the freezing of the waters. When the icy covering has formed their dogs pull their belongings to the moose pastures and caribou ranges of the interior. Here they hunt and trap the long winter through, and after the spring sun has sent the ice booming towards the sea, they sew up their winter skins into boats and drift with dignity to their summer homes. Here the boats are dismantled, and the skins—none the worse for their immersion—are tanned. When their winter's fur catch is traded they can await the autumn salmon run in peace, and so their lives run, sliding gently from spring to winter and from winter to summer, until they take their last long journey to "the happy hunting-ground."

We were not disappointed in our expectations, and when we drew in to the bank at Talkeetna the shore was lined with Indians that had been drawn by the sound of our exhaust. Among them stood our good friend Dyer and some prospectors whom we had not as yet met. The prospectors were headed towards the gravel bars of Valdez

Creek in the interior, where gold had been found in paying quantities.

While our stay in Talkeetna Station was short we made up for lost time in communion with our fellow-men. The Rusk Mount McKinley party had departed for "the outside" some time since. We heard, too, for the first time, that some Indians on whom they had depended to bring them provisions had refused to make the trip, and one who acted as a river guide had been averse to ascending the Tokositna, being obsessed evidently with the olden legends which people the Mount McKinley region with devils and hobgoblins. I had many an interesting talk with old Talkeetna Nicolae, chief of the Talkeetnas. Sitting cross-legged on the floor of his cabin with the smell of tanning moose-hide in my nostrils, I listened to weird stories of the olden days, and it was there that he told me of the Russian trader—possibly one of Malakoff's men—who died in the Kichatna swamps. Later he posed proudly before my camera, his chest liberally decorated with watches—that had long since ceased to work!

A long lazy run took us down to Susitna Station. When the river broadened out sufficiently we could turn the *Explorer*'s head loose and let her go, and we did, with the river pushing behind us while the miles flew by.

We found Susitna Station in a turmoil. A man had been lost in the swamps behind the town, and a searching party was being organised to find him or his remains. We took our places in the long line that filed out into the back-country. A rifle shot was to be the signal of success in our quest.

All day long we moved fan-wise combing the swamp and spruce groves, but the expected rifle shot was not heard, although we strained our ears in the monotonous drone of the mosquito hordes. Later we heard that the man, half-crazed, had reached the banks of the Susitna.

At Beluga we picked up a prospective buyer of the *Explorer* and turned the old boat's bow towards Seldovia. Kussiloff we entered through schools of belugas that were harrying the salmon hordes and stopped at the cannery. On visiting the bunk-houses we found that the scenes of more civilised "Chinatowns" had been transplanted to this northern beach. A night of freezing spray and heavy seas followed, but with the sunrise we came in between the sheltering points of Seldovia harbour, and one more summer of toil and pleasure was finished.

## CHAPTER XV

# The 1912 Expedition

~

***Plans—Difficulties—Preparations for a winter trip—We choose the Seward route and determine to cross the Alaskan Range—Gathering dog teams—Aten and LaVoy commence freighting—We reach Seward—The first days on the trail.***

Immediately after our second failure to climb Mount McKinley Professor Parker and I began to plan a third attempt. We were through with the southern approach—that much we knew—and our next attempt would have to be made from the northern side of the Alaskan Range. The question therefore was which side of the northern approach was the most promising, and we could answer it with our own firsthand knowledge of the great peak. During the night in 1906 that I spent with Dr. Cook on the mountain top west of the Tokositna glacier, I had been able to look along the south-western end of the big mountain. From this point and from the Mount Kliskon country even farther westward I had carefully studied the mountain's contours. Throughout this whole sweep I could not see one promising route. I studied the profile of the Western ridge which dips downward to Peters Glacier. It was at this point that both Judge Wickersham and Dr. Cook had unsuccessfully attacked the big mountain and I could see indications of the cliffs which render this arête difficult.

The northern face we knew was unclimbable, as we had seen both Brooks's and Dr. Cook's photographs of these forbidding ice cliffs.

By a process of elimination therefore our minds centred on the Southern North-eastern Ridge. As I have before stated we did not know as yet that there were three ridges on the north-eastern side, but from what we could see of this approach we were convinced that it offered the best chances of success.*

After deciding on this line of attack the next important question was how we were to reach the ridge. Fairbanks on the Tanana River is the nearest town to Mount McKinley and with the aid of dogs, in the winter time, the journey offers no difficulties, consisting as it does of only 160 miles of excellent snow-travel. Fairbanks is easily reached from the seacoast via the Copper River Railroad and a well travelled trail that crosses the low pass at the head of the Tanana River. This then was our logical route.

But as we thought it over our minds filled with memories of the magnificent stretch of mountains that form the Alaskan Range east of Mount McKinley. Many times we had looked yearningly at the great line of snow peaks, and it was our hearts' desire to explore their unknown cañons. If we could find a pass through the high range we would explore a magnificent mountain wilderness that otherwise might remain unknown for years. The very thought thrilled us and we at once began to perfect our plans.

Now about sixty miles from Mount McKinley the Alaskan Range breaks away, and the mountains become lower and more rounded as you approach the Tanana River. In these lower mountains, eighty miles from Mount McKinley, there is an easy pass called Broad Pass, which has been crossed by a good many prospectors and one survey party.

The only authentic crossing of the range between Broad Pass and Mount McKinley was accomplished by Dr. Cook's expedition, in 1906. In describing it he fails to place it accurately, but states that they crossed it in a single day with pack horses, and that the pass was drained by a large tributary of the Chulitna River.

This description places Dr. Cook's pass in the low part of the Alaskan Range close to Broad Pass, as the only river that enters the Chulitna from that region is the west fork of the Chulitna.

We knew moreover that we would find no pass worthy of the name in the high, ice-bound portion of the range close to Mount McKinley. If we could force a way

*Before our departure we heard of the Central, and Northern North-east Ridge, from Thomas Lloyd of Fairbanks, Alaska; we also gained a general idea of this side of the mountain from a photograph shown to us by Charles Sheldon.—Author

through we would be satisfied. In the glimpses of the range that we had caught from the country south of Mount McKinley we had noticed one promising fact—the range, even in the summer time, was covered with snow. This fact meant that the valleys and cañons would be filled with glaciers which in turn would discharge streams into the Chulitna, and on the frozen surfaces of these rivers and glaciers we hung our hopes of finding a route across the range. While it would be possible for a small party of strong men to ascend the Chulitna during the summer in boats and then pack light loads through the range, the transporting of a large outfit in this manner would require too much time and the accomplishment of this feat in addition to the climbing of Mount McKinley would be an impossibility. We were forced therefore to make a winter trip of it, and to depend for our transportation on the Alaskan dog.

Now the value of dogs in the north fluctuates with the seasons. When the trails begin to harden and winter throws its mantle of snow across the land there is a corresponding boom in the dog market, while in the springtime when the dogs' usefulness vanishes with the melting snows they can be purchased for a song. In order to profit by the spring "slump" we commissioned Arthur Aten to buy dogs for us, and when the summer of 1911 arrived we possessed a strong and well-trained team.

But plans are made but to be broken. With the coming of spring came a call of "Gold!" from the north. With feverish haste we packed and stood ready. Then followed travel-worn letters that told us that "strikes" were being made along the glaciers of Prince William's Sound. Mount McKinley was for the time, forgotten, and we spent our summer among the ice-fed fiords.

With the coming of winter our thoughts drifted back to the big mountain and when the first snow flurry came down from the Kenai Mountains we were ready to advance. Aten and LaVoy were the only men of the old party to join Professor Parker and the writer. Our journey was to be entirely different in character from the work we accomplished in 1910, for speed in dog travel depends on a small party, and we no longer needed the large number of men necessary for relay packing. It was with the keenest regret however that we started on the long trail without our old companions.

As we were to enter the Alaskan Range just east of Mount McKinley our route would lead us up the familiar waterways of the Susitna and Chulitna rivers. But as Cook Inlet was choked with ice during the winter time, we were forced to leave the steamer at Seward.

Seward lies at the head of Resurrection Bay on the south side of the Kenai Peninsula. It is from this port that the incompleted railroad, so often mentioned in the newspapers, starts on its long journey to the interior. Striking directly through the heart of the Kenai Peninsula the railroad winds and tunnels for eighty miles through magnificent mountain scenery to tide-water on Turnagain Arm at the head of Cook Inlet. At this point construction has ceased, but a winter trail leads from the end of the line to Susitna Station via Knik Arm. Beyond Susitna Station a winter trail now leads over the Alaskan Range at the head of the Kichatna to the Kuskoquim and the gold fields of the Iditerod. This three-foot strip of foot-hardened snow is the only link now joining the village that will some day be a city with the wilderness that in days to come will be an inland empire. The road is not operated in the winter time but the grade is too valuable to stand idle, and after the ties and tracks are covered with snow the scream and rumble of the locomotive gives way to the jingle of dog bells.

At intervals of about ten miles, "road-houses" stand offering food and rest to man and dog. They are one of the most important of Alaskan institutions, and on all the winter trails that criss-cross the great land, one will find these resting-places which make rapid travel possible.

Now only one man can drive a dog team. When "the going is bad" an extra man can *help*. But the Seward trail was supposed to be a good trail.

For that reason Professor Parker and I turned over our outfit to Aten and LaVoy in October. They were to relay our supplies to Susitna Station and then up the Susitna as far as they could, returning to Susitna Station to meet us in February. At Seward LaVoy met a "sour-dough" fresh from the Iditerod. He had come over the long trail bound for "the outside" and sold his dogs, sled, and fur sleeping-robe for a ridiculously low price. This addition gave us fourteen dogs for the heavy hauling, and each one had more than earned his cost before our freight rested at Susitna. A telephone line that connected the road-houses was a great help to us. Our companions 'phoned the news of their progress to Brown & Hawkins—the leading merchants of Seward—who kindly forwarded the messages by mail. In this way we were able to keep track of our companions until the day arrived when we too were to start on the long trail.

It was during the last days of January that our steamer drifted in between the fog-draped cliffs of Resurrection Bay. Only ten years before I had been in the same harbour; but now a bustling Alaskan town was scattered over what had then been a green spruce-covered point, and along the water front I could see the trestles of the new railroad whose right of way we were going to follow with our dog teams. The mountains alone were unchanged and looked down through the fog rifts as they did in the old days. To me this is one of the most striking facts in our great country—the rapidity of growth. I have heard an Englishman earnestly comparing (unfavourably) the transportation facilities of a Western city with those of London when I could remember the days when the stumps of forest trees were still obstructing the main avenue of that city! When I first saw Resurrection Bay it was little more than a wilderness fiord. When our little steamer, that, in any other land, would long since have been condemned, came to rest, a canoe came gliding from the shore. The man who paddled it was calling aloud for a minister. The minister was wanted by one Bill or Tom and "he wants to get married *bad*" the canoe-man added, "for he has two kids already!" Such was Seward in the old days, but even then it was historical ground. The Russians had settled there when Alaska belonged to the White Bear, and the first wooden man-o'-war ever launched on the Pacific coast was built by them in this sheltered harbour.

On our sail along the Alaskan coast we had been overcome with forebodings of trouble through the mildness of the winter. No winter like it could be remembered, even by "the oldest inhabitant." Our wildest fears were realised as we walked to our hotel along the Seward streets for the thin glare of ice that covered the ground was melting perceptibly.

Our first task was to find a traveller with a dog-team who was going to Susitna Station, for besides our personal duffle of fifty pounds to the man the invariable forgotten or left-over things had swelled our belongings to a weight of three hundred pounds. Fortune led us to the United States mail-carrier, Vause by name, who was starting over the trail in a few days.

He turned over his second team to us, partly loaded with second-class mail matter—which under his contract he is not forced to deliver. This raised our load to five hundred pounds while he carried an equal bulk of letters on the lead-sled. For a number of days we kicked our heels about the streets of Seward, waiting for the weather to turn cold. In the meanwhile the town was stirred by the arrival of the Iditerod gold shipment.

The gold was packed in small wooden chests—one hundred pounds to the chest—which were handled with grunts and groans by the bank clerks who took them from the dog sleds. The populace stood packed about, but fully one half of their interest was centred on the two magnificent, perfectly matched dog teams that had pulled the treasure from the banks of the Kuskoquim, four hundred miles to the north.

The dogs were owned and driven by "Bob" Griffith, better known as "Dog" Griffith among the trail men. He knew dogs better than a Kentucky horsemen knows horses, and had participated himself in the greatest sporting event of this world—"The Nome Sweepstake"—when men race an unlimited number of wolf-dogs over four hundred miles of frozen Alaskan trail.

We met him later as he wanted tallow to feed to his dogs and I had an over supply to trade. From his lips and those of Mitchell, the driver of Griffith's second team, we heard picturesque but awful things concerning the condition of the Susitna trail. On the theory that the longer we waited the worse things would be, we set the following day for our time of departure.

An earthquake—the precursor possibly of the Katmai eruption that buried Kadiak Island in ashes—rattled the frame houses as we prepared our outfit for the trail.

We said good-by to Seward and its hospitable citizens on the first of February. We crossed a piece of rough trail through the waste of burnt and slashed timber common to Alaskan towns before reaching the shelter of the woods.

In the shelter of the timber we found snow enough to grease our sled runners and before long we were trotting along the line of the railroad.

Vause led with a five-hundred-pound load of mail lashed on a Nome sled, drawn by five dogs. Professor Parker travelled with the lead-sled, while I followed them at the gee-pole of the second Nome sled loaded also with 400 (four hundred) pounds, and drawn by four dogs.

Unless one has been in the north it is hard to realise the importance of the "broken trail." In the winter time the whole country is covered with several feet of soft, powdery snow. This snow is seldom crusted until the spring thaw sets in, and in consequence it is difficult to travel through; even a man on snowshoes may find it arduous work. But after a man has walked over it his snowshoes leave a broad path that freezes hard, and on this narrow strip of frozen crust dogs can pull a loaded sled. As the trail is used it grows broader, firmer, and smoother, until in time it becomes in reality a "winter trail."

After a snow-storm, or a heavy drifting wind, the trail must be rebroken, and at times when it becomes completely effaced you feel your way with a sharpened pole lest you lose the trail and the benefit of its firm foundation.

Now dog-driving, when you have a heavy load and the going is bad, is about as strenuous a job as a man can tackle. Even one week of idleness will allow hardened muscles to become soft, and after many months of city life, no matter how conscientiously one has *exercised* according to civilised standards, the body is in no condition to stand the demands of the trail.

On our first day's run we put twenty-one miles of soft snow behind us. The trail was in execrable condition. The warm weather had rotted the snow, and the sleds in consequence were continually breaking through and turning over into the soft snow beside the trail. Now when a sled turns over or "killapies" its outside runner has a fiendish way of catching under the hard lip of the trail; put five hundred pounds on top of the sled and it is a man-sized job to lift it back onto the trail again. When you have trotted twenty-one long, soft snow miles punctuated frequently with these sled episodes your very bones cry out against your past months of idleness.

Another source of bruises and bad language that we encountered were the numerous trestles. There was a drop of about three feet from the surface of the trail to the ties.

The snow had fallen through between the timbers which were capped with cones of hard ice. We would nurse our dogs as gently as possible to the edge of the trestle and then give them the word to "Mush!" Vause's dogs being under his constant supervision and at the head of our line took the bridges quietly, a thing which few dog teams will do. As I was a stranger to the dogs I drove and as they were behind they took the bridges with a rush. The "gee-pole" or steering-pole is lashed to the right-hand runner of the sled in such a position that the end comes level with your right hand when you stand six feet in front of the sled. When the sled slid from the level of the trail the gee-pole first swept out into space and then plunged down to the level of the ties. As it is absolutely necessary to hold on to the gee-pole to guide the sled, we had to take the drop-off on the run, leap out into space, land, somehow, on the ice-capped ties, and *keep running* while the ice scraped the skin from the knuckles of our right hands. It was dashing, bone-breaking work, and would have made good moving picture "stuff," but when you are wedged between ice-capped ties with the steel runners of a four-hundred-pound sled grinding your back, it's hard to appreciate the picturesque side of things!

About twelve miles from Seward stands the first road-house, and here we got a bite to eat and rested the dogs. Some miles beyond we came to our first trouble; the bridge over Snow River had been washed out by a freshet and the rails and ties hung in midair, held only by the spikes and fish-plates. One look at this aerial route was enough, and we descended to the naked gravel bars of the river bed and by doubling our two dog teams relayed the sleds over a jury-bridge of logs.

When we reached the railroad again it had been transformed by the late freshet into a ridge of ice. On the top of this "ice tight-rope" we juggled with sleds and dogs. Once, my foot slipped and I landed with my sled and dogs in a tangled heap at the base of the ridge. Night overtook us beyond Snow River, and it was inky black when we saw the lights of our night's shelter.

Vause was trail-hardened, having carried mail since the first snow, and to him our day had been only a moderately strenuous one. But to me—fresh from the flesh-pots—it savoured of "hard labour."

With all this work however there goes the invariable recompense; back of all these aches, and strains, and cuts, and bruises lies the knowledge that you are being made over; it is only nature's way of doing the job. It is always hard when you first "hit the trail," but as you think of the days to come, when, with a body as hard as those of the dogs you drive, you can trot unwearied the long day through, the game seems well worth the candle.

CHAPTER XVI

# The Seward Trail

*"Mother White's" road-house—Bad condition of trail—We cross Trail Lake—We reach Turnagain Arm and find it clear of ice—We try the water route—Failure—Crow Creek Pass—Eagle River—We reach Old Knik—News of our companions.*

The road-house where we rested was known as "White's" as it was kept by a nice old couple of that name. "Dad" White supervised the outdoor part of their domain, filling the generous wood-boxes, bringing in the ice-cold water from the mountain streams, and, in the summer time, mending boats and tending the little truck-garden that sloped down to the shore of Kenai Lake.

In the house Mrs. White, or "Mother White" as she was called by all who knew her, reigned supreme. Dressed in the costume of the day she might have stepped from the frame of a Copley or Sir Joshua. Her snow-white hair was the only hint of the weight of years she bore, for her mind and figure were those of a young girl.

They tell the story along the trail of how, in the early days of the railroad, when travelling rates were high, Mother White used to walk the twenty miles to town. But one day an official of the railroad, who was inspecting the track, passed her, and in her next mail she found a pass to Seward.

When we awoke the next morning we looked out over the steel-grey surface of Kenai Lake. In the distance the water blended with the mountain mist. No ice was to be seen, and Dad White told us that it was the first time in the memory of man that the lake had not frozen.

While we were finishing our hot cakes a suspicious murmur from the roof drew our eyes to the windows, and to our dismay we looked out into sheets of warm rain.

Nothing in this world is more disheartening than trotting through rain-rotted snow in a steady downpour, and besides the mail must be kept dry. I own, too, to having felt a secret joy at this unexpected rest. The following day, however, was cooler and we made up for our delay by an early start.

The day was remarkable for the fiendish travel we encountered. Once only were we blessed by a good bit of trail. This was at Trail Lake where we found a mile of clear ice. Jumping on the sleds we went sailing along, and in verity it was more like sailing than sledding, for the dogs were splashing along in several inches of water, and our sleds left long ripples behind that broke the clear reflections of the surrounding mountains. At the end of the lake we paid heavily by running into a piece of trail where we worked for an hour and only made one mile. The trail itself would not bear our weight and we broke through sometimes to our waists.

The conditions held us down to a fourteen-mile day, but the fourth day we trotted eighteen miles, crossing the Kenai Divide and dropping down to the road-house at "Mile 52." The travel was through splendid mountain scenery. We followed, as usual, the railroad line which led us along the timbered mountainsides. When the pitching, sliding sleds allowed us to turn we could look through the ragged tops of the spruce trees to the distant mountainsides that glittered under their mantles of snow and ice.

At the road-houses we learned day by day the history of Aten's and LaVoy's trip across the trail. The miserable winter had changed their trip into a terrific struggle against adverse conditions. At one road-house we would hear that a heavy snow-storm had destroyed the trail and that they had spent two days "breaking" a new one to the next shelter. Farther on we heard that Aten had spent the night, snow-blind in an abandoned cabin, with nothing but the dogs to keep him warm. And again we were told that a fight had occurred among our "huskies" and that our best lead-dog was dead.

As you come out of the Kenai Mountains onto the Cook Inlet side a broad valley opens before you. On the farther side you can see one end of Portage Glacier which runs in a broad ice road across the neck of the peninsula and dips into the Pacific on the southern side. On the left the railroad begins to climb down to the valley floor in a series of curved trestles like a "scenic railroad" at Coney Island. There was a firm crust on the snow—for a wonder—and so we left the line and prepared to coast down to the tracks that we could see winding in big loops below us.

Under the body of a Nome sled there is a thin board capped with steel claws. When you stand on its projecting end and heave up on the handle-bars the steel claws grip the snow and, sometimes, stop the sled. We took our sleds down one at a time. Vause held to the gee-pole with his feet braced straight in front, and I swung on the brake behind. We swept down the long hills in a cloud of snow—our dogs racing madly to escape the leaping sled.

There was little travel at the time we used the trail. Once we met a man who trotted steadily along on long upturned snowshoes. "Going to Seward for medicine for a sick woman at Glacier Creek," he said as he jogged by. We met him six days later at Glacier Creek and found that he had covered the one hundred and fifty-two miles of bad trail in less than five days. On another occasion we saw black specks on the trail ahead that materialised into a team of dogs aimlessly pulling an empty sled. The lead dog had in some manner loosened himself, and as we approached he tried to lead his truant companions around us. We headed them off, however, and tied them firmly to a dead spruce while the surly leader sat at a distance and howled out his sorrow and chagrin. A half-hour later we met a sturdy Swede whose "A ban loose my dogs!" we answered with an account of their capture. From the determined expression on his face as he started after the runaways, it required little imagination to picture what would happen to the lead-dog when our Swede friend caught him.

Beyond the road-house at "Mile 52" the trail leads recklessly along the edge of a precipice, now plunging through tunnels where the dogs panted as they drew the sleds over the bare ties, then hanging over straight drop-offs, where water from the cliffs above had frozen into icicles weighing tons. Here we had to chop grooves in the glare ice lest our sleds should start sliding and drag our dogs into space. Once through the tunnels we dropped down to the Flood River flats at the head of Turnagain Arm and were at sea-level once more.

On the "flats" the glacier winds had been playing their old game, and we were confronted by miles of bare track. But the old saying, "It's always darkest before morn," proved true for we found a battered push-car on a siding. With light hearts we hoisted our two sleds aboard and climbed on top, while the combined dog teams swept us majestically along. "Dog driving on a freight car!" Vause called it, and smiled gleefully as the miles flew by. At nightfall we reached Turnagain Arm and a cabin occupied by a man with a boat. He told us that we could go no farther with the car as rock-slides had covered the track, and that he would take our sleds around the obstructions in his boat the following morning. Unhitching the dogs we led them onward in the darkness. Once they broke away in a strip of timber and chased a wild animal of some kind, but eventually we reached the road-house at "Mile 71" which is "the end of construction."

The road-house at "Mile 71" is on the shore of Turnagain Arm. A rough trail leads along the shore from there to Glacier Creek, a little settlement a few miles farther on. At this point we picked up Muckluck, the right wheel dog of Aten's team, who had been left behind to recuperate from injuries received in a fight. Turnagain Arm was open, and the weather so balmy that a large brown bear had left his hibernating den and wandered to the railroad track, where he was shot by a chance traveller. Early in the morning our friend with the boat arrived and we caught the strong tide and rowed to Glacier Creek.

As far as we could see the "Arm" was open, and the ease of water travel put an idea in my head. If Turnagain Arm was clear, Knik Arm should be open also, and if we could reach Knik by water it would save us hauling our sled over Crow Creek Pass, a 3500-foot gash in the mountains, where we would be forced to back-back our duffle to the summit. It was well worth considering, and later when I met an old friend at Glacier who had a twenty foot boat, the plan began to crystallise. Naimes thought that we could reach Knik without difficulty, so we loaded his boat with Vause's second-class mail matter and our own duffle and put to sea. Vause hitched both teams to his sled and started overland for Knik where we would be reunited. In conception the plan was perfectly feasible, but Cook Inlet has a malevolent temper that cannot be reckoned upon.

At first Naimes's gasoline engine refused to work, it was too cold, but under sail and oars we caught the tide that ran like a river, and made good headway down the "Arm." Then as there was no ice to be seen and the weather was clear we headed for Fire Island twenty-five miles away.

After darkness had settled down we began to see dim masses of ice, and finally when we were only a short distance from Fire Island the floes became so numerous that we could go no farther. As we were afraid of being caught in the ice and swept out into the inlet we had to return to the mainland. This move forced Naimes and me to row all night. After a short rest we started in daylight for our last attempt to reach Knik Arm. After rowing about ten miles we began to encounter more ice-floes, the sky grew black, and snow began to fall. If a storm had come up our chances of escape would have been small. When the floes began to freeze together our failure was written, so we turned and pulled frantically for shore. We rowed for hours in the inky darkness. It was bitterly cold and the snow turned the water to slush. Professor Parker was attacked by a severe chill, and but for a bottle of "hooch," which Naimes had brought, he would have been in a serious predicament. We reached the mainland late at night and a large fire and liberal quantities of moose meat restored our spirits. On the following morning we pulled back thirty miles to Glacier Creek, and our attempt at winter boating was ended.

The important question now was getting a dog team to haul our possessions to Susitna Station. Vause was well on the way, and there were not many dogs for hire at Glacier Creek. With Muckluck as a nest-egg I began to gather a dog team, but my efforts were stopped by joyful news. Bob Griffith and Mitchell, with their two splendid teams, were approaching on their way back to the Iditerod.

MacDonald a Yentna gold miner and a friend of ours in the old days brought the happy tidings. He was on his way to Susitna Station accompanied by his wife, and he added Muckluck to his team until our ways parted.

On the appointed day Griffith arrived and after throwing our freight onto his big sleds we began the climb to Crow Creek Pass. The railroad was now a thing of the past and we followed a regular wood trail that wound steeply upwards through thick groves of Alaska spruce. High above us we could see the snowy crests of rock-ribbed mountain peaks, and on a steep shoulder that had been swept bare of timber by a snow slide, we entered a snow-filled mountain valley. The desolation of the scene was added to by huge piles of worn boulders that choked the frozen bed of a mountain stream. These were the handiwork of man as the coarse gravel held its share of gold.

Travelling behind Griffith's dogs was a different proposition from ordinary dog-driving. In the first place the big Nome sleds were lightly loaded and there were nine dogs in one team and eight in the other. They were all heavy dogs—too heavy for very fast travel, but splendid workers on a long hard pull. Their harness was perfect from the silver bells that jingled so sweetly to the red pom-poms that bobbed gaily on each furry back. The teams were hitched in the regulation Alaskan trail manner—two by two with a single leader.

They pulled on a long pliable "tug-rope" of squared walrus hide which is a luxury on the trail as it doesn't freeze, or cut your moccasin tops into pieces. Almost every dog had been with Griffith since the days of puppyhood, and in handling them he treated them more like children than dogs. On the few occasions when I saw him use a whip he merely pulled it from the bag between the handlebars and then put it back again—the dogs *knew,* and behaved!

On the level mountain benches we could jump on the sleds and take a whiff or two at a pipe or swap a yarn before the trail steepened again. At last on the ragged edge of timber line we came to rest before a snow-covered cabin. This was Sam Capper's road-house and it stood at the mouth of the icy valley that led steeply to the pass.

We took this trail early the next morning. A United States game warden helped us. He had lost most of his fingers on both hands in a winter storm in the Kenai Mountains, but with the stumps he could do more than an average man. After manhandling the sleds over the snow-covered avalanche debris in the valley bed, we came at last to the snow-filled amphitheatre under the wall of the pass. Six hundred feet it rose above us, so straight that it was all we could do to stand in our shoe-packs. "It's here that we begin to sweat," said the game warden. "The dogs *may* be able to pull the empty sleds—but no loaded sleds have crossed the pass this year." But Griffith was studying the slope and made no move to unhitch the dogs. Then turning to the second sled he said, "What do you think, Mitchell?" and Mitchell answered, "Let's take a chance." And we did. First the teams were hitched in one long line, and then came the question of which dog should lead. Now among Griffith's seventeen dogs there was one puppy, a splendid intelligent animal whose fine head and big bones promised well for the days to come. He ran loose a good part of the time, frisking along in the soft snow beside the dignified working dogs. Griffith had taken him on the long trip "just for the experience and to see the world." The puppy at that moment happened to be sitting near by gazing at our activities with the vacuous stare peculiar to puppies, so Griffith, laughing, hitched him at the head of the long line. If we could have understood canine talk we would undoubtedly have heard some indelicate and sarcastic remarks from the old dogs,

"BOB" GRIFFITH'S DOGS PULLING OUR FREIGHT OVER CROW CREEK PASS

but the puppy was already leading up the steep slope, and we were engrossed in the task that confronted us.

Griffith went first—with the dogs; Mitchell and the game warden wrestled with the sled and kept it from swinging pendulum-like on the hard snow; I followed with a shovel poised to brake the sled when it came to rest, while Professor Parker, camera in hand, snap-shotted our progress from the rocks above.

During the rests we gasped for breath, and the panting of men and dogs filled the air. When our breathing had returned to normal, Griffith would shout, "Mush!" Sixty-eight furry feet would tear madly at the snow and the sled would lurch upward, to an accompaniment of gasps and flying snow. In this way with our tendons cracking in the mad rushes we won to the top. Then came a wild slide to the base of the mountain for the second sled. Noon found us eating a light lunch on the top of the pass and shivering in the icy wind. According to Professor Parker's barometer we were 3500 feet above Turnagain Arm. Around us rose a frozen desolation of mountain peaks, the home of the white sheep and goat.

The game warden's eyes were vainly searching the mountainsides for a sled that had been left on the summit, but it had disappeared—blown into one of the rocky gorges below us by the winter wind.

We wasted no time on the summit but said a hasty good-by to the game warden and started downward through a long valley that stretched bare of timber as far as we could see. It was a long, hard, downhill fight. On the first steep pitches we had to double "rough-lock" our sleds or they would have overrun the dogs. We used heavy dog-chains for the purpose and even then we used the brakes freely. But it was in the lower valley that our real troubles began as we found miles of smooth "sideling" trail, where it was impossible to keep the sleds from swinging downhill.

Frequently we were forced to shovel or chop a deep rut for our uphill sled runner in order to hold it in place on particularly steep stretches. But more than once, despite every precaution, the big sleds "killapied" and we landed men, sled, and dogs in a tangled heap below the trail. Chopping trenches for the runners and the general bad conditions held us until night overtook us on the top of the steep hill that slopes down to the valley of Eagle River. Professor Parker had gone ahead, and we knew that food and warmth would be awaiting us in the Raven Creek road-house below, so we left our sleds on the mountainside and stumbled downward with our dogs.

At the "crack o' dawn" we were back at the sleds, and by nightfall we had pulled them twenty miles to the Eagle River road-house. We had crossed the last high divide between Seward and Susitna Station, and the day's travel followed the course of Eagle River towards Knik Arm. Eagle River ran unfrozen and at many of the fords we had to pull our sleds through the water. At first the trail was rough, but as the valley broadened the "going" improved. Soon we began to reach stretches where we could sit on the sleds and enjoy the views about us. These rest "spells" were a relief after the labours of the previous days.

Contentedly puffing our pipes we would watch the country fly past. The aches and bruises of the early days were almost forgotten. Griffith would tell me snatches of his years on the northern trails; of men frozen on the Behring Sea coast; of the great race at Nome, when with victory almost in his hands a blizzard struck him, and his dogs froze stiff in their harness; of the hunt for gold in the early days of the Yukon, and of the old days in the Rockies, when he had driven a stage coach on the turbulent frontier.

Now and then moose tracks in the deep snow would make us search the thickets, but the jingle of the dog-bells was a warning to the forest folk. Stevenson has said that there is no paradise comparable to the deck of a wind-jammer in the "trades," but I have tried both and I would always choose the back of a Nome sled on a northern trail when you can smell the tang of evergreens in the frosty air, and the dogs are running smoothly with their tails tight curled.

Beyond Eagle River we made an easy eighteen-mile day to Old Knik at the head of Knik Arm. Every view now was like a smile from an old friend, for I had hunted in that country before the trail was built. From the sled I could show Griffith the wind-swept tops of snowy mountains where I had followed the white sheep, and several times the dogs smelled moose and we swung hard on the brakes, our ears ringing with the crash of wolf music that followed.

The trails in general were in miserable shape. In the road-houses at night, when we sat around the big stoves drying our steaming clothes, the talk revolved around the mildness of the winter. The belief was general that the Japan current had changed its course, and wild tales of a tropical Alaska filled our evenings. One old prospector with an active imagination said, "Wont it be hell when we have to 'chop-trail' through rubber plants!" But the principal subject of conversation was the trail that we had just crossed on Crow Creek Pass. It had been built, so the trail men told me, by a "government man" at a cost of $50,000.

Now there is not enough travel over the Pass in summer to warrant an expenditure of five thousand dollars, as there is a good water route direct to Knik, and any man who has ever done a winter day's work in the open would know at a glance that no trail could be built over the pass that would not be drifted over by the winter snows.

As you approach Old Knik you drop down to the flats of the Matanuska River. In the summer time it is a beautiful stretch of woodland, meadow, and salt marsh. As you wander through the cottonwood groves you are transported to the farm country of the New England States until you raise your eyes—then the towering snow-capped mountains of the Chugach Range bring you back to Alaska.

The salt meadows were frozen and we "boomed along."

As we entered a strip of familiar woodland the hair on our dogs' backs began to rise and the jingle of our dog-bells was soon answered by the wailing cry of a pack of Indian dogs. "Caches" and scattered cabins began to appear, and as we passed the Indian inmates came to their doors to see us. On seeing the pinched half-clad forms, the rough cabins, and the starved dogs one could not help pondering on the difference between the white and red man.

A Susitna Indian village showing caches for storing food and the cabin where we spent the night

We white men were all the product of civilisation, and everything about our sleds and equipment had been built along the lines laid down by the Indians, and yet what a difference. Our great dogs were sleek and strong and their coats rippled like martin fur over their iron muscles. Our sleds were in perfect condition, varnished against the weather and without one broken brace. We ourselves were warmly and strongly clad and we shouted for the pure joy of life as we flew along the trail. And yet the Indians were products of this wilderness and had taught the white man how to live. As I thought, I remembered the Indian graveyard behind the woods, and the number of fresh graves that I had seen there.

Tuberculosis was their curse when I first visited them, and I still remembered the hopelessness of their struggle. I had called on the Chief of the tribe for aid in finding some goat meat that one of his dogs had stolen from me. The day was bitter cold and as I opened the door of his cabin the thick fetid steam from the interior dimmed the air. The heat was terrific and yet he joined me in the open with a single cotton shirt covering his chest and his legs showing bare through the rents in his trousers. I did not wonder that his body was racked with coughs as I followed him. He was dead when I returned to the village. Again when I was camped by their village a man came to me with a sick child. I have never seen a silent person show more sorrow. The child was in the last stages of consumption, so I gave it bread and maple syrup to make it happy. As the Indian left he said, "White man say Indian sit down long time in cabin get sick—maybe sit down in tent get strong?" I answered in the affirmative and told him that hot cabins were unhealthy, but later when I visited his tent I found it pitched on the *mud* at the edge of a *marsh!* If the missionaries who go among the Indians would talk hygiene in place of religion they could do a great work.

Leaving the Indian village we crossed a second narrow strip of woodland and then the great open flats of the Matanuska lay before us. In the distance we could see Brown's road-house, our shelter for the night, and the dogs raced madly across the level ice and brought us up with a flourish before the door.

The place seemed like home to me. Some years before I had camped close to the spot where the roadhouse now stands. At that time the only white inhabitant of Old Knik was a man called "Scotty" Watson. It was he who had built the road-house, and I had put in my leisure hours helping him. In return for my services he taught me to play "Seven up," and to make catsup from the mushrooms that grew on the marshes.

While we were eating supper a man arrived from Knik who told us that LaVoy and Aten had returned from their trip up the Susitna and were waiting for us at Knik, which was eighteen miles away across the arm. "Red-Jacket," second chief of the Susitna, paid us an official call. I had met him some years before on the Susitna and he told me the gossip of the Indian camps. Talkeetna Nicolae was well and "was looking for a new wife!"

CHAPTER XVII

# The End of the Susitna Trail

~

***The mouth of the Matanuska—Scarcity of dog-salmon—Improvidence of Indians—Knik—We rejoin Aten and LaVoy—Good travelling—We reach Susitna—We leave Griffith and Mitchell—Preparations for the big trip.***

Early to bed and early to rise is a maxim of the trail. As the dogs are fed only once a day, and then at night, it does not do to travel late. Going to sleep early in civilisation may be difficult, but after twenty miles of soft snow travel you need no urging from the Sandman. In fact this sleep-dispensing individual is a tyrant in the northland, and brooks no opposition; when you feel the first touch of his magic wand you fly to your blankets lest sleep overtake you on the way. You notice, also, a difference in the amount of sleep that you need, and you will be surprised to find after the first few days of physical exhaustion are over, that you require less after a hard day on the trail than you do after a strenuous day in your office.

When we left Old Knik it was the beginning of our fourteenth day on the trail, and I was just beginning to feel those first joyous hints of the approach of good physical condition. The really distressing stiffness and soreness resulting from the first pitiless days in the soft snow was just beginning to wear away. Soft muscles were beginning to harden, useless tissue was burning away, raw places on tender feet were being covered with a protecting callous, and sore and swollen hands were beginning to toughen. I knew that many days would pass before I was "fit" according to wilderness standards, but the worst part of this necessary metamorphosis was past. The old trail-hunger, too, had gripped us—that ravenous desire for food that sweeps over one when nature calls aloud for fuel with which to build up the tissues which are being burned up in days of toil. This is the hunger of a famished animal, when table manners are but a dim memory, and table conversation a waste of valuable time.

We swung out over the Matanuska flats in the grey dawn. In places the hard beaten trail was the only snow left, and we could run on the frozen marsh alongside, while a slight pressure of the left hand on the gee-pole kept the sleds on the trail. Men and dogs were in fine fettle and the miles flew by. While we were crossing a salt water "slew" on the rotten ice, we heard the sound of a floe splitting, and turned in time to see Professor Parker struggling in the ice-cold water. During really cold weather this would have been a serious accident, and we would have rushed him to the nearest timber and thawed him out over a spruce fire. As it was he scrambled out before his clothes were wet through, and his warm wool clothing held the heat of his body. On the edge of the marsh we passed two cabins, and a man told us between the howls of a pack of Indian dogs, that we could purchase dog-salmon at a cabin a half-mile from the trail.

Mitchell and I accordingly left the sleds, for there was a dog-food famine throughout the Susitna country, and there had been a corresponding rise in the price of this necessary commodity. Under the circumstances the grumbling of the dog-men was excusable, for in a country where every river is a salmon stream the failure of the Indians to catch enough fish for trade was due to laziness alone. Had any of the Indians who lived along the trail laboured with even the slightest degree of energy, they could have made enough money to supply them with every luxury for the coming year. As it was they were living in want and poverty. The needs of these natives go deeper than a lack of religion or medicine, for I have seen them eating refuse from the beach, when only three days of bidarka paddling would have taken them to mountain ranges teeming with white sheep.

The sight of so many cabins scattered along the Knik shore was a surprise to me, as on my last visit the flats were the uninhabited edge of a great wilderness. In fact the only time that I have heard timber wolves in any numbers was on these same flats six years before. I was camped at the time close to the junction of the Knik and Matanuska rivers and during the evening I heard wolves howling all about me. A tale is told of a prospector who made a trip cross-country from the Matanuska to the Talkeetna. As he was travelling "light" he swung up into the

Talkeetna hills and drifted along above the timber. When he had reached the uplands, so the story runs, a pack of timber wolves joined him. While they did not attempt to harm him they dogged his footsteps day by day. At night he would make his "tea-fire" in an isolated grove of spruce, retiring to the protection of the branches before sleep overcame him. For several days he was followed by his unwelcome escort until at the head of Big Willow Creek they crossed the trail of more promising game and left him.

Another story is told of a dog-driver who was freighting in the Matanuska Valley. He had dropped behind his dog team to roll a cigarette and the team had jogged ahead until about one hundred yards separated them. Suddenly, a pack of wolves broke out of the brush that bordered the trail, and before the man could reach them they had killed, cut out of the traces, and carried off his lead-dog.

While I will not vouch for the truth of these stories, I know that cases somewhat similar have happened in this region. An intimate friend of mine was freighting with dogs on the Skwentna River. On several occasions he was followed by wolves. Usually he was warned of their proximity by the terror of his dogs, for the wolves never showed themselves, but in places where the brush was thick they would approach so close that he could hear them forcing their way through the undergrowth. While he felt uncomfortable at times he was convinced that the wolves were after his dogs and meant him no harm, although the question of what they would do in a time of famine interested him greatly.

Where the Matanuska flats "peter out" you follow the beach under the bluff shores of Knik Arm. At this point the warm winds had turned the trail to ice and we enjoyed excellent travelling. At times even we could ride the sleds and talk or smoke our pipes. The dogs on these occasions seemed to glory in our added weight and would respond to Griffith's cheery commands by curling their tails tighter and pulling with added enthusiasm.

From the tops of our sleds we could look across the ice-packed neck of Knik Arm to the glistening peaks of the Chugach range, and across the foothills we could recognise the rugged country through which we had laboured two days previously.

In this way—now riding where the trail was good, then running at a steady dog-trot across the bad stretches—we came to Knik. The "town" is a tiny settlement of white men and Indian cabins. George Palmer runs the only store, and there the traveller can purchase all the necessities for a wilderness trip. The settlement's excuse for existence is in its location at the entrance to the Matanuska Valley where the Susitna trail crosses.

As we approached the town we were greeted by the howls of countless dogs, and after passing scattered cabins we came to rest among a crowd of men who were gathered outside of the combination store, hotel, and restaurant.

In the tangled mass of dogs and humanity we found Aten, LaVoy, and Vause. It was a joyful reunion, and after answering and asking countless questions we sat down to a hurried luncheon.

Aten and LaVoy each had a team of six dogs. I had known many of them during the previous summer, and we greeted each other affectionately as befitted old friends. They were in magnificent condition, hardened by their work on the trail and full of fire after their short rest.

Aten and LaVoy had accomplished a lot, for under the most difficult conditions they had advanced the bulk of our outfit to a point several miles beyond the mouth of the Tokositna River on the Chulitna. In general they had encountered execrable travelling conditions, but fate at last relented and on the Chulitna River they found miles of glare-ice where they loaded everything onto the sleds and rode behind the leaping dogs. Leaving their outfit on a *supposedly safe* cache they had returned with empty sleds to Susitna Station and thence to Knik.

The easy return journey had hardened our dogs without taxing either their strength or vitality. They were of the small or native variety known as huskies and malamutes. For heavy freighting, such as Bob Griffith was engaged in, the heavy dogs were superior to the small type, but in every other respect the small dogs are more satisfactory. They are faster, quicker on their feet, and will work on less food than the big half-breed dogs. Nature works along certain distinctly drawn lines. In her wisdom she has cast dogs in a certain mould, and when man attempts to improve on it the result is a dog who lacks strength and "snap."

After these northern dogs have had a few days rest they literally radiate strength and vitality. Ours were so obstreperous that we had our hands full when we started to hitch them up. We had to begin operations by anchoring our sled with a bight of rope to the pillars of the store verandah, for as soon as each dog was hitched in place he would begin to howl and pull with all his might on the tug-line.

Vause's, Griffith's, Mitchell's, and our two teams were all bound for Susitna

Station, and they made an imposing picture when they were ready for the trail. Vause being the U.S. mail carrier was given the head of the procession, and as he swept down the trail our dogs howled and threw themselves with savage envy against the traces. When our turn came Professor Parker got into Aten's sled and I into LaVoy's and the straining ropes were loosened. We were off like the wind, swinging around corners on one runner, bouncing over bumps, and sweeping over the straight stretches in a smother of snow. All we could do was to hold on and pray that we wouldn't hit a tree. The man who handles the team holds on to the handle-bars with one foot on the brake and the other on a narrow platform at the rear of the sled. He swings the sled with the brake and by heaving on the handle-bars with all his strength.

I was just beginning to congratulate myself on having escaped without a broken head when the trail plunged down-hill into a wood. The trees flew past in a blurred line and suddenly we saw our Waterloo awaiting us! The dogs were wild with excitement and beyond control, their powerful bodies level with the snow as they dashed along, and beyond was a six-foot drop-off where the trail descended to a lake and turned at a right angle. When the sled bounded into space the dogs turned instantly on the trail and over we went—men, dogs, and sled in a jumbled mass! When we finally got the snow out of our eyes and ears the other dog teams had dwindled to small specks, and above the distant jingle of dog-bells we could hear roars of laughter.

The dogs, chastened by the experience, settled down to their steady trot and we could begin to take in the beauty of the winter landscape. The country between Knik and Susitna Station is flat and our trail took us across the smooth surface of many lakes. The ragged spruce, common to all the muskeg country of the north, added to the desolate aspect of the scene. The trail for some unknown climatic reason was hard and smooth. Hour after hour we slid along, the five teams winding in a sinuous line, while jokes and laughter passed back and forth above the jingle of dog-bells. The miles of bad trail that we had passed were forgotten, for we were at last enjoying winter travel at its best.

As the afternoon wore to its close we struck into a frozen watercourse hemmed in by solid lines of black spruce. It was the Little Susitna River, and the word was passed down the line that there was a road-house close at hand. Vause, Griffith, and Mitchell stopped, as Susitna Station was still twelve miles away, but we kept on as our dogs were fresh and we had no loads. As night came on the cold increased and the jingle of our bells and the grating of the runners were the only sounds in all that great expanse. The sun went down in a deep red sky and still the dogs trotted on. Soon the spruces loomed weirdly against the night sky and the steam of the dog's breath showed light against the blue snow. LaVoy sat behind me on the handle-bars while the cold wind sang past. At times like this, when you have the leisure to think, the spell of the wilderness takes a powerful hold on you.

The spruce-fringed horizons stimulate the imagination, and the monotonous song of the wind and bells has a lulling hypnotic effect on you. You feel as if you had always travelled as you are doing then and always will; that civilisation is only a jumbled dream, and the only things that count are adventures, hard muscles, and food for man and dog.

But suddenly the dogs struck up a faster gait until their trot had changed to run; faster and faster they went, while the sled rolled drunkenly over the broadening trail. Then a light appeared and flashed behind; others came into view and the dogs making a final spurt brought us up before the houses of Susitna Station.

Even in the darkness the houses had a familiar look, and as the doors about us opened we saw the faces of many old friends. Mindful, however, of the hard days to come we saved the news of the trail for the morrow, and after seeing that our dogs were comfortable, we turned in for a much-needed sleep.

We had covered fifty-five miles during the day but the day had been an easier one than any of the days that we had spent on the trail. The brutal, soul-trying days are those when you labour from dawn to twilight and fall asleep with a paltry ten miles to show for your toil.

Our last days in Susitna Station were filled with a thousand interesting details of our coming trip. Odds and ends of every description had to be attended to; ice creepers for river running, raw-hide for mending snowshoes, and letters written, as it was the end of civilisation.

We were joined by Vause, Griffith, and Mitchell on the following day. Vause was planning a trip towards the Talkeetna to recover the body of a man who had drowned in the Susitna the year before. Griffith and Mitchell were resting for a day before beginning their long hard pull to the Iditerod. Among many old friends we met a prospector who gave us the last chapter in the lives of the horses that we had lost at Tyonik in 1906. He had been prospecting the rivers that entered Cook Inlet west of Tyonik. It was in the early part of the winter, and the streams had just been covered with a firm sheet of ice. As he was passing a small Island he was surprised to see a dead animal lying in the snow. On reaching the island he found the carcasses of the other horses and the story of their death was written clear. They had reached the marshy island while searching for fodder and when the ice began to form they were unable to escape. Broken and re-frozen scars in the ice showed where they had attempted to force their way landward, but they had quickly given up the attempt and had died before the ice would bear their weight.

Now Susitna Station is the nearest settlement to the Alaskan Range on the Susitna side. It also forms the only port of entry and departure for the men who have penetrated the great wilderness between the Susitna River and the Tanana. If we could find any knowledge of a pass close to Mount McKinley it would be at Susitna Station. We therefore asked all the prospectors in the town concerning our chances, and Vause, our trail-mate, was the only man who could give us any information. His knowledge, however, was indefinite, and all he knew was that there

Our outfit leaving Susitna Station. All the inhabitants showed the greatest interest in our journey and did everything in their power to aid us.

was a river flowing north below the Chulitna forks, and that he had heard of a prospector who had crossed the range. Vause gave me a rough map of the country as he remembered it which showed the approximate location of the stream that the prospector had described, but as I have never been on the headwaters of the Chulitna I am to this day uncertain as to whether or not the stream we eventually followed was the one indicated. We learned in addition that there was a party of three prospectors freighting towards Talkeetna—two brothers by the name of Wells and their partner Coffee. Coffee and the Wells brothers, we were told, knew more about the Chulitna country than any other men, and LaVoy who had met Coffee told me that it was he who had crossed the range. While it would have added to our peace of mind to have known just where we were going, the uncertainty of our plans made our task the more alluring.

Every one at Susitna Station showed the greatest interest in our venture. We were invited to a "civilised dinner" by McNalley, the A. C. Co., representative—the last we were to enjoy until we reached the Yukon.

## CHAPTER XVIII

# The Beginning of the Wilderness Trail

***We leave Susitna—Rabbits—Arrival at Kroto—"In an Indian Lodge"—We arrive at Talkeetna—We ascend the Chulitna—We meet Stephan and Talkeetna Nicolae—We trade successfully for moose-meat—View of Mount McKinley—We pass the Tokositna River—We arrive at our cache—Wolverines.***

On the 19th of February we were ready for the trail. We drove our dogs into line above the high bluff beneath which we had battled with the churning eddies in our motor-boat days. As we were saying our last farewell an old friend presented us with four quart bottles of rum. Now on all of our previous trips we had placed a ban on alcoholic drinks, and for an instant I thought that it would be wiser to return the gift, but suddenly the memory of Professor Parker's pemmican pudding and the commandeered pint of brandy in 1910 crossed my mind and I thankfully placed the present in a safe place. I am glad now that we took it, for during the months of snow travel that we experienced this rum was the only luxury that we possessed, and used in very small quantities it proved a welcome addition to our evening meal. We used it in our tea, at night only. The first bottle was rationed at the rate of two tablespoonfuls per man per day, the second bottle went at a single tablespoonful a day, the third was dispensed in two teaspoonful lots; while the fourth and last we finished at the base of Mount McKinley by a daily allowance of one teaspoonful a day! While alcohol in any quantity is harmful to men who are leading an active life, we found that rum used in small quantities after a long hard day in the snow acted as an aid to our digestion and circulation.

As we had always left Susitna Station by boat it was a new sensation to slide down onto the frozen surface of the great river and jog away on snowshoes.

In our journey up the Chulitna and Susitna we were always passing places that we remembered from our previous trips—now a smooth snow-covered point where a bad rapid had bothered us, or a spruce-covered island where we had camped in the old days.

We had at last said the final farewell to civilisation, and were dependent on our own resources. The well-travelled trail, with its road-houses was a thing of the past, and we were following a trail that led to an Indian settlement called Kroto, about fifteen miles away. We had reduced our teams to five dogs, respectively, as we had no way of procuring dog food, if we should run short, until we reached a big-game country.

Where an Alaskan town ends the wilderness begins. A short way from Susitna Station the winter silence shut down on us; no sounds but the straining of the dog harness and the rhythmic clicking of our snowshoes broke the absolute silence. Even our dog-bells had been cast aside, for while their jingling was pleasant to hear they were an added weight and might alarm big game. Erratic snowshoe trails grew fewer, and dotted lines in the smooth sweeps of snow told where rabbits had dared the unprotecting opens in frantic leaps.

Had it been a better rabbit year we could have counted on them for dog food and carried less on our sleds. But the Alaskan rabbits die off about every seven years. The character of this epidemic is not known for certain, although I was told by a prospector that an army doctor at Fort Gibbon had found it to be tubercular. The fact remains, however, that the rabbits are practically exterminated at regular intervals, and a man can travel for hundreds of miles without seeing a track in the snow. Were it not for this wise provision of Nature there would not be a willow bush left in Alaska inside of fifteen years. At the time of our journey the rabbits had been on the increase for only three or four years, and yet in favoured localities we saw whole thickets of willow that had been killed by the long-eared pests. When they are really numerous the amount of damage they do is beyond belief, and it is difficult even to get snow with which to make tea, without its tasting of rabbit!

The rabbit crop likewise plays an important part in the economy of the wild, for with the increase in rabbits there is a corresponding increase among the fur-bearing animals. This being particularly true of the lynx. The birds of prey also take their toll of the rabbit hordes, and we often saw the trails of rabbits that ended in a wing-brushed circle of snow with a few drops of blood to show that the cruel talons had reached their mark.

Night began to close in on us as we neared Kroto, and we debated the question as to whether we would invite ourselves into some Indian's cabin or pitch our own tent in the snow. Professor Parker was slightly pessimistic about Indian hospitality in general and Kroto hospitality in particular. But the rest of us rather welcomed the adventure, and after touching on the ethnological value of our proposed call we halted our dogs before the most pretentious cabin. Forcing our way through a yapping rabble of stunted dogs we entered the outer compartment of the cabin and were met by a stalwart Indian by the name of Shilligan. He readily agreed to our demands for a night's shelter, and after bringing our sleds into the outer compartment to protect them from the Indian dogs we entered the inner compartment or "living-room."

The ensuing night can best be described by the word *hectic!* What with prowling Indian babies and puppies our ethnological studies were rudely interfered with, and none of us had to be urged into the open on the following morning!

All day long we jogged over the great flats of smooth snow. Far away lines of black showed where the spruce forests met the river banks. Then new snow came to cover the dim trail, and late at night we camped under a high bank where a fallen spruce furnished us with boughs and fuel.

Our days on the Susitna were much alike. We travelled always over blinding snow flats that stretched away to the black regiments of spruce. Now and then a bluff relieved the monotony, or the snow clouds breaking away would give us glimpses of the icy peaks of the Talkeetna Mountains.

Two days from Susitna we ran gleefully into a fresh broken trail, and a new cache told us that we had overtaken the Wells brothers and Coffee. Following came the call of a dog-driver, and black specks that grew into two men riding empty sleds, who drew aside into the soft snow to let us pass. It was the elder Wells brother and Coffee. They were freighting to Broad Pass they said. Coffee said that he had been across a pass in the Alaskan Range; that he had just gone to take "a look-see"; the pass was short as he crossed over and back, but that "coming back was a damn sight worse than going over!" He had travelled light in the summer time. This was all we heard as our dogs were impatient for the trail and we had a long day ahead of us. As we said "so long," Wells told us that his brother was "keeping camp" a mile up the trail, and later he welcomed us with the splendid hospitality characteristic of the Alaskan prospector.

These men represented the finest type of the Alaskan frontiersmen. Freighting their supplies in the winter time, the spring "break-up" would find them in some distant range of "the interior." Here they would build their cabin, prospect and trap for a year or more, eking out their food supply the while with rifle and fish line. When their food was gone they would raft down some wilderness river, sell their catch of fur at a frontier post, and outfit for another venture. Having found good quartz prospects near the Alaskan Range they were freighting in a two years' outfit, counting optimistically on "the coming of the railroad" to make their embryonic mines valuable. This is the best type of the men who are "opening up" Alaska.

While we were eating a snack with Wells he turned to me and said: "If you tear off anything for the papers about this neck o' the woods tell 'em we need a railroad and need it bad." I promised, and the reader is the witness of my relieved conscience. We left Wells with regret, but it gave us some pleasure to know that they would have the benefit of our trail for many days.

We had little in the way of camp duffle with us; all our regular outfit was in our cache beyond the Tokositna, and we got along as best we could with a tiny mountain tent and a frying-pan or two. We "siwashed" it for two nights until we reached the main fork of the Susitna. Here the upper Susitna, the Talkeetna, and the Chulitna rivers combine to form the main Susitna. The Talkeetna sweeps northward from the unknown fastnesses of the Talkeetna Mountains, while the Chulitna rushes southward from the Alaskan Range and Mount McKinley. In 1910 when the trading-post built by the A. C. Co. was new, there was a tiny settlement at the forks, but now as we trotted into the familiar clearing the cabins stood cold and deserted.

It was at this point that we began our arduous trail-breaking towards the Alaskan Range. We were steadily creeping away from the seacoast, and already the still, intense cold was noticeable. The snow was dry and powdery under our snowshoes and steam was rising from men and dogs as we swung along. We could now see the Alaskan Range standing like a wall of ice against the northern sky; while Mount McKinley's mighty buttresses blended with the haze of distance, so that the great mountain seemed to float cloud-like above the foothills.

Early in the winter an Indian or two had used the Susitna route and left a dim trail, then Aten and LaVoy had broken a relay route through the white drifts. Since then no teams had passed that way, and as we drove our dogs up the Chulitna we had to rebreak our trail. We were encouraged in our added toil by the thought that the wilder the country was, the more interesting it would be.

It was on the Chulitna that we saw the last signs of human habitation. A cache and fresh snowshoe tracks led us to an Indian camp. Pushing through the invariable ring of snarling dogs I entered one of the tents and to my delight found myself in the presence of Talkeetna Nicolae and his two wives. We greeted each other joyfully, for we had met and traded to our mutual benefit in 1910. One of the women thanked me in the sign language for a photograph that I had taken of Talkeetna Nicolae and sent to him. Sitting among a litter of malamute puppies we exchanged the news of the trail. Stephan, Nicolae's son-in-law, had killed a moose, and would trade, I was told; so repairing to the open I began bargaining with the successful hunter. To my question of "How much ketchum moose-meat?" Stephan replied, "Ketchum two bits pound." Now twenty-five cents a pound was next door to piracy, and in addition I had once given Stephan's wife a liberal outfit of food when he had left her destitute and had forgotten to return to her. Stephan's lack of appreciation hardened my heart and I laid the matter before LaVoy who had just joined me. Money is usually a useless encumbrance on a wilderness trail, but we each had a small amount that we had forgotten to spend before leaving Susitna Station. So LaVoy gave Stephan fifty cents, and said, "Let's see if he knows how much a pound is." To our joy Stephan's mind was hazy on weights and he gave us about five pounds of meat. LaVoy then tried again with all his worldly wealth which consisted of forty-five cents, and secured in return an equally large slab of meat. It was now my turn and I tried a piece of "frenzied finance" by giving my only dollar to Stephan and asking him to return the ninety-five cents to LaVoy and give me meat for the difference. Without hesitation he handed the ninety-five cents to LaVoy and gave me about five pounds of hind quarter for my five cents. When we swung out on the trail again we left Stephan chuckling slyly over his business acumen, but we waited until a point of spruce hid the camp before giving vent to our triumphant laughter.

It is not often, however, that the white man comes off victorious in these financial skirmishes, for the Alaskan Indian can, and usually does, drive a hard bargain.

A short distance above the camp we came to the spot where in 1910 the narrowing valley walls had warned us of our approach to the Chulitna cañon. But how different the scene looked now! In place of the rushing waters of the river there lay a smooth expanse of untrodden snow; where, on our first visit the air had trembled to the sullen roar of the rapids we now jogged along through an almost oppressive silence; and where the river banks had been hidden in a tangle of vegetation we looked on rolling snow-drifts and naked rocks.

As we rounded the rock bluff, where on the day long past we had tuned up the *Explorer* for her fight with the rapids, gusts of icy wind began to buffet us. The trail soon disappeared and with heads down we felt our way slowly along. Soon I was forced to use our tent-pole to find the firm foundation, and our progress became so slow that night overtook us between the cañon walls, and we made camp.

The wind subsided during the night and we made faster time the following morning. The cañon had acted as a funnel for the wind and snow, and as soon as the walls began to draw back we began to strike little patches of ice. The "good going" encouraged the dogs and we began to reel off the miles. Soon the cañon bluffs fell behind and towering high into the winter sky stood Mount McKinley. The fact that all the foothills were buried in snow gave the mountain an entirely

THE UPPER CAÑON OF THE CHULITNA RIVER

*We travelled on frozen rivers. In the summer time this cañon is filled by a rushing torrent of glacier water*

different aspect from the views that we had obtained in the summer time; the principal difference being that the snow caused the great ridges that run towards the mountain to blend with the southern buttresses; and in consequence we looked with amused surprise on what appeared to be several climbable routes from the southern approach. Our intimate knowledge of every detail of the mountain's southern formation, alone enabled us to unravel the optical illusion.

The travelling improved as we trotted along, and soon the sight of the frozen entrance of the Tokositna awoke memories of the old days. It seemed that if we were to turn aside and ascend the river we would find our old camp of 1910 standing in the shade of the cottonwoods and hear the voices of our old companions, and the familiar hum of the mosquito horde. As it was we were moving through a land of as savage grandeur and frozen desolation as this world can boast. Our roadway was the mile-wide icy bed of the Chulitna River. It ran flat as a billiard table to the very foot of the Alaskan Range; there the snow smothered foothills began to roll up, two, four, six, eight, and ten thousand feet into the sky, and then behind an interval of blue haze the towering, gleaming form of Mount McKinley rolled up nineteen thousand feet above us.

The Tokosha Mountains, Foraker and Hunter, loomed gigantic to the westward—each one by itself a king but for the overwhelming grandeur of old Bulshaia.

Under the spell of all this beauty we were running with our heads turned towards the range, when suddenly an ominous crack came from under the first sled, and in an instant Aten and the dogs were wallowing ankle deep in the icy water. It was an "over floe" common on all the northern rivers. After a river has frozen solid it often happens that the water will force its way through some weak or open place in the ice. This upper layer of water then freezes, but in our case the new ice was not yet strong enough to bear our weight. It was not very far to the point where Aten and LaVoy had cached our main outfit and we quickly sized up the situation. The cold was not severe enough to render a wetting dangerous, and the only other alternative was to retrace our steps and break a new trail through the soft snow on the edge of the timber. We all decided in favour of the wet route, and for the better part of a mile we dragged our sleds through five inches of water.

In loading a sled a long canvas tarp is first placed on the sled body. The freight is then placed on the tarp whose edges are folded over the load which is then lashed down with much grunting and heaving. These canvas tarpaulins protected our freight from the water, and when we finally reached the grove of spruce that sheltered our cache our dunnage was none the worse for its wet journey.

Now this cache had been our Mecca since the day we had left Knik. For it contained all the pemmican, fuel, and equipment that we were to use in our struggle with the big mountain; but in addition it stood for comfort, warmth, ease, food, and everything that makes life worth while in a snow-bound wilderness. There rested our big tent, stove, axes, bacon, beans, flour, tea, sugar, guns, ammunition, and all the little odds and ends that in civilisation we call necessities but which in the wilderness become luxuries. To protect this treasure trove from wild animals (a cache is sacred to northern men—red or white) Aten and LaVoy had placed it on a platform of logs suspended from a number of trees.

As an added precaution one usually sheathes the trees that hold up the cache with two or more feet of tin from kerosene cans, as it offers no foot- or claw-hold for that Archfiend, the wolverine. This animal boasts the distinction of being the most hated and despised beast on the North American Continent. Woodsmen have a yard long list of descriptive epithets for this animal and of these only two—"Glutton," and "Indian Devil"—would pass the censorship of even the most reckless publisher! For its size it is perhaps as powerfully built an animal as nature has produced. Its iron jaws will splinter the strongest box and its razor-edged claws will carry it up the tallest tree. Its mental attributes consist of a ravenous appetite, a hatred of everything in general and mankind in particular, and a perverted passion for wholesale and wanton destruction.

With the thought of wolverines in a far corner of my brain I had asked Aten and LaVoy when we first met if they had taken the precaution of "tinning our cache." They answered that they had not in view of the fact that the smell of man would linger about and protect the cache until our return. Now the "smell of man" idea will work with *any* animal but a wolverine, and when, as we were approaching our cache, we saw wolverine tracks in the snow we were all decidedly uneasy. On reaching it our worst fears were realised, for the snow was padded down with the track of these animals and the canvas covers of several pemmican packages lay in the snow. Closer scrutiny showed that the trees that formed the posts of our cache were scarred with the claw marks of the Indian Devils. We lost no time in making a thorough investigation, and after lifting off the canvas tarpaulin that covered our provisions we found that a goodly amount of our dog-salmon and bacon had gone.

We were cheered by the thought that the damage might have been greater—but there was more to come! I have already spoken of the wolverine's passion for vindictive and wanton destruction and in a moment we made a discovery that will illustrate why this animal is hated above all other animals.

On starting on our long journey LaVoy had invested in a beautiful and expensive Graflex camera. To protect it on the trail, he had purchased an expensive leather box of the best workmanship. Feeling that it would be perfectly safe in the cache he decided to leave it during his return trip to Susitna. The heavy leather cover being weather proof he hit on a novel plan to protect it from damage. Cutting down a slender cottonwood about thirty feet in length he rove a rope in its end. After lifting the pole into an upright position alongside of the cache he lashed it firmly in place, then tying his camera to the end of the rope he hoisted it to the very top of the pole. Now any one would think that a camera inside of a heavy leather case swinging at the very tiptop of a thirty foot pole would be about as safe as man could make it. A wolverine, however, had climbed the pole, cut off the corners of the shoe-leather case as cleanly as a razor would have done, and then gnawed his way into the camera case! If LaVoy could have corralled the entire wolverine clan the Chulitna Valley would have run with blood! For months afterward when we wanted to rouse his "fighting blood" all we had to do was to mention the word *wolverine!*

## CHAPTER XIX

# Beginning of the Long Relay

~

***Reorganisation at Wolverine Camp—Method of relaying—Trail-breaking—Indications of a pass—The first big glacier—We pass the Chulitna gorge—We find the Chulitna gorge—Advance up the cañon—Dog food—A moose hunt—We find a break in the range—We discover the "unnamed river."***

Despite the visitations of the devilish wolverines our arrival at the cache was a great event in our lives. Outside of the material comfort gained it meant that we were at last "under way" and on a working basis. Heretofore we had been travelling straight away, as we were able to pull all our belongings on the sleds at one time. But from Wolverine Camp onward we had 2500 pounds of duffle to wrestle with which meant that we would have to relay. Furthermore we had no longer even an excuse for a trail, which necessitated the construction or "breaking" of every foot of the path over which we pulled our freight.

No one can realise, without having travelled through a trackless wild, the importance of even the slightest marks to show you the way. On several occasions we lost a full working day by not knowing the lay of the land. The first experience of this kind occurred while breaking our first trail from Wolverine Camp. The main channel of the Chulitna had not frozen in places, and as I was confident that I would soon find a frozen area large enough to allow us to cross with our teams I kept on the edge of the valley.

Now one of the most reliable facts about a river is its unreliability. As soon as I had gotten well within its power the river began to squeeze me towards the bluffs. Finally at the base of an almost perpendicular wall I was forced to stop. One look at the snow cliff sent me on a run to camp for a shovel and then LaVoy and I went to work. At the end of two hours backbreaking work we had shovelled a deep trail around the steep point, and just when we were congratulating ourselves on a clear road we saw a second and steeper bluff come into view ahead, with the perverse river rushing around its base. There was only one thing to do—go back and begin over again. Thereafter we held to the centre of the valley, and just as soon as an unfrozen stream began to lead toward either side we would cross it at all costs and hold to our straight course. By the sweat of our brows we bought experience, which, luckily, is the only way, for in the wilderness, of all things under the sun, human labour is the cheapest!

We were now following the great valley of the Chulitna. It was several miles broad in places and as level as a floor. When unfrozen streams did not complicate our advance our trail would lead as straight as a ruled line for miles. Aten and LaVoy gave all their time to moving our freight, and I shouldered the duties of surveying and breaking our trails. In the broad expanses of the Chulitna one could save an immense amount of time and worry for the dog drivers by breaking an absolutely straight trail, and in this seemingly simple labour one will find that there is lots to learn. A straight trail can be gained only by constant mental concentration. If you let your eyes or mind drift, even for a minute, from the point of spruce trees miles away that you have chosen as a sighting mark, your trail will not run true. It is as if the snowshoes were an electric needle that recorded on the white snow-fields every slight change of the mind. If your mind wanders it will be written in the snow for all to read, and when on your way home you can see your trails stretching away across the snow like a tautened wire you can nod your head in approval at a job well done. There was a great satisfaction in these long cold days on the snow-fields. First came the long tramps straight away when you concentrated your whole mind on the trail and swung your whole weight onto each snowshoe to pack the soft yielding snow. Then came the easier return when your feet flew of themselves treading down automatically the humps left between the snowshoe tracks. Now you could look about you and see the country or follow the flight of great flocks of ptarmigan that rose from the willows as you advanced.

The Chulitna led us always parallel to the Alaskan Range, and on clear days we looked eagerly to the eastward, for it was there that we were going to try to find a way through the ice-bound mountains.

In the abstract, hunting for a pass through an uncharted mountain range might be likened to finding a needle in a haystack, but in reality the finding of a *break* in the range gave us little worry. Any break would be glacier filled and the ice-fields would of necessity throw off large quantities of water which would form rivers. The clew to a pass therefore would be any river of sufficient size to indicate large snow-fields. The finding of a break, however, was in no way a guarantee that we could make a crossing, and it was in the uncertainty of the *kind* of break that we would find that we found cause for worry.

The first indication of a pass east of Mount McKinley is a huge glacier that lies east of the "big glacier" which we followed to Mount McKinley in 1910. It is the largest glacier of the Mount McKinley region; heading under the cliffs of the north-eastern ridges of the big mountain it flows in an easterly direction to the valley of the Chulitna.

Had we been successful in our attempt in 1910 to climb the "great serac" and cross the "12,000-foot col," we would have dropped down onto the upper ice-fields of this great glacier close under the Southern North-East Ridge.

When Doctor Cook made the trip around Mount McKinley in 1903 he rafted down the Chulitna and saw the huge ice river. He gave it the name of "Fidele Glacier," but the name was not adopted by the United States Government. As this body of ice and snow discharges more water into the Chulitna than any other single natural feature an appropriate name for it would be the Chulitna Glacier.

At the time that we were approaching this great river of ice we were hugging the timber on the left-hand or Alaskan Range side of the Chulitna. It was at least a mile to the opposite side of the valley and I took it for granted that the Chulitna ran past close to the end of the ice.

We were having good travelling at the time, and finally succeeded in moving all our duffle up and building a new camp within about five miles of the glacier.

Then came a clear day and LaVoy and I pushed ahead on a combination re-connaissance and trail-breaking trip.

As we approached the glacier we began to search for the opening in the bluffs where the Chulitna came through. The closer we got the more surprised we were, for as far as we could see there was no place where a river could come through the walls. Pushing on ahead I at last reached the eastern wall of the glacier and the truth of the matter lay before me—there was no room for a river as large as the Chulitna between the bluffs; we had passed the cañon where it entered the valley!

At times like this a sense of humour is invaluable and after a lunch around a fire of dry spruce we were able to laugh over our wasted efforts. Looking back across the valley we could see about five miles away, and opposite our camp the merest suggestion of a wooded point that blended cunningly with the higher bluffs behind. "That's her," said LaVoy, "she comes sneaking out behind that point!" And we both drew a breath of relief when we realised that we had only moved up 250 pounds of freight. As we had come so far we decided to take a look-see and we accordingly climbed a part of the terminal moraine. We could not see very much, as the swell of the ice hid the distant horizon, but from the curve in the mountain walls we could tell that the glacier curved towards Mount McKinley. I would have given much to explore its great ice-fields, but it was too big a job to undertake as a side-trip, and the chances of being caught in a huge amphitheatre as we had been in 1910 decided us in pushing farther eastward.

Dame Fortune is always a good old soul at heart and that night she sent a cold frost down from the mountain gorges. It turned the surface of the snow-fields into a hard crust over which we could pull moderately loaded sleds. With light hearts we began freighting our supplies across the valley. As we neared the low timber-screened point that had caused my blunder I saw a low place that promised a route across the neck to the Chulitna. If we could find a good trail across, it would save us about a mile of travel around the point, so Aten and LaVoy waited with their sleds until I could investigate.

It was one of those wonderful winter days when the snow glitters like cut glass and distant snow-covered mountains stand clear-cut against the deep blue sky.

In all that great land there was not a sound to be heard except the creaking of my snowshoes on the dry snow. The stream I was following was spring fed. It ran deep and crystal clear and its bed was green with a kind of aquatic grass. Suddenly I heard a slight noise, and turning quickly I saw a large otter ascend the bank and stretch himself full length in the snow. He was only forty feet away, but he watched me quietly until I began to move forward, when he slipped with scarcely a ripple into the clear stream.

After I had gone a little way, I happened to look back and saw him watching me from the shelter of the bank, craning his long neck from side to side as a sea-lion does and making a sniffing noise.

After I had looked the country over, I went back and got LaVoy, with his Graflex camera, in the hope of securing a picture of the otter. When we reached the stream the otter was not in sight, so we sat down to wait. Before long he appeared swimming up-stream, and then he crawled up the bank and began to roll over and over in the dry snow. Finally he saw us and slipped back into the water. LaVoy did not make an exposure as he hoped for a closer view and I did not shoot the otter, although I had my .30–.40 trained on his shiny body, as I was waiting for the click of LaVoy's camera. He owed his life to our being "camera fiends."

On the edge of this clearing I found a great spruce whose trunk was covered with the claw and tooth marks of the Alaskan brown bear. It was evidently a salmon-fishing spot for the bears, as the tree was still covered with bear hair and dry mud where the great brutes had rubbed themselves after coming out of the river.

The change from open to cañon travel was a relief in some ways, for the scenery was more impressive, although the trail-breaking was more arduous. Aten and LaVoy were the official dog-men. Dogs are far more susceptible than horses to the influence of their drivers, and for this reason it is imperative that each team should be handled by one man. A team driven by different men, even if they are all expert drivers, soon becomes demoralised.

We carried with us two types of snowshoes: the long, graceful, upturned shoes made by the Indians, and the short, strong, "bear-paw" variety made in New Hampshire. The latter we used in rough, steep, climbing, such as we found on the Mount McKinley glaciers, while the long, upturned shoes were used for "breaking-trail" in soft snow.

When Aten or LaVoy accompanied me on my trail-breaking trips I would go well ahead and give the snow a preliminary pounding with my snowshoes. Aten or LaVoy would follow me on snowshoes, with the dog team. We would advance in this order about five miles, when, after dropping our load, we would ride back on the sled, as our weight on the runners improved the trail. These rides to camp were splendid sport.

As we turned the eager dogs' heads towards camp they were yapping with excitement, and the instant the sleds were straightened out in the trail they were off like a shot and we had to jump on quickly or stay behind. After a time they would settle down to their rapid, trail-eating trot, but later when camp came into view they were off again and we would dash up to our tent in grand style. It seemed to be a regular game with the dogs. They would bark and frisk about when their harness was taken off as if to say: "Well! we certainly 'went some' that time!"

The following day, if wind or snow had not damaged our trail we could haul about five hundred pounds to the team over it. We would make two trips in a day, or about twenty miles in all, until our equipment was five miles ahead of our camp. Our camp and personal duffle made a light load for the two teams, and on the following day we would advance ten miles, or five miles beyond our cache, breaking the last half of the trail as we advanced.

If we were uncertain as to our route, both teams would work on the "back-trail," and I would go ahead on a long reconnaissance and trail-breaking trip. It was in this way that we worked our way steadily through the silent wilderness. Everything was done with system; every man knew what his duties were without being told; and, of course, in a life of this kind every one must strive to do even more than his share.

Especially in "making camp" after a long, hard day, does willingness and a knowledge of what to do prove of benefit. When we decided to camp there were two things that we looked for: a *straight*, dead spruce, close to the river bank, and a water hole in the ice. When these two important factors were found, we tramped down a camp-site, flat and hard, with our snowshoes, and went to work. The dogs were fed once a day, at nightfall.

As a rule, smoked salmon—dry feed, as it is called—is the favourite food when fed with tallow. But salmon is too bulky a food for a long wilderness trip.

We were forced to feed corn-meal and "dog-rice," seasoned with salmon and tallow, for the meal and rice swell in cooking and go farther. We cooked it in a large iron pan, and after the mess had cooked we set it in the snow to cool and weighted the cover down to keep the hungry dogs from stealing it. One of our dogs claimed the duty of watching the pan, and any other dog that approached did so at his peril.

The dogs were splendid animals—hard working, faithful, affectionate, and lovable; but among themselves they were savage brutes. Each team was held together by the frail bond of daily companionship and when a fight started each team would back its favourite to the death. We lost some of our most valuable dogs in these savage fights, which were of frequent occurrence.

A CAMP ON THE UPPER CHULITNA SHOWING HOW WE BROKE A YARD AROUND OUR TENT AND TRAILS TO FACILITATE HANDLING OF SLEDS

The upper Chulitna was a beautiful river. Now and then the spruce-crowned walls would draw apart, forming snow-filled amphitheatres, and it was in one of these deep basins that we found our first signs of big game.

It is impossible to convey in words the avalanche of emotions that sweep over a man in the wilderness when he finds himself on the fresh trail of a big game animal. When a man has lived the hard life of the trail for a month or two he not only thinks of and longs for fresh meat during the day, but he dreams of it at night as well. All the camp-fire talk revolves around this one word—*meat!* Now, when you add to this craving the overwhelming excitement of the chase, it is small wonder that your heart beats audibly between your teeth, and that your hands tremble as you pull your rifle from its case.

The track that we saw was made by a fairly large bull moose. Under ordinary conditions I would have waited for a fresh snow or a windy day to stalk him, as there was a thin, brittle crust on the snow. But we were travelling rapidly, and I had to take the chance or leave it. The bull had wandered across the flat, feeding on willow buds, and had then followed a small stream below the towering bluffs that rimmed the valley. In one place he had ventured on to thin ice *and then backed slowly off* on discovering his danger! Then his trail turned and ascended the bluffs.

Hunting the Alaskan moose was an old story to me, and I was conversant with the wonderful climbing ability of the animal, yet this time I could scarcely believe my own eyes, so steep and impassable were the places this moose had climbed. I had to throw my snowshoes ahead of me and dig steps with the butt of my rifle until I reached them. Finally I left the trail where a growth of alders clung to the hillside and drawing myself up, hand over hand, I reached the top after an hour's hard work. As I lashed my snowshoes on I looked over as beautiful a stretch of moose country as I have ever seen.

Rolling, spruce-dotted hills swept away to the very foot of the Alaskan Range, which rose in snowy steps to a line of ice-capped peaks. To the eastward I was overjoyed to see a break in the range that promised a possible route through the mountains. After carefully locating its position in my mind I found the moose trail and began the hunt. But no matter how carefully I advanced the crust broke under my snowshoes. Knowing that I had no chance under these conditions I left the trail, and kept a sharp watch ahead. After some time had passed a murmur swept through the spruce groves and a slight breeze began to shake the ice from the trees. Slowly the rattle of falling ice increased and, overjoyed at what seemed an intervention of providence, I swung back to the bull's trail. Keeping among the spruce trees I again advanced and after going about three hundred yards I came upon the bull's fresh bed. How the beast heard me I will never understand; but hear me he did, for after rising to his feet he had moved slowly away, keeping behind every piece of cover until he had crossed a low ridge, and then he had struck into a slashing run that had sent the brittle crust flying.

Day after day we pushed up the Chulitna River. We never knew monotony, for men who have reached the perfect physical condition that we had attained would find pleasure and enjoyment in anything. The bends of the cañon too beckoned us on, and stimulated our imagination. We always wanted to see what was around the next bend or beyond the next amphitheatre, and we were thinking always of the break in the range which I had seen while following the moose. "Perhaps the next bend will bring us to our river," we would say, and trot onward optimistically, only to find the same stretch of frozen river running between the same unbroken walls.

A few days later I succeeded in breaking a long piece of advance trail and, while Aten and LaVoy were advancing the freight, I made a second attempt to secure meat. Leaving our camp on the Chulitna, I crossed the rolling country to the north until I reached timber line on the Alaskan Range. From this point of vantage I secured a magnificent view of the eastern face of Mount McKinley. During the day I snowshoed about twenty miles through the still snow-smothered woods, and secured a magnificent view of that mountain. It was the first time that I had seen it from the east, and as I studied it through my binoculars I could trace every contour of the eastern side. The Southern and Central North-Eastern ridges joined at an altitude of about 16,000 feet and formed the main Eastern Ridge of the southern or highest summit. The Northern North-East Ridge came down directly from the northern or lower summit. Tracks of wild things dotted the snow—of ermine, wolverine, marten, hare, squirrels, and ptarmigan. Once I saw a marten watching me stealthily from a bole on a gnarled spruce. Great round balls of snow covered the evergreens like turbans and, strange to relate, I heard some bird—a finch, I think—singing as if its throat would burst. I saw no moose sign. The track of the bull that had evaded me was the only sign of big game which I saw on the southern side of the Alaskan Range.

While my moose hunt was a failure from the meat point of view, it was successful as a reconnaissance, for I secured a nearer view of the "break" in the range to the eastward, and I could now see indications of a large stream flowing from the depression, and joining the Chulitna River a few miles above our camp.

The next day Professor Parker and I pushed ahead. The wind was blowing a gale and the river ran alternately through deep cañons and circular amphitheatres. At last we saw some noble peaks of the Alaskan Range topping the timber, and finally we reached a point where the gorge split. The northern or left-hand cañon crossed the line of the valley and turned straight towards the Alaskan Range. Breathlessly we advanced until its size and importance told us that it drained a large part of the range, and that it came from glaciers that might offer us a route to the Yukon side. It was the river of our hopes and fears!

Our thoughts of the future, whether or not we could break through the mountains and where we would come out—if successful—were forgotten. Every anxiety was obliterated by the challenge of the unknown river and the thrill of impending adventures. Racing back to camp we stamped the trail flat and poured out our joyful news, and the following day found us camped in the new cañon.

## CHAPTER XX

# The "Unnamed River"

***Reconnaissance of the "unnamed river"—Beauty of the cañon—We reach the end of the cañon—We see the Alaskan Range—The timber begins to disappear—"Camp-making"—We eat owl—Reconnaissance of the head of the valley—We find a big glacier.***

After we were settled Aten and LaVoy went back for our freight, and I for a long trail-breaking scout ahead. The walls of the cañon were beautifully coloured in warm sienna and umber. Tons of soft snow hung on the cliffs and carpeted the narrow stream bed. Now and then I passed holes in the ice through which I caught glimpses of clear, cold water; the strange snake-like tracks of otters ran here and there and coveys of snow-white ptarmigan flew ahead of me as I advanced. The stream bed was now climbing perceptibly, and large boulders told me that the mountains were near.

There is an indescribable charm in this kind of exploration. In the depths of the cañon I could see no distant landmarks—my compass alone told me that I was going towards the Alaskan Range. I drew a chart of the cañon on the butt of my rifle with a nail and found that it made forty-seven sharp bends in a distance of about five miles. As the time passed the desire to see the mountains grew almost irresistible. From the view that I had secured on my last moose hunt I knew that the cañon was leading me into a great gash in the Alaskan Range—but that was all. I felt like a child at its first theatre party waiting for the curtain to rise. I travelled steadily until my watch told me that I had broken five miles of trail. It was time to find a camping place which was an easy matter as a grove of dead spruce stood on a near-by point. Then there was the stamping down of a tent site to be done so that we would have a firm frozen yard when we arrived on the following day. In hunting for a water hole I advanced to a point beyond our camp, and as I raised my eyes from the snow I saw that the cañon walls were breaking away, and that some of the snow peaks of the Alaskan Range were topping the timber ahead. This was all I wanted to know—that the cañon was leading us *somewhere*, and with a feeling of relief I trotted back to camp.

Our advance up the wild gorge was the pleasantest part of our long journey. I have never seen a spot that symbolised more perfectly the pleasant side of the spirit of winter in the wilderness. Tucked away, as it was, deep down under the protecting flanks of the side ranges it lay steeped in cold sunshine, and silence. Our camps in the tinder-dry spruce groves were protected from every wind, and the still stabbing cold that crept down at nightfall from the ice-capped peaks accentuated the comforts of our warm tent. We had left the unpleasant damp winds of the Pacific behind us and were enjoying for the first time what we called "real winter weather!"

For the first time, too, since leaving Knik we were beginning to encounter

In the Cañon of the Unnamed Tributary of the Chulitna River

rough travel. The mile-broad river flats were giving way to snow-covered rapids and huge drifts that brought our shovels into play.

In the account of our journey over the Susitna-Seward trail I purposely mentioned the use of "Nome sleds." Where one travels over flat snow-fields, or a broken trail, there is no sled superior to the rawhide-lashed basket sleds from the Nome coast. But in a rough journey such as ours the small prospector's, or "Yukon sled," proves its superiority. These are small iron bolted sleds without handle-bars. As they are not large enough to carry a very heavy load we used two sleds behind each team, hitched tandem. When they "killapied" it was easy to right them one at a time, and in particularly steep places we could cast off the rear sled and return for it later, which saved us the unpleasant task of unlashing our loads. The runners being closer together than those of a Nome sled made it unnecessary to break a broad trail.

When we established a camp at the edge of the cañon the snow was firm enough to push on with light loads, so we took our complete camp outfit and moved into the mountains. A mile of snowshoeing took us to a point where the cañon had disappeared for good, and the whole majesty of the Alaskan Range rose before us.

On each side of the valley great side ridges swept down, and through the hollow that they formed we could see a chaotic mass of ice-capped peaks—the "backbone" of the range—blocking our path.

The whole land, peaks, mountain slopes, and valleys were one gleaming sheet of snow, except where the rapidly thinning groves of spruce broke the white mantle in dark lines. In grim solitude and desolate grandeur the scene could not be surpassed by the mountains of the moon. After one look ahead we realised that we were in for a rough time, but as we were expecting a hard trip we could only grin and solace ourselves with the thought that the more difficult the crossing the greater our pleasure would be when we reached the Yukon side.

The thinning spruce told us too that the day was not far away when we would be brought down to alcohol stoves and a pemmican diet. With the idea of enjoying the wood while it lasted we devoted special attention to choosing a camp site.

In the abstract one would naturally suppose that camping in a tent during a northern winter would be cold, uncomfortable work, but I can say in all honesty that I have never enjoyed such rest and comfort as our little Yukon stove and 10 x 12 tent supplied. After we had stamped down a firm foundation in the virgin snow, each man would go to work—there was no division of work as you see among "campers"—but each man did unconsciously the task required at the time. First a large dead spruce would come crashing down into the snow, followed by numerous smaller spruces. The green spruces were quickly stripped of their boughs, and the poles—we used six full lengths and four half-lengths—raised the tent. The boughs were then "woven" into a deep soft mattress and a smooth "foot-log" placed across the tent to divide the beds from the stove and "kitchen." A crib of green logs was then placed under the stove to keep it from melting its way into the snow. Then the kitchen boxes ware brought in, containing all the necessary foods and cooking utensils. Each man's "war bag" and "bed" were placed in a row at the head of the tent; and the snowshoes and everything else eatable—from a dog's point of view—were hung out of reach on the tent-poles. The boughs were then covered with a tarpaulin.

While these activities were under way one of us would be sawing the dead spruce into stove lengths and splitting it, and a generous wood-pile would be ready by the time our tent was pitched.

While the cook was at work trails would be broken to, and water brought from, the nearest water hole, and an out-door kitchen built for cooking dog food. More boughs were brought on which to pile our freight which was covered with our sled-covers.

With the dog food cooking merrily and everything outside stowed away we would repair to the tent. A rope would be stretched along the ridgepole for our wet clothes to dry on, our beds unrolled, and we could surrender to the enjoyment of peace and warmth.

Strangely enough the fur robes in which we slept were all made of a different kind of fur. Professor Parker's was made of the skins of summer killed Lapland reindeer, LaVoy's was made of Australian wombat, Aten's was composed of both summer and winter killed white sheep *(Ovis dalli)*, while mine was made of timber wolf skins. For ordinary winter travel they were all equally good, but in extremely cold weather the wombat was inferior to the other skins, and during our explorations on Mount McKinley LaVoy left his wombat bag with Aten and used the sheep skins.

They were all sewed in the form of a bag. Professor Parker's was arranged with a complicated opening that buttoned over flaps; it was made (at great expense) by a New York outfitter, after the regular New York way. The other three bags were simply sacks with an open end. When you were cold you doubled the top under your head and breathed through a small hole which you made by pushing your hand out of the opening of the bag and withdrawing it. This simple arrangement is warmer, simpler, and cheaper than the New York way and is used almost universally by the men who live in the north. For a hard trip the reindeer and white mountain sheep bags were superior to my wolf skins for the reason that they weighed less. My wolf skin bag complete, including a balloon-silk cover, weighed seventeen pounds, while the sheep skin bag weighed only ten pounds, and the reindeer even less. But weight for weight and warmth for warmth the white sheep bag, roughly made by the Knik Indians, was by far the best. Besides being light and warm the hair on a sheep skin does not hold moisture to any extent, and as our bags were covered with ice, from our breath freezing during the night, this fact was of great value.

While we were making camp Professor Parker had gone ahead to a point of spruce and brought back word that he had seen a glacier winding downward from the centre of the range. We were thrilled by the news, for we knew that we were now on the verge of our struggle with the Alaskan Range. At this time we began to feel the effects of the near-by ice-fields. The streams even in the rapids were frozen from the bottom up; our water pails froze solid beside the stove; and in the mornings our dogs were white with frost.

Knowing that there were hungry days ahead we ate ravenously while there was still wood enough to cook with. Our provisions were of the simplest kind: beans, bacon, flour, sugar, tea, and dried fruits; but in addition we had a liberal supply of sago, and as Aten numbered among his other virtues the ability to concoct savoury dishes from unpromising ingredients we revelled in puddings and desserts. Our breakfast consisted always of the classical sour-dough hot cake, which by the way is superior to all other hot cakes. With a little bacon and liberal quantities of tea they "filled our bunkers" until lunch time. The sour-dough pancake "makes the northern world go round"; it is the universal food of the Alaskan prospector and from it he has received his name of "Sour-dough." As they say in the north, "it sticks to your ribs" and makes an excellent food "to travel on." Lunch was always a potluck affair, and at night we had our big meal of beans, bacon, biscuits, and fruit.

Aten, LaVoy, and I divided the doubtful honour of lighting the fire in the morning. The chilling plunge from the warmth of our sleeping-bags into the frigid air was accomplished with lightning speed, and as each man's turn came around he spent the previous evening in the most elaborate preparation of shavings and kindling wood. When, early in the morning our old battered alarm clock would "go off," the unlucky man, whose turn it was, would leap from his bag, "choke" the alarm clock, open the stove, throw in the bundle of shavings, pile on the kindling, set it afire, put on the water pail, and leap back into bed within the space of a few seconds. No sprinter ever followed the report of the starter's pistol with more feverish energy!

Despite the large quantities of ptarmigans we had secured little or no meat. These birds had, as is usual in the winter time, banded into large flocks, and they were extremely hard to approach. Unless we were able to secure a large number or enough for all hands it was a waste of time. With the Alaskan Range straight in front of us our thoughts clung to the big game ranges of the northern side, and we talked constantly of the meat of sheep, caribou, and moose.

One night we were talking about food in general when Aten stated that owls

Our first view of the Alaskan Range after emerging from the cañon of the unnamed river. Showing otter tracks on left bank of open water.

were good to eat. We listened rather sceptically, but when an owl began to hoot behind our camp I picked up our 22 cal. rifle and went in pursuit. Now a few days previously the ejector of the little arm had broken and without another thought I had put it in my pocket. After locating the owl I took a careful sight and fired. The report of the piece was followed by a heavy blow on my eye and everything went black. Putting my hands to my eyes I could feel blood running through them and I could hear the dogs gathering about me and eating the red snow. After washing my eyes with snow I could see with the left one, and later the surgical ministrations of Aten and LaVoy developed a deep gash beside my right eyeball. A fraction of an inch would have meant the loss of an eye.

In a trip such as ours accidents are bound to happen, and for this purpose we carried one of the Burroughs & Welcome folding surgical cases. It was light and remarkably complete and in the few cases where it was needed it more than paid for its weight. The owl also had been wounded, and later I had the satisfaction of eating some of it, and found it very good. The dogs were very fond of human blood and they fought eagerly for the blood-stained snow whenever we bled from an accident. Their actions at these times have led me to believe that all the tales one hears of men being attacked by their dogs in time of famine, are not fiction.

On the following day Professor Parker and I made a reconnaissance of twenty-five miles. We followed the valley to its head, and found that it split. The western branch wound away between two towering peaks. The eastern branch ended in the glacier that Professor Parker had seen from our camp. It led far into the mountains like a huge white roadway. We could not tell where it went to, although its surface promised a possible sledding route, and I determined to prospect the left-hand cañon before committing ourselves to the glacier route. On the way home we located the last grove of timber, which were cottonwood trees, and broke a straight trail to our camp.

## CHAPTER XXI

# Crossing the Range

*The last timber—Blizzards—The long reconnaissance—A possible "pass"—We move onto the ice—More blizzards—Dog-fights—The Summit—Adventures with our freight on the "big drop-off"—The new glacier—More blizzards—A crevasse—We see timber to the east—Another reconnaissance—We find the Muldrow glacier—Crossing the last pass in a storm.*

To facilitate our reconnaissance trips we advanced our camp the following morning to the last grove of cottonwoods, and their gnarled and twisted trunks bore witness to the savage storms which swept the bleak valley we had entered. Great mountains shot up for thousands of feet and their sides were sheathed with snow and ice. It seemed as if the mountains and elements had joined hands to keep us from going forward.

We were awakened the first morning by the wild shrieking of a mountain gale. The wind sang a grand, deep song among the sharp peaks and desolate gorges, and great spouts of snow shot high into the air where the narrowing mountain walls confined the wind. Aten and LaVoy fought backward through the blizzard to bring up our last relay before the trail was lost. I tried to break a trail ahead to the glacier but my tracks disappeared as soon as I lifted my snowshoes from the snow.

On the following day the "pouderie," as the old *voyageurs* would have called it, still continued. I hunted a possible pass through a deep gorge, where in the choking clouds of snow I had to turn my back to the gale to fill my lungs. My journey was unsuccessful, however, as I saw no indications of a break in the range. This left only the unknown glacier on which we could hang our hopes of reaching, the Yukon side.

MOVING UP TO OUR LAST WOOD CAMP ON THE SOUTH SIDE OF THE RANGE. SUNSHINE BREAKING THROUGH THE CLOUDS AFTER A THREE-DAYS BLIZZARD.

Aten and LaVoy had urged their frightened dogs through the cutting ice-dust, and dropped their loads by some willows below the glacier's snout. This was a good deed, for during the following day and night the blizzard raged so fiercely that we did not leave our straining tent. Finally, as the storm continued, we moved our duffle between blizzards, as it were, and having sledded up some tent-poles we pitched our tent in the last thicket of willows.

We were becoming inured to storms and flying ice-dust, for on the following day we advanced six hundred pounds of equipment to the top of the first steep pitch on the glacier's snout, and it was difficult work, as in places the walls were so steep that the dogs could scarcely keep their feet. Coming down, Aten led the dogs and I coasted on the sled; it was blowing a gale at the time, and I had to shut my eyes against the cutting snow-clouds, but I dropped down to the valley floor like an arrow from a bow—it was exciting sport.

The following day the storm again increased to a blizzard. All day long we lay on our fur robes and listened to the shrieking of the wind between hotly contested games of dominoes.

At last a clear day came, and with the break of dawn I was off in light marching trim to see if I could find where our glacier went to. I climbed the glacier snout slowly, breaking a well-graded trail for the dogs to freight on, and then I hit a fast pace up the glacier. The ice river ran like a Gargantuan road between towering mountain walls; at its head a forbidding line of ice-encrusted precipices barred its course, but to the left, or south, long golden splashes of sunshine slanting down across the blue cliffs told me that there was a break in that direction. This fact cheered me slightly, although I was terror-stricken at the thought that our glacier might prove to be impassable.

As I advanced, a suggestion of a glacial basin on the north, or right, came into view, and I noticed that the main glacier had swung around in a gentle curve until it was running due west. This put an entirely different aspect on the desirability of the left-hand break as a route, for it would lead us south and away from the northern foothills.

The same change made the right-hand basin the only avenue of success, but I had little hope of finding a pass there, as the mountains seemed to rise in perpendicular ice-covered cliffs.

Never in my life have I been filled with such conflicting emotions. If there was no pass our expedition was already an absolute failure, for we would be forced to use our mountain food before reaching Mt. McKinley.

As I advanced through the soft snow more and more of the barrier range came into view. Sometimes the skyline would begin to sweep downward as if it were going to break away, and I would run in my eagerness until the range would begin to climb upwards again, and, panting, I would drop into a walk and curse the snow that made me move so slowly. Close to the northern basin which was still hidden by a mountain shoulder I ate some dog pemmican, and one hardtack biscuit washed down with some water which I melted over a candle in my tin cup. From this point I could see that the left-hand route, where I had seen the promising slants of sunshine, was impossible, while the only break in the barrier range was a mighty glacial amphitheatre with perpendicular walls of solid ice. My only hope was the right-hand basin and, after a short smoke, I started onward. Slowly the mountains broke away and suddenly, as I mounted a moraine, the right-hand basin stretched before me and there lay a smooth snow-field *leading gently to the summit of the range!*

Mad with joy I ran faster and faster, my heart hammering from the exertion and excitement. What would I find on the summit—another impassable range? These and other wild thoughts ran through my mind. As I neared the crest of the range I was almost afraid to look, so much depended on what I would find. I thought of the day in 1906 when Barrill and I reached the summit of this same range one hundred miles to the westward, and then had to retreat after feasting our eyes on the northern "sheep-hills." Here I was again on the very crest, but alone in the blinding glare of unnumbered snow-fields, while on that other day we had toiled upward over sheep pastures spangled with wild flowers.

When only a few feet from the top, I stopped and removed my fur cap—to propitiate the mountain gods—and then I stepped up to the summit. Only a blue void lay below me. I took another step—the void deepened, and with my heart in my mouth I drew gently back—I was standing on a snow cornice that overhung a precipice! For a minute I was completely bewildered, but I finally pulled my scattered senses together and began to think clearly. The first thing to do was to find a place where the cornice was broken so that I could study the country below me. Turning to the left I followed the ridge until, to my delight, I found a point where the cornice broke away, and sitting down on the very summit of the great range I looked out over a gleaming sea of unnamed peaks.

The scene was one of stupendous and awful grandeur. Far below me I saw a tangled system of ice rivers that drained the mighty mountainsides. To my left a narrow arête dropped downward from my eyrie; on the right was the deep glacial basin that I had looked into from the snow cornice; on the left of the arête was a second ice-filled gorge; and both these glacial basins ran northward—separated by the arête—until about four miles beyond they joined a large glacier whose course was hidden by projecting mountain shoulders. The first thing to do was to settle once and for all time whether or not it was possible to descend into either of the glacial basins. Luckily I had my ice axe with me. Taking off my snowshoes I made a *traverse* below the cornice, chopping steps in the hard ice until I reached the crest of the arête.

I could now see that a descent into the left-hand hollow was impossible, as the ridge broke off into great *schruds* and ice walls. Following the arête I descended to the top of a very steep but climbable pitch, and below me I saw gentle snow slopes leading downward to the snowy floor of the right-hand basin—*we could cross the pass!* I tried to yell but the silence of the vast range choked the sound in my throat. I remember wishing that my voice could reach to our camp so that my companions could hear the glad tidings. The next best thing was to hurry home, so reaching the summit I lashed on my snowshoes and started on the ten-mile run to camp.

Now that we had found the pass all our energy and resourcefulness were needed to cross it. During my absence Aten and LaVoy had hauled about 1200 pounds of duffle to the top of the glacier, and on the following day they pushed 350 pounds five miles up the ice-river. Then another blizzard came sweeping across the mountains; our trails were wiped out, and again we spent long hours listening to the noise of the storm and playing dominoes or checkers. But our fighting blood was beginning to rise and we decided to advance despite it.

It shows what mountain equipment can do, for with our alcohol stoves and silk tents we were able to make camp high up on the wind- and snow-lashed back of the glacier. Professor Parker and I slept in our little mountain tent, while Aten and LaVoy swung our old wall tent on a rope stretched between the two trail-sleds. They took the dog teams into the tent with them, thereby securing both warmth

Approaching the Pass in the Alaskan Range

*For 17 days we wormed our way through this chaos of rock and ice.*

and diversion, for a big fight started and the noise was tremendous until the hostile teams were torn apart.

During the night the wind blew with such savage fury that we thought our tents would go to pieces at any moment, but they held splendidly and we soon felt confident of riding out any storm the mountains might send against us. The altitude of our first glacier camp was 3000 feet, or 600 feet above brush line.

The days that followed were a continuous round of toil. I would break trails ahead only to have them lost by a new storm. Aten and LaVoy stuck doggedly to their freighting, and slowly—relay by relay—our pile of freight was moved upward toward the pass. Our second glacier camp was at an altitude of 4200 feet.

While the sun was shining and we were working, the temperature often felt as warm as a sunny spring day, but the instant that the higher peaks began to cast their deep blue shadows the temperature would drop instantly to the neighbourhood of zero. With the fall in temperature the cold air began to move downward toward the valleys, causing savage "glacier winds," which fact probably accounts for the coldest temperatures on the high glaciers occurring in the evening, whereas in the valleys the coldest time is early in the morning.

On the 3d of April we pushed our main camp to a height of 6000 feet. We could stand by our tent and see our trail winding away down the steep slopes of snow like a silver wire until it was lost to view on the lower glacier. When Aten and LaVoy would start on the down trail for a load of freight, the dogs would take the steep grades on the gallop, with the heavy sleds in pursuit.

The temperature in this camp stayed close to zero when the sun was not shining. A gale struck us the first night and our tents could not have stood the strain had it not been for our having dug a deep shelter into the mountainside.

The tents were covered with frost and we suffered much inconvenience as it stuck to our clothes and then melted when we got into our sleeping-bags.

After the storm had subsided I prospected a good route across the summit and down over the steep pitch on the arête, chopping deep steps to facilitate the carrying of heavy loads. To save back-packing our entire outfit down the arête we decided to slide some of our freight down a steep 1000-foot snow slope that forms one wall of the glacier basin, and while Aten and LaVoy were bringing up our remaining freight I packed 400 pounds of equipment across the pass. Later Aten went back for the last load and LaVoy and I soon had the bulk of our belongings on top.

The "big day" of our crossing was set for April 5th, but another blizzard hit us and for twenty-four hours the wind shrieked about our tents. With the coming of the storm I was attacked by a severe case of snow-blindness which—as is often the case—affected my stomach so that I could not eat. It was bitterly cold. Our rubber shoe-packs froze solid and our alarm clock refused to work.

In the evening of our last day on the summit we had a party. Aten broke up an empty pemmican case, which, helped out with a bundle of willows that we had used for marking our trail, gave us enough wood for a fire. After they had set up the camp stove in the big tent they invited Professor Parker and me to "come in and get warm." It certainly was a weird picture! Four men and a pack of wolf-dogs, in a storm battered tent, slung on two sleds 6000 feet up on an icy ridge! The red hot stove cast a crimson glow on the strange gathering. Our party progressed splendidly, until "Laddie," Aten's "leader," backed into the red hot stove. In an instant the tent was filled with a choking, blinding cloud of smoke from the burned hair. A deep growl of disapproval came from the pack of dogs, and Professor Parker went head first through the tent door, and showed good judgment by refusing to come back, although we urged and beseeched him between our fits of laughter and coughing. So ended our only entertainment in the Alaskan Range.

The morning for the crossing of the divide dawned clear and cold. We broke camp early, and soon had all our duffle on the summit. Later on it began to storm, and all day long we worked in clouds of blinding, wind-driven snow.

The question of the day was whether or not our belongings would stand the strain of shooting down over the 1000-foot drop into the glacial hollow. After due deliberation I took a can of hardtack and pushed it over the edge. Away the can sped—slowly at first—but as the slope grew steeper the can gained momentum in leaps and bounds, until, spinning like a pin-wheel, it dropped from sight over the steep slope. Anxiously we waited until after what seemed hours had passed we saw a dark spot shoot out over the white floor of the basin far below us, and a whirring noise came up through the cold air. Slower and more slowly the tiny spot moved until finally it came to rest at the end of the long white line that marked its course. Our experiment was a success!

Emboldened by our first venture, we decided to send over LaVoy's broken sled with a load on it. To keep it from travelling too fast and to hold it straight on its course, I tied two fifty-pound packages of pemmican to a rope and made the drag

The author lowering a loaded sled down the 1000-foot drop-off on the summit of the Alaskan Range

fast to the rear of the sled as a rudder. With considerable apprehension we pushed the sled down to the top of the steep pitch and "let 'er go!" The old sled shot downward like a live thing and dropped out of sight. Anxiously we craned our necks to see it slide out on the glacier far below, but we waited in vain. Professor Parker and Aten had descended the aréte by the steps I had chopped that morning and they yelled to us that the sled had buried itself under an ice cliff, but that it seemed to be intact.

After that we were more cautious. We rolled down the solid stuff piece by piece, and then loading our alcohol and fragile dunnage on a sled we began the most difficult part of our task. We had 300 feet of good rope which included 200 feet of Swiss Alpine rope. Sinking a gee-pole deep in the snow, we lowered the sled as far as it would go. I then went down backwards on the rope, hand over hand, until I reached the sled. As our first sled had upset about one-third of the way down, I decided to cut the second sled loose. Aten had by this time gathered our duffle into a pile—and straight for this cache the sled sped! It must have travelled at the rate of a mile a minute, for from where we were standing, 800 feet above, we could hear it hissing through the air like a one-pound shell. If it had hit the cache it would have smashed everything to bits, but it swerved just in time, the gee-pole ring just touching the edge of the cache, and onward it sped down the valley until the soft snow brought it to rest.

After the excitement was over LaVoy and I chuckled as Aten's remarks reached our ears. Their long journey through the cold air had not cooled them one whit! So partly out of deviltry we cut the second sled loose. We had not the slightest idea that it would go anywhere near the cache—although Aten, to this day, says differently—but the fact remains that the perverse sled did shoot straight for the cache. Aten had just started to put up the mountain tent and was inside arranging the pole when he heard our frantic shouts, and he escaped in the nick of time, for the leaping sled dashed across the tent and crashed into some soft roll of bedding at the end of the cache!

That was the last exciting event in a great day, and we were lucky to get across the pass, for that night another shrieking blizzard struck us and we were held stormbound for thirty-six hours. During the first night a mighty gust of wind tore the wall tent down and LaVoy and Aten, rather than leave their robes in the storm "lay dogo" while the wind drifted them deep in snow.

To our joy we were now through for the present with up-hill work—at least our path lay downwards until we reached the big glacier. The small glacier we were on was only a feeder and it rolled downward so steeply that we were forced to go slowly. On the steep pitches we unhooked the dogs and one man rode the gee-pole while a second braked with a shovel handle. We advanced slowly, now toiling across a level flat and then plunging down some great hill while the snow flew up in clouds. It would have been fine sport with empty sleds; as it was it was hard work. We camped on the edge of the big new glacier that ran east and west. Five minutes' walk below our camp was a snow dome from where we could get a good look down the glacier, which ran eastward, and at its lower end we could see timber—solid black lines of spruce that called to us with promises of game and warm fires. But it was not in the right direction, as our course was westward toward Mount

McKinley, and we realised sadly that we would have to climb again and follow the big glacier westward—if such a thing were possible.

To make sure I made a reconnaissance up the glacier and saw a low pass at its head. According to my observations this pass would lead us to the Muldrow glacier whose snout was mapped by Brooks in 1902. Overjoyed at our good prospects I started homeward, when suddenly the snow broke under my snowshoes and down I dropped. My long Susitna shoe (bless the Indian who made it!) caught on the side of the crevasse and threw me across it, and then the downward pressure forced my foot out of the "siwash hitch" and I jammed it into a crack in the ice; but had the crevasse been a few inches wider I might have had a serious accident. This was the first crevasse that I had broken into since the beginning of our glacier travel, and I made up my mind that henceforward no man should travel over untested snow alone.

The following morning Professor Parker and I started out for the pass that lay about seven miles east of our camp. We were roped in case we found another crevasse. On our way eastward we passed four large ice-feeders that came into our glacier from the south, and on reaching the pass all our worries were swept away, for there below us lay the Muldrow glacier. We knew it by its size and also by its course, as it swept in a great curve to the foothills of Mount McKinley that rose like a great white cloud against the south-west sky.

Our success in crossing the range reminded me of Coffee whom we had met beyond Talkeetna. As he had not reached the Muldrow glacier I am to this day uncertain as to what river he followed, and as he crossed the range in one long day (as Doctor Cook did) the most probable supposition is that he crossed farther to the eastward and came out on one of the tributaries of the Toklat River.

Finding Muldrow glacier meant a lot to us. It made the first part of our journey a success, from the point of view of an exploration. And it also insured our reaching Mount McKinley in fighting trim.

We attacked the big glacier with renewed enthusiasm, and three days later found us pitching our tent on the wind-swept moraine of Muldrow glacier. We were a wild-looking crew, for we had fought our way across the pass in the face of a blizzard. The savage wind drove a solid cloud of ice-dust across the snow and at times we could not see one foot ahead.

Aten and I were delayed on the pass by a top-heavy sled. We had attempted to carry too much as we expected good weather and a down-hill pull. The wind finally reached such terrific force that we had to hold the heavy sled *to keep it from being blown over!* Several times we had to stop and relash our loads and each time the dogs rebelled at facing the storm.

While lashing the sled we had to yell to be heard, and Aten's face through the flying drift looked like a solid piece of ice. Once when we were hauling shoulder to shoulder on a frozen rope he turned and grinned at me and I saw the ice on his face crack open. I had shaved the day before and the ice-dust didn't stick to my face much. We were coated with ice from head to foot when we reached the protection of the moraine of Muldrow glacier and were lucky to pull through with nothing more severe than frozen ears and a few frost bites. We were forced, however, to leave a large cache behind on the summit of the pass.

But these details were instantly forgotten the moment we reached the moraine, for the dream of years had come to pass,—*we were on the northern side of "the range"!*

# CHAPTER XXII

# "The Happy Hunting-Ground"

***Blizzards again—The successful hunt—Death of Muckluck—We return for our cache—Advance towards the foothills—Mountain sheep and caribou—The McKinley Fork of the Kantishna River—Timber at last!***

For years during my wanderings in Alaska I had listened eagerly to the tales told about the northern side of the Alaskan Range. Few men had seen this country, but now and then I met one who had, and always these men spoke of it as a land trampled flat by game! A land where bands of white sheep dotted the upland pastures, where caribou herds drifted across the foothills, and moose browsed in every timber-line valley!

As time went on and I attempted to reach this country something always occurred to keep me from my heart's desire.

First, in 1906 Ed. Barrill and I had to turn back from the Kuskoquim side after having actually feasted our eyes on the sheep pastures of the northern slope.

It was during our retreat, around our foodless campfires in that hungry land that partly on account of its inaccessibility, and partly on account of the longed-for game it harboured, we first spoke of the northern side as "the happy hunting-ground."

In 1910 we were again turned back from swinging Mount McKinley's flank, by the great serac. Here again we reached "bed-rock" with our food, and once more our one topic of conversation was meat, and how we would eat if we could reach "the happy hunting-ground."

They say "the third time never fails," and, with us at least, it was true to its reputation, for it was on the 12th day of April that somewhat battered from our struggle with the storm we pitched our tent beside the Muldrow glacier.

In crossing the range we were seventeen days on the ice without seeing a sign of vegetation and over our pemmican we again talked of the northern game herds.

Now, as we looked northward from the glacier the blizzard was lashing the mountainsides, it was impossible to hunt! I knew the game was there, for from the top of the second pass we had already seen the change that told us game was at hand. The mountains were no longer covered with dense carpets of soft snow, but here and there on the northern slopes were bare patches of brown grass where the winter winds had swept the snow away—and those brown patches meant mountain sheep bands which to us in turn spelled warm white skins to sleep on and juicy steaks and rich stews for the inner man.

The following lines are the entries from my diary made during our first day on the northern side of the range:

"Camp 22, April 13th—Just awake and breakfast is melting. We had to make our tea from melted snow and ice. The blizzard is still raging and all night long the tent rattled and heaved. Aten slept with Parker and me in the mountain tent. Merl rolled up in the wall tent outside, and a mournful picture he made when I awakened him. All you could see was a round form under the snow-drifted canvas and all about; over and under were sleeping dogs covered with snow and ice. I cannot hunt in this weather. *Eight hours later*—grand, big day! This morning (as I said before) we awoke to the roar and thunder of the gale, and the hiss of blizzard-driven sleet.

"After breakfast we sat in our corners and played 'hearts'—for tobacco. About 9:30 A.M. Cliff bundled up and went out to get a report on the weather. He returned in about half an hour blinded by the snow and said that the weather was awful. As he entered the tent door I caught a glimpse of distant mountainsides that looked clear enough to hunt on, so I started to dress although he advised me not to go. But I became desperate and getting into my parka and mittens I went out into the storm. On my left lay the jagged morainal hills of the Muldrow glacier and on my right rose the blizzard-swept flanks of the Alaskan Range. Before long I found sheep sign that had been blown off the mountainsides above me, and as I advanced before the wind I studied the hills above as well as the flying snow clouds would permit. My eyes were weak from an attack of snow-blindness and my smoked glasses were frost covered, and when I finally saw what appeared to be a band of sheep above me I laughed at myself for being deceived by what I thought was an optical illusion. To advance I had to descend into an ice-filled cañon where the wind blew with such fury that I was unable to see, but I soon reached the smooth, frozen surface of an open flat where the gale swept me along as if I was sail-skating. When I came to a stop I glanced up the mountain, and *there, two hundred yards away, was a big band of white sheep just breaking into a run!*

"I had not a second to spare as the band was making around a shoulder of the mountain, but I began to shoot in fear and trembling as I still had a touch of snow-blindness and I could not trust my eyes. After my first shot, however, my coolness came back for I saw a spout of snow just under the band where my bullet had struck.

"Throwing off my snow glasses I fired again and saw the sheep turn and leave the band. I will never again (I fear) feel such a surge of savage triumph as I did when I saw that the sheep was hit. No man who has not felt the cruel hunger that we have felt in this hard land; who has not felt the revolt of living on ice-cold canned things day after day can appreciate the longing with which we looked forward to juicy, steaming, sizzling steaks! Add to this hunger the fact that mountain-sheep meat is the finest meat in the world, and you will understand how I felt."

But fully as great as the desire for flesh is the joy of the successful hunter's return to a "hungry camp"— the triumph of staggering camp-wards under a heavy load of meat. I have often walked buoyantly mile after mile with a heavy meat pack, when without the stimulation of the joyous reception that I knew was awaiting me I would have had to rest many times along the way.

After the wounded sheep turned aside the band swerved away from the ridge and as their white bodies came against the sky I secured two more. Running up the frozen slope I finished the wounded animal and after marking down the others I started on the run for camp.

As I ran I thought of how I could best surprise my companions, as I knew that the sound of my rifle shots had been drowned by the wind. On entering our little tent I began by calling the weather names and grumbling about the difficulties of hunting under such conditions. Then I added that although the weather was bad we really ought to bestir ourselves and get our freight off the mountain. My comrades thought I referred to our dunnage on the pass and as a thick wall of snow was roaring down the pass beyond our protecting mountainside, my remarks were met with contemptuous silence. I then bantered them by saying that they need not go, but that I thought I would take a dog team and try it myself. The atmosphere had by this time reached a point where fireworks were about to begin, so I played my trump card. "If we don't go now," I said, "our freight will spoil."

"What will spoil?" Aten and LaVoy asked together.

"The sheep meat I've got up on the hill," I answered slowly.

For a minute they looked at me wildly and then they decided I was fooling, but they finally hitched up a team and followed me doubtfully down the mountain side; but when we reached the sheep our spirits broke loose and we executed a "Wakamba meat dance" around the bodies.

In cold weather one has a craving for fat, and in the wilderness one is less particular about the way meat is cooked. Our desire for fat was so intense that we tried eating the raw meat, and finding it good beyond words we ate freely of the fresh mutton. I can easily understand now why savage tribes make a practice of

THE AUTHOR SKINNING ONE OF THE WHITE SHEEP KILLED IN THE STORM. THE DOGS WERE GREATLY INTERESTED IN THE OPERATION.

eating uncooked flesh. We slid the sheep down a snow chute to the base of the mountain and after making the tug-line fast to their horns, the happy dogs pulled them to the sled and we were soon in camp. For hours afterwards we fried meat over our alcohol lamp, and ate—each man taking turns at the cooking when his hunger was temporarily satisfied.

I found that the sheep, as far as outward signs were concerned, were in no way different from the sheep of the Chugach or Kenai Mountains. They were (or had been) snow-white all over, but the long winter had left its mark on them and they were badly scarred and weather-beaten.

Their brittle hair had been torn and broken until they had a shaggy or rough appearance, and their pelage was stained to a yellow and brown colour by contact with rocks and gravel.

None of the sheep were fat, but they were in good condition, and at the time that I surprised them they were feeding in the driving snow on a wind-swept patch of winter-cured grass. Their stomachs were well filled with grass, and I found that they had eaten caribou-moss, or lichens, as well.

I found, by back-tracking the band, that they had been down in the flat at the base of the mountain before my arrival, and the experience that I gained in that locality shows that the sheep in the winter time range very low.

At the time that I hunted, the sheep had begun to move upward towards the high mountains, and yet I saw quantities of sheep tracks at an altitude of only 3000 feet. From my own observations I feel sure that in localities where sheep have never been hunted they range much lower than they are supposed to. Even in little hunted regions, they have learned to fear the lowlands.

The next morning the wind had moderated to half a gale so we decided to bring our duffle down from the pass.

When we started to hitch up after breakfast there were only a few dogs around camp. Losing patience over the threatened delay I went down to where we had butchered the sheep, knowing that the dogs would gather there for scraps.

I found two of them and brought them back to camp and started up the glacier on a hunt for the rest, but I returned unsuccessful to find that Aten and LaVoy had left camp on the same quest. About half an hour later they returned and I heard Aten calling to me to come out of the tent. His voice had an unfamiliar sound and I decided that the dogs had killed some wild beast.

As I emerged from the tent a sad sight met my gaze. Muckluck, Aten's left-wheel dog and the best animal we owned, lay dead on the gravel and by his side kneeled Aten with tears coursing down his weather-beaten face. Muckluck was a clean strain malamute, courageous to the point of madness, and willing to fight any number of dogs up to a whole sled team. He had gone down alone to the sheep grounds. There he had encountered LaVoy's team of five dogs, and in the fight that followed he had fallen before a superior number.

It was a great loss to us and after trying to cheer Aten up we started up the pass. As usual we encountered a stinging snow-laden gale, but we forced our way upward through a narrow gully. On the way home I followed the course of our first descent and found a ten-pound box of chocolate, that we had lost during the blizzard. I reached camp ahead of the teams, and by the time Aten had arrived I had buried Muckluck under a great cairn of boulders and placed a sharp shaft of granite at his head.

Aten soon joined me and thanked me with a grip of his hand and we stood over the old dog's grave crying like children. In that savage life so little tenderness or affection enters into the daily grind that a man loves his dogs passionately—and it is well that he does. We named the pass at the base of which the grave lies "Muckluck Pass," in memory of our faithful friend.

After rescuing our cache we turned all our energies to reaching timber. As the snow in the vicinity of the Muldrow glacier had been blown down into the lowlands by the fury of the winds we had difficulty in finding a good sled route.

The Muldrow glacier acted as a huge wind funnel; I have never seen the wind blow with more regularity and fury than it did at our first camp on the northern side of the range. In order to save our tent we were forced to build wind-breaks out of our freight.

Between the moraines and the mountains there were deep hollows in which during the summer time rushing streams led to the lowlands. In the bottom of these miniature cañons we found enough ice and snow to allow us to pull our sleds.

We moved our camp outfit first and after a long day we pitched our camp at the base of the last range of foothills. Along the glacier moraines I saw caribou and bear sign, but it had all been made in the summer time. At this time I knew nothing about the movements of the caribou on the northern side of the range. I had heard from Fred Printz, who was chief packer for Brooks, that caribou were to be found along timber-line in August, but it did not follow that we would find them in the same place in April. I therefore decided to shoot one more sheep before we left the mountains behind us in order that we would have enough meat to last us until we reached moose country. I had no time to spare, as we were camped in the last range of foothills. The mountains about us were beautiful in the extreme and showed variations in form and colouring that I have never seen equalled. To the east of our camp rose a majestic range of a leaden blue colour. It was capped with rugged pinnacles of broken rock and its sides were formed of huge slopes of scree. The pile formed a shoulder or turning point of the main mountain system, and at a distance of two miles I could see through my binoculars trails made by the countless feet of wild sheep during their short migrations or journeys along the range. Surrounding the blue mountains were the typical "sheep-mountains" dear to a hunter's heart.

When, in the north, you see high, eroded mountains splashed here and there with snow-fields between the dead-brown of the mountain pastures, and broken now and then by more rugged peaks that rise still higher into the blue, you can rest assured that sheep are near at hand. I, however, did not need these signs to cheer me, for in the little valley where our tent stood, a broad rut in the snow showed where a band of sheep had passed by.

Leaving camp I climbed a low hill that rose near the centre of a wide valley. From this strategic point I could sweep many miles of mountain pastures with my binoculars. Lying on my stomach with a convenient rock for an elbow rest, I began one of the most interesting operations enjoyed by man—the search for wild game with powerful binoculars on rugged mountainsides. Ranges miles away are brought close to the eye and, fascinated by the secrets of nature that are unfolding before you, you forget everything except the wonderful details that your eyes are drinking in; in imagination you are climbing rugged peaks as you study their ridges and snow-filled couloirs; now you join a great eagle as he soars above some blue void and in imagination you hear the hiss of wind through his broad pinions; or you follow the marmot on his morning constitutional along the talus slopes, and whirr onward with a cock ptarmigan to the side of the demure hen whose love song has lured him. Through it all you have an amusing, guilty feeling of taking advantage of your wild neighbours.

I had been lying thus for probably ten minutes when I saw a sheep. The animal was about two miles away, and I settled myself for the serious work in hand. I had determined that under no consideration would I kill a ewe, so the first fact to settle was whether or not the sheep was a ram. As I looked the ground over I located six more sheep, or seven in all. This was encouraging, for rams often travel in bands of this number, and they all appeared to be of the same size. They were feeding lazily in the shadow of a grassy mountain, and the blue morning haze prevented me from ascertaining how large their horns were.

From their actions and size I finally came to the conclusion that they were rams, and once decided I began the solving of an interesting problem. The sheep were moving slowly, and they were about two miles away and 1500 feet above me. The question was how long it would take me to reach a point ahead of and above the moving band.

It is in the solving of these hunting problems that experience is necessary, for to be able to judge successfully where a certain band of sheep will be after an hour has elapsed, requires an intimate knowledge of their habits, and more hunters have failed by forgetting to study the problem before them than from any other cause. After deciding on the details of the stalk I saw that it would of necessity be a blind approach (that is, that the sheep would be out of sight during the entire stalk), and I was forced to study every distant landmark on the mountain, so that after reaching my desired position I could recognise each rock and gully, although my point of view had changed. This precaution is most necessary in hunting, for the hunter often forgets that the particular rock that he desires to reach will look entirely different to him when he has changed his position, and success often depends on these minute precautions.

As it was early in the morning I knew that the sheep would continue to feed for some time and that in all probability they would feed downward, as they were then near the summit of the mountain.

There were several gullies lying in the path of the band, and after choosing the one which I thought would lead me to a point near my quarry, I started on a trot across the valley. At the base of the mountain I shed all my useless clothing and impedimenta, and began the climb with nothing to bother me but my rifle, knife, camera, and pack-strap. About an hour had passed before I reached a rock that I had chosen as a point of vantage when I planned the stalk, and as I raised my head slowly, watching every point about me, I saw a sheep's horns sticking up above a little knoll thirty yards away. With the thrill of exultation that swept over me came a note of disappointment, for the horns were those of a ewe, and I felt pretty sure that there would be no large rams in the band. Another circumstance that vexed me greatly was, that although the sheep were unaware of my presence, and feeding towards me, the sun was directly behind them and I could not photograph them. Had it not been for this fact I could have secured at least one clear picture of a band of seven sheep less than twenty-five yards away, with Mount McKinley and a large sweep of the Alaskan Range for a background. Although I knew it was hopeless, I waited in the hope that the band might pass me and give me a chance to photograph them. They advanced slowly, eating greedily of the short wind-cured grass, but, unfortunately, they came directly towards me. Several times different sheep raised their heads and stared fixedly at me, but I gave them as good as they sent and held my breath into the bargain, and eventually they would go to feeding again. They finally came so close that I could hear them feeding. If I had been armed with a bow and arrow I could have killed one easily enough. At last an old ewe fixed her eyes on me, and although I lay motionless with my chin in the dirt, I saw her body begin to stiffen with suspicion. When I saw that I was discovered I slowly brought my rifle to my shoulder, and, aiming behind the ear of a young ram, fired. The force of the bullet nearly turned him over, and he almost fell on his back, and so far as I could see, he never moved again. Death was instantaneous and he never knew what had happened to him.

At the report of my rifle the sheep nearly fell over backwards from fright, and then, following the old ewe, they dashed madly up the mountain.

Dropping my rifle I grabbed my camera, and as the sheep turned by a point of rock, I made my first exposure. I had remained in the same position, and as they saw nothing to frighten them, they began to slow down, and I secured several more pictures, the last of which shows the band feeding peacefully out of sight over the top of the mountain.

My victim was a yearling ram. He was in good condition, but had little or no fat on his ribs, although there was enough around the kidneys to fry a few pans full of steak. He weighed close to ninety pounds, and after I had cleaned him I packed him entire to camp, which I reached at 11 A.M. Had I wanted more meat I could have killed the entire band, but during our stay in that country we used the most rigid economy in the use of meat, and we often went without when we were surrounded with game, rather than kill immature animals or females.

MALE ALASKAN WHITE SHEEP (*Ovis dalli*). KILLED BY THE AUTHOR ON THE FOOTHILLS OF MOUNT MCKINLEY.

Every scrap of meat was used, as well as the bones and hides, as rawhide with the hair on is good for the dogs and we fed it to them regularly after cutting it in strips. We saved the best skins and staked them out to dry, and used them to sleep on. These untanned skins were splendid for mountain work, because the fat remaining on the skin kept them from absorbing moisture when laid on the tent floor next to snow or ice, and we carried them to our highest camp on Mount McKinley at 16,615 feet. Aten was the inventor of a method of shortening the hair on the hides so that we could make insoles for use on the mountain. He would first cut the hide into the necessary shape and then singe it on the side of our camp stove until the hair was even and about one-half inch in length. The insoles were a great success, as they were light and easily dried when damp.

As we now had plenty of meat to last us until we reached timber-line, we broke camp the following morning and headed towards the lowlands. As we were leaving camp two cow caribou came around a low point in the stream bed and looked our outfit over thoroughly before breaking into their long, smooth trot. LaVoy ran to the top of a little knoll and brought back word that they had joined a

How we did our marketing. Aten with young caribou.

small band of seven and had left the valley. This was my first view of the caribou of the Mount McKinley region, and during the days I spent in their country I studied them carefully and learned their habits well. This small band of cows was the forerunner of the many bands of females that work their way far into the mountains in the spring to drop their young.

We were now in a wilderness paradise. The mountains had a wild picturesque look due to their bare rock summits, and big game was abundant. We were wild with enthusiasm over the beauty of it all, and every few minutes as we jogged along some one would gaze fondly on the surrounding mountains and ejaculate, "This is sure a white man's country!"

In one of these camps we were awakened by the short excited barks of our dogs, and then we heard a pitiful scream that rose in a shrill crescendo. Aten rushed out of the tent in time to see "Laddie" leap in the air and snap up an Arctic hare that had blundered into camp before discovering its danger.

From the high mountain where I had killed the last sheep I had secured a wonderful view of the great expanse of country below us. I could see a hollow following the eastern wall of the rugged terminal moraine of the Muldrow glacier. One glance at Brooks's map confirmed my opinion that it was the headwaters of the McKinley Fork of the Kantishna. The little stream on which we were camped joined the main gulch about two miles below. Beyond the end of the great moraine began a mile-wide glacier flat which was covered evenly with the snow which the winter winds had blown downward from the mountains. Far beyond were thin dark lines that made my heart leap with expectation, for they were groves of spruce, and after the frigid days among the ice-fields we longed for the crackle and warmth of leaping flames, as a starving man longs for food.

The sight of timber was enough in itself to draw us aside in our advance on Mount McKinley, but we were forced to travel to timber as the nearer foothills were bare of snow. By following timber-line to the next river on the west, the Clearwater, we would find ice which we could follow with our sleds to the very base of Mount McKinley. All this I could see through my binoculars from the mountainside, and as Aten and LaVoy brought up the remainder of our freight during the day, we lost no time in pushing forward. At first we found rough travel. Boulders choked the cañon bed, and over-flows had frozen into steep cascades of ice where we donned "ice-creepers" and "rough-locked" our sleds. But when we entered the main bed of the McKinley Fork we found broad expanses of crusted snow and changing our ice-creepers for snowshoes we made fast time. But the surprise of the day came when we entered the gulch on the edge of the great moraine, for instead of the rough travelling we expected we began to encounter glassy overflows down which we sped behind the galloping dogs. At first we accepted the new conditions stoically—they seemed too good to last—but as point after point flew by and the ice-fields increased in size instead of diminishing we gave way to the exhilaration of the wild ride and urged our flying dogs into a mad race downward.

Had we relayed all our freight two miles farther we would have been able to load it all on our sleds and pull it easily, for the dogs were running hard to keep ahead of our leaping runners and our brakes were throwing up clouds of ice-dust. The splendid speed and the proximity of timber after the stern struggle through the mountains intoxicated us and we yelled with excitement.

As we "boomed along" we at last began to pass patches of stunted willows, and finally a wild cry from Aten drew our eyes to a small clump of dead brush. "Almost enough for a fire!" he shouted and smiles creased our faces from ear to ear. The patches of dead brush increased in number, and as we neared the end of the cañon on the edge of the glacier flat the ice gave way to soft snow and we came to rest beside a small thicket of stunted cottonwoods. To men used to camping in a timbered country it would have been a desolate spot, but the following entry in my diary will show the childish and extravagant delight with which we welcomed our first sight of real wood.

"Camp 25, April 17th—Timber! By all the Red Gods! Timber!! If any one ever reads these scrawled lines I wonder if they will realise what it means to us. First it means success, for we have crossed the Alaskan Range 'from wood to wood.' Secondly, it means that we have added slightly to the world's geographical knowledge—not an easy thing to do in these days—for we have added two new glacier systems to the map. Then comes the delight of warmth and cooked food after seventeen consecutive days' travel through snow and ice smothered mountains. But greater than this is the triumphant feeling of having at last beaten the old mountains themselves; of having withstood their piercing cold, and weathered their savage blizzards; of having dragged our sleds across the faces of their virgin snow-fields and glaciers; and, lastly, of having untangled the route through their twisting cañons and passes."

Besides we are in "God's Country," with the whole majestic sweep of the Alaskan Range towering over us, and culminating in the great, snowy king of mountains—McKinley. Caribou tracks roughen the sand-bars. The air is pulsating with the cackling of unnumbered billions of ptarmigans, and a bushy-tailed old fox is watching our camp from the river bluff.

We are now on the McKinley Fork of the Kantishna River; our struggle with the Alaskan Range is a thing of the past, and five miles below us are dark lines of spruce—real timber—awaiting our arrival!

CHAPTER XXIII

# To the Base of Mount McKinley

~

***Ptarmigan—We reach spruce timber—We find a deserted camp—We find magazines and newspapers—News of another Mount McKinley expedition—I find a spot for a base camp—Professor Parker and Aten go in search of food—Hunting moose—I find a possible pass to the base of Mount McKinley—Professor Parker and Aten successful—We advance to "Base Camp"—Among the caribou herds—Successful reconnaissances.***

As we worked our way into the lowlands, and left the frozen snow-covered ranges behind, we came into the country of the ptarmigan. Words fail me when I try to sing the praises of this noble bird. Without him the barren mountainsides would be as silent as the tomb, for wherever there is a patch of moss or a wind-stunted willow, there you will find the ptarmigan. In the winter time they gather into flocks of from a few birds to several thousands, and when they are found together in large numbers they are difficult to approach. This was the condition of affairs when we entered the Alaskan Range, but when we reached the northern timber-line the mating season was commencing and they were very tame. One of the most impressive experiences of my sojourn on the north side of Mount McKinley had to do with these birds. I had gone down towards the great glacier flat below the moraine to study out the best sledding route through the maze of frozen river channels. It was the first time in months that I found warm, dry grass to lie on. The country about me was still covered with snow, but the sunshine had a hint of spring warmth as I sat on the little hill. There were thousands of ptarmigans about me, and wherever my binoculars rested I could see the white forms of these beautiful birds. When

I first sat down I could hear them cackling on every hand, but as I lay in the sunshine with the whole majestic sweep of the Alaskan Range shining through the spring haze, my ears became attuned to the sounds of the great wilderness about me, and I sat unconscious of all else except the mighty ptarmigan chorus that filled the air. From every knoll and willow, glacier flat and hillside, came the distinctive love song of this bird, and as I listened I became aware of a deep pulsating undertone of sound that filled the whole world about me, and I knew that winter was dead and spring had come. The call of the ptarmigan is not beautiful by itself, but it is so distinctive that once heard it is never forgotten.

A pleasing side of their mating is the habit of the males of uttering their call while they are on the wing. They commence with a guttural cackle which they utter faster and faster until they alight, when they end their song by repeating slowly a call that sounds like *ged-up, ged-up, ged-up, ged-up*, or, *parler vous? parler vous? parler vous?* as they strut proudly about. The males fight constantly and the hens seem to enjoy these battles and sit about clucking among themselves. But once a hen has decided on a mate she comes into her own share of trouble, and is beaten and bullied by the bird she has promised to love and obey. A striking illustration of the cruelty of the males occurred one day when by accident I had shot a female thinking it was a male. As I advanced to pick the hen up a cock rushed out of a clump of willows and pecked and struck the dying hen viciously with his wings, and he had actually dragged her about before I drove him off. The ptarmigan makes delicious eating, and although we seldom killed them we enjoyed the addition they made to our rather restricted menu.

From the mossy hill I decided on a route through the flat valley, to where, five miles away on the northern horizon, I could see a dark line of spruce sentinelling the distant timber-line.

Aten and LaVoy came into camp later with all our freight and enthusiastic over their rapid journey down the frozen river, and the following morning we "hit for the timber." The journey across the blazing snow flats was uneventful.

We pulled our sleds through the broken ice of brittle over-flows but we laughed at the wetting, for the dry spruce grove was drawing nearer. Once in a clear unfrozen pool I saw trout, or grayling darting by, and every exposed bit of river gravel was dotted with mating ptarmigan.

As we neared the timber the dogs broke into a run and with our sleds rocking and leaping over the frozen crust we came to rest among the trees.

A reaction from the weeks of toil came over us and we sat aimlessly on our sleds, laughing and smoking. Aten walked over to a large dead spruce and patted it affectionately, calling it endearing names the while and we grinned appreciatively at each other and the world in general—we were supremely happy.

After we had become used to our new surroundings we began to think of our duties in camp building, and we were looking about us for a suitable camp site when Arthur Aten gave a wild whoop and started on a mad run down the bank. We were after him in an instant for a gleam of white that was different from the surrounding snow had caught our eyes, and as we dashed into a little clearing an old battered tent stood before us. As I ran I noticed also two meat caches, from one of which a great black moose skin hung, swinging in the wind. Nothing stirred nor were our hails answered as we approached, and when Aten looked in he turned to us and said, "No one at home."

The camp was an old hunting camp used occasionally by the miners from the creeks on the lower Kantishna, and a pile of beautiful caribou antlers bore witness to successful hunts in bygone days. The tent was an old 12 x 14 patched in one corner where a conflagration had occurred. There was a raised sleeping platform in the end with plenty of dried caribou skins for mattresses, and an old stove burned through on top and a "grub box" stood in the corner. The invariable pile of dry shavings demanded by the unwritten law of the trail had been placed before the stove by the last occupant before his departure. But the greatest "find" we made was a number of old magazines and newspapers. The latter included some copies of the *Fairbanks Times* wherein we discovered some articles about our own movements that amused us greatly. One of these stated that Tom Lloyd and a party were coming with dog teams to the foothills "to watch us climb the mountain." As I knew Lloyd personally I could picture his facial expression on reading the item!

After we were settled we held a council of war. Even the crossing of the Alaskan Range had been easy compared with the task that now confronted us. The first thing to accomplish was the location of the best spot for the camp that was to be our base while climbing "the big hill." As Mount McKinley towered above a low range of "caribou-hills" only twenty-five miles away in an air line, this task would not be difficult; but the finding of the best route for scaling the great peak was a serious matter, and I determined to devote all my time and energy to solving it. Since reaching the Muldrow glacier we had had many clear views of the big mountain, and on every occasion I had studied every foot of the north-eastern approach through my powerful binoculars. The views from the end of the Muldrow glacier and the headwaters of the Kantishna showed clearly, in every detail, the contours of the three north-eastern ridges. At the first glance that I secured away back on my moose hunt on the Chulitna the Central North-Eastern Ridge had seemed to promise the best route, and every view that we got as we approached nearer and nearer to the mountain confirmed my first opinion.

From Muckluck Pass we had been able to see distinctly a great glacier running up to a high altitude between the Central and Northern North-East ridges. On this glacier we hung our hopes, for the present, and my base camp and climbing-route reconnaissances were made with this glacier as an objective.

Now the *Fairbanks Times* copies that we found in the tent were dated January, and an old trail apparently more than two weeks old led towards Mount McKinley in one direction, and towards Fairbanks via Moose Creek—a river to the eastward—in the other direction. A careful study of the trail convinced me that the men that made it were travelling from, and not towards, Mount McKinley.

Early the next day I followed the trail towards the mountain. It led me across the low caribou-hills from which I obtained a magnificent view of the whole Alaskan Range sweeping in a great arc from the far east or Tanana River side to the western or Peter's glacier side of McKinley. From this point too I saw that a comparatively low range of eroded mountains separated the headwaters of the Clearwater River from the big glacier that separated the Central and Northern North-East ridges. These rounded mountains were the continuation of the Northern North-Eastern Ridge that led to the northern summit of the mountain. The eroded range was gashed by deep valleys drained by the numerous feeders of the Clearwater River, and it was obvious that the best place for a base camp would be at the highest growth of firewood in one of these valleys. Without going farther I was able with my binoculars to locate the last grove of cottonwoods on the central main branch of the Clearwater. From this branch a deep valley ran upward through the eroded mountains towards our promising glacier, and I realised at once that it was my duty to explore this valley at the earliest opportunity. I dismissed the old trail without another thought, for instead of leading towards the promising north-eastern approach at the head of the Clearwater, it continued to spruce timber on the Clearwater on a parallel line with the foothills, and I decided that no party trying to climb the mountain would have passed the north-eastern approach by.

Returning to camp I reported my discoveries, and we began our preparations for an advance to the head of the Clearwater.

While studying our maps at the old tent, we saw two dots on the map that were marked Glacier City and Diamond City. They were a small matter of about forty miles away—a day's run with an empty sled, under good travelling conditions. Not knowing that these towns were deserted we figured that the inhabitants would have broken trails to the heads of Moose Creek and other tributaries during their winter moose hunts. We were badly in need of oatmeal, and we longed for a few simple luxuries such as canned butter and milk. Thinking that Glacier City or its neighbour would certainly boast a store of some kind, it was decided that Professor Parker and Aten would go on a hunt for groceries, while LaVoy and I pushed our freight towards the Clearwater and prospected for a pass to the promising glacier.

But first of all we needed meat and I decided to put in the following day in an effort to kill something.

On our arrival at timber-line we entered the home of the Alaskan moose. Moose, however, range over such a variety of country that one is never quite sure as to what kind of country they are to be found in. Sheep are always near the snow-line, caribou range from the snow-line to timber-line, generally speaking, but moose may be found anywhere, or, as it sometimes seems, *nowhere*. I spent the following day in trying to find a moose, and while I was unsuccessful in securing meat I had a novel experience. For years I had listened to discussions between Alaskan hunters as to whether or not the Alaskan moose utters a call. I have been asked a hundred times for my opinion on this matter and could only answer that, while I had never heard an Alaskan moose call, I believed that they did.

On this occasion I was returning to camp and stopped to leeward of a storm-stunted spruce to take a last look over the country.

Timber-line lay about three hundred feet below me and consisted of two great groves of spruce joined by a narrow line of the same tree. Suddenly, as I stood sweeping the country, I heard a moose call from the narrow connecting line of spruce. I knew it was a cow moose from having heard New Brunswick moose hunters utter the call on a birch-bark horn. The call was loud and reached my ears distinctly; it was a single note. After a wait of about five minutes I heard it again, but this time the sound came from the centre of the large group of spruce. To make sure of the animal's sex, I snowshoed down to the narrow connecting line of timber and there I found the fresh track of the cow leading towards the large grove. The snow was in the condition when the surface for ten feet about me would settle with a loud noise, and as a stalk through the timber was out of the question, and as I would have under no circumstances killed a cow at that time of the year, I returned to camp.

LaVoy had done a good day's work, and after talking of the probable success of our companions' search for food we made plans for the morrow. LaVoy was to continue advancing freight to the top of the range of caribou-hills, while I was to prospect a route to the grove of timber where we were to locate our base camp and, if possible, proceed on a search for a pass to the glacier.

Early on the following day I started out. Leaving the old tent I made good time on the crusted snow across the rolling hills that divide the McKinley Fork from the Clearwater.

As the sun rose the travelling conditions grew worse, for the snow that overlay the willow thickets kept breaking through, and until nightfall I was forced to plough along through heavy water-soaked slush.

Entering the valley that I had chosen as the most promising road to the North-Eastern Ridge, I located a fine grove of alders with a few stunted cottonwoods scattered through it and saw that it would make a splendid camping place. Noon found me well up toward the head of the valley and directly under the snow-covered mountain range that barred our path to the North-Eastern Ridge. Tracks of caribou were abundant, and I also saw a few sheep tracks, but I was moving at top speed and I did not look for game.

The sun was burning down through a clear sky, and as I jogged along on my long shoes I had to keep removing my clothes or night would have found me wet with perspiration. My clothing was finally reduced to first principles and I climbed upward through the snow-buried mountains naked to the waist.

It was a great relief later, when the long, blue shadows began to creep along the mountainsides, to have dry clothes to temper the chill air. At the base of the mountains my valley split into three forks and I chose the left or eastern fork as the most promising. Following an ice-filled gorge where I had to remove my slippery snowshoes, I came up into a desolate mountain amphitheatre, where cast antlers of caribou lay in the snow.

Crossing this silent valley, I climbed the southern wall and suddenly found myself looking down on a huge gleaming glacier, while directly in front of me rose the ice-encrusted flanks of Mount McKinley's Central North-Eastern Ridge.

After one glance, I saw that the glacier was the Muldrow and that it was split by the Central North-Eastern Ridge and flowed in two great streams from the stupendous ice cliffs of Mount McKinley! This was an important discovery, for it filled in a large blank on the map and tied on the snout of the Muldrow Glacier mapped by Brooks, with one of the largest glaciers of the Mount McKinley region. But I was delighted particularly by a second discovery namely, that the northern branch of the Muldrow made a roadway to the very base of Mount McKinley, and with my binoculars I got a view of the North-Eastern Ridge that was more promising even than our previous views.

I was overjoyed, as in one day's travel from the McKinley Fork of the Kantishna River I had actually prospected a route to an altitude of 12,000 feet on the big mountain, and the impressions I got from studying the ridge from 12,000 feet to the summit proved to be correct, as we eventually followed the course that looked most promising to us from this point.

With a light heart I started down from the pass, which was 6000 feet in altitude, and as the sun grew lower I made fast time downward over the long, blue snow slopes. On the way home, I followed a new route to facilitate our freighting. Including side trips I had climbed 6000 feet and covered about thirty-five miles. Due to the soft snow, and my observations, it required fourteen and a half hours, but, except for a pretty keen appetite, I was as fresh as when I left camp.

On reaching home I heard voices and found that Professor Parker and Aten had also been successful on their quest and had purchased some provisions from two generous miners named Clark and Pink who were camped about twenty miles below us. Finding Clark and Pink was a piece of good luck, for Glacier, and Diamond City had long been abandoned. From these men they heard that the sled trail we had seen was made by a party sent out by a Fairbanks newspaper to climb Mount McKinley. This party failed to find a climbable route and returned to Fairbanks before our arrival.

With ample food, plentiful signs of big game, and our route to Mount McKinley decided on, we lost no time in pushing forward. We camped the first day near a little lake in the caribou-hills and pitched our tent on a moss-carpeted hill where the sun had melted the snow.

The following day we reached our base camp on a little stream that ran into one of the four main forks of the Clearwater River.

Seventeen caribou trotted across our line of march and gathered in a picturesque band on a bluff to survey our party. Ptarmigans were about us in millions and rabbits hopped about through the willows, while our eager dogs strained vainly in their attempts to give chase; but it made the sleds go faster, and Aten suggested that "if we could get a rabbit for a 'leader' we would have the fastest dog team on the Kantishna." While we were pitching our tents we saw fourteen caribou feeding up the valley beyond our camp, and the snow was punched through with moose tracks—we were in a big game paradise.

Immediately after our arrival I began a series of long reconnaissance trips among the snow-covered mountains that lay between us and the glacier that we had chosen as a roadway to the base of Mount McKinley. My object was to discover if the left-hand valley that I had explored on my long reconnaissance trip from the McKinley Fork was in reality the best pass. There were several valleys lying west of the one I had seen that might offer a better route for freighting.

On the first day I chose the highest and most westerly valley and it was during these long days spent among the desolate mountains that I became acquainted with the caribou of the region. At this particular time of year (April) most of the bulls were in the lowlands, but almost every high mountain valley sheltered a band of cows. On one occasion I was snowshoeing up a high snow-filled valley when I saw a cow caribou about a mile away. As I advanced I began to see others—some feeding, but most of them lying down, and I used great caution as I thought that there would be some bulls among so large a band.

I spent at least an hour in making the stalk, and finally I reached a point among some boulders where there were caribou all about me except to leeward. Seeing that I could go no farther without being seen, I lay still enjoying my wild surroundings. I have always, when watching wild animals at home, been struck with the seeming peacefulness of their lives. I thought of the years that the animals about me had spent in feeding, lying down, getting up, and feeding again, just as they were doing then. Once in a great while tragedy happens; a snow slide, a rock slide, a bear, a wolf, or a man takes one of their number, and then come more days of absolute quiet and rest. As I lay there watching I sympathised with that curiosity which leads so often to their undoing, and I felt that if I were a caribou I would investigate every interesting or unusual thing that came within my vision. My thoughts were interrupted by the approach of a meddlesome old cow. She must have been a great-great-grandmother at least, for, with her extreme age, she carried herself with a stiff dignity that was amusing.

When she was only twenty feet away and I saw that there was no longer a chance of remaining unseen, rose slowly to my knees and in the most polite manner of which I was capable, said: "Hello, Carrie, where are all the bulls?" I have never seen an animal assume so ludicrous a look of surprise, combined with outraged dignity, and for a moment she stood stiffened in her track, and then, with a deep grunt of disapproval, she turned and trotted stiffly down the valley. The other caribou that had been lying or feeding all about me took a keen interest in the old cow's actions. They evidently thought that anything that could make the old cow run so fast must be terrifying in the extreme, and so in a moment they were all under way. The old cow stopped at times to gather others about her, and at regular intervals the band would stop, as caribou always do, stare indignantly in my direction, and then run on to another band. In this way the individuals gathered into small bands, and these in turn amalgamated until they had formed a large herd that contained twenty-four cows, and after a last long look the herd wound like a great brown snake across a snowy ridge and left me alone to resume my reconnaissance.

On the following day I explored the central valley, and as I snowshoed upward through a narrow cañon, I saw nine caribou lying on a moraine below me.

On returning from the head of the cañon I wormed my way between the rocks until I was within rifle shot of the band, and, getting out my binoculars, settled down for an interesting half-hour.

Through my powerful glasses I could see every detail, and movement of these interesting animals. The thing that interested me most was that they were in a place where in all probability no man ever been, and in a country that is seldom hunted, and yet they were always on the alert. They were lying on gravel or snow, and their siesta time at this time of year seems to be between 11 A.M. and 4 P.M.

They sometimes lie as horses do, with their heads flat on the ground, and I have seen them yawning, as horses do, when the sun was hot. At this time of the year (April 27th) every cow, with the exception of a few very old animals, carried antlers.

Alfred Brooks, in his account of his trip along the range, speaks with surprise of finding a caribou high up among the snow-fields, but after studying these animals I have found that most of the caribou spend the summer among the ruggedest snow-capped mountains; stranger still, were I to take my experiences in the Alaskan Range as representing the usual conditions of affairs, I would be forced to say that the caribou of the region ranged higher than the mountain sheep, for *it so happened* that I saw caribou higher up than I saw sheep, and I likewise saw quantities of caribou tracks higher up than I did those of sheep. But while it is true that the sheep in general range higher on an average than do the caribou, the fact remains that in the Alaskan Range caribou frequently range as high as the mountain sheep. This fact holds good at all seasons and does not depend on their migratory instinct leading them across high passes, as the large quantities of cast antlers and the deep worn caribou trails among the high snow-fields bare witness. In fact, the only accurate descriptive title for these animals is that of *Mountain Caribou*. One must be very careful in studying the habits of animals not to take the actions or habits of One animal as representing its kind, and it is on this account that the value of a statement depends on the experience of the observer. In studying these caribou I had the advantage of an intimate knowledge of other caribou in different ranges, and while I saw many interesting occurrences among these animals, I put them down to individuality unless their frequent re-occurrence warranted their being classed as habits of this species.

While my scouting trips did not swell our larder as I saw nothing but cow caribou, they resulted in the discovery of three passes by which we could reach the glacier. Of these three, the central pass, which we called "Glacier Pass" for purposes of identification, was the best.

## CHAPTER XXIV

# To 11,000 Feet *with a* Dog Team

*We decide to use dogs in our first advance—Aten remains at base camp—Night travel—The first serac—Crevasses—Snow-storms—The big serac—LaVoy falls down a crevasse—We find a snow bridge over a large bergschrund on the big serac—We reach the top of the big serac—Cold—Earthquakes—Avalanches—We reach 11,000 feet—We see the Central North-Eastern Ridge—Our outlook hopeful—We cache our provisions—Return to Glacier Pass—Return to base camp.*

We reached our base camp on the evening of the 24th of April and just four days later our advance on Mount McKinley began. Our idea was to make a reconnaissance in force with a dog team. What we would accomplish would depend entirely on the kind of "going" we found, but we figured that the dogs would be a help in pulling our freight up the glacier.

Our mountain food consisted of:

Pemmican (man): 102 lbs.
Hardtack: 3-32 lb. cans
Sugar: 30 lbs.
Raisins: 30 lbs.
Chocolate: 7 1/2 lbs.
Alcohol: 15 gals.
Pemmican (dog): 75 lbs.

In equipment, we carried one mountain tent, mountain rope, ice-axes, ice-creepers, alcohol lamps, aneroid barometers, hypsometers, thermometers (mercurial and spirit), anemometer, binoculars, prismatic compass, etc. Our outfit complete weighed in the neighbourhood of six hundred pounds. Aten remained at base camp, to feed the extra dogs and look out for things. He also read the thermometer and barometer twice daily.

On reaching the head of "Glacier Pass" we decided to lie over until night came and to do our travelling then as the snow would be firmer. We had our fill of pemmican and tea at 10 P.M. and then we struck out over the frosted surface of the great glacier, which we called the McKinley Glacier. A more appropriate name for this fork of the Muldrow, as well as its sister on the East, would be the Tennally Glacier, as they come directly from the ice-falls of the big mountain, and feed the country of the Kantishna's, whose name for the mountain, as I have stated before, was Tennally. The night travel was picturesque and beautiful in the extreme and as I looked back our procession made a weird picture. We had donned the mountain rope for good as the glacier was badly crevassed. I broke trail, followed by Professor Parker, who was in front of the dogs. LaVoy was at the gee-pole of the sled.

Professor Parker was roped to LaVoy, but we took care to keep the rope free from the sled as its weight was sufficient to carry us with it had it broken through the crust into a crevasse. About 11:30 the moon rose and its light looked almost golden against the deep blue shadows instead of silvery as it does in the Southland.

We crossed tracks of grizzly bears that were leaving their winter dens high up among the ice-falls of the upper glacier. We reached the base of the first serac at 3 A.M. and we were glad to rest as it was bitterly cold and we had made good progress. After a cat-nap LaVoy and I made a trip to the top of the serac. We told Professor Parker that we would return in an hour, but we had not yet begun to appreciate the difficulties of travelling on the McKinley Glacier. There were countless crevasses and I was forced to sound every foot of our trail with my ice-axe, and although I used the greatest caution, I broke through into several ice caverns, but was saved by the rope from any serious accident. After we had been absent from camp for two hours, Professor Parker became worried, and thinking that the trail that LaVoy and I had made would be perfectly safe, he started after us. He had only gone a short distance, however, when the trail itself caved in. Luckily, he caught himself with his hands as the crevasse was not wide, or he might have suffered a dangerous injury, or, probably, come to an end of his climbing career.

In the afternoon LaVoy and I took the dogs and hauled a good load to the summit of the serac. Near the head of the ice-fall we were forced directly under the avalanche-polished walls of the Central North-Eastern Ridge, but when we had to cross areas that were swept by snow-slides we studied our chances carefully and crossed at the most favourable time.

The McKinley Glacier rises in steps, like a giant stairway. We rose about 1000 feet while climbing the first serac and then an almost level plain of snow lay before us. Crossing this blinding ice-field, we pitched our camp at the base of a tremendous serac that rose in two great cliffs with a narrow platform between. It was a wild-looking spot! Great blue cliffs of solid ice, scarred here and there by black rock, rose 4000 feet above us, and while we staked down our tent a snow-storm whirled down from the upper peaks, blotting everything from view and wrapping us in a white mantle. Moving cautiously in the storm, LaVoy and I felt our way to the top of the first bench of the "great serac."

The western walls of this ice-fall were fed by the snow from the north peak of

CLIMBING THE BIG SERAC. THE SMALL SIZE OF THE FIGURES GIVES AND ACCURATE IDEA OF THE SIZE OF THE AVALANCHE DEBRIS.

Mount McKinley, and We were thrilled by catching a glimpse of the main wall of the mountain hanging high above us. On May 3d, we advanced to the top of this first bench and brought up all our belongings. We had now reached an altitude of 8500 feet. We had a hellish morning; our tent was in an accursed spot and we feared to move a step without being tied to the rope.

LaVoy fell into a crevasse when we were about to make camp. I made it a rule to lead as I was used to the treachery of the ice and being light of weight was less of a burden to handle if I broke into a crevasse, That morning, however, I felt an attack of snow-blindness coming on and asked LaVoy to lead. He was very careful at first, but on reaching a level bench he became over-confident and swung rapidly along without sounding with his axe. Suddenly the snow broke through and the fact that he had reached the centre of the crevasse before he fell resulted in his dropping a good distance before the rope became taut. When his weight came on the rope, it did so with crushing force. I was in the middle of the rope and was unable to hold my feet, as my snowshoes slid on the crust. At the time of the shock on the rope Professor Parker was carrying a large coil in his left hand. This hand had been weakened by a gunshot wound on one of our former trips and when the rope came taut with a snap the loose coil was snatched from his hand and he was unable to help. I will never forget the few seconds that followed while LaVoy's weight was pulling me towards the crevasse. I remember straining until my tendons cracked, and jabbing my ice-axe again and again into the hard crust. Just below we had had soft snow, but now, when soft snow would have been a boon, the crust had hardened so that I could not drive my axe home. I then braked with the head of my axe and when only six feet from the edge of the chasm I came to a stop. LaVoy was almost at a standstill at the time and I thought that I had stopped him, but after calling several times, he finally answered and told me to give him more rope, as he was on a ledge of ice that protruded from the ice wall. I will always wonder whether I would have stopped him *without the aid of that ledge!* After anchoring myself firmly I had a talk with LaVoy and he told me that he could follow the ledge upward to a point where he saw light coming through the snow. And while I paid out the rope he made the ascent and it was a welcome sight when he pushed his head through the snow some thirty feet to my left. I examined the crevasse as soon as he joined us; it was about six feet wide and as far as I could tell it extended to China.

This experience did not tend to make us enjoy the glacier work, for we now knew that even with the rope on we were in danger and that a large party would be required to make exploration of this glacier safe. I have heard many men speak of the thoughts that come to one when sudden death is imminent, and there is a popular idea that childhood scenes, or other happy moments, return and fill the mind. I can assure my reader that this is an idle theory for while we were sliding towards "kingdom come" LaVoy was wondering how deep the crevasse was and I was cursing the hard snow that would not grip my axe.

After LaVoy appeared, I took a photograph that shows him emerging from the crevasse, and we advanced thereafter with redoubled caution. We relayed our last load through driving snow and when nightfall came we were happy, for our altitude was now 8500 feet.

THE UPPER STEP OF THE GREAT SERAC

*We climbed on the left-hand slope by crossing a snow-bridge that overhung a large bergschrund.*

The day following was a "big day." The night before we had camped in driving snow and howling wind, surrounded by crevasses and a huge menacing serac rising one thousand feet sheer above us. Our chances of getting our dogs up the avalanche-scarred slopes looked slim indeed. The following day we made a reconnaissance in force and after I had broken into two crevasses we found a snow bridge across a yawning bergschrund, and after making sure that our dogs could cross, we reached the top. Then the sun came out. Our outside shirts were discarded, mitts thrown aside, and our benumbed feet came back to life under the blissful warmth. In the afternoon LaVoy and I hauled two sled-loads to the top of the worst pitch and backpacked three hundred pounds over the bridge that spanned the bergschrund. While climbing the serac, Dewey and Fritz, our two "wheel-dogs," fell into a crevasse and they were unconscious by the time we pulled them out, although they recovered quickly when we loosened their collars. Strange as it may seem, the heat of the sun had little effect on the air temperature. On this day, when our faces were blistering and the glacier was a blinding glare of white, the temperature was 33°, *or only one degree above freezing!*

We were welcomed by another snow-storm when we camped at the summit of the "great serac." We did not know it then, as the driving snow shut out all sight of the surrounding mountains, but our labours to reach the head of the glacier were nearly over. When the clouds broke away on the following morning, we could see the grim walls of Mount McKinley high above our heads, and it was only about three miles to the end of the great amphitheatre where our glacier had its birth. We had risen 1175 feet in climbing the second step of the "great serac" and our camp was now at an altitude of 9675 feet, or nearly half-way up Mount McKinley.

We were not to have everything our own way, however, as a second snow-storm swept down the glacier and the new snow banked up by the ton on the mountainside made our returning under the great cliffs for our equipment a dangerous enterprise. Later, we were glad indeed that we had chosen the wiser course.

To understand the unpleasant side of what happened, one must have gone through the days of anxiety that we had known; we had fallen through treacherous snow into blue-black crevasses and edged breathlessly over precarious snow bridges, until we came to feel that we were never safe and that at any moment the snow might give beneath our feet with the familiar sickening feeling of a dropping elevator. Our position on the edge of the ice cliffs that fall away for more than a thousand feet added also to the terror of what happened. It was after lunch; Professor Parker was sleeping and LaVoy and I were talking in whispers while we listened to the rattle of storm-driven snow across the sides of our frail shelter. Suddenly we felt the glacier under us give a sickening heave and the nearby mountain thundered with avalanches. For an instant I thought that an ice cave had broken in with us, or that the serac was falling and taking us with it! But in a moment we were undeceived for another shock came, and as the thought *earthquake* flashed through my mind and pulsated under the force of the countless avalanches. It was an awful and terrifying sound, and we were glad when the echoes ceased and we once more heard the dreary sound of wind and snow.

The following morning we awoke in a cloudy world, but it was clear enough for LaVoy and myself to go down the back trail for our freight. The tent was thick with frost when we awoke, but we thought little of the cold until we began to travel and then our rubber shoe-packs froze. When we returned to camp an hour later the temperature had risen considerably but the thermometer still registered 10° below zero. We advanced immediately through a heavy snow-storm and broke a trail well up into the great gathering basin, and in the afternoon we hitched up the dogs and relayed a good load forward.

It cleared a little between snow flurries and on reaching the end of our morning's trail we left the dogs and broke forward to the top of the last serac on the McKinley Glacier.

We finally reached a point where we could study the whole sweep of the great North-Eastern Ridge and to our delight we saw a low col, or break in the ridge, that could be reached easily from our glacier and the ridge itself looked climbable all the way to the big basin between the two highest peaks of the big mountain.

We drew the following conclusions: As we had now attained an altitude of 11,000 feet, our camp on the col, or lowest portion of the ridge, would be close to 12,000 feet, which would leave us between three and five thousand feet of climbing before we reached the big basin between the north and south peaks. This meant that we would have to return to our base camp with the dogs. They had been good and faithful servants, but they were already showing the effect of the altitude and we could not risk leaving them on the ice while we were climbing, for if we were held by a storm they would perish.

We were highly elated by the promising appearance of the great ridge, and although we would lose some time in returning with the dogs, our chances were improving as the days were growing longer. Indeed, for the first time we felt confident of conquering the mountain. We were not so foolish as to belittle the task ahead of us, although we could see no natural climbing difficulties that we did not feel able to overcome. It was the "unknown dangers" that filled our minds with vague forebodings of hardships and difficulties. An altitude of 20,000 feet had never been attained so close to the Arctic circle, and we knew from previous experience that the hardships to be undergone at an altitude of only 10,000 feet on this northern giant were far more severe than those encountered in climbing a 20,000-foot peak in the Andes of South America. We knew that the severest weather conditions ever recorded occurred on Mount Washington only 6000 feet above the sea, when a wind of 180 miles an hour was note with an accompanying temperature of 40° below zero! If these conditions could exist at 6000 feet, what might we not expect 20,000 feet up in the sky within 250 miles of the' Arctic circle? It was this feeling of uncertainty as to what might happen that made our attempt on Mount McKinley as exciting a sporting proposition as the heart could desire.

On May 7th we awoke to another day of bitter cold, and snow squalls were sweeping across the glacier. LaVoy and I drove the dogs to 11,000 feet through the storm and there we cached our trail sled, heavily loaded with food and mountain equipment, and securely lashed with ropes tautened over protecting caribou and mountain-sheep skins. As an added precaution I anchored the sled by driving an extra ice-axe between the forward braces deep into the snow.

The weather showed no signs of improving and as we would be unable to advance much farther with the dogs, and as every day of inaction meant just so many more rations of mountain food wasted, we decided to return to base camp at once. After a hasty lunch we packed up our belongings and started down the glacier.

For a short distance we had a faint trail to follow, but it disappeared at the base of the big serac. At first the dogs were able to follow it by scent, but they, too, were soon at fault.

Between the two cliffs of the great serac I had to begin sounding and trail-breaking and for seven hours we struggled against the worst glacier conditions that I have ever experienced. In the seven hours we crept down over six miles of ice and over the whole distance I sounded every foot that we advanced. On the middle serac the clouds closed down on us and then the snow fell, wrapping us in a chilling shroud and blotting out every mountainside and landmark. Crevasses were the least of our troubles. On the edges of the seracs the ice had formed great caverns, and avalanches had covered these caverns with a treacherous layer of rotten snow.

When I had located a crack I would make a hole with my ice-axe large enough for me to see which way the crevasse ran and at which point it "pinched out." The caverns, on the other hand, ran in no definite direction and as LaVoy was following with the sled and dog team, my responsibility was a great one. The last serac we crept over in darkness. We were six miles from Glacier Pass, night had fallen, and the driving snow had turned us—men and dogs alike—to dim, white forms, so we decided to camp. We had only two hardtack and one-eighth pound of pemmican between us. Luckily I had a piece of candle over which I melted a cup of snow water. After dividing our food scraps we rolled into our fur robes.

The next morning was brighter, and as our trail was downhill Professor Parker rode the sled and we jogged down to Glacier Pass in fine style. There we broached our cache and filled up on hardtack, tea, and sugar, and after a nap we struck out for base camp, which we reached in the evening of May 8th!

CHAPTER XXV

# Days at "Base Camp"

***Our dogs chase caribou with a loaded sled—The wild life at the base of Mount McKinley—Photographing caribou and sheep—The band of rams—A grizzly bear visits our camp—"Nervy Nat"—Hunting adventures—Rabbits—LaVoy is injured—The big avalanche—Preparations for the final climb.***

Everything had gone finely with Aten. He had killed one caribou and had fixed up our camp until it was positively luxurious.

After our return to Base Camp the time went by in a succession of delightful days.

It was our first sight of grass and flowers and running water in many months, as the lowlands had still been in the grip of winter when we started up the mountain. We took the most extravagant delight in our new life, for living on the ice is an unnatural and trying ordeal, and experience does not bring immunity from the dislike of it, as a man must steel himself to every new experience.

Judged by civilised standards, our life was anything but lazy; but after our ceaseless struggle against the blizzards and cold of the high snowbound ice-fields everything seemed easy.

We lived largely "off the country" and my days were filled with hunting big game or studying the topographical features of the magnificent mountain country that encircled McKinley. From the first we had been in no hurry to begin our final attack on Mount McKinley. Our early arrival had been due to the necessity of crossing the Alaskan Range while the snow was still in good condition for dog-sledding, but now, with a cache of 300 pounds of mountain provisions at 11,000 feet, we could take our time and wait for the days to lengthen as our chances would be better then.

While we were coming into the main valley on our return from Glacier Pass we were forcibly reminded that the caribou were still living in the vicinity. We had been having a hard time with our sled as most of the snow was gone, and we frequently came to large patches of bare stones where we had to put our shoulders to the sled to help the panting dogs. Suddenly they broke into shrill howls and dashed madly across the valley and as we sprang after them we saw three caribou trotting along the mountainside above us. The dogs' fatigue had disappeared, however, and they continued on their wild stampede until the sled jammed between two large boulders and brought them to a sudden stop. Our sled load was scattered "all over the scenery." Their strength in these moments of excitement was marvellous and they would pull a heavily loaded sled over rough ground and boulders, as if it weighed nothing. This method of "following the hounds" was exciting, but it had its drawbacks.

By the 10th of May, a few caribou cows had dropped their antlers, and the antlers of the bulls were beginning to form. The bulls moved but little while their horns were growing, and my experience leads me to believe that they usually fed at night or very early in the morning.

The caribou cows seemed less regular than the Behring Sea species *(Rangifer granti)* in dropping their antlers, for I saw individuals carrying apparently strong heads as late as the 4th of July. On the 26th of April, Professor Parker climbed one of the mountains near camp, and on his return he told us that high up on the snow-swept ridges he had encountered a cow caribou with a young calf, and photographed them at close quarters. We were greatly interested in the outcome of these photographs, and great was our delight after our return to civilisation to find that the photographs were a success.

On the following day Aten and I had an amusing adventure. We had made it a rule to have only one man hunting for meat, for if two men were hunting and both were successful, we would have a great store of meat in camp at one time and the chances of wasting it would be greater. But on this day we needed meat badly and as Aten and I had hollowed out an elaborate smoke house under the hill we knew that we could take care of an extra animal.

Aten started up the valley and I laid my course along the foothills of the range in a north-easterly direction. I saw no game until I was several miles from camp, and then I located three caribou above me on a steep mountainside. They were too far from camp and in too rough a place to make shooting worth while, and as I had nothing better to do, I began the stalk in the hope of getting a photograph. The animals were moving slowly along in the direction of our base camp, and they crossed in front of my last bit of cover within easy rifle range, and climbed a snow-field where I secured a long range photograph which shows their surroundings well. As they continued to travel towards camp I followed them, taking care that they did not see me. While they were climbing a hill I would lie flat behind a rock or bush, and when they disappeared over the skyline I would trot along in their tracks until I could see them again. We had covered a mile or more playing this exciting game of hide-and-seek when we reached the large valley where our camp lay. The caribou trotted down the long hillside, crossed the rushing stream, and stopped to feed by a little hill within one hundred yards of our tent. The chance was too good to lose, and I ran downward, forded the ice-cold stream, and began to crawl through the low willow brush. I was afraid that the caribou might smell our camp, but the wind held true, and in a short time I was in easy rifle range. Rising to my knees I aimed at the fattest and shot. The animals were standing in thick brush that hid the lower portions of their bodies, and left me only a narrow strip of their backs to aim at, and in consequence I fired several shots before I secured my quarry.

As I stopped shooting I heard a slight noise behind me and turning around, I was surprised to see Arthur Aten. He was standing as I was with his rifle at "the ready" and a disappointed look in his face, which soon turned to one of amusement. He was walking towards camp when he caught sight of the caribou, and as they were crossing the valley and moving in his direction, he hid himself in the brush ahead of their line of march, and was on the point of shooting when I arose from the brush ahead of him and "turned my artillery loose."

We often saw caribou feeding near our camp, and in the evening after the day's labours were done we loved to lie full length in the soft moss on some hilltop and smoke our pipes and watch for game. One day towards the end of our stay a great bull caribou, with his horns in the velvet, walked slowly past our camp in broad day-light, and strangely enough, he paid no attention to us although he was only one hundred yards away, and the wind was blowing towards him. He knew perfectly well that we were there, for he raised his head several times and looked the camp over, but instead of breaking into a run, as we expected him to, he would lower his head and stalk onward at the fast, swinging walk peculiar to caribou.

Although we shot as few animals as possible, I spent all my time wandering through the mountains with my gun and camera. The mountain country at the northern base of Mount McKinley is the most beautiful stretch of wilderness that I have ever seen, and I will never forget those wonderful days when I followed up the velvety valleys or clambered among the high rocky peaks as my fancy led me. In the late evening I have trotted downward through valleys that were so beautiful that I was forced against my will to lie down in the soft grass and drink in the wild beauty of the spot, although I knew that I would be late to supper, and that the stove would be cold.

The mountains were bare of vegetation, with the exception of velvety carpets of green grass that swept downward from the snow-fields; in the centres of the cup-shaped hollows ran streams of crystal clear water; as the sun sank lower and lower the hills would turn a darker blue, until the cold, clean air from the snowfields would remind you that night was come and that camp was far away.

During my wanderings I travelled or studied through my glasses every vale and mountain between the tongues of Peters and the Muldrow glaciers. I know of no joy comparable to that of wandering aimlessly among the mountains. You may lie for an hour watching a ground squirrel trying to build a bear proof burrow, and move off at last filled with amusement at his fright on discovering you, and the abuse that he chatters from the protection of his hole.

As you walk along you may be attracted by the antics of a willow ptarmigan who tries to entice you from the vicinity of his nest. Knowing that his brown mate is setting near by, you allow him to lead you until he flies away with derisive cackles. Then is the time to double back quickly, using your ears and field-glasses, until you hear the happy pair talking over the ease with which you were duped, and if your ears are sharp and you have located the sound aright, you may creep up and see the rare sight of a ptarmigan sitting on her eggs.

I found two nests which I was careful not to disturb, and later LaVoy and I returned and photographed them. Even about camp there was always some wild bird or animal to watch. During our first trip on Mount McKinley, Aten had succeeded in taming a Gambel's sparrow. The little bird formed the habit of flying into our tent at all hours, and he became so bold that Aten named him "Nervy Nat." We always kept a few crumbs on hand, and he would alight on our knees or feet, and make himself at home generally. On one occasion he had a severe lesson, for he made the mistake of *alighting on the hot stove!* Several days went past before he would venture inside the tent, and when he did begin to visit us again, he always gave the stove a wide berth! In time the rabbits grew accustomed to our presence and grew so bold that we had to see that nothing that they would eat was left lying about the camp. We paid a price in learning what they would eat, for we finally came to the conclusion that they would eat anything. Our axe handles were decorated with their tooth-marks, they ate the soap we left by the brook, and on one occasion one of my undershirts which I had just washed and hung on a low willow bush to dry was destroyed during the night.

One day we were all lying in the sun on our little hilltop when a rabbit hopped out into the gravel bar looking for a place to cross the creek. He studied one place critically, and we watched him hopefully, for it was a broad part of the brook and would have made a difficult jump. Odds were offered that he could jump it, when he changed his mind, and choosing another place, gave a tremendous leap and—landed in the water. He went off shaking his wet feet, followed by our laughter. On the same day three big bull caribou and a cow paid us a visit. We saw the first caribou calf on May 16th, and I found that these caribou were not nearly as regular in dropping their young as are the Grant's caribou of the Behring Sea coast, for we saw very young caribou a month or more later; whereas on the coast of Behring Sea the young are usually dropped within a period of two weeks. It is probable, however, that no two seasons are necessarily alike in this respect.

The migrations of this caribou were a matter of great interest to me, and I lost no opportunity to learn what I could on this subject. The results of my observations have convinced me that during the months of April, May, June, and July the caribou of that region do not migrate in any particular direction. Whether some of the bands do or do not later in the year can only be decided by careful observations at some future time, altho' the indications I saw again led me to believe that no general migration occurs. The animals I know, are found all along the northern side of the Alaskan Range during the rut. This would mean that they remain in the vicinity between the month of July, when my observations ceased, and October. In addition to this knowledge I found quantities of bull caribou antlers both at high and low altitudes along the range. While I do not know at just what time the males of this species shed their antlers, they cannot differ greatly in this respect from other caribou, which fact would place this shedding period well on towards the middle of the winter, or later than the time chosen by other caribou for making their general migrations.

On the first day of my arrival in the foothills of Mount McKinley, I found plentiful indications that there had been bears about, and during all my hunting I was constantly on the lookout for bruin. But while they were very scarce during our stay on the Clearwater River, I feel sure that at certain times in the year, probably when the blue-berries are ripe, they are quite plentiful. Our only experience with a bear occurred in camp.

I was washing the breakfast dishes one morning when Aten said: "Hand me the binoculars; I think there is something moving on the mountainside." I did so, and in a moment he added: "Big grizzly! coming this way!"

Excitement reigned and the dishes were forgotten. Aten generously told me to go after the bear, and I refused on the ground that the bear belonged to him, as he had seen it first. He answered that he had no use for a bear skin, and that he wanted me to get the bear. After we had talked it over some more I grabbed up my rifle and, after thanking Aten, started on the run for a little hill that lay in the bear's course. But it proved to be a case of "he who hesitates is lost," for the bear smelled our camp just before he was within good rifle range, and galloped up the mountainside. Now, the bear was very fat, and although I might have been able to hit him, I thought that I would get a better chance by following him. The country was open as far as the west branch of the Clearwater, and having moccasins on my feet I knew that I could make fast time, and I also knew, from two experiences, that I had had on the coast of Behring Sea, that a big bear would not travel very far without resting.

I waited until he had crossed the skyline and then I followed him. There were patches of snow lying over the uplands and the bear's tracks were as easy to follow as the white paper in a game of "hare and hounds."

Every time I crossed a valley I would climb the sky-line slowly and scan the country ahead, but always the tracks lay before me, and, finally, by the west fork of the Clearwater River, the tracks led downward into dense alder thickets and the chase "was up." This bear and the tracks of two grizzlies that we found on the upper glaciers were the only indications that we saw of the presence of these animals in the spring time on the northern face of Mount McKinley. The white sheep ranged everywhere on the northern face of the Alaskan Range. We even found them on the most northern of the north-eastern ridges of Mount McKinley, and on our return from the summit two ewes walked up to our last glacier camp and moved off slowly after satisfying their curiosity. They range low at all times of the year on the mountains near Mount McKinley, as the snow line is lower than it is to the east or west of the great mountain.

My diary for May 19th says: "May 17th was a hazy day, in fact for days past the haze has been growing deeper and deeper, till the mountains have hung like mirages in the sky, with nothing to suggest their rugged frameworks of rock and ice. In the evenings the skies have been the palest of greenish blues, almost grey, and the mountains have stood out very softly in their sunset colours. I started out early in the morning to try to find a bear, and carelessly left my binoculars in camp.

"About two miles from camp I saw some spots on a mountainside. The sun shining through the haze made it difficult for me to make out what kind of animals they were, as the band was a mile distant. Something, a 'hunch' may be, told me that the spots were mountain sheep, but my pessimistic, every day common sense said that they were caribou, for I had frequently seen caribou at a higher elevation on the same mountain.

"From force of habit I was taking in unconsciously every detail of the stalk, while my practical self was urging me to proceed up the valley in search of a bear. Finally my practical self won, and I moved forward, but always my inner self was whispering *Sheep!* and leading my feet behind sheltering hills and away from tell-tale air currents. So distinctly marked were my feelings that I became amused and humoured my inner self, until, on reaching the critical point of the stalk,—which was a shallow snow-filled trench that led upward across the mountainside,—I gave my feet free rein and surrendered to the overwhelming interest of a difficult approach. I should mention here that even if the spots were sheep, the chances were an hundred to one that they would prove to be ewes and lambs—which I would not have molested; but if the animals were rams—I would not have changed places with any man in the Western Hemisphere!

"It so happened that the stalk was blind, as I was forced to keep absolutely hidden during the entire approach, there being no cover on the mountainside. This fact kept me in total ignorance of what kind of beasts I was stalking until I had reached a point within two hundred yards of the point where the animals were lying. On reaching a small rock I took off my cap and raised my eyes slowly. One sheep was in sight—a young ram—and with the idea of at least seeing the rest, and possibly securing a photograph of the band, I dropped back into my little snow trench and began the difficult part of the stalk. It was an unorthodox approach, for I was stalking the sheep from below, but an unfavourable wind and great, smooth mountainsides above cut off all chances in that direction. Lying flat in the snow I wound my way upward. At times, by merely raising my eyes, I could see the young ram, and several times he stared fixedly in my direction, while I lay with my chin in the snow. After about three quarters of an hour creeping I reached a small boulder that proved to be my last cover. Lifting my head carefully I peered over, and then,—my heart pounded audibly in my throat,—for the tops of great curling horns showed above a little knoll, and I knew that I was within rifle shot of a band of rams.

"I sometimes think of the life in civilisation in comparison with the life in the open, for a man can live ten years of the ordinary existence in a large city without once experiencing the intense, overwhelming emotions that ten minutes of life in the wilderness often hold for him.

"After I had recovered my self-possession, I studied the band for the two largest heads, for we could not use more than the meat of two animals. There were six rams in the band; four old, battle-scarred veterans and two six-year-olds. They were lying in a difficult position for a shot, as a little bench cut off the view of the lower parts of their bodies, so that I only had a narrow strip to shoot at. My camera was about twenty feet behind me in the snow-trench.

"Having decided that I could not get closer to the sheep I pushed one foot forward, took a long sight from my knee, fired—and missed!

"With a great bound the band leaped to their feet and dashed up the mountainside. I shot again and missed, but this time I saw my bullet strike high, so holding lower I shot again and the largest ram fell. Turning at once to the rest of the band I singled out the sheep that seemed to carry the largest head, and had the satisfaction of seeing him drop to my first shot. With two large rams to my credit my thoughts flew to my camera, and I dashed back to the snow-gully and returned in time to make three exposures as the sheep crossed over the mountain.

"As I passed the first ram I photographed him as he lay and then proceeded to my second trophy, and after arranging him so that he would show to the best advantage, I exposed my last film. While I was putting my camera away I heard stones rolling on the mountainside above me, and looking up I saw one of the young rams coming back to the scene of the shooting. The first ram I had shot was lying below me and about seventy-five yards away, and the young ram galloped past me and stood by the ram's carcass. As I advanced he stood on the alert watching me. His graceful figure stood out clearly against the snows that draped the distant mountains, and for some time we stood quietly watching each other. He was not more than fifteen yards away, and I could see every movement of his lithe body and the slow rise and fall of his white sides as he regained his breath.

"We stood for a long time and gazed so intently at each other that it became embarrassing, and I was almost relieved when the ram moved and broke the tension. He moved slowly away and seemed to show no fear until I walked up to his fallen companion, and then he seemed to understand, for he turned and passed rapidly over the mountain.

"The heads were the typical shape of the species, as both had a wide spread. They were not large in comparison with other heads I have secured, but were of good size for the sheep of the Mount McKinley region. The largest head measured: outside curve 34 1/2 inches; circumference of base 14 1/2 inches. The second head was slightly smaller. In the cool of the evening LaVoy and I went back for the meat, with a sled and dog team. We pulled over the moss and heather while the sun sank through a crimson sky into the dim blue lowlands. Three caribou, one a great bull with massive velvet horns, swung over the mountain crest, while our dogs bayed furiously and strained at their tug-lines, and their baying echoed back and forth among the mountains until the silence slowly closed in again.

"The northern nights were beautiful beyond words. The sun sank only a short distance below the horizon, leaving a blue twilight that threw a veil of mystery over the valleys and mountains; the cool smell of the snows crept down from the grim ice-barriers of the main range, and the lowlands rolled away to the Yukon like a great blue sea."

Such was our life at the base of North America's highest mountain.

While the days went by we had kept one eye, as it were, on the big mountain, but the time passed so rapidly that the hours had stretched into weeks before we realised it and the day soon arrived that we had decided on as the date for our final attack on the big mountain. Our departure was delayed, however. LaVoy, while stalking a cow caribou and calf with his Graflex camera, fell on a sharp rock and cut his knee open to the bone. The cut was deep and the jagged rock had done such damage that I kept the cut open as long as possible and allowed it to heal by granulation. The delay, however, proved a benefit, for a villainous spell of weather overtook us and we were glad to be in a warm and comfortable camp. While LaVoy's wound healed successfully it gave him much discomfort and his work on Mount McKinley under this handicap redounds greatly to his credit.

Just before our final advance on the big mountain an event occurred that gave us cause for the greatest anxiety. I had been watching a cow and calf caribou on the rolling hills of the east fork of the Clearwater.

On my way home I stopped on a high mountain shoulder to look about me. From my high point of vantage I could look into the big basin at the head of the McKinley glacier and see the upper snow-fields where we had left our sled and its valuable load. I was standing idly studying the great mountain's contours when a white cloud drew my eyes to the stupendous ice walls that rimmed the basin. As I looked the cloud grew larger and larger until it stretched out in a straight line across the cliffs and I knew that I was watching an immense avalanche. When the great mass plunged into the basin a huge cloud of snow shot high in the air until the mountainsides 5000 feet above were hidden by the white pall. It was a larger avalanche even than the great sliding mass of snow that we had seen near the South-West Ridge of the mountain in 1910. Overcome with anxiety for our sled I waited breathlessly until the great cloud had disappeared, and in the interim I could hear the deep thundering of the fall rumbling back and forth among the mountains. When the view was clear I eagerly turned my binoculars towards the head of the glacier and to my inexpressible joy I could see crevasses crossing the snow-fields. If I could see the crevasses the chances were that our sled was not covered up beyond recovery, but when I reported the news to my companions they worried about the fate of our provisions.

## CHAPTER XXVI

# The Conquest of Mount McKinley

*We leave camp with Aten and a dog team—Aten and the dogs leave us—The snow-storms—The big avalanche—LaVoy hurts his knee in a crevasse—We find our sled—We advance to the col—Another blizzard—We advance up the ridge—Difficulties—Soft snow—We establish our ridge camp at 13,600 feet—We return for more food—We advance to 15,000 feet—We are made ill by pemmican—We advance to 16,000 feet—We advance to 16,615 feet—The Big Basin—The North Peak—We attack the Southern Peak, or summit—The storm—We reach 20,300 feet.*

It was on the 5th day of June that we began our final attack on Mt. McKinley. We took Arthur Aten and our dog team with us as far as the base of the first serac. It was a long, hard march and Aten remained all night, sharing my wolf robe. We awoke in a cloudy world and soon we were enveloped in a heavy snowstorm. Aten, fearful that he might be held by the storm, leaped on his sled and faded away into the white mist.

We now turned our minds toward back-packing our supplies to the head of the glacier where our sled and equipment were cached. Although we were travelling as light as we could we had all we could manage under the difficult conditions that we found on the glacier. The snow-storm continued for three days and we lay in our tent eating our valuable food and abusing the weather.

We were dumbfounded by the turn the weather had taken. All the mountains below us that had been practically free of snow when we arrived on the Clearwater River were now buried deep in snow. We knew it could not be the usual state of affairs for these same mountains were grass-covered. If every summer was a repetition of this one no grass could grow.

Under June 8th there is an interesting entry in my diary:

> *The glacier has been very noisy all day; it has groaned and cracked, and at short intervals there have been deep, powerful reports, sounding for all the world like the boom of big guns at a distance. We have been talking about this queer noise but are undecided as to its cause. It must be due to the settling of the great ice caverns under the tremendous weight of new snow.*

It was not until we reached civilisation long afterwards that we found that the unusual booming sound had not come from the glacial caverns, but that it was made by Katmai in eruption three hundred miles away—Katmai, the volcano whose eruption buried Kodiak Island in ashes! Later we found these Katmai ashes in our

SHOVELLING OUT OUR CAMP AFTER A THREE-DAYS BLIZZARD. THE BASE OF THE 1ST SERAC WHERE THE BIG AVALANCHE FELL.

THE GREAT AVALANCHE THAT FELL ABOVE OUR CAMP. IT IS ABOUT A MILE AWAY AND THE SNOW CLOUD SHOWN IN PHOTO IS ABOUT 1000 FEET HIGH.

teapot after we had melted snow, but again we accepted the easiest explanation and decided that the grit in our teacups was merely dust blown from the cliffs.

After the snow ceased falling we were held by good weather, for tons of snow hung poised on the steep cliffs and the route over the seracs under these avalanche-polished slopes was out of the question.

In order to make use of our time, LaVoy and I snowshoed six miles to Glacier Pass and brought back an extra allowance of alcohol, sugar, pemmican, and hard-tack. On our return we saw as fine an avalanche as it has been my luck to witness. It fell from the upper portions of the North-Eastern Ridge, for a distance of about three thousand feet, and when it struck the glacier it threw a snow cloud more than one thousand feet high. It was an awesome sight and we had to lower our tent quickly lest the terrific suction of air caused by the falling snow should do it damage.

We were in our tent at the time waiting for the avalanche to occur in order that we could cross the serac in safety. As the first deep rumbling reached our ears, we scrambled, cameras in hand, out of the tent door and luckily succeeded in getting some good photographs before the snow cloud buried us in its chill embrace. At one o'clock on this day (June 8th) our thermometer registered 46 degrees in the sun. This was the highest temperature recorded by us on Mount McKinley and it is interesting to note that the temperature in the shade at the same moment was only 26 degrees! The big avalanche was followed by countless others, until the very ice shook and the sound blended into the steady rumble of thunder.

After the snow had settled we commenced our arduous advance up the glacier. The new snow made travelling slow, and we were forced to break trail with light loads.

LaVoy's "game knee" gave him trouble, and while climbing the second serac he fell through into a deep crevasse while following in my footsteps, and injured his knee again. But after a good rest he was able to advance once more.

At this time we were under a great nervous strain; the constant lookout for crevasses and avalanches had a depressing effect on us, but we were also in great fear that an avalanche might have buried our cache of mountain equipment. I will never forget the excitement we laboured under as we ploughed slowly up over the last serac. Suddenly a tiny speck of black showed in the snow ahead, and running wildly forward we came to our precious sled. The tip of the ice-axe with which we had anchored it was the only thing in sight, and on shovelling away the snow, we found that the sled had been turned on its side by the terrific wind caused by the avalanche that I had witnessed from the Caribou hills beyond our base camp. The discovery of our cache was a great stimulus to us. Besides the necessary food and equipment we recovered many longed-for luxuries such as mountain sheep and caribou skins to sleep on, reading matter, and a pocket chessboard.

Our cache was on the right-hand side of the final amphitheatre. Looking across the glacier we could see an easy route leading to the col of the North-Eastern Ridge. Where the ridge sagged, its summit was only five hundred feet above the floor of the glacier. We were held once more by a blizzard, but the rest was not unwelcome and when the weather cleared we lost no time in advancing to the top of the col. Here we shovelled deep into the steep snow slopes close to the summit of the ridge. As we dug deeper we made a wall of the blocks of hard snow, and when our labours were completed, we were protected from storms and wind. One of our

THE HEAD OF THE MCKINLEY GLACIER. THE CENTRAL NORTH-EASTERN RIDGE IS SHOWN ON THE LEFT.

chief pleasures was the splendour of the mountain views. The glacier travel had been dangerous, but the dangers had been hidden and we missed the stimulation of being able to look out over the surrounding mountains, for we had been down in a deep ice-rimmed pit, where we were wrapped in chill clouds most of the time. But now everything had changed. Twenty steps from our tent and we could look out from the very top of the great Central North-Eastern Ridge. The first time that we reached the top of the col our breath was taken away by the awesome grandeur of the view. The walls on the southern side were as savage a lot of ice-clad precipices as the mind could picture.

We could not see the depths, for a sea of cold grey clouds rolled ceaselessly one thousand feet below us, and as we stood in awe watching them a shaft of sunlight stabbed the upper clouds and turned the grey sea to fire. Service's lines, "I have stood in some mighty-mouthed hollow, That was plum full of hush to the brim," came into my mind, and later when the clouds drew away we could look down almost straight to cold glacier depths two thousand feet below us.

In addition to the supplies that we had carried up the glacier, we had at our "col camp":

Hardtack: 18 pkgs.
Man pemmican: 11-6 lb. cans
Raisins: 23 lbs.
Sugar: 18 lbs.
Tea (Lipton): 1 lb.
Tea (tabloid): 1 lb.
Alcohol: 9 gals.
Chocolate: 7 lbs.

When we moved our supplies from the glacier to the col camp we had a steep climb of five hundred feet to negotiate, and at this point LaVoy found that on steep slopes of soft snow he could not depend on his knee. Now LaVoy's strength was one of the most important factors in our attempt on the great peak, and as his courage was of the highest quality I knew that his knee was in a serious condition. In all the glacier work I broke trail as a matter of course as my light weight and long

THE COL CAMP. ALTITUDE 11,000 FEET. WE DUG A DEEP HOLE FAR INTO THE SNOW TO PROTECT OUR FRAIL SHELTER FROM THE STORMS.

schooling in this work made it advisable. But LaVoy's help on the great ridge was invaluable and as I looked up over the towering, knife-edged ridge, my heart sank at the possibility of his knee being seriously injured. There was only one thing to be done and that was to make the work as easy as possible for him, so I carried most of the dunnage, although he chafed under the new régime and amply made up for his lack of activity by shovelling out the deep holes in which we set our tent. It was in carrying an eighty-pound load from the glacier to our col camp that I first noticed the effect of our altitude, although it only made itself manifest by a slight acceleration of my breathing.

Our col camp was at an altitude of 11,800 feet, according to Professor Parker's Hicks and my Green aneroid barometer.

On June 19th we made our first reconnaissance on the ridge. Our plan was to climb to the Big Basin between the two great peaks and the reader will see how little we appreciated the immensity of the task that confronted us. We took with us

Looking down on our col camp from 12,000 feet

*On the left is the glacier we ascended; on the right is the great chasm, falling away for 2000 feet to the eastern fork of the Muldrow Glacier.*

ample food for six days, and in addition, extra clothing, films, cameras, glasses, compasses, barometers, a prismatic compass and level, anemometer, etc. The following account of our day's adventure is taken from my diary:

> *June 19th. Back from a very hard trip. We climbed to 13,200 feet through the softest of snow over as sensational a ridge as I have ever been on. Some of the slopes that we traversed were 60° or more, for I measured one that overhung a 2000-foot drop off that measured 50° on the clinometer, and there were many that I could not measure because we were afraid to stay on them longer than necessary. I broke and chopped our trail for five hours, and in places I had to first stamp down platforms in the soft snow before I could reach a firm footing.*
>
> *LaVoy's knee stopped us at 13,200 feet. Now the question is can he travel to-morrow? If he can and it's a good day we will take our camp outfit and climb to the Big Basin, and return for the food that we left on the ridge at 13,200 feet.*

The above entry shows the optimistic view that I held concerning our reaching the basin. It was not until later that we realised to the full the gigantic size of the great mountain, as the next entry in my diary makes clear.

Looking down the great north-eastern ridge from about 13,400 feet

*June 22d. Ridge Camp, altitude 13,600 feet. Much has happened in the last three days. On the morning of the 20th we started out in the firm belief that we would reach the edge of the Big Basin and camp before nightfall. It took us three hours to reach the point where we had left our packs on the first day. It was an impressive spot. The ridge was so sharp that I had to chop off the crest to make room for our feet.*

*On the left the ridge dropped away at a dizzy angle for 5000 feet to the surface of the east fork of the Muldrow Glacier, on the right it fell away almost straight for 2000 feet; you felt as if you were flying. In this narrow ridge we had chopped deep holes to insure the safety of our packs. From the packs onward there were no steps at all, and although I had had to remake a large proportion of our steps during the three preceding hours I started on confidently and we began to creep up the great knife edge of snow. As the time went on I began to feel the effects of the terrific labour. LaVoy despite his willingness could not help me out as the steps were in soft snow and his knee was hurting him. After I had broken trail steadily for an hour, a rock that I had been working towards actually seemed farther away than when I started. As time went on the constant gazing upward along the white ridge into the sun's eye began to tell on me and by the end of the fifth hour I was snow-blind and completely done up. I saw no place level enough to camp and I supposed that we would find hard ice underlying the snow that would prevent our shovelling out a tent-site. I now knew that it would take hours to reach the basin, where we had figured in minutes, in fact I was beginning to realise what the mountain is—it is reared on such a gigantic scale that ice slopes that only look a few hundred feet high may be several thousand! At last I turned to my companions and told them that I was snow-blind and played out, and that I feared that I couldn't chop long enough to reach a camping place. About 100 feet above there was a slight sag in the snow slope below some rocks that were in their turn below the final rise of the ridge where it swoops up a thousand feet to join a rock peak that forms the southern gateway to the Big Basin.*

*After a council of war the Professor said, "Let's try to shovel a site in that sag above us." LaVoy, who was fresh, went to work and to our unbounded joy he struck hard snow instead of ice, and in the course of two*

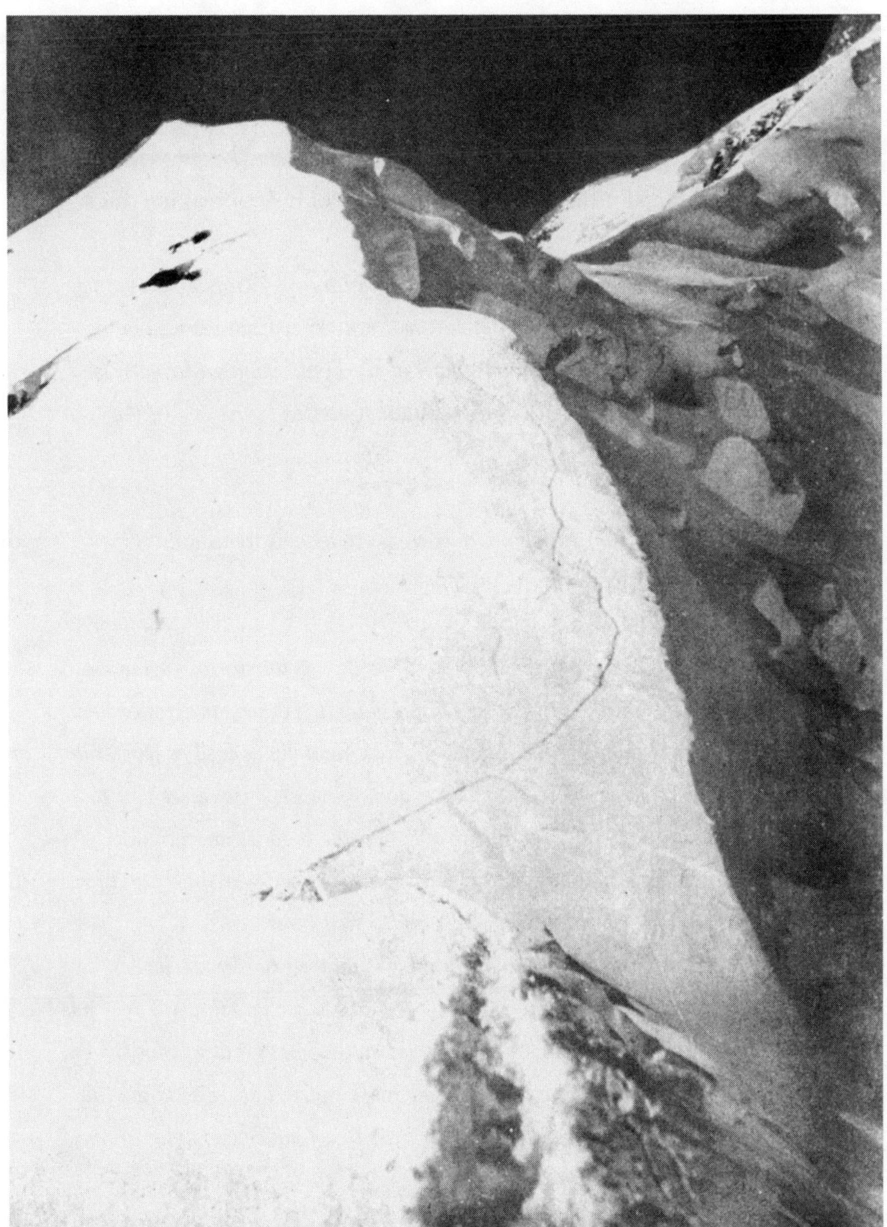

OUR ROUTE UP THE CENTRAL NORTH-EAST RIDGE SHOWING THE TRAIL.
*The making of this trail was heart-breaking work and every storm that swept the peak necessitated our re-breaking and chopping the steps. While the ridge appears to dip in places, the effect is due to the angle at which the camera was held. There are only two level places on the entire ridge.*

> *hours' hard work we had a shelter on the snow slope. We first picked the snow out with our ice-axes and then shovelled it out, the blocks rolling down 2000 feet from the little platform. While LaVoy was finishing up Professor Parker and I descended for the packs we had left on the first day. The distance was close to 500 feet and* it had taken me two hours of heart-breaking toil to lead the way up!
>
> *Went to bed suffering from my eyes, which LaVoy doctored with boracic acid and zinc sulphate, and sick at heart, as I now knew that McKinley was too big for us with our present food supply of six days' rations. Marvellous sunset as we looked over a sea of clouds that stretched to the end of the earth.*

The next entry tells of the final day when we were forced to change our plans and return for more food.

> *June 21st. Ridge Camp. Alt. 13,600 ft. Good day so we started (again) to pack some supplies into the Big Basin. After pounding down steps for an hour we reached hard snow! Oh! what a relief it was mentally as well as physically, for soft snow is treacherous stuff and on many of the steep traverses that we have made we have been afraid to speak for fear the reverberation of our voices would start the snow sliding. LaVoy came forward generously and for eight hours we chopped alternately, each taking half-hour turns.*
>
> *Now one of the strange laws of climbing is that the harder the leader works the easier it is for those who follow, for they can climb upward over five or six laboriously cut steps and then sit down on their axes and rest for five or ten minutes while the leader is chopping others. I enjoyed the rests to the full for it was the first time since I left Glacier Pass that I have been able to enjoy the climbing views.*
>
> *But the work was so difficult that after seven hours of continuous work with LaVoy chopping half the time we rose only 800 feet! We were again forced to leave our packs on a knife-edged ridge at an altitude of 14,400 feet. We were close to the great peak that forms the south gateway and we could just begin to see into the Big Basin!*

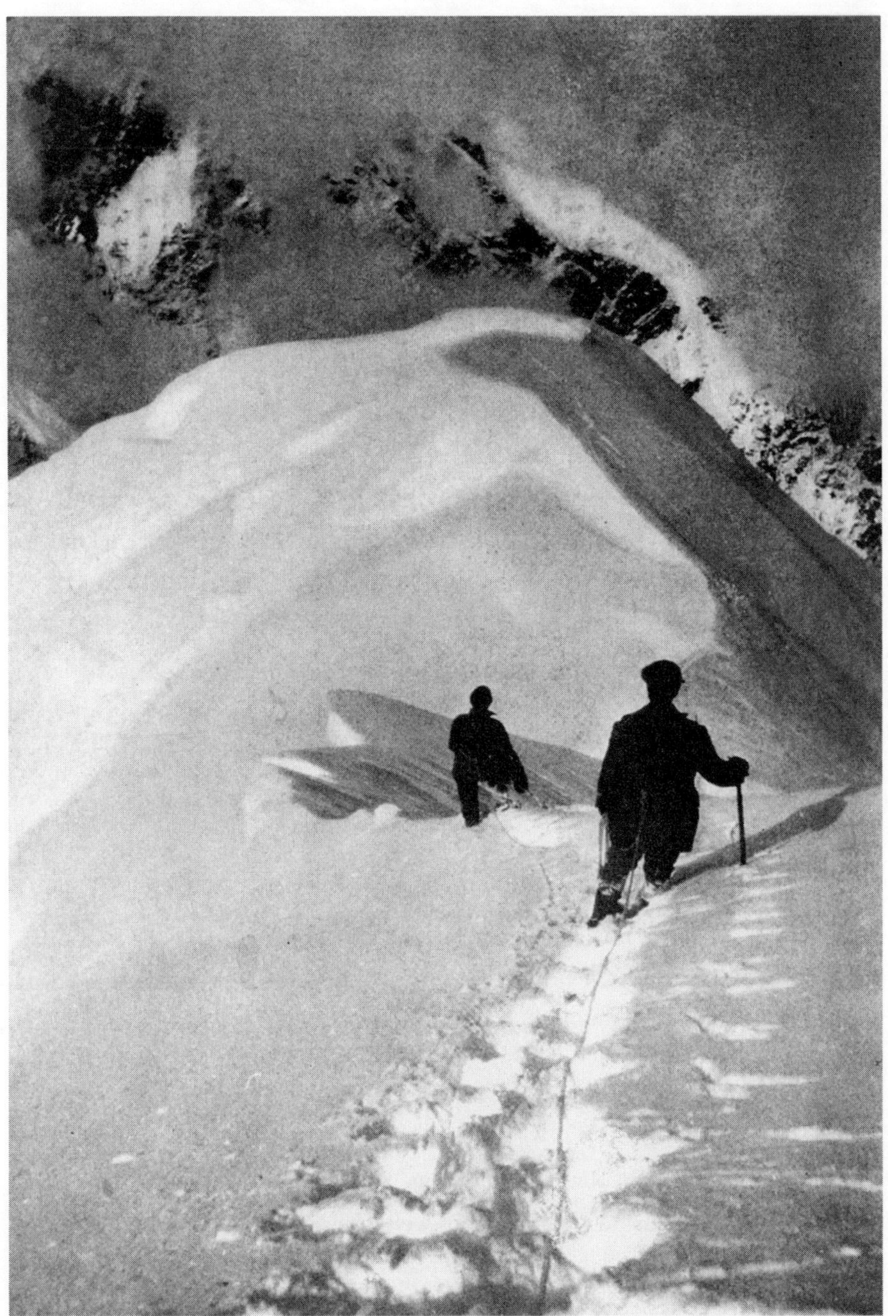

Looking down from 13,500 feet on the north-east ridge to the eastern branch of the Muldrow Glacier 6000 feet below

*On our return to camp we talked the matter over, and we decided that there was only one thing to do—namely to return to our col camp and pack up ten days' rations. It was a hard blow to us as it meant hellish labour, but it had to be done.*

*All day we have been above a sea of clouds—that may mean that we are at last above the bad weather. No ill effects from altitude yet, am enjoying my smoke as usual. Min. tem. June 21st, 4° below zero. June 22d, 3° below zero.*

These entries will give the reader an idea of the difficulty of our climbing, but in return we enjoyed mountain views of the utmost magnificence.

On the following day—June 22d—we were awakened by the howling of the wind, and on emerging from our tent we found clouds about us. As all we had to do to reach our col camp was to follow the steps on the knife-edge ridge we started down for our extra supplies. It was strange to think as we descended through the grey pall that within a few inches of our feet the ridge dropped away between two thousand and four thousand feet. Many of our steps were filled in solidly with drifted snow, but it was far easier to remake them on our way downward than it would have been while ascending with loads. In addition to our supplies at our ridge camp we packed up:

18 lbs. of pemmican
3 gals. of alcohol
9 boxes of hardtack
8 lbs. of sugar
3 lbs. of raisins
1/2 lb. of tea

We also brought our short "climbing" snowshoes as we thought they might be useful in the Big Basin. We figured on twelve days' food from our ridge camp at 13,600 feet. Coming over the narrow arêtes we were struck by heavy "wullies" or wind squalls that blew the snow in clouds off into space. We could hardly see each other at times, and we drove our ice-axes deep into the snow, and moved cautiously; it was spectacular climbing.

By this time we were awful objects to look at; LaVoy and I were always more or less snow-blind, from trail-chopping, and our eyes were swollen to slits and ran constantly; we were all almost black, unshaved, with our lips and noses swollen, cracked, and bleeding, our hands, too, were swollen, cracked, and bloodstained. As LaVoy said, we would have served "to frighten children into the straight and narrow path."

The following day was clear although the usual cloud carpet covered the lowlands. Taking our packs we again attacked the great ridge and nightfall found us triumphant at our ridge camp—we had dropped our loads under the "South Gateway Peak" at an elevation of 15,000 feet.

On the following day we advanced our camp to the shelter of the rocks, where I made the following entry in my diary:

> *"15,000-foot Camp."*
>
> *We have packed up heavy loads from our ridge camp in a little more than three hours as the steps high up were not badly drifted. It was frightfully hard work and glad we are to be camped in the lee of some great granite slabs, with the sun warming our tent. This is the wildest and most desolate spot imaginable. We are on the very edge of the Big Basin that divides the two summits of Mount McKinley. Below us all is mist and clouds; it seems as if the earth, thinking we needed her no more, had withdrawn from our lives.*
>
> *The Big Basin is glacier filled. There are three seracs, and between run easy snow slopes that promise an uneventful route to the base of the South Peak. All we have to do now is to traverse below the cliffs we are camped under, and we will be in the Big Basin.*
>
> *It seems strange to realise that we are camped higher than Mount Tacoma or the Matterhorn! We left enough alcohol and pemmican at ridge camp to last us on our return. We are wearing our snow glasses inside the tent now, and my eyes are so bad that I sleep with glasses on.*

In our 15,000-foot camp we were stormbound. An immense fall of snow occurred, and as we lay in our fur robes our ears were filled with the grandest natural music

View from the 15,000-foot camp

*The northern north-east ridge can be seen falling away into the cloud band that covers the lowlands during the summer months.*

that I have ever heard, for during one entire morning the great amphitheatres thousands of feet below us thundered and boomed under the constant shock of avalanches, and through this awesome bass ran the shrill theme of shrieking wind. McDowell has put the thunder of the surf breaking on jagged reefs into music, but no man yet has written the song of the avalanche and the mountain storm.

Now up to our 15,000-foot camp we had noticed the altitude in one important respect only—Professor Parker and LaVoy had been unable to eat their full ration of pemmican. Occasionally they let a meal go by without tasting it, and they attributed their inability to eat it to the fact that the pemmican was not good. I, however, suffered no inconvenience and ate as much as I wanted until I reached our 15,000-foot camp. On June 26th after the storm had passed we established a camp at 15,800 feet which we called our "16,000-foot camp." In the afternoon of the same day we advanced all our equipment with the exception of our camp outfit. That night I ate my ration of pemmican as usual, but a few hours after I began to suffer from abdominal cramps. The night was one long period of torture, and when morning came I made a vow that I would eat pemmican sparingly in the future. While the physical pain was bad enough the mental worry caused by our inability to eat pemmican was equally serious. Pemmican was our staff of life; on it we depended for strength and heat to carry us through the toil and cold of our high climb. Without it we would be reduced to a diet of tea, sugar, raisins, and a small allowance of chocolate, which was not enough to keep us warm, let alone furnish fuel for the hardest toil.

We were worn down to bone and sinew as it was and needed a strong food to give us strength; while we were as hard as iron we lacked the *rebound* that a well-fed man has—in the language of the training table "we had gone stale." We had learned too that it requires the same kind of energy to withstand bitter cold as is required in the accomplishment of hard physical work. Luckily, the average human being is an optimist; after worrying over the problem for an hour or two we decided that it was *uncooked* pemmican that disagreed with us and we dismissed the question after promising ourselves a pemmican pudding at our 16,000-foot camp.

THE 16,000-FOOT CAMP

*The northern end of the summit can be seen directly over the tent.*

Our progress upward through the Big Basin was uneventful except for the tremendous excitement we were labouring under. The cold too was intense. The leaves of my diary were so cold that I could not write without gloves. At our 16,000-foot camp with an alcohol stove going full blast and the warmth of our three bodies the temperature inside of our tent at 7:30 P.M. on the 26th of June was 5° below zero, and three hours later it was 19° below zero!

It was at this time that we began to devote ourselves to the study of how to conserve our body heat.

I have in the earlier part of my story given the weights of our different sleeping-bags, and as I can speak more accurately of my own experiences I will state the method I followed in trying to get a night's sleep.

My sleeping-bag weighed seventeen pounds. It was large and made of the best blue or "black" wolf fur. When I was ready to sleep I first enclosed my feet in three pairs of the warmest, dry Scotch-wool socks. In addition I wore two suits of heavy woollen under-clothing. Then came heavy woollen trousers covered with canvas "overalls" which keep the wind from penetrating, and the snow from sticking to, the wool trousers. On my upper body I wore two of the heaviest woollen shirts made; they were of grey wool with a double back and large breast pockets that doubled the front thickness. Over these shirts I placed a fine woven Scotch-wool sweater, and around my waist I wrapped a long "muffler" of llama wool. The collars of my shirts were brought close by a large silk scarf, while the ends of wool socks covered my wrists. Over all I wore a canvas "parka," the universal Alaskan wind shield with a hood trimmed with wolverine fur. My head was covered with a musk-rat fur cap which covered my neck and ears and tied under my chin. My hands were protected by heavy Scotch-wool gloves covered with heavy leather gloves, and my feet were enclosed, in addition to the socks, by heavy soft leather moccasins. On retiring we melted the water for our breakfast tea for ice melts much quicker than snow and in this way we were able to warm the tent without a great waste of fuel. Despite the above elaborate precautions I can say in all honesty that *I did not have a single night's normal sleep above 15,000 feet on account of the cold!*

Professor Parker dressed more warmly than either LaVoy or myself. He wore at night a complete suit of double llama wool besides his mountain clothing, and yet he could not sleep for the cold, although Anthony Fiala, leader of the Ziegler Polar Expedition, slept comfortably in a duplicate of Professor Parker's bag, clad only in underclothes when the temperature was 70° below zero! This fact illustrates the comparative effect of cold between sea level and 15,000 feet close to the Arctic circle. This susceptibility to cold, and our inability to eat pemmican, was the only way in which LaVoy and I suffered from the altitude, although Professor Parker was weak and slightly nauseated on our final climb to the edge of the summit.

On the 27th of June we carried our packs in two relays to the top of the second serac between the two great peaks and camped just below the last serac that forms the highest point of the Big Basin. We arrived with our last loads after the sun had gone down, and I have never felt such savage cold as the ice-fields sent down to us. We were in a frigid hollow at an altitude (corrected reading) of 16,615 feet. On the north the great blue ice slopes led up at an almost unclimbable pitch between the granite buttresses of the Northern Peak. On the south frozen snow-fields swept gently to the rock-dotted sky-line of the Central North-East Ridge which led in an easy grade to the final or southern summit of the great mountain. LaVoy went to work with our shovel while I picked away the hard snow with my ice-axe. Despite our labours our feet and hands were beginning to stiffen as we pitched the tent and started our stove, and we were seriously worried for fear Professor Parker would freeze. On the next day we devoted our time to resting and making the most careful preparations for the final climb. My diary entry for the day follows.

> *"17,000-foot Camp" (our barometers placed us close to that altitude but the final readings of our hypsometer compared with our base camp barometer readings placed this camp at an altitude of 16,615 feet). Bitterly cold. Professor Parker feels the altitude. If it is clear we will "hit" the summit to-morrow. We only have 3,500 feet to climb. 3 P.M. same day—June 28th. Splendid loafing day—all well rested, and indications good for a fine climbing day to-morrow, but it has been blowing a gale on the upper snow-fields, although what few clouds have formed have been away below us. We will also be warm to-night as we will not get chilled making camp as we did yesterday. Have put in the spare time getting everything ready for the "big day." Last night was warm, only 8° below zero, so we are not so frightened by the weather, unless a blizzard strikes us, and then anything might happen. We feel somewhat like soldiers on the eve of a battle, for to-morrow promises to be a good day, and if it is it will be the final day of three seasons of endeavour and*

16,615-FOOT CAMP
*The highest camp ever made in North America. It was from this point that we made our two attacks on the summit.*

*several years of thought, planning, and hoping. If we "get there" we will be happy men. There is nothing to stop us except a storm. The route is easy; direct from camp to some rocks that lead to the summit of the ridge 1000 feet above us, thence along the ridge for perhaps a mile to the final dome which will give us perhaps 2000 feet of ice-creeper climbing, and then our dream will be realised. Robert Louis Stevenson says that only one thing in life can be attained—Death; but Robert never climbed a high summit after years of failure! We will rise at 4* A.M. *and start at 6, and we hope to make the climb at the rate of 500 feet an hour, or seven hours in all, and return in two—a nine-hour day.*

*8* P.M. *same day. Beautiful night, have just come in from studying the peak and weather—can look out over the north-east end of the range and see each peak and valley—also blue washes that mean timber 15,000 feet below us; wish we had some here!*

From our camp we saw the northern side of the horse-shoe-shaped summit. The main ridge that we were to follow led up to the northern *heel* of the horseshoe. There it rose to the almost level summit formed by the circular summit ridge. About one hundred yards from the very edge of the summit there was a slight rise, swelling, or hummock on the level ridge and this little hill is in all probability the highest point on the North American continent.

In both our 16,000- and 16,615-foot camps we had tried to eat cooked pemmican without success. We were able to choke down a few mouthfuls of this food but we were at last forced to realise that our stomachs could not handle the amount of fat it contained. The reader will, no doubt, wonder why we placed such dependence on one food and my excuse is that we put it to every proof except altitude in 1910. Fate ordained however that in that year we would not reach an altitude of more than 10,300 feet—close to the exact altitude where the pemmican began to disagree with us in 1912! Had we ascended a little higher we would have discovered this mistake in time to profit by it.

The morning of our final climb dawned clear as crystal. As I came out into the stabbing cold to report on the weather the whole expanse of country to the northeastward stretched like a deep blue sea to where the rising sun was warming the distant horizon.

True to our schedule we left camp at 6 A.M. Not a sound broke the silence of this desolate amphitheatre. At first the snow was hard and required little chopping. We moved very quietly and steadily, conserving our strength for possible exertions to come. At regular half-hour intervals LaVoy and I exchanged places, and the steady strokes of our axes went on with scarcely an intermission.

Between changes both Professor Parker and I checked off our rise in altitude and to our surprise we found that, although we thought we were making fairly good time, we were in reality climbing only 400 feet an hour. Close to the top of the big ridge 1000 feet above our camp we ran into soft snow and we fought against this unexpected handicap at frequent intervals during the day. When we reached 18,500 feet we stopped for an instant and congratulated each other joyfully for we had

A STUDY IN ALTITUDE (FIRST VIEW)
*The Muldrow Glacier and the top of the central north-eastern ridge as seen from 16,000 feet between Mount McKinley's two peaks.*

returned the altitude record of North America to America, by beating the Duke of the Abruzzi's record of 18,000 feet made on Mount St. Elias. Shortly afterward we reached the top of the big ridge. Sentiment, old associations, and a desire for a light second breakfast halted us in the lee of some granite boulders. We had long dreamed of this moment, because, for the first time, we were able to look down into our battle-ground of 1910, and see all the glaciers and peaks that we had hob-nobbed with in the "old days." But the views looking north-eastward along the Alaskan Range were even more magnificent. We could see the great wilderness of peaks and glaciers spread out below us like a map. On the northern side of the range there was not one cloud; the icy mountains blended into the rolling foothills which in turn melted into the dim blue of the timbered lowlands, that rolled away to the north, growing bluer and bluer until they were lost at the edge of the world. On the humid south side, a sea of clouds was rolling against the main range like surf on a rocky shore. The clouds rose as we watched. At one point a cloud would break through between two guarding peaks; beyond, a second serpentine mass would creep northward along a glacier gap in the range; soon every pass was filled with cloud battalions that joined forces on the northern side, and swept downward like a triumphant army over the northern foothills. It was a striking and impressive illustration of the war the elements are constantly waging along the Alaskan Range.

On the southern side hang the humid cloud-banks of the Pacific Coast, the very farthest outpost of the cloud armies of the Japan current; on the north stands the dry, clear climate of the interior, while between, rising like giant earthworks between two hostile armies, stands the Alaskan Range.

We absorbed these beauties as we wound back and forth between the granite boulders on the top of the ridge, and as we advanced the clouds began to thicken on the southern side, but through the deep blue chasms between, the well-remembered contours of the peaks we had explored in 1910—Beard, Hubbard, and Huntington—seemed like the faces of old friends.

A STUDY IN ALTITUDE (SECOND VIEW)

*The Muldrow Glacier from about 18,500 feet altitude on the central north-east ridge. In the left foreground lies the Big Basin. In the centre stands the lower end of the central north-east ridge which splits the Muldrow Glacier into two streams. We ascended the left-hand branch.*

THE SUMMIT OF MOUNT MCKINLEY FROM AN ALTITUDE OF ABOUT 18,600 FEET.
*The left hand end of the long ridge-like summit is lower on account of the foreshortening of the camera. The storm that increased to a blizzard began to blow just before this photo was taken. (From two photos by Belmore Browne)*

As we advanced up the ridge we noticed a shortness of breath and Professor Parker's face was noticeably white but we made fast time and did not suffer in any other way. At a little less than 19,000 feet, we passed the last rock on the ridge and secured our first clear view of the summit. It rose as innocently as a tilted snow-covered tennis-court and as we looked it over we grinned with relief—we *knew* the peak was ours!

Just above us the first swell of the summit rose several hundred feet and we found hard crust and some glare ice where our ice-creepers for the first time began to be of use. Up to our highest camp we had used rubber "shoe-packs" with leather tops, but on our last climb we wore soft tanned moccasins covered with "ice-creapers" of the Appalachian Mountain Club design.

From the time that we had topped the ridge the great northern summit of Mount McKinley had claimed our attention. It rose directly opposite to us and every detail of its ice and rock stood out in bold relief against the northern sky. Report has it that the Lloyd Mount McKinley party had reached this peak or one of its northern shoulders and there raised a pole above a pile of rocks.

On our journey up the McKinley Glacier far below we had begun to study this peak. As we advanced closer and closer each pinnacle of the Northern Ridge stood out in turn against the sky until on the last days close to the southern summit every rock and snow slope of that approach had come into the field of our powerful binoculars. We not only saw no sign of a flag-pole but it is our concerted opinion that the Northern Peak is more inaccessible than its higher southern sister.

During our ascent of the ridge and the first swell of the final summit the wind had increased, and the southern sky darkened until at the base of the final peak we were facing a snow-laden gale. As the storm had increased we had taken careful bearings, and as the snow slope was only moderately steep all we had to do was to "keep going uphill." The climbing was now about of the same steepness as that we encountered in scaling the ridge above our camp, and as the snow was driving in thicker clouds before the strengthening wind we cut good steps. The step chopping reduced our progress once more to the 400-foot an hour speed.

The slope we were attacking was a round dome that came to a point forming the top and beginning of the northern heel. Before the wind and snow blotted the upper snow-fields from view we had had a good view of the inside of the horseshoe which sloped down to wicked-looking seracs that overhung a snow-field far below. Our one thought therefore was to keep well to the north so that in case we got lost in a blizzard there would be less chance of our descending among the crevasses at the top of the drop off. To accomplish our desire we cut our steps in zigzags of about the same length.

When we started up the last slope above the first swell of the final dome we were at an altitude of 19,300 feet. At 19,300 feet LaVoy had begun his turn of chopping and as the lower portion of the summit was less steep than the upper slopes we succeeded in rising 500 feet during our combined turns at leading.

As I again stepped ahead to take LaVoy's place in the lead I realised for the first time that we were fighting a blizzard, for my companions loomed dimly through the clouds of ice-dust and the bitter wind stabbed through my "parka." Five minutes after I began chopping my hands began to freeze and until I returned to 18,000 feet I was engaged in a constant struggle to keep the frost from disabling my extremities. LaVoy's gloves and mine became coated with ice in the chopping of steps.

The storm was so severe that I was actually afraid to get new, dry mittens out of my rucksack for I knew that my hands would be frozen in the process. The only thing to be done was to keep my fingers moving constantly inside of my leather-covered wool mittens.

When my second turn was three fourths finished Professor Parker's barometer registered 20,000 feet. It would have been possible for him to set back the dial and get a higher reading but beyond this point it would have been dangerous to read the instrument had he been able too. The fury of the storm and the lashing clouds of steel-like ice particles would have made it next to impossible to read the dial.

On reaching 19,000 feet my barometer had registered within 100 feet of Professor Parker's, but as we rose higher my instrument—probably due to false compensation—had dropped with great rapidity to 17,200 feet, or little higher than our camp between the two peaks! From then until I returned to camp it was useless, but on the following day it "recovered its composure" and registered the same as Professor Parker's. Professor Parker's barometer behaved with absolute regularity throughout our whole trip, and as we had been able to study the last slopes carefully and could approximate accurately our speed in climbing, our calculations would place the summit at 20,450 feet or 150 feet higher than the United States Government triangulation. On leaving, and returning to, our base camp, both our barometers and a third that Aten had read twice daily during our absence agreed closely; and furthermore all three agreed closely with Brooks's and Reaburn's contour lines.

After passing the 20,000-foot level the cold and the force of the wind began to tell on me. I was forced several times to stop and fight with desperate energy the deadly cold that was creeping up my hands and feet. My estimate at the time for the last quarter of my period was 50 feet. As I stepped aside to let LaVoy pass me I saw from his face as he emerged from the snow cloud that he realised the danger of our position, but I knew too that the summit was near and determined to hold on to the last moment.

As Professor Parker passed me his lips were dark and his face showed white from cold through his "parka" hood, but he made no sign of distress and I will always remember the dauntless spirit he showed in our most trying hour. The last period of our climb on Mount McKinley is like the memory of an evil dream. LaVoy was completely lost in the ice mist, and Professor Parker's frosted form was an indistinct blur above me. I worked savagely to keep my hands warm and as LaVoy's period came to its close we moved slower and more slowly. Finally, I pulled my watch from my neck inside my "parka" hood, and its hands, and a faint hail from above, told me that my turn had come. In LaVoy's period we had ascended about 250 feet.

As I reached LaVoy I had to chop about twenty feet of steps before coming to the end of the rope. Something indistinct showed through the scud as I felt the rope taughten and a few steps more brought me to a little crack or *bergschrund*. Up to this time we had been working in the lee of the north heel of the horseshoe ridge, but as I topped the small rise made by the crack I was struck by the full fury of the storm. The breath was driven from my body and I held to my axe with stooped shoulders to stand against the gale; I couldn't go ahead. As I brushed the frost from my glasses and squinted upward through the stinging snow I saw a sight that will haunt me to my dying day. *The slope above me was no longer steep!* That was all I could see. What it meant I will never know for certain—all I can say is that we were close to the top!

As the blood congealed in my fingers I went back to LaVoy. He was getting the end of the gale's whiplash and when I yelled that we couldn't stand the wind he agreed that it was suicide to try. With one accord we fell to chopping a seat in the ice in an attempt to shelter ourselves from the storm, but after sitting in a huddled group for an instant we all arose—we were beginning to freeze!

I turned to Professor Parker and yelled, "The game's up; we've got to get down!"

And he answered, "Can't we go on? I'll chop if I can." The memory of those words will always send a wave of admiration through my mind, but I had to answer that it was not a question of chopping and LaVoy pointed out our back steps—or the place where our steps ought to be, for a foot below us everything was wiped out by the hissing snow.

Coming down from the final dome was as heartless a piece of work as any of us had ever done. Had I been blind, and I was nearly so from the trail chopping and stinging snow, I could not have progressed more slowly. Every foothold I found with my axe alone, for there was no sign of a step left. It took me nearly two hours to lead down that easy slope of one thousand feet! If my reader is a mountaineer he can complete the picture!

Never in my life have I been so glad to reach a place as I was when I reached the top of the first swell below the summit.

Had the cold that was creeping steathily upward from the tips of LaVoy's and my hands and feet once taken hold we would have frozen in a few minutes, and the worst part of our fight on the summit was the fact that we were fighting a cruel danger that was *unseen!* In the cañon of the Yentna in 1906, where Barrill and I had been forced to take our lives in our hands ten times in less than an hour, it was a fair open fight against the rushing water, but in a fight against a blizzard you are struggling blindfolded against a thousand stabbing ice daggers.

Our troubles were not over, however, when we reached the base of the final dome, for here there were no steps and in descending through the hissing clouds of ice-dust I was led by the wind alone. Again I might have accomplished as much while blinded for my only guide was the icy blast striking my right shoulder. Had the wind shifted we would have perished, but after what seemed hours a dim shape loomed through the storm it was the highest rock on the great ridge and our route was now assured. Finding the first rock ended our first struggle on Mount McKinley's summit, for in descending we kept in the protecting lee of the great ridge. When the gale quieted enough to let us, we talked! We cursed the storm that had driven us back. LaVoy said that we had done enough in getting on top of the mountain, and that we had climbed the peak because it was only a walk of a few minutes from our last steps to the final dome. This was true, but unfortunately there is a technicality in mountaineering that draws a distinction between a mountain top and *the* top of a mountain—we had not stood on *the top*—that was the only difference! We reached camp at 7:35 P.M. after as cruel and heart-breaking a day as I trust we will ever experience.

On the following day we could not climb. Almost all our wearing apparel down to our underclothes was filled with the frost particles that had been driven into our clothing by the gale.

I have spent my life in the open and through the handling of sailing craft have learned to approximate the velocity of wind as accurately as the next man. Professor Parker and LaVoy too were both men who had had much experience in the judging of wind. The *most conservative* of our estimates of the climatic conditions we fought against was a wind of fifty-five miles an hour and a temperature of 15° below zero. During the entire climb LaVoy and I were free from any ill effects from altitude with the exception of moderate shortness of breath, and Professor Parker suffered little more. LaVoy and I both found that the use of our arms in step cutting was far more exhausting than leg work. I rolled and smoked a cigarette at 18,000 and 19,000 feet, and enjoyed the tobacco as I do in lower altitudes. Had the storm allowed me to, I would have smoked on top of the mountain. LaVoy had never used tobacco in any form. Professor Parker is a light smoker and discontinued the use of tobacco while he was at high altitudes.

The drying out of our clothing was a difficult task as we had only one alcohol stove. To add to our difficulties LaVoy and I both developed an attack of snow-blindness from our siege of step cutting and all day long the stabbing pains shot through our temples. Fate too ordained that the peak should be clear, although long "mares' tails" of snow stretching out to the north told us that the gale was still lashing the summit.

## CHAPTER XXVII

# The End of the Long Trail

***We prepare for our second attempt on the summit—We reach 19,300 feet—Again we fight with a blizzard—Our food gone, we retreat to the 15,000-foot camp—We reach the col camp—We retreat down the glacier—We arrive at Glacier Pass—Our anxiety concerning Aten—We reach base camp—We rest after our exertions—The earthquake—We start for the Yukon.***

Throughout the long day after our fight with the summit we talked food and weather conditions. We had now given up all thought of eating pemmican and were living, as in fact we had been living since leaving our 15,000-foot camp, on tea, sugar, hardtack, and raisins. Our chocolate was finished. We had cached our pemmican as we advanced according to the daily amount we were able to choke down, and we found on studying the matter that *we had lost ten days' rations in useless pemmican since leaving our 13,600-foot camp!* In our highest camp alone we had lost four days' rations! We were not only harassed by the thought of the food we had lost, but also by the memory of *the useless weight we had carried*. Moreover, we were forced to eat more of our hardtack and raisins in an attempt to gain the nourishment we had been deprived of by the loss of our pemmican.

This complication reduced us to four meagre day's rations, which meant that we could only make one more attempt on the summit of Mount McKinley, and that attempt must be made on the following day.

The reader will realise with what breathless interest we studied the weather conditions. What had caused the storm on the summit? we asked each other. Was it a general storm sweeping in from the Susitna Valley, or was it a local *tourmente*

THE SUMMIT OF MOUNT MCKINLEY, FROM AN ALTITUDE OF 19,000 FEET.
*The highest point of the mountain can be seen just to the right and apparently below the peak. We were two hours and a quarter reaching our highest point, 20,300 feet, shown by dotted line. This photograph was taken on our second attempt to reach the summit. Clouds of snow and a furious wind turned us back on this attempt after we had reached 19,500 feet. Our steps chopped on the first day's climb could be seen leading to the nearest summit when this photo was taken. In clear weather, perhaps five minutes of easy walking would have taken us to the highest point. (From three photos by Belmore Browne)*

caused by change of temperature? Similar questions filled our minds, and we decided to leave at 3 A.M. on our next attempt.

The following day, strengthened as far as our insipid food would allow, and with our eyes patched up by boracic acid, we started on our final attack.

The steps made on the previous day helped us and in four hours and a half or by 7:30 A.M. we had reached an altitude of 19,300 feet at the base of the final dome. From this point we could see our steps made on the first attempt leading up to the edge of the final dome, and from this point we also secured the photograph of the summit that appears in this book.

But our progress up the main ridge had been a race with a black cloud bank that was rolling up from the Susitna Valley, and as we started towards our final climb the clouds wrapped us in dense wind-driven sheets of snow. We stood the exposure for an hour; now chopping a few steps aimlessly upwards, now stamping backward and forward on a little ledge we found, and when we had fought the blizzard to the limit of our endurance we turned and without a word stumbled downward to our ridge. I remember only a feeling of weakness and dumb despair; we had burned up and lived off our own tissue until we didn't care much what happened! In a crevice on the highest rock of the main ridge we left our minimum thermometer; it, a few cans of frozen pemmican, and our faithful old shovel, are the only traces of our struggle on the Big Mountain.

We reached camp at 3 P.M. and after some hot tea we felt a wild longing to leave the desolate spot. Packing our necessities carefully we shouldered our light loads and struck off down the glacier. I turned on the edge of the glacier bench for a last look at our old camp. Stuck deep in the snow our battered shovel showed black above a foot-trampled blur, while above, the roar of the wind came down from the dark clouds that hid the summit.

The greatest difficulty that we had to overcome on Mount McKinley was the transportation of our tents and equipment. Moreover, we were constantly worried by the thought that we might reach a point on the mountain where it would be impossible to camp. Without a shovel, we could never have reached the dome of Mount McKinley.

The threatening aspect of the sky and the fear of being caught in a blizzard without sufficient food lent wings to our feet, and in about three hours, by the aid of our old trail which still held in places, we reached our 15,000-foot camp.

The drop to a lower altitude combined with a comparatively warm night allowed us to enjoy a delicious night's rest. We had spent seven days above 15,000 feet; six days above 16,000 feet, and four days above 16,615 feet. From the day that we left our 15,000-foot camp we had existed on tea, sugar, hardtack, and raisins. I need hardly add that we were glad to descend.

At our 15,000-foot camp we recovered our snowshoes and at 8 A.M. on the morning of July 2d we started down the Central North-East Ridge. My diary adds that it was a morning of "unmitigated hellishness" as we were enveloped in clouds and wind-driven snow. At 13,400 feet I went snow-blind again and walked off a cornice while leading, but as the thin edge broke under me I drove my axe home in time to keep the strain off the rope. In four and one half hours of continuous work we reached the col camp at 11,800 feet. We were a thankful group of men as we rested luxuriantly in our partly drifted in hollow.

After resting and drinking some hot tea we ate a little pemmican and after a second rest we dropped down to our sled at the head of the glacier. At this point LaVoy stated that he could pull one hundred pounds on the sled more easily than he could carry fifty pounds. I knew the glacier so intimately that I could lead over our back trail through anything but a "black" fog or a blizzard. We therefore loaded the bulk of our necessities on the sled and started down the glacier, LaVoy bringing up the rear with the loaded sled. We came down easily as far as travelling went, but our month's absence had seen a great change in the glacier and large crevasses had appeared all over; these and a heavy fog kept me on a wire edge, until, fearing that I would miss a narrow pass through a bad serac, we camped. As it was 8:30 P.M. we "called it a day's work" and turned, in for a sleep.

When we awoke the following morning we found ourselves in the exact centre of the pass I had hoped to find. Packing up quickly we crossed a second large expanse of snow, and so exact was our course that my axe rang on an empty pemmican tin that we had left on our former ascent of the glacier, and which had been buried by the snows. We came down over the big serac without trouble although numerous new crevasses gashed the steep slopes, but at the base, on the little bench where LaVoy had fallen into the crevasse, I went snow-blind again and we had to camp. Boracic acid and zinc sulphate patched me up once more, but a dense fog kept us in our little tent. We conserved our strength by resting and at 7.30 P.M. the fog lifted and we started downward again.

By this time I was suffering nervously from the constant strain and responsibility of choosing the way, and I made a vow that the next stop we made would be beyond the reach of the accursed crevasses. We travelled slowly but steadily; one by one the well-remembered landmarks passed by. At last at the head of the lowest serac a dim yellow stain in the snow drew my attention. It was so faint that looking down nothing could be seen, but squinting ahead it lay in a dim yellow line. I waited for a well-known crevasse to verify my wild hope, and then I yelled the joyful news to my companions—we had found our old trail! In places it crossed crevasses that had opened since we used it but on the whole it was a Godsend and it led us safely to the base of the last ice-fall.

Nothing remained now but the journey down the "flat" to Glacier Pass and we did not hesitate. The glacier surface had melted down to ice which had overflowed in places so that we broke through into the slush, but not a crevasse appeared. Several large streams rushing through the trenches they had worn in the solid ice gave us some trouble, but soon the bare mountainsides greeted our snow-tired eyes and at 3 A.M. we pulled our sled over the moraine and laid our tired bodies on soft warm earth. It was the first time in 30 days that we had lain on anything but snow or ice!

We finally summoned enough energy to eat a little and pitch our tent and then we slept "like dead men" until the afternoon. When we awoke there was a warm breeze blowing up through the pass, and with it came the smell of grass and wild flowers. Never can I forget the flood of emotions that swept over me; Professor Parker and LaVoy were equally affected by this first "smell of the lowland," and we were wet-eyed and chattered like children as we prepared our packs for the last stage of our journey.

All our thoughts were centred on Arthur Aten. We had told him that we would return in fourteen days and now our absence had stretched to twice that

SLEDDING UNDER DIFFICULTIES. WE USED A SLED WITH WOODEN RUNNERS AS LONG AS WE WERE IN MOSS COUNTRY. AFTER THAT WE PACKED THE DOGS.

number. Vivid pictures of possible accidents flashed through my mind and we made our last preparations in feverish excitement. Two mountain sheep came to within seventy feet of our tent and watched us in surprise before moving away.

LaVoy and I shouldered eighty-pound packs for our trip to camp and in our weakened condition we made "heavy weather" of it. The joy of feeling grass underfoot repaid us for all our troubles, however, and our concern for Aten drove us onward.

When we came out of the Pass into the valley of the Clearwater we encountered a band of fifty caribou and while we rested they trotted excitably about until by a concerted flank movement they caught our scent and floated like a great brown carpet across the mountainsides. So it went, in turns of long packs and short rests while the sinking sun flooded the western sky with gold. At last the old rock above our camp came into view and Professor Parker went ahead.

Then we saw a figure clear cut against the sky. Was it a man or a wild beast? was the thought that flashed through my mind, until a second smaller shape appeared—a dog! And our joyful yells echoed down the valley.

Aten came to meet us, tears of happiness running down his cheeks, and we forgot our stiff-necked ancestry and threw our arms around each other in a wild embrace, while over us, under us, and all around us surged an avalanche of woolly dogs.

Aten's month in the wilderness was a hard ordeal. For many weary days, with a mind tortured by thoughts of possible accidents, he had spent all his spare time on the rock lookout station with his binoculars sweeping the head of the valley where we were to come down out of the snow. We were happy men when we lay on our soft caribou robes in our storm-battered old tent talking of the days of our separation. In my long experience in the North I have never seen men who showed more signs of hardship than we did. My waist line has decreased from 30 in. to 23 1/2 in. during the month we spent on the ice, and Professor Parker and LaVoy were equally emaciated.

Our greatest cause for satisfaction was that whatever we had done had been accomplished by our own unaided efforts.

While we had been trying in vain to scale the *impossible* southern cliffs our friends had been urging us to hire Swiss guides. Not knowing the country as we did, they did not realise that with the exception of the few Swiss guides that had climbed in the Himalayas we could not have found men who knew the game as well as we did, and that guides would refuse to do the work of porters that we were called upon to do. Furthermore, in all the wilderness exploration, the handling of boats, rafts, horses, dogs, and securing meat, they would have been "cheechakos," and an added care.

But aside from this, Professor Parker, LaVoy, and I were moved by a desire to establish as Americans the altitude record of North America; there would have been little credit or satisfaction in paying a man from a foreign country to lead us to our goal. Although on account of climate conditions I am unable to call this book, *The First Ascent of Mount McKinley*, we are equally proud of our conquest of the great peak, for from the point where our ice steps stopped, the climbing ceased; from there onward it was a short walk to the goal we gave so much to reach. If Mount McKinley is ever climbed to the final dome the men who climb it will follow the very trail we pioneered, until, weather permitting, they walk the short

Clark's and Fink's placer mine on the Moose Creek

*From the point where we are sitting to the end of the box, the riffles are yellow with gold.*

distance upward along the gently sloping ridge to the little snow knoll that forms the highest point on the continent. Were it not for this fact we would not have rested from the task we tried so long to accomplish.

In the many strenuous days that we spent on Mount McKinley's ice and snow, we often longed for the peace and comfort of our base camp on the Clearwater. And yet it was in our base camp two days after our return that we were subjected to the strangest and most exciting experience of our entire trip.

It was the evening of July 6th. Professor Parker was resting inside the big tent. LaVoy, Aten, and I had been drying and airing our mountain tent and duffle and doing odd jobs around camp. The sky was a sickly green colour, and the air seemed heavy and lifeless. After finishing our work we rested in the heather and talked of our plans for our coming journey to the Yukon.

The sky reminded me of sinister skies that I had seen on the eastern seacoast before heavy storms, and I turned to Aten and said that were I on a boat I would overhaul the ground tackle and see that everything was snug because it looked like "dirty weather." The words were scarcely out of my mouth before a deep rumbling came from the Alaskan Range. I can only compare the sound to thunder, but it had a deep hollow quality that was unlike thunder, a sinister suggestion of overwhelming power that was terrifying. I remember that as I looked, the Alaskan Range melted into mist and that the mountains were bellowing, and that Aten was yelling something that I could not understand and that the valley above us turned white and then the earth began to heave and roll, and I forgot everything but the desire to stay upright. In front of me was a boulder weighing about two hundred pounds. We had pulled it there with a sled and dog team to anchor our tent; it had sunk into the moss from its own weight, and as I watched, the boulder turned, broke loose from the earth, and moved several feet.

Then came the crash of our falling caches, followed by another muffled crash as the front of our hill slid into the creek, and a lake near by boiled as if it was hot.

The mossy surfaces of the hills were opening all about us, and as the surface opened the cracks filled with liquid mud, and then suddenly everything was still. We stood up dazed and looked about. The Alaskan Range was still wrapped in the haze of avalanche dust, and the country far and near was scarred, and stripped of vegetation where the earth had slid. Our dogs had fled at the beginning of the quake and we could hear them whimpering and running about through the willows.

OUR CAMP ON THE NORTHERN SIDE OF MOUNT MCKINLEY AFTER THE EARTHQUAKE OF JULY 6, 1912

Aten, with his pocket full of tobacco, was asking me impatiently for mine—and then we began to laugh. We ran to the tent to see how Professor Parker had fared, and then we howled again, for as we pulled the flaps aside it seemed as if everything that was movable, including the stove, had fallen in a heap. The stove had overturned and a great flat rock which we used as a base for the stove had moved towards the tent door.

While we were restoring order out of chaos, Aten, who was standing by the tent door, exclaimed: "Good God! Look at Brooks!" As we dashed out of the tent an awe-inspiring sight met our eyes. Just east of Mount McKinley stood a magnificent 12,000-foot peak. It was somewhat like the Matterhorn in shape, and formed the culminating pinnacle in a range some six miles in length that formed the eastern wall of the main eastern fork of the Muldrow Glacier. As this mountain was the finest peak east of Mount McKinley we were anxious to give it a worthy name and we decided to name it after Alfred Brooks, who had led the first survey party through this part of Alaska. While we were uncertain as to whether or not Brooks's name had already been attached to some other Alaskan mountain, we always spoke of the great peak as Mount Brooks. Now, as we reached the open and turned our eyes towards the mountain, we saw that the whole extent of the mountain wall that formed its western flank was avalanching. I have never seen a sight of such overpowering grandeur. The avalanche seemed to stretch along the range for a distance of several miles, like a huge wave, and like a huge wave it seemed to poise for an instant before it plunged downward onto the ice-fields thousands of feet below. The mountain was about ten miles away and we waited breathlessly until the terrific thunder of the falling mass began to boom and rumble among the mountains.

Following the inspiring salvos of nature's artillery came the aftermath we had learned to look for. Beyond the range that rimmed our valley a great white cloud began to rise. As it came into view and began to obscure the Brooks range we could almost check off its growth as it billowed upward with startling rapidity, two—three—four thousand feet until it hung like a huge opaque wall against the main range, and then it fell—the range that rimmed our valley was blotted out and the great wave of avalanche débris came rushing down our valley. We were already at work, strengthening our tent in frantic haste.

We knew that the cloud was advancing at a rate close to sixty miles an hour and that we did not have much time to spare. But with boulders to hold the bottom and tautened guy-ropes, we made the tent as solid as possible and got inside before the cloud struck us. The tent held fast, but after the "wullies" passed, the ground was spangled with ice-dust that only a few minutes before had formed the icy covering of a peak ten miles away!

Before we rolled up in our sleeping-bags, we took a last look about us. In every direction the earth and mountains were seamed and scarred and a great dun-coloured cloud of ice- and rock-dust hid the Alaskan Range. The streams, too, were flooding their banks, and ran chocolate-coloured from the earth-slides that had dammed them. As we compared our adventures and sensations, we thought of the band of fifty caribou that we had seen in the head of the valley—what a sight they must have presented when the earthquake struck them! Fifty wild beasts plunging, falling, and wild-eyed with terror—I would give much to have been on a hillside nearby!

The earthquakes continued at regular intervals for about thirty-six hours. None of them could compare in strength with the first shock, but many of them were severe enough to wreck a modern city. Strangely enough most of the shocks were preceded by a deep detonation. The sound resembled the noise made by exploding steam, and it came always from the same place—Mount McKinley. Experts on seismic disturbances have told me that the sound does not precede the disturbance, but in our case the reverse was true. We would be sitting in our tent, when suddenly the deep, explosive noise would reach our ears. One of us would say, "Here comes another," and if the explosion was of sufficient power we would take the precaution of seeing that our teapot was in a safe place. And then, after a few seconds had elapsed, the quake would reach us. After going through such an experience as the big quake, one realises, for the first time, the gigantic power of the forces of nature, and understands with what ease great mountain ranges have been formed.

My strongest impression immediately after the quake was one of surprise at the elasticity of the earth. We speak of being on "solid ground," but while the earthquake was occurring one felt as if the earth's crust was a quivering mass of jelly.

READY FOR THE 250-MILE TRIP TO THE YUKON
*The poling-boat that we found and repaired on Moose Creek*

With Mount McKinley's farewell salute still ringing in our ears, we turned our faces northward, towards the Yukon. We still had 250 miles of wilderness before us and our days were still full of the joyous incidents of the wild life.

Shouldering as much as we could carry, we put what was left on our faithful dogs, and wandered downward across the foothills looking for a likely stream to carry us to "the outside." We camped with miners on the banks of rushing streams where the gold lay yellow in the sluice-boxes; we drifted down silent rivers where leaping greyling flashed in the air; we camped on birch-covered flats, where moose, wet from the river, stampeded among our crazed dogs; and we floated past sun-drenched banks where Canada geese splashed, honking, from our path.

I would like to tell of the sun-bronzed "sour-doughs" who took us in, and lavished on us the riches of the land, Clark, Fink, Hauselman, and Dalton of Eureka Creek; of Mother McKenzie who built the log palace on Glacier River, and of the broad-backed Tanana that swept us to our journey's end. But I am loath to leave my old companions and our tent in "the happy hunting-ground." My patient reader has followed us over a long trail and it is better that we part there, high up among the caribou hills of the Alaskan Range, where to the southward, cloud-like against the blue, stands the mighty peak named by the Kantishnas in their wisdom—Tennally—The Big Mountain.

# Hudson Stuck: Triumph

*The Ascent of Denali* (1914) is the story of Hudson Stuck's successful ascent of Denali in 1913. At the time, opinions varied as to whether Stuck, Episcopal Archdeacon of the Yukon, had made the first ascent or, with the competing claims of Dr. Cook and the Sourdoughs, perhaps only the second or third triumphant ascent.

By the time Stuck and his companions were packing gear for their 1913 climb, Belmore Browne's book, *The Conquest of Mount McKinley*, had gone a long way toward discrediting Cook. Nevertheless, Cook still clung to his story, and so doggedly that he may have became self-delusional—believing his own fabrications.

The group of Fairbanks miners, who called themselves the Sourdoughs and set off to climb Denali in 1910, were also caught in the backwash of Cook's deceit. Their leader, Tom Lloyd, claimed that they had made the summit in 1910: but in the wake of the Cook scandal—and with no summit photos and some inconsistencies in Lloyd's story—few believed the Sourdoughs had come anywhere near the summit of Denali.

One observer said of this paroxysm of claims and counterclaims: "Lloyd denies Cook. Browne denies Cook and Lloyd. Stuck denies Cook and Lloyd, and, while not denying Browne, repeats over and over that Browne did not reach the top. There is a perfect epidemic of denials. So much so that it would be more accurate to nickname the peak Mount Denial instead of Mount Denali."

In any event, in the spring of 1913 Hudson Stuck was poised to make what he believed would be the first ascent. His quest was not to claim "the top of the continent," or make any sort of "conquest." For Stuck the summit was not so much an end in itself as a means to a greater goal. He hoped his ascent would bolster respect for Native Alaskans by having several of them participate in the climb. In addition to his trusted friend Harry Karstens, Stuck invited three young native men, including the good-natured and indomitable Walter Harper, to join the expedition.

Stuck also hoped to restore the name "Denali," by which Indians of interior Alaska knew this mountain that was such a physical and spiritual presence in their lives. For Stuck this was not an ancillary issue to be taken up with a board of geographic names. It was symbolic of everything that had been stripped from native people. And it went to the heart of why he climbed.

"It may be that the Alaskan Indians are doomed," he wrote. "It may be that the liquor and disease . . . will destroy them off the face of the earth; it is common to meet white men who assume it with complacency. Those who are fighting for the natives with all their hearts and souls do not believe it. But if it be so, let at least the native names of these great mountains remain to show that there once dwelt in the land a simple, hardy race who braved the rigors of its climate and flourished."

Hudson Stuck's *The Ascent of Denali* is a climbing story that rings with the excitement and perils of ascending this magnificent mountain for the first time. As Stuck tackled the final stretch to the summit, he climbed in the footsteps of his young native protégé, Walter Harper, who would be the first human being to set foot upon the top of Denali.

And so it is that within the drama of the ascent, there resonates another story. *The Ascent of Denali* holds us in the spell of Stuck's kind and gentle mind that sought to further the well-being of Alaska natives with his every step up the mountain.

*Art Davidson*

# THE ASCENT OF DENALI

## A Narrative of the First Complete Ascent of the Highest Peak in North America

---

**By Hudson Stuck, D.D.**

*Archdeacon of the Yukon*

*Containing the original diary of Walter Harper*
*First person to achieve Denali's true summit*

# CONTENTS

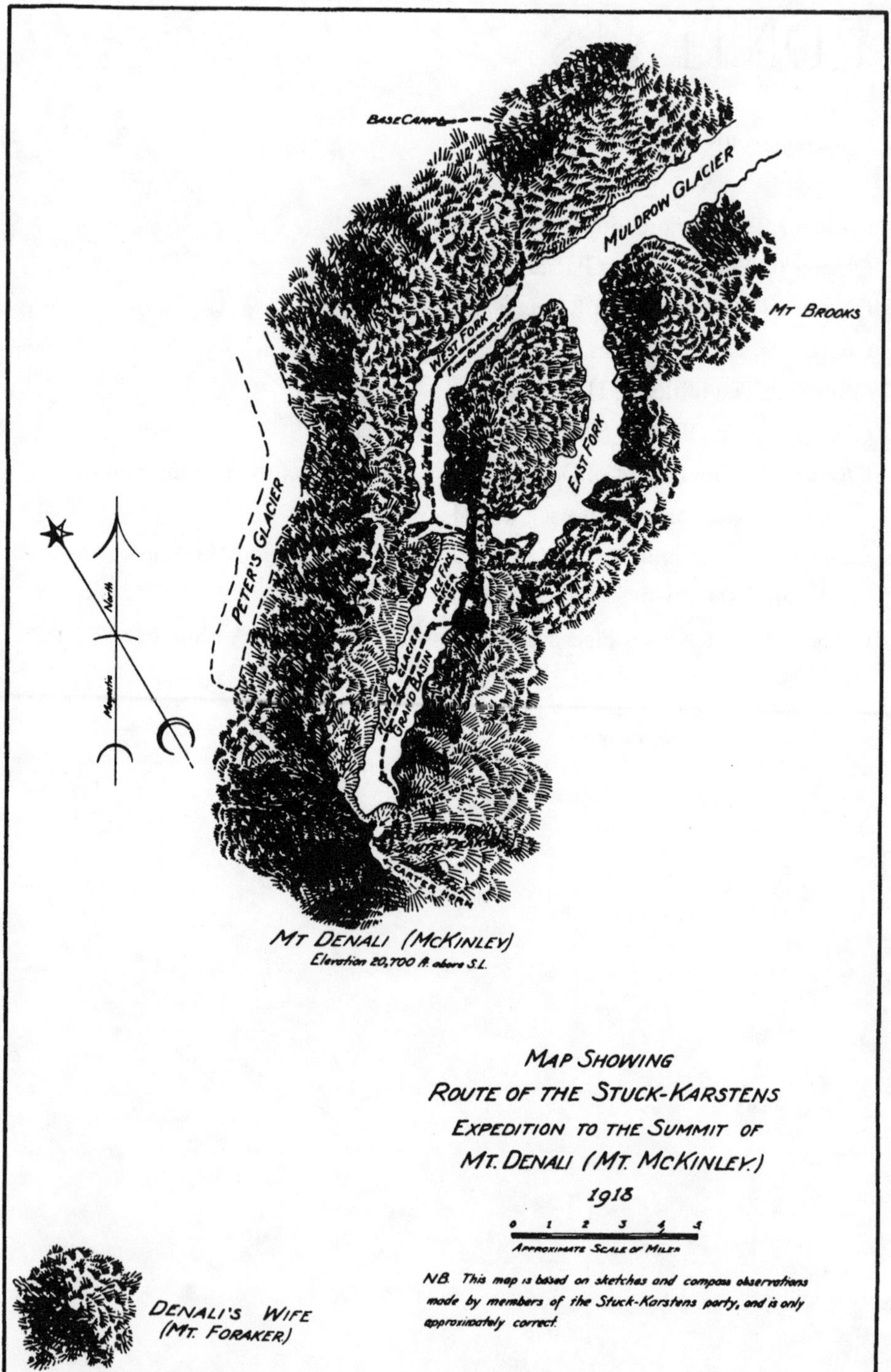

BASE CAMP

MULDROW GLACIER

WEST FORK

EAST FORK

MT BROOKS

PETER'S GLACIER

North

Magnetic

ICE FALL

GRAND BASIN

SOUTH PEAK

CARTER HORN

MT DENALI (MCKINLEY)

Elevation 20,700 ft. above S.L.

MAP SHOWING
ROUTE OF THE STUCK-KARSTENS
EXPEDITION TO THE SUMMIT OF
MT. DENALI (MT. MCKINLEY.)
1918

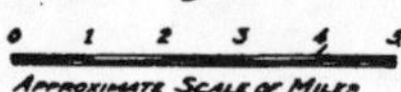


N.B. This map is based on sketches and compass observations made by members of the Stuck-Karstens party, and is only approximately correct.

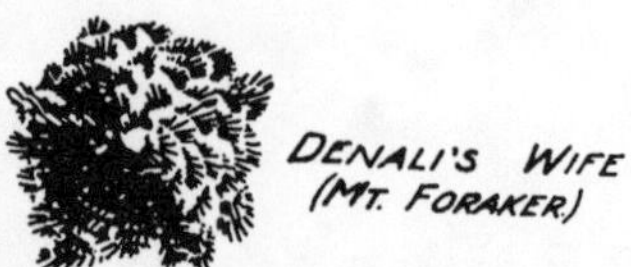

DENALI'S WIFE
(MT. FORAKER)

# PREFACE

Forefront in this book, because forefront in the author's heart and desire, must stand a plea for the restoration to the greatest mountain in North America of its immemorial native name. If there be any prestige or authority in such matter from the accomplishment of a first complete ascent, "if there be any virtue, if there be any praise," the author values it chiefly as it may give weight to this plea.

It is now little more than seventeen years ago that a prospector penetrated from the south into the neighborhood of this mountain, guessed its height with remarkable accuracy at twenty thousand feet, and, ignorant of any name that it already bore, placed upon it the name of the Republican candidate for President of the United States at the approaching election—William McKinley. No voice was raised in protest, for the Alaskan Indian is inarticulate and such white men as knew the old name were absorbed in the search for gold. Some years later an officer of the United States army, upon a reconnoissance survey into the land, passed around the companion peak, and, alike ignorant or careless of any native name, put upon it the name of an Ohio politician, at that time prominent in the councils of the nation, Joseph Foraker. So there they stand upon the maps, side by side, the two greatest peaks of the Alaskan range, "Mount McKinley" and "Mount Foraker." And there they should stand no longer, since, if there be right and reason in these matters, they should not have been placed there at all.

To the relatively large Indian population of those wide regions of the interior of Alaska from which the mountains are visible they have always borne Indian names. The natives of the middle Yukon, of the lower three hundred miles of the Tanana and its tributaries, of the upper Kuskokwim have always called these mountains "Denali" (Den-ah`li) and "Denali's Wife"—either—precisely as here written, or with a dialectical difference in pronunciation so slight as to be negligible.

It is true that the little handful of natives on the Sushima River, who never approach nearer than a hundred miles to the mountain, have another name for it. They call it *Traléika*, which, in their wholly different language, has the same signification. It is probably true of every great mountain that it bears diverse native names as one tribe or another, on this side or on that of its mighty bulk, speaks of it. But the area in which, and the people by whom, this mountain is known as

Denali, preponderate so greatly as to leave no question which native name it should bear. The bold front of the mountain is so placed on the returning curve of the Alaskan range that from the interior its snows are visible far and wide, over many thousands of square miles; and the Indians of the Tanana and of the Yukon, as well as of the Kuskokwim, hunt the caribou well up on its foot-hills. Its southern slopes are stern and forbidding through depth of snow and violence of glacial stream, and are devoid of game; its slopes toward the interior of the country are mild and amene, with light snowfall and game in abundance.

Should the reader ever be privileged, as the author was a few years ago, to stand on the frozen surface of Lake Minchúmina and see these mountains revealed as the clouds of a passing snowstorm swept away, he would be overwhelmed by the majesty of the scene and at the same time deeply moved with the appropriateness of the simple native names; for simplicity is always a quality of true majesty. Perhaps nowhere else in the world is so abrupt and great an uplift from so low a base. The marshes and forests of the upper Kuskokwim, from which these mountains rise, cannot be more than one thousand five hundred feet above the sea. The rough approximation by the author's aneroid in the journey from the Tanana to the Kuskokwim would indicate a still lower level—would make this wide plain little more than one thousand feet high. And they rise sheer, the tremendous cliffs of them apparently unbroken, soaring superbly to more than twenty thousand and seventeen thousand feet respectively: Denali, "the great one," and Denali's Wife. And the little peaks in between the natives call the "children." It was on that occasion, standing spellbound at the sublimity of the scene, that the author resolved that if it were in his power he would restore these ancient mountains to the ancient people among whom they rear their heads. Savages they are, if the reader please, since "savage" means simply a forest dweller, and the author is glad himself to be a savage a great part of every year, but yet, as savages, entitled to name their own rivers, their own lakes, their own mountains. After all, these terms—"savage," "heathen," "pagan"—mean, alike, simply "country people," and point to some old-time superciliousness of the city-bred, now confined, one hopes, to such localities as Whitechapel and the Bowery.

There is, to the author's mind, a certain ruthless arrogance that grows more offensive to him as the years pass by, in the temper that comes to a "new" land and contemptuously ignores the native names of conspicuous natural objects, almost always appropriate and significant, and overlays them with names that are, commonly, neither the one nor the other. The learned societies of the world, the geographical societies, the ethnological societies, have set their faces against this practice these many years past, and to them the writer confidently appeals.

This preface must bear a grateful acknowledgment to the most distinguished of Alaskans—the man who knows more of Alaska than any other human being—Peter Trimble Rowe, seventeen years bishop of that immense territory, for the "cordial assent" which he gave to the proposed expedition and the leave of absence which rendered it possible—one more in a long list of kindnesses which have rendered happy an association of nearly ten years. Nor can better place be found for a tribute of gratitude to those who were of the little party: to Mr. Harry P. Karstens, strong, competent, and resourceful, the real leader of the expedition in the face of difficulty and danger; to Mr. Robert G. Tatum, who took his share, and more than his share, of all toil and hardship and was a most valuable colleague; to Walter Harper, Indian-bred until his sixteenth year, and up to that time trained in not much else than Henry of Navarre's training, "to shoot straight, to speak the truth; to do with little food and less sleep" (though equal to an abundance of both on occasion), who joyed in the heights as a mountain-sheep or a chamois, and whose sturdy limbs and broad shoulders were never weary or unwilling—to all of these there is heartfelt affection and deep obligation. Nor must Johnny be forgotten, the Indian boy who faithfully kept the base camp during a long vigil, and killed game to feed the dogs, and denied himself, unasked, that others might have pleasure, as the story will tell. And the name of Esaias, the Indian boy who accompanied us to the base camp, and then returned with the superfluous dogs, must be mentioned, with commendation for fidelity and thanks for service. Acknowledgment is also made to many friends and colleagues at the mission stations in the interior, who knew of the purpose and furthered it greatly and held their tongues so that no premature screaming bruit of it got into the Alaskan newspapers: to the Rev. C. E. Betticher, Jr., particularly and most warmly.

The author would add, perhaps quite unnecessarily, yet lest any should mistake, a final personal note. He is no professed explorer or climber or "scientist," but a missionary, and of these matters an amateur only. The vivid recollection of a back bent down with burdens and lungs at the limit of their function makes him hesitate to describe this enterprise as recreation. It was the most laborious undertaking with which he was ever connected; yet it was done for the pleasure of doing it, and the pleasure far outweighed the pain. But he is concerned much more with men than mountains, and would say, since "out of the fullness of the heart the mouth speaketh, that his especial and growing concern, these ten years past, is with the native people of Alaska, a gentle and kindly race, now threatened with a wanton and senseless extermination, and sadly in need of generous champions if that threat is to be averted.

## CHAPTER I

# Preparation and Approach

The enterprise which this volume describes was a cherished purpose through a number of years. In the exercise of his duties as Archdeacon of the Yukon, the author has traveled throughout the interior of Alaska, both winter and summer, almost continuously since 1904. Again and again, now from one distant elevation and now from another, the splendid vision of the greatest mountain in North America has spread before his eyes, and left him each time with a keener longing to enter its mysterious fastnesses and scale its lofty peaks. Seven years ago, writing in *The Spirit of Missions* of a view of the mountain from the Pedro Dome, in the neighborhood of Fairbanks, he said: "I would rather climb that mountain than discover the richest gold-mine in Alaska." Indeed, when first he went to Alaska it was part of the attraction which the country held for him that it contained an unclimbed mountain of the first class.

Scawfell and Skiddaw and Helvellyn had given him his first boyish interest in climbing; the Colorado and Canadian Rockies had claimed one holiday after another of maturer years, but the summit of Rainier had been the greatest height he had ever reached. When he went to Alaska he carried with him all the hypsometrical instruments that were used in the ascent as well as his personal climbing equipment. There was no definite likelihood that the opportunity would come to him of attempting the ascent, but he wished to be prepared with instruments of adequate scale in case the opportunity should come; and Hicks, of London, made them nine years ago.

Long ago, also, he had picked out Mr. Harry P. Karstens, of Fairbanks, as the one colleague with whom he would be willing to make the attempt. Mr. Karstens had gone to the Klondike in his seventeenth year, during the wild stampede to

THE AUTHOR AND MR. H. P. KARSTENS

those diggings, paying the expenses of the trip by packing over the Chilkoot Pass, and had been engaged in pioneering and in travel of an arduous and adventurous kind ever since. He had mined in the Klondike and in the Seventy-Mile (hence his sobriquet of "The Seventy-Mile Kid"). It was he and his partner, McGonogill, who broke the first trail from Fairbanks to Valdez and for two years of difficulty and danger—dogs and men alike starving sometimes—brought the mail regularly through. When the stampede to the Kantishna took place, and the government was dilatory about instituting a mail service for the three thousand men in the camp, Karstens and his partner organized and maintained a private mail service of their own. He had freighted with dogs from the Yukon to the Iditerod, had run motor-boats on the Yukon and the Tanana. For more than a year he had been guide to Mr. Charles Sheldon, the well-known naturalist and hunter, in the region around the foot-hills of Denali. With the full vigor of maturity, with all this accumulated experience and the resourcefulness and self-reliance which such experience brings, he had yet an almost juvenile keenness for further adventure which made him admirably suited to this undertaking.

Mr. Robert G. Tatum, of Tennessee, just twenty-one years old, a postulant for holy orders, stationed at the mission at Nenana, had been employed all the winter in a determined attempt to get supplies freighted over the ice, by natives and their dog teams, to two women missionaries, a nurse and a teacher, at the Tanana Crossing. The steamboat had cached the supplies at a point about one hundred miles below the mission the previous summer, unable to proceed any farther. The upper Tanana is a dangerous and difficult river alike for navigation and for ice travel, and Tatum's efforts were made desperate by the knowledge that the women were reduced to a diet of straight rabbits without even salt. The famine relieved, he had returned to Nenana. The summer before he had worked on a survey party and had thus some knowledge of the use of instruments. By undertaking the entire cooking for the expedition he was most useful and helpful, and his consistent courtesy and considerateness made him a very pleasant comrade.

Of the half-breed boy, Walter Harper, the author's attendant and interpreter, dog driver in the winter and boat engineer in the summer of three years previous, no more need be said than that he ran Karstens close in strength, pluck, and endurance. Of the best that the mixed blood can produce, twenty-one years old and six feet tall, he took gleefully to high mountaineering, while his kindliness and invincible amiability endeared him to every member of the party.

The men were thus all volunteers, experienced in snow and ice, though not in high-mountain work. But the nature of snow and ice is not radically changed by lifting them ten or fifteen or even twenty thousand feet up in the air.

A volunteer expedition was the only one within the resources of the writer, and even that strained them. The cost of the food supplies, the equipment, and the incidental expenses was not far short of a thousand dollars—a mere fraction of the cost of previous expeditions, it is true, but a matter of long scraping together for a missionary. Yet if there had been unlimited funds at his disposal—and the financial aspect of the affair is alluded to only that this may be said—it would have been impossible to assemble a more desirable party.

Mention of two Indian boys of fourteen or fifteen, who were of great help to us, must not be omitted. They were picked out from the elder boys of the school at Nenana, all of whom were most eager to go, and were good specimens of mission-bred

TATUM, ESAIAS, KARSTENS, JOHNNY AND WALTER, AT THE CLEARWATER CAMP

native youths. "Johnny" was with the expedition from start to finish, keeping the base camp while the rest of the party was above; Esaias was with us as far as the base camp and then went back to Nenana with one of the dog teams.

The resolution to attempt the ascent of Denali was reached a year and a half before it was put into execution: so much time was necessary for preparation. Almost any Alaskan enterprise that calls for supplies or equipment from the outside must be entered upon at least a year in advance. The plan followed had been adopted long before as the only wise one: that the supplies to be used upon the ascent be carried by water as near to the base of the mountain as could be reached and cached there in the summer, and that the climbing party go in with the dog teams as near the 1st March as practicable. Strangely enough, of all the expeditions that have essayed this ascent, the first, that of Judge Wickersham in 1903, and the last, ten years later, are the only ones that have approached their task in this natural and easy way. The others have all burdened themselves with the great and unnecessary difficulties of the southern slopes of the range.

It was proposed to use the mission launch *Pelican*, which has travelled close to twenty thousand miles on the Yukon and its tributaries in the six seasons she has been in commission, to transport the supplies up the Kantishna and Bearpaw Rivers to the head of navigation of the latter, when her cruise of 1912 was complete. But a serious mishap to the launch, which it was impossible to repair in Alaska, brought her activities for that season to a sudden end. So Mr. Karstens came down from Fairbanks with his launch, and a poling boat loaded with food staples, and, pushing the poling boat ahead, successfully ascended the rivers and carefully cached the stuff some fifty miles from the base of the mountain. It was done in a week or less.

Unfortunately, the equipment and supplies ordered from the outside did not arrive in time to go in with the bulk of the stuff. Although ordered in February, they arrived at Tanana only late in September, just in time to catch the last boat up to Nenana. And only half that had been ordered came at all—one of the two cases has not been traced to this day. Moreover, it was not until late the next February, when actually about to proceed on the expedition, that the writer was able to learn what items had come and what had not. Such are the difficulties of any undertaking in Alaska, despite all the precautions that foresight may dictate.

The silk tents, which had not come, had to be made in Fairbanks; the ice-axes sent were ridiculous gold-painted toys with detachable heads and broomstick handles—more like dwarf halberds than ice-axes; and at least two workmanlike axes were indispensable. So the head of an axe was sawn to the pattern of the writer's out of a piece of tool steel and a substantial hickory handle and an iron shank fitted to it at the machine-shop in Fairbanks. It served excellently well, while the points of the fancy axes from New York splintered the first time they were used. "Climbing irons," or "crampons," were also to make, no New York dealer being able to supply them.

One great difficulty was the matter of footwear. Heavy regulation-nailed alpine boots were sent—all too small to be worn with even a couple of pairs of socks, and therefore quite useless. Indeed, at that time there was no house in New York, or, so far as the writer knows, in the United States, where the standard alpine equipment could be procured. As a result of the dissatisfaction of this expedition with the material sent, one house in New York now carries in stock a good assortment of such things of standard pattern and quality. Fairbanks was ransacked for boots of any kind in which three or four pairs of socks could be worn. Alaska is a country of big men accustomed to the natural spread of the foot which a moccasin permits, but we could not find boots to our need save rubber snow-packs, and we bought half a dozen pairs of them (No. 12) and had leather soles fastened under them and nailed. Four pairs of alpine boots at eleven dollars a pair equals forty-four dollars. Six pairs of snow-packs at five dollars equals thirty dollars. Leather soles for them at three dollars equals eighteen dollars; which totalled ninety-two dollars—entirely ill wasted. We found that moccasins were the only practicable foot-gear; and we had to put *five* pairs of socks within them before we were done. But we did not know that at the time and had no means of discovering it.

All these matters were put in hand under Karstens's direction, while the writer, only just arrived in Fairbanks from Fort Yukon and Tanana, made a flying trip to the new mission at the Tanana Crossing, two hundred and fifty miles above Fairbanks, with Walter and the dog team; and most of them were finished by the time we returned. A multitude of small details kept us several days more in Fairbanks, so that nearly the middle of March had arrived before we were ready to make our start to the mountain, two weeks later than we had planned.

Karstens having joined us, we went down to the mission at Nenana (seventy-five miles) in a couple of days, and there two more days were spent overhauling and repacking the stuff that had come from the outside. In the way of food, we had imported only erbswurst, seventy-two four-ounce packages; milk chocolate, twenty pounds; compressed China tea in tablets (a most excellent tea with a very low percentage of tannin), five pounds; a specially selected grade of Smyrna figs, ten pounds; and sugared almonds, ten pounds—about seventy pounds' weight, all scrupulously reserved for the high-mountain work.

For trail equipment we had one eight-by-ten "silk" tent, used for two previous winters; three small circular tents of the same material, made in Fairbanks, for the high work; a Yukon stove and the usual complement of pots and pans and dishes, including two admirable large aluminum pots for melting snow, used a number of years with great satisfaction. A "primus" stove, borrowed from the *Pelican's* galley, was taken along for the high work. The bedding was mainly of down quilts, which are superseding fur robes and blankets for winter use because of their lightness and warmth and the small compass into which they may be compressed. Two pairs of camel's-hair blankets and one sleeping-bag lined with down and camel's-hair cloth were taken, and Karstens brought a great wolf-robe, weighing twenty-five pounds, of which we were glad enough later on.

Another team was obtained at the mission, and Mr. R. G. Tatum and the two boys, Johnny and Esaias, joined the company, which, thus increased to six persons, two sleds, and fourteen dogs, set out from Nenana across country to the Kantishna on St. Patrick's day.

Travelling was over the beaten trail to the Kantishna gold camp, one of the smallest of Alaskan camps, supporting about thirty men. In 1906 there was a wild stampede to this region, and two or three thousand people went in, chiefly from the Fairbanks district. Town after town was built—Diamond City, Glacier City, Bearpaw City, Roosevelt, McKinley City—all with elaborate saloons and gambling-places, one, at least, equipped with electric lights. But next summer the boom burst and all the thousands streamed out. Gold there was and is yet, but in small quantities only. The "cities" are mere collections of tumble-down huts amongst which the moose roam at will. Interior Alaska has many such abandoned "cities." The few men now in the district have placer claims that yield a "grub-stake" as a sure thing every summer, and spend their winters chiefly in prospecting for quartz. At Diamond City, on the Bearpaw, lay our cache of grub, and that place, some ninety miles from Nenana and fifty miles from the base of Denali, was our present objective point. It was bright, clear weather and the trail was good. For thirty miles our way lay across the wide flats of the Tanana Valley, and this stage brought us to the banks of the Nenana River. Another day of twenty-five miles of flats brought us to Knight's comfortable road-house and ranch on the Toklat, a tributary of the Kantishna, the only road-house this trail can now support. Several times during these two days we had clear glimpses of the great mountain we were approaching, and as we came out of the flat country, the "Sheephills," a foothill range of Denali, much broken and deeply sculptured, rose picturesquely before us. Our travel was now almost altogether on "overflow" ice, upon the surface of swift streams that freeze solidly over their riffles and shallows and thus deny passage under the ice to the water of fountains and springs that never ceases flowing. So it bursts forth and flows *over* the ice with a continually renewing surface of the smoothest texture. Carrying a mercurial barometer that one dare not intrust to a sled on one's back over such footing is a somewhat precarious proceeding, but there was no alternative, and many miles were thus passed. Up the Toklat, then up its Clearwater Fork, then up its tributary, Myrtle Creek, to its head, and so over a little divide and down Willow Creek, we went, and from that divide and the upper reaches of the last-named creek had fine, clear views not only of Denali but of Denali's Wife as well, now come much nearer and looming much larger.

But here it may be stated once for all that the view which this face of the mountains presents is never a satisfying one. The same is true in even greater degree of the southern face, all photographs agreeing with all travellers as to its tameness. There is only one face of the Denali group that is completely satisfying, that is adequate to the full picturesque potentiality of a twenty-thousand-foot elevation. The writer has seen no other view, no other aspect of it, comparable to that of the northwest face from Lake Minchúmina. There the two mountains rise side by side, sheer, precipitous, pointed rocks, utterly inaccessible, savage, and superb. The rounded shoulders, the receding slopes and ridges of the other faces detract from the uplift and from the dignity, but the northwestern face is stark.

DENALI FROM THE MCKINLEY FORK OF THE KANTISHNA RIVER
*Showing the two peaks of the mountain, the one in the rear and to the left (the South Peak) is the higher.*

One more run, of much the same character as the previous day, and we were at Eureka, heart of the Kantishna country, on Friday, 21st March, being Good Friday.

We arrived there at noon and "called it a day," and spent the rest of it in the devotions of that august anniversary. Easter eve took us to Glacier City, and we lay there over the feast, gathering three or four men who were operating a prospecting-drill in that neighborhood for the first public worship ever conducted in the Kantishna camp. Ten miles more brought us to Diamond City, on the Bearpaw, where we found our cache of food in good condition save that the field-mice, despite all precautions, had made access to the cereals and had eaten all the rolled oats.

Amongst the Kantishna miners, who were most kindly and generous in their assistance, we were able to pick up enough large-sized moccasins to serve the members of the party, and we wore nothing else at all on the mountain.

Our immediate task now lay before us: A ton and a half of supplies had to be hauled some fifty miles across country to the base of the mountain. Here the relaying began, stuff being taken ahead and cached at some midway point, then another load taken right through a day's march, and then a return made to bring up the cache. In this way we moved steadily though slowly across rolling country and upon the surface of a large lake to the McKinley Fork of the Kantishna, which drains the Muldrow Glacier, down that stream to its junction with the Clearwater Fork of the same, and up that fork, through its canyon, to the last spruce timber on its banks, and there we made a camp in an exceedingly pretty spot. The creek ran open through a break in the ice in front of our tent; the water-ousels darted in and out under the ice, singing most sweetly; the willows, all in bud, perfumed the air; and Denali soared clear and brilliant, far above the range, right in front of us. Here at the timber-line, at an elevation of about two thousand feet, was the pleasantest camp of the whole excursion. During the five days' stay here the stuff was brought up and carried forward, and a quantity of dry wood was cut and advanced to a cache at the mouth of the creek by which we should reach the Muldrow Glacier.

It should be said that the short and easy route by which that glacier is reached was discovered after much scouting and climbing by McGonogill and Taylor in 1910, upon the occasion of the "pioneer" attempt upon the mountain, of which more will be said by and by. The men in the Kantishna camp who took part in that attempt gave us all the information they possessed, as they had done to the party that attempted the mountain last summer. There has been no need to make reconnoissance for routes since these pioneers blazed the way: there is no other practicable route than the one they discovered. The two subsequent climbing parties have followed precisely in their footsteps up as far as the Grand Basin at sixteen thousand feet, and it is the merest justice that such acknowledgment be made.

At our camp the Clearwater ran parallel with the range, which rose like a great wall before us. Our approach was not directly toward Denali but toward an opening in the range six or eight miles to the east of the great mountain. This opening is known as Cache Creek. Passing the willow patch at its mouth, where previous camps had been made, we pushed up the creek some three miles more to its forks, and there established our base camp, on 10th April, at about four thousand feet elevation. A few scrubby willows struggled to grow in the creek bed, but the hills that rose from one thousand five hundred to two thousand feet around us were bare of any vegetation save moss and were yet in the main covered with snow. Caribou signs were plentiful everywhere, and we were no more than settled in camp when a herd appeared in sight.

Our prime concern at this camp was the gathering and preserving of a sufficient meat supply for our subsistence on the mountain. It was an easy task. First

SOME HEADS OF GAME KILLED AT THE BASE CAMP

Karstens killed a caribou and then Walter a mountain-sheep. Then Esaias happened into the midst of a herd of caribou as he climbed over a ridge, and killed three. That was all we needed. Then we went to work preparing the meat. Why should any one haul canned pemmican hundreds of miles into the greatest game country in the world? We made our own pemmican of the choice parts of this tender, juicy meat and we never lost appetite for it or failed to enjoy and assimilate it. A fifty-pound lard-can, three parts filled with water, was set on the stove and kept supplied with joints of meat. As a batch was cooked we took it out and put more into the same water, removed the flesh from the bones, and minced it. Then we melted a can of butter, added pepper and salt to it, and rolled a handful of the minced meat in the butter and moulded it with the hands into a ball about as large as a baseball. We made a couple of hundred of such balls and froze them, and they kept perfectly. When all the boiling was done we put in the hocks of the animals and boiled down the liquor into five pounds of the thickest, richest meat-extract jelly, adding the marrow from the bones. With this pemmican and this extract of caribou, a package of erbswurst and a cupful of rice, we concocted every night the stew which was our main food in the higher regions.

Here the instruments were overhauled. The mercurial barometer reading by verniers to three places of decimals was set up and read, and the two aneroids were adjusted to read with it. These two aneroids perhaps deserve a word. Aneroid A was a three-inch, three-circle instrument, the invention of Colonel Watkins, of the British army, of range-finder fame. It seems strange that the advantage of the three-circle aneroid is so little known in this country, for its three concentric circles give such an open scale that, although this particular instrument reads to twenty-five thousand feet, it is easy to read as small a difference as twenty feet on it. It had been carried in the hind sack of the writer's sled for the past eight winters and constantly and satisfactorily used to determine the height of summits and passes upon the trails of the interior. Aneroid B was a six-inch patent mountain aneroid, another invention of the same military genius, prompted by Mr. Whymper's experiments with the aneroid barometer after his return from his classic climbs to the summits of the Bolivian Andes. Colonel Watkins devised an instrument in which by a threaded post and a thumb-screw the spring may be relaxed or brought into play at will, and the instrument is never in commission save when a reading is taken. Then a few turns of the thumb-screw bring the spring to bear upon the box, its walls expand until the pressure of the spring equals the pressure of the atmosphere, the reading is taken, and the instrument thrown out of operation again—a most ingenious arrangement by which it was hoped to overcome some of the persistent faults of elastic-chamber barometers. The writer had owned this instrument for the past ten years, but had never opportunity to test its usefulness until now. So, although it read no lower than about fifteen inches, he took it with him to observe its operation. Lastly, completing the hypsometrical equipment, was a boiling-point thermometer, with its own lamp and case, reading to 165° by tenths of a degree.

Then there were the ice-creepers or crampons to adjust to the moccasins—terribly heavy, clumsy rat-trap affairs they looked, but they served us well on the higher reaches of the mountain and are, if not indispensable, at least most valuable where hard snow or ice is to be climbed. The snow-shoes, also, had to be rough-locked by lashing a wedge-shaped bar of hardwood underneath, just above the tread, and screwing calks along the sides. Thus armed, they gave us sure footing on soft snow slopes, and were particularly useful in ascending the glacier. While thus occupied at the base camp, came an Indian, his wife and child, all the way from Lake Minchúmina, perhaps one hundred miles' journey, to have the child baptized. It was generally known amongst all the natives of the region that the enterprise was on foot, and "Minchúmina John," hoping to meet us in the Kantishna, and missing us, had followed our trail thus far. It was interesting to speculate how much further he would have penetrated: Walter thought as far as the glacier, but I think he would have followed as far as the dogs could go or until food was quite exhausted.

Meanwhile, the relaying of the supplies and the wood to the base camp had gone on, and the advancing of it to a cache at the pass by which we should gain the Muldrow Glacier. On 15th April Esaias and one of the teams were sent back to Nenana. Almost all the stuff we should move was already at this cache, and the need for the two dog teams was over. Moreover, the trails were rapidly breaking up, and it was necessary for the boy to travel by night instead of by day on his return trip. Johnny and the other dog team we kept, because we designed to use the dogs up to the head of the glacier, and the boy to keep the base camp and tend the dogs, when this was done, until our return. So we said good-by to Esaias, and he took out the last word that was received from us in more than two months.

The photograph of the base camp shows a mountainous ridge stretching across much of the background. That ridge belongs to the outer wall of the Muldrow

THE BASE-CAMP AT ABOUT 4,000 FEET ON CACHE CREEK
*The Muldrow Glacier flows between the ridge in the background and the peak just beyond it.*

Glacier and indicates its general direction. Just beyond the picture, to the right, the ridge breaks down, and the little valley in the middle distance sweeps around, becomes a steep, narrow gulch, and ends at the breach in the glacier wall. This breach, thus reached, is the pass which the Kantishna miners of the "pioneer" expedition discovered and named "McPhee Pass," after a Fairbanks saloon-keeper. The name should stand. There is no other pass by which the glacier can be reached; certainly none at all above, and probably no convenient one below. Unless this pass were used, it would be necessary to make the long and difficult journey to the snout of the glacier, some twenty miles farther to the east, cross its rough terminal moraine, and traverse all its lower stretch.

On the 11th April Karstens and I wound our way up the narrow, steep defile for about three miles from the base camp and came to our first sight of the Muldrow Glacier, some two thousand five hundred feet above camp and six thousand three hundred feet above the sea. That day stands out in recollection as one of the notable days of the whole ascent. There the glacier stretched away, broad and level—the road to the heart of the mountain, and as our eyes traced its course our spirits leaped up that at last we were entered upon our real task. One of us, at least, knew something of the dangers and difficulties its apparently smooth surface concealed, yet to both of us it had an infinite attractiveness, for it was the highway of desire.

## CHAPTER II

# The Muldrow Glacier

Right opposite McPhee Pass, across the glacier, perhaps at this point half a mile wide, rises a bold pyramidal peak, twelve thousand or thirteen thousand feet high, which we would like to name Mount Farthing, in honor of the memory of a very noble gentlewoman who died at the mission at Nenana three years ago, unless, unknown to us, it already bear some other name.* Walter and our two Indian boys had been under her instruction.

At the base of this peak two branches of the glacier unite, coming down in the same general direction and together draining the snows of the whole eastern face of the mountain. The dividing wall between them, almost up to their head and termination, is one stupendous, well-nigh vertical escarpment of ice-covered rock towering six thousand or seven thousand feet above the glacier floor, the first of the very impressive features of the mountain. The other wall of the glacier, through a breach in which we reached its surface—the right-hand wall as we journeyed up it—consists of a series of inaccessible cliffs deeply seamed with snow gullies and crusted here and there with hanging glaciers, the rock formation changing several times as one proceeds but maintaining an unbroken rampart.

Now, it is important to remember that these two ridges which make the walls of the Muldrow Glacier rise ultimately to the two summits of the mountain, the right-hand wall culminating in the North Peak and the left-hand wall in the South Peak. And the glacier lies between the walls all the way up and separates the summits, with this qualification—that midway in its course it is interrupted by a

* I have since learned that this mountain was named Mount Brooks by Professor Parker, and so withdraw the suggested name.

The Muldrow Glacier. Karstens in the foreground.

pendicular ice-fall of about four thousand feet by which its upper portion discharges into its lower. It will help the reader to a comprehension of the ascent if this rough sketch be borne in mind.

The course of the glacier at the point at which we reached it is nearly northeast and southwest (magnetic); its surface is almost level and it is free of crevasses save at its sides. For three or four miles above the pass it pursues its course without change of direction or much increase in grade; then it takes a broad sweep toward the south and grows steep and much crevassed. Three miles farther up it takes another and more decided southerly bend, receiving two steep but short tributaries from the northwest at an elevation of about ten thousand feet, and finishing its lower course in another mile and a half, at an elevation of about eleven thousand five hundred feet, with an almost due north and south direction (magnetic).

A week after our first sight of the glacier, or on the 15th April, we were camped at about the farthest point we had been able to see on that occasion—just round the first bend. Our stuff had been freighted to the pass and cached there; then in the usual method of our advance, the camp had been moved forward beyond the cache on to the glacier, a full day's march. Then the team worked backward, bringing up the stuff, to the new camp. Thus three could go ahead, prospecting and staking out a trail for further advance, while two worked with the dog team at the freighting.

For the glacier difficulties now confronted us in the fullest degree. Immediately above our tent the ice rose steeply a couple of hundred feet, and at that level began to be most intricately crevassed. It took several days to unravel the tangle of fissures and discover and prepare a trail that the dogs could haul the sleds along. Sometimes a bridge would be found over against one wall of the glacier, and for the next we might have to go clear across to the other wall. Sometimes a block of ice jammed in the jaws of a crevasse would make a perfectly safe bridge; sometimes we had nothing upon which to cross save hardened snow. Some of the gaps were narrow and some wide, yawning chasms. Some of them were mere surface cracks and some gave hundreds of feet of deep blue ice with no bottom visible at all. Sometimes there was no natural bridge over a crevasse, and then, choosing the narrowest and shallowest place in it, we made a bridge, excavating blocks of hard snow with the shovels and building them up from a ledge below, or projecting them on the cantilever principle, one beyond the other from both sides. Many of these crevasses could be jumped across by an unencumbered man on his snow-shoes that could not have been jumped with a pack and that the dogs could not cross at all. As each section of trail was determined it was staked out with willow shoots, hundreds of which had been brought up from below. And in all of this pioneering work and, indeed, thenceforward invariably, the rope was conscientiously used. Every step of the way up the glacier was sounded by a long pole, the man in the lead thrusting it deep into the snow while the two behind kept the rope always taut. More than one pole slipped into a hidden crevasse and was lost when vigor of thrust was not matched by tenacity of grip; more than once a man was jerked back just as the snow gave way beneath his feet. The open crevasses were not the dangerous ones; the whole glacier was crisscrossed by crevasses completely covered with snow. In bright weather it was often possible to detect them by a slight depression in the surface or by a faint, shadowy difference in tint, but in the half-light of cloudy and misty weather these signs failed, and there was no safety but in the ceaseless prodding of the pole. The ice-axe will not serve—one cannot reach far enough forward with it for safety, and the incessant stooping is an unnecessary added fatigue.

For the transportation of our wood and supplies beyond the first glacier camp, the team of six dogs was cut into two teams of three, each drawing a little Yukon sled procured in the Kantishna, the large basket sled having been abandoned. And in the movement forward, when the trail to a convenient cache had been established, two men, roped together, accompanied each sled, one ahead of the dogs, the other just behind the dogs at the gee-pole. This latter had also a hauling-line looped about his breast, so that men and dogs and sled made a unit. It took the combined traction power of men and dogs to take the loads up the steep glacial ascents, and it was very hard work. Once, "Snowball," the faithful team leader of four years past, who has helped to haul my sled nearly ten thousand miles, broke through a snow bridge and, the belly-band parting, slipped out of his collar and fell some twenty feet below to a ledge in a crevasse. Walter was let down and rescued the poor brute, trembling but uninjured. Without the dogs we should have been much delayed and could hardly, one judges, have moved the wood forward at all. The work on the glacier was the beginning of the ceaseless grind which the ascent of Denali demands.

How intolerably hot it was, on some of these days, relaying the stuff up the glacier! I shall never forget Ascension Day, which occurred this year on the 1st May. Double feast as it was for SS. Philip and James falls on that day—it was a day of toil and penance. With the mercurial barometer and a heavy pack of instruments and cameras and films on my back and the rope over my shoulder, bent double hauling at the sled, I trudged along all day, panting and sweating, through four or five inches of new-fallen snow, while the glare of the sun was terrific. It seemed impossible that, surrounded entirely by ice and snow, with millions of tons of ice underfoot, it *could* be so hot. But we took the loads right through to the head of the glacier that day, rising some four thousand feet in the course of five miles, and cached them there. On other days a smother of mist lay all over the glacier surface, with never a breath of wind, and the air seemed warm and humid as in an Atlantic coast city in July. Yet again, starting early in the morning, sometimes a zero temperature nipped toes and fingers and a keen wind cut like a knife. Sometimes it was

ASCENSION DAY, 1913

bitterly cold in the mornings, insufferably hot at noon, and again bitterly cold toward night. It was a pity we had no black-bulb, sun-maximum thermometer amongst our instruments, for one is sure its readings would have been of great interest.

It was a pity, also, that we had no means of making an attempt at measuring the rate of movement of this glacier—a subject we often discussed. The carriage of poles enough to set out rows of them across the glacier would have greatly increased our loads and the time required to transport them. But it is certain that its rate of movement is very slow in general, though faster at certain spots than at others, and a reason for this judgment will be given later.

The midway cache between our first and last glacier camps was itself the scene of a camp we had not designed, for on the day we were moving finally forward we were too fatigued to press on to the spot that had been selected at the head of the glacier, and by common consent made a halt at the cache and set up the tent there. This is mentioned because it had consequences. If we had gone through that day

Hard work for dogs as well as men on the Muldrow Glacier

and had established ourselves at the selected spot, a disaster that befell us would, in all probability, not have happened; for the next day, instead of moving our camp forward, we relayed some stuff and cached it where the camp would be made, covering the cache with the three small silk tents. Then we sat around awhile and ate our luncheon, and presently went down for another load. Imagine our surprise, upon returning some hours later, to see a column of smoke rising from our cache. All sorts of wild speculations flew through the writer's mind as, in the lead that day, he first crested the serac that gave view of the cache. Had some mysterious climber come over from the other side of the mountain and built a fire on the glacier? Had he discovered our wood and our grub and, perhaps starving, kindled a fire of the one to cook the other? Was there really, then, some access to this face of the mountain from the south? For it is fixed in the mind of the traveller in the north beyond eradication that *smoke* must mean *man*. But ere we had gone much farther the truth dawned upon us that our cache was on fire, and we left the dogs and the sleds and hurried to the spot. Something we were able to save, but not much, though we were in time to prevent the fire from spreading to our far-hauled wood. And the explanation was not far to seek. After luncheon Karstens and the writer had smoked their pipes, and one or the other had thrown a careless match away that had fallen unextinguished upon the silk tents that covered the cache. Presently a little wind had fanned the smouldering fabric into flame, which had eaten down into the pile of stuff below, mostly in wooden cases. All our sugar was gone, all our powdered milk, all our baking-powder, our prunes, raisins, and dried apples, most of our tobacco, a case of pilot bread, a sack full of woollen socks and gloves, another sack full of photographic films—all were burned. Most fortunately, the food provided especially for the high-mountain work had not yet been taken to the cache, and our pemmican, erbswurst, chocolate, compressed tea, and figs were safe. But it was a great blow to us and involved considerable delay at a very unfortunate time. We felt mortification at our carelessness as keenly as we felt regret at our loss. The last thing a newcomer would dream of would be danger from fire on a glacier, but we were not newcomers, and we all knew how ever-present that danger is, more imminent in Alaska in winter than in summer. Our carelessness had brought us nigh to the ruining of the whole expedition. The loss of the films was especially unfortunate, for we were thus reduced to Walter's small camera with a common lens and the six or eight spools of film he had for it.

The next day the final move of the main camp was made, and we established ourselves in the cirque at the head of the Muldrow Glacier, at an elevation of about eleven thousand five hundred feet, more than half-way up the mountain. After digging a level place in the glacier and setting up the tent, a wall of snow blocks was built all round it, and a little house of snow blocks, a regular Eskimo igloo, was built near by to serve as a cache. Some details of our camping may be of interest. The damp from the glacier ice had incommoded us at previous camps, coming up through skins and bedding when the tent grew warm. So at this camp we took further precaution. The boxes in which our grub had been hauled were broken up and laid over the whole portion of the floor of the tent where our bed was; over this wooden floor a canvas cover was laid, and upon this the sun-dried hides of the caribou and mountain-sheep we had killed were placed. There was thus a dry bottom for our bedding, and we were not much troubled thenceforward by the rising moisture, although a camp upon the ice is naturally always a more or less sloppy place. The hides were invaluable; heavy as they were, we carried them all the way up. So soon as we were thus securely lodged, elated when we thought of our advance, but downcast when we recalled our losses, we set ourselves to repair the damage of the fire so far as it was repairable. Walter and Johnny must go all the way down to the base camp and bring up sled-covers out of which to construct tents, must hunt the baggage through for old socks and mitts, and must draw upon what grub had been left for the return journey to the extreme limit it was safe to do so.

Karstens, accustomed to be clean-shaven, had been troubled since our first glacier camp with an affection of the face which he attributed to "in-growing whiskers," but when many hairs had been plucked out with the tweezers and he was nothing bettered, but rather grew worse and the inflammation spread to neck and temple, it was more correctly attributed to an eczema, or tetter, caused by the glare of the sun. So he was not loath to seclude himself for a few days in the tent while we set about the making of socks and mitts from the camel's-hair lining of the sleeping-bag. Walter's face was also very sore from the sun, his lips in particular being swollen and blistered. So painful did they become that I had to cut lip covers of surgeon's plaster to protect them. Then the boys returned with the sorry gleanings of the base camp, and the business of making two tents from the soiled and torn sled-covers and darning worn-out socks and mittens, was put in hand. Our camp looked like a sweat-shop those days, with its cross-legged tailormen and its litter of snippets. In addition to the six-by-seven tent, three feet six inches high, in which we were to live when we left the glacier, we made a small, conical tent in which to read the instruments on the summit. And all those days the sun shone in a clear sky!

Here, since reference has just been made to the effect of the sun's glare on the face of one member of the party, it may be in place to speak of the perfect eye protection which the amber snow-glasses afforded us. Long experience with blue and smoke-colored glasses upon the trail in spring had led us to expect much irritation of the eyes despite the use of snow-glasses, and we had plentifully provided ourselves with boracic acid and zinc sulphate for eye-washes. But the amber glasses, with their yellow celluloid side-pieces, were not a mere palliative, as all other glasses had been in our experience, but a complete preventive of snow-blindness. No one of us had the slightest trouble with the eyes, and the eye-washes were never used. It is hard for any save men compelled every spring to travel over the dazzling snows to realize what a great boon this newly discovered amber glass is. There is no reason anywhere for any more snow-blindness, and there is no use anywhere for any more blue or smoked glasses. The invention of the amber snow-glass is an even greater blessing to the traveller than the invention of the thermos bottle. No test could be more severe than that which we put these glasses to.

We were now at the farthest point at which it was possible to use the dogs, at our actual climbing base, and the time had come for Johnny and the dogs to go down to the base camp for good. We should have liked to keep the boy, so good-natured and amiable he was and so keen for further climbing; but the dogs must be tended, and the main food for them was yet to seek on the foot-hills with the rifle. So on 9th May down they went, Tatum and the writer escorting them with the rope past the crevasses as far as the first glacier camp, and then toiling slowly up the glacier again, thankful that it was for the last time. That was one of the sultriest and most sweltering days either of us ever remembered, a moist heat of sun beating down through vapor, with never a breath of breeze—a stifling, stewing day that, with the steep climb added, completely exhausted and prostrated us.

It is important that the reader should be able to see, in his mind's eye, the situation of our camp at the head of the glacier, because to do so is to grasp the simple orograpy of this face of the mountain, and to understand the route of its ascent, probably the only route by which it can be ascended. Standing beside the

Ice-fall of nearly 4,000 feet by which the upper or Harper Glacier discharges into the lower or Muldrow Glacier

tent, facing in the direction we have journeyed, the great highway of the glacier comes to an abrupt end, a cul-de-sac. On the right hand the wall of the glacier towers up, with enormous precipitous cliffs incrusted with hanging ice, to the North Peak of the mountain, eight or nine thousand feet above us. About at right angles to the end of the glacier, and four thousand feet above it, is another glacier, which discharges by an almost perpendicular ice-fall upon the floor of the glacier below. The left-hand wall of the glacier, described some pages back as a stupendous escarpment of ice-covered rock, breaks rapidly down into a comparatively low ridge, which sweeps to the right, encloses the head of the glacier, and then rises rapidly to the glacier above, and still rises to form the left-hand wall of that glacier, and finally the southern or higher peak of the mountain.

So the upper glacier separates the two great peaks of the mountain and discharges at right angles into the lower glacier. And the walls of the lower glacier sweep around and rise to form the walls of the upper glacier, and ultimately the summits of the mountain. To reach the peaks one must first reach the upper glacier, and the southern or left-hand wall of the lower glacier, where it breaks down into the ridge that encloses the head of the glacier, is the only possible means by which the upper basin may be reached. This ridge, then, called by Parker and Browne the Northeast Ridge (and we have kept that designation, though with some doubt as to its correctness), presented itself as the next stage of our climb.

Now just before leaving Fairbanks we had received a copy of a magazine containing the account of the Parker-Browne climb, and in that narrative Mr. Browne speaks of this Northeast Ridge as a steep but practicable snow slope and prints a photograph which shows it as such. To our surprise, when we first reached the head of the glacier, the ridge offered no resemblance what ever to the description or the photograph. The upper one-third of it was indeed as described, but at that point there was a sudden sharp cleavage, and all below was a jumbled mass of blocks of ice and rock in all manner of positions, with here a pinnacle and there a great gap. Moreover, the floor of the glacier at its head was strewn with enormous icebergs that we could not understand at all. All at once the explanation came to us "the earthquake"! The Parker-Browne party had reported an earthquake which shook the whole base of the mountain on 6th July, 1912, two days after they had come down, and, as was learned later, the seismographic instruments at Washington recorded it as the most severe shock since the San Francisco disturbance of 1906.

THE NORTHEAST RIDGE SHATTERED BY EARTHQUAKE IN JULY 1912
*The earthquake cleavage is plainly shown half-way down the ridge in the background. The Browne Tower is the uppermost point in the picture. The Parker Pass is along its base.*

There could be no doubt that the earthquake had disrupted this ridge. The huge bergs all around us were not the normal discharge of hanging glaciers as we had at first wonderingly supposed; they were the incrustation of ages, maybe, ripped off the rocks and hurled down from the ridge by this convulsion. It was as though, as soon as the Parker-Browne party reached the foot of the mountain, the ladder by which they had ascended and descended was broken up.

What a wonderful providential escape these three men, Parker, Browne, and LeVoy had! They reached a spot within three or four hundred feet of the top of the mountain, struggling gallantly against a blizzard, but were compelled at last to beat a retreat. Again from their seventeen-thousand-foot camp they essayed it, only to be enshrouded and defeated by dense mist. They would have waited in their camp for fair weather had they been provided with food, but their stomachs would not retain the canned pemmican they had carried laboriously aloft, and they were compelled to give up the attempt and descend. So down to the foot of the mountain they went, and immediately they reached their base camp this awful earthquake shattered the ridge and showered down bergs on both the upper and lower glaciers. Had their food served they had certainly remained above, and had they remained above their bodies would be there now. Even could they have escaped the avalanching icebergs they could never have descended that ridge after the earthquake. They would either have been overwhelmed and crushed to death instantly or have perished by starvation. One cannot conceive grander burial than that which lofty mountains bend and crack and shatter to make, or a nobler tomb than the great upper basin of Denali; but life is sweet and all men are loath to leave it, and certainly never men who cling to life had more cause to be thankful.

The difficulty of our task was very greatly increased; that was plain at a glance. This ridge, that the pioneer climbers of 1910 went up at one march with climbing-irons strapped beneath their moccasins, carrying nothing but their flagpole, that the Parker-Browne party surmounted in a few days, relaying their camping stuff and supplies, was to occupy us for three weeks while we hewed a staircase three miles long in the shattered ice.

It was the realization of the earthquake and of what it had done that convinced us that this Muldrow Glacier has a very slow rate of movement. The great blocks of ice hurled down from above lay apparently just where they had fallen almost a year before. At the points of sharp descent, at the turns in its course, at the points where tributary glaciers were received, the movement is somewhat more rapid. We saw some crevasses upon our descent that were not in existence when we went up. But for the whole stretch of it we were satisfied that a very few feet a year would cover its movement. No doubt all the glaciers on this side of the range are much more sluggish than on the other side, where the great precipitation of snow takes place.

We told Johnny to look for us in two weeks. It was thirty-one days ere we rejoined him. For now began the period of suspense, of hope blasted anew nearly every morning, the period of weary waiting for decent weather. With the whole mountain and glacier enveloped in thick mist it was not possible to do anything up above, and day after day this was the condition, varied by high wind and heavy snow. From the inexhaustible cisterns of the Pacific Ocean that vapor was distilled, and ever it rose to these mountains and poured all over them until every valley, every glacier, every hollow, was filled to overflowing. There seemed sometimes to us no reason why the process should not go on forever. The situation was not without its ludicrous side, when one had the grace to see it. Here were four men who had already passed through the long Alaskan winter, and now, when the rivers were breaking and the trees bursting into leaf, the flowers spangling every hillside, they were deliberately pushing themselves up into the winter still, with the long-expected summer but a day's march away.

The tedium of lying in that camp while snowstorm or fierce, high wind forbade adventure upon the splintered ridge was not so great to the writer as to some of the other members of the expedition, for there was always Walter's education to be prosecuted, as it had been prosecuted for three winters on the trail and three summers on the launch, in a desultory but not altogether unsuccessful manner. An hour or two spent in writing from dictation, another hour or two in reading aloud, a little geography and a little history and a little physics made the day pass busily. A pupil is a great resource. Karstens was continually designing and redesigning a motorboat in which one engine should satisfactorily operate twin screws; Tatum learned the thirty-nine articles by heart; but naval architecture and even controversial divinity palled after a while. The equipment and the supplies for the higher region were gone over again and again, to see that all was properly packed and in due proportion.

As one handled the packages and read and reread the labels, one was struck by the meagre English of merchandisers and the poor verbal resources of commerce generally. A while ago business dealt hardly with the word "proposition." It was the universal noun. Everything that business touched, however remotely, was a "proposition." When last he was "outside" the writer heard the Nicene Creed described as a "tough proposition"; the Vice-President of the United States as a "cold-blooded proposition," and missionaries in Alaska generally as "queer propositions." Now commerce has discovered and appropriated the word "product" and is working it for all it is worth. The coffee in the can calls itself a product. The compressed medicines from London direct you to "dissolve one product" in so much water; the vacuum bottles inform you that since they are a "glass product" they will not guarantee themselves against breakage; the tea tablets and the condensed pea soup affirm the purity of "these products"; the powdered milk is a little more explicit and calls itself a "food product." One feels disposed to agree with Humpty Dumpty, in "Through the Looking-Glass," that when a word is worked as hard as this it ought to be paid extra. One feels that "product" ought to be coming round on Saturday night to collect its overtime. The zwieback amuses one; it is a West-coast "product," and apparently "product" has not yet reached the West Coast—it does not so dignify itself. But it urges one, in great letters on every package, to "save the end seals; they are valuable!" Walter finds that by gathering one thousand two hundred of these seals he would be entitled to a "rolled-gold" watch absolutely free! This zwieback was the whole stock of a Yukon grocer purchased when the supply we ordered did not arrive. The writer was reminded of the time when he bought several two-pound packages of rolled oats at a little Yukon store and discovered to his disgust that every package contained a china cup and saucer that must have weighed at least a pound. One can understand the poor Indian being thus deluded into the belief that he is getting his crockery for nothing, but it is hard to understand how the "gift-enterprise" and "pre-mmm-package" folly still survives amongst white people—and Indians do not eat zwieback. What sort of people are they who will feverishly purchase and consume one thousand two hundred packages of zwieback in order to get a "rolled-gold" watch for nothing? A sack of corn-meal takes one's eye mainly by the enumeration of the formidable processes which the "product" inside has survived. It is announced proudly as "degerminated, granulated, double kiln-dried, steam-ground"! But why, in the name even of an adulterous and adulterating generation, should rice be "coated with talcum and glucose," as this sack unblushingly confesses? It is all very well to add "remove by washing"; that is precisely what we shall be unable to do. It will take all the time and fuel we have to spare to melt snow for cooking, when one little primus stove serves for all purposes. When we leave this camp there will be no more water for the toilet; we shall have to cleanse our hands with snow and let our faces go. The rice will enter the pot unwashed and will transfer its talcum and glucose to our intestines. Nor is this the case merely on exceptional mountain-climbing expeditions; it is the general rule during the winter throughout Alaska. It takes a long time and a great deal of snow and much wood to produce a pot of water on the winter trail. That "talcum-and-glucose" abomination should be taken up by the Pure Food Law authorities. All the rice that comes to Alaska is so labelled. The stomachs and bowels of dogs and men in the country are doubtless gradually becoming "coated with talcum and glucose."

It was during this period of hope deferred that we began to be entirely without sugar. Perhaps by the ordinary man anywhere, certainly by the ordinary man in Alaska, where it is the rule to include as much sugar as flour in an outfit, deprivation of sugar is felt more keenly than deprivation of any other article of food. We watched the gradual dwindling of our little sack, replenished from the base camp with the few pounds we had reserved for our return journey, with sinking hearts. It was kept solely for tea and coffee. We put no more in the sour dough for hot cakes; we ceased its use on our rice for breakfast; we gave up all sweet messes. Tatum attempted a pudding without sugar, putting vanilla and cinnamon and one knows not what other flavorings in it, in the hope of disguising the absence of sweetness, but no one could eat it and there was much jeering at the cook. Still it dwindled and dwindled. Two spoonfuls to a cup were reduced by common consent to one, and still it went, until at last the day came when there was no more. Our cocoa became useless—we could not drink it without sugar; our consumption of tea and coffee diminished there was little demand for the second cup. And we all began to long for sweet things. We tried to make a palatable potation from some of our milk chocolate, reserved for the higher work and labelled, "For eating only." The label was accurate; it made a miserable drink, the milk taste entirely lacking, the sweetness almost gone. We speculated how our ancestors got on without sugar when it was a high-priced luxury brought painfully in small quantities from the Orient, and assured one another that it was not a necessary article of diet. At last we all agreed to Karstens's laconic advice, "Forget it !" and we spoke of sugar no more. When we got on the ridge the chocolate satisfied to some extent the craving for sweetness, but we all missed the sugar sorely and continued to miss it to the end, Karstens as much as anybody else.

Our long detention here made us thankful for the large tent and the plentiful wood supply. That wood had been hauled twenty miles and raised nearly ten thousand feet, but it was worthwhile since it enabled us to "weather out the weather" here in warmth and comparative comfort. The wood no more than served our need, indeed, we had begun to economize closely before we left this camp.

We were greatly interested and surprised at the intrusion of animal life into these regions totally devoid of any vegetation. A rabbit followed us up the glacier to an elevation of ten thousand feet, gnawing the bark from the willow shoots with which the trail was staked, creeping round the crevasses, and, in one place at least, leaping such a gap. At ten thousand feet he turned back and descended, leaving his tracks plain in the snow. We speculated as to what possible object he could have had, and decided that he was migrating from the valley below, overstocked with rabbits as it was, and had taken a wrong direction for his purpose. Unless the ambition for first ascents, have reached the leporidæ, this seems the only explanation.

At this camp at the head of the glacier we saw ptarmigan on several occasions, and heard their unmistakable cry on several more, and once we felt sure that a covey passed over the ridge above us and descended to the other glacier. It was always in thick weather that these birds were noticed at the glacier head, and we surmised that perhaps they had lost their way in the cloud.

But even this was not the greatest height at which bird life was encountered. In the Grand Basin, at sixteen thousand five hundred feet, Walter was certain that he heard the twittering of small birds familiar throughout the winter in Alaska, and this also was in the mist. I have never known the boy make a mistake in such matters, and it is not essentially improbable. Doctor Workman saw a pair of choughs at twenty-one thousand feet, on Nun Kun in the Himalayas.

Our situation on the glacier floor, much of the time enveloped in dense mist, was damp and cold and gloomy. The cliffs around from time to time discharged their unstable snows in avalanches that threw clouds of snow almost across the wide glacier. Often we could see nothing, and the noise of the avalanches without the sight of them was at times a little alarming. But the most notable discharges were those from the great ice-fall, and the more important of them were startling and really very grand sights. A slight movement would begin along the side of the ice, in one of the gullies of the rock, a little trickling and rattling. Gathering to itself volume as it descended, it started ice in other gullies and presently there was a roar from the whole face of the enormous hanging glacier, and the floor upon which the precipitation descended trembled and shook with the impact of the discharge. Dense volumes of snow and ice dust rose in clouds thousands of feet high and slowly drifted down the glacier. We had chosen our camping-place to be out of harm's way and were really quite safe. We never saw any large masses detached, and by the time the ice reached the glacier floor it was all reduced to dust and small fragments. One does not recall in the reading of mountaineering books any account of so lofty an ice-fall.

## CHAPTER III

# The Northeast Ridge

Some of the photographs we succeeded in getting will show better than any words the character of the ridge we had to climb to the upper basin by. The lowest point of the ridge was that nearest our camp. To reach its crest at that point, some three hundred feet above the glacier, was comparatively easy, but when it was reached there stretched ahead of us miles and miles of ice-blocks heaved in confusion, resting at insecure angles, poised, some on their points, some on their edges, rising in this chaotic way some 3,000 feet. Here one would have to hew steps up and over a pinnacle, there one must descend again and cut around a great slab. Our wisest course was to seek to reach the crest of the ridge much further along, beyond as much of this ice chaos as possible. But it was three days before we could find a way of approach to the crest that did not take us under overhanging icebergs that threatened continually to fall upon our heads, as the overhanging hill threatened Christian in the "Pilgrim's Progress." At last we took straight up a steep gully, half of it snow slope, the upper half ice-incrusted rock, and hewed steps all the five hundred feet to the top. Here we were about half a mile beyond the point at which we first attained the crest, with that half mile of ice-blocks cut out, but beyond us the prospect loomed just as difficult and as dangerous. We could cut out no more of the ridge; we had tried place after place and could reach it safely at no point further along. The snow slopes broke off with the same sharp cleavage the whole ridge displayed two thousand five hundred feet above; there was no other approach.

So our task lay plain and onerous, enormously more dangerous and laborious than that which our predecessors encountered. We must cut steps in those ice-blocks, over them, around them, on the sheer sides of them, under them—

The shattered Northeast Ridge

whatever seemed to our judgment the best way of circumventing each individual block. Every ten yards presented a separate problem. Here was a sharp black rock standing up in a setting of ice as thin and narrow and steep as the claws that hold the stone in a finger-ring. That ice must be chopped down level, and then steps cut all round the rock. It took a solid hour to pass that rock. Here was a great bluff of ice, with snow so loose and at such a sharp angle about it that passage had to be hewed up and over and down it again. On either side the ridge fell precipitously to a glacier floor, with yawning crevasses half-way down eagerly swallowing every particle of ice and snow that our axes dislodged: on the right hand to the west fork of the Muldrow Glacier, by which we had journeyed hither; on the left to the east fork of the same, perhaps one thousand five hundred feet, perhaps two thousand feet lower. At the gap in the ridge, with the ice gable on the other side of it, the difficulty and the danger were perhaps at their greatest. It took the best part of a day's cutting to make steps down the slope and then straight up the face of the enormous ice mass that confronted us. The steps had to be made deep and wide; it was not merely one passage we were making; these steps would be traversed again and again by men with heavy packs as we relayed our food and camp equipage along this ridge, and we were determined from the first to take no unnecessary risks whatever. We realized that the passage of this shattered ridge was an exceedingly risky thing at best. To go along it day after day seemed like tempting Providence. We were resolved that nothing on our part should be lacking that could contribute to safety. Day by day we advanced a little further and returned to camp.

The weather doubled the time and the tedium of the passage of this ridge. From Whitsunday to Trinity Sunday, inclusive, there were only two days that we could make progress on the ridge at all, and on one of those days the clouds from the coast poured over so densely and enveloped us so completely that it was impossible to see far enough ahead to lay out a course wisely. On that day we toppled over into the abyss a mass of ice, as big as a two-story house, that must have weighed hundreds of tons. It was poised upon two points of another ice mass and held upright by a flying buttress of wind-hardened snow. Three or four blows from Karstens's axe sent it hurling downward. It passed out of our view into the cloud-smother immediately, but we heard it bound and rebound until it burst with a report like a cannon, and some days later we saw its fragments strewn all over the flat two thousand feet below. What a sight it must have been last July, when the whole ridge was heaving, shattering, and showering down its bergs upon the glacier floors! One day we were driven off the ridge by a high wind that threatened to sweep us from our footholds. On another, a fine morning gave place to a sudden dense snow-storm that sent us quickly below again. Always all day long, while we were on that ridge, the distant thunder of avalanches resounded from the Great Basin far above us, into which the two summits of Denali were continually discharging their snows. It sounded as though the King of Denmark were drinking healths all day long to the salvoes of his artillery—that custom "more honored in the breach than in the observance." From such fancy the mind passed easily enough to the memory of that astonishing composition of Grieg's, "In the Hall of the Mountain King," and, once recalled, the stately yet staccato rhythm ran in one's ears continually. For if we had many days of cloud and smother of vapor that blotted out everything, when a fine day came how brilliant beyond all that lower levels know it was! From our perch on that ridge the lofty peaks and massive ridges rose on every side. As little by little we gained higher and higher eminence the view broadened, and ever new peaks and ridges thrust themselves into view. We were within the hall of the mountain kings indeed; kings nameless here, in this multitude of lofty summits, but that elsewhere in the world would have each one his name and story.

And how eager and impatient we were to rise high enough, to progress far enough on that ridge that we might gaze into the Great Basin itself from which the thunderings came, the spacious hall of the two lords paramount of all the mountains of the continent—the north and south peaks of Denali! Our hearts beat high with the anticipation not only of gazing upon it but of entering it and pitching our tent in the midst of its august solitudes. To come down again—for there was as yet no spot reached on that splintered back-bone where we might make a camp—to pass day after day in our tent on the glacier floor waiting for the bad weather to be done that we might essay it again; to watch the tantalizing and, as it seemed, meaningless fluctuations of the barometer for encouragement; to listen to the driving wind and the swirling snow, how tedious that was!

At last when we had been camped for three weeks at the head of the glacier, losing scarce an hour of usable weather, but losing by far the greater part of the time, when the advance party the day before had reached a tiny flat on the ridge where they thought camp could be made, we took a sudden desperate resolve to move to the ridge at any cost. All the camp contained that would be needed above was made up quickly into four packs, and we struck out, staggering under our loads. Before we reached the first slope of the ridge each man knew in his heart that we were attempting altogether too much. Even Karstens, who had packed his "hundred and a quarter" day after day over the Chilkoot Pass in 1897, admitted that he was "heavy." But we were saved the chagrin of acknowledging that we had undertaken more than we could accomplish, for before we reached the steep slope of the ridge a furious snow-storm had descended upon us and we were compelled to return to camp. The next day we proceeded more wisely. We took up half the stuff and dug out a camping-place and pitched the little tent. Every step had to be shovelled out, for the previous day's snow had filled it, as had happened so many times before, and it took five and one-half hours to reach the new camping-place. On Sunday, 25th May, the first Sunday after Trinity, we took up the rest of the stuff, and established ourselves at a new climbing base, about thirteen thousand feet high and one thousand five hundred feet above the glacier floor, not to descend again until we descended for good.

We were now much nearer our work and it progressed much faster, although as the ridge rose it became steeper and steeper and even more rugged and chaotic, and the difficulty and danger of its passage increased. Our situation up here was decidedly pleasanter than below. We had indeed exchanged our large tent for a small one in which we could sit upright but could not stand, and so narrow that the four of us, lying side by side, had to make mutual agreement to turn over; our comfortable wood-stove for the little kerosene stove; yet when the clouds cleared we had a noble, wide prospect and there was not the sense of damp immurement that the floor of the glacier gave. The sun struck our tent at 4:30 A.M., which is nearly two and one-half hours earlier than we received his rays below, and lingered with us long after our glacier camp was in the shadow of the North Peak. Moreover, instead of being colder, as we expected, it was warmer, the minimum ranging around zero instead of around 10° below.

The rapidity with which the weather changed up here was a continual source of surprise to us. At one moment the skies would be clear, the peaks and the ridge standing out with brilliant definition; literally five minutes later they would be all

Camp at 13,000 feet on Northeast Ridge

blotted out by dense volumes of vapor that poured over from the south. Perhaps ten minutes more and the cloud had swept down upon the glacier and all above would be clear again; or it might be the vapor deepened and thickened into a heavy snow-storm. Sometimes everything below was visible and nothing above, and a few minutes later everything below would be obscured and everything above revealed.

This great crescent range is, indeed, our rampart against the hateful humidity of the coast and gives to us in the interior the dry, windless, exhilarating cold that is characteristic of our winters. We owe it mainly to this range that our snowfall averages about six feet instead of the thirty or forty feet that falls on the coast. The winds that sweep northward toward this mountain range are saturated with moisture from the warm waters of the Pacific Ocean; but contact with the lofty colds condenses the moisture into clouds and precipitates most of it on the southern slopes as snow. Still bearing all the moisture their lessened temperature will allow, the clouds pour through every notch and gap in the range and press resolutely onward and downward, streaming along the glaciers toward the interior. But all the time of their passage they are parting with their moisture, for the snow is falling from them continually in their course. They reach the interior, indeed, and spread out triumphant over the lowlands, but most of their burden has been deposited along the way. One is reminded of the government train of mules from Fort Egbert that used to supply the remote posts of the "strategic" telegraph line before strategy yielded to economy and the useless line was abandoned. When the train reached the Tanana Crossing it had eaten up nine-tenths of its original load, and only one-tenth remained for the provisioning of the post. So these clouds were being squeezed like a sponge; every saddle they pushed through squeezed them; every peak and ridge they surmounted squeezed them; every glacier floor they crept down squeezed them, and they reached the interior valleys attenuated, depleted, and relatively harmless.

The aneroids had kept fairly well with the mercurial barometer and the boiling-point thermometer until we moved to the ridge; from this time they displayed a progressive discrepancy therewith that put them out of serious consideration, and one was as bad as the other. Eleven thousand feet seemed the limit of their good behavior. To set them back day by day, like Captain Cuttle's watch, would be to depend wholly upon the other instruments anyway, and this is just what we did, not troubling to adjust them. They were read and recorded merely because that routine had been established. Says Burns:

*"There was a lad was born in Kyle,*
*But whatna' day o' whatna' style,*
*I doubt it's hardly worth the while*
*To be sae nice wi' Robin."*

So they were just aneroids: aluminum cases, jewelled movements, army-officer patented improvements, Kew certificates, import duty, and all—just aneroids, and one was as bad as the other. Within their limitations they are exceedingly useful instruments, but it is folly to depend on them for measuring great heights.

Perched up here, the constant struggle of the clouds from the humid south to reach the interior was interesting to watch, and one readily understood that Denali and his lesser companions are a prime factor in the climate of interior Alaska.

Day by day Karstens and Walter would go up and resume the finding and making of a way, and Tatum and the writer would relay the stuff from the camp to a cache, some five hundred feet above, and thence to another. The grand objective point toward which the advance party was working was the earthquake cleavage—a clean, sharp cut in the ice and snow of fifty feet in height. Above that point all was smooth, though fearfully steep; below was the confusion the earthquake had wrought. Each day Karstens felt sure they would reach the break, but each day as they advanced toward it the distance lengthened and the intricate difficulties increased. More than once a passage painfully hewn in the solid ice had to be abandoned, because it gave no safe exit, and some other passage found. At last the cleavage was reached, and it proved the most ticklish piece of the whole ridge to get around. Just below it was a loose snow slope at a dangerous angle, where it seemed only the initial impulse was needed for avalanche bear it all below. And just before crossing that snow slope was a wall of overhanging ice beneath which steps must be cut for one hundred yards, every yard of which endangered the climber by disputing the passage of the pack upon his shoulders.

Late in the evening of the 27th May, looking up the ridge upon our return from relaying a load to the cache, we saw Karstens and Walter standing, clear-cut, against the sky, upon the surface of the unbroken snow *above* the earthquake cleavage. Tatum and I gave a great shout of joy, and, far above as they were, they heard us and waved their response. We watched them advance upon the steep slope of the ridge until the usual cloud descended and blotted them out. The way was clear to the top of the ridge now, and that night our spirits were high, and congratulations were showered upon the victorious pioneers. The next day, when they would have gone on to the pass, the weather drove them back. On that smooth, steep, exposed slope a wind too high for safety beat upon them, accompanied by driving snow. That day a little accident happened that threatened our whole enterprise—on such small threads do great undertakings hang. The primus stove is an admirable device for heating and cooking superior, one thinks, to all the newfangled "alcohol utilities"—but it has a weak point. The fine stream of kerosene which, under pressure from the air-pump, is impinged against the perforated copper cup, heated to redness by burning alcohol, and is thus vaporized—first passes through several convolutions of pipe within the burner, and then issues from a hole so fine that some people would not call it a hole at all but an orifice or something like that. That little hole is the weak spot of the primus stove. Sometimes it gets clogged, and then a fine wire mounted upon some sort of handle must be used to dislodge the obstruction. Now, the worst thing that can happen to a primus stove is to get the wire pricker broken off in the burner hole, and that is what happened to us. Without a special tool that we did not possess, it is impossible to get at that burner to unscrew it, and without unscrewing it the broken wire cannot be removed. Tatum and I turned the stove upside down and beat upon it and tapped it, but nothing would dislodge that wire. It looked remarkably like no supper; it looked alarmingly like no more stove. How we wished we had brought the other stove from the launch, also! Every bow on an undertaking of this kind should have two strings. But when Karstens came back he went to work at once, and this was one of the many occasions when his resourcefulness was of the utmost service. With a file, and his usual ingenuity, he constructed, out of the spoon-bowl of a pipe cleaner the writer had in his pocket, the special tool necessary to grip that little burner, and soon the burner was unscrewed and the broken wire taken out and the primus was purring away merrily again, melting the water for supper. We feel sure that we would have pushed on even had we been without fire. The pemmican was cooked already, and could be eaten as it was, and one does not die of thirst in the midst of snow; but calm reflection will hardly allow that we could have reached the summit had we been deprived of all means of cooking and heating.

On this ridge the dough refused to sour, and since our baking-powder was consumed in the fire we were henceforth without bread. A cold night killed the germ in the sour dough, and we were never again able to set up a fermentation in it. Doubtless the air at this altitude is free from the necessary spores or germs of ferment. Pasteur's and Tyndall's experiments on the Alps, which resulted in the overthrow of the theory of spontaneous generation, and the rehabilitation of the old dogma that life comes only from life, were recalled with interest, but without much satisfaction. We tried all sorts of ways of cooking the flour, but none with any success. Next to the loss of sugar we felt the loss of bread, and in the food longings that overtook us bread played a large part.

On Friday, 30th May, the way had been prospected right up to the pass which gives entrance to the Grand Basin; a camping-place had been dug out there and a first load of stuff carried through and cached. So on that morning we broke camp, and the four of us, roped together, began the most important advance we had made yet. With stiff packs on our backs we toiled up the steps that had been cut with so much pains and stopped at the cache just below the cleavage to add yet further burdens. All day nothing was visible beyond our immediate environment. Again and again one would have liked to photograph the sensational-looking traverse of some particularly difficult ice obstacle, but the mist enveloped everything.

Just before we reached the smooth snow slope above the range of the earthquake disturbance lay one of the really dangerous passages of the climb.

It is easier to describe the difficulty and danger of this particular portion of the ascent than to give a clear impression to a reader of other places almost as hazardous. Directly below the earthquake cleavage was an enormous mass of ice, detached from the cleavage wall. From below, it had seemed connected with that wall, and much time and toil had been expended in cutting steps up it and along its crest, only to find a great gulf fixed; so it was necessary to pass along its base. Now from its base there fell away at an exceedingly sharp angle, scarcely exceeding the angle of repose, a slope of soft, loose snow, and the very top of that slope where it actually joined the wall of ice offered the only possible passage. The wall was in the main perpendicular, and turned at a right angle midway. Just where it turned, a great mass bulged out and overhung. This traverse was so long that with both ropes joined it was still necessary for three of the four members of the party to be on the snow slope at once, two men out of sight of the others. Any one familiar with Alpine work will realize immediately the great danger of such a traverse. There was, however, no avoiding it, or, at whatever cost, we should have done so. Twice already the passage had been made by Karstens and Walter, but not with heavy packs, and one man was always on ice while the other was on snow. This time all four must pass, bearing all that men could bear. Cautiously the first man ventured out, setting foot exactly where foot had been set before, the three others solidly anchored on the ice, paying out the rope and keeping it taut. When all the first section of rope was gone, the second man started, and when, in turn, his rope was paid out, the third man started, leaving the last man on the ice holding to the rope. This, of course, was the most dangerous part of this passage. If one of the three had slipped it would have been almost impossible for the others to hold him, and if he had pulled the others down, it would have been quite impossible for the solitary man on the ice to have withstood the strain. When the first man reached solid ice again there was another equally dangerous minute or two, for then all three behind him were on the snow slope. The beetling cliff, where the trail turned at right angles, was the acutely dangerous spot. With heavy and bulky packs it was exceedingly difficult to squeeze past this projection. Ice gives no such entrance to the point of the axe as hard snow does, yet the only aid in steadying the climber, and in somewhat relieving his weight on the loose snow, was afforded by such purchase upon the ice-wall, shoulder high, as that point could effect. Not a word was spoken by any one; all along the ice-wall rang in the writer's ears that preposterous line from "The Hunting of the Snark"—"Silence, not even a shriek" It was with a deep and thankful relief that we found ourselves safely across, and when a few minutes later we had climbed the steep snow that lay against the cleavage wall and were at last upon the smooth, unbroken crest of the ridge, we realized that probably the worst place in the entire climb was behind us.

Steep to the very limit of climbability as that ridge was, it was the easiest going we had had since we left the glacier floor. The steps were already cut; it was only necessary to lift one foot after the other and set the toe well in the hole, with the ice-axe buried afresh in the snow above at every step. But each step meant the lifting not only of oneself but of one's load, and the increasing altitude, perhaps

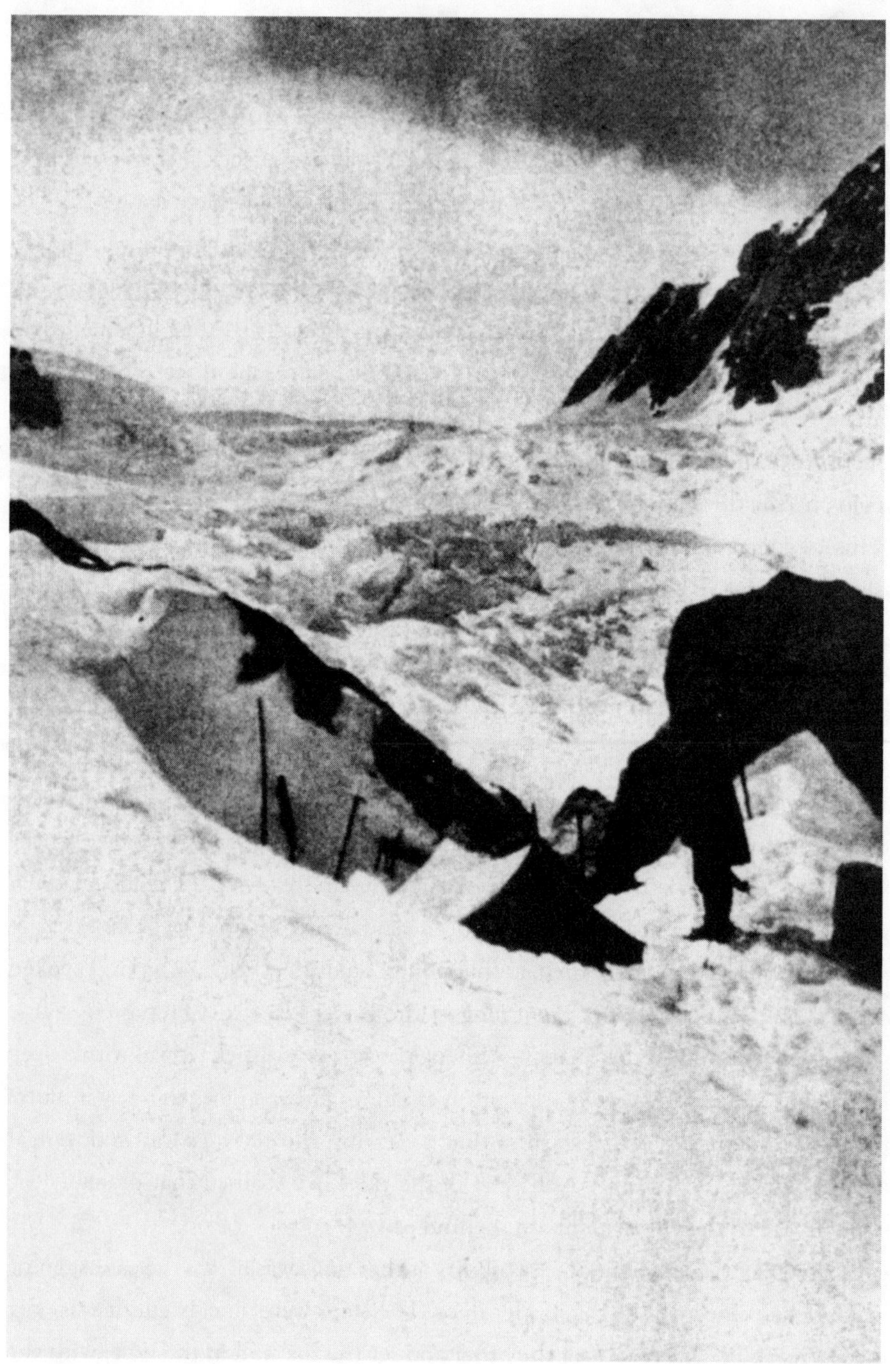

THE UPPER BASIN REACHED AT LAST. OUR CAMP AT THE PARKER PASS AT 15,000 FEET.

aggravated by the dense vapor with which the air was charged, made the advance exceedingly fatiguing. From below, the foreshortened ridge seemed only of short length and of moderate grade, could we but reach it—a tantalizingly easy passage to the upper glacier it looked as we chopped our way, little by little, nearer and nearer to it. But once upon it, it lengthened out endlessly, the sky-line always just a little above us, but never getting any closer.

Just before reaching the steepest pitch of the ridge, where it sweeps up in a cock's comb, we came upon the vestiges of a camp made by our predecessors of a year before, in a hollow dug in the snow—an empty biscuit carton and a raisin package, some trash and brown paper and discolored snow—as fresh as though they had been left yesterday instead of a year ago. Truly the terrific storms of this region are like the storms of Guy Wetmore Carryl's clever rhyme that "come early and avoid the *rush*." They will sweep a man off his feet, as once threatened to our advance party, but will pass harmlessly over a cigarette stump and a cardboard box; our tent in the glacier basin, ramparted by a wall of ice-blocks as high as itself, we found overwhelmed and prostrate upon our return, but the willow shoots with which we had staked our trail upon the glacier were all standing.

Long as it was, the slope was ended at last, and we came straight to the great upstanding granite slabs amongst which is the natural camping-place in the pass that gives access to the Grand Basin. We named that pass the Parker Pass, and the rock tower of the ridge that rises immediately above it, the most conspicuous feature of this region from below, we named the Browne Tower. The Parker-Browne party was the first to camp at this spot, for the astonishing "sourdough" pioneers made no camp at all above the low saddle of the ridge (as it then existed), but took all the way to the summit of the North Peak in one gigantic stride. The names of Parker and Browne should surely be permanently associated with this mountain they were so nearly successful in climbing, and we found no better places to name for them.

There is only one difficulty about the naming of this pass; strictly speaking, it is not a pass at all, and the writer does not know of any mountaineering term that technically describes it. Yet it should bear a name, for it is the doorway to the upper glacier, through which all those who would reach the summit must enter. On the one hand rises the Browne Tower, with the Northeast Ridge sweeping away beyond it toward the South Peak. On the other hand, the ice of the upper glacier plunges to its fall. The upstanding blocks of granite on a little level shoulder of the ridge lead around to the base of the cliffs of the Northeast Ridge, and it is around the base of those cliffs that the way lies to the midst of the Grand Basin. So the Parker Pass we call it and desire that it should be named.

And while names are before us, the writer would ask permission to bestow another. Having nothing to his credit in the matter at all, as the narrative has already indicated, he feels free to say that in his opinion the conquest of the difficulties of the earthquake-shattered ridge was an exploit that called for high qualities of judgment and cautious daring, and would, he thinks, be considered a brilliant piece of mountaineering anywhere in the world. He would like to name that ridge Karstens Ridge, in honor of the man who, with Walter's help, cut that staircase three miles long amid the perilous complexities of its chaotic ice-blocks.

When we reached the Parker Pass all the world beneath us was shrouded in dense mist, but all above us was bathed in bright sunshine. The great slabs of granite were like a gateway through which the Grand Basin opened to our view.

The ice of the upper glacier, which fills the Grand Basin, came terracing down from some four thousand feet above us and six miles beyond us, with progressive leaps of jagged blue sérac between the two peaks of the mountain, and, almost at our feet, fell away with cataract curve to its precipitation four thousand feet below us. Across the glacier were the sheer, dark cliffs of the North Peak, soaring to an almost immediate summit twenty thousand feet above the sea; on the left, in the distance, was just visible the receding snow dome of the South Peak, with its two horns some five hundred feet higher. The mists were passing from the distant summits, curtain after curtain of gauze draping their heads for a moment and sweeping on.

We made our camp between the granite slabs on the natural camping site that offered itself, and a shovel and an empty alcohol-can proclaimed that our predecessors of last year had done the same.

The next morning the weather had almost completely cleared, and the view below us burst upon our eyes as we came out of the tent into the still air.

The Parker Pass is the most splendid coigne of vantage on the whole mountain, except the summit itself. From an elevation of something more than fifteen thousand feet one overlooks the whole Alaskan range, and the scope of view to the east, to the northeast, and to the southeast is uninterrupted. Mountain range rises beyond mountain range, until only the snowy summits are visible in the great distance, and one knows that beyond the last of them lies the open sea. The near-by peaks and ridges, red with granite or black with shale and gullied from top to bottom with snow and ice, the broad highways of the glaciers at their feet carrying parallel moraines that look like giant tram-lines, stand out with vivid distinction. A lofty peak, that we suppose is Mount Hunter, towers above the lesser summits. The two arms of the Muldrow Glacier start right in the foreground and reveal themselves from their heads to their junction and then to the terminal snout, receiving their groaning tributaries from every evacuating height. The dim blue lowlands, now devoid of snow, stretch away to the northeast, with threads of stream and patches of lake that still carry ice along their banks.

And all this splendor and diversity yielded itself up to us at once; that was the most sensational and spectacular feature of it. We went to sleep in a smother of mist; we had seen nothing as we climbed; we rose to a clear, sparkling day. The clouds were mysteriously rolling away from the lowest depths; the last wisps of vapor were sweeping over the ultimate heights. Here one would like to camp through a whole week of fine weather could such a week ever be counted upon. Higher than any point in the United States, the top of the Browne Tower probably on a level with the top of Mount Blanc, it is yet not so high as to induce the acute breathlessness from which the writer suffered, later, upon any exertion. The climbing of the tower, the traversing to the other side of it, the climbing of the ridge, would afford pleasant excursions, while the opportunity for careful though difficult photography would be unrivalled. Even in thick weather the clouds are mostly below; and their rapid movement, the kaleidoscopic changes which their coming and going, their thickening and thinning, their rising and falling produce, are a never-failing source of interest and pleasure. The changes of light and shade, the gradations of color, were sometimes wonderfully delicate and charming. Seen through rapidly attenuating mist, the bold crags of the icy ridge between the glacier arms in the foreground would give a soft French gray that became a luminous mauve before it sprang into dazzling black and white in the sunshine. In the sunshine, indeed, the whole landscape was hard and brilliant, and lacked half-tones, as in the main it lacked color; but when the vapor

Above all the range except Denali and Denali's Wife

drew the gauze of its veil over it there came rich, soft, elusive tints that were no more than hinted ere they were gone.

Here, with nothing but rock and ice and snow around, nine thousand feet above any sort of vegetation even in the summer, it was of interest to remember that at the same altitude in the Himalayas good crops of barley and millet are raised and apples are grown, while at a thousand feet or so lower the apricot is ripened on the terrace-gardens.

Karstens and Walter had brought up a load each on their reconnoissance trip; four heavy loads had been brought the day before. There were yet two loads to be carried up from the cache below the cleavage, and Tatum and Walter, always ready to take the brunt of it, volunteered to bring them. So down that dreadful ridge once more the boys went, while Karstens and the writer prospected ahead for a route into the Grand Basin.

The storms and snows of ten or a dozen winters may make a "steep but practicable snow slope" of the Northeast Ridge again. One winter only had passed since the convulsion that disrupted it, and already the snow was beginning to build up its gaps and chasms. All the summer through, for many hours on clear days, the sun will melt those snows and the frost at night will glaze them into ice. The more conformable ice-blocks will gradually be cemented together, while the fierce winds that beat upon the ridge will wear away the supports of the more egregious and unstable blocks, and one by one they will topple into the abyss on this side or on that. It will probably never again be the smooth, homogeneous slope it has been; "the gable" will probably always present a wide cleft, but the slopes beyond it, stripped now of their accumulated ice so as to be unclimbable, may build up again and give access to the ridge.

The point about one thousand five hundred feet above the gable, where the earthquake cleavage took place, will perhaps remain the crux of the climb. The ice-wall rises forty or fifty feet sheer, and the broken masses below it are especially difficult and precipitous, but with care and time and pains it can be surmounted even as we surmounted it. And wind and sun and storm may mollify the forbidding abruptness of even this break in the course of time.

With the exception of this ridge, Denali is not a mountain that presents special mountaineering difficulties of a technical kind. Its difficulties lie in its remoteness, its size, the great distances of snow and ice its climbing must include the passage of, the burdens that must be carried over those distances. We estimated that it was twenty miles of actual linear distance from the pass by which we reached the Muldrow Glacier to the summit. In the height of summer its snow-line will not be higher than seven thousand feet, while at the best season for climbing it, the spring, the snow-line is much lower. Its climbing is, like nearly all Alaskan problems, essentially one of transportation. But the Northeast Ridge, in its present condition, adds all the spice of sensation and danger that any man could desire.

## CHAPTER IV

# The Grand Basin

The reader will perhaps be able to sympathize with the feeling of elation and confidence which came to us when we had surmounted the difficulties of the ridge and had arrived at the entrance to the Grand Basin. We realized that the greater and more arduous part of our task was done and that the way now lay open before us. For so long a time this point had been the actual goal of our efforts, for so long a time we had gazed upward at it with hope deferred, that its final attainment was accompanied with no small sense, of triumph and gratification and with a great accession of faith that we should reach the top of the mountain.

The ice of the glacier that fills the basin was hundreds of feet beneath us at the pass, but it rises so rapidly that by a short traverse under the cliffs of the ridge we were able to reach its surface and select a camping site thereon at about sixteen thousand feet. It was bitterly cold, with a keen wind that descended in gusts from the heights, and the slow movement of step-cutting gave the man in the rear no opportunity of warming up. Toes and fingers grew numb despite multiple socks within mammoth moccasins and thick gloves within fur mittens.

From this time, during our stay in the Grand Basin and until we had left it and descended again, the weather progressively cleared and brightened until all clouds were dispersed. From time to time there were fresh descents of vapor, and even short snow-storms, but there was no general enveloping of the mountain again. Cold it was, at times even in the sunshine, with "a nipping and an eager air," but when the wind ceased it would grow intensely hot. On the 4th June, at 3 P.M. the thermometer in the full sunshine rose to 50° F.—the highest temperature recorded on the whole excursion—and the fatigue of packing in that thin atmosphere with the sun's rays reflected from ice and snow everywhere was most exhausting. We

TRAVERSE UNDER THE CLIFFS OF THE NORTHEAST RIDGE TO ENTER THE GRAND BASIN

were burned as brown as Indians; lips and noses split and peeled in spite of continual applications of lanoline, but, thanks to those most beneficent amber snow-glasses, no one of the party had the slightest trouble with his eyes. At night it was always cold, 10° below zero being the highest minimum during our stay in the Grand Basin, and 21° below zero the lowest. But we always slept warm; with sheep-skins and caribou-skins under us, and down quilts and camel's-hair blankets and a wolf-robe for bedding, the four of us lay in that six-by-seven tent, in one bed, snug and comfortable. It was disgraceful overcrowding, but it was warm. The fierce little primus stove, pumped up to its limit and perfectly consuming its kerosene fuel, shot out its corona of beautiful blue flame and warmed the tight, tiny tent. The primus stove, burning seven hours on a quart of coal oil, is a little giant for heat generation. If we had had two, so that one could have served for cooking and one for heating, we should not have suffered from the cold at all, but as it was, whenever the stew-pot went on the stove, or a pot full of ice to melt, the heat was immediately absorbed by the vessel and not distributed through the tent. But another primus stove would have been another five or six pounds to pack, and we were "heavy" all the time as it was.

Something has already been said about the fatigue of packing, and one would not weary the reader with continual reference thereto; yet it is certain that those who have carried a pack only on the lower levels cannot conceive how enormously greater the labor is at these heights. As one rises and the density of the air is diminished, so, it would seem, the weight of the pack or the effect of the weight of the pack is in the same ratio increased. We probably moved from three hundred to two hundred and fifty pounds, decreasing somewhat as food and fuel were consumed, each time camp was advanced in the Grand Basin. We could have done with a good deal less as it fell out, but this we did not know, and we were resolved not to be defeated in our purpose by lack of supplies. But the packing of these loads, relaying them forward, and all the time steeply rising, was labor of the most exhausting and fatiguing kind, and there is no possible way in which it may be avoided in the ascent of this mountain. To roam over glaciers and scramble up peaks free and untrammelled is mountaineering in the Alps. Put a forty-pound pack on a man's back, with the knowledge that to-morrow he must go down for another, and you have mountaineering in Alaska. In the ascent of this twenty-thousand-foot mountain every member of the party climbed at least sixty thousand feet. It is this going down and doing it all over again that is the heart-breaking part of climbing.

It was in the Grand Basin that the writer began to be seriously affected by the altitude, to be disturbed by a shortness of breath that with each advance grew more distressingly acute. While at rest he was not troubled; mere existence imposed no unusual burden, but even a slight exertion would be followed by a spell of panting, and climbing with a pack was interrupted at every dozen or score of steps by the necessity of stopping to regain breath. There was no nausea or headache or any other symptom of "mountain sickness." Indeed, it is hard for us to it understand that affection as many climbers describe it. It has been said again and again to resemble seasickness in all its symptoms. Now the writer is of the unfortunate company that are seasick on the slightest provocation. Even rough water on the wide stretches of the lower Yukon, when a wind is blowing upstream and the launch is pitching and tossing, will give him qualms. But no one of the four of us had any such feeling on the mountain at any time. Shortness of breath we all suffered from, though none other so acutely as myself. When it was evident that the progress of the party was hindered by the constant stops on my account, the contents of my pack were distributed amongst the others and my load reduced to the mercurial barometer and the instruments, and, later, to the mercurial barometer alone. It was some mortification not to be able to do one's share of the packing, but there was no help for it, and the other shoulders were young and strong and kindly.

FIRST CAMP IN THE GRAND BASIN—16,000 FEET, LOOKING UP

With some hope of improving his wind, the writer had reduced his smoking to two pipes a day so soon as the head of the glacier had been reached, and had abandoned tobacco altogether when camp was first made on the ridge; but it is questionable if smoking in moderation has much or any effect. Karstens, who smoked continually, and Walter, who had never smoked in his life, had the best wind of the party. It is probably much more a matter of age. Karstens was a man of thirty-two years, and the two boys were just twenty-one, while the writer approached fifty. None of us slept as well as usual except Walter—and nothing ever interferes with his sleep—but, although our slumbers were short and broken, they seemed to bring recuperation just as though they had been sound. We arose fresh in the morning though we had slept little and light.

On the 30th May we had made our camp at the Parker Pass; on the 2d June, the finest and brightest day in three weeks, we moved to our first camp in the Grand Basin. On the 3d June we moved camp again, out into the middle of the glacier, at about sixteen thousand five hundred feet.

Here we were at the upper end of one of the flats of the glacier that fills the Grand Basin, the sérac of another great rise just above us. The walls of the North

Second camp in the Grand Basin—looking down, 16,500 feet

Peak grow still more striking and picturesque here, where they attain their highest elevation. These granite ramparts, falling three thousand feet sheer, swell out into bellying buttresses with snow slopes between them as they descend to the glacier floor, while on top, above the granite, each peak point and crest ridge is tipped with black shale. How comes that ugly black shale, with the fragments of which all the lower glacier is strewn, to have such lofty eminence and granite-guarded distinction, as though it were the most beautiful or the most valuable thing in the world? The McKinley Fork of the Kantishna, which drains the Muldrow, is black as ink with it, and its presence can be detected in the Tanana River itself as far as its junction with the Yukon. It is largely soluble in water, and where melting snow drips over it on the glacier walls below were great splotches, for all the world as though a gigantic ink-pot had been upset.

While we sat resting awhile on our way to this camp, gazing at these pinnacles of the North Peak, we fell to talking about the pioneer climbers of this mountain who claimed to have set a flagstaff near the summit of the North Peak—as to which feat a great deal of incredulity existed in Alaska for several reasons—and we renewed our determination that, if the weather permitted when we had reached our goal and ascended the South Peak, we would climb the North Peak also to seek for traces of this earliest exploit on Denali, which is dealt with at length in another place in this book. All at once Walter cried out: "I see the flagstaff!" Eagerly pointing to the rocky prominence nearest the summit—the summit itself is covered with snow—he added: "I see it plainly!" Karstens, looking where he pointed, saw it also and, whipping out the field-glasses, one by one we all looked, and saw it distinctly standing out against the sky. With the naked eye I was never able to see it unmistakably, but through the glasses it stood out, sturdy and strong, one side covered with crusted snow. We were greatly rejoiced that we could carry down positive confirmation of this matter. It was no longer necessary for us to ascend the North Peak.

The upper glacier also bore plain signs of the earthquake that had shattered the ridge. Huge blocks of ice were strewn upon it, ripped off the left-hand wall, but it was nowhere crevassed as badly as the lower glacier, but much more broken up into sérac. Some of the bergs presented very beautiful sights, wind-carved incrustations of snow in cameo upon their blue surface giving a suggestion of Wedgwood pottery. All tints seemed more delicate and beautiful up here than on the lower glacier.

On the 5th June we advanced to about seventeen thousand five hundred feet right up the middle of the glacier. As we rose that morning slowly out of the flat in which our tent was pitched and began to climb the steep sérac, clouds that had been gathering below swept rapidly up into the Grand Basin, and others swept as rapidly over the summits and down upon us. In a few moments we were in a dense smother of vapor with nothing visible a couple of hundred yards away. Then the temperature dropped, and soon snow was falling which increased to a heavy snow-storm that

THIRD CAMP IN THE GRAND BASIN—17,000 FEET—SHOWING THE SHATTERING OF THE GLACIER WALLS BY THE EARTHQUAKE

*The rocks at the tip of the picture are about 19,000 feet high and are the highest rocks on the south peak of the mountain.*

raged an hour. We made our camp and ate our lunch, and by that time the smother of vapor passed, the sun came out hot again, and we were all simultaneously overtaken with a deep drowsiness and slept. Then out into the glare again, to go down and bring up the remainder of the stuff, we went, and that night we were established in our last camp but one. We had decided to go up at least five hundred feet farther that we might have the less to climb when we made our final attack upon the peak. So when we returned with the loads from below we did not stop at camp, but carried them forward and cached them against to-morrow's final move.

On Friday, the 6th June, we made our last move and pitched our tent in a flat near the base of the ridge, just below the final rise in the glacier of the Grand Basin, at about eighteen thousand feet, and we were able to congratulate one another on making the highest camp ever made in North America. I set up and read the mercurial barometer, and when corrected for its own temperature it stood at 15.061. The boiling-point thermometer registered 180.5, as the point at which water boiled, with an air temperature of 35°. It took one hour to boil the rice for supper. The aneroids stood at 14.8 and 14.9, still steadily losing on the mercurial barometer. I think that a rough altitude gauge could be calculated from the time rice takes to boil—at least as reliable as an aneroid barometer. At the Parker Pass it took fifty minutes; here it took sixty. This is about the height of perpetual snow on the great Himalayan peaks; but we had been above the perpetual snow-line for forty-eight days.

We were now within about two thousand five hundred feet of the summit and had two weeks' full supply of food and fuel, which, at a pinch, could be stretched to three weeks. Certain things were short: the chocolate and figs and raisins and salt were low; of the zwieback there remained but two and one-half packages, reserved against lunch when we attacked the summit. But the meat-balls, the erbswurst, the caribou jelly, the rice, and the tea—our staples—were abundant for two weeks, with four gallons of coal-oil and a gallon of alcohol. The end of our painful transportation hither was accomplished; we were within one day's climb of the summit with supplies to besiege. If the weather should prove persistently bad we could wait; we could advance our parallels; could put another camp on the ridge itself at nineteen thousand feet, and yet another half-way up the dome. If we had to fight our way step by step and could advance but a couple of hundred feet a day, we were still confident that, barring unforeseeable misfortunes, we could reach the top. But we wanted a clear day on top, that the observations we designed to make could be made; it would be a poor success that did but set our feet on the highest point. And we felt sure that, prepared as we were to wait, the clear day would come.

As so often happens when everything unpropitious is guarded against, nothing unpropitious occurs. It would have been a wonderful chance, indeed, if, supplied only for one day, a fine, clear day had come. But supplied against bad weather

THE NORTH PEAK, 20,000 FEET HIGH

*Our last camp in the Grand Basin, at 18,000 feet: the highest camp ever made in North America.*

for two or three weeks, it was no wonder at all that the very first day should have presented itself bright and clear. We had exhausted our bad fortune below; here, at the juncture above all others at which we should have chosen to enjoy it, we were to encounter our good fortune.

But here, where all signs seemed to promise success to the expedition, the author began to have fears of personal failure. The story of Mr. Fitzgerald's expedition to Aconcagua came to his mind, and he recalled that, although every other member of the party reached the summit, that gentleman himself was unable to do so. In the last stage the difficulty of breathing had increased with fits of smothering, and the medicine chest held no remedy for blind staggers.

CHAPTER V

# The Ultimate Height

We lay down for a few hours on the night of the 6th June, resolved to rise at three in the morning for our attempt upon the summit of Denali. At supper Walter had made a desperate effort to use some of our ten pounds of flour in the manufacture of "noodles" with which to thicken the stew. We had continued to pack that flour and had made effort after effort to cook it in some eatable way, but without success. The sour dough would not ferment, and we had no baking-powder. *Is* there any way to cook flour under such circumstances? But he made the noodles too large and did not cook them enough, and they wrought internal havoc upon those who partook of them. Three of the four of us were unwell all night. The digestion is certainly more delicate and more easily disturbed at great altitudes than at the lower levels. While Karstens and Tatum were tossing uneasily in the bedclothes, the writer sat up with a blanket round his shoulders, crouching over the primus stove, with the thermometer at -21°F. outdoors. Walter alone was at ease, with digestive and somnolent capabilities proof against any invasion. It was, of course, broad daylight all night. At three the company was aroused, and, after partaking of a very light breakfast indeed, we sallied forth into the brilliant, clear morning with not a cloud in the sky. The only packs we carried that day were the instruments and the lunch. The sun was shining, but a keen north wind was blowing and the thermometer stood at -4°F. outdoors. We were rather a sorry company. Karstens still had internal pains; Tatum and I had severe headaches. Walter was the only one feeling entirely himself, so Walter was put in the lead and in the lead he remained all day.

We took a straight course up the great snow ridge directly south of our camp and then around the peak into which it rises; quickly told but slowly and most

The South Peak from about 18,000 feet

*The ridge with two peaks in the background is shaped like a horseshoe, and the highest point on the mountain is on another little ridge just beyond, parallel with the ridge that shows, almost at the middle point between the two peaks.*

laboriously done. It was necessary to make the traverse high up on this peak instead of around its base, so much had its ice and snow been shattered by the earthquake on the lower portions. Once around this peak, there rose before us the horseshoe ridge which carries the ultimate height of Denali, a horseshoe ridge of snow opening to the east with a low snow peak at either end, the centre of the ridge soaring above both peaks. Above us was nothing visible but snow; the rocks were all beneath, the last rocks standing at about 19,000 feet. Our progress was exceedingly slow. It was bitterly cold; all the morning toes and fingers were without sensation, kick them and beat them as we would. We were all clad in full winter hand and foot gear—more gear than had sufficed at 50° below zero on the Yukon trail. Within the writer's No. 16 moccasins were three pairs of heavy hand-knitted woollen socks, two pairs of camel's-hair socks, and a pair of thick felt socks; while underneath them, between them and the iron "creepers," were the soles cut from a pair of felt shoes. Upon his hands were a pair of the thickest Scotch wool gloves, thrust inside huge lynx-paw mitts lined with Hudson Bay duffle. His moose-hide breeches and shirt, worn all the winter on the trail, were worn throughout this climb; over the shirt was a thick sweater and over all the usual Alaskan "parkee" amply furred around the hood; underneath was a suit of the heaviest Jaeger underwear—yet until nigh noon feet were like lumps of iron and fingers were constantly numb. That north wind was cruelly cold, and there can be no possible question that cold is felt much more keenly in the thin air of nineteen thousand feet than it is below. But the north wind was really our friend, for nothing but a north wind will drive all vapor from this mountain. Karstens beat his feet so violently and so continually against the hard snow to restore the circulation that two of his toe-nails sloughed off afterward. By eleven o'clock we had been climbing for six hours and were well around the peak, advancing toward the horseshoe ridge, but even then there were grave doubts if we should succeed in reaching it that day, it was so cold. A hint from any member of the party that his feet were actually freezing—a hint expected all along—would have sent us all back. When there is no sensation left in the feet at all it is, however, difficult to be quite sure if they be actually freezing or not—and each one was willing to give the attempt upon the summit the benefit of the doubt. What should we have done with the ordinary leather climbing boots? But once entirely around the peak we were in a measure sheltered from the north wind, and the sun full upon us gave more warmth. It was hereabouts, and not, surely, at the point indicated in the photograph in Mr. Belmore Browne's book, that the climbing party of last year was driven back by the blizzard that descended upon them when close to their goal. Not until we had stopped for lunch and had drunk the scalding tea from the thermos bottles, did we all begin to have confidence that this day would see the completion of the ascent. But the writer's shortness of breath became more and more distressing as he rose. The familiar fits of

THE CLIMBING-IRONS

panting took a more acute form; at such times everything would turn black before his eyes and he would choke and gasp and seem unable to get breath at all. Yet a few moments' rest restored him completely, to struggle on another twenty or thirty paces and to sink gasping upon the snow again. All were more affected in the breathing than they had been at any time before—it was curious to see every man's mouth open for breathing—but none of the others in this distressing way. Before the traverse around the peak just mentioned, Walter had noticed the writer's growing discomfort and had insisted upon assuming the mercurial barometer. The boy's eager kindness was gladly accepted and the instrument was surrendered. So it did not fall to the writer's credit to carry the thing to the top as he had wished.

The climbing grew steeper and steeper; the slope that had looked easy from below now seemed to shoot straight up. For the most part the climbing-irons gave us sufficient footing, but here and there we came to softer snow, where they would not take sufficient hold and we had to cut steps. The calks in these climbing-irons were about an inch and a quarter long; we wished they had been two inches. The creepers are a great advantage in the matter of speed, but they need long points. They are not so safe as step-cutting, and there is the ever-present danger that unless one is exceedingly careful one will step upon the rope with them and their sharp calks sever some of the strands. They were, however, of great assistance and saved a deal of laborious step-cutting.

At last the crest of the ridge was reached and we stood well above the two peaks that mark the ends of the horseshoe.*

Also it was evident that we were well above the great North Peak across the Grand Basin. Its crest had been like an index on the snow beside us as we climbed,

---

* The dotted line on the photograph opposite page 346 of Mr. Belmore Browne's book, "The Conquest of Mt. McKinley," does not, in the writer's opinion, represent the real course taken by Professor Parker, Mr. Belmore Browne, and Merl Le Voy in their approach to the summit, and it is easy to understand the confusion of direction in the fierce storm that descended upon the party. (See page 481 in this book.) If, as the dots show, the party went to the summit of the right-hand peak, they went out of their way and had still a considerable distance to travel. "Perhaps five minutes of easy walking would have taken us to the highest point," says Mr. Browne. It is probably more than a mile from the summit of the snow peak shown in the picture to the actual summit of the mountain. One who took that course would have to descend from the peak and then ascend the horseshoe ridge, feet above the summit of the snow peak. In the opinion that Professor Parker expressed to the writer, the dotted lines should bear much more to the left, making directly for the centre of the horseshoe ridge, which is the obvious course. But it should again be said that men in the circumstances and condition of this party when forced to turn back, may be pardoned for mistaking the exact direction in which they had been proceeding.

and we stopped for a few moments when it seemed that we were level with it. We judged it to be about five hundred feet lower than the South Peak.

But still there stretched ahead of us, and perhaps one hundred feet above us, another small ridge with a north and south pair of little haycock summits. This is the real top of Denali. From below, this ultimate ridge merges indistinguishably with the crest of the horseshoe ridge, but it is not a part of it but a culminating ridge beyond it. With keen excitement we pushed on. Walter, who had been in the lead all day, was the first to scramble up; a native Alaskan, he is the first human being to set foot upon the top of Alaska's great mountain, and he had well earned the lifelong distinction. Karstens and Tatum were hard upon his heels, but the last man on the rope, in his enthusiasm and excitement somewhat overpassing his narrow wind margin, had almost to be hauled up the last few feet, and fell unconscious for a moment upon the floor of the little snow basin that occupies the top of the mountain. This, then, is the actual summit, a little crater-like snow basin, sixty or sixty-five feet long and twenty to twenty-five feet wide, with a haycock of snow at either end—the south one a little higher than the north. On the southwest this little basin is much corniced, and the whole thing looked as though every severe storm might somewhat change its shape.

So soon as wind was recovered we shook hands all round and a brief prayer of thanksgiving to Almighty God was said, that He had granted us our hearts' desire and brought us safely to the top of His great mountain.

This prime duty done, we fell at once to our scientific tasks. The instrument-tent was set up, the mercurial barometer, taken out of its leather case and then out of its wooden case, was swung upon its tripod and a rough zero established, and it was left awhile to adjust itself to conditions before a reading was attempted. It was a great gratification to get it to the top uninjured. The boiling-point apparatus was put together and its candle lighted under the ice which filled its little cistern. The three-inch, three-circle aneroid was read at once at thirteen and two-tenths inches, its mendacious altitude scale confidently pointing at twenty-three thousand three hundred feet. Half an hour later it had dropped to 13.175 inches and had shot us up another one hundred feet into the air. Soon the water was boiling in the little tubes of the boiling-point thermometer and the steam pouring out of the vent. The thread of mercury rose to 174.9° and stayed there. There is something definite and uncompromising about the boiling-point hypsometer; no tapping will make it rise or fall; it reaches its mark unmistakably and does not budge. The reading of the mercurial barometer is a slower and more delicate business. It takes a good light and a good sight to tell when the ivory zero-point is exactly touching the surface of the mercury in the cistern; it takes care and precision to get the vernier exactly level with the top of the column. It was read, some half-hour after it was set up, at 13.175 inches. The alcohol minimum thermometer stood at 7° F. all the while we were on top. Meanwhile, Tatum had been reading a round of angles with the prismatic compass. He could not handle it with sufficient exactness with his mitts on, and he froze his fingers doing it barehanded.

The scientific work accomplished, then and not till then did we indulge ourselves in the wonderful prospect that stretched around us. It was a perfectly clear day, the sun shining brightly in the sky, and naught bounded our view save the natural limitations of vision. Immediately before us, in the direction in which we had climbed, lay—nothing: a void, a sheer gulf many thousands of feet deep, and one shrank back instinctively from the little parapet of the snow basin when one

Denali's Wife from the summit of Denali

had glanced at the awful profundity. Across the gulf, about three thousand feet beneath us and fifteen or twenty miles away, sprang most splendidly into view the great mass of Denali's Wife, or Mount Foraker, as some white men misname her, filling majestically all the middle distance. It was our first glimpse of her during the whole ascent. Denali's Wife does not appear at all save from the actual summit of Denali, for she is completely hidden by his South Peak until the moment when his South Peak is surmounted. And never was nobler sight displayed to man than that great, isolated mountain spread out completely, with all its spurs and ridges, its cliffs, and its glaciers, lofty and mighty and yet far beneath us. On that spot one understood why the view of Denali from Lake Minchúmina is the grand view, for the west face drops abruptly down with nothing but that vast void from the top to nigh the bottom of the mountain. Beyond stretched, blue and vague to the south-west, the wide valley of the Kuskokwim, with an end of all mountains. To the north we looked right over the North Peak to the foot-hills below, patched with lakes and lingering snow, glittering with streams. We had hoped to see the junction of the Yukon and Tanana Rivers, one hundred and fifty miles away to the north-west, as we had often and often seen the summit of Denali from that point in the winter, but the haze that almost always qualifies a fine summer day inhibited that stretch of vision. Perhaps the forest-fires we found raging on the Tanana River were already beginning to foul the northern sky.

It was, however, to the south and the east that the most marvellous prospect opened before us. What infinite tangle of mountain ranges filled the whole scene, until gray sky, gray mountain, and gray sea merged in the ultimate distance! The near-by peaks and ridges stood out with dazzling distinction, the glaciation, the drainage, the relation of each part to the others all revealed. The snow-covered tops of the remoter peaks, dwindling and fading, rose to our view as though floating in thin air when their bases were hidden by the haze, and the beautiful crescent curve of the whole Alaskan range exhibited itself from Denali to the sea. To the right hand the glittering, tiny threads of streams draining the mountain range into the Chulitna and Sushitna Rivers, and so to Cook's Inlet and the Pacific Ocean, spread themselves out; to the left the affluents of the Kantishna and the Nenana drained the range into the Yukon and Bering Sea.

Yet the chief impression was not of our connection with the earth so far below, its rivers and its seas, but rather of detachment from it. We seemed alone upon a dead world, as dead as the mountains on the moon. Only once before can the writer remember a similar feeling of being neither in the world or of the world, and that was at the bottom of the Grand Cañon of the Colorado, in Arizona, its savage granite walls as dead as this savage peak of ice.

Above us the sky took a blue so deep that none of us had ever gazed upon a midday sky like it before. It was a deep, rich, lustrous, transparent blue, as dark as a Prussian blue, but intensely blue; a hue so strange, so increasingly impressive, that to one at least it "seemed like special news of God," as a new poet sings. We first noticed the darkening tint of the upper sky in the Grand Basin, and it deepened as we rose. Tyndall observed and discussed this phenomenon in the Alps, but it seems scarcely to have been mentioned since.

It is difficult to describe at all the scene which the top of the mountain presented, and impossible to describe it adequately. One was not occupied with the thought of description but wholly possessed with the breadth and glory of it, with its sheer, amazing immensity and scope. Only once, perhaps, in any lifetime is such vision granted, certainly never before had been vouchsafed to any of us. Not often in the summer time does Denali completely unveil himself and dismiss the clouds from all the earth beneath. Yet we could not linger, unique though the occasion, dearly bought our privilege; the miserable limitations of the flesh gave us continual warning to depart; we grew colder and still more wretchedly cold. The thermometer stood at 7° in the full sunshine, and the north wind was keener than ever. My fingers were so cold that I would not venture to withdraw them from the mittens to change the film in the camera, and the other men were in like case; indeed, our hands were by this time so numb as to make it almost impossible to operate a camera at all. A number of photographs had been taken, though not half we should have liked to take, but it is probable that, however many more exposures had been made, they would have been little better than those we got. Our top-of-the-mountain photography was a great disappointment. One thing we learned: exposures at such altitude should be longer than those below, perhaps owing to the darkness of the sky.

When the mercurial barometer had been read the tent was thrown down and abandoned, the first of the series of abandonments that marked our descent from the mountain. The tent-pole was used for a moment as a flagstaff while Tatum hoisted a little United States flag he had patiently and skilfully constructed in our

Robert Tatum raising the Stars and Stripes on the highest point in North America

*This photograph was exposed upon a previous exposure.*

camps below out of two silk handkerchiefs and the cover of a sewing-bag. Then the pole was put to its permanent use. It had already been carved with a suitable inscription, and now a transverse piece, already prepared and fitted, was lashed securely to it and it was planted on one of the little snow turrets of the summit—the sign of our redemption, high above North America. Only some peaks in the Andes and some peaks in the Himalayas rise above it in all the world. It was of light, dry birch and, though six feet in length, so slender that we think it may weather many a gale. And Walter thrust it into the snow so firmly at a blow that it could not be withdrawn again. Then we gathered about it and said the Te Deum.

It was 1:30 P.M. when we reached the summit and two minutes past three when we left; yet so quickly had the time flown that we could not believe we had been an hour and a half on top. The journey down was a long, weary grind, the longer and the wearier that we made a détour and went out of our way to seek for Professor Parker's thermometer, which he had left "in a crack on the west side of the last boulder of the north-east ridge." That sounds definite enough, yet in fact it is equivocal. "Which is the last boulder?" we disputed as we went down the slope. A long series of rocks almost in line came to an end, with one rock a little below the others, a little out of the line. This egregious boulder would, it seemed to me, naturally be called the last; Karstens thought not—thought the "last boulder" was the last *on* the ridge. As we learned later, Karstens was right, and since he yielded to me we did not find the thermometer, for, having descended to this isolated rock, we would not climb up again for fifty thermometers. One's disappointment is qualified by the knowledge that the thermometer is probably not of adequate scale, Professor Parker's recollection being that it read only to 60° below zero, F. A lower temperature than this is recorded every winter on the Yukon River.

A thermometer reading to 100° below zero, left at this spot, would, in my judgment, perhaps yield a lower minimum than has ever yet been authentically recorded on earth, and it is most unfortunate that the opportunity was lost. Yet I did not leave my own alcohol minimum—scaled to 95° below zero, and yielding, by estimation, perhaps ten degrees below the scaling—there, because of the difficulty of giving explicit directions that should lead to its ready recovery, and at the close of such a day of toil as is involved in reaching the summit, men have no stomach for prolonged search. As will be told, it is cached lower down, but at a spot where it cannot be missed.

However, for one, the writer was largely unconscious of weariness in that descent. All the way down, my thoughts were occupied with the glorious scene my eyes had gazed upon and should gaze upon never again. In all human probability I would never climb that mountain again; yet if I climbed it a score more times I would never be likely to repeat such vision. Commonly, only for a few hours at a time, never for more than a few days at a time, save in the dead of winter when climbing is out of the question, does Denali completely unveil himself and dismiss the clouds from all the earth beneath him. Not for long, with these lofty colds contiguous, will the vapors of Cook's Inlet and Prince William Sound and the whole North Pacific Ocean refrain from sweeping upward; their natural trend is hitherward. As the needle turns to the magnet so the clouds find an irresistible attraction in this great mountain mass, and though the inner side of the range be rid of them the sea side is commonly filled to overflowing.

Only those who have for long years cherished a great and almost inordinate desire, and have had that desire gratified to the limit of their expectation, can enter into the deep thankfulness and content that filled the heart upon the descent of this mountain. There was no pride of conquest, no trace of that exultation of victory some enjoy upon the first ascent of a lofty peak, no gloating over good fortune that had hoisted us a few hundred feet higher than others who had struggled and been discomfited. Rather was the feeling that a privileged communion with the high places of the earth had been granted; that not only had we been permitted to lift up eager eyes to these summits, secret and solitary since the world began, but to enter boldly upon them, to take place, as it were, domestically in their hitherto sealed chambers, to inhabit them, and to cast our eyes down from them, seeing all things as they spread out from the windows of heaven itself.

Into this strong yet serene emotion, into this reverent elevation of spirit, came with a shock a recollection of some recent reading.

Oh, wisdom of man and the apparatus of the sciences, the little columns of mercury that sling up and down, the vacuum boxes that expand and contract, the hammer that chips the highest rocks, the compass that takes the bearings of glacier and ridge—all the equipage of hypsometry and geology and geodesy—how pitifully feeble and childish it seems to cope with the majesty of the mountains! Take them all together, haul them up the steep, and as they lie there, read, recorded, and done for, which shall be more adequate to the whole scene—their records?—or that simple, ancient hymn, "We praise Thee, O God!—Heaven and earth are full of the majesty of Thy Glory!" What an astonishing thing that, standing where we stood and seeing what we saw, there are men who should be able to deduce this law or that from their observation of its working and yet be unable to see the Lawgiver!—who should be able to push back effect to immediate cause and yet be blind to the Supreme Cause of All Causes; who can say, "This is the glacier's doing and it is marvellous in our eyes," and not see Him "Who in His Strength setteth fast the mountains and is girded with power," Whose servants the glaciers, the snow, and the ice are, "wind and storm fulfilling His Word"; who exult in the exercise of their own intelligences and the play things those intelligences have constructed and yet deny the Omniscience that endowed them with some minute fragment of Itself! It was not always so; it was not so with the really great men who have advanced our knowledge of nature. But of late years hordes of small men have given themselves up to the study of the physical sciences without any study preliminary. It would almost seem nowadays that whoever can sit in the seat of the scornful may sit in the seat of learning.

A good many years ago, on an occasion already referred to, the writer roamed through the depths of the Grand Cañon with a chance acquaintance who described himself as "Herpetologist to the Academy of Sciences" in some Western or Mid-Western State, and as this gentleman found the curious little reptiles he was in search of under a root or in a cranny of rock he repeated their many-syllabled names. Curious to know what these names literally meant and whence derived, the writer made inquiry, sometimes hazarding a conjectural etymology. To his astonishment and dismay he found this "scientist," whom he had looked up to, entirely ignorant of the meaning of the terms he employed. They were just arbitrary terms to him. The little hopping and crawling creatures might as well have been numbered, or called x, y, z, for any significance their formidable nomenclature held for him. Yet this man had been keenly sarcastic about the Noachian deluge and had jeered from the height of his superiority at hoary records which he knew only at second-hand reference, and had laid it down that if the human race became extinct the birds would stand the best chance of "evolving a primate"! Since that time other scientists have been encountered, with no better equipment, with no history, no poetry, no philosophy in any broad sense, men with no letters—illiterate, strictly speaking—yet with all the dogmatism in the world. Can any one be more dogmatic than your modern scientist? The reproach has passed altogether to him from the theologian.

The thing grows, and its menace and scandal grow with it. Since coming "outside" the writer has encountered a professor at a college, a Ph.D. of a great university, who confessed that he had never heard of certain immortal characters of Dickens whose names are household words. We shall have to open Night-Schools for Scientists, where men who have been deprived of all early advantages may learn the rudiments of English literature. One wishes that Dickens himself might have dealt with their pretensions, but they are since his day. And surely it is time some one started a movement for suppressing illiterate Ph.D.'s.

Of this class, one feels sure, are the scientific heroes of the sensational articles in the monthly magazines of the baser sort, of which we picked up a number in the Kantishna on our way to the mountain. Here, in a picture that seems to have obtruded itself bodily into a page of letter-press, or else to have suffered the accidental irruption of a page of letter-press all around it, you shall see a grave scientist looking anxiously down a very large microscope, and shall read that he has transferred a kidney from a cat to a dog, and therefore we can no longer believe in the immortality of the soul; or else that he has succeeded in artificially fertilizing the ova of a starfish—or was it a jellyfish ?—and therefore there is no God; not just in so many bald words, of course, but in unmistakable import. Or it may be—so commonly does the crassest credulity go hand in hand with the blankest skepticism—he has discovered the germ of old age and is hot upon the track of another germ that shall destroy it, so that we may all live virtually as long as we like; which, of course, disposes once for all of a world to come. The Psalmist was not always complaisant or even temperate in his language, but he lived a long time ago and must be pardoned; his curt summary stands: "Dixit insipiens!" But the writer vows that if he were addicted to the pursuit of any branch of physical knowledge he would insist upon being called by the name of that branch. He would be a physiologist or a biologist or an anatomist or even a herpetologist, but none should call him "scientist." As Doll Tearsheet says in the second part of "King Henry IV": "These villains will make the word as odious as the word 'occupy'; which was an excellent good word before it was ill-sorted." If Doctor Johnson were compiling an English dictionary to-day he would define "scientist" something thus: "A cant name for an experimenter in some department of physical knowledge, commonly furnished with arrogance and dogmatism, but devoid of real learning."

Here is no gibe at the physical sciences. To sneer at them were just as foolish as to sneer at religion. What we could do on this expedition in a "scientific" way we did laboriously and zealously. We would never have thought of attempting the ascent of the mountain without bringing back whatever little addition to human knowledge was within the scope of our powers and opportunities. Tatum took rounds of angles, in practice against the good fortune of a clear day on top, on every possible occasion. The sole personal credit the present writer takes concerning the whole enterprise is the packing of that mercurial barometer on his back, from the Tanana River nearly to the top of the mountain, a point at which he was compelled to relinquish it to another. He has always had his opinion about mountain climbers who put an aneroid in their pocket and go to the top of a great, new peak and come down confidently announcing its height. But when all this business is done as closely and carefully as possible, and every observation taken that there are instruments devised to record, surely the soul is dead that feels no more and sees no further than the instruments do, that stirs with no other emotion than the mercury in the tube or the dial at its point of suspension, that is incapable of awe, of reverence, of worshipful uplift, and does not feel that "the Lord even the most mighty God hath spoken, and called the world from the rising of the sun even to the going down of the same," in the wonders displayed before his eyes.

We reached our eighteen-thousand-foot camp about five o'clock, a weary but happy crew. It was written in the diary that night: "I remember no day in my life so full of toil, distress, and exhaustion, and yet so full of happiness and keen gratification."

The culminating day should not be allowed to pass without another tribute to the efficiency of the amber glasses. Notwithstanding the glare of the sun at twenty thousand feet and upward, no one had the slightest irritation of the eyes. There has never been an April of travel on the Yukon in eight years that the writer has not suffered from inflammation of the eyes despite the darkest smoke-colored glasses that could be procured. A naked candle at a road-house would give a stab of pain every time the eyes encountered it, and reading would become almost impossible. The amber glasses, however, while leaving vision almost as bright as without them, filter out the rays that cause the irritation and afford perfect protection against the consequences of sun and glare. There is only one improvement to make in the amber glasses and that is some device of air-tight cells that shall prevent them from fogging when the cold on the outside of the glass condenses the moisture of perspiration on the inside of the glass. We use double-glazed sashes with an air space between on all windows in our houses in Alaska and find ourselves no longer incommoded by frost on the panes; some adaptation of this principle should be within the skill of the optician and would remove a very troublesome defect in all snow-glasses.

If some one would invent a preventive against shortness of breath as efficient as amber glasses are against snow-blindness, climbing at great altitudes would lose all its terrors for one mountaineer. So far as it was possible to judge, no other member of the party was near his altitude limit. There seemed no reason why Karstens and Walter in particular should not go another ten thousand feet, were there mountain in the world ten thousand feet higher than Denali, but the writer knows that he himself could not have gone much higher.

## CHAPTER VI

# The Return

The next day was another bright, cloudless day, the second and last of them. Perhaps never did men abandon as cheerfully stuff that had been freighted as laboriously as we abandoned our surplus baggage at the eighteen-thousand-foot camp. We made a great pile of it in the lee of one of the ice-blocks of the glacier—food, coal-oil, clothing, and bedding—covering all with the wolf-robe and setting up a shovel as a mark; though just why we cached it so carefully, or for whom, no one of us would be able to say. It will probably be a long time ere any others camp in that Grand Basin. While yet such a peak is unclimbed, there is constant goading of mountaineering minds to its conquest; once its top has been reached, the incentive declines. Much exploring work is yet to do on Denali; the day will doubtless come when all its peaks and ridges and glaciers will be duly mapped, but our view from the summit agreed with our study of its conformation during the ascent, that no other route will be found to the top. When first we were cutting and climbing on the ridge, and had glimpses, as the mists cleared, of the glacier on the other side and the ridges that arose from it, we thought that perhaps they might afford a passage, but from above the appearance changed and seemed to forbid it altogether. At times, almost in despair at the task which the Northeast Ridge presented, we would look across at the ice-covered rocks of the North Peak and dream that they might be climbed, but they are really quite impossible. The south side has been tried again and again and no approach discovered, nor did it appear from the top that such approach exists; the west side is sheer precipice; the north side is covered with a great hanging glacier and is devoid of practicable slopes; it has been twice attempted. Only on the northeast has the glacier cut so deeply into the mountain as to give access to the heights.

June 8th was Sunday, but we had to take advantage of the clear, bright day to get as far down the mountain as possible. The stuff it was still necessary to pack made good, heavy loads, and we knew not what had happened to our staircase in our absence.

Having said Morning Prayer, we left at 9.30 A.M., after a night in which all of us slept soundly—the first sound sleep some had enjoyed for a long time. Contentment and satisfaction are great somnifacients. The Grand Basin was glorious in sunshine, the peaks crystal-clear against a cloudless sky, the huge blocks of ice thrown down by the earthquake and scattered all over the glacier gleamed white in the sunshine, deep-blue in the shadow. We wound our way downward, passing camp site after camp site, until at the first place we camped in the Grand Basin we stopped for lunch. Then we made the traverse under the cliffs to the Parker Pass, which we reached at 1:30 P.M. The sun was hot; there was not a breath of wind; we were exceedingly thirsty and we decided to light the primus stove and make a big pot of tea and replenish the thermos bottles before attempting the descent of the ridge. While this was doing a place was found to cache the minimum thermometer and a tin can that had held a photographic film, in which we had placed a record of our ascent. Above, we had not found any distinctive place in which a record could be deposited with the assurance that it would be found by any one seeking it. One feels sure that in the depth of winter very great cold must occur even at this elevation. Yet we should have liked to leave it much higher. Without some means, which we did not possess, of marking a position, there would, however, have been little use in leaving it amid the boulders where we hunted unsuccessfully for Professor Parker's instrument. We had hoped to be able to grave some sign upon the rocks with the geological hammer, but the first time it was brought down upon the granite its point splintered in the same exasperating way that the New York dealer's fancy ice-axes behaved when it was attempted to put them to practical use. "Warranted cast steel" upon an implement ought to be a warning not to purchase it for mountain work. Tool-steel alone will serve.

Our little record cache at the Parker Pass, placed at the foot of the west or upward-facing side of the great slab which marks the natural camping site, should stand there for many years. It is not a place where snow lies deep or long, and it will surely be found by any who seek it. We took our last looks up into the Grand Basin, still brilliant in the sunshine, our last looks at the summit, still cloudless and clear.

There was a melancholy even in the midst of triumph in looking for the last time at these scenes where we had so greatly hoped and endeavored—and had been so amply rewarded. We recalled the eager expectation with which we first gazed up between these granite slabs into the long-hidden basin, a week before, and there was sadness in the feeling that in all probability we should never have this noble view again.

Before the reader turns his back upon the Grand Basin once for all, I should like to put a name upon the glacier it contains—since it is the fashion to name glaciers. I should like to call it the Harper Glacier, after my half-breed companion of three years, who was the first human being to reach the summit of the mountain. This reason might suffice, but there is another and most interesting reason for associating the name Harper with this mountain. Arthur Harper, Walter's father, the pioneer of all Alaskan miners, "the first man who thought of trying the Yukon as a mining field so far as we know," as William Ogilvie tells us in his "Early Days on the Yukon"* (and none had better opportunity of knowing than Ogilvie), was also the first man to make written reference to this mountain, since Vancouver, the great navigator, saw it from the head of Cook's Inlet in 1794.

Arthur Harper, in company with Al. Mayo, made the earliest exploration of the Tanana River, ascending that stream in the summer of 1878 to about the present site of Fairbanks; and in a letter to E. W. Nelson, of the United States Biological Survey, then on the Alaskan coast, Harper wrote the following winter of the "great ice mountain to the south" as one of the most wonderful sights of the trip."** It is pleasant to think that a son of his, yet unborn, was to be the first to set foot on its top; pleasantly also the office of setting his name upon the lofty glacier, the gleam from which caught his eye and roused his wonder thirty years ago, falls upon one who has been glad and proud to take, in some measure, his place.

Then began the difficulty and the danger, the toil and the anxiety, of the descent of the ridge. Karstens led, then followed Tatum, then the writer, and then Walter. The unbroken surface of the ridge above the cleavage is sensationally steep, and during our absence nearly two feet of new snow had fallen upon it. The steps that had been shovelled as we ascended were entirely obliterated and it was necessary

* Ottawa: Thorburn & Abbott, 1913, p. 87.
** "Mt. McKinley Region": Alfred H. Brooks, Washington, 1911, p. 25.

Beginning the descent of the ridge; looking down 4,000 feet upon the Muldrow Glacier

to shovel new ones; it was the very heat of the day, and by the canons of climbing we should have camped at the Pass and descended in the early morning. But all were eager to get down, and we ventured it. Now that our task was accomplished, our minds reverted to the boy at the base camp long anxiously expecting us, and we thought of him and spoke of him continually and speculated how he had fared. One feels upon reflection that we took more risk in descending that ridge than we took at any time in the ascent. But Karstens was most cautious and careful, and in the long and intensive apprenticeship of this expedition had become most expert. I sometimes wondered whether Swiss guides would have much to teach either him or Walter in snow-craft; their chief instruction would probably be along the line of taking more chances, wisely. If the writer had to ascend this mountain again he would intrust himself to Karstens and Walter rather than to any Swiss guides he has known, for ice and snow in Alaska are not quite the same as ice and snow in the Alps or the Canadian Rockies.

The loose snow was shovelled away and the steps dug in the hard snow beneath, and the creepers upon our feet gave good grip in it. Thus, slowly, step by step, we descended the ridge and in an hour and a half had reached the cleavage, the most critical place in the whole descent. With the least possible motion of the feet, setting them exactly in the shovelled steps, we crept like cats across this slope, thrusting the points of our axes into the holes that had been made in the ice-wall above, moving all together, the rope always taut, no one speaking a word. When once Karstens was anchored on the further ice he stood and gathered up the rope as first one and then another passed safely to him and anchored himself beside him, until at last we were all across. Then, stooping to pass the overhanging ice-cliff that here also disputed the pack upon one's back, we went down to the long, long stretch of jagged pinnacles and bergs, and our intricate staircase in the masonry of them. Shovelling was necessary all the way down, but the steps were there, needing only to be uncovered. Passing our ridge camp, passing the danger of the great gable, down the rocks by which we reached the ridge and down the slopes to the glacier floor we went, reaching our old camp at 9.30 P.M., six and a quarter hours from the Parker Pass, twelve hours from the eighteen-thousand-foot camp in the Grand Basin, our hearts full of thankfulness that the terrible ridge was behind us. Until we reached the glacier floor the weather had been clear; almost immediately thereafter the old familiar cloud smother began to pour down from above and we saw the heights no more.

The camp was in pretty bad shape. The snow that had fallen upon it had melted and frozen to ice, in the sun's rays and the night frosts, and weighed the tent down to the ground. But an hour's work made it habitable again, and we gleefully piled the stove with the last of our wood and used the last spoonfuls of a can of baking-powder to make a batch of biscuits, the first bread we had eaten in two weeks.

Next day we abandoned the camp, leaving all standing, and, putting our packs upon a Yukon sled, rejecting the ice-creepers, and resuming our rough-locked snow-shoes, we started down the glacier in soft, cloudy weather to our base camp. Again it had been wiser to have waited till night, that the snow bridges over the crevasses might be at their hardest; but we could not wait. Every mind was occupied with Johnny. We were two weeks overstayed of the time we had told him to expect our return, and we knew not what might have happened to the boy. The four of us on one rope, Karstens leading and Walter at the gee-pole, we went down the first sharp descents of the glaciers without much trouble, the new, soft snow making a good brake for the sled. But lower down the crevasses began to give us trouble. The snow bridges were melted at their edges, and sometimes the sled had to be lowered down to the portion that still held and hauled up at the other side. Sometimes a bridge gave way as its edge was cautiously ventured upon with the snow-shoes, and we had to go far over to the glacier wall to get round the crevasse. The willows with which we had staked the trail still stood, sometimes just their tips appearing above the new snow, and they were a good guide, though we often had to leave the old trail. At last the crevasses were all passed and we reached the lower portion of the glacier, which is free of them. Then the snow grew softer and softer, and our moccasined feet were soon wet through. Large patches of the black shale with which much of this glacier is covered were quite bare of snow, and the sled had to be hauled laboriously across them. Then we began to encounter pools of water, which at first we avoided, but they soon grew so numerous that we went right through them.

The going grew steadily wetter and rougher and more disagreeable. The lower stretch of a glacier is an unhandsome sight in summer: all sorts of rock débris and ugly black shale, with discolored melting ice and snow, intersected everywhere with streams of dirty water—this was what it had degenerated into as we reached the pass. The snow was entirely gone from the pass, so the sled was abandoned—left standing upright, with its gee-pole sticking in the air that if any one else ever chanced to want it, it might readily be found. The snow-shoes were piled around it, and we resumed our packs and climbed up to the pass. The first thing that struck our eyes as we stood upon the rocks of the pass was a brilliant trailing purple moss flower of such gorgeous color that we all exclaimed at its beauty and wondered how it grew clinging to bare rock. It was the first bright color that we had seen for so long that it gave unqualified pleasure to us all and was a foretaste of the enhancing delights that awaited us as we descended to the bespangled valley. If a man would know to the utmost the charm of flowers, let him exile himself among the snows of a lofty mountain during fifty days of spring and come down into the first full flush of summer. We could scarcely pass a flower by, and presently had our hands full of blooms like schoolgirls on a picnic.

But although the first things that attracted our attention were the flowers, the next were the mosquitoes. They were waiting for us at the pass and they gave us their warmest welcome. The writer took sharp blame to himself that, organizing and equipping this expedition, he had made no provision against these intolerable pests. But we had so confidently expected to come out a month earlier, before the time of mosquitoes arrived, that although the matter was suggested and discussed it was put aside as unnecessary. Now there was the prospect of a fifty or sixty mile tramp across country, subject all the while to the assaults of venomous insects, which are a greater hindrance to summer travel in Alaska than any extremity of cold is to winter travel.

Not even the mosquitoes, however, took our minds from Johnny, and a load was lifted from every heart when we came near enough to our camp to see that some one was moving about it. A shout brought him running, and he never stopped until he had met us and had taken the pack from my shoulders and put it on his own. Our happiness was now unalloyed; the last anxiety was removed. The dogs gave us most jubilant welcome and were fat and well favored.

What a change had come over the place! All the snow was gone from the hills; the stream that gathered its three forks at this point roared over its rocks; the stunted willows were in full leaf; the thick, soft moss of every dark shade of green and yellow and red made a foil for innumerable brilliant flowers. The fat, gray conies chirped at us from the rocks; the ground-squirrels, greatly multiplied since the wholesale destruction of foxes, kept the dogs unavailingly chasing hither and thither whenever they were loose. We never grew tired of walking up and down and to and fro about the camp—it was a delight to tread upon the moss-covered earth after so long treading upon nothing but ice and snow; it was a delight to gaze out through naked eyes after all those weeks in which we had not dared even for a few moments to lay aside the yellow glasses in the open air; it was a delight to see joyful, eager animal life around us after our sojourn in regions dead. Supper was a delight. Johnny had killed four mountain-sheep and a caribou while we were gone, and not only had fed the dogs well, but from time to time had put aside choice portions expecting our return. But what was most grateful to us and most extraordinary in him, the boy had saved, untouched, the small ration of sugar and milk left

JOHNNY FRED, WHO KEPT THE BASE-CAMP AND FED THE DOGS AND WOULD NOT TOUCH THE SUGAR

for his consumption, knowing that ours was all destroyed; and we enjoyed coffee with these luxurious appurtenances as only they can who have been long deprived of them. There are not many boys of fifteen or sixteen of any race who would voluntarily have done the like.

The next day there was much to do. There were pack-saddles of canvas to

"MUK," THE AUTHOR'S PET MALAMUTE

make for the dogs' backs that they might help us carry our necessary stuff out; our own clothing and footwear to overhaul, bread to bake, guns to clean and oil against rust. Yet withal, we took it lazily, with five to divide these tasks, and napped and lay around and continually consumed biscuits and coffee which Johnny continually cooked. We all took at least a partial bath in the creek, cold as it was, the first bath in—well, in a long time. Mountain climbers belong legitimately to the great unwashed.

It was a day of perfect rest and contentment with hearts full of gratitude. Not a single mishap had occurred to mar the complete success of our undertaking—not an injury of any sort to anyone, nor an illness. All five of us were in perfect health. Surely we had reason to be grateful; and surely we were happy in having Him to whom our gratitude might be poured out. What a bald, incomplete, and disconcerting thing it must be to have no one to thank for crowning mercies like these!

On Tuesday, the 10th June, we made our final abandonment, leaving the tent standing with stove and food and many articles that we did not need cached in it, and with four of the dogs carrying packs and led with chains, packs on our own backs and the ice-axes for staves in our hands, we turned our backs upon the mountain and went down the valley toward the Clearwater. The going was not too bad until we had crossed that stream and climbed the hills to the rolling country between it and the McKinley Fork of the Kantishna. Again and again we looked back for a parting glimpse of the mountain, but we never saw sign of it any more. The foot-hills were clear, the rugged wall of the glacier cut the sky, but the great mountain might have been a thousand miles off for any visible indication it gave. It is easy to understand how travellers across equatorial Africa have passed near the base of the snowy peaks of Ruwenzori without knowing they were even in the neighborhood of great mountains, and have come back and denied their existence.

The broken country between the streams was difficult. Underneath was a thick elastic moss in which the foot sank three or four inches at every step and that makes toilsome travelling. The mosquitoes were a constant annoyance. But the abundant bird life upon this open moorland, continually reminding one as it did of moorlands in the north of England or of Scotland, was full of interest. Ptarmigan, half changed from their snowy plumage to the brown of summer, and presenting a curious piebald appearance, were there in great numbers, cackling their guttural cry with its concluding notes closely resembling the "ko-ax, ko-ax" of the Frogs'

Chorus in the comedy of Aristophanes; snipe whistled and curlews whirled all about us. Half-way across to the McKinley Fork it began to rain, thunder-peal succeeding thunder-peal, and each crash announcing a heavier downpour. Soon we were all wet through, and then the rain turned to hail that fell smartly until all the moss was white with it, and that gave place to torrents of rain again. Dog packs and men's packs were alike wet, and no one of us had a dry stitch on him when we reached the banks of the McKinley Fork and the old spacious hunting tent that stands there in which we were to spend the night. Rather hopelessly we hung our bedding to dry on ropes strung about some trees, and our wet clothing around the stove. By taking turns all the night in sitting up, to keep a fire going, we managed to get our clothes dried by morning, but the bedding was wet as ever. Fortunately, the night was a warm one.

The next morning there was the McKinley Fork to cross the first thing, and it was a difficult and disagreeable task. This stream, which drains the Muldrow Glacier and therefore the whole north-east face of Denali, occupies a dreary, desolate bed of boulder and gravel and mud a mile or more wide; rather it does not occupy it, save perhaps after tremendous rain following great heat, but wanders amid it, with a dozen channels of varying depth but uniform blackness, the inky solution of the shale which the mountain discharges abundantly tingeing not only its waters but the whole Kantishna, into which it flows one hundred miles away. Commonly in the early morning the waters are low, the night frosts checking the melting of the glacier ice; but this morning the drainage of yesterday's rain-storm had swollen them. Channel after channel was waded in safety until the main stream was reached, and that swept by, thigh-deep, with a rushing black current that had a very evil look. Karstens was scouting ahead, feeling for the shallower places, stemming the hurrying waters till they swept up to his waist. The dogs did not like the look of it and with their packs, still wet from yesterday, were hampered in swimming. Two that Tatum was leading suddenly turned back when half-way across, and the chains, entangling his legs, pulled him over face foremost into the deepest of the water. His pack impeded his efforts to rise, and the water swept all over him. Karstens hurried back to his rescue, and he was extricated from his predicament, half drowned and his clothes filled with mud and sand. There was no real danger of drowning, but it was a particularly noxious ducking in icy filth. The sun was warm, however, and after basking upon the rocks awhile he was able to proceed, still wet, though he had stripped and wrung out his clothes—for we had no dry change—and very gritty in underwear, but taking no harm whatever. I think Tatum regretted losing, in the mad rush of black water, the ice-axe he had carried to the top of the mountain more than he regretted his wetting.

On the further bank of the McKinley Fork we entered our first wood, a belt about three miles wide that lines the river. Our first forest trees gave us almost as much pleasure as our first flowers. Animal life abounded, all in the especially interesting condition of rearing half-grown young. Squirrels from their nests scolded at our intrusion most vehemently; an owl flew up with such a noisy snapping and chattering that our attention was drawn to the point from which she rose, and there, perched upon a couple of rotten stumps a few feet apart, were two half-fledged owlets, passive, immovable, which allowed themselves to be photographed and even handled without any indication of life except in their wondering eyes and the circumrotary heads that contained them. Moose signs and bear signs were every where; rabbits, now in their summer livery, flitted from bush to bush. That belt of wood was a zoological garden stocked with birds and mammals. And we rejoiced with them over their promising families and harmed none.

From the wood we rose again to the moorland—to the snipe and ptarmigan and curlews, some yet sitting upon belated eggs—to the heavy going of the moss and the yet heavier going of niggerhead. Our journey skirted a large lake picturesquely surrounded by hills, and we spoke of how pleasantly a summer lodge might be placed upon its shores were it not for the mosquitoes. The incessant leaping of fish, the occasional flight of fowl alone disturbed the perfect reflection of cliff and hill in its waters. At times we followed game trails along its margin; at times swampy ground made us seek the hillside.

Thus, slowly covering the miles that we had gone so quickly over upon the ice of the lake two months before, we reached Moose Creek and the miners' cabins at Eureka late at night and received warm welcome and most hospitable entertainment from Mr. Jack Hamilton. It was good to see men other than our own party again, good to sleep in a bed once more, good to regale ourselves with food long strange to our mouths. Here we had our first intimation of any happenings in the outside world for the past three months and sorrowed that Saint Sophia was still to remain at Mohammedan temple, and that the kindly King of Greece had been murdered. Here also Hamilton generously provided us with spare mosquito netting for veils, and we found a package canvas gloves I had ordered from Fairbanks long before, and so were protected from our chief enemies. From Moose Creek we went over the hills to Caribou Creek and again were most kindly welcomed and entertained by Mr. and Mrs. Quigley, and discussed our climb for a long while with McGonogill of the "pioneer" party. Then, mainly down the bed of Glacier Creek, now on lingering ice or snow-drift, with the water rushing underneath, now on the rocks, now through the brush, crossing and recrossing the creek, we reached the long line of desolate, decaying houses known as Glacier City, and found convenient refuge in one of the cabins therein, still maintained as an occasional abode. On the outskirts of the "city" next morning a moose and two calves sprang up from the brush, our approach over the moss not giving enough notice to awake her from sleep until we were almost upon her.

Instead of pursuing our way across the increasingly difficult and swampy country to the place where our boat and supplies lay cached, we turned aside at midday to the "fish camp" on the Bearpaw, and, after enjoying the best our host possessed from the stream and from his early garden, borrowed his boat, choosing twenty miles or so on the water to nine of niggerhead and marsh. But the river was very low and we had much trouble getting the boat over riffles and bars, so that it was late at night when we reached that other habitation of dragons known as Diamond City. While we submerged our cached poling boat to swell its sun-dried seams, Walter and Johnny returned the borrowed boat, and, since the stream had fallen yet more, were many hours in reaching the fish camp and in tramping back.

But the labor of the return journey was now done. A canvas stretched over willows made a shelter for the centre of the boat, and at noon on the second day men, dogs, and baggage were embarked, to float down the Bearpaw to Kantishna, to the Tanana, to the Yukon. The Bearpaw swarmed with animal life. Geese and ducks, with their little terrified broods, scooted ahead of us on the water, the mothers presently leaving their young in a nook of the bank and making a flying détour to return to them. Sometimes a duck would simulate a broken wing to lure us away from the little ones. We had no meat and were hungry for the usual early summer diet of water-fowl, but not hungry enough to kill these birds. Beaver dropped noisily into the water from trees that exhibited their marvellous carpentry, some lying prostrate, some half chiselled through. It seemed, indeed, as though the beaver were preparing great irrigation works all through this country. Since the law went into effect prohibiting their capture until 1915 they have increased and multiplied all over interior Alaska. They are still caught by the natives, but since their skins cannot be sold the Indians are wearing beaver garments again to the great advantage of health in the severe winters. One wishes very heartily that the prohibition might be made perpetual, for only so will fur become the native again. It is good to see the children, particularly, in beaver coats and breeches instead of the wretched cotton that otherwise is almost their only garb. Would it be altogether beyond reason to hope that a measure which was enacted to prevent the extermination of an animal might be perpetuated on behalf of the survival of an interesting and deserving race of human beings now sorely threatened? Or is it solely the conservation of commercial resources that engages the attention of government? There are few measures that would rebound more to the physical benefit of the Alaskan Indian than the perpetuating of the law against the sale of beaver skins. With the present high and continually appreciating price of skins, none of the common people of the land, white or native, can afford to wear furs. Such a prohibition as has been suggested would restore to Alaskans a small share in the resources of Alaska. Is there any country in the world where furs are actually needed more?

Not only beaver, but nearly all fur and game animals have greatly increased in the Kantishna country. In the year of the stampede, when thousands of men spent the winter here, there was wholesale destruction of game and trapping of fur. But the country, left to itself, is now restocked of game and fur, except of foxes, the high price of which has almost exterminated them here and is rapidly exterminating then throughout interior Alaska. They have been poisoned in the most reckless and unscrupulous way, and there seems no means of stopping it under the present law. We saw scarcely a fox track in the country, though a few years ago they were exceedingly plentiful all over the foot-hills of the great range. Mink, marten, and muskrat were seen from time to time swimming in the river; a couple of yearling moose started from the bank where they had been drinking as we noiselessly turned a bend; brilliant kingfishers flitted across the water. So down these rivers we drifted, sometimes in sunshine, sometimes in rain, until early in the morning of the 20th

June, we reached Tanana, and our journey was concluded three months and four days after it was begun. When the telegraph office opened at 8 o'clock a message was sent, in accordance with promise, to a Seattle paper, and it illustrates the rapidity with which news is spread to-day that a ship in Bering Sea, approaching Nome, received the news from Seattle by wire-less telegraph before 11 A.M. But a message from the Seattle paper received the same morning asking for "five hundred more words describing narrow escapes" was left unanswered, for, thank God, there were none to describe.

CHAPTER VII

# The Height of Denali, With a Discussion of the Readings on the Summit and During the Ascent

The determination of the heights of mountains by triangulation is, of course, the method that in general commends itself to the topographer, though it may be questioned whether the very general use of aneroids for barometric determinations has not thrown this latter means of measuring altitudes into undeserved discredit when the mercurial barometer is used instead of its convenient but unreliable substitute.

The altitude given on the present maps for Denali is the mean of determinations made by triangulation by three different men: Muldrow on the Sushitna* side in 1898, Raeburn on the Kuskokwim side in 1902, and Porter, from the Yentna country in 1906. In addition, a determination was made by the Coast and Geodetic Survey in 1910, from points near Cook's Inlet. "The work of the Coast Survey," writes Mr. Alfred Brooks, "is more refined than the rough triangulation done by our men; at the same time they were much further away." "It is a curious coincidence," he adds, "that the determination made by the Coast Survey was the mean which we had assumed from our three determinations" (twenty thousand three hundred feet).

---

*"Sushitna" represents unquestionably the native pronunciation and the "h" should be retained. The reason for its elision current in Alaska is too contemptible to be referred to further. Perhaps the same genius removed this "h" who removed the "'s" from "Cook's Inlet" of the British admiralty. One is not surprised when a post-office at Cape Prince of Wales is named "Wales" because one is not surprised at any banalities of the postal department—Alaska or elsewhere, but one expects better things from the cultured branches of the government service. It is interesting to speculate what will happen to Revillegigedo Island, which Vancouver named for the viceroy of Mexico who was kind to him, when the official curtailer of names finds time to attend to *it*. If there be a post-office thereon it is probably already named "Gig."

There are, however, two sources of error in the determination of the height of this mountain by triangulation—a general one and a particular one. The general one lies in the difficulty of ascertaining the proper correction to be applied for the refraction of the atmosphere, and the higher the mountain the greater the liability to this error; for not much is positively known about the angle of refraction of the upper regions of the air. The officers of the Trigonometrical Survey of India have published their opinion that the heights of the great peaks of the Himalayas will have to be revised on this account. The report of the Coast Survey's determination of the height of Denali claims a "co-efficient of refraction nearer the truth" than the figure used on a previous occasion; but a very slight difference in this factor will make a considerable difference in the result.

The particular source of error in the case of this mountain lies in the circumstance that its summit is flat, and there is no culminating point upon which the cross-hairs of the surveying instrument may intersect.

The barometric determination of heights is, of course, not without similar troubles of its own. The tables of altitudes corresponding to pressures do not agree, Airy's table giving relatively greater altitudes for very low pressures than the Smithsonian. All such tables as originally calculated are based upon the hypothesis of a temperature and humidity which decrease regularly with the altitude, and this is not always the case; nor is the "static equilibrium of the atmosphere" which Laplace assumed always maintained; that is to say an equal difference of pressure does not always correspond to an equal difference of altitude. There is, in point of fact, no absolute way to determine altitude save by running an actual line of levels; all other methods are approximations at best. But there had never been a barometric determination of the height of this mountain made, and it was resolved to attempt it on this expedition.

To this end careful arrangements were made and much labor and trouble undergone. The author carried his standard mercurial mountain barometer to Fort Gibbon on the Yukon in September, 1912, and compared it with the instrument belonging to the Signal Corps of the United States army at that post. A very close agreement was found in the two instruments; the reading of the one, by himself, and of the other, by the sergeant whose regular duty it was to read and record the instrument, being identical to two places of decimals at the same temperature.

Arrangements were made with Captain Michel of the Signal Corps at Fort Gibbon, when the expedition started to the mountain in March, 1913, to read the barometer at that post three times a day and record the reading with the reading of the attached thermometer. Acknowledgment is here made of Captain Michel's courtesy and kindness in this essential co-operation. The reading at Fort Gibbon which most nearly synchronizes with the reading on top of the mountain is the one taken at noon on the 7th June. The reading on top of the mountain was made at about 1:50 P.M., so that there was an hour and fifty minutes difference in time. The weather, however, was set fair, without a cloud in the sky, and had been for more than twelve hours before and remained so for thirty-six hours afterward. It would seem, therefore, that the difference in time is negligible. The reading at Fort Gibbon, a place of an altitude of three hundred and thirty-four feet above sea-level, at noon on the 7th June, was 29.590 inches with an attached thermometer reading 76.5° F. The reading on the summit of Denali at 1:50 P.M. on the same day, was 13.617. The writer is greatly chagrined that he cannot give with the same confidence the reading of the attached thermometer on top of the mountain, but desires to set forth the circumstances and give the readings in his note-book records.

The note-book gives the air temperature on the summit as 7° F., taken by a standard alcohol minimum thermometer, and it remained constant during the hour and a half we were there. The sun was shining, but a bitter north wind was blowing. But the reading of the thermometer attached to the barometer is recorded as 20° F. I am unable to account for this discrepancy of 13°. The mercurial barometer was swung on its tripod inside the instrument tent we had carried to the summit, a rough zero was established, and it was left for twenty minutes or so to adjust itself to conditions before an exact reading was taken. It was my custom throughout the ascent to read and record the thermometer immediately after the barometer was read, but it is almost certain that on this momentous occasion it was not done. Possibly the thermometer was read immediately the instrument was taken out of its leather case and its wooden case and set up, while it yet retained some of the animal heat of the back that had borne it, and the reading was written in the prepared place. Then when the barometer was finally read, no temperature of the attached thermometer was noted. This is the only possible explanation that occurs, and it is very unsatisfactory. It was not until we were down at the base camp again that I looked at the figures, and discovered their difference, and I could not then recall in detail the precise operations on the summit. It is hard to understand, ordinarily, how any man could have recorded the two readings on the same page of the book without noticing their discrepancy, but perhaps the excitement and difficulty of the situation combined to produce what Sir Martin Conway calls "high altitude stupidity."

It is indeed impossible to convey to the reader who has never found himself circumstanced as we were an understanding of our perturbation of mind and body upon reaching the summit of the mountain: breathless with excitement—and with the altitude—hearts afire and feet nigh frozen. What should be done on top, what first, what next, had been carefully planned and even rehearsed, but we were none of us schooled in stoical self-repression to command our emotions completely. Here was the crown of nearly three months' toil—and of all those long years of desire and expectation. It was hard to gather one's wits and resolutely address them to prearranged tasks; hard to secure a sufficient detachment of mind for careful and accurate observations. The sudden outspreading of the great mass of Denali's Wife immediately below us and in front of us was of itself a surprise that was dramatic and disconcerting; a splendid vision from which it was difficult to withdraw the eyes. We knew, of course the companion peak was there, but had forgotten all about her, having had no slightest glimpse of her on the whole ascent until at the one stroke she stood completely revealed. Not more dazzling to the eyes of the pasha in the picture was the form of the lovely woman when the slave throws off the draperies that veiled her from head to foot. Moreover, problems that had been discussed and disputed, questions about the conformation of the mountain and the possibilities of approach to it, were now soluble at a glance and clamored for solution. We held them back and fell at once to our scientific work, denying any gratification of sight until these tasks were performed, yet it is plain that I at least was not proof against the disturbing consciousness of the wonders that waited.

It was bitterly cold, yet my fingers, though numb, were usable when I reached the top; it was in exposing them to manipulate the hypsometrical instruments that they lost all feeling and came nigh freezing. And breathlessness was naturally at its worst; I remember that even the exertion of rising from the prone position it was necessary to assume to read the barometer brought on a fit of panting.

With these circumstances in mind we will resume the discussion of the readings taken on the summit and their bearing upon the altitude of the mountain. It seems right to disregard the temperature recorded for the attached thermometer, and to use the air temperature, of which there is no doubt, in correcting the barometric reading. So they stand:

| Bar. | Temp. |
|---|---|
| 13.617 in. | 7° F. |

The boiling-point thermometer stood at 174.9° F. when the steam was pouring out of the vent.

They stand therefore:

| *Gibbon* (334 feet altitude) | | *The Summit of Denali* | |
|---|---|---|---|
| Bar. | Ther. | Bar. | Ther. |
| 29.590 | 76.5° F. | 13.617 | 7° F. |

Now, the tables accessible to the writer do not work out their calculations beyond eighteen thousand feet, and he confesses himself too long unused to mathematical labors of any kind for the task of extending them. He was, therefore, constrained to fall back upon the kindness of Mr. Alfred Brooks, the head of the Alaskan Division of the United States Geological Survey, and Mr.Brooks turned over the data to Mr. C. E. Giffin topographic engineer of that service, to which gentleman thankful acknowledgment is made for the result that follows.

Ignoring a calculation based upon a temperature of 20° F. on the summit, and another based upon a temperature of 13.5° F. on the summit (the mean of the air temperature and that recorded for the attached thermometer) and confining attention to the calculation which takes the air temperature of 7° F. as the proper figure for the correction of the barometer, a result is reached which shows the summit of Denali as twenty-one thousand and eight feet above the sea. It should be added that Mr. Giffin obtained from the United States Weather Bureau the barometric and thermometric readings taken at Valdez on 7th June about the same length of time after our reading on the summit as the reading at Gibbon was before ours. From these readings Mr. Giffin makes the altitude of the mountain twenty thousand three hundred and seventy-four feet above Valdez, which is ten feet above the sea-level. From this result Mr. Giffin is disposed to question the accuracy of the reading at Gibbon, though the author has no reason to doubt it was properly and carefully made. Valdez is much farther from the summit than Fort Gibbon and is in a different climatic zone. The calculation from the Valdez base should, however, be taken into consideration in making this barometric determination, and the mean of the two results; twenty thousand six hundred and ninety-six feet, or, roundly, *twenty thousand seven hundred feet*, is offered as the contribution of this expedition toward determining the true altitude of the mountain.

The figures of Mr. Giffin's calculations touching the altitude of this mountain and also determining the altitudes of various salient points or stages of the ascent of the mountain are printed below:

## DENALI (MOUNT McKINLEY)

### Using air thermometer reading +7° and the reading at Fort Gibbon for same date

| | | |
|---|---|---|
| Mount McKinley, barometric reading | 13.617 in. | |
| Barometer reduced to standard temperature | +.027 in. | Temp. 7° |
| | 13.644 in. | |
| Fort Gibbon, barometric reading | 29.590 in. | |
| Barometer reduced to standard temperature | –.128 in. | Temp. 76.5° |
| | 29.462 in. | |
| Mount McKinley, corrected barometer | 13.644 in. | 21,324 ft. |
| Fort Gibbon, corrected barometer | 29.462 in. | 400 ft. |
| | | 20,924 ft. |
| Mean temperature, 41.7°—approximate difference in elevation | 20,924 ft. | –356 ft. |
| Latitude, 64°—approximate difference in elevation | 20,568 ft. | +15 ft. |
| Mean temperature, 41.7°—approximate difference in elevation | 20,568 ft. | +71 ft. |
| Elevation lowest, 400—approximate difference in elevation | 20,568 ft. | +20 ft. |
| Elevation above Fort Gibbon | | 20,674 ft. |
| Elevation of Fort Gibbon | | 334 ft. |
| *Elevation above sea* | | 21,008 ft. |

### Using the Thermometric Reading of 7° at Mount Mckinley and the U. S. Weather Bureau Reading at Valdez for Same Date

| | | |
|---|---|---|
| Mount McKinley, barometric reading | 13.617 in. | |
| Barometer reduced to standard temperature | +.027 in. | Temp. 7° |
| | 13.644 in. | |
| Valdez, barometric reading | 29.76 in. | |
| Barometer reduced to standard temperature | .068 in. | |
| | 29.692 in. | Temp. 54° |
| Mount McKinley, corrected barometric reading | 13.644 in. | 21,324 ft. |
| Valdez, corrected barometric reading | 29.692 in. | 190 ft. |
| | | 21,134 ft. |
| Mean temperature, 30.5°—approximate difference in elevation | 21,134 ft. | –840 ft. |
| Latitude, 62°—approximate difference in elevation | 20,295 ft. | +18 ft. |
| Mean temperature, 30.5°—approximate difference in elevation | 20,295 ft. | +42 ft. |
| Elevation lowest, 190—approximate difference in elevation | 20,295 ft. | +20 ft. |
| Elevation above Valdez | | 20,374 ft. |
| Elevation of Valdez | | 10 ft. |
| *Elevation above sea* | | 20,384 ft. |

## ALTITUDES OF CAMPING STATIONS

### First Glacier Camp

| | | |
|---|---|---|
| Glacier Camp, barometric reading | 22.554 in. | Temp. 81° |
| Barometer reduced to standard temperature | –106 in. | |
| | 22.448 in. | |
| Fort Gibbon, barometric reading | 29.110 in. | Temp. 74° |
| Barometer reduced to standard temperature | –.120 in. | |
| | 28.990 in. | |
| Glacier Camp, corrected barometer | 22.448 in. | 7,791 ft. |
| Fort Gibbon, corrected barometer | 28.990 in. | 840 ft. |
| | | 6,951 ft. |

| | | |
|---|---|---|
| Mean temperature, 77.5°—approximate difference in elevation | 6,951 ft. | +393 ft. |
| Latitude, 64°—approximate difference in elevation | 7,343 ft. | +5 ft. |
| Mean temperature, 77.5°—approximate difference in elevation | 7,343 ft. | +74 ft. |
| Elevation lowest, 840—approximate difference in elevation | 7,343 ft. | +3 ft. |
| Elevation above Fort Gibbon | | 7,426 ft. |
| Elevation of Fort Gibbon | | 334 ft. |
| *Elevation above sea* | | 7,760 ft. |

**Head of Muldrow Glacier**

| | | |
|---|---|---|
| Muldrow Glacier, barometric reading | 19.640 in | Temp. 36° |
| Barometer reduced to standard temperature | –.013 in. | |
| | 19.627 in. | |
| Fort Gibbon, barometric reading | 30.065 in. | Temp. 71° |
| Barometer reduced to standard temperature | –.115 in. | |
| | 29.950 in. | |
| Muldrow Glacier, corrected barometer | 19.627 in. | 11,441 ft. |
| Fort Gibbon, corrected barometer | 29.950 in. | (–)45 ft. |
| | | 11,486 ft. |
| Temperature, 53.5°—approximate difference in elevation | 11,486 ft. | +79 ft. |
| Latitude 65°—approximate difference in elevation | 11,565 ft. | +8 ft. |
| Mean temperature, 53.5°—approximate difference in elevation | 11,565 ft. | +63 ft. |
| Elevation lowest, 45—approximate difference in elevation | 11,565 ft. | +6 ft. |
| Elevation above Fort Gibbon | | 11,642 ft. |
| Elevation of Fort Gibbon | | 334 ft. |
| *Elevation above sea* | | 11,976 ft. |

**Parker Pass**

| | | |
|---|---|---|
| Parker Pass, barometric reading | 17.330 in. | Temp. 43° |
| Barometer reduced to standard temperature | –.023 in. | |
| | 17.307 in. | |
| Fort Gibbon, barometric reading | 30.050 in. | Temp. 69.5° |
| Barometer reduced to standard temperature | –.111 in. | |
| | 29.939 in. | |
| Parker Pass, corrected barometer | 17.307 in. | 14,861 ft. |
| Fort Gibbon, corrected barometer | 29.939 in. | (–)35 ft. |
| | | 14,896 ft. |
| Mean temperature, 56.25°—approximate difference in elevation | 14,896 ft. | +185 ft. |
| Latitude, 64°—approximate difference in elevation | 15,091 ft. | +11 ft. |
| At temperature of 56.25°—approximate difference in elevation | 15,091 ft. | +92 ft. |
| Elevation lowest, –35—approximate difference in elevation | 15,091 ft. | +11 ft. |
| Elevation above Fort Gibbon | | 15,195 ft. |
| Elevation of Fort Gibbon | | 334 ft. |
| *Elevation above sea* | | 15,529 ft. |

**Last Camp**

| | | |
|---|---|---|
| Last Camp, barometric reading | 15.220 in. | Temp. 40° |
| Barometer reduced to standard temperature | –.016 in. | |
| | 15.204 in. | |
| Fort Gibbon, barometric reading | 29.660 in. | |
| Barometer reduced to standard temperature | –120 in. | Temp. 73.5° |
| | 29.540 in. | |
| Last Camp, corrected barometer | 15.204 in. | 18,382 ft. |
| Fort Gibbon corrected barometer | 29.540 in. | 329 ft. |
| | | 18,053 ft. |

| | | |
|---|---|---|
| Mean temperature, 56.75°—approximate difference in elevation | 18,053 ft. | +248 ft. |
| Latitude, 64°—approximate difference in elevation | 18,301 ft. | +17 ft. |
| Mean temperature, 56.75°—approximate difference in elevation | 18,301 ft. | +112 ft. |
| Elevation lowest, 329—approximate difference in elevation | 18,301 ft. | +16 ft. |
| Elevation above Fort Gibbon | | 18,446 ft. |
| Elevation of Fort Gibbon | | 334 ft. |
| *Elevation above sea* | | 18,780 ft. |

CHAPTER VIII

# Explorations of the Denali Region and Previous Attempts at its Ascent

The first mention in literature of the greatest mountain group in North America is in the narrative of that most notable navigator, George Vancouver. While surveying the Knik Arm of Cook's Inlet, in 1794, he speaks of his view of a connected mountain range "bounded by distant stupendous snow mountains covered with snow and apparently detached from each other." Vancouver's name has grown steadily greater during the last fifty years as modern surveys have shown the wonderful detailed accuracy of his work, and the seamen of the Alaskan coast speak of him as the prince of all navigators.

Not until 1878 is there another direct mention of these mountains, although the Russian name for Denali, "Bulshaia Gora," proves that it had long been observed and known.

In that year two of the early Alaskan traders, Alfred Mayo and Arthur Harper, made an adventurous journey some three hundred miles up the Tanana River, the first ascent of that river by white men, and upon their return reported finding gold in the bars and mentioned an enormous ice mountain visible in the south, which they said was one of the most remarkable things they had seen on their trip.

In 1889 Frank Densmore, a prospector, with several companions, crossed from the Tanana to the Kuskokwim by way of the Coschaket and Lake Minchúmina, and had the magnificent view of the Denali group which Lake Minchúmina affords, which the present writer was privileged to have in 1911. Densmore's description was so enthusiastic that the mountain was known for years among the Yukon prospectors as "Densmore's mountain."

Though unquestionably many men traversed the region after the discovery of gold in Cook's Inlet in 1894, no other public recorded mention of the great mountain was made until W. A. Dickey, a Princeton graduate, journeyed extensively in the Sushitna and Chulitna valleys in 1896 and reached the foot of the glacier which drains one of the flanks of Denali, called later by Doctor Cook the Ruth Glacier. Dickey described the mountain in a letter to the New York *Sun* in January, 1907, and guessed its height with remarkable accuracy at twenty thousand feet. Probably unaware that the mountain had any native name, Dickey gave it the name of the Republican candidate for President of the United States at that time—McKinley. Says Mr. Dickey: "We named our great peak Mount McKinley, after William McKinley, of Ohio, the news of whose nomination for the presidency was the first we received on our way out of that wonderful wilderness."

In 1898 George Eldridge and Robert Muldrow, of the United States Geological Survey, traversed the region, and Muldrow estimated the height of the mountain by triangulation at twenty thousand three hundred feet.

In 1899 Lieutenant Herron crossed the range from Cook's Inlet and reached the Kuskokwim. It was he who named the lesser mountain of the Denali group, always known by the natives as Denali's Wife, "Mount Foraker," after the senator from Ohio.

In 1902 Alfred Brooks and D. L. Raeburn made a remarkable reconnoissance survey from the Pacific Ocean, passing through the range and along the whole western and northwestern faces of the group. They were the first white men to set foot upon the slopes of Denali. Shortly afterward, in response to the interest this journey aroused among Alpine clubs, Mr. Brooks published a pamphlet setting forth what he considered the most feasible plan for attempting the ascent of the mountain.

The next year saw two actual attempts at ascent. After holding the first term of court at Fairbanks, the new town on the Tanana River that had sprung suddenly into importance as the metropolis of Alaska upon the discovery of the Tanana gold-fields, Judge Wickersham (now delegate to Congress) set out with four men and two mules in May, 1903, and by steamboat ascended to the head of navigation of the Kantishna. Heading straight across an unknown country for the base of the mountain, Judge Wickersham's party unfortunately attacked the mountain by the Peters Glacier and demonstrated the impossibility of that approach, being stopped by the enormous ice-incrusted cliffs of the North Peak. Judge Wickersham used to say that only by a balloon or a flying-machine could the summit be reached; and, indeed, by no other means can the summit ever be reached from the north face. After a week spent in climbing, provisions began to run short and the party returned, descending the rushing, turbid waters of that quite unnavigable and very dangerous stream, the McKinley Fork of the Kantishna, on a raft, with little of anything left to eat, and that little damaged by water. Judge Wickersham was always keen for another attempt and often discussed the matter with the writer, but his judicial and political activities thenceforward occupied his time and attention to the exclusion of such enterprises. His attempt was the first ever made to climb the mountain.

## DOCTOR COOK'S ATTEMPTS

About the time that Judge Wickersham was leaving the north face of the mountain an expedition under Doctor Frederick A. Cook set out from Tyonek, on Cook's Inlet, on the other side of the range. Doctor Cook was accompanied by Robert Dunn, Ralph Shainwald (the "Hiram" of Dunn's narrative), and Fred Printz, who had been chief packer for Brooks and Raeburn, and fourteen pack-horses bore their supplies. The route followed was that of Brooks and Raeburn, and they had the advantage of topographical maps and forty miles of trail cut in the timber and a guide familiar with the country. Going up the Beluga and down the Skwentna Rivers, they crossed the range by the Simpson Pass to the south fork of the Kuskokwim, and then skirted the base of the mountains until a southwesterly ridge was reached which it is not very easy to locate, but which, as Doctor Brooks judges, must have been near the headwaters of the Tatlathna, a tributary of the Kuskokwim. Here an attempt was made to ascend the mountain, but at eight thousand feet a chasm cut them off from further advance.

Pursuing their northeast course, they reached the Peters Glacier (which Doctor Cook calls the Hanna Glacier) and stumbled across one of Judge Wickersham's camps of a couple of months before. Here another attempt to ascend was made, only to find progress stopped by the same stupendous cliffs that had turned back the Wickersham party. "Over the glacier which comes from the gap between the eastern and western peaks" (the North and South Peaks as we speak of them), says Doctor Cook, "there was a promising route." That is, indeed, part of the only route, but it can be reached only by the Muldrow Glacier. "The walls of the main mountain rise out of the Hanna (Peters) Glacier," Cook adds. The "main mountain" has many walls; the walls by which the summit alone may be reached rise out of the Muldrow Glacier, a circumstance that was not to be discovered for some years yet.

The lateness of the season now compelled immediate return. Passing still along the face of the range in the same direction, the party crossed the terminal moraine of the Muldrow Glacier without recognizing that it affords the only highway to the heart of the great mountain and recrossed the range by an ice-covered pass to the waters of the Chulitna River, down which they rafted after abandoning their horses. Doctor Cook calls this pass "Harper Pass," and the name should stand, for Cook was probably the first man ever to use it.

The chief result of this expedition, besides the exploration of about one hundred miles of unknown country, was the publication by Robert Dunn of an extraordinary narrative in several consecutive numbers of *Outing*, afterward republished in book form, with some modifications, as "The Shameless Diary of an Explorer," a vivid but unpleasant production, for which every squabble and jealousy of the party furnishes literary material. The book has a curious, undeniable power, despite its brutal frankness and its striving after "the poor renown of being smart," and it may live. One is thankful, however, that it is unique in the literature of travel.

Three years later Doctor Cook organized an expedition for a second attempt upon the mountain. In May, 1906, accompanied by Professor Herschel Parker, Mr. Belmore Browne, a topographer named Porter, who made some valuable maps, and packers, the party landed at the head of Cook's Inlet and penetrated by motor-boat and by pack-train into the Sushitna country, south of the range. Failing to cross the range at the head of the Yentna, they spent some time in explorations along the Kahilitna River, and, finding no avenue of approach to the heights of the mountain, the party returned to Cook's Inlet and broke up.

With only one companion, a packer named Edward Barrille, Cook returned in the launch up the Chulitna River to the Tokositna late in August. "We had already changed our mind as to the impossibility of climbing the mountain," he writes. Ascending a glacier which the Tokositna River drains, named by Cook the Ruth Glacier, they reached the amphitheatre at the glacier head. From this point, "up and up to the heaven-scraped granite of the top," Doctor Cook grows grandiloquent and vague, for at this point his true narrative ends.

APPROACHING THE RANGE

The claims that Doctor Cook made upon his return are well known, but it is quite impossible to follow his course from the description given in his book, "To the Top of the Continent." This much may be said: from the summit of the mountain, on a clear day, it seemed evident that no ascent was possible from the south side of the range at all. That was the judgment of all four members of our party. Doctor Cook talks about "the heaven-scraped granite of the top" and "the dazzling whiteness of the frosted granite blocks," and prints a photograph of the top showing granite slabs. There is no rock of any kind on the South (the higher) Peak above nineteen thousand feet. The last one thousand five hundred feet of the mountain is all permanent snow and ice; nor is the conformation of the summit in the least like the photograph printed as the "top of Mt. McKinley." In his account of the view from the summit he speaks of "the ice-blink caused by the extensive glacial sheets north of the Saint Elias group," which would surely be out of the range of any possible vision, but does not mention at all the master sight that bursts upon the eye when the summit is actually gained—the great mass of "Denali's Wife," or Mount Foraker, filling all the middle distance. We were all agreed that no one who had ever stood on the top of Denali in clear weather could fail to mention the sudden splendid sight of this great mountain.

But it is not worth while to pursue the subject further. The present writer feels confident that any man who climbs to the top of Denali, and then reads Doctor Cook's account of his ascent, will not need Edward Barrille's affidavit to convince him that Cook's narrative is untrue. Indignation is, however, swallowed up in pity when one thinks upon the really excellent pioneering and exploring work done by this man, and realizes that the immediate success of the imposition about the ascent of Denali doubtless led to the more audacious imposition about the discovery of the North Pole—and that to his discredit and downfall.

## THE PIONEER ASCENT

Although Cook's claim to have reached the summit of Denali met with general acceptance outside, or at least was not openly scouted, it was otherwise in Alaska. The men, in particular, who lived and worked in the placer-mining regions about the base of the mountain, and were, perhaps, more familiar with the orography of the range than any surveyor or professed topographer, were openly incredulous. Upon the appearance of Doctor Cook's book, "To the Top of the Continent," in 1908, the writer well remembers the eagerness with which his copy (the only one in Fairbanks) was perused by man after man from the Kantishna diggings, and the acute way in which they detected the place where vague "fine writing" began to be substituted for definite description.

Some of these men, convinced that the ascent had never been made, conceived the purpose of proving it in the only way in which it could be proved—by making the ascent themselves. They were confident that an enterprise which had now baffled several parties of "scientists," equipped with all sorts of special apparatus, could be accomplished by Alaskan "sourdoughs" with no special equipment at all. There seems also to have entered into the undertaking a naïve notion that in some way or other large money reward would follow a successful ascent.

The enterprise took form under Thomas Lloyd, who managed to secure the financial backing of McPhee and Petersen, saloon-keepers of Fairbanks, and Griffin, a wholesale liquor dealer of Chena. These three men are said to have put up five hundred dollars apiece, and the sum thus raised sufficed for the needs of the party. In February, 1910, therefore, Thomas Lloyd, Charles McGonogill, William

Taylor, Peter Anderson, and Bob Horne, all experienced prospectors and miners, and E. C. Davidson, a surveyor, now the surveyor-general of Alaska, set out from Fairbanks, and by 1st March had established a base camp at the mouth of Cache Creek, within the foot-hills of the range.

Here Davidson and Horne left the party after a disagreement with Lloyd. The loss of Davidson was a fatal blow to anything beyond a "sporting" ascent, for he was the only man in the party with any scientific bent, or who knew so much as the manipulation of a photographic camera.

The Lloyd expedition was the first to discover the only approach by which the mountain may be climbed. Mr. Alfred Brooks, Mr. Robert Muldrow, and Doctor Cook had passed the snout of the Muldrow Glacier without realizing that it turned and twisted and led up until it gave access to the ridge by which alone the upper glacier or Grand Basin can be reached and the summits gained. From observations while hunting mountain-sheep upon the foot-hills for years past, Lloyd had already satisfied himself of this prime fact; had found the key to the complicated orography of the great mass. Lloyd had previously crossed the range with horses in this neighborhood by an easy pass that led "from willows to willows" in eighteen miles. Pete Anderson had come into the Kantishna country this way and had crossed and recrossed the range by this pass no less than eleven times.

McGonogill, following quartz leads upon the high mountains of Moose Creek, had traced from his aerie the course of the Muldrow Glacier, and had satisfied himself that within the walls of that glacier the route would be found. And, indeed, when he had us up there and pointed out the long stretch of the parallel walls it was plain to us also that they held the road to the heights. From the point where he had perched his tiny hut, a stone's throw from his tunnel, how splendidly the mountain rose and the range stretched out!

These men thus started with the great advantage of a knowledge of the mountain, and their plan for climbing it was the first that contained the possibility of success.

From the base camp Anderson and McGonogill scouted among the foot-hills of the range for some time before they discovered the pass that gives easy access to the Muldrow Glacier. On 25th March the party had traversed the glacier and reached its head with dogs and supplies. A camp was made on the ridge, while further prospecting was carried on toward the upper glacier. This was the farthest point that Lloyd reached. On 10th April, Taylor, Anderson, and McGonogill set out about two in the morning with great climbing-irons strapped to their moccasins and hooked pike-poles in their hands. Disdaining the rope and cutting no steps, it was "every man for himself," with reliance solely upon the *crampons*. They went up the ridge to the Grand Basin, crossed the ice to the North Peak, and proceeded to climb it, carrying the fourteen-foot flagstaff with them. Within perhaps five hundred feet of the summit, McGonogill, outstripped by Taylor and Anderson, and fearful of the return over the slippery ice-incrusted rocks if he went farther, turned back, but Taylor and Anderson reached the top (about twenty thousand feet above the sea) and firmly planted the flagstaff, which is there yet.

This is the true narrative of a most extraordinary feat, unique—the writer has no hesitation in claiming—in all the annals of mountaineering. He has been at the pains of talking with every member of the actual climbing party with a view to sifting the matter thoroughly.

For, largely by the fault of these men themselves, through a mistaken though not unchivalrous sense of loyalty to the organizer of the expedition, much incredulity was aroused in Alaska touching their exploit. It was most unfortunate that any mystery was made about the details, most unfortunate that in the newspaper accounts false claims were set up. Surely the merest common sense should have dictated that in the account of an ascent undertaken with the prime purpose of proving that Doctor Cook had *not* made the ascent, and had falsified his narrative, everything should be frank and aboveboard; but it was not so.

A narrative, gathered from Lloyd himself and agreed to by the others, was reduced to writing by Mr. W. E. Thompson, an able journalist of Fairbanks, and was sold to a newspaper syndicate. The account the writer has examined was "featured" in the New York Sunday *Times* of the 5th June, 1910.

In that account Lloyd is made to claim unequivocally that he himself reached both summits of the mountain. "There were two summits and we climbed them both"; and again, "When I reached the coast summit" are reported in quotation marks as from his lips. As a matter of fact, Lloyd himself reached neither summit, nor was much above the glacier floor; and the south or coast summit, the higher of the two, was not attempted by the party at all. There is no question that the party *could* have climbed the South Peak, though by reason of its greater distance it is safe to say that it could not have been reached, as the North Peak was, in one march from the ridge camp. It must have involved a camp in the Grand Basin with all the delay and the labor of relaying the stuff up there. But the men who accomplished the astonishing feat of climbing the North Peak, in one almost superhuman march from the saddle of the Northeast Ridge, could most certainly have climbed the South Peak too.

They did not attempt it for two reasons, first, because they wanted to plant their fourteen-foot flagstaff where it could be seen through a telescope from Fairbanks, one hundred and fifty miles away, as they fondly supposed, and, second, because not until they had reached the summit of the North Peak did they realize that the South Peak is higher. They told the writer that upon their return to the floor of the *upper* glacier they were greatly disappointed to find that their flagstaff was not visible to them. It is, indeed, only just visible with the naked eye from certain points on the upper glacier and quite invisible at any lower or more distant point. Walter Harper has particularly keen sight, and he was well up in the Grand Basin, at nearly seventeen thousand feet altitude, sitting and scanning the sky-line of the North Peak, seeking for the pole, when he caught sight of it and pointed it out. The writer was never sure that he saw it with the naked eye, though Karstens and Tatum did so as soon as Walter pointed it out, but through the field-glasses it was plain and prominent and unmistakable.

When we came down to the Kantishna diggings and announced to the men who planted it that we had seen the flagstaff, there was a feeling expressed that the climbing party of the previous summer must have seen it also and had suppressed mention of it; but there is no ground whatever for such a damaging assumption. It would never be seen with the naked eye save by those who were intently searching for it. Professor Parker and Mr. Belmore Browne entertained the pretty general incredulity about the "Pioneer" ascent, perhaps too readily, certainly too confidently; but the men themselves must bear the chief blame for that. The writer and his party, knowing these men much better, had never doubt that *some* of them had accomplished what was claimed, and these details have been gone into for no other reason than that honor may at last be given where honor is due.

To Lloyd belongs the honor of conceiving and organizing the attempt but not of accomplishing it. To him probably also belongs the original discovery of the route that made the ascent possible. To McGonogill belongs the credit of discovering the pass, probably the only pass, by which the glacier may be reached without following it from its snout up, a long and difficult journey; and to him also the credit of climbing some nineteen thousand five hundred feet, or to within five hundred feet of the North Peak. But to Pete Anderson and Billy Taylor, two of the strongest men, physically, in all the North, and to none other, belongs the honor of the first ascent of the North Peak and the planting of what must assuredly be the highest flagstaff in the world. The North Peak has never since been climbed or attempted.

In the summer of the same year, 1910, Professor Parker and Mr. Belmore Browne, members of the second Cook party, convinced by this time that Cook's claim was wholly unfounded, attempted the mountain again, and another party, organized by Mr. C. E. Rusk, of Portland, Oregon, also endeavored the ascent. But both these expeditions confined themselves to the hopeless southern side of the range, from which, in all probability, the mountain never can be climbed.

## THE PARKER-BROWNE EXPEDITION

To a man living in the interior of Alaska, aware of the outfitting and transportation facilities which the large commerce of Fairbanks affords, aware of the navigable waterways that penetrate close to the foot-hills of the Alaskan range, aware also of the amenities of the interior slope with its dry, mild climate, its abundance of game and rich pasturage compared with the trackless, lifeless snows of the coast slopes, there seems a strange fatuity in the persistent efforts to approach the mountain from the southern side of the range.

It is morally certain that if the only expedition that remains to be dealt with—that organized by Professor Parker and Mr. Belmore Browne in 1912, which came within an ace of success —had approached the mountain from the interior instead of from the coast, it would have forestalled us and accomplished the first complete ascent.

The difficulties of the coast approach have been described graphically enough by Robert Dunn in the summer and by Belmore Browne himself in the winter. There are no trails; the snow lies deep and loose and falls continually, or else the whole country is bog and swamp. There is no game.

The Parker-Browne expedition left Seward, on Resurrection Bay, late in January, 1912, and after nearly three months' travel, relaying their stuff forward, they crossed the range under extreme difficulties, being seventeen days above any vegetation, and reached the northern face of the mountain on 25th March. The expedition either missed the pass near the foot of the Muldrow Glacier, well known to the Kantishna miners, by which it is possible to cross from willows to willows in eighteen miles, or else avoided it in the vain hope of finding another. They then went to the Kantishna diggings and procured supplies and topographical information from the miners, and were thus able to follow the course of the Lloyd party of 1910, reaching the Muldrow Glacier by the gap in the glacier wall discovered by McGonogill and named McPhee Pass by him.

Mr. Belmore Browne has written a lucid and stirring account of the ascent which his party made. We were fortunate enough to secure a copy of the magazine in which it appeared just before leaving Fairbanks, and he had been good enough to write a letter in response to our inquiries and to enclose a sketch map. Our course was almost precisely the same as that of the Parker-Browne party up to seventeen thousand feet, and the course of that party was precisely the same as that of the Lloyd party up to fifteen thousand feet. There is only one way up the mountain, and Lloyd and his companions discovered it. The earthquake had enormously increased the labor of the ascent; it had not altered the route.

A reconnoissance of the Muldrow Glacier to its head and a long spell of bad weather delayed the party so much that it was the 4th June before the actual ascent was begun—a very late date indeed; more than a month later than our date and nearly three months later than the "Pioneer" date. It is rarely that the mountain is clear after the 1st June; almost all the summer through its summit is wrapped in cloud. From the junction of the Tanana and Yukon Rivers it is often visible for weeks at a time during the winter, but is rarely seen at all after the ice goes out. A close watch is kept by friends at Tanana (the town at the confluence of the rivers) discovered the summit on the day we reached it and the following day (the 7th and 8th June) but not for three weeks before and not at all afterward; from which it does not follow, however, that the summit was not visible momentarily, or at certain hours of the day, but only that it was not visible for long enough to be observed. The rapidity with which that summit shrouds and clears itself is sometimes marvelous.

As is well known, the Parker-Browne party pushed up the Northeast Ridge and the upper glacier and made a first attack upon the summit itself, from a camp at seventeen thousand feet, on the 29th June. When within three or four hundred feet of the top they were overwhelmed and driven down, half frozen, by a blizzard that suddenly arose. On the 1st July another attempt was made, but the clouds ascended and completely enveloped the party in a cold, wind-driven mist so that retreat to camp was again imperative. Only those who have experienced bad weather at great heights can understand how impossible it is to proceed in the face of it. The strongest, the hardiest, the most resolute must yield. The party could linger no longer; food supplies were exhausted. They broke camp and went down the mountain.

The falling short of complete success of this very gallant mountaineering attempt seems to have been due, first to the mistake of approaching the mountain by the most difficult route, so that it was more than five months after starting that the actual climbing began; or, if the survey made justified, and indeed decided, the route, then the summit was sacrificed to the survey. But the immediate cause of the failure was the mistake of relying upon canned pemmican for the main food supply. This provision, hauled with infinite labor from the coast, and carried on the backs of the party to the high levels of the mountain, proved uneatable and useless at the very time when it was depended upon for subsistence. There is no finer big-game country in the world than that around the interior slopes of the Alaskan range; there is no finer meat in the world than caribou and mountain-sheep. It is carrying coals to Newcastle to bring canned meat into this country—nature's own larder stocked with her choicest supplies. But if, attempting the mountain when they did, the Parker-Browne party had remained two or three days longer in the Grand Basin, which they would assuredly have done had their food been eatable, their bodies would be lying up there yet or would be crushed beneath the débris of the earthquake on the ridge.

CHAPTER IX

# The Names Placed Upon the Mountain by the Author

There was no intent of putting names at all upon any portions of this mountain when the expedition was undertaken, save that the author had it in his mind to honor the memory of a very noble and very notable gentlewoman who gave ten years of her life to the Alaskan natives, set on foot one of the most successful educational agencies in the interior, and died suddenly and heroically at her post of duty a few years since, leaving a broad and indelible mark upon the character of a generation of Indians. Miss Farthing lies buried high up on the bluffs opposite the school at Nenana, in a spot she was wont to visit for the fine view of Denali it commands, and her brother, the present bishop of Montreal, and some of her colleagues of the Alaskan mission, have set a concrete cross there. When we entered the Alaskan range by Cache Creek there rose directly before us a striking pyramidal peak, some twelve or thirteen thousand feet high. Not knowing that any name had been bestowed upon it, the author discharged himself of the duty that he conceived lay upon him of associating Miss Farthing's name permanently with the mountain range she loved and the country in which she labored. But he has since learned that Professor Parker placed upon this mountain, a year before, the name of Alfred Brooks, of the Alaskan Geological Survey. Apart from the priority of naming, to which, of course, he would immediately yield, the author knows of no one whose name should so fitly be placed upon a peak of the Alaskan range, and he would himself resist any effort to change it.

Having gratified this desire, as he supposed, there had meantime arisen another desire—upon reading the narrative of the Parker-Browne expedition of the previous year, a copy of which we were fortunate enough to procure just as we were starting for the mountain. It was the feeling of our whole company that the names of Professor Parker and Mr. Belmore Browne should be associated with the mountain they so very nearly ascended.

When the eyes are cast aloft from the head of the Muldrow Glacier the most conspicuous feature of the view is a rudely conical tower of granite, standing sentinel over the entrance to the Grand Basin, and at the base of that tower is the pass into the upper glacier which is, indeed, the key of the whole ascent of the mountain. (See illustration on page 536.)

We found no better place to set these names; we called the tower the Browne Tower and the pass the Parker Pass. The "pass" may not, it is true, conform to any strict Alpine definition of that term, but it gives the only access to the glacier floor. From the ridge below to the glacier above this place gives passage; and any place that gives passage may broadly be termed a pass.

It was when this pass had been reached, after three weeks' toil, that the author was moved to the bestowal of another name by his admiration for the skill and pluck and perseverance of his chief colleague in the ascent. Those who think that a long apprenticeship must be served under skilled instructors before command of the technique of snow mountaineering can be obtained would have been astonished at Karstens's work on the Northeast Ridge. But it must be kept in mind that, while he had no previous experience on the heights, he had many years of experience with ice and snow—which is true of all of us except Tatum, and *he* had two winters' experience. In the course of winter travel in the interior of Alaska most of the problems of snow mountaineering present themselves at one time or another.

The designation "Northeast," which the Parker-Browne party put upon the ridge that affords passage from the lower glacier to the upper, is open to question. Mr. Charles Sheldon, who spent a year around the base of the mountains studying the fauna of the region, refers to the *outer* wall of the Muldrow Glacier as the Northeast Ridge, that is, the wall that rises to the North Peak. Perhaps "East Ridge of the South Peak" would be the most exact description. But it is here proposed to substitute Harry Karstens's name for points-of-the-compass designations, and call the ridge, part of which the earthquake shattered, the dividing ridge between the two arms of the Muldrow Glacier, soaring tremendously and impressively with ice-incrusted cliffs in its lower course, the Karstens Ridge. Regarded in its whole extent, it is one of the capital features of the mountain. It is seen to the left in the picture on page 518, where Karstens stands alone. At this point of its course it soars to its greatest elevation, five or six thousand feet above the glacier floor; it is seen again in the middle distance of the picture on page 607.

Not until this book was in preparation and the author was digging into the literature of the mountain did he discover the interesting connection of Arthur Harper, father of Walter Harper, narrated in another place, with Denali, and not until that discovery did he think of suggesting the name Harper for any feature of the mountain, despite the distinction that fell to the young man of setting the first foot upon the summit. Then the upper glacier appeared to be the most appropriate place for the name, and, after reflection, it is deemed not improper to ask that this glacier be so known.

It has thus fallen out that each of the author's colleagues is distinguished by some name upon the mountain except Robert Tatum. But to Tatum belongs the honor of having raised the stars and stripes for the first time upon the highest point in all the territory governed by the United States; and he is well content with that distinction. Keen as the keenest amongst us to reach the top, Tatum had none the less been entirely willing to give it up and go down to the base camp and let Johnny take his place (when he was unwell at the head of the glacier owing to long confinement in the tent during bad weather), if in the judgment of the writer that had been the wisest course for the whole party. Fortunately the indisposition passed, and the matter is referred to only as indicating the spirit of the man. I suppose there is no money that could buy from him the little silk flag he treasures. It was also while this book was preparing that the author found that he had unwittingly renamed Mount Brooks, and the prompt withdrawal of his suggested name for that peak left the one original desire of naming a feature of the mountain or the range ungratified, and his obligation toward a revered memory unfulfilled.

Where else might that name be placed? For a long time no place suggested itself; then it was called to mind that the two horns at the extremities of the horseshoe ridge of the South Peak were unnamed. Here were twin peaks, small, yet lofty and conspicuous—part of the main summit of the mountain. The naming of one almost carried with it the naming of the other; and as soon as the name Farthing alighted, so to speak, from his mind upon the one, the name Carter settled itself upon the other. In the long roll of women who have labored devotedly for many years amongst the natives of the interior of Alaska, there are no brighter names than those of Miss Annie Farthing and Miss Clara Carter, the one forever associated with Nenana, the other with the Allakaket. To those who are familiar with what has been done and what is doing for the Indians of the interior, to the white men far and wide who have owed recovery of health and relief and refreshment to the ministrations of these capable women, this naming will need no labored justification; and if self-sacrifice and love, and tireless, patient labor for the good of others be indeed the greatest things in the world, then the mountain top bearing aloft these names does not so much do honor as is itself dignified and ennobled. These horns of the South Peak are shown in the picture on page 563; they are of almost equal height; the near one the author would name the Farthing Horn, the far one the Carter Horn.

And now the author finds that he has done what, in the past, he has faulted others for doing—he has plastered a mountain with names. The prerogative of name-giving is a dangerous one, without definite laws or limitations. Nothing but common consent and usage ultimately establish names, but he to whom falls the first exploration of a country, or the first ascent of a peak, is usually accorded privilege of nomenclature. Yet it is a privilege that is often abused and should be exercised with reserve. Whether or not it has been overdone in the present case, others must say. This, however, the author will say, and would say as emphatically as is in his power: that he sets no store whatever by the names he has ventured to confer comparable with that which he sets by the restoration of the ancient native names of the whole great mountain and its companion peak.

It may be that the Alaskan Indians are doomed; it may be that the liquor and disease which to-day are working havoc amongst them will destroy them off the face of the earth; it is common to meet white men who assume it with complacency. Those who are fighting for the natives with all their hearts and souls do not believe it, cannot believe it, cannot believe that this will be the end of all their efforts, that any such blot will foul the escutcheon of the United States. But if it be so, let at least the memorial of their names remain. When the inhabited wilderness has become an uninhabited wilderness, when the only people who will ever make their homes in it are exterminated, when the placer-gold is gone and the white men have gone also, when the last interior Alaskan town is like Diamond City and Glacier City and Bearpaw City and Roosevelt City; and Bettles and Rampart and Coldfoot; and Cleary City and Delta City and Vault City and a score of others; let at least the native names of these great mountains remain to show that there once dwelt in the land a simple, hardy race who braved successfully the rigors of its climate and the inhospitality of their environment and flourished, until the septic contact of a superior race put corruption into their blood. So this book shall end as it began.

# WALTER HARPER

**By Yvonne Mozée**

It's just a small, rather beat-up, once-blue notebook, perhaps intended for accounts, with vertical red lines like a mini-ledger. The pages are bound with top stitching, and the cover's layers are peeling apart.

On one cover, now so faint that most of it is just an imprint, is handwritten:

*Diary of Mt. McKinley*
*Walter Harper*
*1 June 1913*

I wonder where it traveled on that climb. In Walter's hip pocket? In a body pack?

And I wonder where he kept it after that first-of-all-time climb, and how it came to his sister Jessie, my mother.

Walter Harper was a handsome, strong, appealing fellow of 20 when he scrambled to the highest peak of Mt. McKinley/Denali and stood on its summit. It was June 7, 1913, and young Harper was the first man ever to set foot on the top of North America's highest mountain.

Half Athabascan, half Irish, he was matched to the honor by both birth and ability. His parents were Arthur and Jennie Harper—she of the Indian people of the Koyukuk, and he of the tribe of the Irish.

Arthur Harper was born in Belfast to a shipbuilding family. He left Ireland as a young man and made his way to western Canada.

He was "the first man who thought of trying the Yukon as a mining field, so far as we know . . . ," William Ogilvie wrote in *Early Days on the Yukon*.[1]

Pondering Arrowsmith's map of that region of North America, Harper became convinced that there must be gold in the Yukon basin. After a trip down the Peace

1. William Ogilvie, *Early Days On the Yukon*, John Lane Company, New York, 1913. p. 87

and Mackenzie Rivers, he arrived at Fort Yukon in 1872. In the next years, his explorations for gold were intermixed with trading, and his travels took him the length of the Yukon to St. Michael. He thoroughly explored the Tanana, Fortymile, Sixtymile, and Stewart Rivers. In most of these years he was closely linked with Jack McQuesten and Alfred Mayo. The three names are top-of-the-totem in all accounts of that pre-Klondike era.

On one of his trips, perhaps in 1878, Arthur Harper met Jennie Albert (her Indian name sounded like "Seyn-dahn," pronounced with clipped syllables) at Nulato on the lower Yukon. They were married there, and according to one acquaintance they spent their honeymoon poling up the Yukon 1050 miles to Ft. Selkirk.[2]

In the next years Harper and his growing family—there were ultimately eight children of whom Walter was the youngest—lived at Eagle, at Nuklukayet (Old Station) where the Tanana River meets the Yukon and where Walter was probably born, at Ft. Selkirk, possibly at Ft. Reliance, and at their trading posts at the mouths of the Stewart and the Fortymile Rivers (the latter four in Canadian territory).

Though Arthur Harper never made a strike himself, his conviction that gold could be found, his explorations, and his letters to friends in British Columbia mining camps all played a key role in the opening up of the Yukon. In *Blazing Alaska's Trails*, Alfred H. Brooks says, "Harper was, therefore, the discoverer of gold on the Yukon and the pioneer prospector whose efforts directly led to the discovery of Forty-mile, the Klondike, and Fairbanks."[3] (McQuesten's extension of credit to the early prospectors, and his fair distribution of provisions when shortages existed, were major contributions as well, Brooks said.)

When the Klondike strike was finally made in 1896, Arthur Harper and his then-partner Joe Ladue staked a town-site at what became Dawson. Today, on a par with King, Queen, and Princess Streets, there is Harper Street. He and Ladue had a sawmill—a gold mine in itself—and the aging Harper finally made a small fortune, although Ogilvie says Harper was penniless when he died.

But by the Dawson years, Arthur and Jennie had parted ways. He had sent

---

2. Andrew Kokrine, Sr., quoted in a letter from Orie Shade, Tanana, to Margaret Harper Burke, Dec. 27, 1950, in possession of the author.
3. Alfred Hulse Brooks, *Blazing Alaska's Trails*, University of Alaska Press, Fairbanks, 1973. p. 318

each child to California for schooling, and this was a sorrow to Jennie. When they split up, she kept little Walter, and he was raised to learn the Indian ways which were to serve him in superb stead in the coming years.

Walter was already a teenager when he went to school for the first time. Until then he had lived an Indian village life, knew little English, and could not read or write. It was here at the Nenana Mission School, perhaps in 1909, that the English churchman Hudson Stuck first met the 16-year old. Stuck had already had a number of native aides in his traveling ministry. They served in the combined roles of interpreter, guide, pilot/mechanic for the mission launch and dogteam driver-handler.

Walter became Stuck's next companion, and of him the Archdeacon wrote: "He was adept in all wilderness arts. An axe, a rifle, a flaying knife, a skin needle with its sinew thread—with all these he was at home; he could construct a sled or a pair of snow-shoes, going to the woods for his birch, drying it and steaming it and bending it; and could pitch camp with all the native comforts and amenities as quickly as anybody I ever saw."[4]

He had also acquired a naturalist's close, accurate knowledge of birds and beasts, Stuck wrote. "He would have made the most valuable field-assistant to anyone engaged in a description of Alaskan fauna . . . ."[5]

Stuck took on Walter's education, now interrupted after only one year, which " . . . his active intelligence had made such quick use of . . . that it was a good foundation to build upon; and our desultory lessons in camp—reading aloud, writing from dictation, geography and history in such snippets as circumstances permitted—were eagerly made the most of, and his mental horizon broadened continually."[6]

The two read aloud a great deal, from *Treasure Island* to Shakespeare. Stuck stressed literature, history, and writing. This training continued through their entire association. In the diary Walter kept on the McKinley climb, there are lists of the Presidents, the books of the Old Testament, the States, and the names of the week from Norse and Latin mythology.

---

4. Hudson Stuck, *Ten Thousand Miles With a Dog Sled*, Charles Scribner's Sons, New York, 1914. p. 315.
5. Hudson Stuck, *A Winter Circuit of Our Arctic Coast*. Charles Scribner's Sons, New York, 1920. p. 227
6. Stuck, *Ten Thousand Miles*. p. 315

Beyond Waiter's native skills and stamina, and his intelligence and mental outreach, Walter impressed his mentor with his qualities of character and personality. "He spoke the naked truth," Stuck wrote of his teenage charge. Yet, he noted, Walter's manner was "gentle and unobtrusive" and he was a welcome guest everywhere.[7]

"Wherever he went he made friends and aroused admiration, for with all (his) splendid physique and virility, with his capacity and resourcefulness, there went a modesty, a courtesy, a deference, that marked him a gentleman in any company and a sweetness of temper and an amiability that attracted people to him . . ." Stuck noted.[8]

Years later, his sister Margaret put it another way: "Walter had personality—scads of it. Everybody liked him. The girls were crazy about him."

Stuck illustrated Walter's "self-reliance and ingenuity" in an incident which happened on one of their early trips in the mission launch *Pelican*. One of the cylinders broke when they were far from any machine stop. Walter carved a new bracket out of the only chunk of hard wood available, the shotgun stock, and wired it into place. ". . . the Indian pilot we had picked up at Chena was so much impressed that when he returned home he told his friends that 'when engine break, Walter he make new engine out of wood."[9]

During a winter in Kuskokwim country with a dogteam, Stuck had released their local guide a day's travel away from the next roadhouse. But after breaking camp next morning, the two could not find the trail. They had passed a Native encampment some miles back, but without their interpreter, could not have gotten information there. Much of the course ahead lay across open country, and there were absolutely no signs of trail anywhere. Then off in the distance they saw two stray dogs making a beeline for them. "The explanation, full of hope, sprang at once to the boy's mind. The dogs must belong to the native encampment some six miles back, and they had been to the roadhouse for what scraps they could pick up, and were returning." Sure enough, Stuck and Walter followed their trail, though it

7. Ibid.
8. Hudson Stuck, address delivered at St. Stephen's Church, Fort Yukon, Nov. 1, 1918, reprinted in the *Fairbanks Daily News-Miner*, Dec. 4, 1918.
9. Hudson Stuck, *Voyages on the Yukon and Its Tributaries*, Charles Scribner's Sons, New York, 1917. p. 301

grew ever fainter under falling snow, across open country and across two lakes. It led them eight miles on to the roadhouse?[10]

By the time of the McKinley climb in the summer of 1913, Stuck and Harper had been closely associated for three years. The father-son, tutor-pupil, confidante and friend relationship was to total nine years. It must have been an interesting combination—the middle-aged English man-of-the-cloth and the young Native lad, born to the bush. Early in the McKinley climb, Walter wrote his sister Margaret from Base Camp, sending the letter back with the youngster Esaias. Dated April 14, it reflects a competent basic literacy, a down-to-earth practicality: "Esaias killed three caribou yesterday and I killed a sheep and we are now boiling down meat making our own pemmican to eat on the high altitude.[11]

After that historic climb, Stuck took Walter on a journey and entered him as a student at Mount Hermon School in Massachusetts. In his application to the school, Walter described himself as 23 years of age and his occupation as trapper, dog musher, guide, and woodchopper. He said he wanted to become a physician, and that he could provide only pocket money for himself.

One of his letters to his sister Jessie in February 1914 reflects a certain *savoir faire* among his new peers: "I received the cap and gloves mother sent me. I was tickled to death with them. I went over to Northfield today to a funeral of our pastor. Everybody thought the cap I had on a queer style. I told them it was a new style I was getting out."[12]

School records show that he was "a satisfactory student and also a man of excellent citizenship and fine character. . . ."[13]

Walter spent three years at Mount Hermon. Then Stuck suggested he return north, and Walter eagerly did so. Presumably in the winter of 1916-17, the two resumed their journeys to the villages and missions.

In 1917-18, the final year of Walter's life, he and Stuck made a six-month trip by dog team from Fort Yukon west to Kotzebue Sound, then northward along the Arctic Coast to Point Hope and Point Barrow, on to Flaxman and Herschel

---

10. Stuck, *Ten Thousand Miles*. p. 320
11. Walter Harper, letter to his sister Margaret, April 14, 1913, in possession of her son, Frank O'Farrell.
12. Walter Harper, letter to his sister Jessie, Feb. 13, 1914, in possession of the author.
13. Lester P. White, letter from Mount Hermon to Bradford Washburn, April 20, 1951.

Islands, and back to Fort Yukon. As the ptarmigan flies, it was at least 1800 miles. The two men must have covered well over 2200.

The trip was unexpectedly imperiled before it began when Walter was hospitalized in Fort Yukon's Mission Hospital with typhoid fever. The wife of the doctor who treated him says it was apparently contracted from eating peaches brought from Dawson by a riverboat steward.[14] But Walter recuperated far faster than the doctor prophesied, and they left on November 7. Walter's anticipations for the trip zeroed in on a possible chance to hunt polar bear, since moose, caribou, sheep, and bear were, for him, old hat.

Stuck felt compelled to pursue Walter's education to prepare him for college and medical school. So Walter's studies continued. Both men kept diaries. Walter also kept the accounts, making all purchases and payments on the trip.

When they reached Point Hope, where they spent some weeks, the missionary there, Rev. William Archibald Thomas, gave Walter a daily hour of math and another of Latin, while Stuck required the writing of a daily theme. In exchange for his daily instruction, Thomas had his housework done by the other two! The three were prior friends, having traveled across the continent together and backpacked through Yellowstone Park the summer of Walter's return.

At Point Hope, Walter decided he should learn how to flense seals since they were a major item in feeding the dogs. Thomas decided to learn with him. Stuck notes that the seal should be skinned before the carcass freezes without cutting into the thick layer of blubber just beneath the skin. "The latter is no easy job, nor was it successfully performed; and the two men, and the back kitchen where the deed was done, reeked with blood and oil. Walter had it set down in his diary that day, 'Mr. Thomas and I skinned a seal; the archdeacon stood around and made remarks. . . .'"[15] Walter and Thomas also went out for polar bear, but with no luck.

At Point Hope they celebrated Christmas and, soon afterwards, Walter's 25th birthday, the latter with a feast including a roast ptarmigan apiece. Of course the celebration included some reading: *Romeo and Juliet* was finished, and *The Merchant of Venice* was begun. Somewhere along the way, they finished it "by candle

---

14. Clara Heintz Burke, *Doctor Hap*, Coward-McCann, Inc., New York, 1961. p. 226
15. Stuck, *A Winter Circuit*. p. 123

light in igloos."[16] Later, far to the east on Flaxman Island, they continued with *A Midsummer Night's Dream*.

However, earlier in the trip, *Othello* didn't pass the test with Walter and was read only once. "I could not bring Walter to a re-reading because Iago's continual ribaldry and obscenity were so offensive to him."[17]

It was during the weeks in Point Hope that the child Howard Rock, later famous as the founder and editor of Alaska's first Native newspaper *Tundra Times*, encountered the pair. Years later Rock wrote of their visit, "I have clear memory that the young Indian was fine looking and had a nice smile."[18] Rock remembers having his picture taken by Stuck, whose mustache and beard were a rare sight to him then.

The two were traveling with two dog teams, and a sled and a toboggan. Before they left Point Hope, Walter had built a new sled to replace the toboggan. When they reached Barrow, Walter designed and built a new, smaller sled. "A natural-born mechanic," said Barrow pioneer Charlie Brower.[19]

And at Barrow Walter learned that two of Brower's sons, half-Eskimo, were serving in the Armed Forces. The war was still on, but the summer before, anyone with Indian, Eskimo, or Aleut blood was excluded from military registration, and Walter had been hurt by the discrimination. At Barrow he was encouraged again in his interest to serve. He'd long been interested in aviation, and Stuck surmised that his sights were set on the aviation corps.

The continuing journey was exhausting: full of perils, discomfort, slogging and hard work. It was the dead of winter, and the weather was often against them. Some days were sheer struggle.

Often Walter was too tired to stay awake, but Stuck read aloud at least a little each night, or recited poetry. So there in the remote and winder-bludgeoned arctic night could be heard excerpts from *The Lady of the Lake* or *Elegy Written in a Country Churchyard* or *Henry V.* Sometimes the two would sing hymns or songs they knew by heart.

At Flaxman Island they stayed in the cabin left by early surveyor Ernest de

---

16. *Fairbanks Daily News-Miner* (see note 8.)
17. Stuck, *A Winter Circuit*. p. 31
18. Howard Rock, *Tundra Times*, Aug. 9, 1956 (reprinted Feb. 5, 1975)
19. Stuck, *A Winter Circuit*.

Koven Leffingwell. Other passersby had ripped up the books nearest the stove to start their fires. From the remaining books, Stuck and Walter each took a souvenir—Walter chose a primer of French literature!

And here at Flaxman, Walter at last comes in for some censure from the Archdeacon. "George Leavitt, their Barrow guide and I had brought our harness indoors; Walter had thoughtlessly left his lying where it was taken off," Stuck wrote.[20] Their departure was delayed while the harness for Walter's dog team was dug out of three or four feet of hard-packed snow, and carefully so as not to chop it up as well.

When the two men finally turned south along what Stuck calls the Herschel Island River (perhaps the Firth), the journey was on its homeward leg. By then they were traveling alone. Walter lent Stuck his diary and thus shared with him his engagement to marry the girl who'd been his nurse while he had typhoid. Walter also confirmed his intention to enlist. Both plans cut across Stuck's hopes for his immediate medical training, but the two men were brought closer by the sharing of these confidences. Stuck was also glad to note that the diary was well written!

By now spring was coming with warmer weather, mushy snow, and overflowing lakes. Traveling was even more difficult. Stuck broke trail on snowshoes while Walter managed both sleds and all the dogs—an exhausting task. But "it was under just such circumstances that Walter shone. . . never irritated or impatient, always cheerful though with not much to say. Stress of any kind added to his customary taciturnity."[21]

By night both men were now too bushed for any study. The book work finally lapsed completely.

Then, six months minus ten days from the day they left Fort Yukon, they were back. It was the last winter trip they would make together. Summer saw them making the mission rounds in the *Pelican* once again.

In August, they left Nenana in the *Pelican*, planning to fulfill several commissions along the 200-mile trip to Tanana—a marriage, a baptism, delivery of mail and parcels. Leaving Nenana at noon, they arrived at Tolovana about 5 P.M. to find a telegraph message that an Indian youngster had been badly scalded at a camp further along. Unless he could be given medical attention, he would die.

---

20. Ibid. p. 300
21. Ibid. p. 344

"It looks as if it's up to us," Stuck told Walter, and Walter, "never loath at any sort of adventure or special stress, responded, 'All right, I'm with you.'"

It was dark and stormy when they reached the Indian camp three hours later and took on the father and the child, burned when he had backed into a boiling pot set on the ground. Then began a night-long run through blackness, wind, and rain, along a winding channel full of shoals and sandbars. Walter was at the wheel all night.

"No one save a man with eyes like an owl and reading water as who should read a book; no one, I think who has not spent his boyhood in a birch-bark canoe and so come to an intuitive *feeling* of water, could have brought that launch one hundred miles lickety-split down the Tanana River in the pitch dark and the driving rain, and have touched bottom but once—and then only for an instant."

They arrived at the hospital in Tanana at five o'clock in the morning. But the only physician was at the Army post three miles away, so it was another two hours before they'd roused him and taken him back in the launch. Stuck then went to bed; Walter, after the night-long run—and a trip that had begun half a day before that, "took a bath and walked down town to see his married sisters. . . ."[22] (Alas, the child died late that morning.)

In early September, Walter and the nurse, Frances Wells, were married by Stuck at Fort Yukon in the chapel decorated with autumn leaves. After the wedding reception, the two went in the doctor's launch up the Porcupine River to camp. Then they took the riverboat to a point somewhere along the Yukon where Walter went hunting and bagged two moose, two caribou, and three bear (presumably for mission use, since he and Frances were leaving for the States).

From Fort Yukon they took the last boat of the season heading ultimately for Philadelphia, where they planned to be at her father's home in Germantown until they could sort out their own plans. Frances wanted to do Red Cross work. Walter's goals were still the aviation corps and medicine. A legacy which Frances had inherited would help see him through medical school, and he planned to return as a doctor to the Indian people of the Yukon. Once on their winter circuit, Walter and Stuck had been reminiscing about the McKinley climb, and Walter exclaimed how much he hoped to climb Denali's Wife (Mt. Foraker) before he went Outside again.

---

22. Archdeacon Stuck, "A Wild Ride," *Spirit of Missions*, November 1918.

"His heart had always been set on that companion peak," wrote Stuck. "But I said, 'You will have to save that for a vacation when you are in charge of the hospital in Tanana'—and we laughed it off."[23]

Walter and Frances reached Skagway, probably by railway after a river trip to Whitehorse, and sailed from there on October 22. The ship was the *Princess Sophia*.

In the night, the *Sophia* hit Vanderbilt Reef in Lynn Canal. The weather was stormy and the passengers and crew were not taken off, though rescue vessels stood by. Then the storm worsened, and 38 hours after she struck the reef, the ship foundered. All aboard were lost.

Walter Harper was 25. He and his bride were buried together in Juneau.

"I think the basis of his character was an intense self-respect," Stuck wrote. "He has left behind him a sweet memory and the light of a bright example."[24]

---

23. Stuck, A *Winter Circuit*. p.284
24. Stuck, letter from St. Michael, Alaska, to Mount Hermon School, Mar. 15, 1919.

*Yvonne Mozée, independent writer-photographer, was born in Anchorage, Alaska, daughter of Ben Mozée, educator, reindeer superintendent, and U.S. Marshal, and of Jessie Harper, teacher, artist, and sister to Walter Harper. After her mother's death, Yvonne found Harper's diary among her papers.*

# DIARY OF WALTER HARPER

## APRIL 15$^{TH}$ 1913, TUESDAY

Esias left this morning for Nenana at half past eight, and Johnnie and I stayed in camp till noon cutting some wood into blocks and getting it ready to be hauled up to the Muldrow Glacier. After lunch we hitched up the dogs and went down three or four miles below our camp and brought up some willows for fire wood while the Archdeacon and Mr. Tatum stayed in camp and made some biscuit and Mr. Karstens worked on the creepers.

## APRIL 16$^{TH}$ 1913, WEDNESDAY

Johnnie and I took each a load of freight over the divide on the Muldrow Glacier, each having three dogs to one sled, and while Mr. Karstens and Mr. Tatum went on up the glacier breaking and marking out the trail we came home. Soon after lunch we started out after a bunch of caribou we had seen this morning. We went up the right fork of the Clear Water to its very head, and from there got a splendid view of Minchúmina and the McKinley Fork where it winds into the Kantishna.

## APRIL 17$^{TH}$ 1913, THURSDAY

We made another trip up to the glacier this morning; our loads contained mostly fire wood and coming back we tobogganned most of the way. After lunch we made a trip down the creek for some willows and it was quite windy till we got close to the camp. Soon after supper we fed the dogs and retired.

## APRIL 18$^{TH}$ 1913, FRIDAY

We got up at five o'clock this morning, had breakfast and were ready to go at eight for the camp on the Muldrow Glacier. It was about two in the afternoon when we got to the end of the trail which Mr. Karstens and Mr. Tatum had previously broken and marked. After having some sour-dough hot cakes Mr. Karstens took his sounding pole and went ahead cautiously testing every step of the way, and one mile

[Editor's Note: All spellings are as in the original diary.]

April 16th. 1913
Wednesday

Johnnie and I took each a load of freight over the divide on the Muldrow Glacier, each having three dogs to one sled, and while Mr. Karstens and Mr. Tatum went on up the glacier breaking and marking out the trail we came home. Soon after lunch we started out after a bunch of caribou we had seen this morning. We went up the right fork of the Clear Water to its very head, and from there got a splendid view of Minchumina and the McKinley Fork where it winds into the Kantishna.

Second day's entry in the diary (Courtesy Yvonne Mozée)

further we decided to camp. So Johnnie and I threw off the stuff we had on the sled and went back to get some more from the lower glacier, making the trip four hours.

## APRIL 19TH 1913, SATURDAY

Johnnie and I went back to the glacier cache this morning for some more provision. We got back at twelve o'clock. Soon after lunch we went back for another load and came five. It has been very windy today. We saw clouds way down below us. While Johnnie and I were freighting the Archdeacon and Mr. Karstens and Mr. Tatum went up the glacier, and while making their way over a crevass lost the sounding pole in the crevass.

## APRIL 20TH 1913, SUNDAY

It has been a clear bright day today. Johnnie and I went down to base-camp this morning. We stayed there feasting on the choicest parts of the caribou. The sun was shining there while way up high on the mountain it was storming, making it invisible. We started from there at two o'clock and when we got to the glacier Johnnie turned back while I came on to the camp on the glacier.

## APRIL 21ST 1913, MONDAY

I started down to the glacier cache this morning at nine o'clock and got there at ten. I saw that Johnnie had made a trip up there and went back so I thought I would take a run down there and see Johnnie. I stayed till two in the afternoon and then took a load of wood and started back. Johnnie came as far as the glacier with me with a load of wood and turned back. I met the snow about a mile from our camp on the Muldrow Glacier. I got back I saw Mr. Tatum in bed with a stomack trouble.

## APRIL 22ND 1913, TUESDAY

It was very cloudy this morning. The ridges on both sides are invisible. We waited till noon before we attempted to go up the glacier, then each tied the climbing rope around him stringing into a long line; the first time I have ever been on the line. The work was very interesting and exciting for awhile but after standing around and getting one's feet cold one gets very weary. We got home and Mr. Tatum set to work making stew while I set to work making pie and some dumplings for the stew. Right after supper we went to bed with intention of rising early.

## APRIL 23RD 1913, WEDNESDAY

We got up at half past three; had breakfast and started up the glacier at half past seven. After going over several crevasses we got to one which we could not cross. The snow bridge on which we previously had crossed gave away and fell about ten or twelve feet into the crevass; but fortunately there were some drifted underneath it so we went to work and built up a snow bridge. We passed several other crevasses after that but we had no trouble in crossing them. We were out twelve hours today. After we came back I took the dogs and went down to the base-camp where Johnnie was.

## APRIL 24TH 1913, THURSDAY

Johnnie and I got up at half past five o'clock. Johnnie took a load of dry wood while I took a load of green willows. We reached our camp on the glacier at one, and soon after lunch we went back to the cache on the glacier and brought back a load apiece of dry wood.

## APRIL 25TH 1913, FRIDAY

The alarm went off at half past three this morning and when I got up to make fire and to cook breakfast I found that Johnnie in his sleep had kicked the syrup pot over and was spilled all over the canvis which we had under us and one corner of a blinket that was over us. After breakfast Johnnie went back to the glacier cache for a load of wood while four of us went up the glacier. Up till noon the day has been a splendid one, and on our way back after been at the twelveth thousand feet we were enveloped in mist and as we got near the mist grew thicker and if it weren't for the willows with which we marked the trail we would have had a considerable trouble in finding our way back.

## APRIL 26TH 1913, SATURDAY

We took two loads of wood up the glacier this morning Mr. Karstens, Mr. Tatum, Johnnie and I. We had little trouble in crossing some of the crevasses with the dogs, and one place poor old Snow Ball fell through and Mr. Karstens tried to pull him out but the harness on him broke and he fell to the bottom so they let me down with a rope and I tied a rope around his body and we were both hoisted up by the others. Coming we made several snow bridges, and we got home about half past six.

## APRIL 27TH 1913, SUNDAY

We made one trip half way up the glacier this morning before noon, and we lay up for the rest of the day. We had a little service in the afternoon. The sun has been shining all day and Mt. Denali stood out in the clear blue sky splendidly.

## APRIL 28TH 1913, MONDAY

We made two trips up to our cache on the glacier; one in the morning and one in the afternoon and when we came back from the trip in the afternoon Johnnie and I went down to the base camp and stayed there that night. It has been a fine day today, just such a day as yesterday.

## APRIL 29TH 1913, TUESDAY

We left the base-camp this morning at ten o'clock for the willow cache for some rabbits, the skins of which we want for inside of our mittens and moccasins to keep them warm. But the skins were a disappointment, for the hair was all coming off. After we came back to the base-camp we took lunch, loaded our sleds with the things necessary to us on the glacier camp and came on. After we got about half way up the summit we met the wind blowing great guns, and we were compelled to put on our sweaters and parkas. We reached our camp on the glacier at half past eight o'clock.

## APRIL 30TH 1913, WEDNESDAY

We took two loads of freight up to the head of the Muldrow Glacier. We also picked out a place for our camp. The weather has been very disagreeable today. It has been snowing all day.

## MAY 1ST 1913, THURSDAY

When I got up this morning to cook breakfast the tent was sacking in. It had about two or three inches of snow on top of it, and after the fire was going for awhile it began to melt, and though I tried to get the snow off it was soaking wet. We moved our camp today, and the trail was very heavy with last night's snow and we only got half way up to the head of the glacier. It has been snowing off and on all day long.

## MAY 2ND 1913, FRIDAY

We made one trip to the head of the glacier before noon where we previously had cached some stuff, and in the afternoon we made another trip, and to our great disappointment we found the stuff that we had cached in the morning was burning. All the sox and stockings, all the sugar and the Archdeacon's films and three silk tents which were proposed for up above were burnt, and two shovels, an axe, some dog fish, all the milk, some butter and some baking powder, one or two overalls and Mr. Karstens fur parka.

## MAY 3RD 1913, SATURDAY

We moved our camp this morning up to the head of the glacier. The sun was very hot and we made a slow time doing it. After we pitched the tent we broke up all the boxes we had and put the boards on the snow underneath us to serve as a floor. After this was all done we set to work making a cache of hard snow blocks, putting one on top of another in a shape similar to an igloo. Just as soon as the sun went behind the north ridge of the north peak of Denali the thermometer went down to 26 below zero.

## MAY 4TH 1913, SUNDAY

The Archdeacon, Mr. Tatum, Johnnie and myself went down and got the last load at our last camp on the glacier while Mr. Karstens stayed in camp at the head of the Muldrow Glacier. It took us four hours to make the round trip, and at five o'clock in the afternoon Johnnie and I started down to the base-camp for some dog feed and few of other things.

## MAY 5TH 1913, MONDAY

Johnnie and I slept a little too much this morning. We got up at nine o'clock, and it took us quite a long time to get ready. It was past eleven before we got started, and it was half past eight when we got to our camp on the head of the Muldrow Glacier.

## MAY 6TH 1913, TUESDAY

I took Johnnie and went up the northeast ridge this morning with the expectation of getting a fine view but from where we were we did not see much for the ridge was low at that point. After we came back Mr. Karstens cut up a canvis for a little tent to use when we get above here, and the Archdeacon cut up one of our blinkets for socks while Mr. Tatum baked some biscuits and dried them to get the moisture out of them. Johnnie and the Archdeacon sewed on the socks while Mr. Karstens and I sewed on the tent till nine in the evening, and left it to finish tomorrow.

## MAY 7TH 1913, WEDNESDAY

We set to work again soon after breakfast on the tent while the Archdeacon and Mr. Tatum tried to find a way up the northeast ridge to get our stuff up. They were gone for five hours without success, and while they were gone Mr. Karstens, Johnnie and I finished the tent that we started to make yesterday. We also cut up another canvis for one more but smaller tent for the top of Denali to read the instruments in. We saw the finest avalanches this morning coming down from the north ridge of Mt. Denali one after another shaking the whole Muldrow Glacier as it struck it. I rushed out with the Archdeacon's camera and mine and took snap-shots of them as they were falling.

## MAY 8TH 1913, THURSDAY

The sun shone brightly all day. Mr. Karstens, Johnnie and I went up on the northeast ridge trying to find a way by which we could get up to the col with packs on our backs. We got just half way to it cutting steps every foot of the way. Cutting steps is a long, tiresome business. The Archdeacon and Mr. Tatum stayed in camp getting things ready to take up the mountain.

## MAY 9TH 1913, FRIDAY

Johnnie went down this morning; the Archdeacon and Mr. Tatum went as far as our first glacier camp to see that he gets over the bad crevasses without harm. Mr. Karstens and I went up on the ridge still trying to find a way up to the col. We did not go much further than we went the previous day for it was step chopping all the way, and a place up there, sort of a low saddle which we saw from our camp on the glacier and which looked to be the easiest going was the most difficult place to go over. It was nothing but broken up chunks of ice just balancing on the ridge.

## MAY 10TH 1913, SATURDAY

It blew a gale all day, and we had to stay in camp waiting for it to subside but it continued all day and night. Mr. Karstens experimented with an alcohol stove, which was a success. The stove burns long enough to boil a pot of tea. We have been burning the coal oil Primus stove all day to save wood as we have but few sticks left.

## MAY 11TH 1913, SUNDAY

This morning when we got up the sun was shining brightly and with the exception of some clouds which were below us on the glacier the sky was clear. After we breakfasted we started up on the ridge intending to get up on the col. We had heavy packs on our backs and we toiled up the ridge gasping for breath, and we were about half way up when the clouds that we saw down on glacier began to move up and in a short time we were enveloped in a mist so we were compelled to cache our stuff there and retreast our steps back to our camp on the Muldrow Glacier. It had snowed about four inches in our absances.

## MAY 12TH 1913, MONDAY

It has been just such another day as yesterday; the clouds being down below us and later when we were up on the ridge it came up as it did yesterday, hovering the whole ridge and the surrounding peaks. We were forced to leave the ridge and return to our camp down below on the glacier. The steps we made going up were all filled in with snow for it was snowing heavily and we were soaking wet down our necks and backs.

## MAY 13TH 1913, TUESDAY

We went to bed at half past eight last night and got up at eight o'clock this morning. We lay in our tent all day as it was very cloudy both below and above us and we did not dare venture upon the ridge for fear of the avalanches. This new fall of snow will surely create avalanches.

## MAY 14TH 1913, WEDNESDAY

The weather is still uncertain. The clouds from down below are moving up as usual and the ridges on both sides of us are invisible in places. We saw very little of the sun all day. We had nothing to do today so the Archdeacon gave me dictation lesson from one of Shakespeare's small pocket edition. Mr. Tatum had neuralgia in his jaw all day and I think if we can go out tomorrow he will be unable to go with us.

## MAY 15TH 1913, THURSDAY

We got up at five o'clock this morning. The sky was cloudless and the sun shone out brightly, beating down on the ice ridges and the snow slopes, causing many avalanches. We went up on the ridge today, cleaned out our old steps and went beyond our old trail toward Parker's Col, an altitude of thirteen thousand feet.

## MAY 16TH 1913, FRIDAY

Mr. Tatum is still unable to get out with the neuralgia in his jaw. The Archdeacon, Mr. Karstens and I went up on the ridge and cut some more steps up toward the col. We hope tomorrow we will get to the col if it's clear and still.

## MAY 17TH 1913, SATURDAY

Mr. Karstens and I went up on the ridge this morning with the expectation of reaching the col but when we got upon the ridge it began to get cloudy and windy so we waited there where our cache was. The clouds got denser and denser until the sky over us was all black so we decided to return to our camp on the glacier as it was not safe for us to go up the knife-edged ridge in the smother. Just before we went to bed we heard an avalanche so we rushed out of the tent to see where it was coming from. It was coming from the hanging glacier at the head of the Muldrow Glacier and it was very interesting watching it rolling down the mountain side like a roaring thunder and afterwards raising a cloud one thousand feet or more up in the air.

## MAY 18TH 1913, SUNDAY

It has been cloudy all day and also snowing heavily. We had morning service and the rest of the day we put in the best we could. Today is Trinity Sunday. It has been two months and two days since we left Nenana. It is very tedious staying in the tent all day waiting for the weather to clear.

## MAY 19TH 1913, MONDAY

It has been just such another day as yesterday. It is heavily overcast, and every now and then the sun tries to shine but it gets smothered in a short time. We hope tomorrow will be a fine day, although that has been our hope for the last week. All we want now is one good day to reach the col and we hope from there it won't be so hard.

## MAY 20TH 1913, TUESDAY

We have been here on the glacier for a month and two days and doubtless will be here for some time yet as the weather shows no evidence of clearing up. Yesterday morning I saw a bird flying across the glacier over our tent. Just think of a bird being up here at an altitude of twelve thousand feet.

## MAY 21ST 1913, WEDNESDAY

Mr. Karsten and I went up on the ridge this morning for it looked promising; the sky was clear and the clouds managed to keep off the ridge till we were finished. But Oh! How hard the work was of clearing the steps. It took us six solid hours to make one mile.

## MAY 22ND 1913, THURSDAY

We lay inactive in our tent all day, listoning to the snow falling our tent and hugging the little coal oil primus stove to keep warm, and hoping tomorrow will be a good day.

## MAY 23RD 1913, FRIDAY

We took and packed up all our belongings this morning and started up the ridge intending to pitch our little tent on the ridge at an altitude of twelve thousand feet. We weren't two hundred yards from our tent when we saw that we could not make to the top of the ridge with the loads we had on our backs so we turned back putting it off till tomorrow.

## MAY 24TH 1913, SATURDAY

We took a portion of our mountain camping outfit and cooking utensils and picked up our little tent on the ridge and pitched it about halfway between our camp on the glacier and col. After that we came back part way down the ridge and brought up a cache we made there before to the little tent, and tomorrow we will come up to it rain or shine.

## MAY 25TH 1913, SUNDAY

We took all our belongings and started up to the camp on the ridge this morning with a great deal of pleasure and satisfaction that we won't have to come down the old ridge which we were all tired of, and I specially for I am at the head always cleaning out the steps. I think I know every step of the way nearly. After we had lunch Mr. Karstens and I went up the ridge toward the col, and after a hard work of seven hours we returned failing to reach the col.

## MAY 26TH 1913, MONDAY

Mr. Tatum and I went up on the ridge this morning expecting surely to reach the col this time but it was very foggy and we had lot of chopping to do and didn't make it. I wanted to go on, no matter how late it was but Mr. Tatum got cold and so we turned. We got back to our tent just before seven where the Archdeacon and Mr. Karstens had dinner waiting for us.

## MAY 27TH 1913, TUESDAY

Mr. K. and I went up the ridge this morning at eight o'clock and we got to the unbroken snow slope around twelve and about fifty further up we found P.P. and B.'s camp which looked as though it had been left yesterday. There were empty cracker boxes and raisin boxes. We were pretty well tired so we went back to our tent about fifteen hundred feet below us. While we were up doing this work the Archdeacon and Tatum made a trip up about halfway with some grub.

## MAY 28TH 1913, WEDNESDAY

Mr. Karstens and I went up the ridge. We took with us enough grub to last four days so that if we should have to move our camp up higher we wouldn't have to carry any as it is all we could do to carry our bedding and the tent and the coal oil primus stove. We did not get to the col today for it was so cloudy and windy that we did not know where we were going and had to turn back.

## MAY 29TH 1913, THURSDAY

Karstens and I succeeded in reaching the col today. The distances around here are so deceptive that the comb which lay between us and the col seemed endless to me going up over it. From the col we saw the north peak and the south was just hidden behind a snow peak of the northeast ridge. We are all happier tonight than we have been for three weeks just because we reached the col which we have been working hard to get to for the last three weeks.

### MAY 30TH 1913, FRIDAY

We broke camp this morning and moved up to the col and pitched our tent in the lee of a granite slab from where if it were a good day we could get a fine view but its been misty and cloudy for three weeks.

### MAY 31ST 1913, SATURDAY

Tatum and I went down the ridge to our last camp on the ridge and got the creepers and caribou skins and when we got to our second cache on the ridge we took some more things and also at the third cache few hundred feet above we took some more and had lunch there. When we started up from there I had so much on my back that I had to make a head band to help my back. The Archdeacon and Karstens went up the basin of the north and south peaks of Denali breaking and cutting steps for our next movement.

### JUNE 1ST 1913, SUNDAY

Tatum and I went down the ridge this morning and got the last load. We made the trip in three and a half hours. The Archdeacon and Karstens took each a load of food up above and also picked and shoveled out a place to pitch our tent. After making lunch on pea soup K. and T. and I took some more stuff up. When Mr. Tatum and I came up the ridge the wind was so strong that in several places on the narrow ridge I nearly lost my balance with the heavy pack on my back. We had morning service before we went down the ridge and tonight while we were having our evening service it was so cold that we had to ware our parkas.

### JUNE 2ND 1913, MONDAY

We broke camp this morning at eight o'clock and got to the next camping place at twelve, eight hundred feet higher. After we pitched the tent and had lunch Karstens and I went up into the basin and we used the creepers for the first time on this trip. Hitherto we had been packing them. We made a good time on them on the hard snow crest and we went up to the seventeen thousand feet. We saw Parker and Browne's tracks up one of the slopes which had been tramped one year ago.

## JUNE 3RD 1913, TUESDAY

We moved camp up nine hundred feet higher this morning. It blew all night and part of the day. For the first time on this trip I suffered with my feet. They were so cold that I thought they were going to freeze. This morning while we were moving the camp we sat down to take a rest about half way to our next camping place, and while resting we began to talk about the flag staff that was supposed to have been put up on the north peak of Denali by Anderson and Taylor, and as we were talking about it I suddenly looked up to the ridge that was running down from the north peak and to our great surprise I saw it standing out against the blue sky. The pole was about twelve or fourteen feet long. It has been there for three years. For the first time today it has been absolutely clear for three weeks.

## JUNE 4TH, JUNE 5TH, JUNE 6TH

[All empty pages, undated, and unwritten.]

## JUNE 7TH 1913, SATURDAY

We went to bed last night seven o'clock with the intention of rising at one or two in the morning and get started for the summit. We lay in bed till ten but could not go to sleep so we got up, lit the primus stove and sat around it. Mr. K. had a headache and Tatum had another and the Archdeacon could not move without losing his breath and our spirits were all pretty low, for we knew what a tremindus task it was to get to the top and back in one day. However, we stayed up till four, then started for the top, and soon after we started the grade got so steep that we were compelled to zigzag, and although we had our creepers we had to chop steps. After a long and tedious grind we reached the first level about half way to the top, and there we ate our second breakfast, and from there we plotted slowly but steadily. It was one o'clock when we got to the top. I was ahead all day and was the first ever to set foot on Mt. Denali. We lost no time in setting up the little instrument tent and while the Archdeacon was reading the mercurial barometer I boiled the boiling point thermometer. It was extremely cold and a keen wind blowing and could not stay long.

## JUNE 8TH 1913, SUNDAY

We took a last glimpse at the north and south peaks of Mt. Denali and turned our faces toward the lowlands and as we had the creepers on the footing was good

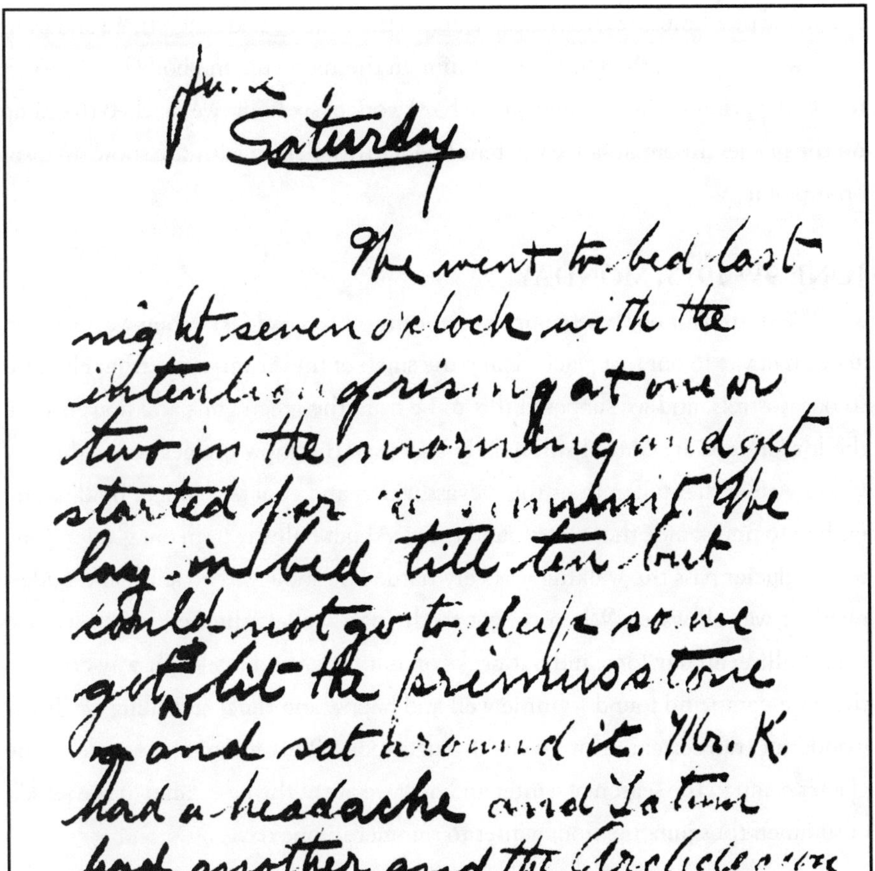

June

Saturday

We went to bed last
night seven o'clock with the
intention of rising at one or
two in the morning and get
started for the summit. We
lay in bed till ten but
could not go to sleep so we
got up lit the primus stove
and sat around it. Mr. K.
had a headache and Tatum
had another and the Archdeacon
could not move without losing
his breath and our spirits were
all pretty low, for we knew
what a tremendous task it was
to get to the top and back
in one day. However, we stayed
up till four, then started for

BEGINNING OF THE ENTRY THE DAY HE REACHED THE SUMMIT (COURTESY YVONNE MOZÉE)

and made fine time down to the camp above the col. We had lunch there and went on down to the col, there we left a minimum thermometer and boiled a big pot of tea on the primus oil stove, and after a hard work of six hours we reached the camp on the glacier. In our absance the tent had partly fallen in with the snow that was on top of it.

### JUNE 9TH 1913, MONDAY

We started for our base-camp this morning at ten o'clock. When we got down about halfway to our first glacier camp the smell of the air was some what changed to our nostrels, and we supposed this to be from the green grass and flowers from the lowlands. Our old trail still held but some of the snow bridges across the crevasses were either fallen in or the crevass widen and could no longer hold us and we had to find some other way around them. About halfway from our glacier camp to the glacier pass the walking was very hard. The snow was all slush and underneath it was all water. When we got to the pass we left the sled which we had been pulling all day long and put packs on our backs and made our way down to the base-camp and found Johnnie well and happy, and the dogs rolling fat. It is a wonderful transformation we went through today. This morning we were at the glacier camp in the season of winter and now we are at the base camp in the season of summer, thus jumping from winter to summer in one day.

### JUNE 10TH 1913, TUESDAY

We rested all day for our long journey to Diamond during which Johnnie made some biscuits for the trip and Mr. K. and I made some dog packs and Tatum washed his underware a handkerchief for each of us. The mosquitoes are so thick that we have to use our handkerchiefs instead of mosquito netting of which we have none. We heard thunder today for the first time this year and it also rained.

### JUNE 11 1913, WEDNESDAY

We left our tent standing, left most of our things in it and taking just what was necessary for the trip, we took a last glimpse at the surrounding hills and started. The going was fine and we made a fine time, and at reaching the Clear Water we lunched and went on to Lloid's tent on the McKinley Fork. We had heavy thunderstorm and it also rained heavily, soaking us to the skin. When we got to Lloid's tent we cutt lots of wood and had fire all night staying up and keeping fire alternately.

## JUNE 12TH 1913, THURSDAY

(Dated but unwritten.)

## JUNE 13TH 1913, FRIDAY

We left Eureka at half past ten o'clock.

## JUNE 14TH 1913, SATURDAY

We left Quakiley's at eleven this morning. The sun was roasting hot and we made slow progress walking. We rested often and when we got about half way to Glacier we stopped and had lunch. While having lunch I took my fly hook and fished for a while but caught nothing. There were some gralings but they would not bite. When we arrived at Glacier we made ourselves at home in Taylor's house.

# Afterword

Where I live in Alaska, Denali is always a presence on the horizon. Sometimes, watching clouds move over the mountain, I imagine Judge Wickersham and Belmore Browne, Hudson Stuck, Walter Harper, Billy Taylor and the others looking up at these same wind-swept slopes above the clouds—when they were young, their legs strong, their hearts pounding with a hunger for adventure.

Looking back, we see that more often than not their lives were marked by a combination of triumphs and defeats—and that wherever deceit appeared it had a way of unraveling otherwise worthy reputations and lives. The three books in this trilogy do a wonderful job of bringing to life these men and their times. But their lives would, of course, go on, taking many twists and turns as a result of their experiences on Denali. So, too, would some of the mysteries continue for years.

One lingering question was how far had the Sourdoughs climbed in 1910. Hudson Stuck's *The Ascent of Denali* became widely accepted as an accurate account of the first ascent. Yet, among some mountaineers a nagging thought persisted: perhaps in the midst of the Cook scandal, the Sourdoughs had been unfairly dismissed. Maybe they had climbed to Denali's higher south summit.

The only firsthand account of the Sourdough ascent was that of their leader, Tom Lloyd, who said they had made it. The other Sourdoughs had either died or, following their visions of streams full of gold, had long since disappeared into the Alaska bush.

Then in mid-July of 1937, a waitress at the McKinley Park roadhouse noticed a young man, Norman Bright, reading *The Ascent of Denali*. She nudged him and pointed out a burly, good-natured miner who looked to be in his sixties. It was Billy Taylor, a member of the 1910 Sourdough Expedition; he and Pete Anderson were the ones who had lugged a spruce pole to the north summit for their friends in Fairbanks to see. Amazed to find one of the old Sourdoughs still alive and not yet senile, Bright asked Taylor about his climb:

NB: *How long did you stay on top of the north summit?*

BT: *Between two and two and a half hours, if I remember rightly. Sunshine on top, but cloudy below us.*

NB: *Did you know the other summit was higher?*

BT: *Looking across the two of them, it didn't seem to have any elevation more, but they claim it's 300 feet higher.*

NB: *What was the reason that you did not climb the South Peak?*

BT: *We set out to climb the North Peak. That's the toughest peak to climb—the North.*

NB: *What can you tell me about Lloyd?*

BT: *He was fine in his own way, but he was lookin' for too much fame. He conflicted his stories by telling his intimate friends he didn't climb it, and told others he was at the top. We didn't get out til June, and then they didn't believe any of us had climbed it . . . We never dreamed he wouldn't give a straight story.*

Billy Taylor cleared up the lingering mystery: their leader, Tom Lloyd, had lied about reaching the south summit. Taylor also shed light on one of the great ironies in all of mountaineering. As Stuck himself said, "The men who accomplished the astonishing feat of climbing the North Peak, in one superhuman march . . . could most certainly have climbed the South Peak too."

What Billy Taylor and Pete Anderson accomplished is almost unimaginable in this era when climbers use light, high-tech gear and usually launch their summit attempts from a 17,000 foot high-camp. Their ascent with primitive gear and a 14-foot spruce pole, from 11,000 feet to the north summit and back in one day is one of the most amazing climbs in American mountaineering. Unfortunately, during their lifetimes their remarkable feat went virtually unnoticed, undermined by the deceit of their leader.

The Cook controversy should have ended when Belmore Browne located the snowy knoll miles from Denali's summit where Cook had taken his "summit" photo. But it didn't. Cook's supporters wrote articles and books defending their hero. They formed the Frederick A. Cook Society to clear the doctor's name, complaining about "those who continue to denigrate his achievements and his character."

One of Cook's most persistent critics has been Bradford Washburn, the leading expert on Denali. In 1956, he used high-resolution photographic equipment to locate the exact spot where Cook took his infamous "summit" photo. Washburn's evidence was conclusive. But it wouldn't silence the prattle of Cook's defenders. Said Washburn, "Nobody ever likes to face the facts of a gigantic lie or hoax."

In 2001, nearly a hundred years after Cook's first trip to Alaska, Washburn and Peter Cherici would write *The Dishonorable Dr. Cook*, a book that drives a decisive spike into the coffin of Cook's reputation. Yet, how easily Cook could have left a legacy of accomplishment. His remarkable 1903 circumnavigation of Denali is all but forgotten in the shadow of his grand deceit. As David Roberts observes in *Great Exploration Hoaxes*, "Cook was no mere bungler or incompetent. The abiding irony of his career is that had he taken credit only for the geographic feats he actually accomplished, he would be esteemed today as an explorer of no mean significance."

In any event, Cook's life continued to spiral out of control. After some success as a businessman, he was convicted of fraud for overvaluing oil properties in 1923 and sentenced to fourteen years in Leavenworth. In yet another ironic twist in his vexed life, Cook was now being punished for fraud he didn't commit: The lands in question later gushed with oil.

Cook must have experienced a moment of relief, if not some moral vindication, when the great explorer Roald Amundsen, who had been with Cook in the Antarctic, visited him in prison. Amundsen said, "Remembering his kindness to me and recalling that I owed my life indeed to his resourcefulness . . . I felt I could do no less than make a short journey to the prison and call upon my former benefactor in his present misfortune."

After spending seven years in prison, Cook was paroled in 1930. He would live the last ten years of his life in poverty, supported primarily by his daughter Helene from a second marriage. On his deathbed in 1940, Cook was pardoned by President Franklin Roosevelt. The name of another of Cook's daughters, Ruth, still graces Denali's majestic Ruth Glacier.

In contrast to the desultory unwinding of Cook's life, Belmore Browne's life blossomed after the publication of his book, *The Conquest of Mount McKinley*. He married, had children, and became well known for his paintings of the American West. However, even with the passage of time, the reverberations of Cook's deceit touched his life.

"In looking back on that remarkable controversy," Browne said, "I am still filled with astonishment at the incredible amount of vindictive and personal spite that was shown by the partisans of Dr. Cook. Men who had never seen an ice axe . . . accused us of untold crimes because we dared to question Cook's honesty."

Belmore Browne would live to the age of 73, painting right up to his death in 1953. He is remembered for his three expeditions to Denali—first with Cook and then twice with Herschel Parker—but his life was filled with other adventures as well. Bradford Washburn recalls that Browne, "dogteamed and rafted a thousand miles from Seward to the Yukon . . . fought the Chulitna's rocky rapids in an open boat and floated down the Stikine in a Tlingit canoe. He panned for gold on the gravel bars of the Kantishna and hunted seals and whales in bidarkhas with the Aleuts . . . and he had what all men most desire: a devoted wife and a happy family."

In 1947, thirty-five years after Belmore Browne came so agonizingly close to reaching the summit of Denali, his son George went to the mountain. With some friends, and his father very much in mind, he made the fourth successful ascent.

After their triumph on Denali in 1913, Hudson Stuck and Walter Harper remained close, their relationship much like that of a father and son. Stuck encouraged Harper to continue his education and took him to Massachusetts to enroll in college. On his application Harper described himself as "a trapper, dog musher, guide, and woodchopper."

After graduating in 1917, Harper returned to Alaska to make a six-month, twenty-two-hundred-mile dogsled trip with Stuck. They headed out from Fort Yukon in November, stopping at villages as they worked their way westward to Kotzebue, then up the Arctic coast to Point Hope and Barrow, before returning to Fort Yukon.

It would be the last trip the two would make together. That fall, in Fort Yukon, Harper married a nurse named Francis Wells. The young couple headed for Philadelphia, where Walter planned to enter medical school. He wanted to return to Alaska as a doctor to help the native people of the Yukon. In Skagway they boarded the *Princess Sophia*. In the night a storm came up. The *Sophia* struck a reef, and everyone aboard perished.

Stuck's triumph on Denali would be forever tempered by the untimely death of Walter Harper, who he loved as a man loves his only son. Stuck returned to his life's work among native people in the small villages scattered across northern Alaska. He died in 1920. Though his own life was marked by success, even greatness, he must, at times, have felt discouraged by the continuing struggles of native people to survive in a rapidly changing world.

Recalling the glorious moments atop Denali with Harper, Stuck wrote a fitting epitaph for their grand adventure—and for others who seek the solace of mountains: "There was no pride of conquest, no trace of that exultation of victory some enjoy upon the first ascent of a lofty peak, no gloating over good fortune that had hoisted us a few hundred feet higher than others who had struggled and been discomfited. Rather was the feeling that a privileged communion with the high places of the earth had been granted."

Whether or not we shoulder a pack to climb Denali ourselves, I think that many of us, in our own way, follow in the footsteps of Belmore Browne, Hudson Stuck, and the other pioneers. How these hardy and heartfelt men dealt with triumph and defeat—and, like Cook and Lloyd, were sometimes tempted to deceit—speaks to us as clearly today as it did when they set out for Denali.

I see more clearly now, than when I was young and lived to climb, that there are many mountains in our lives. We don't have to be blazing routes up unclimbed peaks to hear Belmore Browne's words ringing in our ears—"We shouted for the pure joy of life as we flew along the trail."

*Art Davidson*
*Alaska*
*April 2001*

THE MOUNTAINEERS, founded in 1906, is a nonprofit outdoor activity and conservation club, whose mission is "to explore, study, preserve, and enjoy the natural beauty of the outdoors. . . ." Based in Seattle, Washington, the club is now the third-largest such organization in the United States, with 15,000 members and five branches throughout Washington State.

The Mountaineers sponsors both classes and year-round outdoor activities in the Pacific Northwest, which include hiking, mountain climbing, ski-touring, snowshoeing, bicycling, camping, kayaking and canoeing, nature study, sailing, and adventure travel. The club's conservation division supports environmental causes through educational activities, sponsoring legislation, and presenting informational programs. All club activities are led by skilled, experienced volunteers, who are dedicated to promoting safe and responsible enjoyment and preservation of the outdoors.

If you would like to participate in these organized outdoor activities or the club's programs, consider a membership in The Mountaineers. For information and an application, write or call The Mountaineers, Club Headquarters, 300 Third Avenue West, Seattle, WA 98119; 206-284-6310.

The Mountaineers Books, an active, nonprofit publishing program of the club, produces guidebooks, instructional texts, historical works, natural history guides, and works on environmental conservation. All books produced by The Mountaineers Books fulfill the club's mission.

***Send or call for our catalog of more than 500 outdoor titles:***

The Mountaineers Books is proud to be a corporate sponsor of Leave No Trace, whose mission is to promote and inspire responsible outdoor recreation through education, research, and partnerships. The Leave No Trace program is focused specifically on human-powered (nonmotorized) recreation.

Leave No Trace strives to educate visitors about the nature of their recreational impacts, as well as offer techniques to prevent and minimize such impacts. Leave No Trace is best understood as an educational and ethical program, not as a set of rules and regulations.

For more information, visit www.LNT.org, or call 800-332-4100.

*Other titles you might enjoy from The Mountaineers Books:*

**THE DISHONORABLE DR. COOK: Debunking the Notorious Mount McKinley Hoax,** *Bradford Washburn and Peter Cherici*
An exploration of Dr. Cook's life and character and why he staked his reputation on such a flimsy story. Contains side-by-side comparisons of Cook's original photos with Washburn's identical ones, taken from locations very different than Cook alleged.

**DENALI: A Literary Anthology,** *Bill Sherwonit, editor*
A literary collection about Denali (a.k.a. Alaska's Mount McKinley) and the broad shadow it casts in history, culture, and nature. Spans over 100 years—from native tales and myths to early exploration to modern day adventure.

**DENALI'S WEST BUTTRESS: A Climber's Guide to Mount McKinley's Classic Route,** *Colby Coombs; Bradford Washburn, photographer*
A step-by-step expert handbook to the West Buttress Route, by a long-time Denali climbing guide. Includes photos by the legendary Bradford Washburn and route overlays.

**THE WILDEST DREAM, The Biography of George Mallory,**
*Peter and Leni Gillman*
An intimate, well-rounded portrait of George Mallory, offering a wealth of insight into the man behind the myth and the controversy, written by two investigative journalists.

**THE FALLING SEASON: Inside the Life and Death Drama of Aspen's Mountain Rescue Team,** *Hal Clifford*
An insider's account of one of North America's premier mountain rescue organizations. Includes intimate profiles of team members and why they routinely risk their lives to help others, interspersed with dramatic rescue stories.

**MOUNT McKINLEY: The Pioneer Climbs,** *Terris Moore*
Highlights early climbs on Mount McKinley, from initial explorations to the 1940s; illustrated with maps and historic photos.

**MOUNT McKINLEY: Icy Crown of North America,** *Fred Beckey*
Portrait of a great climbing challenge, from its natural history to its influence on natives, prospectors, and climbers.

**THE MYSTERY OF MALLORY & IRVINE,** *Tom Holzel and Audrey Salkeld*

This thorough exploration of mountaineering's greatest mystery has been fully revised in light of the discovery of Mallory's body on Mount Everest and offers a complete history of expeditions from 1924 to 1999.

**HIGH ACHIEVER: The Life and Climbs of Chris Bonington,** Jim Curran
This biography of one of the world's best-known climbers examines Bonington's deepest motives and reveals the joys and occasional despair of living a life as a high-profile climber.

**55 WAYS TO THE WILDERNESS IN SOUTHCENTRAL ALASKA, Fourth Edition,** *Helen Nienhueser and Nancy Wolfe*
The classic guide to year-round hiking, skiing, and snowshoeing.